Introduction to Unity 3D with C#

The Exodus Adventure

3rd Edition

By

Kris Murray & Philip Conrod

BIBLEBYTE BOOKS

PO Box 701

Maple Valley, WA 98038

www.BibleByteBooks.com

www.BibleByteGames.com

Published by:
BibleByte Books (a publishing division of Kidware Software LLC)
PO Box 701
Maple Valley, Washington 98038
1.425.413.1185
www.BibleByteBooks.com
www.BibleByteGames.com

Printed in the United States of America

ISBN-13: 978-1-951077-26-6 (Printed Edition)
ISBN-13: 978-1-951077-27-3 (Electronic Edition)

This guide was developed for the course, "Introduction to Unity 3D with C#: The Exodus Adventure", produced by BibleByte Books, Maple Valley, Washington. It is not intended to be a complete reference to the Visual C# language or Unity 3D. Please consult the Microsoft website or Unity's website for detailed reference information.

About The Authors

Philip Conrod holds a bachelor's degree in Computer Information Systems and a master's certificate in Business Development from Regis University. Philip was one of the early pioneers in developing Christian video games back in 1982. Since then, Philip has published over two dozen Computer Bible Games. Philip has authored, co authored and edited numerous computer programming books for students of all ages. Philip has also held various Information Technology leadership roles in companies like Sundstrand Aerospace (acquired by Raytheon Technologies), Safeco Insurance Companies, FamilyLife (CRU), Kenworth Truck Company, PACCAR Inc., and served as the Senior Vice President, Information Technology & CIO for Darigold for over a decade. Philip currently serves as the President & Publisher of BibleByte Books & Games and Kidware Software LLC. He also attends weekly worship services and leads a Men's Bible Study Fellowship group at his local church.

Kris Murray currently resides in Folsom California. He graduated from Oregon Institute of Technology in 2004 with a double-degree in Computer Hardware and Software Engineering. He was hired right afterwards by Intel Corporation as a Software Engineer programming in C/C++ for embedded applications. He has since changed roles multiple times writing internal tools as well as released Windows kernel drivers. He is currently a leader for his team and helps role model and mentor the junior engineers. Since 2009 he's been passionate about helping using Christian games to spread the message of Jesus Christ. He attends weekly worship services at a local church where he helps out with music, playing violin and viola. He is also a member of Bible Study Fellowship where he volunteers teaching the Bible in the children's program.

Acknowledgements by Philip Conrod

I want to thank my best friend Jesus, who has always been there by my side giving me wisdom and guidance. Without you, this book would have never been published. I also want to thank my three wonderful daughters - Stephanie, Jessica and Chloe, who helped with beta testing and target audience feedback. I want to especially thank Chloe Conrod for copy editing this version of the tutorial. I could not have accomplished this without all your hard work, love and support. I also want to thank Vlado žabiačan for creating most of the amazing Egyptian themed 3D Environment Models you see in this tutorial. I also want to thank Virtualware for creating many of the original Egyptian 3D Character Models, various creature 3D Models and several of the 3D environment models. I also want to thank Steve Finney for all the custom UMA Egyptian costume conversions he did for this project I also want to thank Vertigo Games for the awesome music soundtrack and the young Moses 3D Character Model. I want to thank Andrzej Dobrowolski for the Universal Footsteps. I also want to thank Jon Collins for helping with the initial Introduction to the Unity 3D section. I also want to thank so many others who contributed assets to this tutorial textbook for students. You can find a complete list of credits for each of the creators in the Game Design Document found in Appendix B. I also want to thank Unity for helping democratize game development by creating an economical and powerful game engine for beginning game developers.

I also want to thank my many students high school students who play tested this textbook and let me experiment with them on how best to teach it to students. I want to give special thanks to some very special high school and college interns: Sibo Zhang, Brennan Snodgrass, Chloe Conrod, Joel Abraham and Anita Daniel for serving as devoted multi-year interns testing this course several times as we updated it for newer versions of Visual Studio Visual C# and Unity 3D.

Last and certainly not least I want to thank my co-author, Kris Murray, for doing most of the hard work in writing this beginning Unity 3D C# tutorial. Thank you so much for collaborating with me on this tutorial textbook project and on the 3D "Exodus Vigil" Puzzle Maze Adventure Game which can be purchased on Steam or on our website.

Acknowledgements by Kris Murray

I give thanks to the God of Abraham, Isaac, and Jacob and I give Him all the glory for the work I do. I recognize that Jesus working in my life through the Holy Spirit all my work would be fruitless It is from him that my life has meaning. From him, through him, and to him are all things. I also thank my wife and son, whom I love and are a motivation for my endeavors. I also thank God for giving me this opportunity to help teach others how to make Christian games through Phil Conrod.

Foreword by Ken B. Mitchell

For over 24 years I have known Philip Conrod as a best friend, fellow Christian, and my personal IT guy for a variety of computer issues that have come my way. Philip's technological expertise mixed with his spiritual gifts of knowledge and teaching have given him not only a unique set of skills for working in the Information Technology field for over 30 years but also for serving Jesus in the church. He has saved his home church thousands of dollars in needed upgrades, understanding networks intricacies and teaching staff members needed computer skills.

The "other side" of Philip's gifts lie in his amazing ability to teach. Simply put, he makes the "hard concepts" easy to understand! Whether it's doctrinal, devotional or day to day living from the Bible, student after student have grown tremendously from Philip's teaching at New Community Church. Recently I was leading a group of young adults and asked, "Which mentor has influenced you the most?" Not surprisingly, Philip Conrod's name quickly rose to the top! He has, for years been a favorite Sunday school teacher for many students in our church, including my own son.

Of course, the highlight of each year is when a crowded house of teenagers and college graduates, of "Mr. Phil", play hours of computer games intertwined with Christian fellowship in his home every year for over 20 years. It is this very combination that makes Philip the perfect co-author for the Introduction to Unity 3D C#: Exodus Adventure Game programming book. Making the Bible fun, intriguing and filled with learning enables all of us to grow in our biblical knowledge. Sit back and be prepared to be challenged, captivated and without knowing it, grow in your knowledge and understanding of the Bible!

Ken B. Michell

Sr. Pastor

New Community Church

Maple Valley, Washington USA

www.newcommunity.us

Foreword by Scott Adams

Greetings Adventurer!

My name is Scott Adams and I am honored to be writing the forward to this incredible 3D game programming tutorial. I am one of the earliest founders of the home computer gaming industry. My experience with computer Adventure type games dates back to 1978 when I created the first commercially available adventure for home computers.

I am writing this in 2018 and a lot has changed in the last 40 years in computers. Obviously, a lot more can be done with our current technology than the primitive games of the past. Luscious artwork and full-scale animation have become the norm. Today's game studios spend hundreds of thousands of dollars on artists and designers to create modern games.

So how does one go about creating such a game on their own? Or learning the tools that the studios use?

That is where this textbook comes in. It opens up the world of Unity 3D and provides all the game assets of art and scripting to create a real masterpiece of a game. As a nascent game creator, you will be shown how to take full advantage of the Unity 3D system to build the game, then you will also have all the assets of that game to use in your own creations later.

You are starting an incredible journey where you are going to learn the tools you need to make games. Once you have that foundation, you will be limited only by your own imagination! You have a great deal of fun waiting for you in the pages of this book. So, go ahead, turn the page, and get started now.

Happy Adventuring!

Scott Adams

www.clopas.net

www.msadams.com

Table of Contents

Chapter 1 – Introduction 9
Chapter 2 – Game Design Document 35
Chapter 3 – 3rd Person Controller 47
Chapter 4 – User Control in the 3rd Person 71
Chapter 5 – Maps and Zones 99
Chapter 6 – Actor Animation Controller 121
Chapter 7 – Dialogue System 137
Chapter 8 – Cinematics and Cut-scenes 157
Chapter 9 – Menu System and UI 179
Chapter 10 – Inventory Management 197
Chapter 11 – Building Levels 213
Chapter 12 –Music and Miscellaneous 229
Chapter 13 – Skybox Controller 237
Chapter 14 – Saving Player State 247
Chapter 15 – Quest Journal 259
Chapter 16 – Sheep Corralling Minigame 281
Chapter 17 – Populating the Game World 291
Chapter 18 – The Unity Multipurpose Avatar (UMA) 303
Chapter 19 – Finishing Touches 349
Chapter 20 – Deploying your Game 365
Appendix A – Troubleshooting 371
Appendix B – Game Design Document 375
Other Self-Study and/or Instructor-Led Programming Tutorials By BibleByte Books 405

Chapter 1 – Introduction

Hi, my name is Teacher Phil. I'm glad you decided to come with me on this journey to learn C#.

And I'm Teacher Steph. I can't wait to get busy making a Unity game with you.

So, after hours and hours of playing RPGs, FPSs, MUDs, MOBAs, TBSs, TPSs (That reminds me, I need to finish that TPS report for work), and MMOs you've decided to start making your own games. Good for you! Few things in life give as much satisfaction as building a project from the ground up.

However, making a game's not so easy, especially if you're doing it all by yourself. What will the player do in the game? Is the graphics going to be 2D or 3D? What about 2.5D, what is that? What kind of music and sound effects are you going to have? Is there going to be a story? What about the user interface? All these things and more go into a game and can overwhelm even the best of us. In this book, not only will you learn how to make a game, but also how to manage all these things into something you feel you can accomplish.

In this chapter, I'll introduce the Unity 3D game authoring tool. Subsequent chapters will teach you how to manage your game features, load the provided base assets (stuff that goes in your game), write all the code you need, and then integrate it all together into a fun and playable game.

For this book, I've crafted a fun adventure game that we'll make called *The Exodus Adventure*. This non-violent game is a point-and-click adventure that takes the player through the story of the Exodus through the eyes of Moses (That is, third person eyes. Would that make you a guardian angel?). We'll be making our game while learning C# at the same time. Sound like fun? Of course, it will be!

Here is a list of features you'll learn to develop in this book:

- Zoom the camera
- Play Sounds/Music
- Vary footsteps on terrain
- Code a script to move a boat
- Panning World Map
- Generate UMA characters from a script
- Interact with actors
- Play cut scenes
- Program actors to do different things
- Manage items in an inventory
- Control day and night
- Save Player state
- Quests

There is a truckload of assets included for you to make this game including 3D models, music, sound effects, 2D drawn art, and more. The best part is that after you're done making this game you can use all the included assets to make your own "non-commercial" games for your friends and families!

If you experience any issues with the assets in this book, then check out Appendix A. This has some troubleshooting methods you can use to get things to work.

The assets for you to start with are located here: /Initial-Assets/

If one of the scripts that you wrote, or something else, just isn't working then you can view the fully made game and see if it helps you fix your issue here: /Final-Assets/

Introducing Unity

There are a lot of different game authoring tools out there right now. In addition to Unity there is Unreal ™, CryEngine ™, GameMaker ™, and many more. Each of them has their pros and cons. Since you're new to making games, I recommend that you start with one engine and get good at that before learning others. And hey! Since you've already bought this book, learning Unity 3D sounds like a great place to start.

Unity is a good tool to start with for several reasons. It is free to use to make games until you start raking in the cash. It does limit some advanced features on the free version like customizable splash screens. Most of the features are easy to learn and use. Unity has a great community with many books, forums, YouTube videos, as well as a treasure trove of assets you can buy (or find for free) in their asset store.

Unity used to be called Unity 3D, somewhat of a misnomer. While Unity is great for 3D games, you can make 2D games just as easily with it. You can also do 2.5D where the graphics is 3D, but gameplay happens in 2D. But The Exodus Adventure project for this tutorial will be full-blown 3D.

In the early-1980's, there were many 'toy' computers being introduced to the computing world. Names like VIC-20, Commodore 64, Apple II, Texas Instruments 99/4A, Atari 400, Coleco Adam, Sinclair, and the IBM PC Jr., were finding their way to market. This market created many home and hobbyist programmers who enjoyed writing computer programs they could use at home. These programs were written in BASIC, a language included for free with the computers being sold. Since that time, the complexity of even the most basic computer platform has exceeded those early hobbyists' expectations to where sophisticated virtual 3d arenas spring into life at the touch of a button, and game players can explore never before envisioned wildernesses solving complex puzzles and vanquishing foes. With this level of sophistication, the ability to create games was taken out of the hands of the hobbyist, where most of the current big players originally started from and turned into a multi-million-dollar industry.

In 2004 David Helgason, Nicholas Francis & Joachim Ante set out to change this, recognizing the need for a platform that would once again make game development an accessible past time or even career for the individual at an affordable price. They established Unity with this philosophy and made it a goal to provide the tools needed to as broad a base of developers and potential developers as possible. Over the next 20 years the Unity platform has grown to become one of the major development environments for game studios.

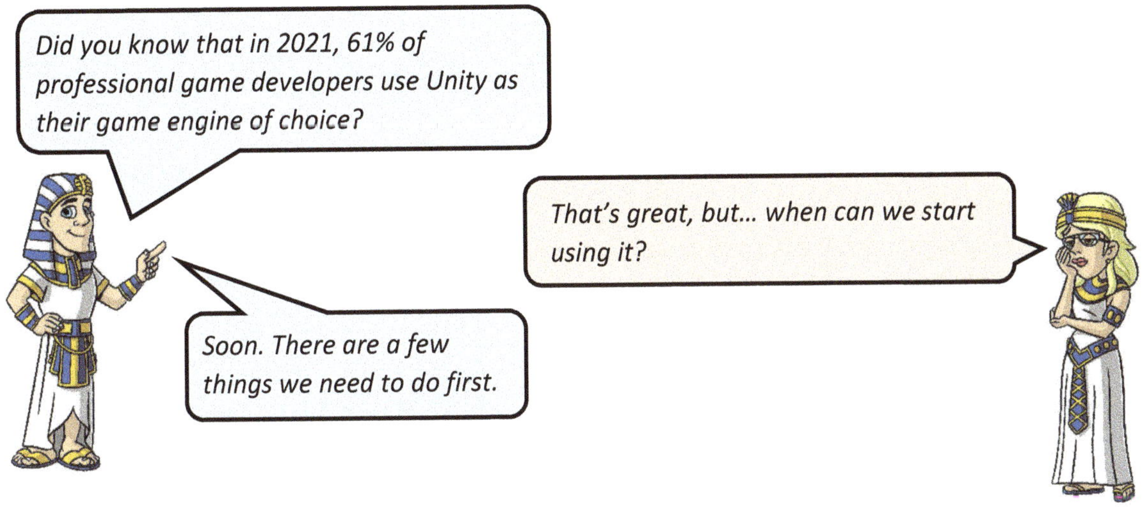

Requirements for Unity 3D

You can make games using Unity on Windows or Apple OSX. You can still build for any OS (Operating System) or platform, this is just whatever OS you want to do development on. Unity supports Windows 10+ 64-bit, Mac OS X 10.13+, and Linux Ubuntu 16.04, 18.04, and CentOS 7. You'll need a GPU (Graphics Processing Unit, which is on your graphics card, we recommend a minimum of GeForce 1050) with DX9 (DX is short for DirectX which is one way of displaying graphics) or DX11 with feature level 9.3 capabilities and at least 16 GB of RAM. Most other requirements depend on the game you want to make. Of course, the faster and better your development platform the better your development experience will be.

The first step is to download the Unity Hub from here: https://unity.com/download.

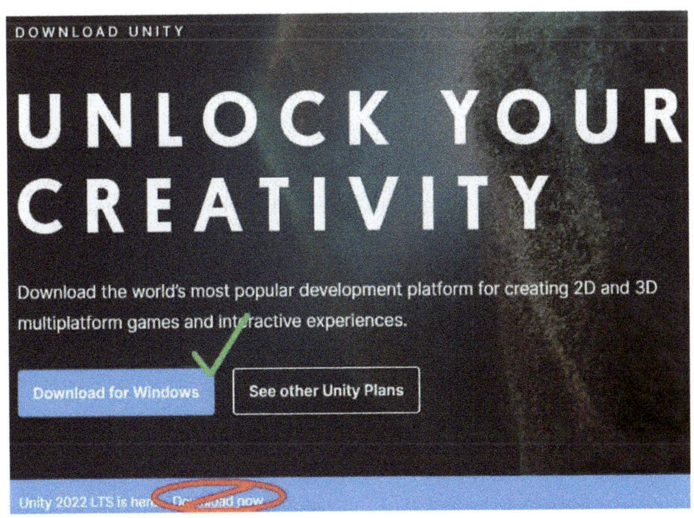

Figure 1

You will be greeted by the screen in Figure 1. Do not click the blue ribbon on the bottom that says, "Download now". That downloads the editor directly. Click "Download for Windows" to get Unity Hub. This software package manages your Unity installed versions, projects, and even has opportunities to take your learning further. If you use Mac OS or Linux then you need to scroll down and find the download link to your Operating System. Once downloaded, go to your system's download folder, and run "UnityHubSetup.exe" or equivalent for Mac OS and Linux (i.e.,

Ubuntu or CentOS). If your OS asks you "Do you want to allow this app to make changes to your device?" then click "Yes". The installation process will begin!

The first window to pop up will be the License agreement shown in Figure 2, which comes with all software you will use. License agreements are like a rulebook. When you're playing a game or sport with your friends you have rules that say what you are allowed to do and what you aren't allowed to do. License Agreements tend to be long and hard to read because of the language used. Please note that if you are under the age of 13 then, by US law, your parent or guardian to agree for you. To accept the terms in the legal agreement, click the button, "I Agree".

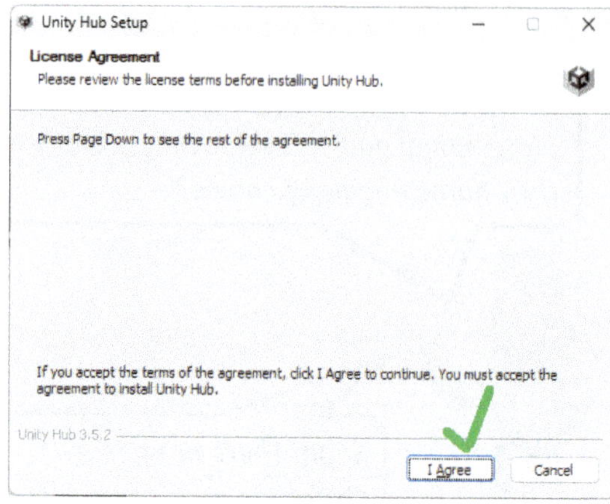

Figure 2

The install location shown in Figure 3, tells Unity Hub where to live on your computer. If you're computer savvy and have a particular place in mind then you can change the default. Otherwise click the button "Install". You will see the green bar going forward on the screen as the installation progresses.

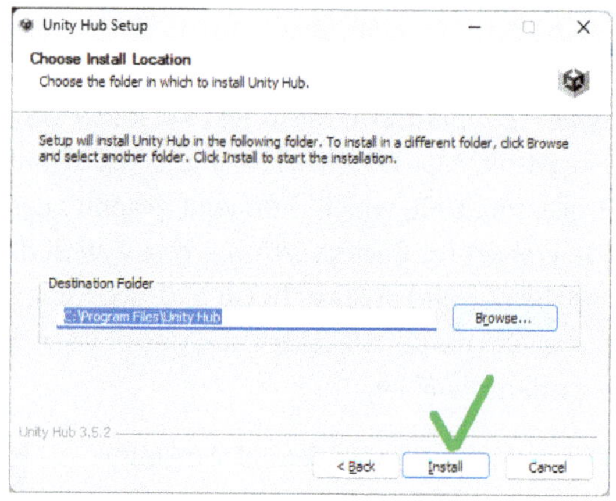

Figure 3

Once it's completed then you'll see the window in Figure 4. Ensure the checkbox for "Run Unity Hub" is checked and click the button "Finish".

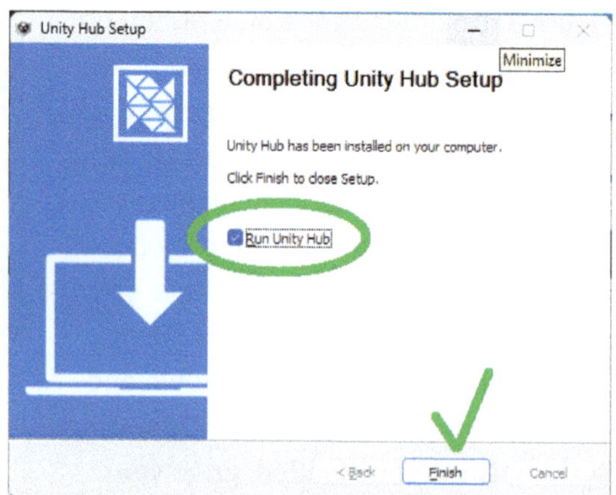

Figure 4

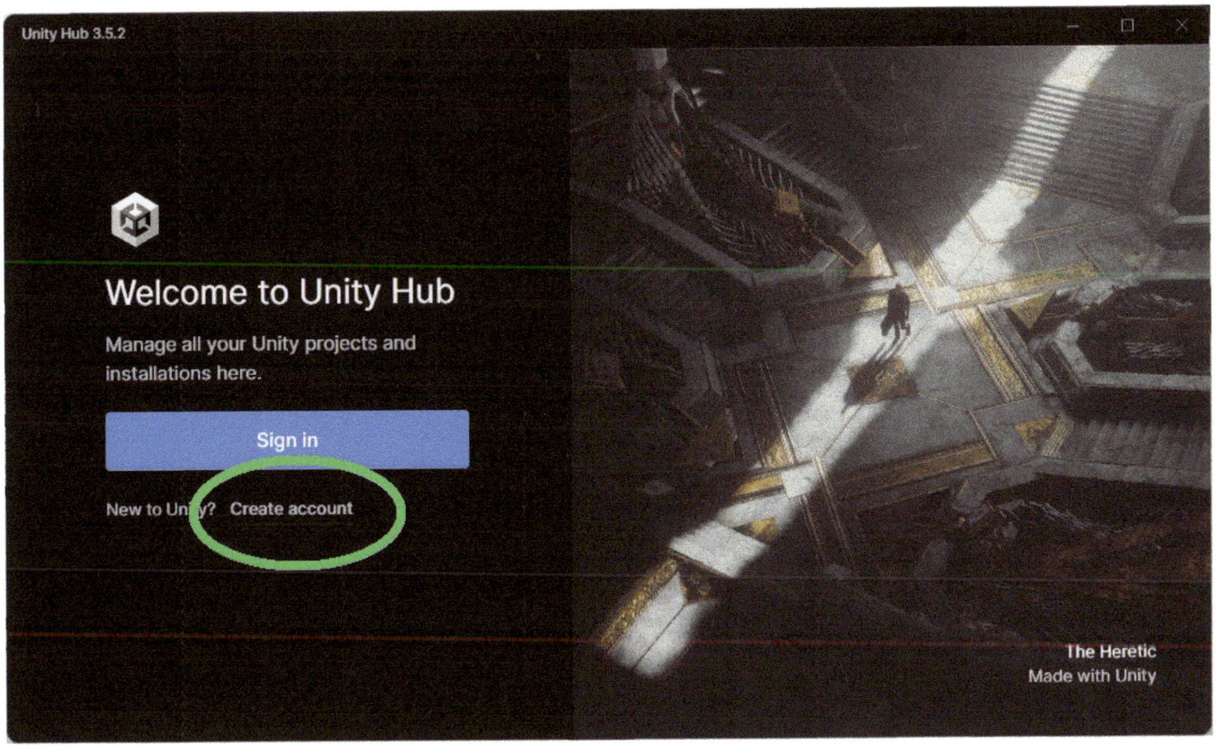

Figure 5

When Unity runs, you'll see the welcome screen shown in Figure 5. On the right you can see a screenshot from a short film that Unity Technologies created to show off how well Unity can render graphics called "The Heretic". It is a science fiction story and doesn't relate to the Bible in any way.

To get started with Unity Hub, you need an account. If you already have one you can sign in, but this tutorial will assume you don't and walk you through the steps to create one. Click the "Create account" link from Figure 5 and it will open your internet browser and take you to a page to do just that.

In Figure 6 on the next page, you'll see something like the webpage you just linked to. Type your email address (or a parent/guardian's email address if you don't have one), a strong password using the guidelines the webpage provides you, a unique username for the community forums, and your full name.

On the bottom-right, you will also see a checkbox that verifies "I'm not a robot". This is a security feature to help prevent abuse from spam bots. If you are a robot, then do not check it.

The lift-side has three more check boxes. The first is for the Terms of Service. You can click the link to read those and check the box when you agree. The second checkbox is another agreement to Unity's privacy policy. You can click the link to read and check the box when you agree. Finally, if you want to know more about Unity's promotions and receive emails you may check that box but you do not have to. After that, click the green button "Create a Unity ID".

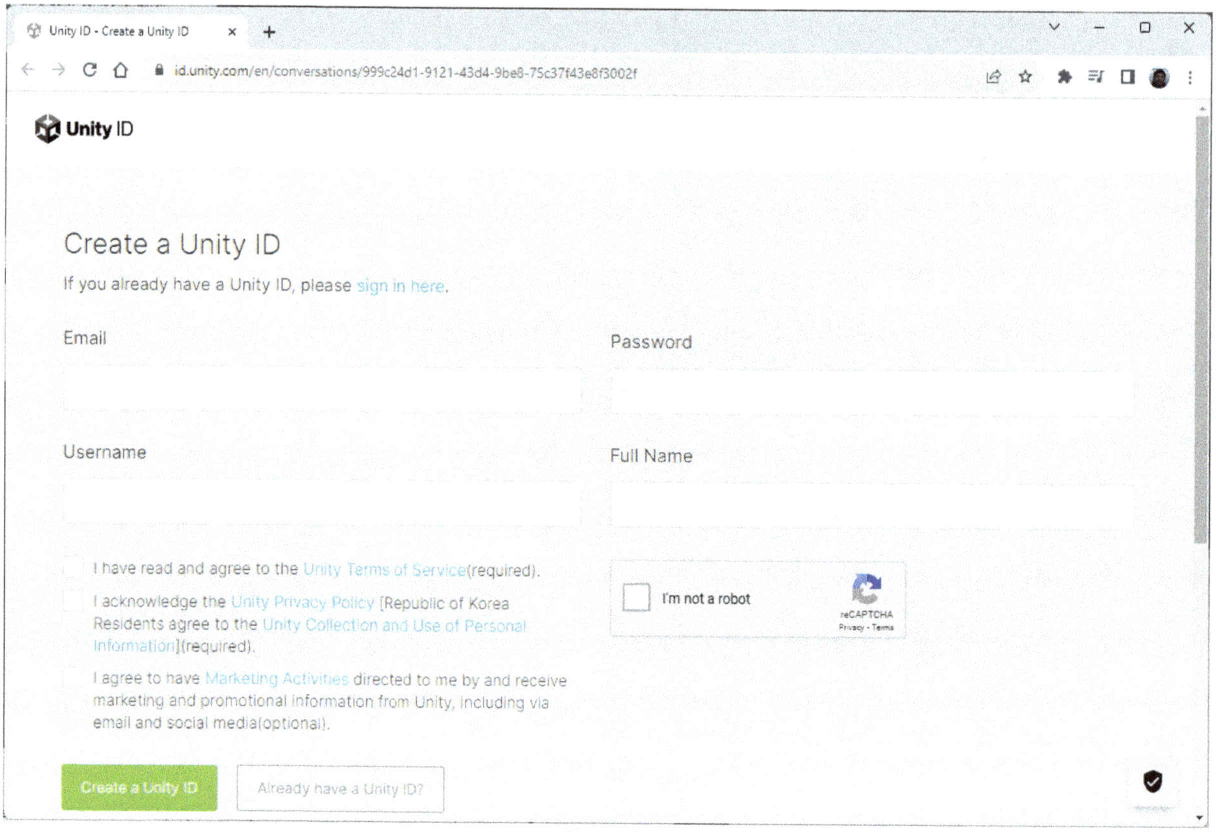

Figure 6

After the Unity website has finished processing the information and creating your account, it will ask you to confirm your email as shown in Figure 7.

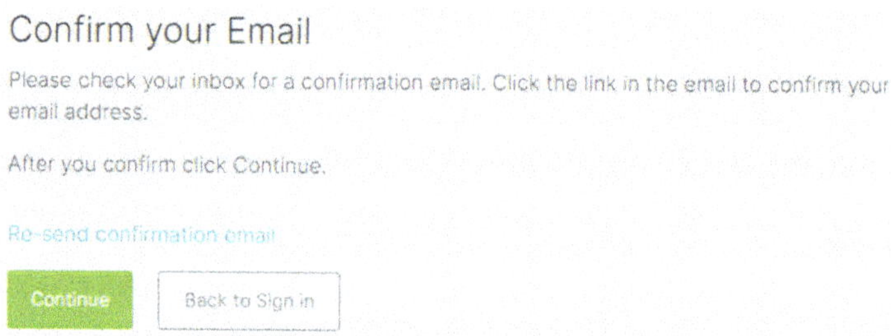

Figure 7

To complete the confirmation, go to your email and find the email from "Unity Technologies" and click the "Link to confirm email" from that email as shown in Figure 8.

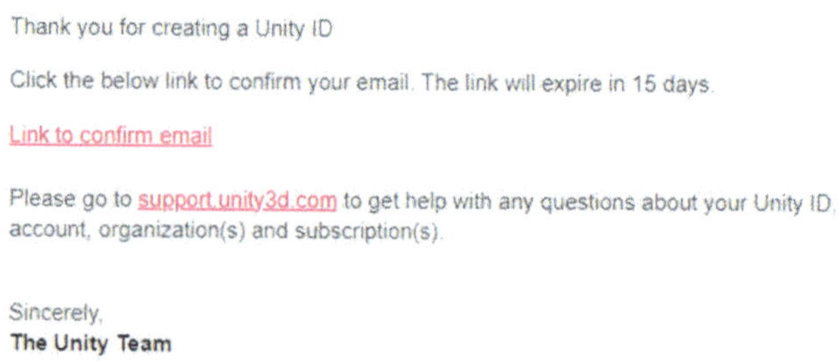

Figure 8

Once you click the email, it asks you to complete the security exercise to prove that you're not a spam bot (seriously though, if you are a spam bot then don't click it. Then click the blue "verify" button.

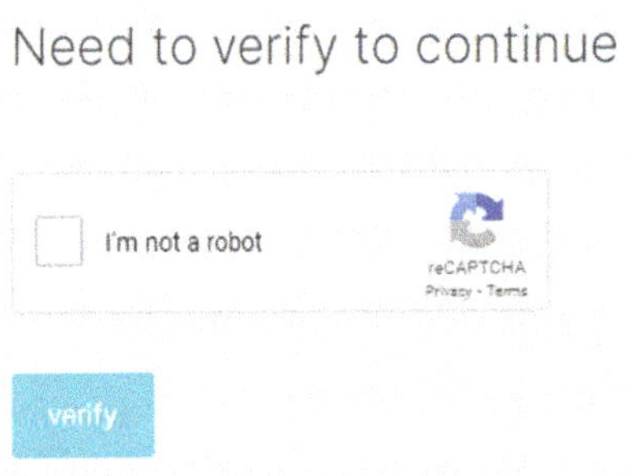

Figure 9

Congratulations, you have now created your very own Unity account! While this does feel like a very long process just to use Unity, once we get in, you'll see just how much it allows you to do. Go back to the Unity Hub application from Figure 5 and sign in using your (or your parent/guardian's email).

Unity is constantly updated for new features and bug fixes. The Unity version we verified with the assets for this revision of the textbook is **Unity 2022.3 (LTS)**. This textbook features screenshots taken from the Microsoft Windows version of Unity 2022.3.9f1. Newer versions of the Unity 3D Engine may change the way Unity 3D works and the location of menus and features. The MAC version of Unity 3D will work slightly different especially when working with the file system and using special COMMAND KEYS. You can download the latest version of Unity 3D at www.unity3d.com. You are NOT required to buy the Plus or Pro plans for Unity 3D for personal Academic Use. You just need to download the Free Personal plan. Once downloaded, execute the installation package and Unity 3D will install to the default location.

IMPOTANT NOTE: This tutorial and all the software included are licensed for Academic & Education Use only. Students can only use this package in personal projects. Students are not allowed to re-distribute, give away, re-sell, or share this tutorial or the associated software packages anywhere. Please Contact BibleByte Books directly at our website if you wish to obtain special permission and purchase a special license to distribute or sell a commercial game using any of the assets or source code contained in this tutorial!

Getting Started

You've got Unity Hub installed and which has a lot of different knobs, gears, widgets, and do-dads. Don't get nervous. Remember, we're stronger together when we have unity. I wonder how many times I can make that joke before it gets old. Let's find out!

After you login, you will be greeted with the welcome screen shown in Figure 10. On the left-hand side there is a list:

Figure 10

- **Projects:** These are the game source files that you'll make.
- **Installs:** Tracks Unity Editor versions in case you have different versions for different games.
- **Learn:** Great places to go after you're finished with this tutorial to continue your fun.
- **Community:** Place online to get you answers, assets, and help for your future games.

Before we can embark on our exciting journey into the depths of game development, we need an install which is kind of like our ship that we use to navigate those treacherous waters. Click "Installs" on the left panel and you'll be shown which editors have been installed like in Figure 11. Right now, you have none. Let's fix that! Click "Install Editor" in the bottom-right.

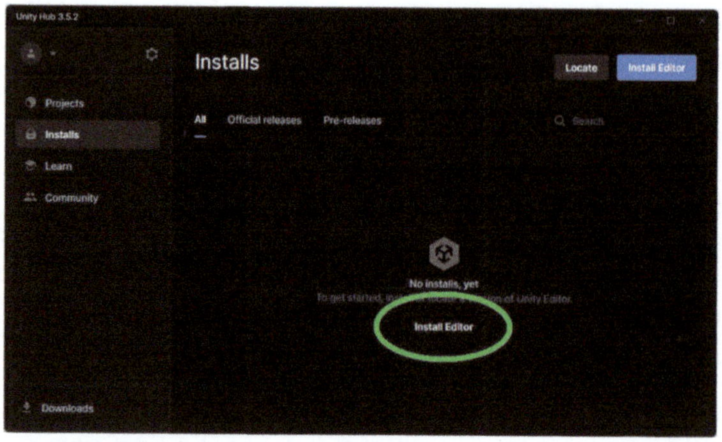

Figure 11

This brings up the editor selection screen that you can see in Figure 12. It defaults to show you the "Official releases", but you can also choose versions that haven't been released yet as "Pre-releases" to test if it works with your game, as well as versions that are no longer supported and "Archived". We will use the 2022.3 Official Release. This is marked as LTS or Long-Term-Support so that game developers know they can use it for a long time. The version number may differ on the digits at the end, but it should be 2022.3.something. If a newer version that starts with something like Unity 6 shows up at the top of the list, then just search down until you find the 2022 LTS version. Click the blue "Install" button to get the install started.

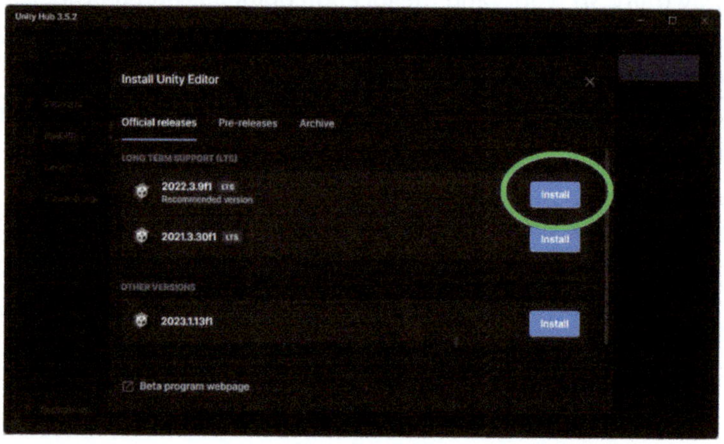

Figure 12

Now we get to the configuration options for the installation. Here is where Unity really shows its versatility. You can build for different platforms like mobile (iOS and Android), PC, MacOS, Linux, and more! Just make sure the box for "Microsoft Visual Studio Community 2022" is checked and click the blue "Continue" button at the bottom-right.

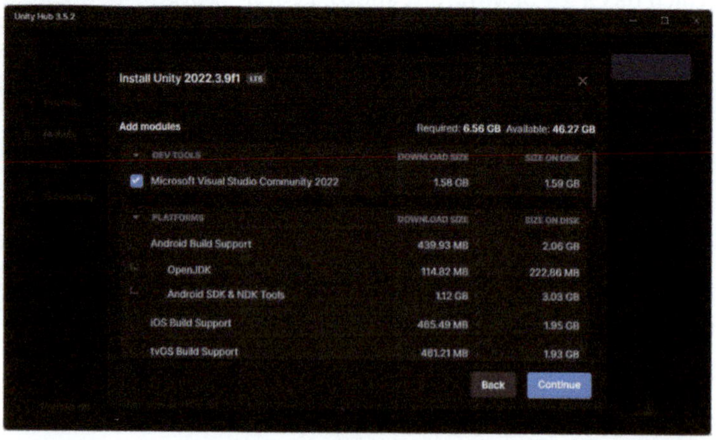

Figure 13

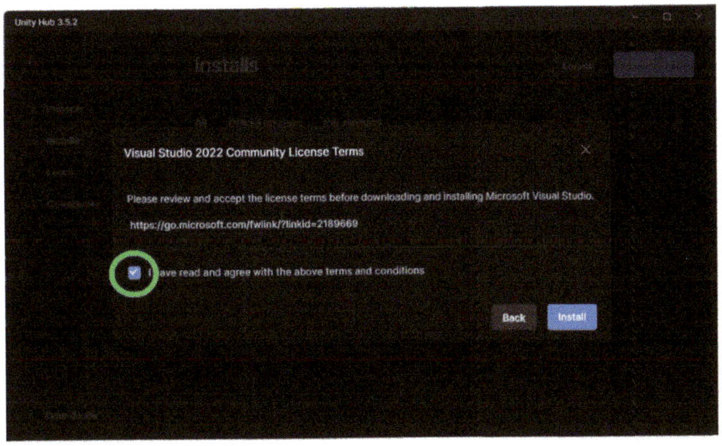

Figure 14

We've dealt with license agreements before and there's one more we need to agree to. Microsoft already develops some very good tools to edit code called "Visual Studio". Instead of re-inventing the wheel, Unity has decided to reuse what Microsoft has already done. But that means that you also need to agree to Microsoft's License to use Visual Studio. You may click the link to view the License terms and, when ready you (or your parent/guardian) may check the box "I have read and agree…". Then Click the blue "Install" button to continue.

As soon as you do, the window will disappear, and you'll see a list of active downloads. This will take a bit of time. So go grab your favorite beverage and sit back to wait. While you're waiting, this would be a good time to read my book "Exodus: God of the Slaves" or play the game "Exodus Vigil" which are companions to this tutorial. The game is based on the historical fiction novel that follows the familiar events of the Exodus from an Egyptian perspective. As you play the game, just imagine that using this tutorial YOU TOO can make something like that. Pretty cool, huh?

Figure 15

There is one little gotcha with installing Visual Studio. During installation, it will prompt you for some input. The sneaky part about it is that the pop-up may not… pop up. Periodically check your task bar for an icon that looks like what you see in the top-left of Figure 15. If you see it, then click on it and you will see the pop-up shown on the right. Click "Continue" and installation of the Visual Studio code editor will commence.

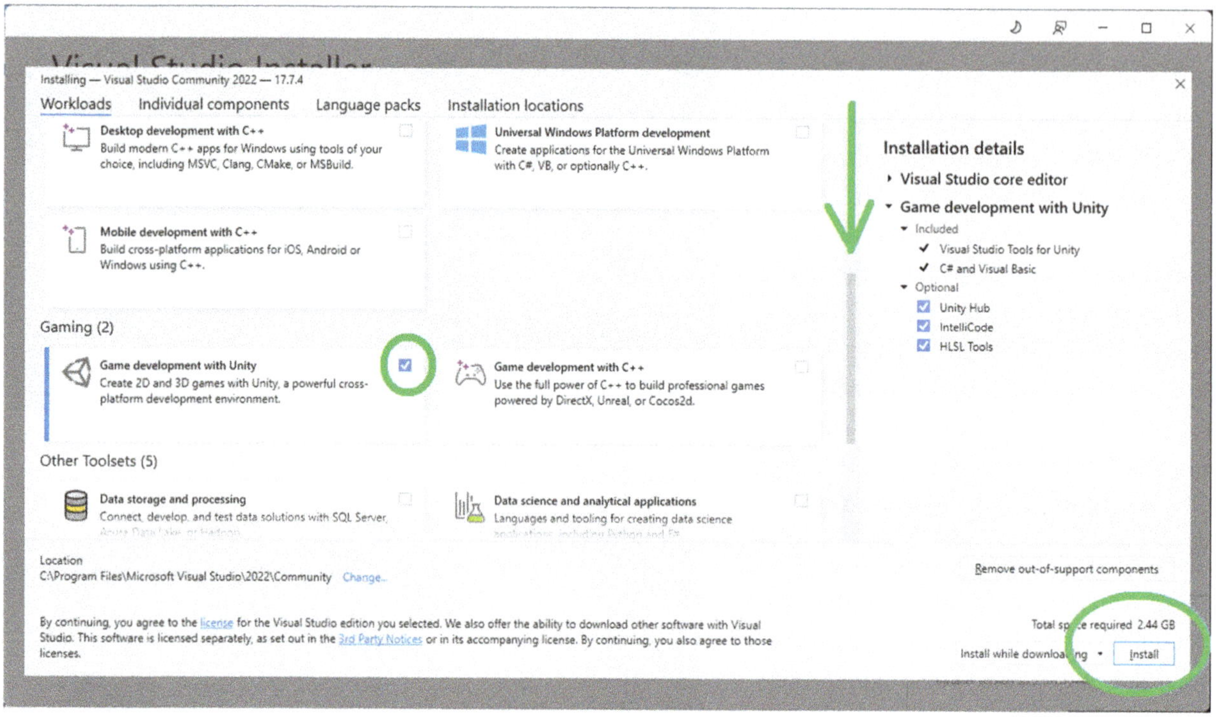

Figure 16

After a short time of downloading and installing, the screen shown in Figure 16 will pop-up to configure the Visual Studio install. Only one component needs to be added. Scroll down to the "Gaming" section and check the box for "Game development with Unity". Then click the "Install" button on the bottom-right. This will continue downloading and installing Visual Studio and the components needed to edit scripts for your Unity game projects.

When it's done installing, Visual Studio will prompt you to sign in. There are some advantages to creating an account and signing in. For purposes of this tutorial, we do not need to do that. For now, as shown in Figure 17, click the link "Skip this for now."

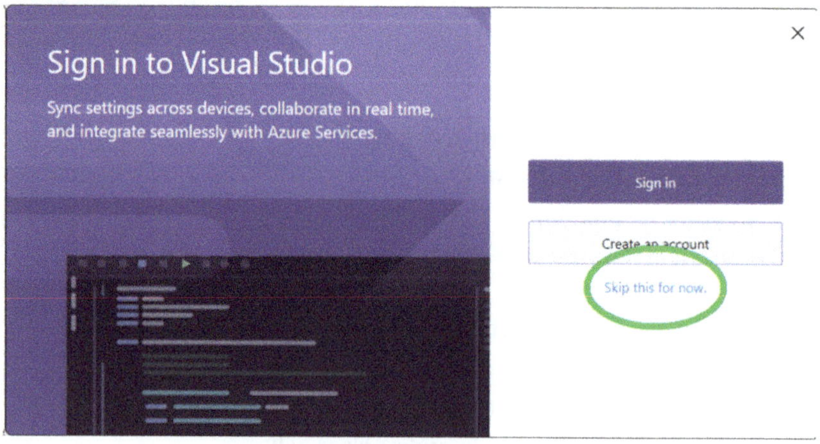

Figure 17

Next, Visual Studio wants you to personalize how you want to code as you can see in Figure 18. Since we'll be coding in C#, set the "Development settings" to "Visual C#". After that is the theme, you can choose whichever one you prefer. I like Blue. After you're done personalizing your experience click the purple button to "Start Visual Studio".

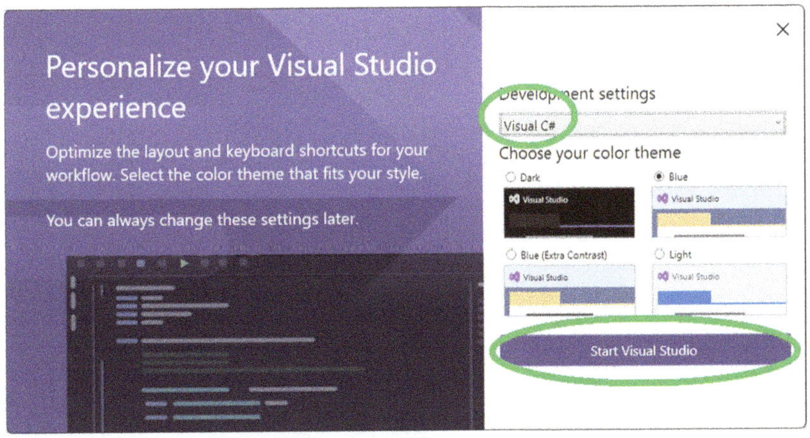

Figure 18

At this point, we're done configuring Visual Studio and you can close that window. Now go back to Unity Hub and you will see the version we installed appear in the list like in Figure 19.

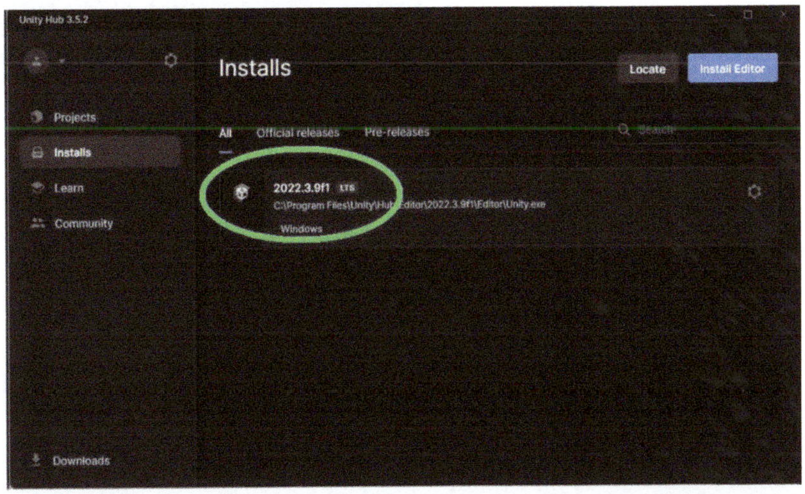

Figure 19

Now we're ready to begin. In, Figure 20 Select the "Projects" panel. It's still empty but will not be soon. Click the blue "New Project" button.

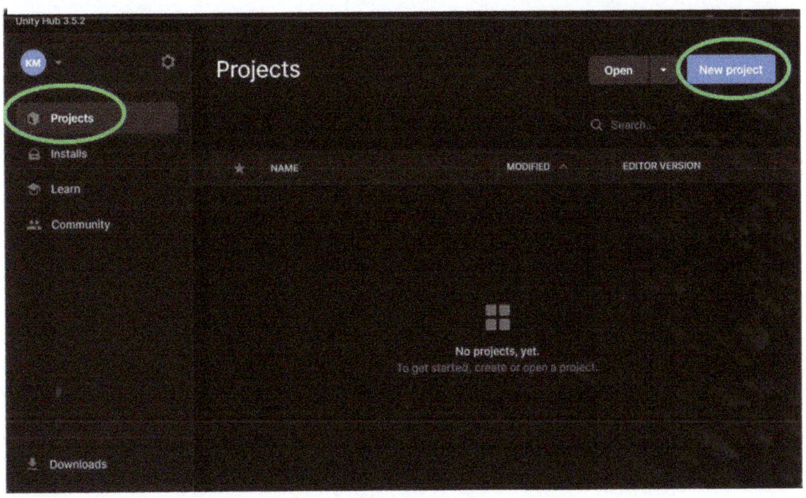

Figure 20

This takes you to the screen shown in Figure 21. The options in this screen give you power to configure what kind of project you're going to make and which version of the Unity editor Later on, if you want to create a 2D game you can select it. Changing this optimizes the project with those settings. For example, the camera will be perspective in 3D but isometric in 2D. Perspective lets things farther away from you look smaller. With isometric, the distance from you doesn't change how small it gets. For this tutorial we won't need to change any of them. You want the template set to "3D Core" as shown. Set the "Project name" to "Exodus Adventure" as circled in the bottom right of the figure. The click the blue button "Create project". When it's done loading, you will be greeted by the IDE with a gray and blue horizon as far as the eye can see.

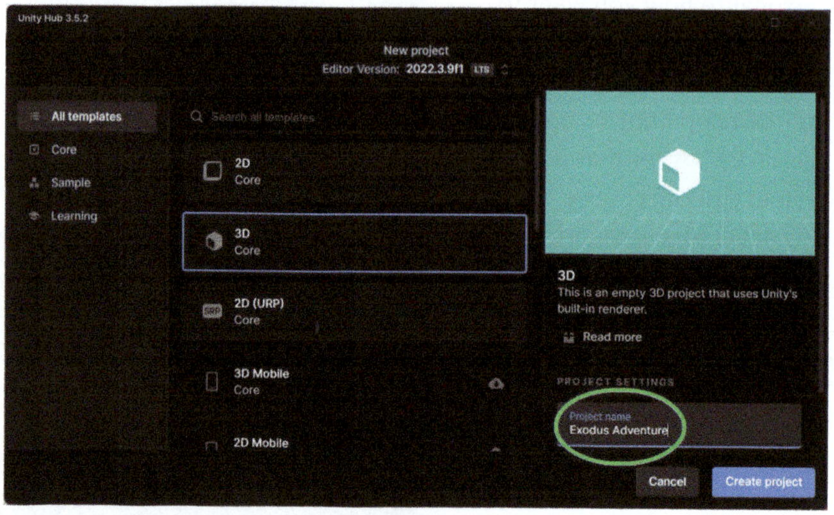

Figure 21

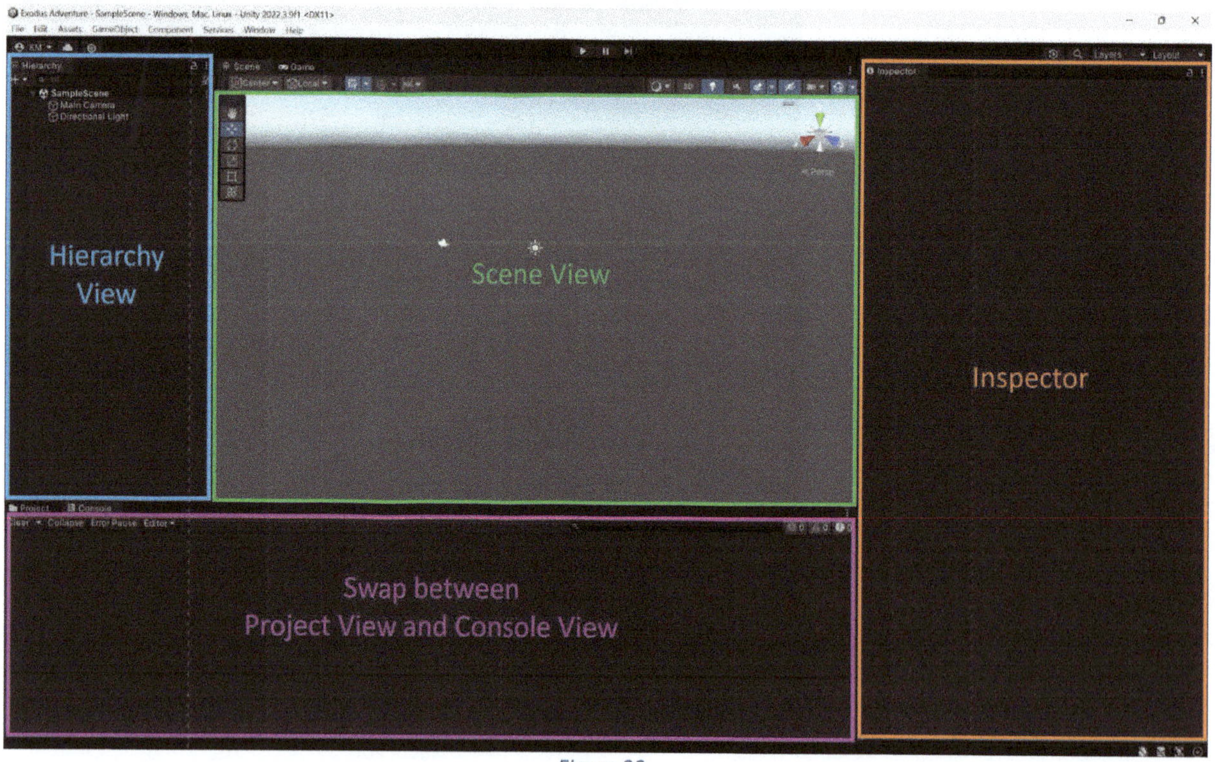

Figure 22

Integrated Development Environment (IDE)

The IDE is just a fancy way to say the program used to make the game. Now that you've installed and launched Unity, I'm going to explain What you now see. In Figure 22 on the previous page, I color-coded the different views. Green is the "Scene View" and shows you what is in your game and allows you to modify the scene.

The "Hierarchy View" is shown in blue on the left. This lists all the objects in the scene. Right now, it has a Main Camera and a Directional Light. Left-click the Main Camera, you'll see a "Camera Preview" appear in the bottom-right of the Scene View. Cameras show the player all of the cool graphics and art that's in your game.

Now, cameras are like your eyes, they need light to work. To illustrate this, go to a room with no windows. Close the door and turn off the light. What do you see? Nothing. The directional light is there so that we can see objects in our game. Click it in the Hierarchy View. It shows you what direction the light is pointing in the Scene View.

Above the camera and light is the name of the Scene. You can also see the name of the scene in the middle of the title bar. It's just "Sample scene. Very boring. Once we load the pre-generated scene from the provided assets, we'll dump this sample into the bit bucket (that's another way of saying it will be gone forever).

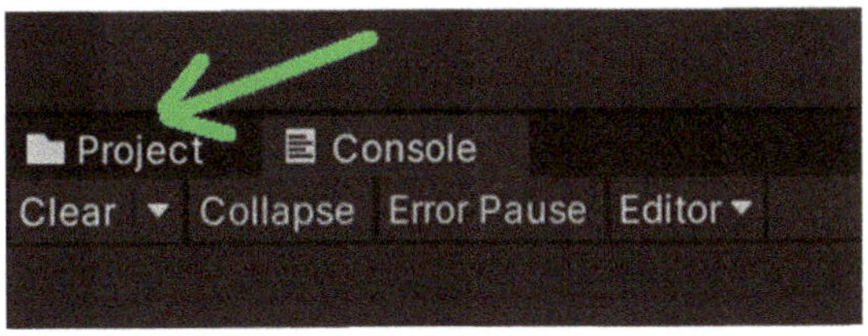

Figure 23

Below the Hierarchy View is a multi-purpose panel that is used for both the "Project View" and the "Console" Which I colored in purple. Right now it's showing you the "Console". This area will be where you find out about errors and other information in your game. Let's check out the "Project View" by clicking "Project" as shown in Figure 23. This shows all the assets in your game. Right now all you have is a folder named "Scenes" which contains this empty sample scene. We will load the pre-generated assets provided with this tutorial that will fill this out.

On the right-hand side of the screen is the "Inspector View" colored in orange. We'll spend a lot of time in the Inspector. This shows all the knobs and dials for an object we can change and mess up. These knobs and dials are organized into groups called Components. We'll talk more about these components later.

Lights... Camera... What?

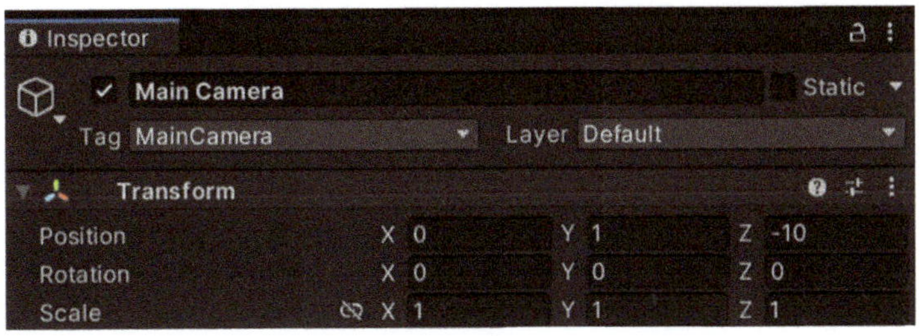

Figure 24

If you don't see the "Main Camera" in the inspector like in Figure 24, then click on it again in the "Hierarchy View". You can see it has a few different components. The first one is the Transform. This has 3 things: 1) Position of the object in 3D space, 2) Rotation of where the object is facing, and 3) Scale for how big the object is. Cameras use the position and rotation. Scale gets ignored.

It also has a Camera component with a lot more stuff. I'm not going to go over all of it here, but enough to get you an idea. The "Clear Flags" mean what gets shown when no object is in view. The default is a skybox. A skybox is just a box with images on all 6 sides where the player sits in the middle and no matter where they look, they will always see something.

Try it out in the Scene View. Hold the right-mouse button and move the mouse. This rotates the camera so you can see all around. Notice that the mouse icon changes to an eye. Here's looking at you kid.

Left click on the Directional Light in the Hierarchy View again. You can see in the Inspector that it also has a Transform. Change the X Rotation from 50 to 60. Did you see that? The sun moved at your command! You can undo it by pressing CTRL+Z. Try changing the position and you can see it moving around. Now try changing the scale. Did you notice any change? Nope. Lights only use Position and Rotation.

Left click on the Main Camera in the Hierarchy View. In the Inspector, go back to the Camera component and change the "Clear Flags" to Solid Color. Notice in the Camera Preview that the blue and gray horizon off to nowhere is gone and replaced by just solid blue. The "Background" setting adjusts what color to show. We'll use more camera settings later. Change the "Clear Flags" back to Skybox.

Creating your First Object

Now that we've learned about the camera and light, let's create an object. There are a lot of different objects to choose from but we're going to just make a cube so we can get a handle on how things work in 3D space. In the main menu select GameObject > 3D Object > Cube as shown in Figure 25.

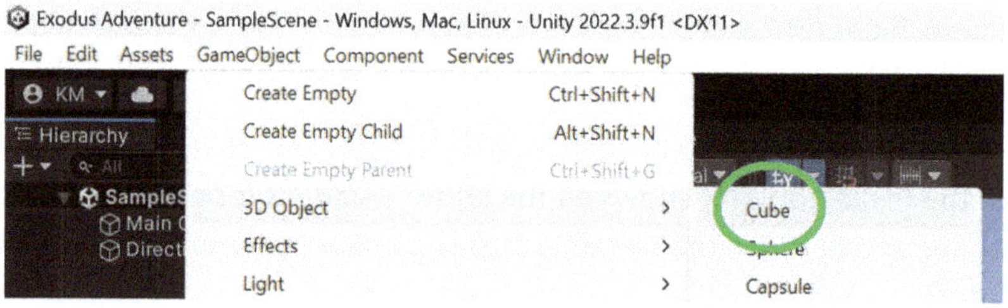

Figure 25

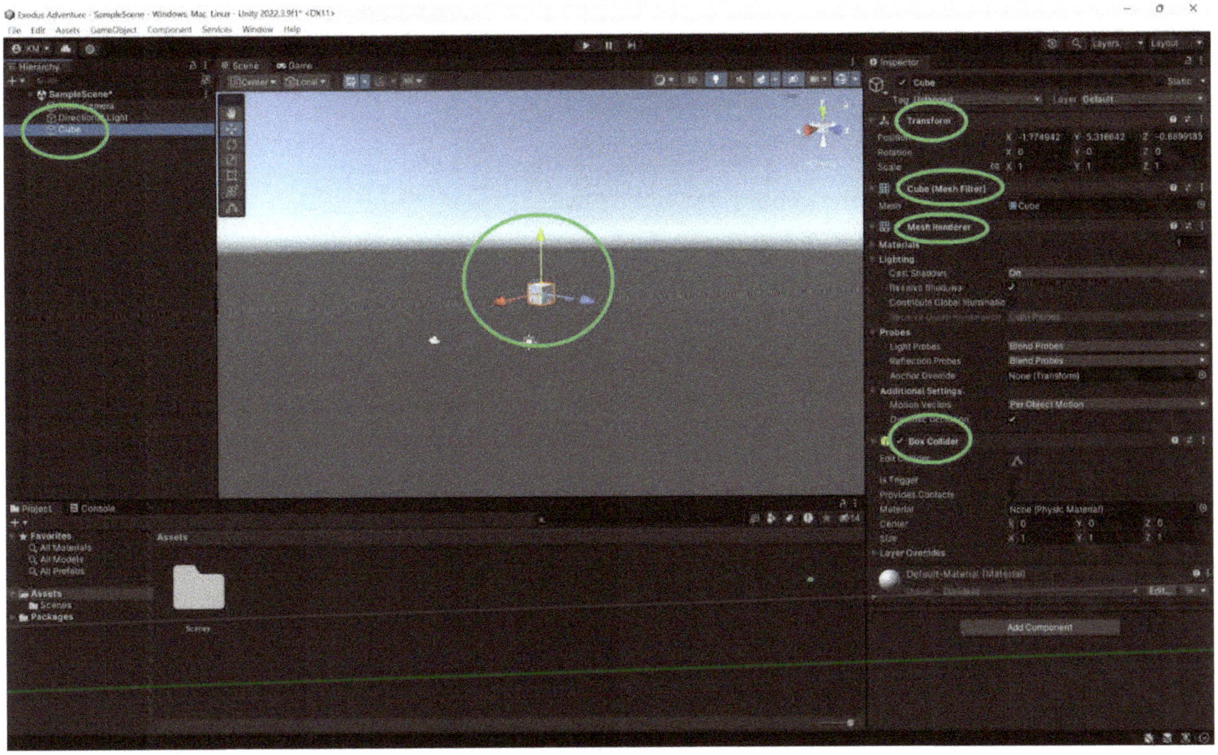

Figure 26

A white cube was created in the middle of our scene in Figure 26. You can see that "Cube" is also in the Hierarchy View. You see 3 sides of the cube and each one has a different color. This is because of the direction of the light. Left click on the "Cube" in the Hierarchy View and you can see its components in the inspector. It has a Transform, a Cube (Mesh Filter), a Mesh Renderer, and a Box Collider.

The "Cube (Mesh Filter)" tells Unity the shape of the object. The "Box Collider" is used for 3D physics. Unity will keep objects with colliders on them from passing through each other. Now that is what it's like when objects collide. The Mesh Renderer tells Unity how to display the object.

You Got to Move it!

Next, we're going to move it around. But first we need to understand how 3D space works. Take your right hand and extend your first two fingers with your thumb up to look like a gun. Whoa! Watch where you're pointing that thing. Now pay attention. If you're left-handed just use your right-hand anyway. If you're missing your right-hand then find someone with a spare and use theirs. Then move your middle finger to point sideways so each finger is pointing 90 degrees in different directions.

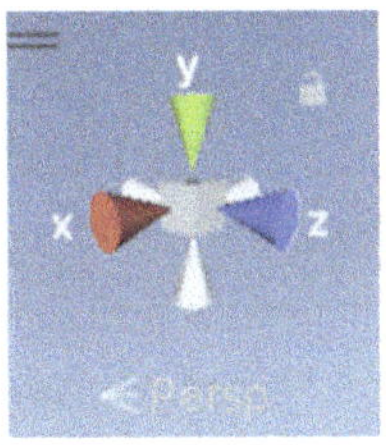

Figure 27

You can see that your hand looks like the Directional Gizmo in Figure 27. This is the same gizmo in the top-right of the Scene View. In 3D space there are 3 axes: X (red), Y (green), and Z (blue). Tap your middle finger; that is the x-axis. Going counterclockwise your thumb is the Y-axis and your pointer finger is the z-axis. At the bottom the 'Persp' label lets you know that you're in Perspective View.

Rotate the camera in Scene View by moving the mouse while hold down the right mouse button. You can see that this gizmo rotates around too. This will always tell you where the axes are no matter how the Scene View looks.

Now we're ready to mess with the cube. There are a few different things we can do with it. In Figure 28, you can see the four main ways we can change the cube. Moving, rotating, and scaling change the properties in the transform component in the inspector. In the top-left just below the main menu a toolbar with the 5 icons from Figure 28.

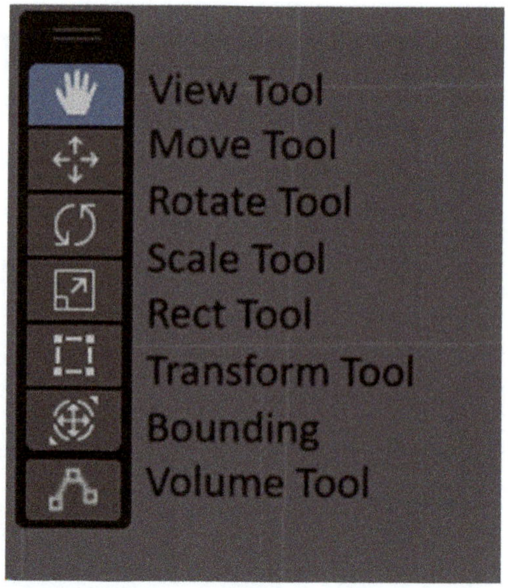

Figure 28

Press 'W' to go into move mode. When you click and hold the left mouse button on the red arrow you can move the cube along the x-axis. The blue moves it along the z-axis and the green moves it along the y-axis. Notice the values for X, Y, and Z of Position will update in the Inspector.

Quaternions track an object's rotation inside Unity, but is displayed in X, Y, and Z format. This is called Euler (pronounced oi-ler). When scripting, we'll need to translate between Quaternions and Euler. The reason Unity uses Quaternions is complicated but necessary to properly rotate objects.

Now press 'E' to go into rotate mode. If you click on the cube itself, you can rotate it around freely. Clicking on the colored lines rotates it around the respective axis. You can also see the rotation values update in the inspector.

Next press 'R' to adjust the scale of the cube. You can make the cube really big or really small. Again, values are updated in the inspector. When you press 'Y' you get into a special mode where you can adjust all three. Just click the line, box, or arrow you want to change. Be careful to watch where you click. Since they are so close together it is easy to select one you didn't intend.

Try creating some of the other 3D objects in the GameObject menu and see how you can translate, rotate, and scale them. Rotate the camera around and look at them from different sides.

From Figure 28, you can see there is also a hand button. You can click on it or press the 'Q' key. When you left click the Scene View it pans side-to-side and up-and-down. If you hold the ALT key, then the hand changes to an eye. Hold Left-click and move the mouse while ALT is held will move the Scene View around a point. Holding right-click while moving the mouse and ALT is held will zoom the camera. It may be easier to zoom by using the mouse scroll wheel, but sometimes people prefer the hard way to do something.

The last button looks like a square with a circle in it. This is the Rect Tool used for rect or rectangle transforms commonly seen on GUI objects. This feature won't be covered in this guide and when we get to the User Interface section in Chapter X then we'll change the rect transform by hand.

Another way to move the scene view is using Flythrough mode. Simply hold down the right mouse button in the Scene View and press the WASDQE keys on the keyboard. You can fly through the scene like Superman!

Click on the cube again in the Hierarchy View. Now press 'F' and you'll see the Scene View will "Focus" on the object. If you try the ALT and Left-click thing while moving the mouse you can rotate around all sides of it.

The Birds and the Bees

Now we're going to talk about how to make children with Unity. No, not like that! We're going to use the Hierarchy View. From the main menu, create a Sphere using GameObject > 3D Object > Sphere. Then use the translation tool to move it to the side of the cube. You should see something like Figure 29.

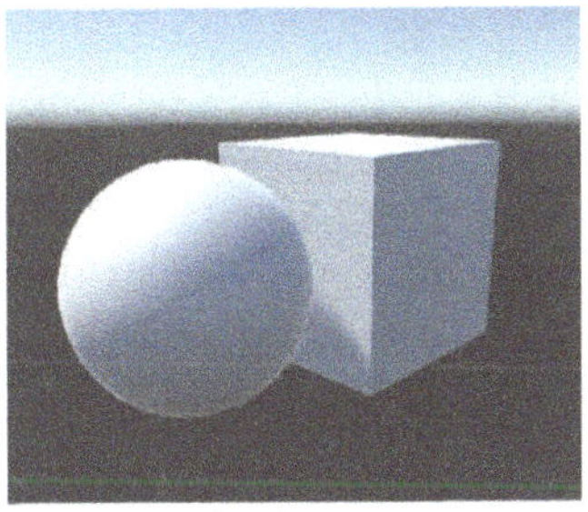

Figure 29

Now go to the Hierarchy View and click the "Sphere". Staying in the Hierarchy View, drag the "Sphere" onto the "Cube". The name "Sphere" will move to the right and the Cube will get one of those upside-down triangles as shown in Figure 30. The Sphere is now a child of the Cube. The Cube is now a Parent of the Sphere. If you change the transform of the cube the sphere changes too. You can also drag the Sphere so it is no longer a child of the Cube, but why break a family apart?

Figure 30

Any object can have children. The object can have as many children as you want. I have a son and know parenting can be tough, but don't worry the parent object can handle it. Even the child objects can have children! Another way to make children is to right-click on the object and create another 3D Object as shown in Figure 31.

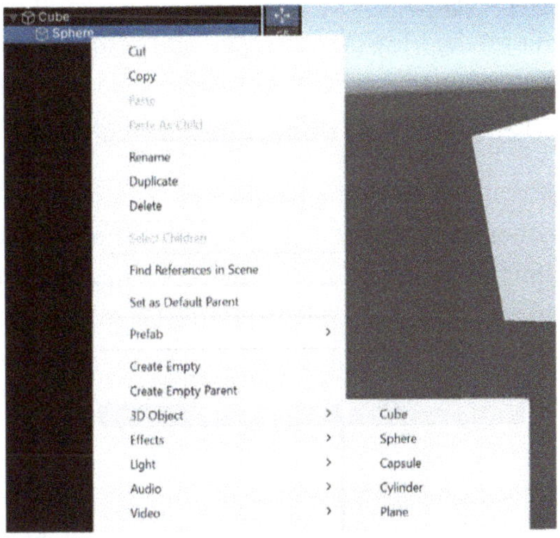

Figure 31

Having a parent/child relationship for your object are useful for treating those collections of objects as a single unit. This can make doing operations on objects (like hiding or deleting) much easier.

Prefabricated Objects

Creating objects is great! Moving, rotating, and scaling them can be fun. Making them into children and parents can feel a little weird but at least we understand why we do it. But do we have to do it every time we want to make something? Not when you have copy and paste!

Just like when your mom asks you to copy your older sister's behavior, you can press CTRL+C on your Cube and then CTRL+V to have an exact duplicate created. Do you see it? Not really. That's because what you copied is also in the exact spot as the other object. Use the Translation tool to move it and you can see it is indeed an exact copy as shown in Figure 32.

Figure 32

This can save you a lot of time. You can keep pasting more and more cubes. You can also press the Delete key and delete them. However, if you delete your last copy of the cube then it's gone for good!

Enter the prefab. The Prefab is a prefabricated object that you save in your assets so that you can use it even when it's not in the scene to copy from. Think of it as a way to copy and save something permanently so you can keep copying it later.

Drag "Cube" from the Hierarchy View onto the right pane of the Project View. You should see "Cube" now appear next to the "Scenes" folder like in Figure 33.

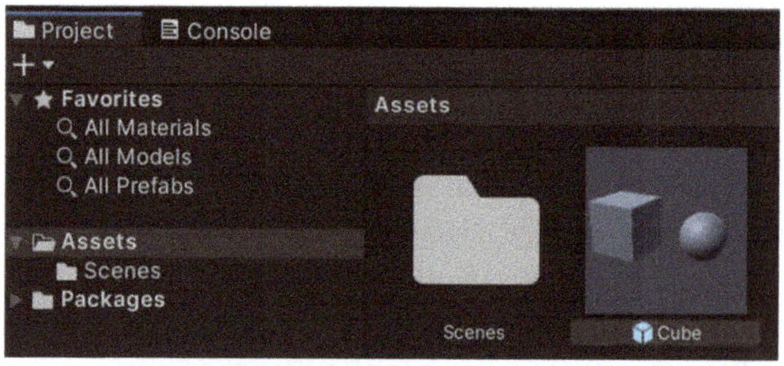

Figure 33

You will also see that the "Cube" object in the Hierarchy View has changed color from white to blue. You can use this color-coding to see which objects in your scenes are prefabs and which are not.

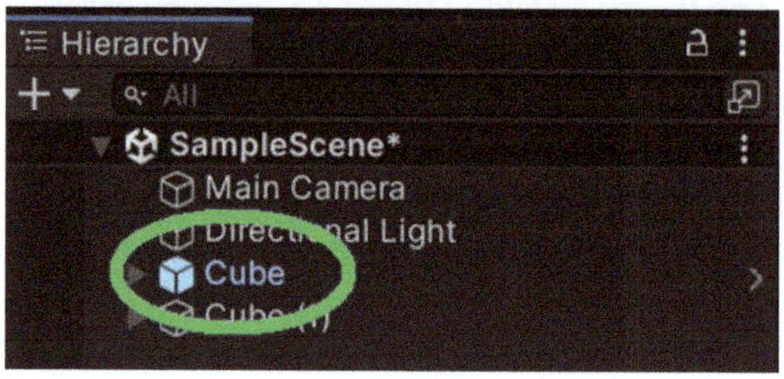

Figure 34

If you delete all the families of cubes and spheres and other objects you've created, like the evil overlord that you are, you don't have to worry about creating them again. You only need to drag it from the Project View onto the Scene View or the Hierarchy View.

Now... Action!

Now doing all this stuff is well and good, but what does this have to do with an actual game? Well, I'm glad you asked. We're going take this and put it together so you can actually make a game you can play (sort of).

Click on the Cube and then look at the main menu for "Component" and click it. Then select Physics > Rigidbody as shown in Figure 35.

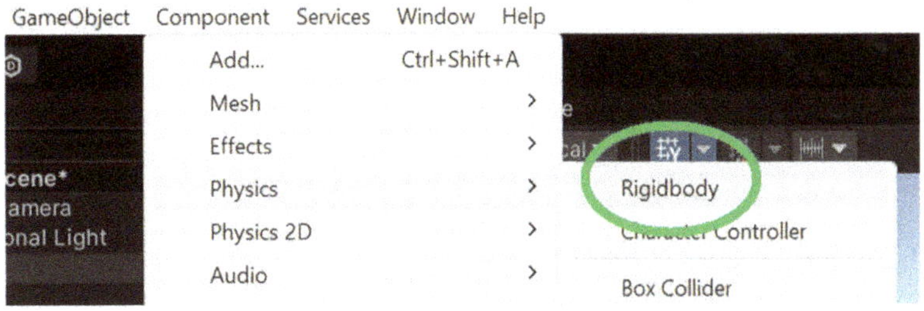

Figure 35

The Rigidbody Component tells Unity that it can apply 3D physics to this object. It has a bunch of parameters that I'll briefly describe. *Mass* is similar to weight and affects how much the object moves when other forces act on it (forces like gravity or when other objects collide into it). The bigger the *Mass* the less it is affected. *Drag* is how quickly the object slows down when no forces are acting on it. *Angular Drag* is the same thing except for rotation. Obvious *Use Gravity* is obvious. And we won't worry about the rest right now.

Bringing your attention to the Game View, it is in the same area as the Scene View tab as shown in Figure 36, you just need to click on it. On the right, the 'Maximize On Play" button if depressed will show the game in the window. If you press it then the game will run full screen.

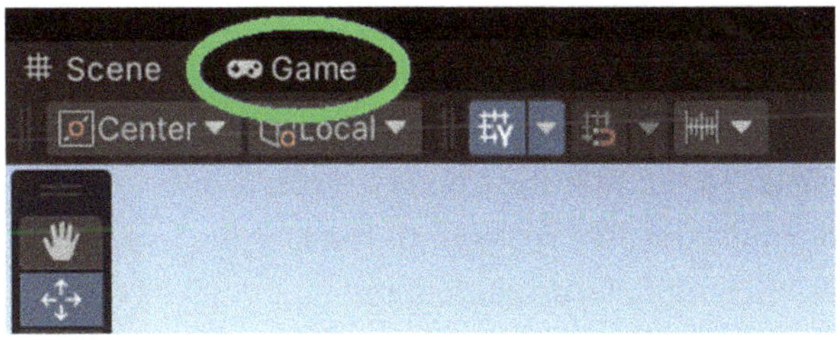

Figure 36

Now you can see through the same camera that the player will see through. If you click "Display 1" on the left you can see a long list of display numbers. This is for showing different cameras in your scene, we won't use this. Next is "Free Aspect". When you click this you get a list of display proportions. If you're targeting a specific platform (like an android phone or iPhone) then you can see what it will look like in these different perspectives. Scale zooms in toward the center. Go back to the Scene View.

Figure 37

In the top-center of the screen you can see a toolbar with 3 buttons as shown in Figure 37. The sideways triangle on the left is the play button. This will start the game, so try it out by left-clicking on it. When the game loads you'll see your objects start falling down and down and down.

When playing, left click the right-most button, the sideways triangle with a line next to it, a few times. This single-steps the game so you can see things happen in S-L-O-W M-O-T-I-O-N.

Like I said before, the Rigidbody tells Unity to apply 3D physics and now the object suffers from gravity and falls into the endless abyss below. Press the play button again to stop the game. Now we're going to try something a little different. Press play again, but before the objects fall off the screen press the middle button with the 2 vertical lines shown in Figure 37. This is the pause button and you'll notice that not only do your objects stop falling, but you've been thrust back into Scene View. It's useful to make changes that will be overwritten when the game is stopped.

Get Grounded

To keep your object from an existence of endless falling down without a satisfying splat, we're going to make some ground. Create a Plane by selecting GameObject > 3D Objects > Plane as you can see in Figure 38.

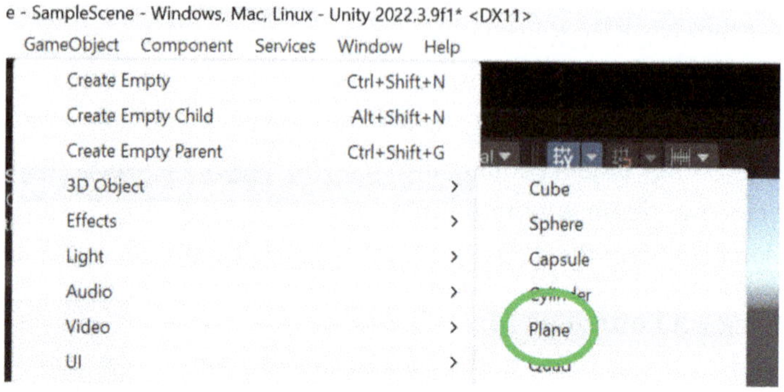

Figure 38

In the Inspector, set the plane's position to 0, 0, as shown in Figure 39. Then set the scale to 20, 1, 20. So it's easier to tell that this cube isn't just a normal cube, we're going to rename it to "Ground". To do that, in the inspector, right above the transform, there is another little section. You'll see "Plane" with a "Tag" and then a "Layer" underneath it as shown in Figure 39. Click the field that shows "Plane" and change it to "Ground". This renames the object. You can see the change reflected in the Hierarchy View as well.

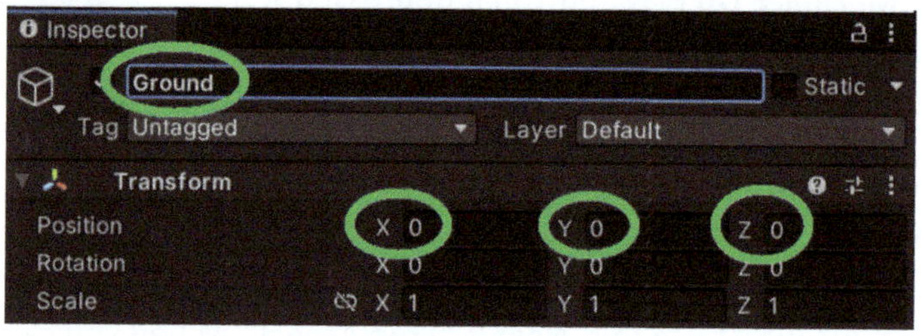

Figure 39

Click the Tag and you'll see a bunch of options pop up like "MainCamera", "Player", and others that you can see in Figure 40. If you've ever moved to a new house and had to box all your stuff up, sometimes you'll put different colored stickers or tags on the boxes so the movers will know where to put each box. Blue goes in the bathroom. Red goes in the kitchen. Green goes in the living room. And hot pink goes in your bedroom. Hot pink was all that was left so that's the color you get. The tag is like the colored sticker on the box. You can put these stickers on your objects so that we can easily and quickly tell what to do with each object. Later, we're going to use this to figure out if a player bumps into a character so we can start a conversation. On the right of tag is layer which we'll talk about it later.

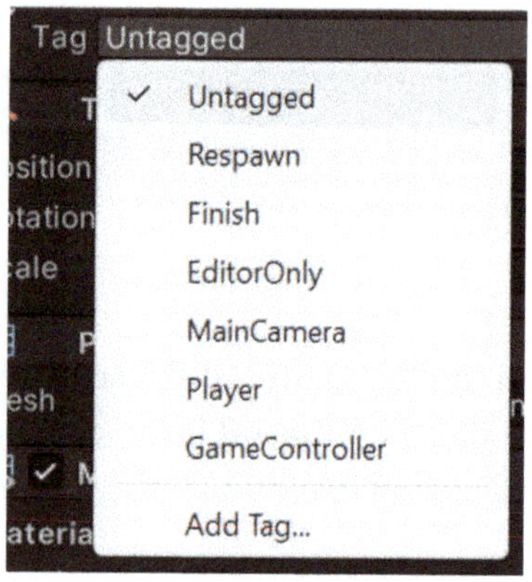

Figure 40

Now, when you glance at the Scene View, you should see something like Figure 41. Make sure the prefab is above the ground and move it up if it isn't. Otherwise, it's a long ways down. Looks great! Except everything is all dressed in white like little angels. If it weren't for the shadows cast by the light then we would have a hard time seeing the objects at all. Well, the real world is dirty and grimy, so we're going to change the color of the ground.

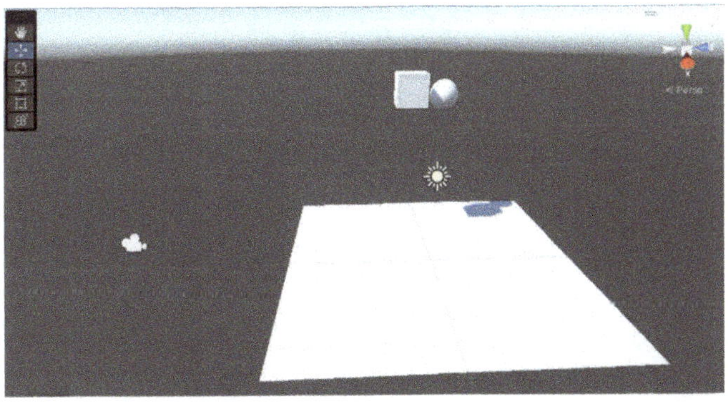

Figure 41

When you look back at the inspector, you can see the very bottom component shows "Default-Material" like in Figure 42. Unity hands each object one of these when it's created.

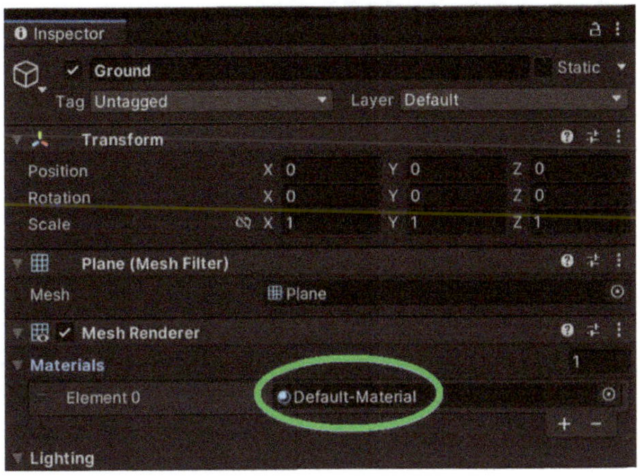

Figure 42

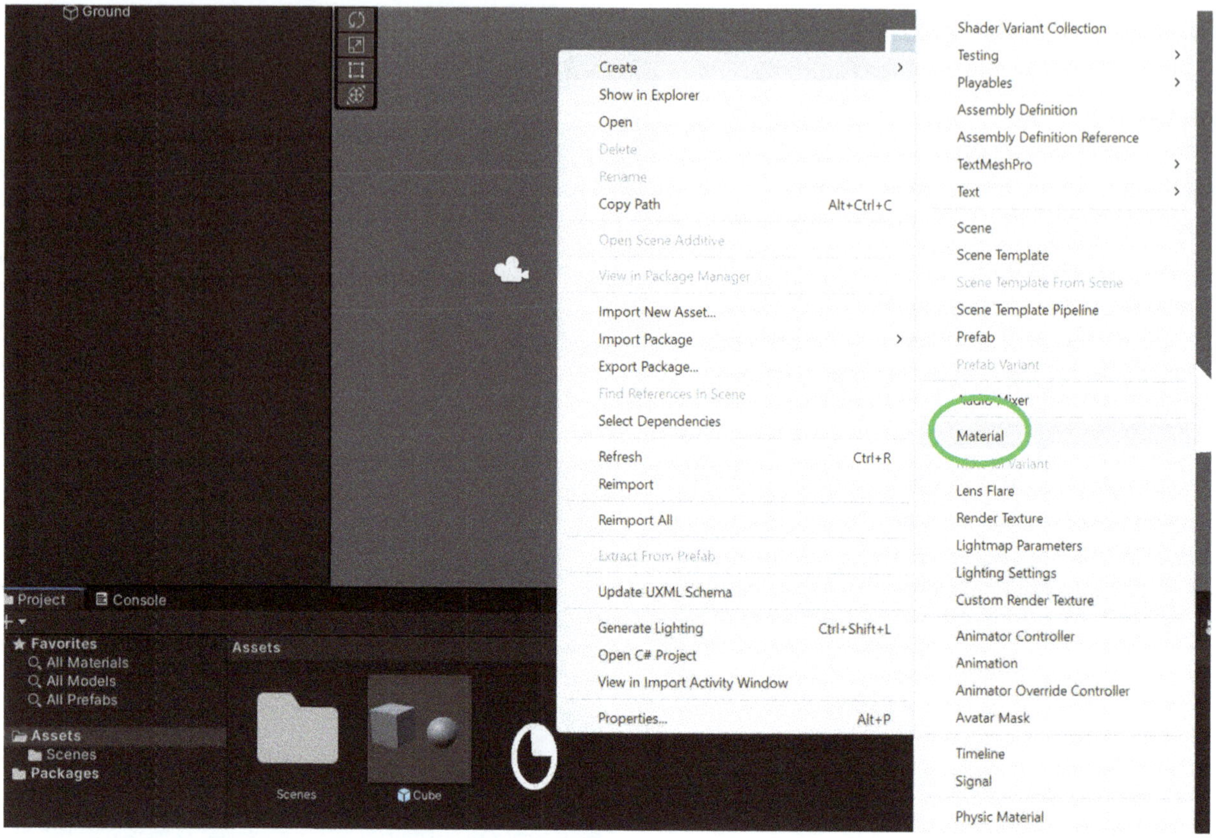

Figure 43

Go to the Project View and right-click in the open space in the Assets Panel as shown in Figure 43. Right-click, select Create > Material. Name it "Ground Material".

When you look over at the inspector, you see a bunch of new things in Figure 44. The only thing we care about is Albedo. Albedo is a fancy name which means some fancy things, but all you need to know is that it's the color of the material. Click on the white bar to the right of it and a Color Window pops up. Choose any color you want. I'm going to choose a particularly drab shade of brown. The Hexadecimal value at the bottom is the numerical representation of that color.

Then from the Project View, in the Assets Pane, where you see your material, hold the left-mouse button and drag the material into the scene view and onto the big white space that is your ground object. We could have dragged it onto the object in the Hierarchy view. Or, if the object was selected, we could have dragged it onto the inspector as well.

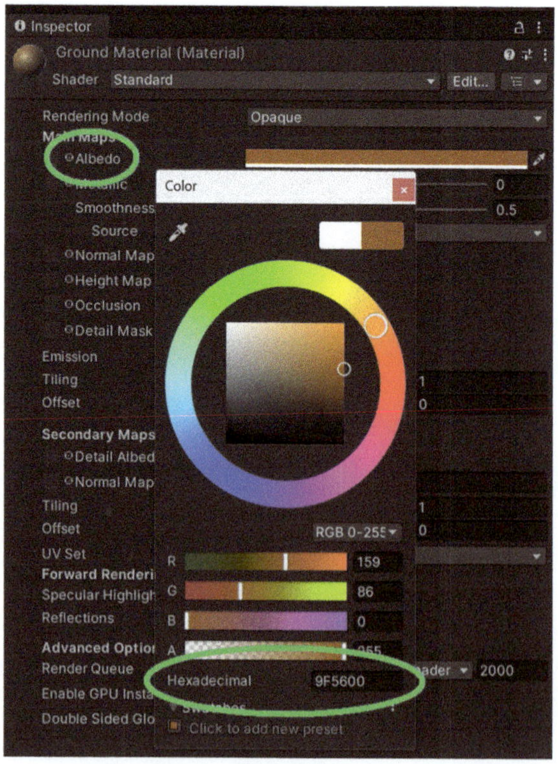

Figure 44

Click on Ground in the Hierarchy View. You'll see that the white sphere under the Mesh Renderer has changed to your chosen color. Now click the play button and you'll see something like Figure 45. Depending on you moved and parented the objects, your view may look different. The object no longer falls into infinite nothingness, but rests comfortably upon the cold hard ground. Very entertaining.

Figure 45

The Script

We've come a long way in this chapter. We started with the infinite void and have filled it with some objects using a few clicks of the mouse. The last thing we're going to do here is move around the object we've created and learned to love with the arrow keys on the keyboard. To do that, we need something called a script.

You may be familiar with the word, script. Movies use scripts. The actors read and say the lines in the script and, if the director is lucky, they don't go off-script too often. Objects use a script too. The script is in a special language called C#. Don't be afraid! We'll talk about C# more in later chapters, so just follow along and resist the urge to touch the giant man-eating plants along the edge of the path.

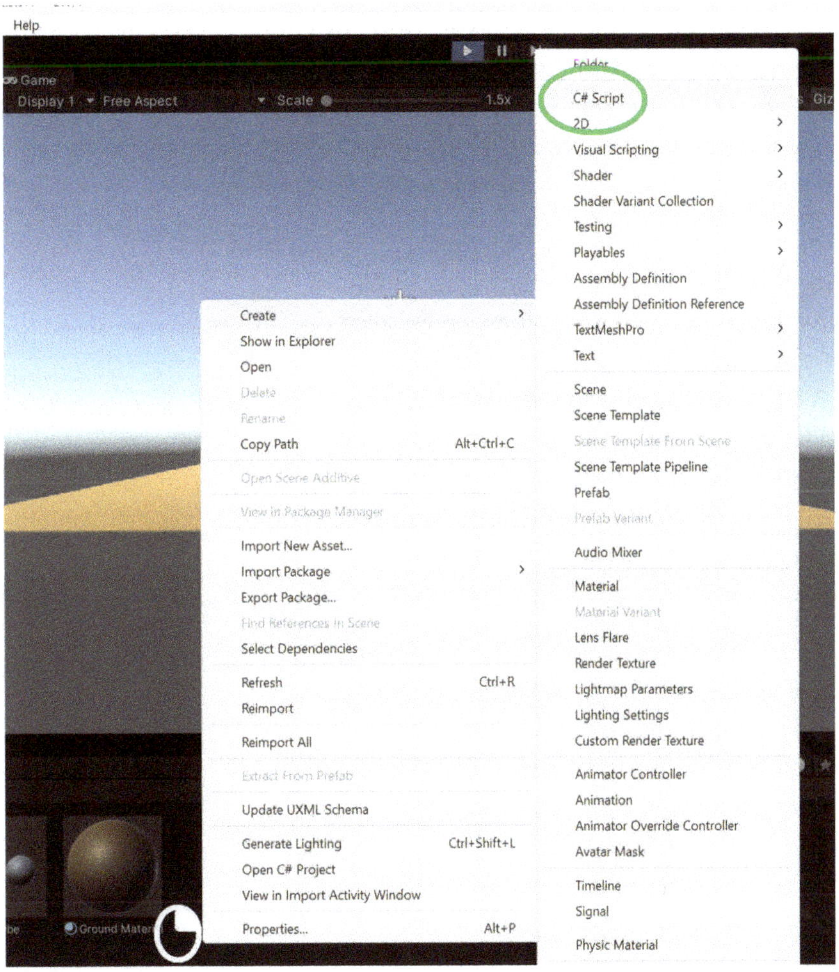

Figure 46

In the Assets Pane of the Project View, right-click and select Create > C# Script as you can see in Figure 46. Name it "PlayerController". Next, click on the "Cube" in the Hierarchy View so that its components are visible on the inspector at the right. Now drag the "PlayerController" C# script from the Assets Pane in the Project View onto the blank space at the bottom of the inspector.

You will see the "Player Controller (Script)" added below the Rigidbody but above the "Default-Material" as shown in Figure 47. The script has now been added to the object. This means that the object will follow the script when the game is played, like an actor follows the script in a movie. Except you don't have to worry about the object going off-script. It also means that the object does EXACTLY, what you tell it to. So that means if you tell it to do something that you don't mean, or you make a mistake telling it, the object won't do what you want. In the software world, this is called a ~~feature,~~ I mean, bug.

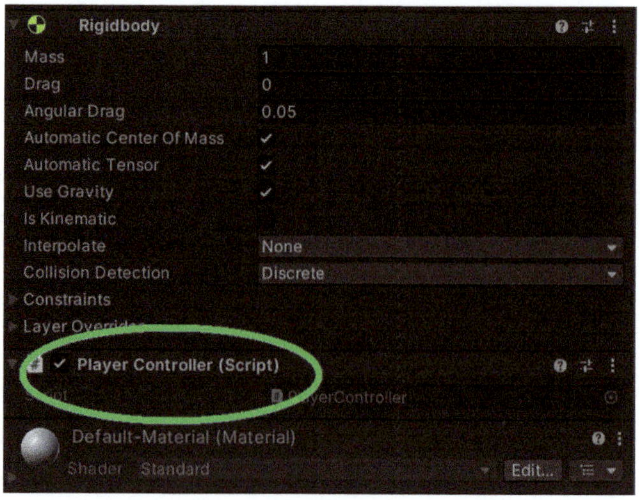

Figure 47

Now, in the Assets Pane of the Project View, double-click the Player Controller. This will bring up the script in an editor called Visual Studio. This is a tool developed by Microsoft to help people like you and I to write scripts and program code. If you want to change editors, then in the Main Menu select Edit > Preferences. In the pop-up menu select "External Tools" and in "External Script Editor" you can choose which editor you want to use. If any of the highlighting in the screenshots shown for the scripts are not in your Visual Studio window, follow the steps in Appendix A – Troubleshooting to resolve.

You may see a popup from Windows Security Alert after you open the script file that looks like Figure 48. When we installed Visual Studio, it has the option to sign-in, which requires going to the internet. Windows is checking with you to make sure it's ok to allow Visual Studio to do that. You can click "Allow access" at the bottom in case you decide you want to create an account with Visual Studio in the future.

Also, if this happens, your Visual Studio may appear without the script file you double-clicked on. This is just a one-time thing because of the security alert. Just close Visual Studio and open the script again.

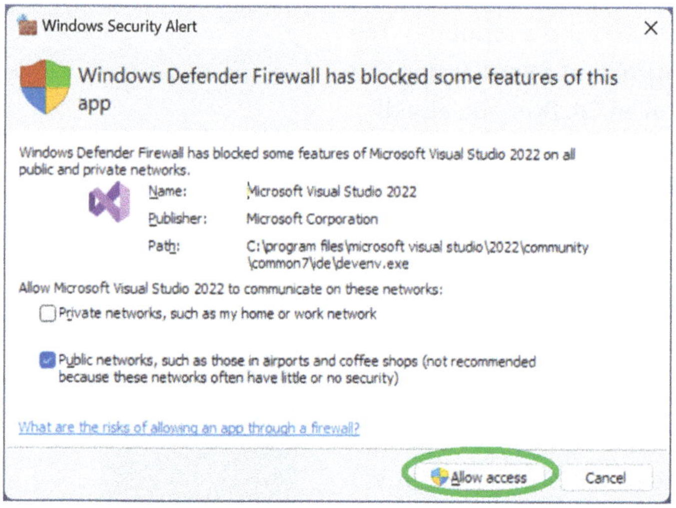

Figure 48

The script file you opened should look like Figure 49. This is how all new scripts look. Except that "PlayerController" on line 5 is the name you gave to the file. This may look like nonsense to you, but that's ok. That why it's call "code". We'll demystify all this stuff as we go.

```
1   using System.Collections;
2   using System.Collections.Generic;
3   using UnityEngine;
4
    Unity Script | 0 references
5   public class PlayerController : MonoBehaviour
6   {
7       // Start is called before the first frame update
        Unity Message | 0 references
8       void Start()
9       {
10
11      }
12
13      // Update is called once per frame
        Unity Message | 0 references
14      void Update()
15      {
16
17      }
18  }
```

Figure 49

Type these lines into your script at the exact spot you see in Figure 50. Be sure you type it in exactly, even matching lower and upper case. If you see any tooltips popup then just ignore them for now. Later chapters will explain C# and scripting in detail, but I'll explain what this is doing.

```
13  // Update is called once per frame
    Unity Message | 0 references
14  void Update()
15  {
16      Vector3 newPos = transform.position;
17      newPos.x += Input.GetAxis("Horizontal") * Time.deltaTime;
18      newPos.z += Input.GetAxis("Vertical") * Time.deltaTime;
19      transform.position = newPos;
20  }
```

Figure 50

Remember when you pushed the single-step button and saw the game progress in S-L-O-W M-O-T-I-O-N? Every time you pressed that button it followed the instructions under "Update" on line 12. These lines run from the top line under "Update" to the last, in order. Line 13 saves the current position the object is at in 3D space. Lines 14 and 15 change the position when the up, down, left, or right keys on the keyboard are pressed. And Line 16 changes the object's position with the saved position. This script will move the object around whenever you press the arrow keys on the keyboard. Press CTRL+S to save or go to File > Save so we don't lose our changes.

If you already know a little bit about scripting you may be wondering, "Why do we need to save the current position? Wouldn't it be easier to change the object's position directly?" Well, you would be right. But because of how Unity works with objects the entire position must be changed at the same time. You can't just change the 'X' or 'Z' value.

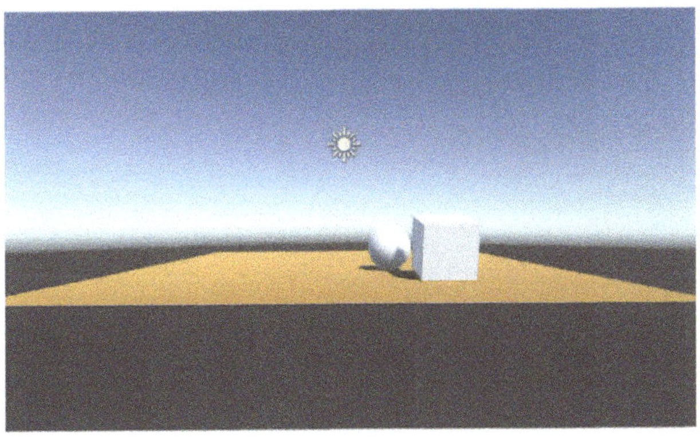

Figure 51

Now we're ready to try it out. Click the play button again. If you mistyped the script then some red text will appear at the bottom of the

Unity window. Check your script with and try again. Now when you press the arrow keys on the keyboard the object you created will move around the screen like you see in Figure 51.

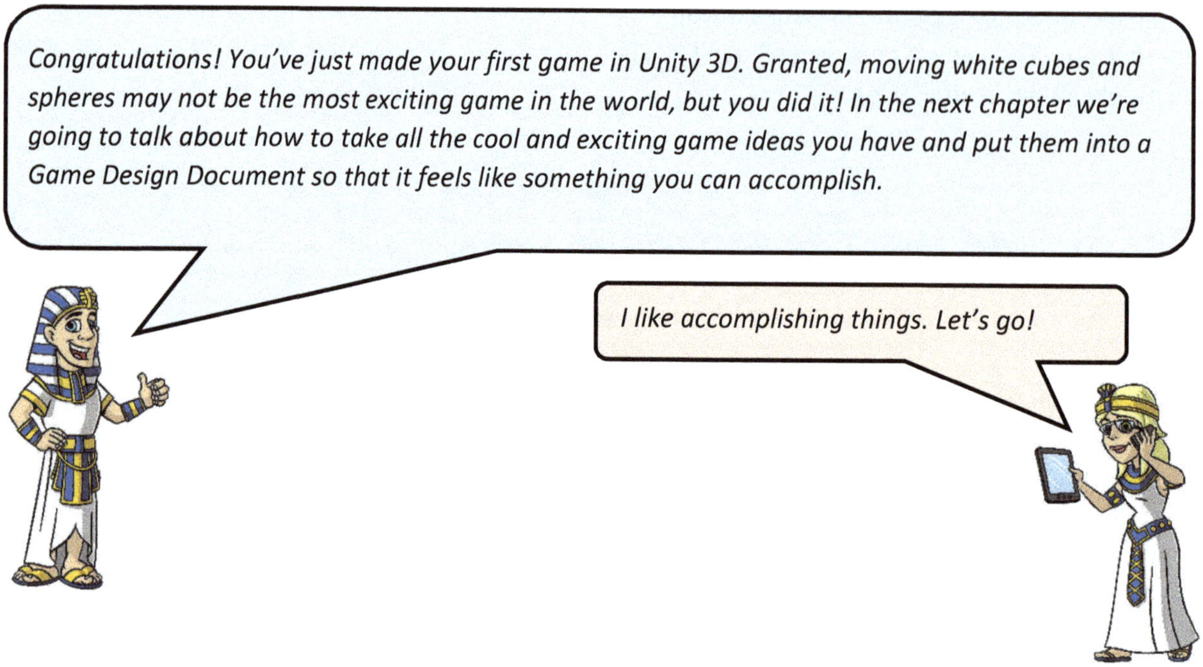

Chapter 2 – Game Design Document

You may or may not know about interior design, but we've all done some of it. Think of it like this, you just moved to a new house and need to figure out where to put stuff in your bedroom. There are certain

things you need to have like a bed and a dresser. Maybe you get to choose what kind of covers go on the bed. What about the curtains? Will there be curtains? What color and pattern are they? Why are we talking about curtains anyway?

Think of game design like designing the interior of your room. You have certain things that need to be there like graphics, input, music, and sound effects. You can customize pretty much everything and in many different ways. As the game designer, your job is to "walk into the room" take a look at it and what you have and then figure out how to arrange everything.

You may be wondering, "Why spend time on a document when that time will be better spent actually making the game?" That's a good. There are several big killers of projects that, unless dealt with, will make you feel like locusts came and ate the years you spent working on your project.

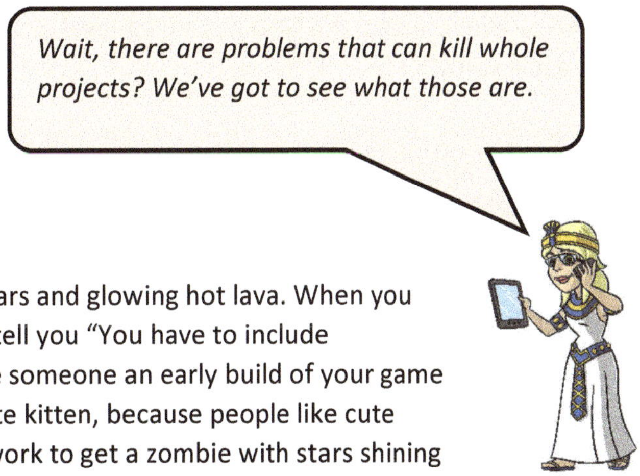

Project Killers:

- *Scope Creep:* There are a lot of cool features and widgets you can add to your game. When you work on the game, you'll think of more like shining stars and glowing hot lava. When you tell your friends about the game, they'll tell you "You have to include exploding zombies!" Then when you give someone an early build of your game to test, they'll say you need to have a cute kitten, because people like cute kittens. So, then you've spent a year of work to get a zombie with stars shining over his head walking on glowing hot lava holding a cute kitten before he explodes into tiny bits. But you're still no closer to actually finishing the game.
- *Ambiguity:* Ambiguity is a long word that means you don't really know about something. You have an idea that you want your main character to look sort of like that one game but better. Better how? Not sure, but it's going to be better! If you don't know where you're going, then you could end up anywhere.
- *Priority:* So, you decide your game to make a game. Where do you start? What do you work on first? Should you add all the features or design all the levels first? When should you start testing and polishing the game? Should you fix those bugs you found or let them go while you work on finishing the game?

The GDD will help with all these problems. It is a requirements document. A requirement is something that must be in your game, and you can't release the game without it. If something isn't in your GDD then don't add it into the game. There may be times when you feel a feature is important enough to add it into the GDD. But make sure you give the feature a lot of consideration before you do that. Making requirements as specific as possible, with as much detail as you can add, will fend off much of the ambiguity.

Having a design/requirements document is useful for any software project, not just games.

Being good at deciding priority comes by doing more and more projects. The GDD will help you look at everything you have to do so you can make the decision yourself. Remember, the goal is to finish your game. You can get a lot of motivation by getting something that is playable as quickly as you can and then adding onto it. Then, iteration by iteration, you work on the requirements in the GDD until you've added the last one. And you're done.

The Drawing Board

If you've ever flown on a plane and sat at the window seat, then you know you can see a lot from high up in the sky. You can see a bunch of houses over here, shopping areas over there, and then maybe some farmland as you fly over the countryside. This is a high-level view of the area. In addition to requirements, the GDD has a high-level picture of your game. Below is a list of things included in a GDD.

- Overview
- Platform(s)
- Target Market
- Game Pillars
- Gameplay
- Graphics
- User Interface
- Story
- Music
- Sound Effects

You can customize the GDD to meet your needs, adding and changing sections as you think is best. Since the GDD has requirements and high-level ideas it usually isn't the best place to have code.

The overview is a summary of your game. It should be between 1-3 paragraphs. You can think of it this way. You're in an elevator with the CEO of a big game company and he asks you to tell him about your game. You only have the time it takes for the elevator to go from the first floor to the top floor to tell him how cool your game is. You should tell him how the game works and why it will be fun for the player. Focus on what the player will do in the game and how the player feels in the game.

The Platform refers to PC, consoles like Xbox or PlayStation, Android, iPhone, etc. Unity can build games for almost any platform. See this link for the current supported platforms: https://unity3d.com/unity/multiplatform. While you can build for all these platforms using Unity, starting out you probably want to choose 1 of them and focus on that. Different platforms have different characteristics. Screen size is an obvious difference. You will need to make sure your user interface is visible and readable on every platform you support. So, if you just start off with one platform it makes ensuring your game looks good on that platform much easier. I recommend adding additional platforms after you have more experience under your belt.

If you go to a firing range or an archery range, you'll see that at the end of the range is a sheet of paper or cardboard with alternating white and red circles inside each other. This is the target. Your goal is to fire and hit as close to the middle as possible. When making games, you need to think about what kind of people your players are. People who play PC adventure games usually care a lot about graphic quality and storyline while people who play matching puzzle games on their phone like to feel the accomplishment of solving the puzzles. Considering the genre of your game try to think about what the characteristics are of the people who will play your game and things they care about. This will help when determining the priority of what things to work on.

Large buildings use giant sturdy metal beams to hold the next story or roof up. In ancient times, these pillars were often made of stone or bricks. If these pillars break, then the building comes crashing down. The same can happen in your game without pillars. These are wide and sweeping themes that guide your every design decision.

Put all the different things the player can do or that happen to the player in the gameplay section. Sometimes it can be useful to break this section up into sections about each feature so you can put as much detail as you can.

You've heard "A picture is worth a thousand words" but we're going to try and shoot for something a little more effective for the graphics section. Here is where you specify if the graphics will be 3D models or 2D hand-drawn or some mix in-between. Will it be realistic or cartoony? Try and think of a theme all the graphics will follow. Having high quality graphics is great, but it's better to have graphics that fit together.

Take some time to describe how the player will interact with the game. Talk about the menus or dialogue boxes and how they pop up and go away. Will there be an options menu? What options can the player set?

The story section doesn't have to be an entire book describing the entire story of your game. That should be in a separate document if you want to write it all down. This should be a high-level outline (airplane view) of the story.

Consider the genre, platform, and characteristics of the player when thinking about the music. What kind of music does this group of people like? Also talk about all the different parts of the game that need music (i.e. Title screen, playing through levels, victory screen, defeat screen) and describe what you want the music to sound like and how the music should make the player feel.

Sound effects are similar to music. You may have footsteps for walking and then a jump sound just to name a couple. List as many as you can. Also, describe how you want them to sound. Are you going for funny or serious? Will it be recorded effects or beeps and boops?

Exodus Adventure GDD

You may find it helpful to have both the book and the GDD open for you to look at, at the same time.

We've got a lot of work ahead of us for *The Exodus Adventure* game. But fear not! I've already got you covered by writing the GDD for you. The rest of this chapter will go over it.

You will find *The Exodus Adventure* GDD in Appendix A. Browse down to the Table of Contents. You'll see some of the sections are in the list of sections I wrote about earlier and some different ones. I took a lot of the features that would be in the gameplay section and gave them their own sections. Instead of a story section, since the game will be quest-based, I have a Quests section where you can read the high-level outline of the story.

We'll start with the Overview section. Go ahead and read it to yourself now. Pretend you are in that elevator with the CEO and you're giving him this pitch, so he'll want to fund your game. Take your time, I'll wait.

Done yet? Good. So, it may not be the best elevator pitch, but it does give you a good idea of what the game is all about. It talks about all the major parts, tries to make the game sound fun and exciting, and says why the player will want to keep playing.

The target market describes who the game is designed for and why they will want to play it, as well as their expectations. Genre expectations should be here too. The target platform also includes player expectations of for that platform. It is important to consider the expectations of your players. If you don't include an important feature, they expect then it can easily translate into lots of negative feedback about your game.

I've also included a list of the 3rd party packages required for making this game. You probably won't need this section in your game. This is more for your [the reader's] benefit so you can keep track of all the assets provided by this tutorial.

The Exodus Adventure has 3 pillars that everything in the game is built around. Being targeted to Christians it is important that the game be Bible-based. The storytelling should not only tell the story of the Exodus but also immerse the player in the culture with the people. All the puzzles and gameplay should be challenging to the player and fun. Typically, you start easy and get harder as the player learns how to play. All of the features should be looked at through these 3 things, so the player has a feeling of unity.

Plotting Against You

For me, the story of a game or movie (or piece of art in general) can be the most important thing about it. If it doesn't have good characters or plot, then I get bored. Different people focus on different things like graphics or gameplay. But a lot of people are like me. That doesn't mean people like don't care about graphics or gameplay, we do. It just means story is the primary thing we look for.

When working on the story, it is important to figure out how you want the story to function in the game. There are typically three primary focus areas: 1) Plot, 2) Characters, and 3) World. It's easy to say, "well, we want all three to be great!" But that is much harder in practice than you think. Especially for your first game, just choose one and let the others point back to that.

If you're not sure which you want to focus on then here are some questions to ask yourself to help: "Do I have a cool story to tell with lots of twists and turns?", "Do I have a cool character in mind and want the player to feel how cool the character is?", and "Have I been thinking a lot about the world, places, and history of the area and just want the player to have fun in there?" Odds are, once you think about it, you'll find yourself gravitating to one of them.

For our game, the story follows the events in the Bible from the book of Exodus from chapters two through seven (Exodus 2-7).

Game Loops

I like riding on roller coasters. My son does too. I remember the first time taking him on a big ride. He was scared at first. But he had a great time and wanted to ride it over and over and over and over and over again.

The game loop is kind of like a short roller coaster ride. For example, with FPS games you look at the screen and decide what you want to shoot. That is the shortest loop. The player does that most often. Then they may think about dodging incoming projectiles. Then they may think about where they need to move on the map. But the core game loop is finding something to shoot.

It is very important to identify what the core game loop is in your game. If your core game loop isn't fun, then players won't think your game is fun. That is why all the successful FPS games have really cool-looking weapons and great firing sound effects, those make the experience of looking at the screen and firing at something more fun.

When determining your gameplay, think about the game loops. For *The Exodus Adventure* game, we have several. The core game loop is looking at the screen and finding an actor to click on to talk to. That is why I begin by talking about interacting with the actors. To make this core game loop more fun the player is given some different rewards.

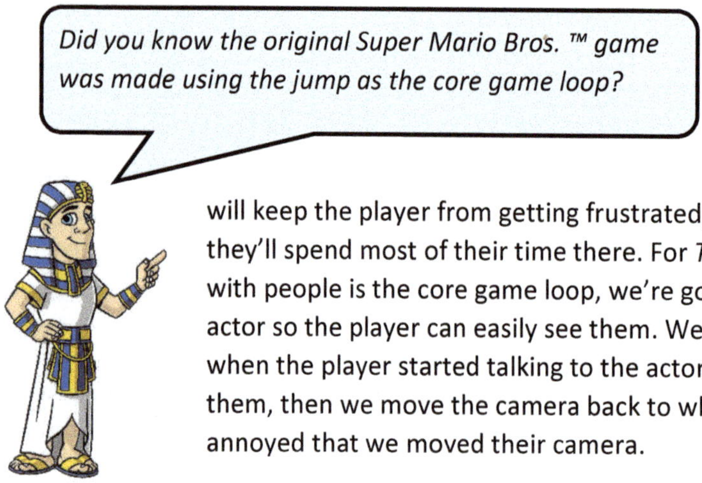

It is also important to note things that will keep the player from getting frustrated, especially in the core game loop since they'll spend most of their time there. For *The Exodus Adventure*, since interacting with people is the core game loop, we're going to show Moses together with the actor so the player can easily see them. We'll move the camera from where it was when the player started talking to the actor to another location showing both of them, then we move the camera back to where it was. This way user doesn't get annoyed that we moved their camera.

I'm not a Doctor, but I play one on TV

When we think of actors in movies and on TV, we normally think about all people that you see moving about, talking to, and interacting with each other. But anything can be an actor, even an inanimate object. In fact, we have a number of inanimate object actors in *The Exodus Adventure* game. Why? Because they aren't paid as much as models of people. But the player will be able to interact with them just the same.

You'll also notice that Moses has an identical twin. His twin is like his stunt double for cut scenes. We'll talk more about cut scenes later in Chapter 8. The Moses the player controls just plain behaves differently than how we need him to behave in cut scenes. For cut scenes, we need everything to be controlled and have the flexibility to move around actors based on what we think looks good. It also mentions animators, which you may be wondering about. I'll talk about it in the next section.

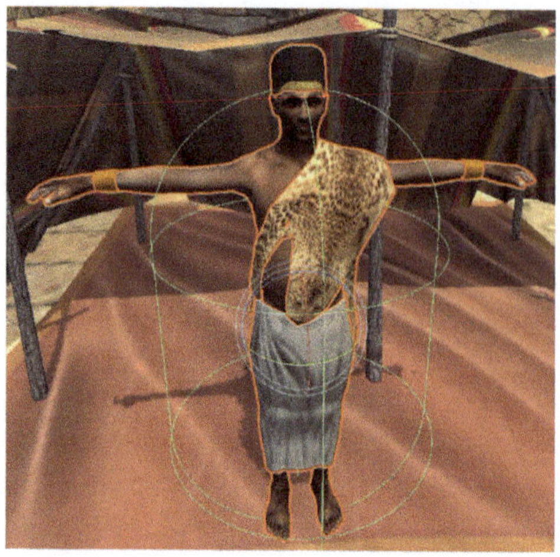

Next in the GDD, you'll read a complete list of the character and object actors needed for the game. Making this list is very important in planning for the graphics for the game. Every actor will need some kind of graphical representation. When you read through, you'll see how each of the actors maps to a graphical representation.

One question you may have thought of is "How much can I reuse graphics?" It's a difficult question to answer and the best answer may change from genre to genre and from time to time. Many games use the same basic graphic (2D or 3D) and recolor it to make it look different. You'll notice some model reuse in the character actor list of the GDD. For this kind of game there is a careful balance for reuse. You don't want the player to see the same character model every time they turn around. But at the same time, a model for each person can get time-consuming or expensive to make.

Cut Scenes and Cinematics

Some quick definitions here. A cut scene just refers to any sequence that is not interactive. That means that while a cut scene is going on the player won't be doing anything except maybe clicking to progress dialogue. A cinematic is basically the same thing. For purposes of our game, cinematics will be just like cut scenes only longer.

Many games use pre-rendered videos for their cinematic cut scenes. That means they had a separate very high-powered computer do all the hard work and calculations as actors moved around the scene for every frame. Then they put all those together, slap a music track on it, maybe some voice acting and then they have a very nice little movie.

But we're not going to do that. We're going to render all our cut scenes real-time. That means the computer the player is playing on will play the cut scene. We need to determine what actors we will use and how they will move. To do that, I'll show you how to write a cut scene engine from scratch in chapter 8.

So I started off by saying that cut scenes are not interactive but now I'm going to tell you that we'll be implementing some interaction in our cut scenes. Now, before you start sending off angry tweets and posts, let me explain myself.

This was a design decision after looking hard at how the implementation worked. At first, I decided there would be dialogue separate from cut scenes. After all, cut scenes are supposed to be non-interactive while dialogue requires interaction. For example, with dialogue the player can be given choices about how to respond to an actor's question.

However, there are things that I wanted to do in both cut scenes and dialogue. For instance, moving the camera around, having additional actors created and moving around, and having the actors perform animations. For this reason, I decided to combine how I implemented cut scenes and dialogue so that I wouldn't have to do the work twice.

Next, I describe the two cinematics the game will have. The opening cinematic helps get the player more interested in the game while the ending cinematic provides closure on the story and rewards the player for completing the game. Notice how the outlines of the cinematics are written like shots in a movie.

You can also read through the planned cut scenes. The descriptions are less detailed than the cinematics. You can put as much detail as you have time for, but I decided to spend more time adding specifics to the cinematics because I saw them as more important.

Taking Inventory

As a puzzle adventure game, we'd be remiss if we didn't have some kind of inventory management system. You can read about the requirements of the inventory management system, but they're pretty standard if you've played the genre before.

There are a couple things I want to highlight. First, notice that it says the items will have 2D icons that will be 256x256 (the 'x' reads 'by') 2D art. This means the image for the items presented to the player will be 256 pixels high and 256 pixels long. It is important to specify how big the icons are and other information like style or theme. That way you can give this to the artist (if you're not drawing the art yourself) who will draw something more in-line with what you want. Alternatively, if you want to buy the art this can be your guide when looking through assets.

I also included the full list of items with details on how what images will be used as the icon like we did for the 3D models. Again, having a full list is important for planning. If you need to buy the models and budget is a problem then having a full list will help you determine what you can afford.

Maps and Menus

The map is feature of the game to help keep the player from getting stuck or annoyed. The player can look at the map, see where they are and then where they need to go and get a better idea of how to get there. If they don't know where to go or how to get there then they'll get frustrated.

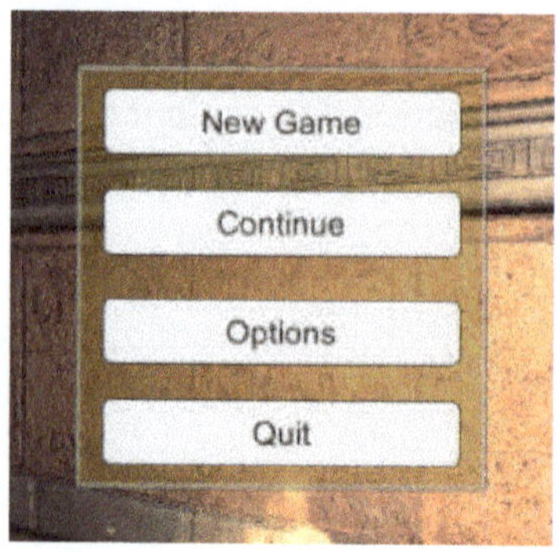

Now, the way I've talked about player frustration so far is that it's always a bad thing. However, especially as a puzzle game, we will want the player to be frustrated sometimes. The question is, what is causing the player to get frustrated. We want the player to get frustrated on the puzzles, not the other parts of the game.

The menu and other user interface is similar. You don't want to frustrate the player by having the interface get in the way of what the player wants to do. Interface design is another one of those "more of an art than a science" kind of things and programmers are notoriously bad at designing user interfaces. That's why command-based applications like Linux are popular among hard-core programmers.

The map for the player is kind of like the GDD for game developers. They help us know where to go.

Unless you've got a good eye for user design then you need to figure it out the hard way like me. Trial and error. That means you do your best the first time and then give it some people to try out. Watch them closely. Look at their facial expressions and wait for that dirty look. That's your cue to see what they're trying to do in the game. This is the part that you need to improve. Jot it down and be sure to ask the person about it later. A lot of times they'll have some different ideas you hadn't considered.

Quests and the journal is another feature to help keep the player from getting frustrated. The map helps the player get to where they want to go. But talking with the actors will tell the player where that is. This isn't a memory game, it's a puzzle game. So don't require them to remember.

Dream the Impossible Dream

Whether you want to fight the unbeatable foe without question or pause, or run where the brave dare not go, you need something to help you march into hell for a heavenly cause. But don't run off chasing windmills just yet because we're going to talk about quests and the journal.

You'll see there is quite a lot of detail describing how the journal works. Again, we want the player frustration to be when solving problems, not trying to figure out what the objective is. Remember, the more detail you add to something is how important you think it is. I thought that it was very important to keep the player from getting frustrated here.

Like the list of items and actors, I include a full list of quests. The Quests section acts as the story section in the list I gave earlier. When you read through the quests, you'll see I put the information about each quest in 5 categories: Actors, Location, Items, Description, and Details. State what the actors, location, and items associated with this quest will help you developing the quests in the game. The description is intended to be the actual text shown to the player about the quest. The details give all the information about the quest and story behind it so you can go develop.

You will see the quest section is quite long. The story of the game follows Moses as he returns to Egypt to convince Pharaoh to let the Israelites go so, they can start Exodusing (is that a word? Oh well, I'm going to go with it!) Egypt. Don't worry, you won't be required to implement all the quests to get through this tutorial. I'll take you through 2 of them: 1) The Meeting of Moses and Aaron and 2) Signs for the Israelites. Once you're done with the tutorial you have the choice of coming back to implement the rest of the quests on your own. You can also look at the example game to see how I implemented them.

In addition to the main quest, I added a couple lines of side quests for Egyptian and Hebrew culture. The main quest line is very important, but side quests give your game more depth. It also gives the player more choices for what to do. The little things in your game, often the things that go unnoticed, are usually the things that really immerse the player.

Finally, we get to the meat of the game, the puzzle section. The table here is a numbered list of all the puzzles with a comprehensive description. I gave each puzzle a number so they can be easily differentiated in the quests. If you've read them through, you probably noticed how I referred to puzzle numbers.

A good exercise to do would be to think about how the puzzle would look like in your mind and draw it on paper or using a paint program. This is very helpful to keep you from getting stuck when making puzzles.

As you read through the puzzles, you'll see I try to give as much information about the puzzle itself and how it is solved. I bring in actors, locations, and items only as they relate to the puzzle. Staying focused on the actual puzzle helped me to spend my time on the right things and finish the GDD quicker. There is still a balancing act for what details to include and what not to include. For example, in puzzle 4 I describe a jumping puzzle. I don't say exactly where the things are that the player jumps on but describe how the puzzle is to be built.

Asset Lists

We've already talked a bit about assets (and tried very hard not to crack the obvious jokes about them). Now, I've included a list of the assets here in the GDD, but I don't have it in the list of GDD sections above. I find it useful, especially for projects with a large amount of assets, to compile a list so I can see what I've got. This helps when doing level design and choosing what to put where. I'll talk about level design later in chapter 11, but having these lists lets you close your eyes and really visualize what you want the level to look like.

You may also find it helpful to list out all your assets for planning purposes already mentioned. If a 3D artist charges $X for a model and you have $Y budget for this game (which also includes 2D art, music, etc) then you have a good idea how many 3D models you can afford. But by no means do you have to include asset lists into your GDD.

The lists I include are 3D art, 2D art, animation, music, and sound effects. Feel free to skim through them now. But we'll be looking at them later on in the level design chapter.

Loading the Assets

Now you may be wondering why we're 2 chapters into a coding book and haven't really talked about programming yet. Very good question. I'm reminded by that old Greek fable where a guy named Daedalus crafted his son Icarus a pair of wings made of wax. Too bad for him, he flew too close to the sun (because everybody knows the sun is at the top of the sky), his wings melted, and he fell into the sea below him with a big splash. What does that have to do with anything? I'm not sure, but it's an interesting little story.

Actually, there are some good reasons that I've touched on already. There's programming and then there is software engineering. Programming is, of course, writing code. Software engineers do a lot of programming but that is only a part of what we do. What else do we do? Well, requirements and design documents are another big part. In addition to just teaching you how to code, I intend to teach you how to design your code as you work through this project. A lot of times there is more than one way to code something. I'll talk about some of those ways, the pros and cons, and different situations where you may choose one over the other.

Part of engineering is figuring out the "corner cases" before they actually happen. A corner case is a special kind of issue that only happens when other seemingly normal things happen. Think about a square. You've got four lines. But when two of them come together, you have a corner.

Importing the Assets

So where were we? Ah yes, loading our assets. There are actually quite a lot of really high-quality assets that come with this tutorial. In this chapter we will talk about each of them and some of the issues you may see along the way.

Way back in chapter 1 we created a project for *The Exodus Adventure* game. We're going to reuse that. To load the assets into the project we need to copy those assets into the project's "Assets" folder. Assuming you followed the steps in that chapter for creating the project then we know where to copy them. For Windows, the destination folder is "Documents > UnityProjects > Exodus Adventure > Assets". **To download a copy of all the assets to your computer your teacher or parent will need to register this textbook at the website link shown in Appendix A.**

Next, take the file InitialAssets.unitypackage and copy it to the "Documents > UnityProjects > Exodus Adventure > Assets". This will take a while to copy. As I said before, there are A LOT of really high-quality assets that come with this tutorial. These assets are licensed for you (and only you) to use in any game you want to make or even sell. Sharing or posting them to anywhere is not allowed.

While waiting for the assets to copy, I want to talk a little about the goal of this chapter. By the end of this chapter, you should have all of the assets needed for *The Exodus Adventure* game loaded into Unity without any errors which show up as a red stop-sign exclamation marks on the console. Warnings that show up as a yellow yield-sign exclamation mark are ok. See Figure 52 for examples. Errors are things you HAVE to fix and warnings are things you may want to fix, depending on what the warning is.

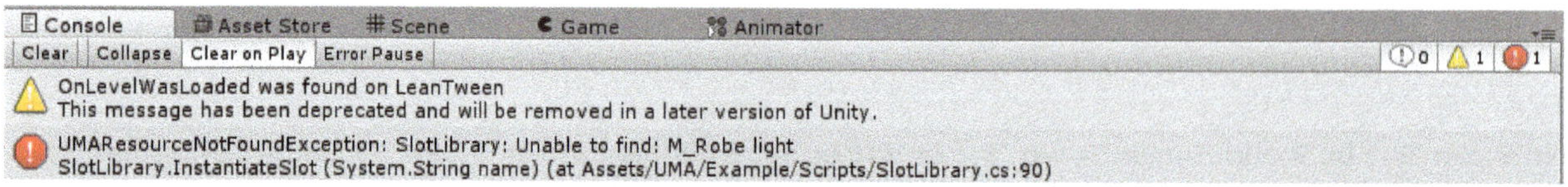

Figure 52

Once the copy is finished Unity will need to load it. To do that just put the focus on the Unity window and it will figure out you added the new "unitypackage" file. From the Project View, click on the Assets folder like what is shown in Figure 53 and you'll see "EAT Initial 3rdEd" pop up in the pane to the right. Double-click the file "EAT Initial 3rdEd" to and Unity will start preparing the package. This will take a while since it's such a big package. In the meantime, pick up "Exodus: God of the Slaves" and continue reading, or launch "Exodus Vigil". I'm totally not biased but I think those are some really great pieces of entertainment.

Figure 53

Once the "Import Unity Package" window pops up like in Figure 54, then you're ready to import. The middle pane has all the high-quality file and folder goodness that will be imported. To start the process, click the "Import" button at the bottom-right of the window. Chill out one more time with your favorite game or book (hint, hint) while all these great assets are importing.

After Unity is done loading all the assets you will be able to interact with the Unity Window again. You will now see a bunch of folders listed under the Assets in the Project View. There will likely be some warnings and a few errors. These are not going to block us on anything.

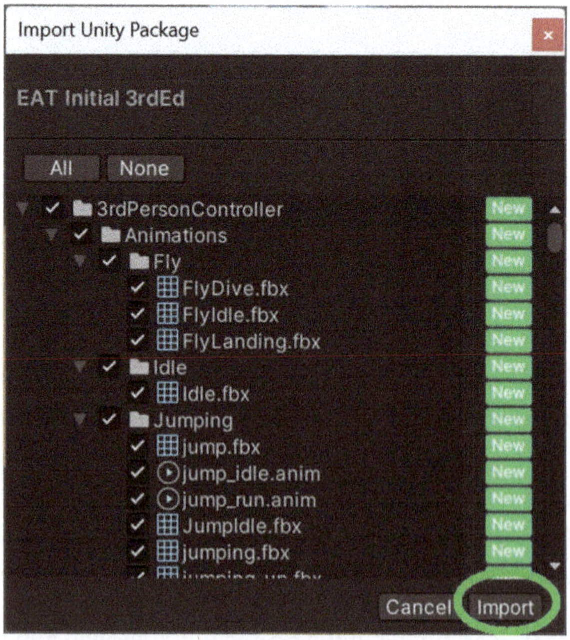

Figure 54

Chapter 3 – 3rd Person Controller

The hour has now come. You've been introduced to Unity and learned how to get around. You've also learned how to design a project and have loaded the required assets. It is now time to start learning C# and have fun making our game.

Before we begin, let's see just where the C# language fits in the history of some other computer languages. You'll see just how new C# is! In the early 1950's, most computers were used for scientific and engineering calculations. The programming language of choice in those days was called **FORTRAN**. FORTRAN was the first modern language and is still in use to this day (after going through several updates). In the late 1950's, bankers and other businesspeople got into the computer business using a language called **COBOL**. Within a few years after its development, COBOL became the most widely used data processing language. And, like FORTRAN, it is still being used today.

In the 1960's, two professors at Dartmouth College decided that "everyday" people needed to have a language they could use to learn programming. They developed **BASIC** (**B**eginner's **A**ll-Purpose **S**ymbolic **I**nstruction **C**ode). BASIC (and its successors, GW-Basic, Visual Basic, Visual Basic Express) is probably the most widely used programming language. Many (including myself, but I'm not biased one bit!) dismiss it as a "toy language," but BASIC was the first product developed by a company you may have heard of – Microsoft! And, BASIC has been used to develop thousands of commercial applications.

C# had its beginnings in 1972 when AT&T Bell Labs developed the **C** programming language. It was the first, new scientific type language since FORTRAN. If you've ever seen a C program, you will notice many similarities between C# and C. Then, with object-oriented capabilities added, came **C++** in 1986 (also from Bell Labs). This was a big step.

In 2001, Microsoft introduced its .NET platform and a new language as well – C#. It represented a streamlined version of C and C++, with a little Java thrown in. If you've ever used another programming language, you will see equivalent structures in the language of C#.

Variables

Before we get started, we need to cover some basic C# concepts. Variables are used by C# to hold information needed by an application. I called captain obvious and asked how they got their name, and this is what he said, "They're called variables because they can vary". Thanks a lot! So, the information in the variables changes. Sometimes you change the variable and other times something else changes it.

There are some rules when naming variables. If you don't follow these rules, then the compiler will give you an error. Here are the rules:

- No more than 40 characters
- They may include letters, numbers, and underscore (_)
- The first character must be a letter which, by convention, is usually lower-case
- You cannot use a reserved word (keywords used by Visual C#)

With large projects, sometimes it is easy to forget what a variable is for. Use meaningful variable names that help you understand what it is for. Also, if you give your code to someone else, then they will have an easier time understanding what your code does.

Examples of acceptable variable names:

startingTime	interest_Value	letter05
johnsAge	number_of_Days	timeOfDay

Data Types

The kind of information variables store is of a particular **type** of data. C# has a lot of different data types. Whenever you declare that you're going to use a variable, you say what the type is. The type of the variable always goes with the name of the variable.

bool (short for Boolean) variables can have one of two different values: **true** or **false** (reserved words in Visual C#). Boolean variables are helpful in making decisions. There is one possible point of confusion when working with Boolean values. Note some control properties are Boolean, for example, the Enabled property. When setting such a property at design time, the choices are **True** or **False** (using upper case letters). When setting Boolean values in code (either setting control properties or some other variable), the choices are **true** or **false** (using lower case letters). Be aware of this when writing code. A common error is to use upper case values, rather than the proper lower-case values.

If a variable stores a whole number (no decimal), there are three data types available: **short**, **int,** or **long**. Which type you select depends on the range of the value stored by the variable:

Data Type	**Range**
short	-32,678 to 32,767
int	-2,147,483,648 to 2,147,483,647
long	-9,223,372,036,854,775,808 to 9,223,372,036,854,775,807

We will forsake short and long and only use **int** for our projects.

If we need to store a number with a decimal, then we have two options: **float** or **double**. The double uses twice as much storage as float, providing more precision and a wider range.

Examples:

Data Type	Value
float	3.14
double	3.14159265359

Strings can be fun to play with, especially for kittens. You can tie things like ribbons and bells together on the same string and watch it play for hours. Or better yet, post it online and let me watch for hours. They're fun in C# too! You tie letters together like words. But unlike words, you can put any combination of letters, numbers, and symbols together.

C# is a popular language for strings and changing them around. Changing strings using code is called string manipulation. These manipulations are performed on variables of type **string**. A string variable is just that - a string (list) of various characters. In C#, you use double-quotes to indicate string variables. Examples of strings:

C# offers a powerful set of methods to work with string type variables. You can do cool stuff like adding strings together and even replacing letters! We'll talk about this in a later chapter.

"C# Language"   "012345"   "Title   Author"

Single character string variables have a special type, type **char**, for character type. A character is one of any letter, number, or other symbols (like what you see on your keyboard). A character variable is enclosed in single-quotes. Examples of characters:

'a' '1'   'V'   '*'

Variable Declaration

Now that we have the variable name and type, we're ready to declare it. Declaring a variable in your scripts lets you access that variable so you can change it or check the value. See Figure 55 for some examples of variable declarations.

```
7    int myInt;
8    double myDouble;
9    string myString, yourString;
```

Figure 55

Line 7 declares an integer named "myInt". The next line declares a double (remember: double the value of a float) called "myDouble". And the last line declares 2 variables, both of the string type. The first one is named "myString" and the second one is named "yourString". Notice that there is a semicolon at the end of each line. Semicolons are like the end of a sentence, use them instead of periods.

Egypt Nile Scene

Now let's get into some really fun stuff. Going deep into C# is fun too! But we need to get some more things ready in our project before doing more C# scripting.

In the project view go to Assets > Ancient Egypt as you see in Figure 56. To change the view to list out everything instead of showing you thumbnails, move the slider bar in the bottom-right of the screen all the way to the left. Then double click on "Egypt_Nile Scene". This is a scene asset that contains instances of objects, their positions, and components.

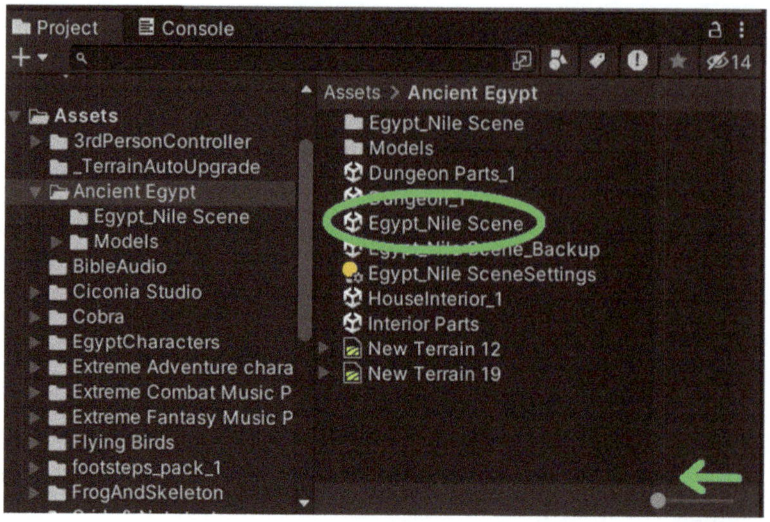

Figure 56

There will be a few warnings and errors, but those won't impede our game-making progress. It won't stop Unity from playing the scene and will go away when the scene is loaded again.

In the Hierarchy View, click the "FPSController", move the mouse to the Scene View, and press the 'F' key to see it. You should see a white camera gizmo and a white sound listener gizmo with some lines going out like in Figure 57.

Go ahead and press the play button. You'll see a view of the city gate in the Game View. The game is now running and you can use standard FPS controls to move around the map. Moving the mouse will rotate the camera. You can use the arrow keys or 'W', 'A', 'S', 'D' to move around. Pressing the space bar will jump.

Feel free to explore the map as much as you want. You'll use this later to make the game. We will be making changes to the "Egypt_Nile_Scene" so if something happens then we have an "Egypt_Nile_Scene_Backup" all ready for you.

Figure 57

Third Person Controller

Ok, now that you've had a lot of fun with the FPS Controller, delete it. Seriously! If you remember in our GDD we're making a 3rd person game, not a 1st person game. In the Project View, browse to Assets > Extreme Adventure character pack > Characters > Characters. You will see a "Model_Civilian" in that folder. Click and drag it onto the terrain where the FPS controller was in Scene View. Then press 'F' to focus on it. Click on the hand tool in the top-right of the screen and hold ALT. When you left click and drag you can rotate around this guy and can look at him from every angle.

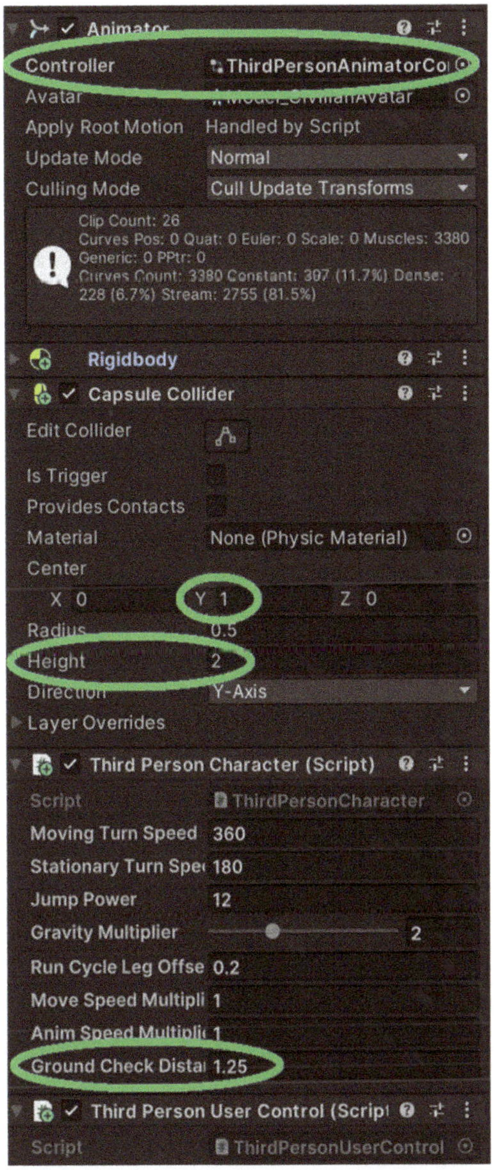

Figure 58

This guy is going to be the young Moses who the player will be moving around. The next step is to add the right components and C# scripts to let the player move him. Go to the inspector on the right and click "Add Component". Select "Physics" and then "Capsule Collider". Set the Center 'Y' value to 1 and the Height to 2. Right-click the "Model_Civilian" and select "Open Prefab Asset". In the Project View, add ThirdPersonUserControl from the path: Standard Assets > Characters > ThirdPersonCharacter > Scripts. Adding this component will automatically add a Rigidbody component and a Third Person Character script. From Assets > Standard Assets > Characters > ThirdPersonCharacter > Animator, drag "ThirdPersonAnimatorController" to the Controller field in the Animator component. Refer to Figure 58.

In the inspector's Third Person Character component change the "Ground Check Distance" to "1.25". I'll go over all the fields here in a bit, but while we're here I'll explain what this one does. It is to determine if the player is touching the ground or not so we can do the correct animation. If we left this as "0.1" then the script wouldn't look far enough underneath the 3D model and think it was in the air. Then we would have a funny-looking pose of Moses hovering over the ground, and I don't think that was one of the miracles God told him to do.

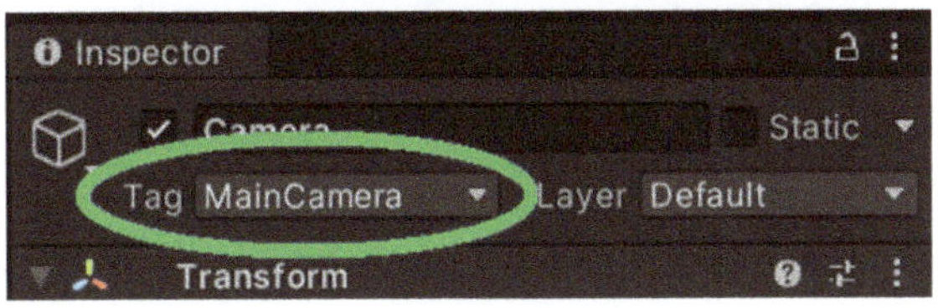

Figure 59

To see Moses we need to add a camera. In the Hierarchy View, highlight "Model_Civilian" right-click and select "Camera". This adds a camera GameObject as a child under Moses. We want the camera as a child because that means whenever Moses moves the camera will follow him. Leaving it named "Camera" is fine. In the inspector, we need to change the Tag to "MainCamera" so our scripts will work as shown in Figure 59. Then drag and drop the "ThirdPersonOrbitCam" C# script onto the camera's inspector from the path: Assets > 3rdPersonController > Scripts > LevelScripts. Finally, drag the "Model_Civilian" from the Hierarchy View onto the "Player" field in the "ThirdPersonOrbitCam" script.

With that we're ready to go into the game and play what we have so far. Click that sideways Triforce let's save the princess! Er... I mean... save the Israelites. The controls to move Moses are the same as with the FPS Controller that we deleted. As you've probably already noticed, you can rotate the camera by moving the mouse. It also changes the direction that Moses is running. When you click the play button again to stop playing then everything will go back to where it was before you started playing.

"If" only...

One question that you may have had burning in the back of your mind while playing through is, "If the player uses the mouse to move the camera around, then how will they use items?" That is a very good point! It would be very awkward for the player to have to keep moving around the camera when they try to use the mouse to select an item to use. So, we're only going to move the camera around if the player holds down the right mouse button. To do that, we need to learn about "if" statements.

The concept of an "if" statement for making a decision is very simple. We check to see if a particular Boolean condition is true or false. If it is true, then we take a certain action or set of actions. If not, we may do something else or even nothing at all.

The simplest form of the "if" statement:

```
if (condition)
      [process this line of code]
```

In this statement, if condition is true, then the single statement following the statement will be executed. If condition is false, nothing is done, and program execution continues following this line of code. You can see an example below of some code that may run when you try and buy a new game at your favorite game store.

Example:

```
if (balance - purchase < 0)
   trouble = true;
```

Brace yourselves! We need to break out some math. We subtract purchase from balance and if it is less than zero then we can't afford it and your card is declined.

If there is more than one line of code to process following an "if" statement, we use another form of it:

```
if (condition) {
      [process this code]
      [and this code too!]
}
```

Here, if the condition is true then the code between the two curly braces is executed. If the condition is false, then nothing happens and code execution continues after the closing right brace.

Example:

```
if (balance - purchase < 0) {
      trouble = true;
      AskMomForMoney("puppy-dog face");
}
```

Again, we subtract the purchase from our card balance and if that is less than zero then two lines of information are processed: trouble is set to true and a method request more money (along with our best puppy dog face, because she can't resist the puppy-dog face) is sent to mom so we can buy the game. Notice the indentation of the code between the two braces. Visual Studio automatically indents the code for you. It makes understanding (and debugging) your code much easier.

These cool new "if" statements are one way a computer program can "branch". Think of a branch like following a path. The computer's CPU (Central Processing Unit) is walking along, but then the path veers off to the left and right. The CPU needs to figure out which way to go.

What if you want to do one thing if a condition is true and another if it is false? Use an if/else block:

```
if (condition) {
    [process code here]
} else {
    [process code there]
}
```

In this block, if the condition is true, the code between the first two braces is executed. If the condition is false, the code between the second set of braces is processed.

Example:

```
if (balance - purchase < 0) {
      trouble = true;
      AskMomForMoney("puppy-dog face");
} else {
      trouble = false;
}
```

Here, the same two lines are executed if you don't have enough money to buy the game (balance - purchase < 0), but if you do (else) then you're not in trouble and you can buy the game.

Lastly, we can test multiple conditions by adding the "else if" statement:

```
if (condition1) {
        [process code in a house]
} else if (condition2) {
        [process code with a mouse]
} else if (condition3) {
        [process code in a box]
} else {
        [process code with a fox]
}
```

In this block, if condition1 is true, the code between the "if" and first "else if" line is executed. If condition1 is false, condition2 is checked. If condition2 is true, the indicated code is executed. If condition2 is not true, condition3 is checked. Each subsequent condition in the structure is checked until a true condition is found, an else statement is reached, or the last closing brace is reached.

Example:

```
if (balance - purchase < 0) {
        trouble = true;
        AskMomForMoney("puppy-dog face");
} else if (balance - purchase == 0) {
        trouble = false;
        SendDadText("Ca$h 4 Chorz?");
} else {
        trouble = false;
}
```

Now, one more condition is added. If your balance equals the price of the game [else if (balance - purchase == 0)], you're still not in trouble, but you'll need to do some chores for your dad to earn more money.

Time to make a Decision

With "if" statements in our box of tools we're ready to implement the feature. Remember, we only want the camera to move when we hold down the right mouse button. In the Project View, go to Assets > 3rdPersonController > Scripts > LevelScripts and double-click the file ThirdPersonOrbitCam to open it in Visual Studio.

```
void LateUpdate()
{
    if (Input.GetMouseButton(1))
    {
        // Get mouse movement to orbit the camera.
        angleH += Mathf.Clamp(Input.GetAxis("Mouse X"), -1, 1) * horizontalAimingSpeed * Time.deltaTime;
        angleV += Mathf.Clamp(Input.GetAxis("Mouse Y"), -1, 1) * verticalAimingSpeed * Time.deltaTime;
    }

    // Set vertical movement limit.
    angleV = Mathf.Clamp(angleV, minVerticalAngle, targetMaxVerticalAngle);
```

Figure 60

Go to line 53 in the file, make a new line, and add in the text "if (Input.GetMouseButton (1))" and then on the next line put an opening curly brace '{'. Then on line 57 make another new line and in just a single closing curly brace "}". The new code should look like Figure 60.

Now push the play button again. You'll see that you can move the mouse around freely and the camera won't move until you hold down the right mouse button.

Making Comments

Comment statements begin with the two slashes (**//**).

Example:

```
// This is a comment
x = 2 * y; // another way to write a comment
```

You, as a programmer, should decide how much to comment your code. Consider such factors as reuse, your audience, and the legacy of your code. In our notes and examples, we try to insert comment statements when necessary to explain some detail. You can also have a multiple line comment. Begin the comment with **/*** and end it with ***/**.

Example:

```
/*
 * This is a very long
 * comment over
 * a few lines
 */
```

Putting an asterisk (*) on each line is not required but is encouraged for comments that explain the code. You can also "comment out" code to keep it from running. This can be a useful debugging strategy.

Example:

```
if (balance - purchase < 0) {
     trouble = true;
     AskMomForMoney("puppy-dog face");
} else if (balance - purchase == 0) {
     /*
     trouble = false;
     SendDadText("Ca$h 4 Chorz?");
     */
} else {
     trouble = false;
}
```

Statements and Expressions

Before going further, we need to talk. Well, more specifically, we need to make statements. Like when you open your mouth to make a statement, you can make statements in C# too. Now, some of you may be like, Hey! What about non-verbal statements like facial expressions? You'll be glad to hear that C# has expressions too. Expressions combine variables, constant numbers, and other interesting things.

The simplest (and most common) statement in C# is the assignment statement. It consists of a variable name, followed by the assignment operator (=), followed by some sort of expression, followed by a semicolon (;). The expression on the right-hand side is evaluated, then the variable on the left hand side of the assignment operator is replaced by that value of the expression.

Examples:

```
startTime = now;
explorer = "Captain Spaulding";
bitCount = byteCount * 8;
energy = mass * lightSpeed * lightSpeed;
netWorth = assets - liabilities;
```

The assignment statement stores information.

Statements normally take up a single line. Since C# ignores white space, statements can be stacked using a semicolon (;) to separate them.

Example:

```
startTime = now; endTime = startTime + 10;
```

The above code is the same as if the second statement followed the first statement. The only place we tend to use stacking is for quick initialization of like variables.

If a statement is very long, it may be continued to the next line without any kind of continuation character. Again, this is because C# ignores white space. It keeps processing a statement until it finally sees a semicolon.

Example:

```
months = Math.Log(final * intRate / deposit + 1)

           / Math.Log(1 + intRate);
```

This statement, though on two lines, will be recognized as a single line. We usually write each statement on a single line. Be aware that long lines of code in the notes many times wrap around to the next line (due to page margins).

Visual C# Arithmetic Operators

Operators modify values of variables. The simplest operators carry out arithmetic operations. There are five arithmetic operators in C#.

Addition is done using the plus (+) sign and subtraction is done using the minus (-) sign.

Operation	**Example**	**Result**
Addition	7 + 2	9
Addition	3.4 + 8.1	11.5
Subtraction	6 - 4	2
Subtraction	11.1 – 7.6	3.5

Multiplication is done using the asterisk (*) and division is done using the slash (/).

Operation	**Example**	**Result**
Multiplication	8 * 4	32
Multiplication	2.3 * 12.2	28.06
Division	12 / 2	6
Division	45.26 / 6.2	7.3

The last operator is the remainder operator represented by a percent symbol (%). This operator divides the whole number on its left side by the whole number on its right side, ignores the main part of the answer, and just gives you the remainder. It may not be obvious now, but the remainder operator is used a lot in computer programming.

Operation	**Example**	**Division Result**	**Operation Result**
Remainder	7 % 4	1 Remainder 3	3
Remainder	14 % 3	4 Remainder 2	2
Remainder	25 % 5	5 Remainder 0	0

Did you know you can actually use computer programs to do your math homework? It's true! Once you know C# or another language, you can use these arithmetic operators to create equations in the statements so you don't have to write it out by hand. Next, we'll learn about methods that will make this super easy to do.

The mathematical operators have the following precedence indicating the order they are evaluated without specific groupings:

1. Multiplication (*) and division (/)
2. Remainder (%)
3. Addition (+) and subtraction (-)

If multiplications and divisions or additions and subtractions are in the same expression, they are performed in left-to-right order.

You can use parentheses around expressions to force your own precedence.

Example:

```
(7 + 3) * (4 + 6)
```

In the above example the 7 +3 and 4 + 6 are calculated before they are multiplied together for 10 * 10 resulting in 100.

A Method to the Madness

You added some code in an "if" statement and are now conditionally rotating the camera. But we probably ought to understand what we did. But first we need to learn about methods.

A method is a group of code that runs together from the top of the method to the bottom. Like a variable, methods have declarations.

Method Declaration:

```
type MethodName(Parameters)
```

The "type" is the same type that is in a variable. It can be an int, float, bool, or other types that we make up! Methods also have a special type called "void". This is where we reach into the void to pull something out. What do we pull out? Nothing. Because there's nothing in the void. So functions with a "void" type return nothing. Just don't look into it or the void will look into you. Oh wait, never mind. That's the abyss.

Way back in the good old days when I trudged to school in the snow, up-hill both ways, methods were called "subroutines". These subroutines let programmers write much fewer lines of code. This concept has also been called a procedure or function.

"MethodName" is the name we use when we want to call the method and run the code in the method. Inside parentheses are parameters to the method. A parameter is something that the method needs to do its job. This needs a type and a name just like a variable. Let's look at an example.

Example:

```
int AskMomForMoney(string FaceName)
```

Like the "if" statement, you show what code runs inside a method using curly braces:

```
type MethodName (Parameters)
{
        [process this code]
}
```

Methods can also have multiple parameters. Use a comma to separate each parameter.

Example:

```
bool DoChoreForDad(int Difficulty, int MoneyReward)
{
        if (Difficulty > MoneyReward)
                return false;
        else
                return true;
}
```

In the example above you can see there are two parameters separated by a comma. These two parameters are used by the "if" statement in the method. Inside the "if" statement you see a new word, "return". This tells C# that we stop running code in this method and send back the value after the "return" statement.

You can also return a variable. This sends back whatever value was stored in the variable.

Example:

```
int AskMomForMoney(string FaceName)
{
        int money = 10;

        if (FaceName == "puppy-dog face")
        {
                money = 20;
        }

        return money;
}
```

In this example, we declare the variable money at the top of the method. Mom normally gives us $10 when we ask. But if we give her our best puppy-dog face then we can get $20. Then we return the variable "money" at the bottom of the method.

Finally, we learn how to call a method and run the code grouped underneath it.

Example:

```
if (balance - purchase < 0) {
      balance += AskMomForMoney("puppy-dog face");
} else if (balance - purchase == 0) {
      SendDadText("Ca$h 4 Chorz?");

      if (DoChoreForDad(difficulty, reward)
            balance = reward;
}
```

You can see in the above example that we have 3 method calls. If we don't have enough money to make the purchase, then we ask mom with our best puppy-dog face. The "+=" is a special symbol that means we add what is on the right to the variable on the left. So, we take the return value from the method and add it to the balance.

It may be fun and profitable to use C# to do your math homework for you by coding methods and statements. You can try something easy at first like calculating a multi-variable equation like this: $5X + 3X^2 + X^3/10$. Set 'X' as the input parameter, call it for different values of 'X', and use Debug.Log(X) to print the answer in the console. That's pretty neat!

If we're left with no money after we buy the game, then we need to earn some. So, we send our dad a text asking to do chores to earn money. This method has a void type, so we just call it like normal. Then we call the method "DoChoreForDad" inside the "if" statement with the parameter's "difficulty" and reward". Notice that there aren't any other conditions in the "if" statement. Since the method already returns a "bool" type then the code underneath will run if the method returns true. So, if the work is worth the reward, then we do it and set our balance to the reward.

Going back to the code we wrote earlier; you can see that we added the "if" statement in the "LateUpdate" method as shown in Figure 60 on page 57. And that we called a method named "GetMouseButton" inside the "if" statement with the argument "1". We're not putting any other conditionals in the "if" statement, so we know the return type of the method is a "bool".

But you may be wondering what that "Input" thing with the dot after it is? Well, I'm glad you asked because we're going to talk about it next.

A Language with a lot of Class

Scroll up to the top of the file in Visual Studio for "ThirdPersonOrbitCam.cs" and you'll see something that looks like Figure 61. Below the first two lines that

```
using UnityEngine;
using System.Collections;

Unity Script (2 asset references) | 4 references
public class ThirdPersonOrbitCam : MonoBehaviour
{
```

Figure 61

start with "using", the 2nd word on the 4th line is "class".

I know what you're thinking. You still have homework you need to do for your math class but hang with me here for a little bit. Kind of like how a class at school is a group of students, a class in C# groups up variables and methods. To access these variables and methods, you go through the class.

Classes are the foundational element of something called "Object Oriented Programming" or OOP for short, as in, oops created a class again. Up to this point, we've talked about "Procedural Programming" (NOT abbreviate as PP for short because of the obvious reason).

Way back in the dark ages of computers, before C# was created as a language, programmers etched their code on stone tablets using languages like Fortran, COBOL, and BASIC. They used methods but called them procedures. You can call procedures. You can call procedures from within procedures. And you can even call procedures from within procedures from within procedures! That's why they called it "procedural".

Classes were originally introduced in a language called Smalltalk in the 1970s. As OOP became more popular in the mid-1990s, other languages like C++ added support for classes.

But OOP is the cool new thing that everyone is doing. It is a different way of thinking about how to code. It's best explained by looking at an example. Let's say you want to share stuff with your friends online. The first thing we do is figure out what all the entities that interact with each are.

Entities:

- Person
- Comment

Entities also have attributes and behaviors. An easy way to understand those is that attributes are nouns (things they have or are) and behaviors are verbs (things they do). Next, we get a list of attributes and behaviors for each entity.

Attributes and Behaviors:

Person

- Attribute: Name
- Attribute: Gender
- Behavior: Make comments to themselves
- Behavior: Make comments to other people
- Behavior: Make comments on their own comments
- Behavior: Make comments on someone else's comments
- Behavior: Like other peoples' comments

- Behavior: Flag other peoples' comments as offensive
- Behavior: Edit or delete their own comments

Comment

- Attribute: What was said or the text
- Attribute: Who made the comment
- Attribute: Number of likes
- Attribute: Is this comment flagged as offensive

Ok, now we have everything we need to get started writing our code. We turn Person and Comment into classes. The attributes get implemented as variables in those classes. And the behaviors are methods contained in the classes.

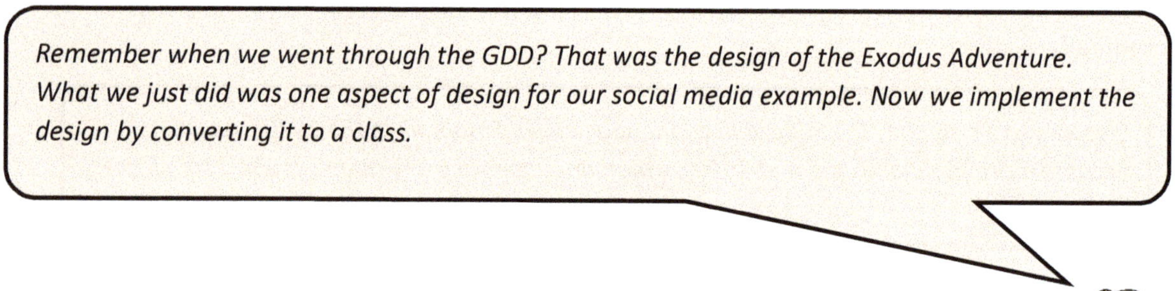


```
scope class ClassName
{
      [Attributes]
      [Methods]
}
```

The first thing we do is determine who has access to the attributes and behaviors in the class. This is called the scope and there are three types of scope. Both classes and their variables and methods have a scope.

- public: any other code is able to access this class
- private: Used for variables and methods in the class, not the class itself
- protected: Used for inheritance which we will talk about later

Example:

```
public class Comment
{
      public string Text;
      public Person Speaker;
      public bool Offensive;
      public int likes;
}
```

We have our comment class, and you can see that it is public. You can also see that the variables are public as well. One thing that may look confusing is the "Speaker" variable where we use the type

"Person", but that isn't one of the types we've mentioned before. That's because when you declare a class then it becomes a new type that you can use for variables and method arguments.

Sometimes, when you create a class, there are attributes about the class that need to be set when the class is created. To do that we use a special method called a constructor. You leave off the type for the constructor because it uses the class name as the type.

```
scope class ClassName
{
      [Variables]

      Public ClassName (Arguments)
      {
            [Set Variables from the Arguments]
      }
}
```

With that, we can define the Person class here:

```
public class Person
{
      private string NameOfPerson;
      private string GenderOfPerson;

      public Person (string name, string gender)
      {
            NameOfPerson = name;
            BirthdayOfPerson = birthday;
      }

      public string GetName()
      {
            return NameOfPerson;
      }

      public dateTime GetGender()
      {
            return GenderOfPerson;
      }

      public void MakeComment (string Text, Person Listener)
      { … }

      public void Edit Comment (Comment cmt)
      { … }

      public void DeleteComment (Comment cmt)
      { … }

      public void LikeComment (Comment cmt)
      { … }
```

```
        public void FlagComment (Comment cmt)
        { … }
}
```

This one is quite a bit bigger because a person does a lot more things than a comment. In this class, the two variables "NameOfPerson" and "GenderOfPerson" are private. This prevents other code from accessing these variables.

Sometimes we want to keep other code from accessing certain variables and methods because it helps prevent bugs. If something isn't supposed to be accessed, but it accidentally is being accessed then it can cause problems. This helps save us debug work down the road.

Now, people don't often change their names or gender. So, by preventing other code from accessing those variables we keep bugs from coming into our system. But you may ask, if other code can't access these variables then how do we set them? I'm glad you asked.

The three methods following the driver will allow code to set the variables and get them. We have our constructor which sets the two private variables. Then we have two methods that return the value of the variables. So, once you set the person's name and birthday, you can't change it.

For the other methods, notice that we mark them as public so other code can call them. For methods that should only be called inside the class, use "private" like with the variables. So, if any code tries to access those variables or methods an error will pop up in the compiler.

Instantiating Classes

We've defined what it means to be a person and a comment in the example so far. But in order to use them we need to create instances, and we do that by using the "new" keyword.

```
ClassName InstanceName;
InstanceName = new ClassName(Parameters);
```

First we create a variable with the type as the name of the class, since creating a new class also creates a new type you can use for variables. Now, you may be familiar with "=" for math operations. Here, we use the equals symbol to set the variable to the "new" instance of the class we're instantiating. The "new" keyword creates the instance of the class so we can start using it.

Example:

```
Person personInst;
personInst = new Person("Grace", "Female");
```

Unlike some other languages like C++, C# doesn't require you to delete objects you created using "new". C# figures out when you're done and calls the garbage collector to take out the trash.

Here, we say there is a new variable of type "Person" whose name is "personInst". Then we create a "new" person with the name "Grace" and the gender "Female". We access this person using the variable "personInst" with the "." (or dot) operator.

```
InstanceName.method(Parameters);
InstanceName.variables
```

You can see that both methods and variables in the class are accessed using the dot operator. Now let's look at the code we modified and try to understand what is going on back on Page 63 in Figure 61. On line 53 we added our "if" statement. You can see that we're accessing the method "GetMouseButton" from the class "Input" and passing in the argument "1".

The Input class is a special class defined by Unity that is used for user input like the mouse, keyboard, and other devices. Unity stuffed the Input class with a bunch of other useful things as well. We used one of them back in Chapter 1! If you recall, in the script we created, we called the method "GetAxis". An axis is like a number line that goes from -1, through 0, to 1. By default, the horizontal axis goes to -1 when the left arrow is pressed and then to 1 when the right arrow is pressed. If no arrow is pressed, then it is 0. The vertical axis works the same way with the up and down arrows. Unity allows you to setup other keys and axes as well, but we don't need them for this game.

Shocked by the Static!

You may be surprised to see that we're accessing a method from the "Input" class which wasn't instantiated using the "new" keyword. Every day is a surprise when you're coding C#! There is another keyword that allows you to access a class's variables and methods, and that is "static".

You probably thought of static electricity when you read that. Static electricity is when there is an electrical charge stored in the surface of some object. You slide down a slide at a playground and suddenly your hair wants to stand straight up. The charge wants to go somewhere but it can't. It's static. Then you touch your friend and shock the living daylights out of them. The charge has moved and is no longer static. Your hair goes back to normal.

Static objects in C# are created when the code first runs and is cleaned up by the garbage collector when the program ends. It doesn't change. As a result, no other instances of this class can be created. You can't use the "new" keyword on a "static class".

```
static scope class ClassName
{
      [Static Variables]
      [Static Methods]
}
```

In static classes, the variables and methods need to be static too. We'll talk more about static objects in later chapters. But know that it exists and that you don't need to create instances of classes to access their variables and methods.

Zoom!

The last thing we need to add to the 3rd person controller is the ability to zoom the camera. Zooming out lets the player get a larger view of their surroundings while zooming in lets the player move the camera easier in tight spaces like tunnels. The player will zoom in by scrolling their mouse wheel. We've got some code to add, so strap your seatbelts on and get ready for the ride of your life!

Go back to the ThirdPersonOrbitCam.cs in Visual Studio. All the changes we need to make are in that file. Make a couple new lines and add the code as shown in Figure 62. These three new public variables in the class control our zoom feature.

```
public float minVerticalAngle = -60f;

public float ZoomSensitivity = 0.5f;
public float MinZoom = 2;
public float MaxZoom = 10;

private float angleH = 0;
```

Figure 62

- zoomSensitivity: how much each scroll tick will zoom the camera
- minZoom: the closest zoom to the player
- maxZoom: the farthest zoom from the player

Also note that at the end of the variable declaration that we set them to a value. These are the default values for the variable. By default, numbers like ints and floats are initialized to '0', unless we set the default ourselves. Go back to Unity and click on the camera that the "ThirdPersonOrbitCam.cs" script is attached to. You'll see that these variables show up in the inspector with the default values. You can change the values here and Unity will use them over the defaults we wrote in the script.

```
72        // Set FOV.
73        cam.GetComponent<Camera>().fieldOfView = Mathf.Lerp (cam.GetComponent<Camera>().fieldOfView, targetFOV,  Time.deltaTime);
74
75        if (((Mathf.Abs(targetCamOffset.z) > MinZoom) && (Input.mouseScrollDelta.y > 0)) ||
76            ((Mathf.Abs(targetCamOffset.z) < MaxZoom) && (Input.mouseScrollDelta.y < 0)))
77        {
78            targetCamOffset.z += Input.mouseScrollDelta.y * ZoomSensitivity;
79        }
```

Figure 63

Going back to Visual Studio, there is one more piece of code to add, and this is the critical section that actually does the zooming. While the code itself isn't that long, getting it in the right place is critical. Make a couple new lines and type in the code from lines 74 through 78 as shown in Figure 63.

We have a number of things going on here and I'll explain each of them. But first we need to learn about comparison and logical operators.

Comparison and Logical Operators

There are six comparison operators in C# used to compare the value of two expressions (the expressions must be of the same data type). These are the basis for making decisions:

Operator	**Comparison**
>	Greater than
<	Less than
>=	Greater than or equal to
<=	Less than or equal to
==	Equal to
!=	Not equal to

The comparison operators provide a Boolean result. They are either true or false.

Examples:

```
a = 9.6    b = 8.1    a > b  returns true
a = 14     b = 14     a < b  returns false
a = 14     b = 14     a >= b returns true
a = 7      b = 11     a <= b returns true
a = 7      b = 7      a == b returns true
a = 7      b = 7      a != b returns false
```

Logical operators operate on bool data types and also provide a Boolean result. They are also used in decision making. We will use three logical operators

Operator	**Operation**
`!`	`Logical Not`
`&&`	`Logical And`
`||`	`Logical Or`

The Not (!) operator simply negates a Boolean value. It is very useful for 'toggling' Boolean variables. Toggling them means changing from true to false or from false true.

Examples:

```
if a = true     then !a = false
if a = false    then !a = true
```

The And (&&) operator checks to see if two different bool data types are both true. If both are true, the operator returns a true. Otherwise, it returns a false value.

Examples:

```
a = true, b = true     then a && b = true
a = true, b = false    then a && b = false
a = false, b = true    then a && b = false
a = false, b = false   then a && b = false
```

The Or (||) operator (typed as two "pipe" symbols) checks to see if either of two bool data types is true. If either is true, the operator returns a true. Otherwise, it returns a false value.

Examples:

```
a = true, b = true     then a || b = true
a = true, b = false    then a || b = true
a = false, b = true    then a || b = true
a = false, b = false   then a || b = false
```

```
// Set FOV.
cam.GetComponent<Camera>().fieldOfView = Mathf.Lerp (cam.GetComponent<Camera>().fieldOfView, targetFOV,  Time.deltaTime);

if (((Mathf.Abs(targetCamOffset.z) > MinZoom) && (Input.mouseScrollDelta.y > 0)) ||
    ((Mathf.Abs(targetCamOffset.z) < MaxZoom) && (Input.mouseScrollDelta.y < 0)))
{
    targetCamOffset.z += Input.mouseScrollDelta.y * ZoomSensitivity;
}
```

With all of that under our seatbelts, let's unpack the "if" statement we wrote. We have an outer condition, and each part has a condition.

The outer condition uses an OR operation.

```
Expression || Expression
```

The inner conditions use AND operations.

```
Expression && Expression
```

So the whole thing together looks like this:

```
(Expression && Expression) || (Expression && Expression)
```

This sort of "if" statement is perfect to make sure some value is within a certain range, which is what we're doing. We want to change the zoom (Z-axis offset) of the camera when the mouse Scroll is moved but we don't want the player to zoom too far in or too far out.

Math Functions

I know, you saw the section heading and were reminded about your math homework again. There is quite a lot of math that goes into programming. But you can use these math functions for homework the same way as before and put them in statements.

Good thing for you C# handles all the calculations, you just need to tell it what to do. C# provides a set of functions that perform tasks such as square roots, trigonometric relationships, and exponential functions. In the code we wrote, we used the math library below:

```
Mathf.Abs(targetCamOffset.z)
```

Each of the C# math functions comes from the Mathf class of the Express framework (an OOP concept). All this means is that each function name must be preceded by "Mathf." (say Math-F-dot) to work properly. The methods and the returned values are:

Math Function	Value Returned
Mathf.Abs	Returns the absolute value of a specified number
Mathf.Acos	Returns a double value containing the angle whose cosine is the specified number
Mathf.Asin	Returns a double value containing the angle whose sine is the specified number
Mathf.Atan	Returns a double value containing the angle whose tangent is the specified number
Mathf.Cos	Returns a double value containing the cosine of the specified angle
Mathf.Clamp	Returns a float from an input that is "clamped" between 2 numbers
Mathf.Clamp01	Returns a float from an input that is "clamped between 0 and 1
Mathf.Max	Returns the larger of two numbers
Mathf.Min	Returns the smaller of two numbers
Mathf.PI	A constant that specifies the ratio of the circumference of a circle to its diameter
Mathf.Pow	Used to raise a number to a specified power – an exponentiation operator
Mathf.Round	Returns the number nearest the specified number of decimal points
Mathf.Sign	Returns an Integer value indicating the sign of a number
Mathf.Sin	Returns a Double value containing the sine of the specified angle
Mathf.Sqrt	Returns a double value specifying the square root of a number
Mathf.Tan	Returns a double value containing the tangent of an angle

Examples:

Math.Abs(-5.4)	returns the absolute value of –5.4 (returns 5.4)
Math.Cos(2.3	returns the cosine of an angle of 2.3 radians
Math.Max(7, 10)	returns the larger of the two numbers (returns 10)
Math.Sign(-3)	returns the sign on –3 (returns a –1)
Math.Sqrt(4.5)	returns the square root of 4.5

Take a Test-drive

The statement inside the "if" modifies the target Z-Axis offset for the camera based on the mouse scroll wheel. It also takes into account the zoom sensitivity we added so you have control over how quickly the camera is zoomed. Now that we can zoom let's go for a test-drive. Click the Play button.

Go ahead and move the camera around by holding down the right mouse button and dragging the mouse. Then use the middle scroll wheel on your mouse. You can see the camera gets closer and farther away from our player model.

Try this little experiment. Zoom out the camera all the way. Then rotate the camera toward the ground. You'll see that the camera automatically zooms back into the player model so we aren't looking up at him from below the ground. This is because our orbit camera script is equipped with some methods that detect solid objects like the ground. This is called collision detection, and we'll talk about that later.

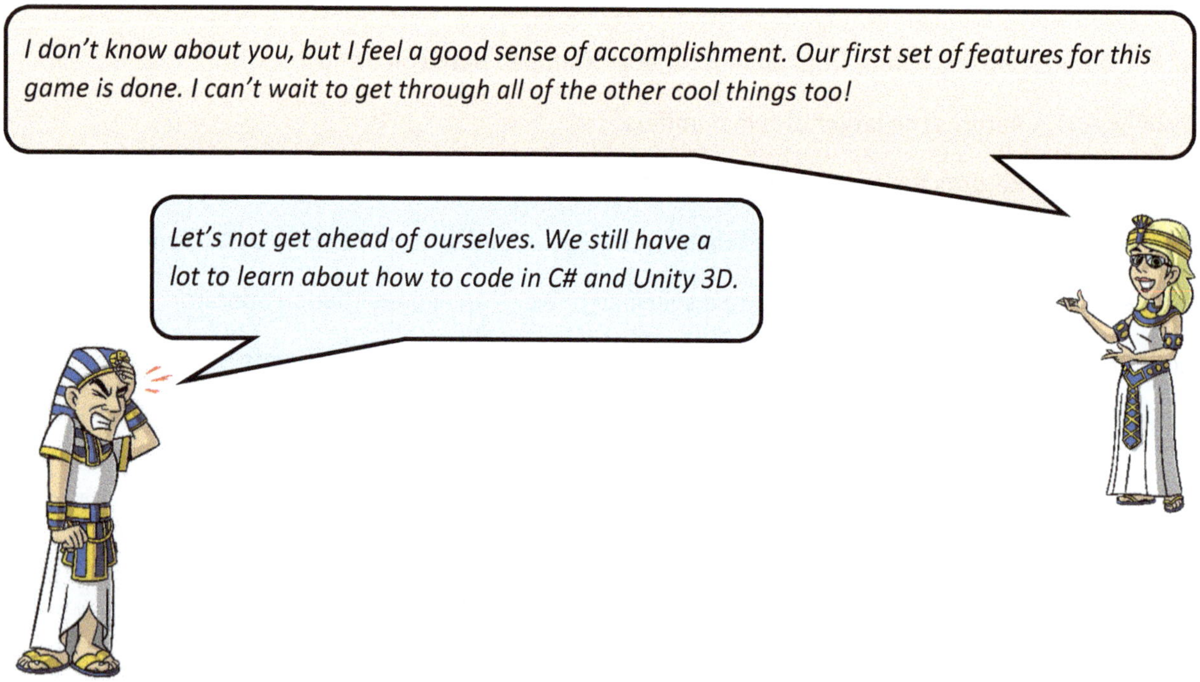

Chapter 4 – User Control in the 3rd Person

We had a lot of fun last chapter. We got our camera working right so we can see everything that's going on and learned a bit of C# as well. We're going to continue learning C# while we add some cool features to our 3rd person user controller. But first, let's organize our asset space.

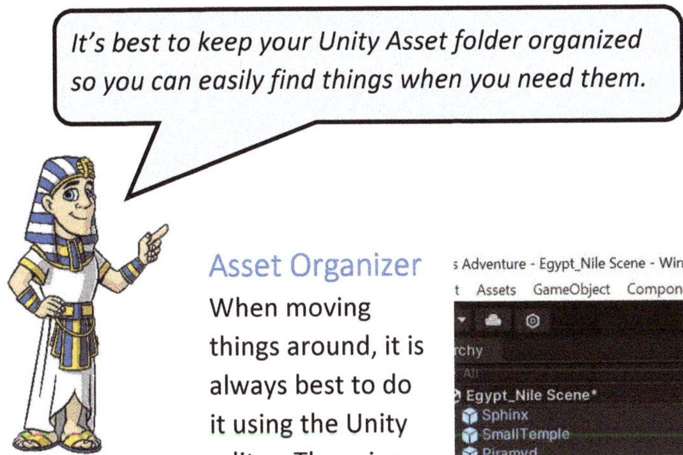

Asset Organizer

When moving things around, it is always best to do it using the Unity editor. There is a lot of "glue" that Unity provides for attaching components like scripts to objects. If you change the location from the file explorer, then Unity cannot find it and marks it missing. But if you do it using the Project View of the editor then Unity will automatically update all the objects using whatever you moved.

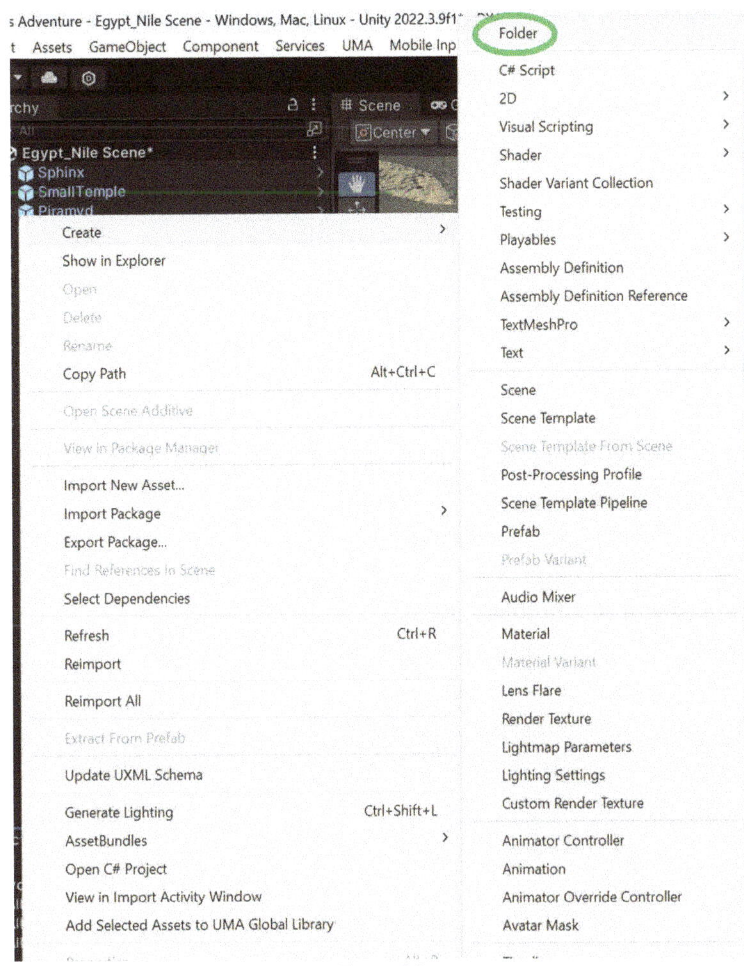

Figure 64

First, right-click on the Assets folder and select: Create > Folder, as you can see in Figure 64. Type "Models", without the double-quotes, as the name of the folder and press Enter. You'll see it automatically sorts itself in the middle, so everything is in alphabetical order. Drag and drop the following folders inside it: Ancient Egypt, Cobra, EgyptCharacters, Extreme Adventure characters pack, Flying Birds, FrogAndSkeleton, Herdsim, Rustic_Pack, and Sickleadz Props.

Don't worry if you accidentally move something else in there. Just take what you put there by mistake and drag it back to the Assets folder. What we've done here is put all our 3D Models into a single folder.

Next create another folder and name it "Animations". Move the Raw Mocap Data into this folder. Create another folder called "Scripts". Put 3rdPersonController inside it. While these packages include more than just scripts, we'll categorize them as scripts because it the provide functionality. Create a "Materials" folder that we'll leave empty for now. Create a "Music" folder and move Extreme Combat Music Pack and Extreme Fantasy Music Pack inside it. Create "Prefabs" which we'll use later.

Create a "Sound Effects" folder and move the footsteps_pack_1 folder inside it. In the Images folder create 2 more folders named "Logos" and "Icons". Move the BibleByteBooks_logo.gif and ExodusAdventureTitle.png into the Logos folder. Put all the other images in the Icons folder. Then, in the root Assets folder, move the "RPG GUI" folder into the Images folder. Also in the root Assets folder, move the "RPG_inventory_icons" folder into Assets > Images > Icons.

Create a folder named "Textures". Move the folders metal_06, Grids & Nets textures pack, and Mage recolor original textures into it. Finally, we create some folders that will be empty now which we'll fill later: Prefabs and Scenes. At this point your folder structure should look like the list below:

- **_TerrainAutoUpgrade**
- **Animations**
    - Raw Mocap Data
- **BibleAudio**
- **Ciconia Studio**
- **Images**
    - Logos
    - Icons
        - RPG_inventory_icons
    - RPG GUI
- **Materials**
- **Models**
    - Ancient Egypt
    - Cobra
    - Egypt Characters
    - Extreme Adventure characters pack
    - Flying Birds
    - FrogAndSkeleton
    - Herdsim
    - Rustic_Pack
    - Sickleadz Props
- **Music**
    - Extreme Combat Music Pack
    - Extreme Fantasy Music Pack
- **PostProcessing**
- **Prefabs**
- **Scenes**
- **Scripts**
    - 3rdPersonController
- **Sound Effects**
    - footsteps_pack_1
- **Standard Assets**

- **Textures**
    - metal_06
    - Grids & Nets textures pack
    - Mage recolor original textures
- **UMA**

Saving Moses

The Bible doesn't say whether God saved a prefab of Moses, but it would be best for us to. If you recall, prefabs let you save an object with all its attributes and child objects so we don't have to create them again. So that we know that this is our player prefab, rename the GameObject in the Hierarchy View from "Model_Civilian" to "MosesPlayer" by right-click and selecting Rename. In the Project View, navigate to Assets > Prefabs. Drag the newly named "MosesPlayer" object from the Hierarchy View onto the open space in the right pane of the Project View as shown in Figure 65. Select "Original Prefab", when asked.

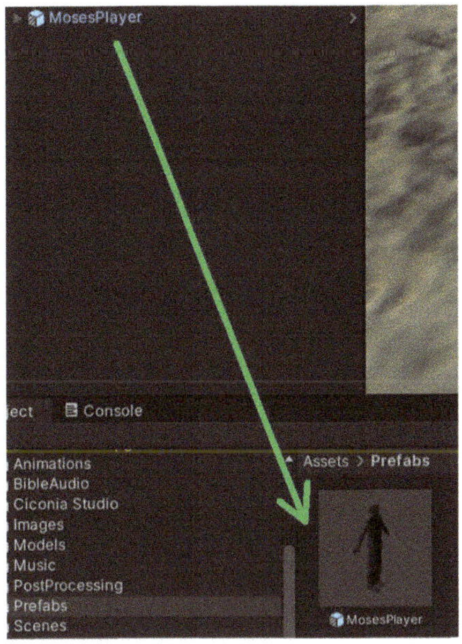

Figure 65

The Sound of Footsteps

In video games, it's important to get the big things right. But it's the sum of the little things that really immerse a player into the game. One of those small things is being able to hear your footsteps as you walk around. Now, playing the same exact footstep over and over again can get kind of boring, so we're going to play a variety of footsteps that sound similar but different, so the player feels like they're actually walking around.

Also, when you walk on different materials you have different footsteps. Carpet sounds different from wood and grass sounds different from rock. We're going to play different sounds based on what kind of material the player is walking on. Before we start making these changes we need to learn about arrays and random numbers.

Figure 66

Arrays

An array is a lining up or range of a particular thing. In Figure 66 you can see a lining up or array of statues. This array has 5 statues in it. Each statue is a little bit different but is still a statue.

C# has powerful facilities for handling arrays, which provide a way to store a large number of variables under the same name. Each variable, called an element, in an array must have the same data type, and they are distinguished from each other by an array index.

Arrays are declared in a manner similar to that used for regular variables but with a couple of differences. After the type of the array put opening and closing brackets "[]". Then we need to use the "new" statement, similar to classes, and say how big the array is.

Example:

```
int[] item;

item = new int[9];
```

The index on an array variable begins at 0 and ends at the dimensioned value minus one. So the item array in the above examples has nine items, ranging from item[0] to item[8]. You use array variables just like any other variable - just remember to include its name and its index.

When talking about which one of an array, we use the term "element". You may be thinking about The Elements like fire, water, and so on. Or maybe you're thinking of the Table of Elements from science class. An element is a basic unit of something. In C#, an element is the basic unit of an array. In the above example, an element is an integer.

It is also possible to have arrays of classes. For example, to have 20 Person classes available use:

```
Person[] personArray = new Person[20];
```

You can initialize arrays similar to variables. You can (optionally) delete the explicit array number and let C# figure it out by counting the number of elements used to initialize the array.

Example:

```
int[] item = new int[] {0, 1, 2, 3, 4, 5, 6, 7, 8};
```

C# will know this array has 9 elements.

To use an array in a statement use the brackets to say which element in the array you want to use:

```
item[5] = 7 * 70;
```

So then, C# will know you're referring to element number 5 or the 6th element in the array.

Multiple Dimensions

Figure 67

Like your favorite sci-fi games, movies, and books, arrays can also have with multiple dimensions. We have statues arranged in a grid in Figure 67. This array is 5 statues long and 4 statues deep to make a total of 5 * 4 = 20 statues.

One way to implement this in C# is to make an array of arrays. You have a number of elements long and a number of elements wide. The example below shows how to declare, instantiate this.

Example:

```
int[][] Statues;

Statues = new int[][4];

Statues[0] = new int[5];

Statues[0][3] = 12;
```

There are 2 sets of brackets on the first line to declare this array of arrays. For every dimension of the array, you add another set of brackets. When initializing the array, you always initialize one dimension at a time, which is what you see on line 2. Line 3 uses the method to refer to an element of the first dimension of the array on the left-hand of the equals sign. On the right side we create the next dimension of statues. Finally, on the fourth line we set the third element of the first dimension, denoted by [0] then [3], to the value 12.

Another way to declare this is with a 2D array by putting commas into the brackets. Each comma increases the number of dimensions by one.

Example:

```
int[,] Statues = new int[4,5];
```

You can use the same concept to create additional dimensions for your arrays. You just add another set of brackets. Please note that the more dimensions you add to your arrays, the more complicated your code will be. Sometimes this complexity is warranted if, for example, you want a 3D array of coordinates in space.

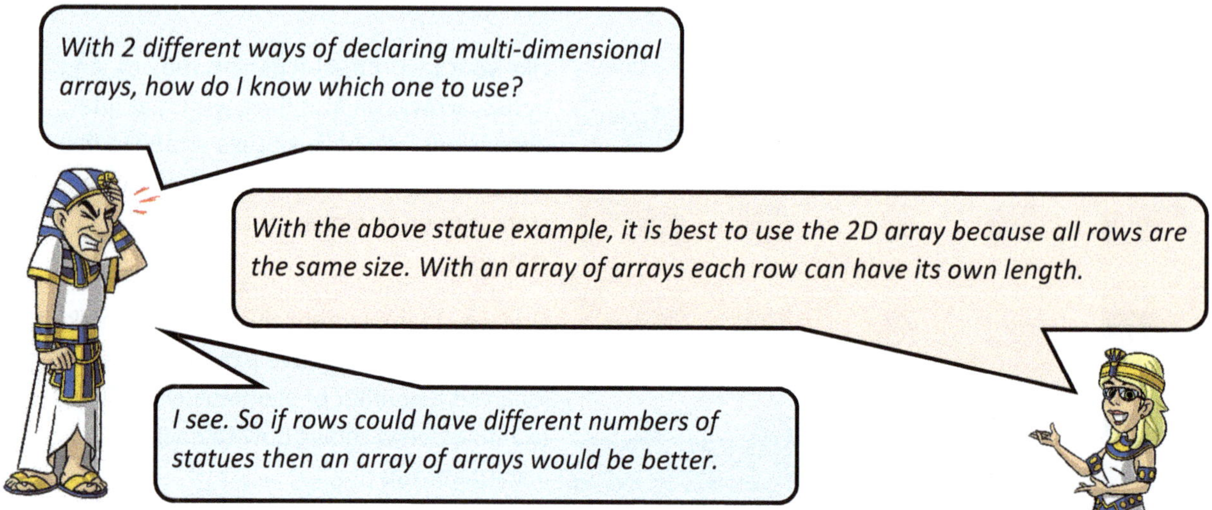

Inspecting Dimensions

For our footstep feature, we need to use a 2-dimensional array so we can have a variety of footsteps for each type of terrain. The plan is to make it easy to use so we can just drag our footsteps right onto the inspector. But there is one problem. Unity doesn't support showing multi-dimensional arrays in the inspector. So, we need a different way to write our 2D array.

For this new way, we're going to create a class inside the ThirdPersonUserControl class inside the script, "ThirdPersonUserControl.cs". It is embedded deep in the StandardAssets folder. Instead of having you try and search for it, we're going to find it using a slick method.

In the Hierarchy View, click on our "model_civilian" so that we can see his components in the inspector. Next, scroll down until you find the script "ThirdPersonUserControl". Then click on the box to the right of "Script" that is grayed out. This will automatically take you to the script in the Project View. You should see something similar to Figure 68. Now all you have to do is double-click the script and it in the Project View and it will open in Visual Studio.

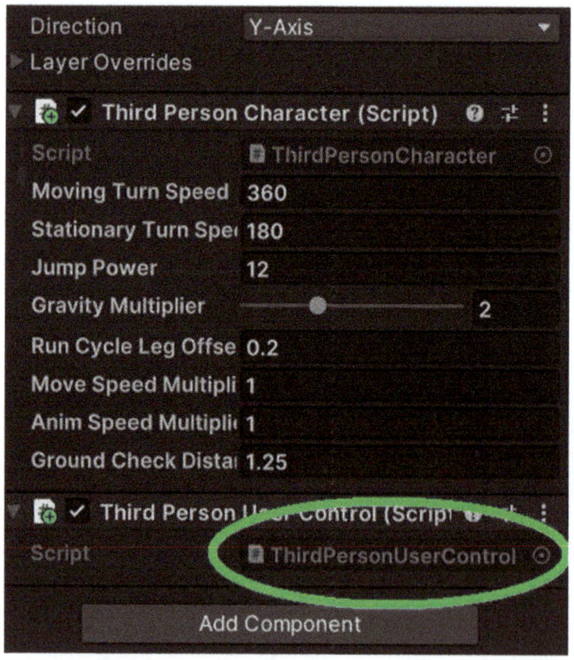

Figure 68

Type in the code as shown in Figure 69. The [System.Serializable] line above the class declaration tells C# that this class is something that can be shown in the inspector. This class has only one variable, which is an array of AudioClips. This array will hold the actual bits of audio to play when Moses is walking around. The AudioClip is a class defined in Unity, remember that classes are types and can be used in variable declaration, for sound and music to play using the computer's audio system. Whether or not the computer has speakers or headphones, you don't have to worry about that. It is handled for you.

```
public class ThirdPersonUserControl : MonoBehaviour
{
    [System.Serializable]
    2 references
    public class _footstep_sounds
    {
        public AudioClip[] footsteps;
    }

    public _footstep_sounds DefaultFootsteps;
    public _footstep_sounds[] TerrainFootsteps;
```

Figure 69

After the class is defined with its array, we create some variables below it. The "DefaultFootsteps" variable holds the footstep sounds that will be played when the player is not on the terrain. Maybe they've jumped on a rock or are walking on one of the blocks of stone or building. The next variable, "TerrainFootsteps", is our multi-dimensional array. Essentially, what we've done is used our class to wrap around the array. Then we just make an array of that class. We'll use it a bit differently than a 2D array, but it functions just the same.

Adding Audio

We're going to add another variable, but this time it will be private. Remember, that means this can only be accessed from inside the class. This line goes after the other private variables as shown in Figure 70 on line 25.

```
19        private ThirdPersonCharacter m_Character;
20        private Transform m_Cam;
21        private Vector3 m_CamForward;
22        private Vector3 m_Move;
23        private bool m_Jump;
24
25        private AudioSource m_Audio;
```

Figure 70

Make a new line and type:

```
private AudioSource m_Audio;
```

This variable will let us interact with the object's AudioSource component so we can play sounds. You may be asking, "What Audio Source Component? There isn't one attached to our MosesPlayer object." Good question! We'll go add it now.

Go back to Unity and make sure the "MosesPlayer" object is selected in the Hierarchy View. Going over to the inspector scroll to the very bottom and you'll see an "Add Component" button. Click it and select Audio > Audio Source. Update the prefab by dragging Moses onto the prefab from before.

The Audio Source component has a whole bunch of public variables that can be tweaked here. The next step is to link the variable "m_AudioSource" we declared in the code to the component we added to the object. To do that we need to add some code to the script's "Start" method.

Scroll down just a little bit and find the "Start" method. At the bottom of the method, create a new line and write the code shown in Figure 71.

This code gets the instance of the Audio Source component attached to the object so we can play sounds using it in the rest of the script.

```
else
{
    Debug.LogWarning(
        "Warning: no main camera found. Third perso
    // we use self-relative controls in this case,
}

// get the third person character ( this should nev
m_Character = GetComponent<ThirdPersonCharacter>();
m_Audio = GetComponent<AudioSource>();
```

Figure 71

Walking the Terrain

We're going to get pretty deep into C# for this next part. We will add 3 new methods to this class. The first one will determine if the player is standing on the terrain. At the bottom of the file, add the method as shown in Figure 72. Be sure to add it before 2 of the curly braces at the end of the file but after the first one. **Placement of the method in the right set of curly braces is critical.**

```
        private bool IsOnTerrain()
        {
            bool onTerrain = false;
            RaycastHit hitInfo;

            // Find out what is under the player
            if (Physics.Raycast(transform.position + new Vector3(0, 0.5f, 0),
                transform.TransformDirection(Vector3.down),
                out hitInfo))
            {
                if (hitInfo.transform.tag == "Terrain")
                {
                    onTerrain = true;
                }
            }

            return onTerrain;
        }
    }
}
```

Figure 72

The method "IsOnTerrain" can only be called from inside this class (private), returns a true or false value (bool), and has no parameters. At the top of the method, we declare a bool called "onTerrain" and initialize it to false. So, we assume the player is not on the terrain unless we find out otherwise.

The next variable and the "if" statement after it is what we use to find out if the player is on the terrain. RaycastHit is a class in Unity that is set to the instance of an object.

Next, we ask Unity's Physics engine if there is anything underneath the player. To do that, we access the Physics class. Specifically, we call the Raycast method. What does this do? Well, we learn from the Sound of Music that a ray is a "drop of golden sun". It basically starts at a certain place (like the sun) and travels in a direction for a specified distance. You can think of casting like casting fishing nets over the water, it's like throwing something. So, we basically throw this ray out there and see if it hits anything.

The ray starts at "transform.position" plus some Vector3 as indicated by the first parameter of the method. The "transform" is an instance of the Transform class of the object the script is attached to (which is the player). Vector3 is the class Unity uses to represent 3D space. This adds to the 'Y' position that we will start our Ray. If we don't do this then our ray will start below the player's feet and miss whatever he's standing on.

The second parameter is the direction of the ray. Since we're trying to determine what the player's walking on, the direction is down.

Raycasting is useful for a lot of different things. Later on, we'll learn how to use it to figure out what object a player clicked on with the mouse.

The last argument is the "hitInfo" that we declared earlier. But it uses the keyword "out" before it. Up until now, all the parameters we used go into the method. This parameter actually comes out of the method. The return value also comes out of the method, but there is only 1 return. If you want to have multiple things returned, then you need to create "out" parameters. See below for how to do it.

```
Return MethodName(Type Input, out Type Output1, out Type,
Output2)
{
      [Code to do something]
}
```

We've called the Raycast method now, which returns a bool. If it is true, then that means the ray hit something. If it is false, then the ray didn't hit anything. If it hit something, then we want to know if it is the terrain. To figure that out, we check the object's tag.

Now we need to take a moment to give the Terrain the right tag. Click on "Terrain" in the Hierarchy View and in the Inspector click the box next to Tag that says "Untagged". We want to set this to "Terrain". So, click "Add Tag…" as shown in Figure 73.

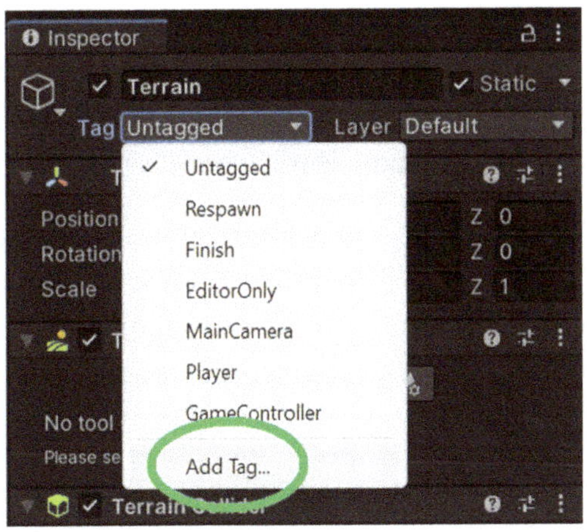

Figure 73

Under the Tags section click the plus sign and you'll be prompted to enter the name of the new tag. Type in "Terrain" and click Save. You'll see the new tag appear as shown in Figure 74.

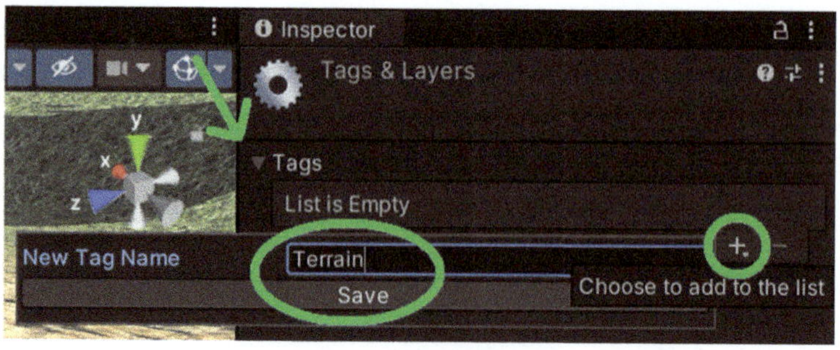

Figure 74

Click back on the Terrain object in the Hierarchy View and when you click the Tag box, you'll see that "Terrain" has been added. Select it, and now when we try to check for it in the "if" statement we'll be able to see it and set the "onTerrain" bool to true. After that, the method returns the "onTerrain" bool back to whoever called it, and life goes on.

The Loop of Life

As life goes on, the next method we need to add requires running the same code a bunch of times. We could either, write all the code and have a huge method, or we can shorten it significantly by putting that code in a loop. There are many applications that call for the repetition of certain code segments. For example, you may want to roll a die (simulated die of course) until it shows a six. Or, you might generate financial results until a certain sum of returns has been achieved. This idea of repeating code is called iteration or looping.

In C#, looping is done with one of three formats. The first is the while loop:

```
while (condition)
{
        [process this code]
}
```

In this structure, the code block in braces is repeated 'as long as' the Boolean expression condition is true. Note that a while loop structure will not execute even once if the while condition is false the first time through. If we do enter the loop, it is assumed at some point the condition will become false so we can exit the loop. Notice there is no semicolon after the while statement.

This brings up a very important point – if you use a loop, make sure you can get out of the loop!! As long as your code is operating in some loop, nothing else can run in the game. In addition to making the condition false, you can exit a loop using the break statement. This will get you out of a loop so other code can run. Of course, you need logic in a loop to decide when a break is appropriate.

Example:

```
counter = 1;
while (counter <= 1000)
{
        counter += 1;
}
```

This loop repeats as long as (while) the variable counter is less than or equal to 1000.

The second looping structure in C# is a do/while structure:

```
do
{
        [process this code]
}
while (condition);
```

This loop repeats 'as long as' the Boolean expression condition is true. The loop is always executed at least once. Somewhere in the loop, the condition must be changed to false to allow exiting. Notice there is a semicolon after the while statement.

Example:

```
sum = 0;
do
{
        sum += 3;
}
while (sum <= 50);
```

In this example, we increment a sum by 3 until that sum exceeds 50 (or while the sum is less than or equal to 50).

The third kind of loop is a counting loop. This kind of loop is useful for adding items to a list or summing a number of values to find an average.

C# counting is accomplished using the "for" loop:

```
for (initialization; expression; update)
{
        [process this code]
}
```

The initialization step is executed once and is used to initialize a counter variable. The expression step is executed before each repetition of the loop. If the expression is true then the code is executed; if false, the loop is exited. The update step is executed after each loop iteration. It is used to update the counter variable.

Example:

```
for (degrees = 0; degrees <= 360; degrees += 10)
{
        // convert to radians
        r = degrees * Math.PI / 180;
        a = Math.Sin(r);
        b = Math.Cos(r);
        c = Math.Tan(r);
```

```
}
```

In this example, we compute trigonometric functions for angles from 0 to 360 degrees in increments of 10 degrees. It is assumed that all variables have been properly declared.

Yet another way to code a loop is using "foreach". This is great for doing operations on an array or list (we'll talk about these later).

```
foreach (type variable in ArrayName)
{
      [Do processing on variable]
}
```

Example:

```
float[] myValues = new float[100];
sum = 0;
foreach (float val in myValues)
{
      sum += val;
}
average = sum / 100;
```

This code finds the average value of 100 numbers stored in the array myValues. It first sums each of the values in a "for" loop. That sum is then divided by the number of terms (100) to yield the average. Note the use of the increment operator. Also, notice the counter is declared in the initialization step. This is a common declaration in a loop or block of code. Such loop or block level variables lose their values once the loop is completed.

With so many kinds of loops it can be hard trying to figure out which one to use. Use "for" loops when you have to count something or go through an array or list. Use a "while" loop when you want to loop until something happens. And use a "do while" loop if you want to make sure you go through the loop at least once.

You may exit a "for" loop early using a break statement. This will transfer program control to the statement following the closing brace. Use of a continue statement will skip all statements remaining in the loop and return program control to the "for" statement.

You can also use a "continue" statement within a loop. When a "continue" is encountered, all further steps in the loop are skipped and the program operation is transferred to the top of the loop.

Again, make sure you can always get out of a loop! Infinite loops are never nice. Sometimes the only way out is rebooting your machine!

Standing on Solid Ground?

We're done with our method to determine if the player is on the terrain, now we need to figure out what that terrain is. To do that, we need to go down into the depths of the TerrainData class. First, we find where on the terrain the player currently is. Once we've got the player's coordinates we get the texture mix at that point. A texture is a picture that Unity wraps around objects. For terrain, you can have multiple textures on the terrain and mix them so that they transition into each other more naturally. See in Figure 75 where there is a rocky texture on the cliff to the right, then it gets sandy at the top, then transitions to grassy going toward the left.

Figure 75

Since we can mix textures like that, in order to play the right sound, we need to find out which texture is most dominant at the spot where the player is currently standing or walking.

```
private int GetTerrainTextureIndex(Vector3 pos)
{
    TerrainData terrainData = Terrain.activeTerrain.terrainData;
    Vector3 terrainPos = Terrain.activeTerrain.transform.position;
    float[,,] alphaMaps;
    float textureMaxMix = 0;
    int textureMaxIndex = -1;

    // Determine terrain coordinates
    int terPosX = (int)(((pos.x - terrainPos.x) / terrainData.size.x) * terrainData.alphamapWidth);
    int terPosZ = (int)(((pos.z - terrainPos.z) / terrainData.size.z) * terrainData.alphamapHeight);

    // Get the texture mix
    alphaMaps = terrainData.GetAlphamaps(terPosX, terPosZ, 1, 1);

    // Determine the texture with the biggest mix
    for (int i = 0; i < alphaMaps.GetUpperBound(2) + 1; i++)
    {
        if (alphaMaps[0, 0, i] > textureMaxMix)
        {
            textureMaxIndex = i;
            textureMaxMix = alphaMaps[0, 0, i];
        }
    }

    return textureMaxIndex;
}
```

Figure 76

The function in Figure 76 is a private method that returns an integer and gets a Vector3 passed as a parameter named "pos". That is short for position. At the beginning of the method, we declare a TerrainData variable and initialize it. To set the variable we use the Terrain static class. From it, we find what the active terrain is and get its data. Both Terrain and TerrainData are Unity specific classes.

The "terrainPos" variable we'll use to offset against to find the terrain coordinates to get the texture mix at that spot. Next, we come to "float[,,]" which is one of the ways to declare a multi-dimensional array. In this case, we have a 3D array of float types. This "alphaMap" will store the actual texture mix for the terrain.

The "textureMix" array of floats will hold the actual texture mix at the current location of the player. Since we're trying to find the texture with the largest mix, we need to store "textureMaxMix" so we know what largest mix is. Then the "textureMaxIndex" actually holds the index into the array of which texture has the largest mix.

The next two lines (on 119 and 120) get the coordinates on the terrain of the player's current location using. We use X and Z because, if you remember, Y is the vertical axis. The code on line 123 gets the "Alpha Map" of the specified position. In digital graphics, "alpha" refers to transparency. Think about it this way. You have a pair of sunglasses that tint everything blue. If you look at a red car, then it will seem purple. The same idea is used for the terrain. You've got some grass-colored texture on top, but you can see through it a little to some of the sand texture on the bottom.

Now we loop through the texture mix of the player's coordinate. Since we're counting up through the elements of the texture mix array it is easiest to code using a "for" loop. The "if" statement checks if the current texture's mix is higher than what we've already found as the max. Since textureMaxMix is initialized to 0 the first texture in the loop (or element 0) will always start off as the max. If another one is higher, we set the "textureMaxMix" to its value and the "textureMaxIndex" to the index of the current texture (which we found to be higher).

At the end of the loop, we've found which texture has the highest mix and we're done! We can return that texture's index.

Casting Lots

The next method we'll add will choose which array of footstep sounds from which to randomly pick. But before we add that, we need to learn about random numbers. Random numbers introduce unpredictability. This ensures different results each time you go through your code. C# has a few ways to generate random numbers. The generator uses the C# Random object in the Unity Engine. You can get either random integers or floats. C# uses the type of the parameters to tell it which.

Integer Example:

```
int randomInt = Random(0, 5);
```

This statement generates integer that is greater than or equal to the lower limit and less than the upper limit. The possible values will be 0, 1, 2, 3, and 4.

To roll a six-sided die, the number of spots would be computed using:

```
numberSpots = Random(0, 5) + 1;
```

The random number generator doesn't really give us numbers at random. It runs an equation that uses the system clock to start with, called the seed. Since the clock always changes, the numbers are random enough. If you seed the random number generator with the same number then you end up with the same set of "random" numbers. This is "pseudo-random".

To randomly choose a number between 100 and 200, use:

```
number = myRandom.Next(101) + 100;
```

Float Example:

```
float randomFloat = Random(0.0f, 5f);
```

This statement generates a float that is greater than or equal to the lower limit and less than or equal to the upper limit. So, you can get values ranging anywhere between 0 and 5. But the likelihood you'll get exactly 0 or 5 is very very VERY small.

Letting the foot fall

With a good understanding of how random numbers work we can get started on our method to choose random footsteps. We will call both methods we just coded.

```
private void PlayFootstepSound()
{
    if (m_Audio.isPlaying == false)
    {
        _footstep_sounds selSteps = DefaultFootsteps;

        if (IsOnTerrain())
        {
            int terrainTexInd = GetTerrainTextureIndex(transform.position);

            if ((terrainTexInd < TerrainFootsteps.Length) && (TerrainFootsteps[terrainTexInd] != null))
            {
                selSteps = TerrainFootsteps[terrainTexInd];
            }
        }

        m_Audio.clip = selSteps.footsteps[UnityEngine.Random.Range(0, selSteps.footsteps.Length)];
        m_Audio.Play();
    }
}
```

Figure 77

See Figure 77 for the new method to insert into the class. The very first thing we do is check the "isPlaying" variable of the Audio Source. We only want to start a new footstep sound if there are no footsteps already playing. Otherwise, the audio will get clogged with footsteps and the player won't know what's going on. Inside the "if" statement we declare a variable of the class we created before. This variable will store the array of footsteps from which we will choose. We initialize it to the default array.

Next, we call the method "IsOnTerrain" and if the player is over terrain, then call the "GetTerrainTextureIndex" method to get the dominant texture. Once we have the dominant texture, we use that texture index to select one of the arrays in the 2D terrain footstep array.

Finally, we randomly select one of the footsteps in the array as the clip in the audio source and play it. Now we're almost done so we have this feature working. There are 3 more lines of code we need to add. Find the method "FixedUpdate" and enter lines 80-84 from Figure 78 near the bottom of the function but before the last two lines. If the player is moving, then the "m_Move" variable will be non-zero. If the player is moving, then we want to hear footsteps.

```
76 #if !MOBILE_INPUT
77             // walk speed multiplier
78             if (Input.GetKey(KeyCode.LeftShift)) m_Move *= 0.5f;
79 #endif
80 
81             if (m_Move != Vector3.zero)
82             {
83                 PlayFootstepSound();
84             }
85 
86             // pass all parameters to the character control script
87             m_Character.Move(m_Move, crouch, m_Jump);
88             m_Jump = false;
```

Figure 78

With that last bit of code, the feature is now done. But we're not quite ready to test it yet. We've got the code done to select random footsteps from the public arrays and now we need to fill those arrays up with footsteps.

Figure 79

Heading back into the Unity editor, go back to the inspector for the "Model_Civilian". In the "Third Person User Control" script, you'll see two variables here with triangles to the left of them as shown in Figure 79. Click the triangle next to "Default Footsteps" to reveal the footstep class. Expand that and you'll see the array with a Size set to '0'. We're going to add some footsteps clips in this array.

Figure 80

In the Project View, under assets, expand the Sound Effects folder and then expand footsteps_pack_1. You'll see a whole bunch of different types of footstep sounds. Click the "ground folder and you'll see there are 50 variations of the standard ground footstep. Now, you can set the size of the array up to 50 and drag each footstep sound over but we should be able to get away with 5 variations. You can drag each sound onto the "Footsteps" and when you let go, you'll see the number go up. When you expand, it should look like Figure 80.

Next is the terrain 2D array. But there is one little problem. You don't know what index the different textures like grass and sand are. To find that out you need to walk on the terrain and print out each index in the console. But don't fret! I've already done the hard work for you.

Terrain Textures:

0. Sand
1. Stones
2. Gravel
3. Sand
4. Grass Dry
5. Stones

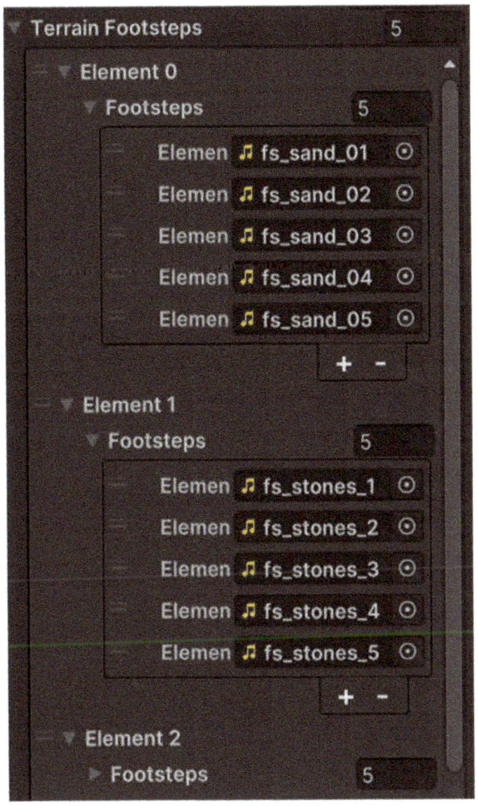

Figure 81

So now you can go through and setup the Terrain Footstep 2D array. Set the size of the Terrain Footsteps array to 6 (because there are 6 textures on the terrain). Then go through each element and set the size to 5. The next part will get a little tedious. Go to the folder for each texture listed above and drag the first 5 textures into each of them.

Notice that sand and stones are both in the list twice. To make those textures sound different, use footsteps 6-10. These will look similar to Figure 81 but with all 6 elements in the 2D array filled out.

Unity connects the audio to the variables in the array like glue. Once you put it there it stays until you change it. With all that work on the player let's save him again. Drag the "Model_Civilian" onto the Prefab we created earlier named "MosesPlayer" in the Prefabs folder under Assets in the Project View. If you get a prompt asking whether or not to replace, just click replace.

Now we're ready to try out our footstep feature. Click the play button and give it a test drive. Having the footsteps play as we walk and change depending on what we're walking on really helps draw the player into the game. But you may have noticed a couple odd things. The footsteps on the grass don't line up with Moses' actual steps on the ground and if you try jumping, the footsteps still play.

Fix the footsteps

We'll fix the problem of footsteps while jumping a little later. Right now, we'll try and line up the footstep audio to the animation as best as we can. There are a few different ways to do it, but we need to catch our breath from all the coding we did in the last section, so we'll do it the easy way.

If you remember, the Audio Source has a pitch variable. Now, back when your grandparents were kids, instead of playing MP3 music files on your phone, they had something called a record player. This record player was a really early music player. You put this big black frisbee, called a record, on the player, put the cartridge in the middle, and it would play the music on the record. But there was an interesting little knob on the record player. It controlled the speed the record was played at. If you cranked up the speed, then not only would the record play faster but it would also sound higher in pitch. In this way, the Audio Source is like a record player.

What we're going to do is add a speed knob to our Audio Source (record player) which we will use to change the pitch. As a result, the footstep will either play faster or slower. Then, all we need to do is watch the footsteps and listen so that we can line them up.

In order to do this, we need to make modifications in a couple different places. First, add a new public float in the "_footstep_sounds" class named "Speed" as seen in Figure 82. With track speed with each array of footsteps. That means the footsteps in each array should be about the same length, but now we can have different lengths between different arrays. Note that "= 1" gives a default value of '1' to this variable.

```
[System.Serializable]
3 references
public class _footstep_sounds
{
    public float Speed = 1;
    public AudioClip[] footsteps;
}
```

Figure 82

```
155 m_Audio.clip = selSteps.footsteps[UnityEngine.Random.Range(0, selSteps.footsteps.Length)];
156 m_Audio.pitch = selSteps.Speed;
157 m_Audio.Play();
```

Figure 83

To change the Audio Source's pitch to match the speed of the footsteps, add the code shown in line 156 of Figure 83.

Finally, we need to set the "Speed" values for each footstep array in the inspector. As you go back to Unity, the script changes will be imported, and you'll see the "Speed" variable added to the array. Because we set the default to '1', you can see that they all have been set in the inspector. However, we want to speed up the grass footstep so it better matches Moses' footstep animation. Set it to "1.5" for Element 4 as you can see in Figure 84.

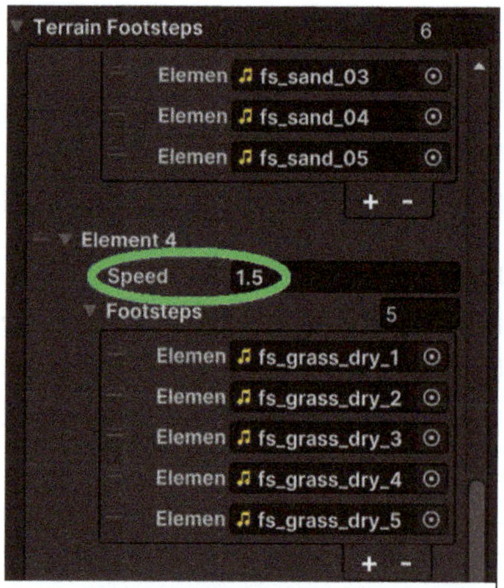

Figure 84

Footsteps in the Air?

Next, we're going to fix the problem where footsteps are heard while the player is jumping. To do that, we need to know if the character is on the ground and only play footsteps then. Luckily, we don't have to check ourselves, the "ThirdPersonCharacter" script already holds that information, but we can't use it because it is not public. As you can see in Figure 85, right-click on the "ThirdPersonCharacter" type that is just below where we declared our footstep variables and click "Go

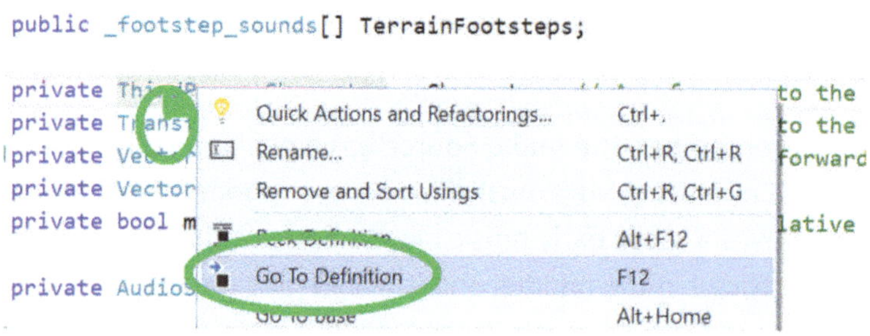

Figure 85

to Declaration". This will take you directly into the "ThirdPersonCharacter" script, so we don't have to search for it in the Project View.

Inside the class, if you search down the variables, you can find the one, we're looking for named "m_IsGrounded". Now, it is not marked as private, but any class variable without a scope keyword (i.e., public, private, or protected) is set to private by default. So, all we need to do is make it public as you can see in Figure 86. Save the file and go back to the "ThirdPersonUserControl" script.

```
Rigidbody m_Rigidbody;
Animator m_Animator;
public bool m_IsGrounded;
float m_OrigGroundCheckDistance;
```

Figure 86

Scroll down to the "FixedUpdate" method and find where we inserted our footstep code. Add code as shown in Figure 87 on line 82 to check if the player is on the ground. Now go back into the game. Walk around a bit and then try jumping. You'll hear that the footsteps now correctly stop playing while Moses is in the air.

```
82  if ((m_Move != Vector3.zero) && m_Character.m_IsGrounded)
83  {
84      PlayFootstepSound();
85  }
```

Figure 87

The Sound of Jumping

To add sound effects for jumping and landing, start with adding public variables above our footstep arrays like in Figure 88.

```
public AudioClip JumpSound;
public AudioClip LandSound;
public _footstep_sounds DefaultFootsteps;
public _footstep_sounds[] TerrainFootsteps;
```

Figure 88

To figure out when we've landed, we need to store a copy of the "IsGrounded" variable. We'll name it, as shown in Figure 89 on line 29, as "m_LastGrounded". This variable stores the last state of this boolean. Having this last state around will let us figure out when the character changes from NOT being on the ground TO being on the ground.

```
28  private AudioSource m_Audio;
29  private bool m_LastGrounded;
```

Figure 89

Now we add the C# code to play the jump and land sounds at the right times. Scroll down to the "Update" method and add the code as shown in Figure 90. We'll go over the second "if" statement first. Line 61 above was already written and gets whether the player pressed the jump button. Later in the script, this "m_Jump" variable gets sent to the "ThirdPersonCharacter" script to actually make Moses jump.

```
51          private void Update()
52          {
53              if (!m_LastGrounded && m_Character.m_IsGrounded)
54              {
55                  m_Audio.clip = LandSound;
56                  m_Audio.Play();
57              }
58
59              if (!m_Jump)
60              {
61                  m_Jump = CrossPlatformInputManager.GetButtonDown("Jump");
62
63                  if (m_Jump && m_Character.m_IsGrounded)
64                  {
65                      m_Audio.clip = JumpSound;
66                      m_Audio.Play();
67                  }
68              }
69
70              m_LastGrounded = m_Character.m_IsGrounded;
71          }
```

Figure 90

On line 63, the if statement checks if the player pressed the jump button and we also make sure that Moses is still on the ground. If so, then we play the jump sound. We want to make sure they aren't jumping already, or the sound will play every frame and sound like a glitch and every time the button is pressed. After this "if" statement we set what the current grounded state to the last one, so we have that history.

Back to the first "if" statement on line 53, we check if Moses was last seen OFF the ground but is currently on the ground. This allows us to find out the exact moment when he lands. At that moment we play the "LandSound".

Minor Tweaks

There are still a couple things a little off about our player character. First, Moses can jump really high. There is a knob that is very easy to adjust for this. Clicking on the "MosesPlayer" in the Hierarchy View, scroll down in the Inspector until you can see the "Third Person Character" script. One of the variables is Jump Power and it is currently set to '12'.

Try different values of jump power. Set it really high, something like '50' so Moses can jump over walls. I find that a jump power of '9' looks best to me.

Figure 91

Another problem Moses has is walking up stairs. Give it a try. In play mode, run Moses inside the gate and turn into one of the corridors. You'll see steps leading upward but if you try to walk up them it's like Moses is hitting a wall.

To fix that, we need to adjust one of the variables among the "MosesPlayer" components. In the Capsule Collider, change the "Radius" variable to 0.9. Since the capsule collider has that curved shape, as seen in Figure 91, when it hits against an edge there is a natural tendency to move up. But, for these steps, the curve isn't big enough so increasing the radius makes the curve bigger so Unity's physics will allow the player to climb the steps.

Now, if you click play, then the stairs are much easier to climb. Overwrite our "MosesPlayer" prefab to save this change.

Moving the Mountains

Figure 92

There is another little thing that could get in the way of our player enjoying the game. Click the play button and go back through the gate and into the city. To the left, is a big building that looks like an Egyptian Temple.

Go over there and try to get on the platform. Doesn't work, does it? If you go into the Scene view and focus on the "MosesPlayer" then you can see why. The green lines are his collider are only just above the blocks as shown in Figure 92. Unity's physics engine won't let us climb that no matter how big we make the radius.

To solve this problem, we're going to lower the whole temple, with the foundation. Exit play mode and in the Hierarchy View click on the "Big Temple". You can see the whole structure gets highlighted in orange.

In the inspector, set the 'Y' value of the transform's position to '84.35'. This lowers the whole structure so that Moses can climb onto the structure's foundation as easily as a stair. Save the scene and go back into play mode to give it a try.

Walking in Water?

Another fun thing to try is to go swimming! Outside the city is the Nile River which runs deep and wide. Well, maybe not quite to scale, but you get the idea. You can take Moses in the river and see what happens. I was playing around, and in Figure 93, you can see I've got Moses peeking out of the water like a Navy Seal.

Figure 93

But we're not going to launch any amphibious assaults on the city in this game. One of the tricky things with games is giving the player boundaries. From a player perspective, you don't really want them so you can explore wherever you want to go. But from a game development perspective, we don't have the resources to make a world where the player can explore indefinitely. To compromise, we

try to make the boundaries look as natural as possible. We're going to use the river as a boundary for the player.

First, in the Hierarchy View, click the "WaterProDayTime" object. We need a new tag again. So, click the Tag in the inspector and select "Add Tag...". The new tag's name will be "Water". Next, Add a Box Collider component from the Physics section. Set the Y Center to '-0.05' and set the size's X/Y/Z values to 1.25, 0.1, 1.25 respectively. The collider will make it so the player will be able to walk on the water. But since that particular miracle was reserved for Jesus, we need to keep Moses from stepping on it.

Now we need to do something once the player is on the water. What we're going to do is, if the player is on the water, we move the player off the water. So, open the "ThirdPersonUserControl" script again in Visual Studio because we have some C# scripting to do.

A Time for Timers

I love cookies. I love white chocolate and macadamia nut cookies more. But I probably love white chocolate and macadamia nut cookies that are freshly baked the most. When baking cookies, it is important to make sure the cookie dough stays in the oven for the right amount of time. If you let them stay in too long, they get burned but if you take them out too early, they are too gooey.

An easy way to make sure you know the right time to take the cookies out of the oven is by using a timer. Well, we can make use of timers in C# too. There is a handy method named "Invoke" that will wait an amount of time we tell it and then call any method we want in the class.

```
Invoke("TakeOutCookies", 10.4f);
```

The above statement will wait for 10.4 seconds and then call the method TakeOutCookies(). This also means that you need to define the method that you want it to call, otherwise you'll get an error. Arguments can't be passed with Invoke().

If you want to call that method repeatedly, there's something for that too!

```
InvokeRepeating("ReadBook", 5f, 28.7);
```

This method will call ReadBook() the first time after 5 seconds. After that it will call it every 28.7 seconds. This way you'll never stop reading books. Your mom will be happy. Let's say you want to stop reading books or you changed your mind about taking out the cookies because they need to cook longer. The below method call will stop both "Invoke" and "InvokeRepeating" in their tracks.

```
CancelInvoke("ReadBook");
```

No Swimming

Let's add some more private variables. Add "lastPos" as shown in Figure 94 on line 30. The Vector3 "lastPos" variable will hold the last valid position of the player. This will be on ground that isn't tagged as water.

```
28        private AudioSource m_Audio;
29        private bool m_LastGrounded;
30        private Vector3 lastPos;
```

Figure 94

We could just update "lastPos" every time "Update" is called, but since we need to do a ray cast operation for it, we don't want that slowing things down. Instead, we'll do it every quarter of a second to keep performance impact minimal. Add the code on line 49 of Figure 95 which is inside the Start method.

```
46            // get the third person character ( this should never
47            m_Character = GetComponent<ThirdPersonCharacter>();
48            m_Audio = GetComponent<AudioSource>();
49            InvokeRepeating("PreventWaterWalk", 0.25f, 0.25f);
```

Figure 95

At the of the class, on line 180, add the method in Figure 96. It first sets the "lastPos" if the player is on the ground but not on water. Then, if the player is on water it reverts to the "lastPos".

```
180       private void PreventWaterWalk()
181       {
182           if (m_Character.m_IsGrounded && !IsOverWater(transform.position))
183           {
184               lastPos = transform.position;
185           }
186
187           if (IsOverWater(transform.position))
188           {
189               transform.position = lastPos;
190           }
191       }
```

Figure 96

```
193     private bool IsOverWater(Vector3 pos)
194     {
195         bool overWater = false;
196         RaycastHit rcHit;
197 
198         if (Physics.Raycast(pos + new Vector3(0, 1, 0), Vector3.down * 2, out rcHit))
199         {
200             if (rcHit.transform.tag == "Water")
201             {
202                 overWater = true;
203             }
204         }
205 
206         return overWater;
207     }
```

Figure 97

After the method that prevents the player from walking on water, we need to add another method that will detect if the player got onto the water. Write the code on line 193 shown in Figure 97. Like the footstep method, we're casting a ray downward to see what we hit. If we hit "Water" then return true, otherwise return false.

With this feature implemented you can go to the water all you want and never actually go in. You can even try jumping into the water and you'll end it wherever you started your jump.

Before we're done here, let's tag Moses as the "Player". Click the "MosesPlayer" and in the inspector, set the Tag to "Player". This will let other scripts we write know how to find the player. Go ahead and overwrite the "MosesPlayer" prefab to save our work so far.

Boat Sailing

To end this chapter, we're going to go sailing on the Nile! We're going to create a brand-new script, but first, let's get our boat. In Figure 98, type "SailingBoat" in the search bar. You can see a model of the same name appear in the bottom pane. Drag it onto the blank space at the bottom of the Hierarchy View.

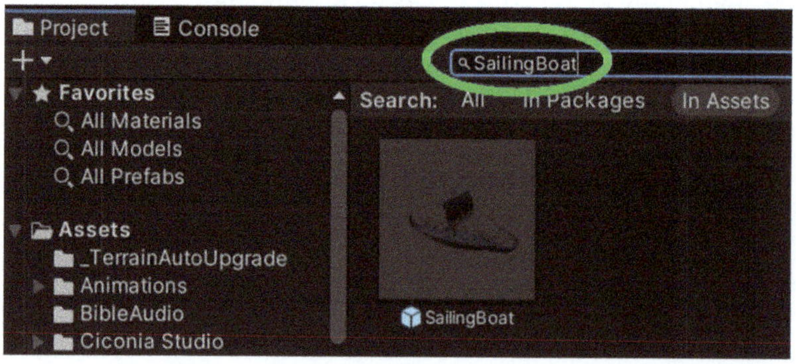

Figure 98

Set the transform's "Position" and "Rotation" values as shown in Figure 99. You don't need to change the Scale. This places the boat in the water nearby where we put Moses.

Figure 99

Next we need to add a couple physics components. First, add a RigidBody to it and set the variables to: Drag = 0.2, Angular Drag = 0.2, and Use Gravity = False (uncheck). In the Constraints section ensure only the Y position is checked and the X and Z rotation is checked. Now add a Box Collider where the Center has the Y set to '-8.5' and the size is set to: 'X = 7', 'Y = 0.5', 'Z = 35'. See Figure 100 to check your values and checkboxes.

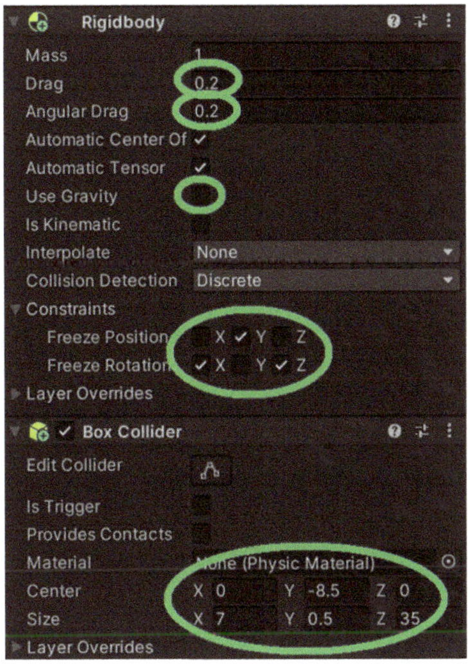

Figure 100

With the ship object all setup, now we need a script to control it. Batten down the hatches and get ready to set sail! Navigate to Assets > Scripts in the Project View and right-click on the blank space, selecting Create > C# Script. Name it "BoatController". Then drag the "BoatController" C# script onto the "PlayerShip" object in the Hierarchy View.

First, add the variables shown in Figure 101. "CamTrans" is a reference to a GameObject's transform we can use to place the camera so the player can see the ship moving. The "ForwardSpeed" is how fast the boat moves along, and the "RotateSpeed" is how fast it will turn. The "IsBoating" Boolean tracks whether or not we're sailing the boat or walking around as Moses. Finally, the Player variable will refer to the "MosesPlayer" so we can make sure that when we move the boat it doesn't move the player.

```
public Transform CamTrans;
public float ForwardSpeed;
public float RotateSpeed;
public bool IsBoating;
public GameObject Player;
```

Figure 101

Create a new method to "EnableBoating" similar to the method shown in Figure 102. First, we access the "main" camera. In Unity scenes, it is possible to have multiple cameras. You do this when you want to switch between them or show the player different parts of the scene. We'll use this later for the world map. But we can always use the "main" variable to access the main camera. This is the camera with the Tag "Main Camera". Just make sure there is only one camera tagged as main.

```
private void EnableBoating()
{
    Camera.main.transform.SetParent(transform);
    Camera.main.transform.position = CamTrans.position;
    Camera.main.transform.rotation = CamTrans.rotation;
    Camera.main.GetComponent<ThirdPersonOrbitCam>().enabled = false;
    Player.SetActive(false);
}
```

Figure 102

Now, we will change the parent of the main camera from Moses to the boat. Remember how the camera follows Moses along because it is a child object of him? Well, now the camera will follow the boat because it is a child object of it.

Next, we set the player to inactive by coding "SetActive(false)". This means the player's update method won't get called and the object will no longer show up in the game or scene views. The object will also be grayed out in the Hierarchy View. We want to do this so that when we move the boat, we don't move Moses too.

After that, we set the position and rotation of the main camera to the public variables we defined above. Then we disable the ThirdPersonOrbitCam script by setting enabled to false. Like disabling the player object, just disabling the script will stop the script from getting Update and other method calls.

To disable boating we just undo what we did as seen in Figure 104. Enable the player, set Moses back as the parent, and enable the ThirdPersonOrbitCam.

```
private void DisableBoating()
{
    Player.SetActive(true);
    Camera.main.transform.SetParent(Player.transform);
    Camera.main.GetComponent<ThirdPersonOrbitCam>().enabled = true;
}
```

Figure 104

```
void Update()
{
    if (Input.GetKeyDown(KeyCode.B))
    {
        IsBoating = !IsBoating;

        if (IsBoating)
        {
            EnableBoating();
        }
        else
        {
            DisableBoating();
        }
    }

    if (IsBoating)
    {
        Vector3 force = transform.forward * Input.GetAxis("Vertical") * ForwardSpeed;
        GetComponent<Rigidbody>().AddForce(force);
        transform.Rotate(Vector3.up, Input.GetAxis("Horizontal") * RotateSpeed);
    }
}
```

Figure 103

To switch between boating and walking we add code from Figure 103 to the "Update" method. If the 'B' key is pressed, then we make the switch. We use our "IsBoating" Boolean to track it. Remember, the '!' operator changes Boolean values between true and false. After that, we either call the methods for Enable or Disable boating, depending on what is the Boolean.

In the bottom "if" statement, we have our controller to do the boating. It's simple but has some new code for us. We're going to use the same vertical axis to row forward and backward as with Moses. But we don't want to just change the position of the boat because that's not how boats work in water. You row forward and even when you stop rowing you still go forward. To get the same effect, we use the Unity physics engine to add force to our object. We use the "Rigidbody" component that we created earlier to add the force to the object. Force comes in the form of a Vector3.

We apply force going to the forward side of the model to go forward. Then we multiply that by the Vertical axis (i.e., player pressing 'W' or 'S' the keys) and then our forward speed so we can control how fast the boat goes. Finally, we rotate the boat based on the Horizontal axis (i.e., player pressing left or right keys) and the speed to rotate. When we rotate, we need to specify not only the angle but the axis we want to rotate on. Selecting "Vector3.up" uses the Y-axis which makes the boat turn left and right.

Figure 105

There's just a couple more things to do back in Unity we need to do to setup our script. In the Hierarchy View, right-click on the "PlayerShip" and select "Create Empty" named "CamLoc". It should show up as a child of "PlayerShip". Set the transform to what you see in X. Then left click "PlayerShip" so the "BoatController" shows up in the inspector and drag "CamLoc" into the "CamTrans" field. The camera will move to it when the boat controller is enabled.

Figure 106

While the "PlayerShip" is selected. In the "BoatController" script, set Forward Speed to "10" and Rotate Speed to 0.5. Drag "MosesPlayer" onto the Player field so it looks like Figure 106. Now click the play button and get ready to set sail. Pressing the 'B' button will let you board the boat. Go sailing for a little bit and press 'B' again to go back to Moses. He's right where you left him. Feel free to play around with the settings on the boat controller to go faster, slower, or change the camera position.

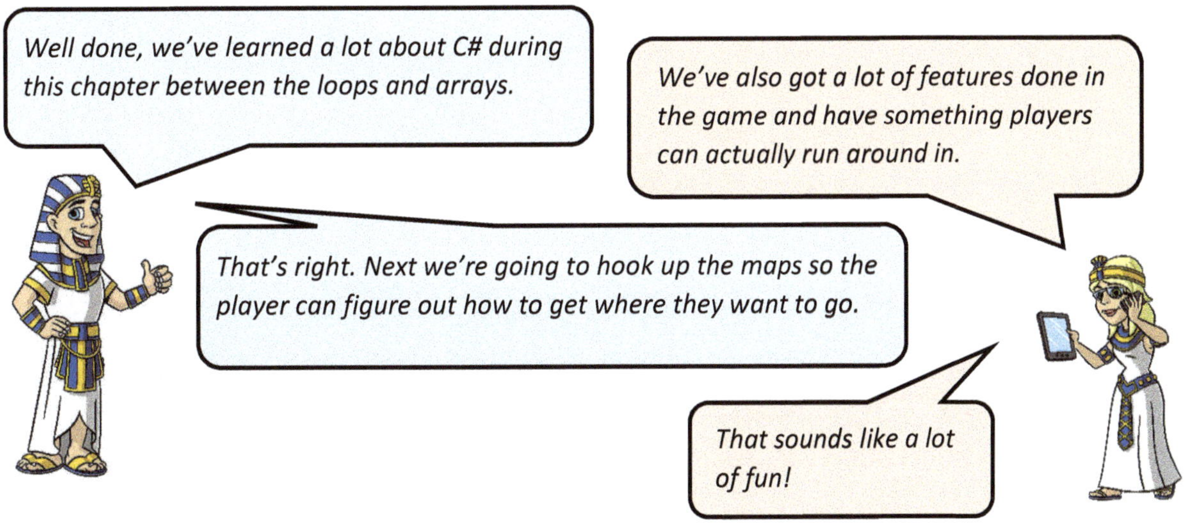

Chapter 5 – Maps and Zones

In this chapter we're going to create 2 kinds of maps, a mini map, and a world map. I called captain obvious to ask what a mini map was, and he said, "A mini map is like a normal map, only smaller." Thanks a lot!

The mini map shows the map around the player so they know where they are. It is usually takes up a small amount of screen space in one of the corners, like the upper-right. Then they know how to get to places that are close-by them.

To find places that are far away, you need the world map. The world map takes up most or all the screen and shows much more area than the mini map.

Mini map for Moses

There are two options to make makes. The first option is to look at the layout of the land or area and start drawing. While that may be fun, we're going to go with the second option which is to use cameras. We talked about cameras back in Chapter 1 and setup our 3rd person camera in Chapter 3.

Create a new camera by selecting GameObject > Camera and then rename it to "MiniMapCam". Set the 'Y' Position in the transform to '600' and the 'X' Rotation to 90 to make the camera look down.

Set the Projection to Orthographic. The projection of the camera is how it presents what it sees to the player and there are a couple different ways to do that. A perspective projection displays what the camera sees from a specific point as though it were there in 3D space. Orthographic projection displays what the camera sees as though it were in 2D space which results in a flat-looking screen. For the world map, orthographic projection is what we want.

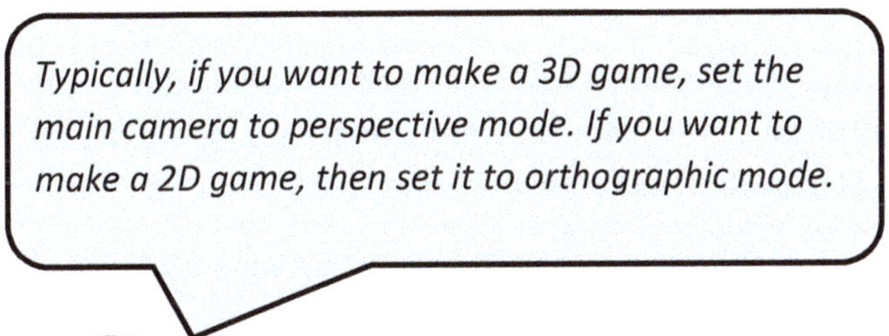

Notice that when you change the camera to orthographic that the lines coming out from the camera change from a pyramid-shape to a box. These lines show you what the camera is currently looking at. To see a little bigger area, change the size to '60'.

Next, we'll change the viewport of the camera. The viewport is the player's screen, what the player sees. In the Viewport Rect variables, we can change where, on the screen, the camera displays what it sees. Set the Viewport Rect to X=0.7, Y=0.7, W=0.25, and H=0.25. Having a viewport smaller than the screen will still allow us to see some of the main camera around the edges of the world map. Finally, to see the map's camera we need to set the depth higher than the camera on Moses. Set 'Depth' to '1'.

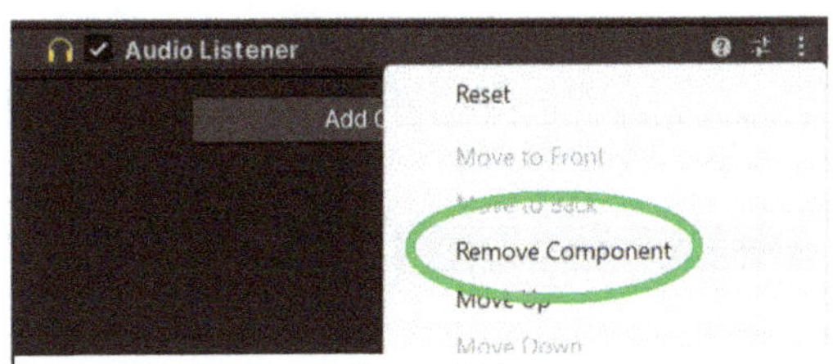

Figure 107

Now delete the Audio Listener at the bottom of the inspector for the camera. Like your ears, Audio Listeners are what allows the player to hear sound in the game scene. But we only need 1 audio listener for the whole scene, so we'll remove the one on our new camera that comes on it by default. To do that, click the three dots on the right of the Audio Listener component and select "Remove Component" as shown in Figure 107.

We've got the basics setup for the mini map, let's click play and check it out. You should see it show up in the upper-right hand of the screen as seen in Figure 108. Even though you move Moses around, the mini map stays in the same place on the screen. This is because of the viewport we set above.

Figure 108

You Get a File... And you Get a File... Everyone Gets a File!

By now you've probably noticed that, generally, whenever we have a class there is a separate script file for that class. There are some exceptions, but this is generally good software design practice.

A little while back we talked about creating objects for our social media program. We came up with 2 classes: 1) Person and 2) Comment. Each of these classes should get its own file. This separation of the objects helps prevent bugs where changes to one object don't cause problems in another object. Objects that are separated are easier to reuse and test because the other object doesn't need to be included or changed.

However, when we were creating our array of arrays for the footsteps, we created another class in the same file and even inside another class. That was because the class we created was intended to be used inside and only inside that class for the purpose of providing the array of arrays to the inspector.

Unity requires that any script files include a class with the same name as the file. This means that if you decide to change the name of a class, you need to change the name of the file too.

```
public class Zone : MonoBehaviour
{
    public string ZoneName;
    public GameController gc;

    Unity Message | 0 references
    private void OnTriggerEnter(Collider other)
    {
        if (other.transform.tag == "Player")
        {
            gc.EnterZone(ZoneName);
        }
    }
}
```

Figure 109

Getting in the Zone

Now that we have our mini map showing up, we're going to divide it up a bit so it is easier for the player to know where they are. A zone is a part of the map that includes important actors. We will make the zones that the player can go to. But first, we need to create a game controller script. This will be a C# script that controls the flow of the game so all our objects can live together in Unity.

Create these 3 new C# scripts under the "Scripts" folder: GameController, Zone, and ZoneText. Double-click the "Zone" script to open it in Visual Studio, we'll add code for it first as seen in Figure 109. Add a public string variable named "ZoneName" and another public variable 'gc' to store a reference to the "GameController" we will create next. This class won't use the "Start" and "Update" methods, so go ahead and delete them.

When the Update method is present, it will get called every frame by Unity. Removing the Update method when you don't need it will both clean up your code and streamline performance.

After that is a special method named "OnTriggerEnter". Triggers are like colliders that we learned about in Chapter 1 except they don't collide. Triggers are used to find out when something enters or exits. We'll check if the player was the object that entered the trigger. If so, then that means they entered... the zone. So we call the "EnterZone" method that we'll code up next.

The GameController script is next. Double-click to open it in Visual Studio. Then add the code as shown in Figure 110. The "ZoneTextObj" is an instance of the text object we'll use to actually show the player what zone they entered. The next array of Zones will be set with all the zones we create for the game and will be entered using the inspector.

The "Start" and "Update" methods are empty for now. But keep it around because we'll use it later. Make a new public void method named "EnterZone". This is the method we called in the Zone script. In this script we make another method call to "SplashZone" which we'll define in the next script "ZoneText".

```
public class GameController : MonoBehaviour
{
    public ZoneText ZoneTextObj;
    public Zone[] ZoneObjects;

    // Start is called before the first frame update
    void Start()
    {

    }

    // Update is called once per frame
    void Update()
    {

    }

    public void EnterZone(string zoneName)
    {
        ZoneTextObj.SplashZone(zoneName);
    }
}
```

Figure 110

A Space for your Names

I'd like to interrupt our regularly scheduled coding of zones to bring you an announcement from our sponsor, namespaces. In addition to cooking and cleaning for you, namespaces allow you to group multiple classes together. In essence, it is a space where you can put all your names (i.e. classes and variables).

Here is how you declare a namespace:

```
namespace Name
{
	class ClassName
	{
		[Class Stuff]
	}
}
```

It's pretty much the same as how you declare a class. Everything you want inside that namespace goes inside the curly braces. You can put as many classes and variables as you like in a namespace, as long as they have different names.

Example:

```
namespace Animals
{
	class Cat
	{
		public Vector3 FindCatnip()
		{
			...
		}
	}
}


namespace Animals
{

	public class Dog
	{
		public Vector3 WalkTheHuman()
		{
			...
		}
	}
}
```

You use classes and variables in your namespace with the dot (.) operator.

Example:

```
Animals.Dog.WalkTheHuman();
Animals.Cat.FindCatnip();
```

Enumerated Types

We've talked about the built-in types for variables (i.e., int, float, and string) and then how creating classes make a new type. There is another way of making a new type called "Enumerations". Here is how you create it:

```
scope enum EnumName
{
        Option1,
        Option2,
        Option3,
        OptionN
}
```

Enumerated types are great for when you have specific options for a variable.

Example:

```
public enum _pet
{
        Dog,
        Cat,
        Fish,
        Lizard
}
```

In the above example, Dog, Cat, Fish, and Lizard are types of pets you can have. Enumerated types have a scope like other variables and classes.

To declare a variable of an enumerated type, just declare it like normal. Then to set your variable, you use the dot (.) operator like with classes and methods.

Example:

```
private_pet MyPet;
public _pet YourPet;

YourPet = _pet.Cat;
MyPet = _pet.Lizard;
```

In this example, we declare 2 variables of the enumerated type. Then, we set them. Maybe you have a cat, but I have a lizard. A lizard?! What kind of crazy guy has a lizard?

Don't forget, both the enumerated type's declaration and the variable declaration need to have scope assigned to them.

Zoning out

To help you remember which variables are for instances or prefabs, put an "Object", "obj", or "Prefab" in the name. It helps prevent bugs when you know what is supposed to be in a variable.

Now open the "ZoneText" script. This script will be a bit longer. It controls the text shown to the player. Just making the text appear and disappear could be done using simple timers that you know how to do. But we can do better than that! We're going to make the name of the zone fade in, stay visible for a time, and then fade out. It's going to look very cool!

Code the public and private variables as shown in Figure 111. We have two TextmeshProNGUI variables. The "TMPro" is the namespace where it lives. These two texts are the white text and shadow text.

But this Shadow will be pretty cool. We'll have the normal zone name show up in white and then behind it will be this shadow which provides 2 benefits: 1) Looks awesome and 2) helps the player see it better against light backgrounds. It will behave the exact same as the regular text, just appear behind it.

The other public variable is the "AlphaDelta". This tells the code to fade in and out the text and how fast to do the fading. You could just leave out the public variable and put the number you want to use instead. This is called "hard coding" the number.

```
public class ZoneText : MonoBehaviour
{
    public TMPro.TextMeshProUGUI ZoneTextObj;
    public TMPro.TextMeshProUGUI ZoneShadowObj;
    public float AlphaDelta;

    8 references
    private enum _zone_state
    {
        None,
        FadeIn,
        Solid,
        FadeOut
    }

    private _zone_state zoneState;
    private float curAlpha;
```

Figure 111

It can be frustrating to hard-code numbers into your methods and later realize they need to change. Use public variables and set them in the inspector!

After that we have an enumerated type for the state of the zone text. It is either: 1) doing nothing, 2) fading in, 3) remaining solid, or 4) fading out. This "_zone_state" enumeration will be used for a state machine. We'll talk about state machines later on, but basically, we'll start off doing nothing, then when we need to splash up text we transition to the "FadeIn" state. Then we transition to "Solid" and then "Fadeout". Once the whole thing is done the state machine goes back to "None and waits for the next time it needs to splash up text.

Then we declare our variable to track the zone state. The "curAlpha" variable tracks the current value of the zone text transparency. The "solidTimeout" is a timer that makes sure we keep the zone text solid for the right amount of time.

Code the 2 lines shown in Figure 112 in the "Start" method. This initializes our Zone State variable, so it isn't doing anything at the beginning. Then we call a function that we haven't coded yet. But when we do, it will initialize the text that displays the zone name to be totally transparent.

```
void Start()
{
    zoneState = _zone_state.None;
    SetAlpha(0);
}
```

Figure 112

Which switch is which?

In addition to if/then/else type statements, the "switch" structure can be used when there are multiple selection possibilities. The "switch" structure is used to make decisions based on the value of a single variable. The structure is:

```
switch (variable)
{
case [variable has this value]:
      [process this code]
      break;
case [variable has that value]:
      [process that code]
      break;
default:
      [process some other code]
      break;
}
```

The way this works is that the value of variable is examined. Each case statement is then sequentially examined until the value matches one of the specified cases. Once found, the corresponding code is executed. If no case match is found, the code in the default segment (if there) is executed.

The "break" statements transfer program execution to the line following the closing right brace. These statements are optional but will almost always be there. If a break is not executed, all code following the case processed will also be processed (until a break is seen or the end of the structure is reached). This is different behavior than "if" statements where only one 'case' could be executed.

As an example, say we've written this code using the "if" statement:

```
if (age == 5)
{
      category = "Kindergarten";
}
else if (age == 6)
{
      category = "First Grade";
}
else if (age == 7)
{
      category = "Second Grade";
}
```

```
else
{
      category = "Older Child";
}
```

This will work, but it is ugly code and difficult to maintain.

The corresponding code with "switch" is much cleaner:

```
switch (age)
{
case 5:
      category = "Kindergarten";
      break;
case 6:
      category = "First Grade";
      break;
case 7:
      category = "Second Grade";
      break;
default:
      category = "Older Child";
      break;
}
```

Zoning In

Now add code to the "Update" method as shown in Figure 113. Basically, the whole method switches on the "zoneState" variable. The code run in this method changes depending on the state.

If we're fading the text in, then we'll add "AlphaDelta" modified by the "deltaTime" to the "curAlpha" variable. Then we set the alpha (or transparency) of the text to whatever the current alpha is.

An alpha value of '1' means the text is totally solid. So then we move to the next state, which is "Solid". At that point we invoke "SetFadeOutState" after 2 seconds.

```
void Update()
{
    switch (zoneState)
    {
        case _zone_state.FadeIn:
            curAlpha += AlphaDelta * Time.deltaTime;
            SetAlpha(curAlpha);

            if (curAlpha >= 1)
            {
                curAlpha = 1;
                zoneState = _zone_state.Solid;
                Invoke("SetFadeOutState", 2);
            }
            break;
        case _zone_state.FadeOut:
            curAlpha -= AlphaDelta * Time.deltaTime;
            SetAlpha(curAlpha);

            if (curAlpha <= 0)
            {
                zoneState = _zone_state.None;
            }
            break;
    }
}

0 references
private void SetFadeOutState()
{
    zoneState = _zone_state.FadeOut;
}
```

Figure 113

When fading out, we subtract the "AlphaDelta" modified by the "deltaTime" to the "curAlpha" variable. Then we set the alpha of the text to whatever the current alpha is, like what we did before. However, this time if the alpha is 0 or less (it could be negative!) then we're done fading out and the text is completely transparent. In this case we are now done fading and reset the state machine so we can start again if the player enters a zone again.

In the Splash Zone

Next add the "SetAlpha" method into the class as shown in Figure 114. This method sets the alpha (or transparency) of the white and shadow text objects to the given value.

```
private void SetAlpha(float alpha)
{
    // Update the white text
    Color tempColor = ZoneTextObj.color;
    tempColor.a = Mathf.Clamp01(alpha);
    ZoneTextObj.color = tempColor;

    // Upadate the shadow text
    tempColor = ZoneShadowObj.color;
    tempColor.a = Mathf.Clamp01(alpha);
    ZoneShadowObj.color = tempColor;
}
```

Figure 114

The color of text is another one of those variables where we can't just set the alpha individually. We need to get the color, set the alpha, and then set the color back.

The Mathf method to clamp the value between 0 and 1 is used to make sure we don't go outside those bounds since the alpha must be between these values. After that we set the color of the text to the one with the updated alpha value.

We're finally ready to get wet and add the method "SplashZone". We won't have trained dolphins swimming around in this method. But it is very important to the feature.

```
public void SplashZone(string zoneName)
{
    zoneState = _zone_state.FadeIn;
    curAlpha = 0f;
    ZoneTextObj.text = zoneName;
    ZoneShadowObj.text = zoneName;
}
```

Figure 115

Add the method shown in Figure 115. This is the method that the "GameController" calls when it figures out that the player enters a zone. The term "Splash" means just throwing it up on the screen for a while until it "washes off". We start the state machine by setting the state to "_zone_state.FadeIn" and make sure the current alpha is set to '0f' which means transparent. The 'f' helps C# know that the '0' we're talking about is a float and not an int. The next two lines set the name of the zone that we want to splash onto both the normal and shadow texts.

Splashing Text

We're almost ready to sign off on this feature. The C# scripting is done and now we need to hook everything up with the Unity glue that makes it work. Go back into Unity and click the Canvas in the Hierarchy View. Right-click and select UI > Text - TextMeshPro. Two objects are created, a "Canvas" and a "Text(TMP)". TMP means Text Mesh Pro. Rename "Text(TMP)" to "ZoneText". There is a "TMP Importer" window that pops up which looks something like Figure 116. It has two parts, TMP Essentials which includes... essential... parts for using it. The other are examples. We'll just need the essentials, click the "Import TMP Essentials" button and close the window by clicking 'X'.

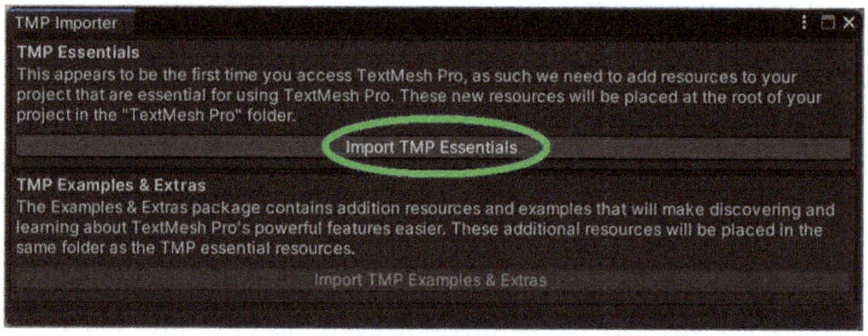

Figure 116

In the Rect Transform, set the Pos X to 0, Pos Y to 0, Width to '400', and Height to '60' in the Rect Transform as you can see in Figure 117.

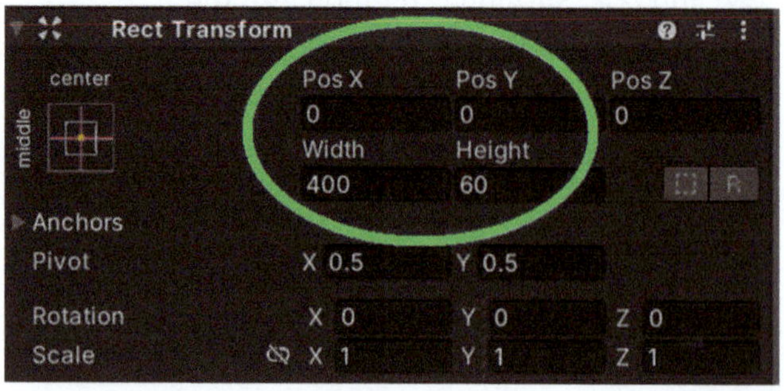

Figure 117

In the "TextMeshPro – Text (UI)" component, set the Font Style to 'B' for Bold and the Font Size to '40'. Under Alignment, check the button to center the text like what you see in Figure 118. Don't worry about it showing up as "New Text", we'll change that in the script.

Now, left-click on the component and create a copy of it by pressing CTRL+C and then CTRL+V. Rename the new component to "ZoneTextShadow" and drag it right above the "ZoneText". The order is important as UI objects are displayed to the player in this order. So with objects that overlap, the last object will partially or fully cover the others up.

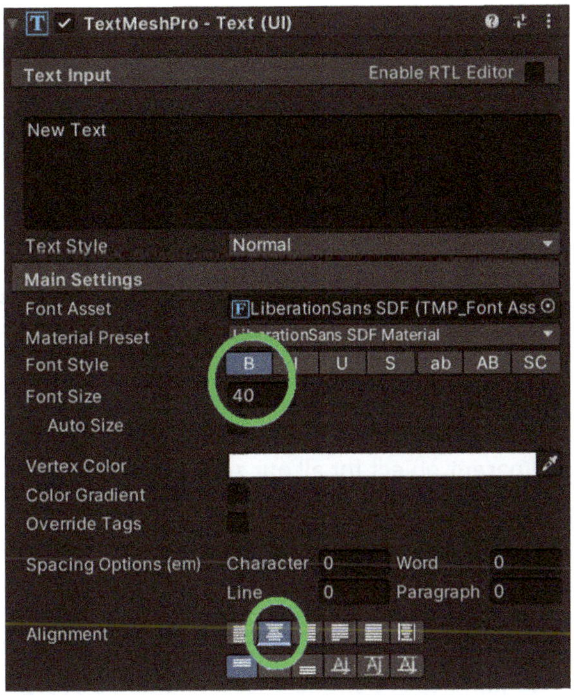

Figure 118

Click the colored part to the right of the "Vertex Color". This is the color that the text will show up as. The default is white. When you click it a new window will pop up that looks like Figure 119. This allows you to choose from all the different possible colors. We're going to choose black which is hexadecimal code "000000". Plug that code into the Hexadecimal field shown in the figure.

To make the shadow actually look like a shadow, we'll change the position. Scroll up to the top to the Rect Transform and set Pos X to "-3" and Pos Y to "3". This puts the black text up and to the left, making it really look like a shadow of the original text. You can see it by pressing the 'F' key to focus on the "ZoneTextShadow" put together with the "ZoneText".

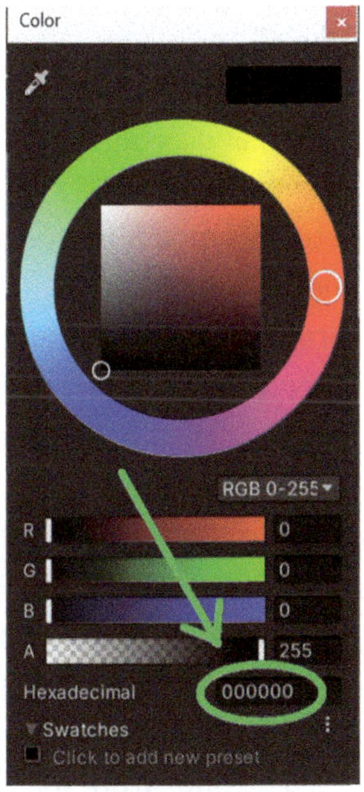

Figure 119

Let's add the script now. Go into the Project View and under Assets > Scripts drag the ZoneText script onto the inspector for the "ZoneText" object. To set the Shadow variable, drag the "ZoneText" from the Hierarchy into the box to the right of Shadow. Do the same with the "ZoneTextShadow". Then set the Alpha Delta to '0.25'. Later, if the fading feels to fast or slow to you then you can adjust it here. It should look like Figure 120.

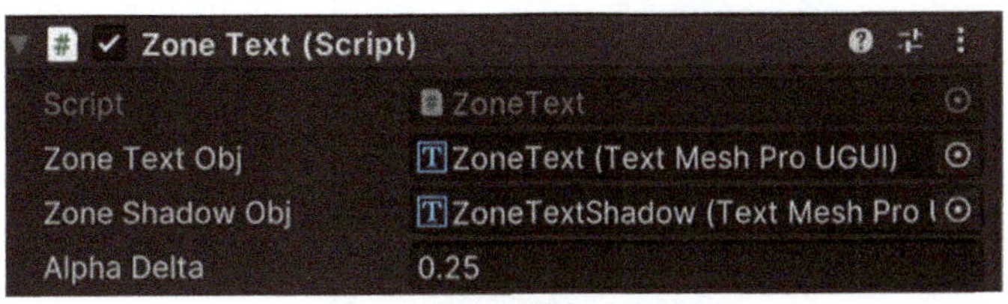

Figure 120

This sets up the splash text to display the zone. Now we need to create the "GameController" object. In the menu on the top-left of the screen select GameObject > Create Empty. This makes a new object named "GameObject" at the bottom of the Hierarchy View. Rename it to "GameController" and also set its Tag to "GameController". Then go to Assets > Scripts in the Project View and drag the GameController script onto it. We'll use our special "Unity Glue" to simply drag "ZoneText" from the Hierarchy View onto the "Zone Text Obj" like you see in Figure 121. Now, the only thing left to do is create the actual zone.

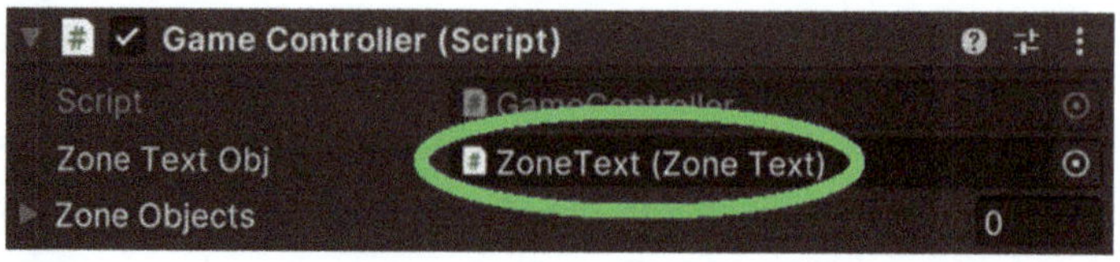

Figure 121

Create another empty object using the same method above and name it "MapZones". This object will be the parent object for all our zones. Set the Position in the transform to be all '0's. Right-click it and select "Create Empty". This is another way of doing the same thing, except now the object is a child object of the "MapZones" object. Rename the child object to "PalaceZone". Set the Position in the Transform to be X=1302, Y=36, and Z=1545.

The position of the palace zone is dead center in that "Big Temple" we moved earlier so the player didn't have jump to get on the bricks. Pharaoh's decided to re-purpose it for his palace. So, when the player enters the area around the palace, we're going to splash up some text so the player knows it.

Add a Box Collider component to the "PalaceZone" object. Set the size to X=130, Y=100, and Z=60. Check the trigger box. We've used colliders before, but this one is in trigger mode. In this mode, the physics engine will not prevent colliders to pass through each other but still calls a method when the colliders... well... collide. The method called is "OnTriggerEnter" which was coded in the Zone script. Then add the Zone script to the "PalaceZone" object. Give it the name "Pharaoh's Palace". This is the actual text that will show up on the screen. The inspector for the "PalaceZone" object should look like Figure 122. Finally, to add this zone to our list of zones, click the "GameController" and drag the "PalaceZone" from the Hierarchy View onto the "Zone Objects" in the Inspector.

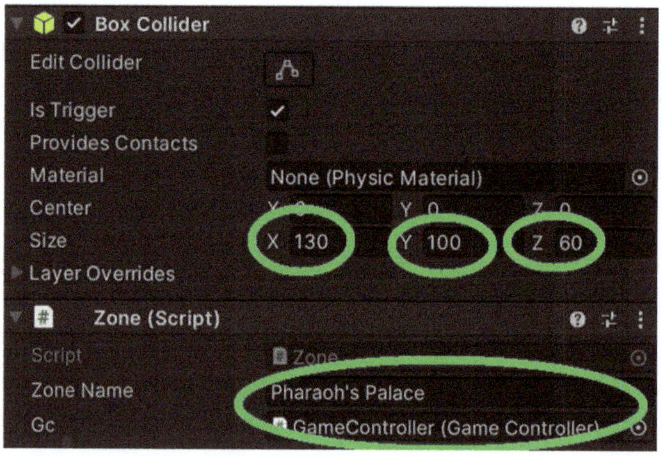

Figure 122

Figure 123

Our feature is now done! Go back into play mode and run up to the palace. You will see the text "Pharaoh's Palace" splash onto the screen, remain there for a couple seconds, and then wash off like in Figure 123.

The World Map

Imagine you're an eagle soaring over the land. After you're done looking for a nice juicy rabbit to eat, notice how small everything looks from so high up in the air, but you can see a lot more. You'll get the similar thing from looking out the window of an airplane in-flight.

If you want to go further, you can use the ways given above to add all the other zones described in the GDD. Play around with different colliders like the sphere to get different shapes that better match the locations.

The world map will look down at the land, so the player can see locations that are normally far away from each other. We'll also let the player pan the map by dragging it using the mouse. The player will be able to enable and disable the world map by pressing the 'M' key on the keyboard.

Create a new camera by selecting GameObject > Camera and then rename it to "WorldMapCam". Set the 'Y' Position in the transform to '600' and the 'X' Rotation to 90 to make the camera look down.

Set the Projection to Orthographic. The projection of the camera is how it presents what it sees to the player and there are a couple different ways to do that. A perspective projection displays what the camera sees from a specific point as though it were there in 3D space. Orthographic projection displays what the camera sees as though it were in 2D space which results in a flat-looking screen. For the world map, orthographic projection is what we want.

Typically, if you want to make a 3D game, set the main camera to perspective mode. If you want to make a 2D game, then set it to orthographic mode.

Notice that when you change the camera to orthographic that the lines coming out from the camera change from a pyramid-shape to a box. These lines show you what the camera is currently looking at. To see a bigger area, change the size to '200'.

Next, we'll change the viewport of the camera. The viewport is the player screen, what the player actually sees. In the Viewport Rect variables, we can change where, on the screen, the camera displays what it sees. Set the Viewport Rect to X=0.1, Y=0.1, W=0.8, and H=0.8. Set 'Depth' to '1' and then remove the Audio Listener like we did before for the mini map.

Let's test it out by entering play mode. You'll see something like Figure 124. You can see how the new camera overlays what it sees on top of the main camera. We can still see the mini map and Moses can still move around, but don't worry, we'll address that in the upcoming sections.

Figure 124

Making a List

We've all made lists before. Maybe you've made a list of groceries you need to get, video games to buy, or something else. You can make lists in C# too! They are very similar to arrays in that they hold any number of variables of one type. However, lists have a bonus, you don't need to specify how big it is when you declare it.

Here is how you declare and instantiate a list:

```
List<type> ListName;
ListName = new List<type> ();
```

Lists have methods to help you add and remove elements from it:

```
ListName.Add(ElementName);
ListName.Remove(ElementName);
ListName.RemoveAt(Index);
```

The "Add" method puts the new element at the end of the list. The "Remove" method scratches off the first instance of that element in the list. The "RemoveAt" method takes away the element at the given integer index.

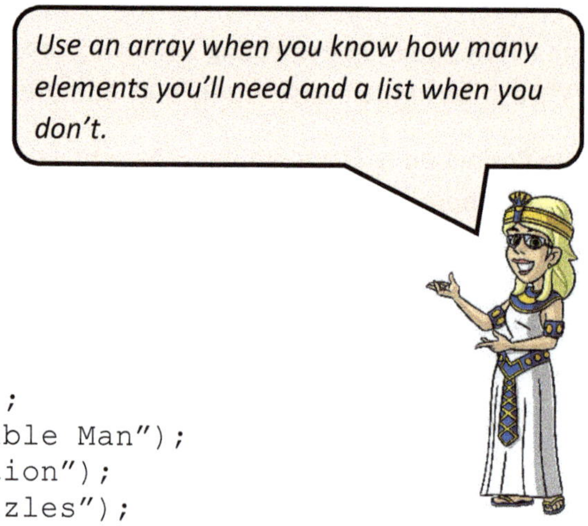

Example:

```
List<string> GamesToBuy;
GamesToBuy = new List<string> ();
GamesToBuy.Add("Adventures of Bible Man");
GamesToBuy.Add("Disciple Demolition");
GamesToBuy.Add("Prodigal Pig Puzzles");
GamesToBuy.Add("Grand Theft Aero");
GamesToBuy.Add("Exodus Adventure");

// How did that get on the list?
GamesToBuy.Remove("Grand Theft Aero");
```

Controlling the World

Open the "GameController" script and add the public and private variables as shown in Figure 125. The "ZoneTextObj" and "ZoneObjects" are already there, so you don't need to add them again. The next variable has a long name "ZoneWorldMapTextPrefab". This holds the prefab we'll use to instantiate zone names for the world map.

```
public ZoneText ZoneTextObj;
public Zone[] ZoneObjects;
public GameObject ZoneWorldMapTextPrefab;
public GameObject PlayerPos;
public GameObject MinimapObj;
public GameObject WorldMapObj;
public GameObject Player;

2 references
private enum _ui_state
{
    None,
    WorldMap
}
private _ui_state uiState;
private List<GameObject> ZoneWorldMapTextObjList;
```

Figure 125

The next two public variables hold references to the player and to the object we'll use to show the player position on the map. This will be the same icon that is used for the player on the mini map. The last 2 public variables hold the instances to the mini-map and the world map camera.
Next, we have another enumeration. This one tracks the state of our UI. We'll talk about UI in Chapter 9 - Menu System and UI, but the purpose of this code is to not show both maps to the player at the same time. Then we have a list of the world map text names that we'll display on the map. We keep track of this list so we can delete the text names when the player turns the world map off.

```
    void Start()
    {
        ZoneWorldMapTextObjList = new List<GameObject>();
        foreach(Zone zone in ZoneObjects)
        {
            GameObject zoneTextObj = Instantiate(ZoneWorldMapTextPrefab);
            Vector3 tPos = zoneTextObj.transform.position;
            tPos.y = 99f;
            zoneTextObj.transform.position = tPos;
            zoneTextObj.GetComponent<TMPro.TextMeshPro>().text = zone.ZoneName;
            zoneTextObj.name = zone.ZoneName;
            ZoneWorldMapTextObjList.Add(zoneTextObj);
        }
        uiState = _ui_state.None;
        WorldMapSetActive(false);
    }
```

Figure 126

In the "Start" method, add code shown in Figure 126. We initialize the list and populate it with all the zones. The "Instantiate" method is a new one for us. This method creates a new instance of the object in the scene. It will show up on the bottom of the Hierarchy View when we're playing the game. It is saved in "zoneTextObj". Then we set the position to match where we put the zone in the scene and update the name. We also set the transform name (transform.name) to the name of the zone. This is the name that will appear for the object in the Hierarchy View. After that we add the zone text to the list.

Then we initialize the UI state machine and handle set the world map UI components to inactive if they exist. Doing this will mean they won't be shown in the scene until we activate them. At the end, we get the player instance the same way we did in the boat controller.

```
void Update()
{
    if (Input.GetKeyUp(KeyCode.Escape))
    {
        // Disable any window when the player presses Escape
        if (uiState == _ui_state.WorldMap)
        {
            WorldMapSetActive(false);
            uiState = _ui_state.None;
        }
    }

    //Check to enable the World Map
    if (Input.GetKeyUp(KeyCode.M))
    {
        WorldMapHandler();
    }

    // Update player position and rotation on the world map
    if (uiState == _ui_state.WorldMap)
    {
        Vector3 tPos = Player.transform.position;
        tPos.y = PlayerPos.transform.position.y;
        PlayerPos.transform.position = tPos;
        PlayerPos.transform.rotation = Quaternion.Euler(90, Player.transform.eulerAngles.y, 0);
    }
}
```

Figure 127

We'll fill out the "Update" method for the "GameController" now. Add the code as shown in Figure 127. There 3 "if" statements we need every frame. When the player presses the ESCAPE key, we want to disable any windows they have open. And so, if the UI state is in the "World Map" mode then we disable it and reset the state.

The next "if" statement checks if the player pressed the 'M' key. And when that happens, we call the method "WorldMapHandler" if the world map objects exist. This method will determine if the world map needs to be shown or hidden. Will talk about this method next.

Notice we're using the method "GetKeyUp" for when the player releases the key. But "GetKeyDown" returns true when the player presses the key down.

The last "if" statement makes sure the player position object we use for the world map matches the player. The way we're going to implement this is to put an object high in the air above the player so that when our orthographic world map camera looks down it will see it instead of the player. We could have used the UI system to show the player position image, like we did for the splash screen, but this way simplifies the code to move the map around so we can see faraway places.

After the "Update" method, skip over the "EnterZone" method and write the code as shown in Figure 128. In here we decide whether to display the world map or hide it. If the UI is currently displaying the world map and the user presses 'M' then we want to hide it and set the UI state accordingly. If there is nothing displayed on the UI (remember, there will be more things to display than just the world map), then we show the world map and set the UI state to say we're showing the world map.

```
public void WorldMapHandler()
{
    if (uiState == _ui_state.WorldMap)
    {
        WorldMapSetActive(false);
        uiState = _ui_state.None;
    }
    else if (uiState == _ui_state.None)
    {
        WorldMapSetActive(true);
        uiState = _ui_state.WorldMap;
    }
}
```

Figure 128

Figure 129 shows the last method we need to add for the "GameController". This method handles both activating and deactivating the world map. At the top, we set the "WorldMapObj" and "PlayerPos" objects' active state to the "active" parameter that was passed in.

Then we set the mini map to do the opposite of that. **DON'T FORGET the '!' before "active" on line 93.** This means whenever the world map is shown, the mini map will hide. Then when the world map hides, the mini map is shown. If we're setting the world map to active, then move the camera to center on the player.

```
89  public void WorldMapSetActive(bool active)
90  {
91      WorldMapObj.SetActive(active);
92      PlayerPos.SetActive(active);
93      MinimapObj.SetActive(!active);
94
95      foreach (GameObject zoneText in ZoneWorldMapTextObjList)
96      {
97          zoneText.SetActive(active);
98      }
99
100     if (active)
101     {
102         Vector3 tPos = Player.transform.position;
103         tPos.y = WorldMapObj.transform.position.y;
104         WorldMapObj.transform.position = tPos;
105     }
106 }
```

Figure 129

Moving the World

Ok, we won't really "move the world", but we move the camera so that it looks like it. Create a new C# script under the Assets > Scripts folder and name it "WorldMapCam". This script will let the player pan the camera so they can view the entire map.

```
public float Granularity;
public float Top, Bot, Left, Right;

private Vector3 lastLoc;
```

Figure 130

Add the variables shown in Figure 130. The "Granularity" is how fast the map moves when the player drags it. The "Top", "Bot, "Left", and "Right" variables tell the script when to stop panning so the player won't move the camera off the terrain. We can't let them stare into the endless abyss! The "lastLocation" is for the mouse position, so we can update the map as the player moves the mouse. You'll notice we're putting all 4 panning variables on the same line separated by commas. This little trick helps us save space while keeping variables used for the same thing, together.

Leave the "Start" method empty for this script. You can delete it if you want, it won't change the behavior of the script and it makes the file shorter. But if, it turns out, we need to put something there then keeping it around will make things easier.

```
    void Update()
    {
        // Check for mouse input
        if (Input.GetMouseButtonDown(0))
        {
            lastLoc = Input.mousePosition;
        }

        if (Input.GetMouseButton(0))
        {
            Vector3 newPos = transform.position;
            newPos.x += (lastLoc.x - Input.mousePosition.x) * Granularity;
            newPos.z += (lastLoc.y - Input.mousePosition.y) * Granularity;

            if (newPos.x < Left)
            {
                newPos.x = Left;
            }
            if (newPos.x > Right)
            {
                newPos.x = Right;
            }
            if (newPos.z < Top)
            {
                newPos.z = Top;
            }
            if (newPos.z > Bot)
            {
                newPos.z = Bot;
            }

            transform.position = newPos;

            // Update Last Mouse Position
            lastLoc = Input.mousePosition;
        }
    }
```

Figure 131

Now stuff all the code into the "Update" method that you see in Figure 131. The first "if" statement checks if the left mouse button has been pressed. It only returns true once for each down press. If so, then we update the mouse's last location.

The next "if" statement checks if the mouse button is being held. The "GetMouseButton" method returns true while the button is being held and will continue to return true until the button is released. This is important because we'll use this to let the player drag the map.

We start off by getting the new position of the camera using some math. We get the difference (subtraction) between the mouse's last location and its current location. Then we multiply that by the granularity, or the amount we want to move the map when the player drags it. After we set the new position we need to make sure it is within the boundaries. We need to check each direction individually to make sure we haven't gone over.

After the boundary checks we update the camera to the new position and last location the mouse was to the current location. This is all the scripting we need to do for this feature.

A Granularity of '1' will make the map move with the mouse. If you put a value of '2' then it will move twice as fast as the mouse.

Map Objects and Prefabs

We've already created the camera for the world map. Now let's add the script to it. Click the "WorldMapCam" object in the Hierarchy View. Then browse to Assets > Scripts in the Project View. Drag the WorldMapCam script onto the inspector panel and set the values shown in Figure 132.

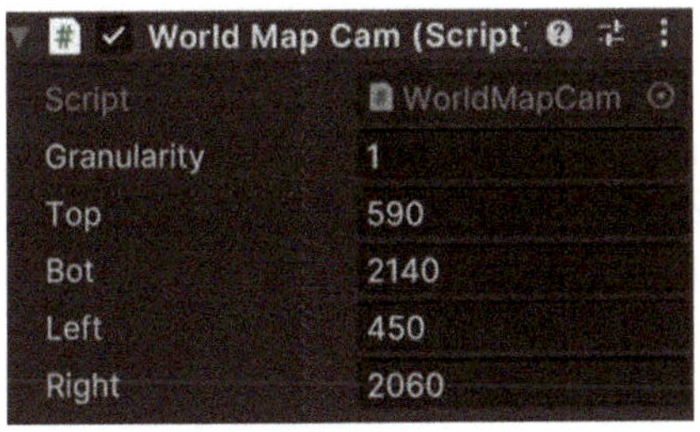

Figure 132

Next, we'll create the object that shows where the player is, on the map as well as the prefab for the 3D text that will display the zone names. Since the mini map already has a nice icon for player position, we're going to reuse that. To find out where it is, in the Hierarchy View, expand the Canvas and click the "Minimap". Under the Map script click the Settings button.

Now, we need to show the icon on the map that represents the Moses so the player can easily spot him. We're going to re-purpose a gold coin for that, the player won't suspect a thing! In the Project View, type "Money" and then drag it up to the Hierarchy View as shown in Figure 133. Rename it to "PlayerPos" and set the position's Y to '100' to be really high in the air. We'll rotate it sideways by setting the rotation's X to '90'. Then set the 'X', 'Y', and 'Z' variables of the Scale to '30'.

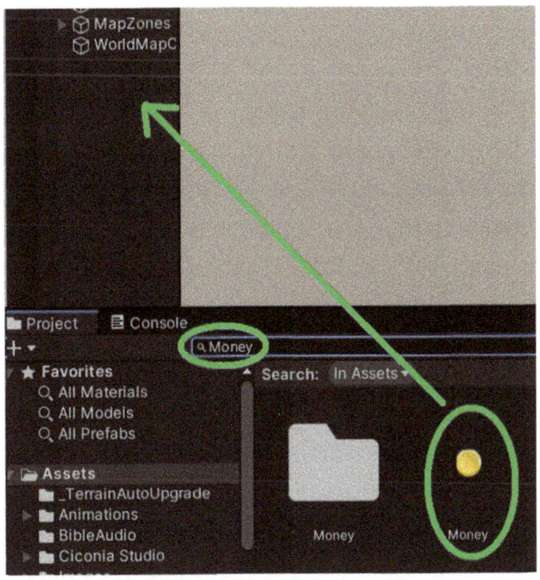

Figure 133

Now let's create the prefab for the text to show the zone names on the world map. In the Project View create a new folder under Prefabs named "UI". This will keep all of our UI prefabs for this game. Create another TextMeshPro by going to the main menu and selecting GameObject > 3D Object > Text – TextMeshPro. Name it "ZoneWorldMapText".

A mesh is how 3D artists talk about the actual 3D model. For text, Unity creates the mesh for the model to match the text you want to display.

In the rect transform, set the Width to '100' and the Rotation's 'X' value to '90'. Then, in the Text Mesh component, change the Font Style to Bold, Font Size to 100, and Alignment to Center. Now you can drag this object in the "UI" folder we created above. We don't need the 3D Text object in the hierarchy view anymore so just delete it.

Now let's glue everything together to the "GameController". In the Project View's Assets > Prefabs > UI, drag the ZoneWorldMapText prefab into the "Zone World Map Text" variable in the inspector. In the Hierarchy View, drag "PlayerPos" object to the "Player Pos" variable in the inspector. Drag "MosesPlayer" to the player field. Under the Canvas, drag "MiniMapCam" to the "Minimap Obj" variable. Finally, drag the "WorldMapCam" object to "World Map Obj". The Game Controller should look like Figure 134.

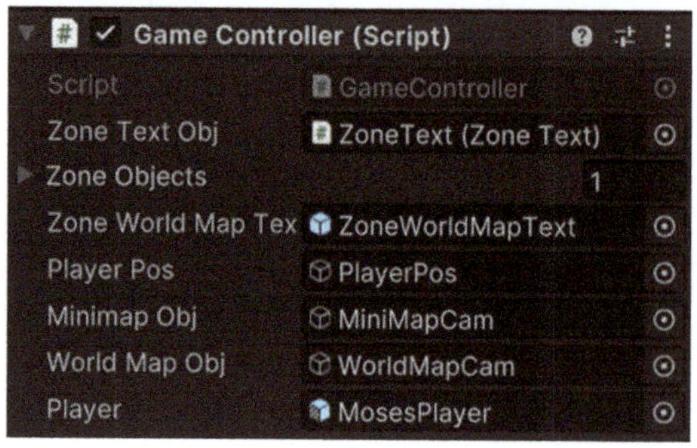

Figure 134

With that done, click play and try out your new world map feature. Press the 'M' key and the world map will appear. The mini map will also disappear. Left click on the map and drag it around. Then press 'M' again and the world map will disappear while the mini map re-appears. The World map will now show Moses moving with the icon we used. However, the mini map doesn't move yet. So, let's hook it up!

Moving the Mini map

The whole benefit for a mini map is to show the area around the player. Suffice to say, a mini map that doesn't move is pretty useless. Let's fix that! Create a new script named "MiniMapCam" and type the code from .

```
    public Transform Player;

    // Start is called before the first frame update
    Unity Message | 0 references
    void Start()
    {

    }

    // Update is called once per frame
    Unity Message | 0 references
    void Update()
    {
        Vector3 tPos = transform.position;
        tPos.x = Player.position.x;
        tPos.z = Player.position.z;
        transform.position = tPos;
    }
```

Figure 135

Speaking the Word

The last feature we'll implement in this chapter is playing audio from the spoken World English Bible. The recording of Exodus chapters 1-10 included in this tutorial is a public domain LibriVox recording. The entire Old Testament recording is here: https://librivox.org/old-testament-world-english-bible/. Since the audio comes as all 10 chapters, we'll need to play only a small part of it at a time.

The first thing we need to do is add an Audio Source component to our "GameController" object. You can do this in the inspector by clicking "Add Component" and selecting Audio > Audio Source. In the Project View, go to Assets > BibleAudio and drag the "oldtestament_007_worldenglishbible" file onto the AudioClip variable in the "GameController" object's new Audio Source. Then uncheck the block to "Play On Awake". We only want to play this sound when the player enters a zone. The fields in the component should look like Figure 136.

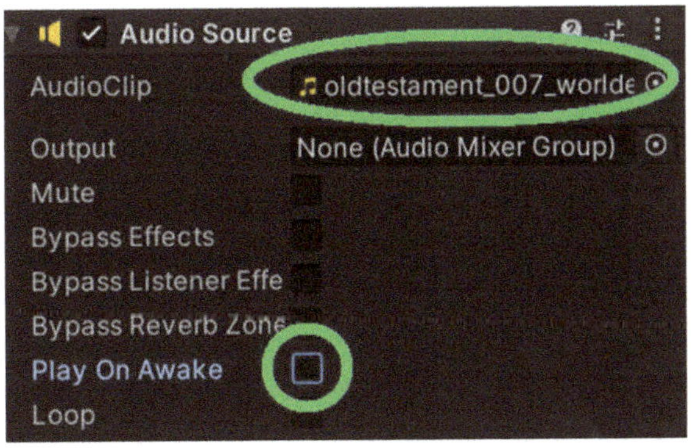

Figure 136

Now we need to update a couple scripts. Go back to the "GameController" script. Scroll to the "EnterZone" method and change it to look like Figure 137. We need to add a couple more parameters. The offset tells us the location in the audio to start playing. The length tells us how much of the audio to play. Taken together, we can play very specific passages in the Bible audio. These are both in seconds. Then we need to stop the audio at the right time. We'll invoke a method "StopAudio" to do that.

```
public void EnterZone(string zoneName, float offset, float length)
{
    ZoneTextObj.SplashZone(zoneName);
    GetComponent<AudioSource>().time = offset;
    GetComponent<AudioSource>().Play();
    Invoke("StopAudio", length);
}

0 references
public void StopAudio()
{
    GetComponent<AudioSource>().Stop();
}
```

Figure 137

We're done editing the Game Controller script, but there are a couple changes we need to make in the Zone script, so open that up. Before the "GameController" we need to add 2 public float variables, one for the offset into the audio and the other for the length of the audio to play. You can call them "AudioOffset" and "AudioLength".

```
public string ZoneName;
public float AudioOffset, AudioLength;
public GameController gc;

Unity Message | 0 references
private void OnTriggerEnter(Collider other)
{
    if (other.transform.tag == "Player")
    {
        gc.EnterZone(ZoneName, AudioOffset, AudioLength);
    }
}
```

Figure 138

Now we just need to pass them to the Game Controller script. To do that, go to the "OnTriggerEnter" method and find the call to "EnterZone". Add the "AudioOffset" and then the "AudioLength" parameters separated by a comma. It should look like Figure 138.

All that's left is to set the offset and length variables on the zone object. In the Hierarchy View, click the "PalaceZone" that is a child of "MapZones". You'll see the two new variables we added. Now, to find the offset and length, you need to go through and listen to the audio and find the exact moment in time where the passage we want starts and ends. This can be a tedious process, but then again, it may not be a bad idea to listen to the Bible.

From the GDD, we see that the passage we want for Pharaoh's Palace is Exodus 5:2. Lucky for you, though, I've already done the hard work. I found that the start of the passage is 13 minutes and 54 seconds while the end is 14 minutes and 4 seconds. To get the offset in seconds we use the equation below:

```
Minutes * 60 + Seconds = Total Seconds
```

This means our start time is:

```
13 * 60 + 54 = 834
```

Likewise, the end time is:

```
14 * 60 + 4 = 844
```

So, the start time is 834 and the length is the difference (834 - 844) which is 10. So, we plug those numbers in and get what you see in Figure 139.

Now let's click play and hear what happens. Walk Moses right onto the platform and when you see the text appear you should also hear the passage being spoken.

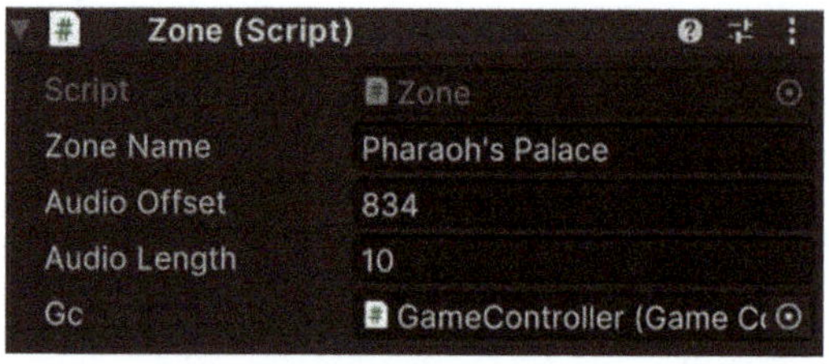

Figure 139

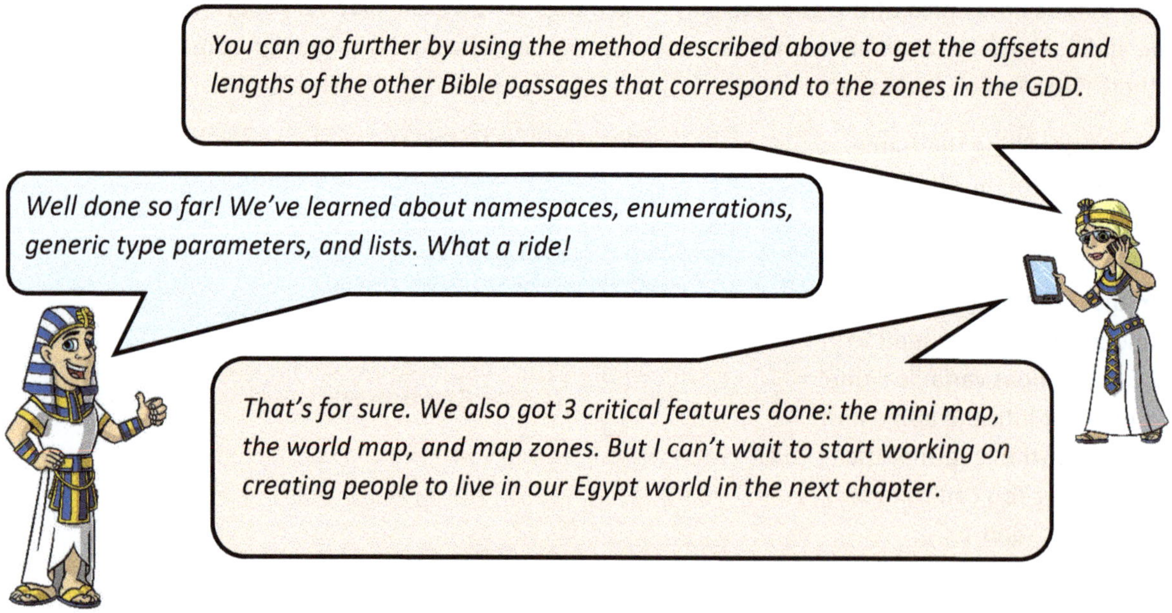

Chapter 6 – Actor Animation Controller

Populating our Egypt land and making the people move around is one of the fun parts of making a game. Looking at the nice landscape, entering zones, and doing things by the menu is great, but the character actors really pull the player.

We've got a number of them that we can use in our game. In the Project View, go to Assets > Models > EgyptCharacters > Prefabs. This folder has the list of actor characters we'll use for the game. Click on the first one, Embalmer. Notice that in the bottom-right of the screen, underneath the inspector, the 3D model appears like Figure 140 in the standard 'T' pose. Most 3D models of people you'll see will be in this pose.

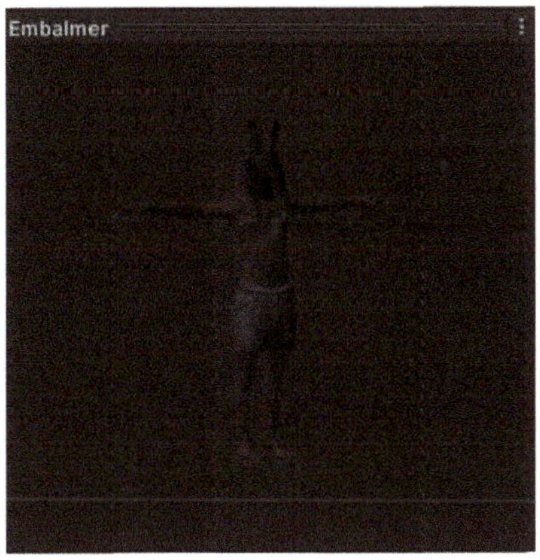

Figure 140

Let's take and drag him onto the scene. Holding your arms out like that gets tiring, but don't worry, he'll start moving once you start the game. That is done using an Animator component which you can see in the inspector. This is how Unity connects 3D models with animations.

The default Controller is "Animator" which just shows some of the demo animations in a loop. If you want to see them then click the play button. Don't worry about trying to find the Embalmer in the Game View. Just switch over to the Scene View and you should see him. The animations, especially the idle animations, can take a while, so if you want to see all of them, you'll need to wait. Or if you're impatient, like me, then just get out of play mode and we'll continue.

Click on the circle to the right of "Animator" in the Controller field like you see in Figure 141 and type in "ThirdPersonAnimatorController" into the Select Runtime Animation Controller window and select it. This animation controller is in the Standard Assets like the third person player controller we used for the player. And this is, in fact, the same animation controller that the player uses.

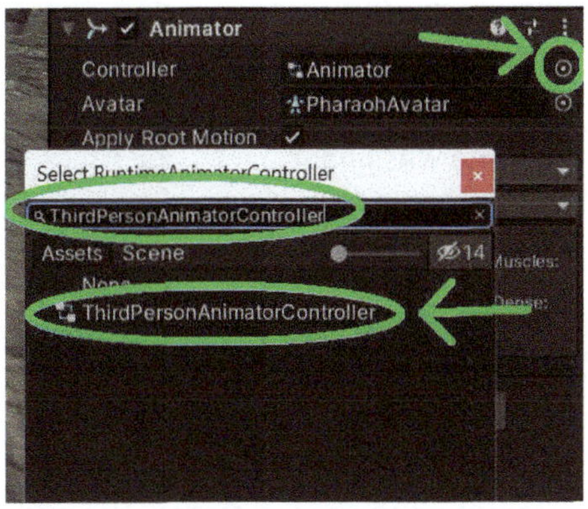

Figure 141

The process of putting joints and bones on 3D models is called "rigging". If you want a model to animate it needs to be rigged first.

The Avatar is a special translation file that helps Unity to glue the animations and the models together. For humanoid models (that is, 3D models of people), there are standard ways to do animation. Animation is done around moving parts like knees, elbows, heads, etc. The Avatar tells Unity where all these moving parts are so that Unity can apply the animations. The end result is a moving person like the Moses player we already have.

Sometimes, the animation causes the model to move in a certain direction. For example, a jump animation would cause the model to go up. This is called the root motion of the animation. In many cases we want to use it because it makes sense for the model to move in that direction and Unity will take care of everything. If, however, there is some weird movement going on, it can be due to animations moving the model in a way you don't want. Try unchecking the "Apply Root Motion" box and see if it fixes your issue. The "Update Mode" and "Culling Mode" are more advanced, and we won't discuss here.

Click on the "ThirdPersonAnimatorController" to find it in the Project View and then click the file. If the Animator View is in one of the tabs, then click to see what the animator looks like. If you can't see it, then it's probably hidden. Unity has a lot of different windows and features to help with game development. Many are advanced and aren't shown by default when the project first loads. To see the Animator View go to the main menu and select Window > Animation > Animator as shown in Figure 142. It should show up in the center panel next to the Scene View.

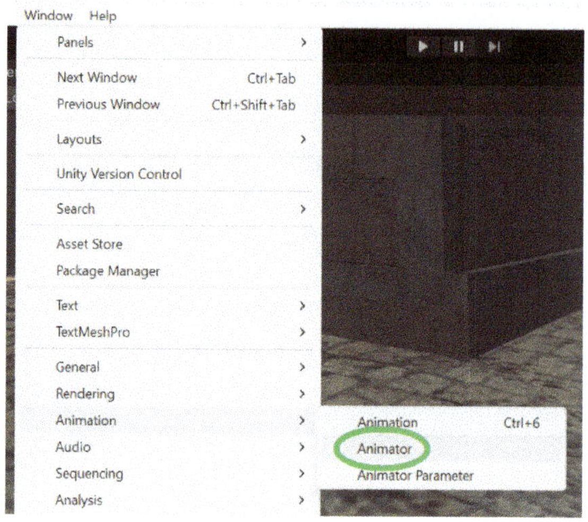

Figure 142

You should see the diagram in Figure 143. This state machine is quite a bit more complicated than our fading state machine. That one was linear, meaning you could draw the state machine diagram in a line, if you wanted to. Before I get into the details of this state machine, we need to talk about the parameters. All the arrows you see are state transitions that use parameters to change states. The middle mouse button will pan around the diagram and scroll wheel will zoom.

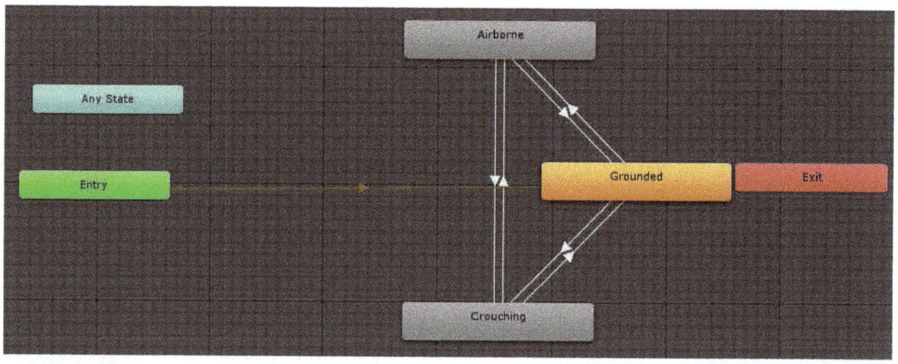

Figure 143

You're looking at the layers right now. We won't need to use those in this tutorial. Click the "Parameters tab and you can see them as shown in Figure 144. These parameters are set by the script and used by the animator. There are 4 kinds of parameters: 1) Float – for decimal numbers, 2) Int – for whole numbers, 3) Bool – shown as

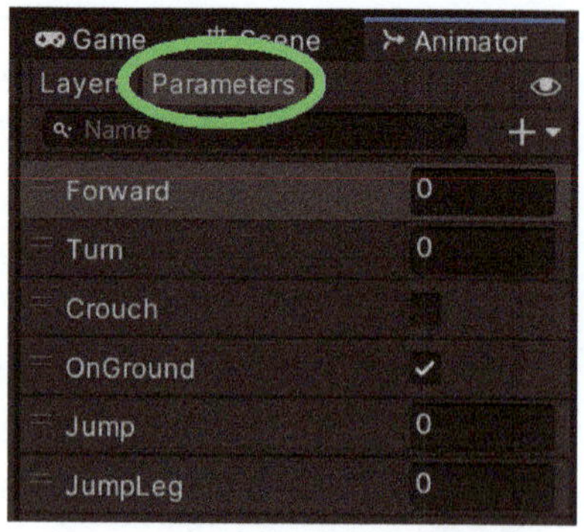

Figure 144

check box for true or false, and 4) Trigger – also shown as a check box but as soon as it is checked it gets handled and set to false right away.

You can add more actions for characters like reaching for objects and other animations by making more states and adding transitions in the animator. We'll do that in later chapters.

First, we have "Forward" which is a float. It gives the speed the person is going '0.5' is a walk and '1' is a run. If it is negative, then the person needs to walk backward. Next is "Turn", which is a float, where negative is turn left, positive is turn right, and 0 is straight ahead. "Crouch" is a Boolean, the character is either crouching down or not. Same thing with "OnGround", the character is either on the ground or not.

The "Jump" float tracks the characters velocity in the 'Y' (or up and down) direction. Positive is up and negative is down. That means when the player presses the key and jumps, this value will be in the positive direction. As gravity takes hold the player slows down and this value decreases until it gets to '0'. At that point, the player starts falling to the ground and has a negative value. The "JumpLeg" float just tracks with which leg the character jumped. The left leg is '1' and the right leg is '-1'.

Now let's look back at the state machine in Figure 143. The green "Entry" state is where Unity starts the state machine. It immediately sets the state to "Grounded". So, the character starts on the ground. If you click the arrow going from the "Grounded" state to the "Airborne" state in the inspector, you'll see what is shown in Figure 145. This arrow tells Unity when to transition the states. What we really care about are the "Conditions" at the bottom. You can see that if "OnGround" is false, meaning if we're not on the ground, then we go airborne, and Unity will play a nice-looking falling animation for the character.

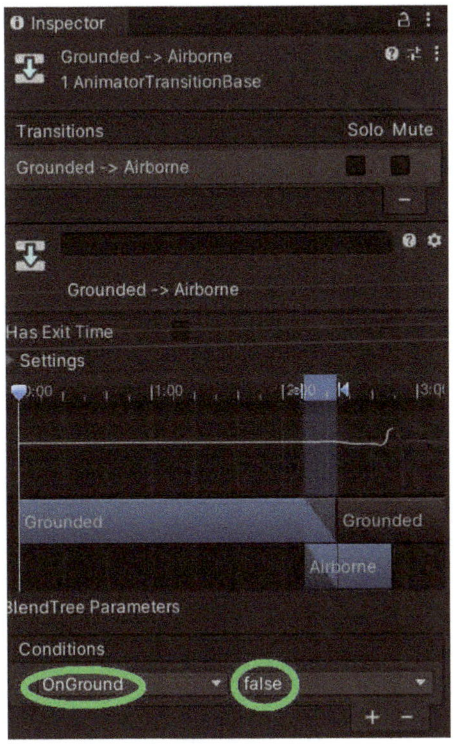

Figure 145

Now click the arrow going the other way. You'll see the conditions has 2 items. The first is when "OnGround" is true, we're back on the ground.

Makes sense. Next, the "Jump" float must also be greater than '-2'. What's that about? Notice that there is also an arrow going from "Airborne" to "Crouching". This is related. If you jump and land, then you're going to crouch a bit when you land. However, with small amounts of time being airborne (like if you just walk down a flight of stairs" you don't crouch down. So the animator is modeling how things would happen in real life. Go ahead and take a look at the other state transitions to see how the state machine flows.

Let's check out what's going on under the hood in the "Grounded" state by double-clicking on it. You'll see a "Blend Tree" with lines going to a bunch of other states as shown in Figure 146.

The Unity blend trees are simply, really cool! But there's nothing simple about how they work. Basically, they take a bunch of different animations for 3D models of the same type (like a humanoid) and blend them together using parameters to control how much they are blended. This is how the player character can smoothly transition between walking forward and turning different directions.

You can see in the blend tree here that all the animations for a humanoid to move around are listed in the blend tree. To the right, in the inspector, is a very complicated mapping for how the blend tree works. We're not going to get into that as it is a more advanced feature but know that blend trees help get the smooth animation transitions that make games feel more polished.

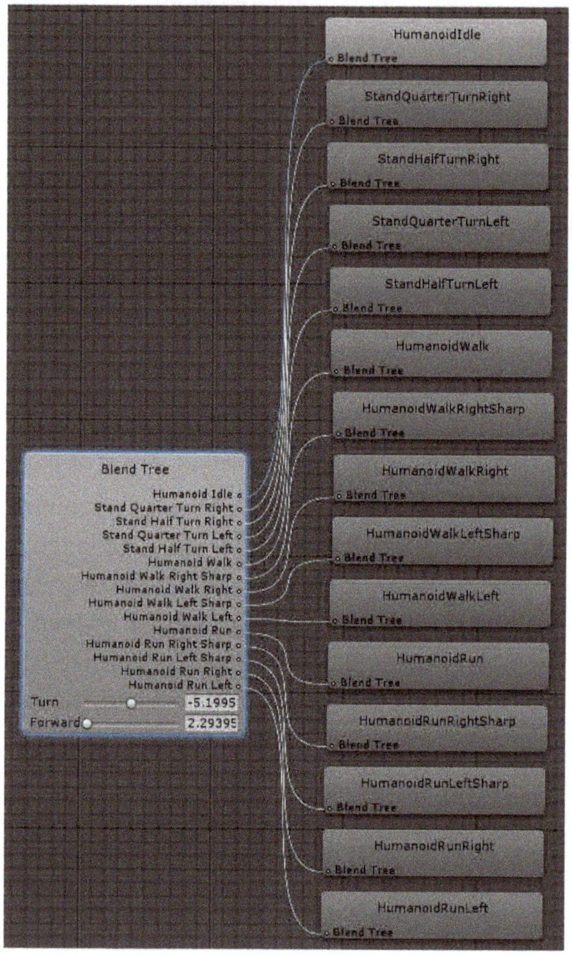

Figure 146

Generic Type Parameters

The next method we're going to implement calls another method using something we haven't looked at yet. The generic type parameter is something you use when you want to declare a variable, method, or class but want the type for it to be able to change when you run your program or play your game.

We won't spend much time on them, since we won't be making any generic type parameters, but it is very common to use them. Here is the basic form for to call methods that use generic type parameters:

```
MethodName <type> (Parameters);
```

This would call the method "MethodName" using the specified type and passing in the given parameters.

Example:

```
GetComponent <BoxCollider> ();
```

Using generic type parameters is useful for lists of objects, which we'll talk about later.

The above example calls a method named "GetComponent". The type passed in is a "BoxCollider" and there are no parametes given for this method.

You can also use this for classes and variables.

Controlling Actors

Let's go back to our Embalmer friend now. We want him to be treated the same as the player character by the physics engine (no discrimination here). To make sure the animation looks right, we need to separate it from the physics. Right-click on the Embalmer in the Hierarchy View and select "Rename" and change the name to "Guard". We'll have a bunch of these embalmer guys with the headdress running around guarding the city. Add a capsule collider component and set the Center 'Y' to '0.9', Radius to '0.3', and the Height to '1.75' like you see in Figure 147.

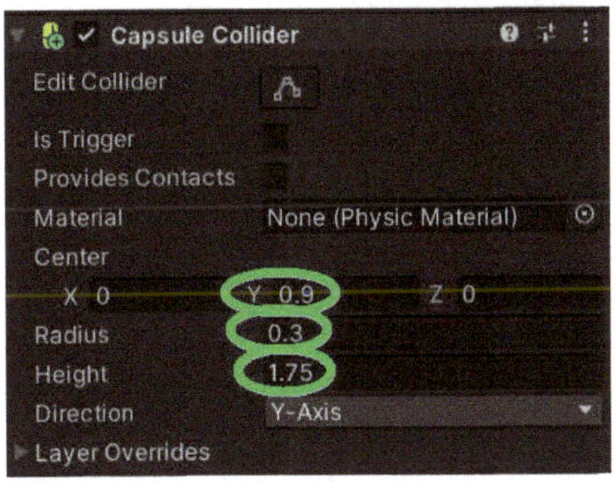

Figure 147

For the real work in telling the actor to do what he's supposed to, we create a script. So create a new C# script named "ActorController" and open it up in Visual Studio. Add the variables shown in Figure 148 at the top of the class. The enumerated type here has the different actions that an actor can take. They are either not doing anything (idle), walking around (WaypointWalk), or is moving about with an animation (Animation).

```
public enum _action_type
{
    Idle,
    WaypointWalk,
    Animation
}
public _action_type ActionType;
public Transform[] Waypoints;
public float Speed;
public string Animation;
public bool DontHighlight;

private Animator m_Animator;
private Renderer[] m_Renderers;
private bool inDialogue;
private int waypointIndex;
private bool waypointDir;
private List<Shader> savedShaders;
private Shader highlightShader;
private Vector3 moveLoc;
private bool activeActor;
```

Figure 148

Public Variable Descriptions:

- ActionType: Which kind of action to do (discussed above)
- Waypoints: Array of the waypoints the actor will walk between
- Speed: How fast the actor will walk between waypoints
- Animation: This string is the animation to play if that is the chosen action

- DontHighlight: One cool feature games have is to highlight actors when you move the mouse over them. We're going to do that in this game too. But for some actors, like water, you don't want to highlight them.

You can do more complicated things with the scripting like walking somewhere, doing an animation like talking to someone or peering into the distance to look for something, and then walking somewhere else that would add more interest to the actor. But we're going to keep it simple for this game.

Private Variable Descriptions:

- m_Animator: Store this object's animator component
- m_Renderers: Stores this object's texture renderers
- inDialogue: We'll get to dialogue later, but this will track if the actor is in a dialogue with the player
- waypointIndex: If the action is walking between waypoints then this variable tracks which waypoint the actor is currently walking towards
- waypointDir: Once we get to the last waypoint, the actor walks backward through the list. This Bool tracks which direction through the list the actor is walking.
- savedShaders: When highlighting an actor, the mouse is hovering over, save the current shaders on the actor so we can restore them
- moveLoc: Place to move the actor. Will be used for cut scenes.
- activeActor: Active actors get to be interacted with by the player. Will use later when we deactivate actors for various reasons so the player cannot interact with them anymore.

Next, code up the "Start" method as shown in Figure 149. We start by initializing our local handles to the animator component. Next, we get an array of all the renderer components in all the children. This is for the actor highlight feature, so we can restore the actor to normal after the mouse moves away from them.

```
30    void Start()
31    {
32        m_Animator = GetComponent<Animator>();
33        m_Renderers = GetComponentsInChildren<Renderer>();
34
35        savedShaders = new List<Shader>();
36        highlightShader = Shader.Find("Unlit/Texture");
37        waypointIndex = 0;
38        waypointDir = true;
39        activeActor = true;
40
41        if (ActionType == _action_type.Animation)
42        {
43            SetAnimation(Animation, Random.Range(0f, 5f));
44        }
45    }
```

Figure 149

We do some more initialization stuff and then at line 41 we setup the animation if the action was set for that. The first argument to the method is the name of the animation, but the second argument is the offset into that animation. This means that the actor may start in the middle of the animation. This prevents large crowds of actors doing the same animation from looking like a flash mob.

```
void Update()
{
    if (!inDialogue)
    {
        UpdateAction();
    }
    else if (Speed > 0)
    {
        float curDistance = Vector3.Distance(transform.position, moveLoc);
        m_Animator.SetFloat("Forward", Speed, 0.1f, Time.deltaTime);

        if (curDistance < 0.1f)
        {
            Speed = 0;
            m_Animator.SetFloat("Forward", 0, 0, Time.deltaTime);
            moveLoc.y = transform.position.y;
            transform.position = moveLoc;
        }
    }
}
```

Figure 150

Let's fill out the "Update" method now according to Figure 150. The method "UpdateAction" is normally called except during cut scenes (which we'll work on later).

If there is a cut scene going on then we check if the actor needs to move somewhere. To summarize this block of code, we need to check if the actor has arrived at the location. If the distance to where the actor is trying to go is very small (i.e., less than 0.1 units) then we'll say that's close enough. Using animations, trying to get actors to get to exactly a certain location (i.e., zero distance) is very difficult.

The new thing here is the "SetFloat" method on the animator. We saw that "Forward" was a parameter in the "ThirdPersonAnimatorController" and makes the model animate to walk forward. This is the way, in C# code, to communicate with the animator. We'll see more of this later.

After the "Update" method add the "UpdateAction" method shown in Figure 151. The only action that requires constant processing is walking between waypoints. Writing the code this way lets us easily add more "else if" blocks if we decide to add more actions that need constant processing.

The first thing we do is make sure that we have at least 2 waypoints because walking between only 1 waypoint isn't very fun (I dare you to it). We get the current position of the waypoint but use the 'Y' position of the actor. This makes the calculation to see if we've reached the waypoint much easier.

The Vector3 object has a neat static method you can call to get the distance between two points in 3D space called… "Distance". We use this to get how far away the actor is from the current waypoint. Then we point the actor toward the waypoint and tell him to move forward using the animator.

```
    private void UpdateAction()
    {
        if ((ActionType == _action_type.WaypointWalk) && (Waypoints.Length > 1))
        {
            Vector3 tObj = Waypoints[waypointIndex].position;
            tObj.y = transform.position.y;

            float curDistance = Vector3.Distance(tObj, transform.position);
            transform.LookAt(tObj);
            m_Animator.SetFloat("Forward", Speed, 0.1f, Time.deltaTime);

            if (curDistance < 0.1f)
            {
                if (waypointDir)
                {
                    waypointIndex++;

                    if (waypointIndex >= Waypoints.Length)
                    {
                        waypointDir = false;
                        waypointIndex = Waypoints.Length - 2;
                    }
                }
                else
                {
                    waypointIndex--;

                    if (waypointIndex < 0)
                    {
                        waypointDir = true;
                        waypointIndex = 1;
                    }
                }
            }
        }
    }
```

Figure 151

Lastly, we see if we're close enough to the waypoint to claim the actor has reached it and to move on to the next one. Then, depending on which direction we're going through the waypoint list, we move on to the next (or previous) waypoint. If we've reached the end or the beginning of the list, then we need to toggle the direction.

Add the method in Figure 152 which will be used by the cut scene engine (discussed later) to move actors. They give us the location to move the actor and how fast the actor should move (i.e., walk or run). If the speed given is greater than zero, then we setup the variables so that the code we wrote in the "Update" method will make sure the actor gets to that location. Otherwise, the actor needs to be at the location immediately.

```
public void MoveActor(Vector3 loc, float speed)
{
    if (speed > 0)
    {
        moveLoc = loc;
    }
    else // If zero or less then transport the actor
    {
        transform.position = loc;
    }

    Speed = speed;
    inDialogue = true;
    transform.LookAt(moveLoc);
}
```

Figure 152

At the end we call the "LookAt" method, which we also called in "UpdateAction". This method will rotate the transform so that it faces whatever 3D point you give it. Then when we tell the animator to move "Forward" it will walk (or run) towards it.

These next methods handle highlighting the actor when the player moves the mouse over it. Add the methods shown in Figure 153. The methods, "OnMouseOver" gets called when the mouse hovers over the collider attached to the object, and "OnMouseExit" gets called when the mouse stops hovering over it.

```
private void OnMouseOver()
{
    if (!DontHighlight && activeActor && (savedShaders.Count == 0))
    {
        foreach(Renderer rend in m_Renderers)
        {
            savedShaders.Add(rend.material.shader);
        }

        foreach (Renderer rend in m_Renderers)
        {
            rend.material.shader = highlightShader;
        }
    }
}

Unity Message | 0 references
private void OnMouseExit()
{
    if (!DontHighlight && activeActor)
    {
        for (int i = 0; i < m_Renderers.Length; i++)
        {
            m_Renderers[i].material.shader = savedShaders[i];
        }
        savedShaders.Clear();
    }
}
```

Figure 153

For "OnMouseEnter" if the actor is marked to NOT highlight then we don't. As mentioned before, if the actor is marked as not active then the player cannot interact with it and so we don't want to highlight it either.

The last check has to do with how Unity processes events for moving the mouse over objects. It will make numerous calls to this method when the player mouser-overs the actor, but we only want to run this code once. So, we use the "savedShaders" list to tell if we've already run this code. If it has no shaders in it (i.e., length of zero) then that means this is the first time the player moused-over the actor.

If all these conditions are met, then we highlight the actor. The first thing we do is initialize the "savedShaders" list. This indicates we've processed the mouse-over already. Then we save the names of the shaders currently on the renderers for the model. We replace them with a shader named "Unlit/Texture" which we found earlier in the Start method and stored.

Shaders are bits of code Unity uses to tell it how to display the textures on models and can be used for a lot of different purposes. They can make models look bumpy even though it really is smooth. They can make the textures look shiny or dull.

In the "OnMouseExit" method we need to restore the shaders to what they were previously. Then we clear the list and set the "savedRenderers" to null so that the next time the player moves the mouse over the actor it will highlight.

The second to last method in this file to add is "SetAnimation" shown in Figure 154. This is a "helper method" for the class to help make coding quicker.

```
public void SetAnimation(string animName, float offset)
{
    m_Animator.SetFloat("AnimOffset", offset);
    m_Animator.SetTrigger(animName);
}

Unity Message | 0 references
private void OnAnimatorMove()
{
    transform.position += m_Animator.deltaPosition;
}
```

Figure 154

The last method is shown in Figure 154 and named "OnAnimatorMove". This method gets called when the animator attached to the object is doing something. So, when the animator is moving, we make sure the actor stays in sync. We don't need a bunch of bad actors running around.

Patrolling with Waypoints

First up, we'll give our guard a patrol route. Go back to Unity and, in the Hierarchy View, and click the "Guard" object. Drag the "ActorController" script from Asset > Scripts in the Project View onto the inspector panel for it. To make the waypoints, right-click on the "Guard" object and create an Empty object named "Waypoint1". Copy and paste it and rename the new object "Waypoint2". Move "Waypoint2" away from the guard similar to Figure 155. Clicking back on the guard, set the Speed to '0.5' which will be a nice brisk walking pace.

Figure 155

The last thing he's going to need is a "Rigidbody" component. Add one like you did way back in chapter 1. This will make sure that he stays on the ground. You may notice that the terrain isn't flat. This depth adds more immersion to the levels. However, this means there is nothing from keeping our actor from walking off a cliff and staying in the air like those old cartoons. A Rigidbody will fix that. Make sure "Use Gravity" is checked and the Constraints to "Freeze Position" and "Freeze Rotation" are checked like you see in Figure 156. Constraining the position and rotation will limit how physics works on the actor so he'll stay upright and won't get into some weird position or start spinning forever.

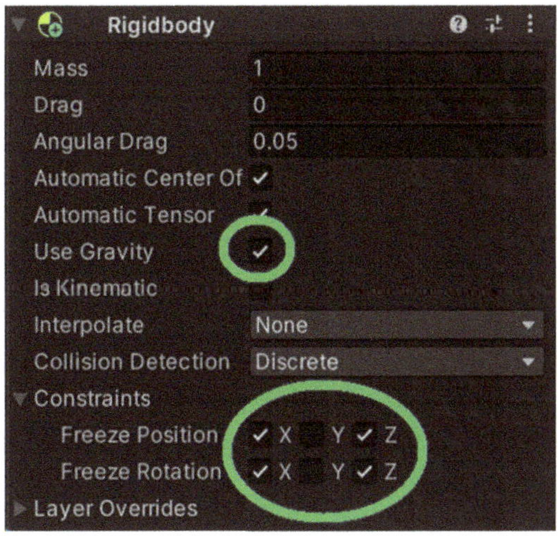

Figure 156

Figure 157

That's all the glue we need right now. Click the play button and let's see what happens. If your player object isn't close to the guard, then you can just use the Scene View to see what happens. But you should see something like Figure 157. The guard will walk between to one of the game objects we created, turn around, walk to the other one, and then repeat.

Because of the way we implemented the code, we can add as many waypoints as we want and make the route as complicated as we want, and the guard will still walk one way and then follow it back.

If you get in the guard's way and try to block him from his route, then he'll keep going and try to push you. Notice, that no matter where you push him, he'll try his best to get to the next waypoint.

Very good work. Exit play mode and let's save him in a prefab so we don't lose him. First, set the Action Type back to Idle, set the Size of the Waypoints array to 0, and set the Speed to 0. This puts him back to an initial state so it's easier to create him. Then drag him to the Project View under Assets > Prefabs with "MosesPlayer" as an Original Prefab. We're going to make some Egyptian slaves next and will reuse him.

If you want to go further, try adding a new action to walk the waypoints in a circle. So, instead of walking backward through the waypoint list, just walk to the first waypoint.

Slave Labor

We are, however, done with the "Embalmer" object, so you can delete him and the two waypoints you created to test your code. Let's get a model that looks more like an Egyptian slave. In the Project View, go to the folder Assets > Models > Egypt Characters > Prefabs and drag "Man_01" onto the Scene View near Moses. Add Rigidbody and Capsule colliders like you did with the Embalmer guy and set the fields to the same values.

Set the Animator to "ThirdPersonAnimatorController" and add the "ActorController" as well. Set the Action Type of the "ActorController" to "Animation" because he's going to be hard at work. At work doing what? Painting! Well, not really. The second painting animation has the actor crouching on the ground, so it looks like he's being oppressed. We'll just use that. In the Animation field, put "Painting2".

To add a new animation, go to Assets > Models > EgyptCharacters > Source > Anims and drag "Painting_02" onto the Animator View, just above the "Grounded" state. Now, right-click on the "Grounded" state and select "Make Transition". A white line with an arrow following the mouse appears. Click on the new "Painting_02" state and we've now got a transition to it.

Click on the line or the arrow you just made to view the properties of it in the inspector. The Conditions are blank, but we need something to tell us when to enter this state. This is the perfect situation for a trigger parameter! In the top-left of the Animator View, look at the Parameters panel displaying all the different parameters for our animator as shown in Figure 158.

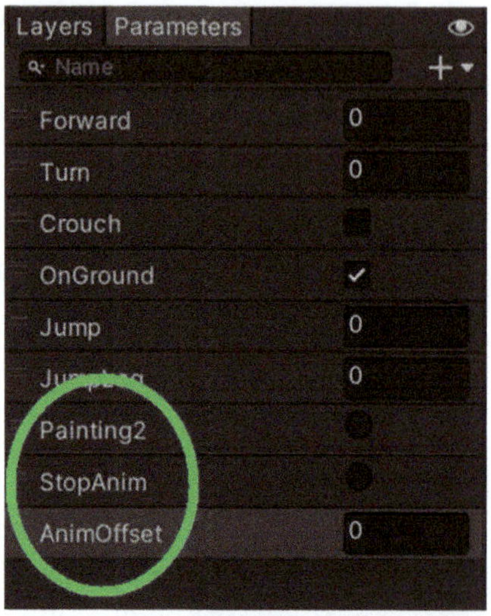

Figure 158

On the right side of the panel is a plus sign '+'. Click it and select "Trigger". This is how you create new parameters we can use from our scripts. Name the trigger "Painting2", the same text we put in the Animation field in the Actor script. Add another "Trigger" parameter and name it "StopAnim". We'll use this parameter later on so that when the player talks to the actor doing an animation, they will stop and engage in dialogue. The last parameter to add is "AnimOffset" which will be a Float.

Click back on the transition line you made before and we're going to add a new condition for it. Click the '+' sign at the bottom-right of the Conditions area. If you want to delete a condition just click the condition you want to delete and press the '-' sign.

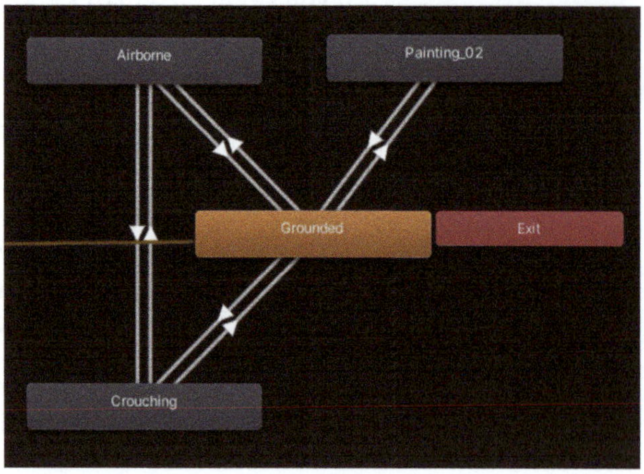

Figure 159

When the drop-down box appears, click it and select "Painting2". Now, whenever this trigger gets set the state will transition from "Grounded" to "Painting_02" and play the new animation. Also, uncheck "Has Exit Time". This is when you want the animation to stop when it is done, but we want it to loop. Create another transition going the other way, from "Painting_02" to "Grounded". Add a condition for when the "StopAnim" trigger gets set. Uncheck the "Has Exit Time" box again. The new animation state machine should look like Figure 159.

Finally, click on the "Painting_02" state. Find the "Cycle Offset" field and check the box to the right of it that says "Parameter". Then, in the drop-down to the left, select the "AnimOffset" so it looks like the bottom-right of Figure 160. This sets the "AnimOffset" parameter to control where the animation will start playing. Now we're ready to check this out in play mode. After a short delay, you should see the actor quickly crouch down and start doing something. Rename him to "EgyptianSlave" and save a prefab of him.

Figure 160

There are some more animations we'll need to use for the game. Go to the Assets > Animations > Raw Mocap Data > Animations > Interacting folder and add these animations to the animator in the same way: "IdleGrab_FrontHigh", "IdleGrab_LowFront", and "IdleGrab_Neutral". These will be useful when we want to show the player or an actor grabbing something. You can name the parameter triggers as "GrabHigh", "GrabLow", and "GrabNeutral". You don't need to add "StopAnim" to the condition for the transition back to "Grounded" on these. They will transition automatically because of "Has Exit Time".

Additionally, you can go through the animations in the folder Assets > Models > EgyptCharacters > Source > Anims and add them to the "ThirdPersonAnimatorController" like we did for the "Painting_02" animation. Giving the actors in the world a variety of animations will help them feel more natural and better immerse the player into the game. Be sure to delete the "EgyptianSlave" object from the Hierarchy View when you're done. These were just for creating the prefabs we'll need, and we don't want a player finding them.

You can use this process to create other character actors listed in the GDD. Be sure to create separate prefabs for each of them in the Assets > Prefabs > Actors folder. This will make populating the world with actors very easy. At the very least, make the Aaron actor. We'll need to use him later.

Guards and Slaves

With all the building blocks in place, we're ready to start populating our city with guards and slaves. In Figure 161 you can see a map of the city. I've circled the city gates in red. These will need some guards to look after them. Then, circled in green are some ruined structures. We'll put some slaves here, cleaning up the mess.

We'll start by adding guards to the gates. It doesn't matter which gate you start at; they are both exactly the same. And we'll add the guards in similar positions there too.

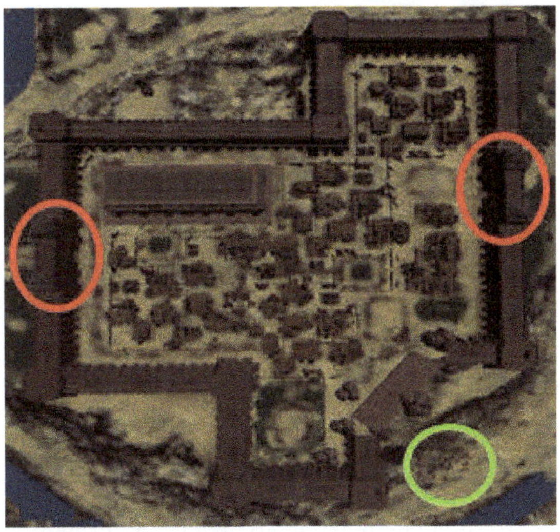

Figure 161

Figure 162 shows a close-up of one of the gates. We'll put an idle guard on either side of the gate, both inside and outside. So that's 4 guards total here. We'll have 4 guards standing watch between the gaps on top of the gate. Then we'll have a guard patrolling across the top.

Figure 162

In the Project View, go to Assets > Prefabs > Actors, and drag the "Guard" prefab out to the corners of the gate. As you put each guard out, be sure to rotate the guard to face away from the gate. To save time, you can just copy and paste the first guard, to move the second into position. Then highlight both guards, copy and paste them, move them to the other side of the gate, and then rotate them to face the right direction.

Now, let's add guards up on top of the gate. Drag a guard to each of the gaps on the side of the gate opposite of the city and rotate them so they look out, over the wall. Be sure and place them close to the edge or it will be hard for the player to see the guards from the ground.

Position and rotation of character actors doesn't need to be precise. People tend to be imprecise as a rule, so it's ok if they aren't totally lined up. In fact, unless you're showing strict military ranks, totally lined up people can look a bit unnatural.

We'll add the patrolling guard next. Drag another guard onto the gate and put him on the side closest to the city. Give a little room from the stone blocks at the side of the gate. It doesn't matter where he is, length-wise along the gate, however. We don't need to worry about rotating this guy because he'll rotate himself to face his waypoints.

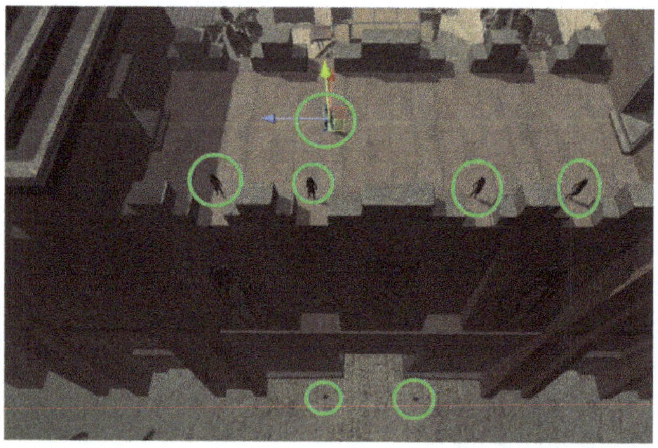

Figure 163

Create the waypoints again, like in the previous section, by creating the empty objects as child objects of the guard. Click the "Embalmer" child object of that guard and add the 2 waypoints to the list. Then set the Action Type to "Waypoint Walk" and change the speed to '0.5'. Then move the waypoints out to the length of the gate. Don't put them right up against the way, but close to it. Finally, move the waypoints out of the Guard object so they are no longer children. They should be similar to Figure 163. Click Play and... play around.

Exit play mode and let's go to the other gate and put some guards there. You can do the same thing that we did at this gate or you can do something completely different. Again, this is where you can show your creativity. Maybe you want some of the guards to circle up, like they're talking. Or maybe you want a couple more guards on patrol.

Let's add the poor Egyptians slaving away at the ruins in the hot sun. Move the Scene View over to the ruins highlighted in green back up on Figure 161. Now, this will be populated much different than how the guards at the gate were. At the gate, we placed characters where we thought guards ought to be. But here, we're going to just put slaves out randomly.

Grab our "EgyptianSlave" prefab that we created earlier, and put it out, on or nearby the ruins. Then rotate him around to face some random direction. Do it again. Then do it again. Let's put 10 slaves out working at cleaning up the ruins.

Now, I'll show you another neat little trick. In the Hierarchy View, click the first "EgyptianSlave" that appears. Then, hold down the SHIFT key, and click on the last "EgyptianSlave" object. It will likely be named "EgyptianSlave (9)". With them all highlighted, set the Action Type to "Animation" and set the Animation to "Painting2".

Wasn't that easy? Prefabs, and well-designed C# code, really help save a lot of time. Go into play mode and let's see those Egyptian slaves at work. Again, if you don't feel like running all the way over to the ruins, you can use the Scene View to look at all the hard-working slaves. As before, they will all start animating after a few seconds.

That was super fun! Populating the city with people really adds a lot to the game. We could even go further and put people in the market and other areas of the city, as well as the Hebrew camp.

Most definitely. But I'm really stoked about the next section. We're going to take these actors and let our player interact with them. There are still lots of new things to learn!

Chapter 7 – Dialogue System

Now that we've got actors populating, animating, and walking around in our Egyptian city it's time to let the player interact with them. You've probably seen the really big games have actors speaking. It's like a big movie production! We won't have that kind of dialogue, but we will have the kind you can read.

This will be a little bit complicated, so let me explain. Even better, let me show you a picture! Take a look at the diagram in Figure 164. The Actor is going to hold onto the dialogue. The dialogue itself is built from a list of elements. These elements will describe who is speaking, what they're saying, and other details.

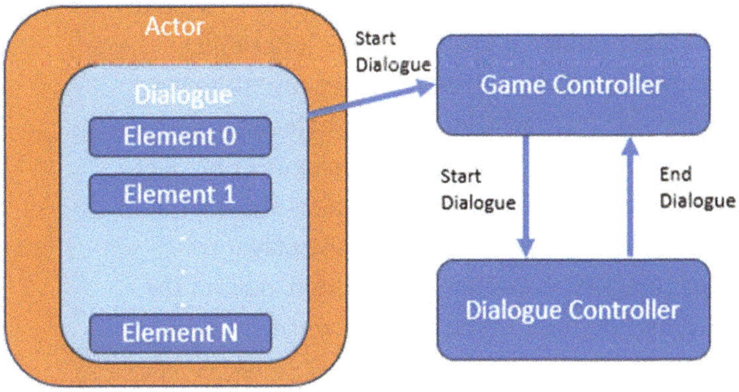

Figure 164

When the actor figures out that they are having a dialogue with the player, they will tell the Game Controller to start a dialogue with the one it encapsulates. The Game Controller will tell the player to stop moving, close any open windows, and then pass the dialogue to the Dialogue Controller so that it can officially start the dialogue. When the dialogue has run its course then the Game Controller is notified.

In programming lingo, when you want to say that an object has other objects, you use the word 'encapsulate'. You may have heard the term "Time Capsule". It is a container that has things from a year long ago. In the same way, objects are containers and encapsulate variables and methods.

The diagram really helps to put what we want to do into perspective. It also gives us a head start for how the code needs to be written. We'll need a class for the Dialogue Controller and then another two classes for the Dialogue and its elements. The existing classes for the Actor Controller and Game Controller will also need to be modified. It's not shown here, but we will need to write a small amount of code in the "ThirdPersonUserControl" script again.

Now that we know what to do, let's go write some code!

Writing the Script's Scripts

In general, writing dialogue requires a script. To manage all those scripts, we need to write a script. In fact, when I was sitting down to write this section, I was writing a script to talk about writing a script for the scripts. Make sense? If so, that's one of us.

Anyways, create a new C# script named "DialogueElement" and open it up in Visual Studio. Change the file to look like what you see in Figure 165. This script is a little bit different from others we've written. Line 5 is an attribute or meta data about the class which will allow us to use it, we did something similar in Chapter 4. The inheritance from Monobehavior is removed because this class will not be attached directly to an object.
The response types will tell the Dialogue Controller what to do after the line of dialogue is shown. If it is "None" then it simply prompts the player to "Press any Key to Continue". Let them look for the "Any Key" on their keyboard for a while.

They also can type a string on the keyboard as "Input" as well as choose from a list of options we call "Choices".

```
5      [System.Serializable]
       6 references
6      public class DialogueElement
7      {
8          public string LineName;
9          public string Speaker;
10         public string Text;
11
           6 references
12         public enum _response_type
13         {
14             None,
15             Input,
16             Choice,
17             End
18         }
19         public _response_type Response;
20
21         public string[] Choices;
22     }
```

Figure 165

The code will use these choices and inputs to change the outcome of the script. While not quite as sophisticated as Artificial Intelligence, this will give your actors some life.

The code will use these choices and inputs to change the outcome of the script. While not quite as sophisticated as Artificial Intelligence, this will give your actors some life.

To encapsulate the Dialogue Element class, create another script named "Dialogue". Add the code from Figure 166. In addition to the array of "DialogueElements" for the lines of the dialogue, there is a helper method that will be used by the Dialogue Controller we'll create next. This method loops through each of the lines to find the given name. This will help to make more complicated and interesting dialogue for our actors.

```
public DialogueElement[] Lines;

1 reference
public int GetIndexFromDialogueName(string name)
{
    int ret = -1;

    for (int i = 0; i < Lines.Length; i++)
    {
        if (Lines[i].LineName == name)
        {
            ret = i;
            break;
        }
    }

    return ret;
}
```

Figure 166

Create another new script named "DialogueController" and start off by "using TMPro" on line 4 from Figure 167. Then fill in the public and private variables starting on line 8. The Dialogue Controller will decide when our user interface objects are shown and what the text will read. One thing to call out is on line 13 is a prefab reference. Since both object instances and prefabs use the "GameObject" type, naming them differently is a good way to remember which variable is a prefab and which is not.

```
4   using TMPro;
5
    Unity Script (1 asset reference) | 1 reference
6   public class DialogueController : MonoBehaviour
7   {
8       public TextMeshProUGUI SpeakerText;
9       public TextMeshProUGUI DialogueText;
10      public GameObject DialoguePanel;
11      public GameObject InputWindow;
12      public GameObject ContinueText;
13      public GameObject ButtonPrefab;
14      public GameObject Player;
15      public GameController gc;
16
17      private Dialogue curDia;
18      private List<GameObject> buttonList;
19      private int diaIndex;
20      private bool waitForClick;
21      private bool uiClicked;
```

Figure 167

In Figure 168 you can see the Start method. Go ahead and code it up. All those dialogue UI objects start as not shown, where their active attribute is set to false.

```
void Start()
{
    DialoguePanel.SetActive(false);
    InputWindow.SetActive(false);
    ContinueText.SetActive(false);

    buttonList = new List<GameObject>();
    curDia = null;
    waitForClick = false;
    uiClicked = false;
}
```

Figure 168

The "curDia" variable holds the dialogue it is playing right now. Since there is no dialogue at the very beginning, it is set to null. There are a couple variables about clicking. The bool "waitForClick" will let us know when the player clicked the mouse or pressed a key to advance the dialogue. There is another bool named "uiClicked" which will make sure we don't skip when the player clicks buttons.

Next up is the Update method. Add the code for it from Figure 169. This is where we handle the case when we display a line of dialogue to the player and then wait for them to continue and advance the dialogue.

If the previous line of dialogue had the player click a button to make a choice, then we make sure we don't double-process it by checking the "uiClicked" bool.

Once they advance the dialogue then we check if the dialogue was supposed to end. If so, we end it, if not, then we process the next element of the dialogue.

```
void Update()
{
    if (waitForClick)
    {
        if (CheckContinue() && !uiClicked)
        {
            if (curDia.Lines[diaIndex].Response ==
                DialogueElement._response_type.End)
            {
                EndDialogue();
            }
            else
            {
                waitForClick = false;
                ProcessNextElement();
            }
        }
    }

    uiClicked = false;
}
```

Figure 169

At the end, we set "uiClicked" to false. You'll see in our code to handle the button press, this variable is set to true. If we didn't have this variable then there would be a bug that when the player presses one of the dialogue buttons, it will also think the player clicked to advance to the next dialogue element, thus skipping the next dialogue. Adding this Boolean allows us to ignore that mouse click so that we play each line of dialogue.

These next couple of methods are to help us out. Add them from Figure 170. The method "CheckContinue" helps to keep our if statement clean. To advance dialogue, we want to check the mouse left-click as well as a few keys on the keyboard.

The method "IsInDialogue" will be helpful later on to let other scripts know that a dialogue is going on. To determine if that's the case, we put a conditional statement as part of the return. This statement will get evaluated and the result returned. So, if our current dialogue (aka. curDia) refers to a dialogue then we're in a dialogue. If it is null, or nothing, then it doesn't.

```
public bool CheckContinue()
{
    bool ret = false;

    if (Input.GetMouseButtonDown(0) ||
        Input.GetKeyDown(KeyCode.KeypadEnter) ||
        Input.GetKeyDown(KeyCode.Return) ||
        Input.GetKeyDown(KeyCode.Space))
    {
        ret = true;
    }

    return ret;
}

0 references
public bool IsInDialogue()
{
    return curDia != null;
}
```

Figure 170

If you remember our diagram, the Game Controller tells the Dialogue Controller when to start. Then the Dialogue Controller tells the Game Controller when dialogue ends. That's the code we'll type next in Figure 171.

Starting a dialogue needs a reference to a dialogue which is passed in as an argument on line 79. But we'll only start a dialogue if one currently is not started. The statement "!curDia" is short for "curDia != null". So, if there is no current dialogue then we'll set it to the dialogue that's passed in so we can refer to it later, we reset our index that points to the element of the dialogue we're working on, show the dialogue window so the player can see the dialogue, and then start processing the line of dialogue.

```
79      public void StartDialogue(Dialogue dia)
80      {
81          if (!curDia)
82          {
83              curDia = dia;
84              diaIndex = 0;
85              DialoguePanel.SetActive(true);
86              ProcessElement();
87          }
88      }
89
        2 references
90      public void EndDialogue()
91      {
92          if (curDia)
93          {
94              DialoguePanel.SetActive(false);
95              InputWindow.SetActive(false);
96              ContinueText.SetActive(false);
97
98              CleanUpButtons();
99              curDia = null;
100             waitForClick = false;
101             gc.EndDialogue();
102         }
103     }
```

Figure 171

To end the dialogue, we need to first make sure there is a dialogue to end. We'll hide the user interface objects, delete the buttons, set the current dialogue to null, and tell the Game Controller that the dialogue has ended.

```
105     public void ProcessElement()
106     {
107         if (curDia)
108         {
109             if (diaIndex < curDia.Lines.Length)
110             {
111                 SpeakerText.text = curDia.Lines[diaIndex].Speaker + ":";
112                 DialogueText.text = curDia.Lines[diaIndex].Text;
113 
114                 switch(curDia.Lines[diaIndex].Response)
115                 {
116                     case DialogueElement._response_type.None:
117                         waitForClick = true;
118                         ContinueText.SetActive(true);
119                         break;
120                     case DialogueElement._response_type.Input:
121                         InputWindow.GetComponent<TMP_InputField>().text = "";
122                         InputWindow.SetActive(true);
123                         break;
124                     case DialogueElement._response_type.Choice:
125                         float xAdd = -100;
126                         foreach(string choice in curDia.Lines[diaIndex].Choices)
127                         {
128                             GameObject button = Instantiate(ButtonPrefab, DialoguePanel.transform.parent);
129                             button.GetComponentInChildren<TextMeshProUGUI>().text = choice;
130                             Vector3 tPos = InputWindow.GetComponent<RectTransform>().position;
131                             tPos.x += xAdd;
132                             button.GetComponent<RectTransform>().position = tPos;
133                             string arg = choice;
134                             button.GetComponent<UnityEngine.UI.Button>().onClick.AddListener(() => SelectChoice(arg));
135                             buttonList.Add(button);
136                             xAdd += 200;
137                         }
138                         break;
139                     case DialogueElement._response_type.End:
140                         waitForClick = true;
141                         ContinueText.SetActive(true);
142                         break;
143                 }
144             }
145             else
146             {
147                 EndDialogue();
148             }
149         }
150     }
```

Figure 172

The method above in Figure 172 is the main workhorse for the dialogue controller. This is a big method, so pay careful attention to the code. After we've determined a dialogue is in-progress, we check the index on line 109. We want to process lines until the last one. On lines 111 and 112 we set the text components for the speaker and dialogue panel.

After that we use the handy switch statement, we learned about earlier to find out what to do based on what kind of response this line of dialogue elicits. We will create the user interface for these later.

- "None": Or no response means just putting up the prompt to press any key.
- "Input": Will show the input window for the player to type in text from the keyboard.
- "Choice": Instantiates some buttons for the player to press. We'll cover this more.
- "End": Similar to "None" except when the player advances the dialogue will end.

The code in the "Choice" case is a little complicated, I'll unpack it for you. First, we prepare a float named "xAdd" which will help in putting the buttons in different locations, so they aren't stacked on top of each other. The 'x' in that variable refers to the X-Axis. The for loop iterates on each of the choices to instantiate a button for them.

The next block of code after the instantiate configures the button so it will work within our dialogue subsystem. Each button has a child object with a "TextMeshProUGUI" component which tells the player the text on the button. We set that text to the choice. Lines 129 to 131 change the position of the button using the "xAdd" float for the corresponding Y position.

Lines 132 and 133 help connect the button to this Dialogue Controller script. You see that on line 134 that we get the button component and add a listener to its "onClick" attribute. When a button is clicked, methods added as listeners get called. The funky "() => SelectChoice(arg)" means that we're going to define a method here named "SelectChoice" which has 1 argument that gets passed in. Whenever the button is clicked then "SelectChoice" will get called with whatever "arg" is. On line 133, we set "arg" to whatever the choice was.

Passing methods as arguments are a flexible way to change behavior. It's treating the method as a variable. Don't be scared! Just see it as one thing.

For the last code in this block, we add the button to our list of buttons and increment our "yAdd" variable. Now, when we use yAdd the next iteration of the loop it will be ready with the next position of the button.

Finally, we get to the else block on line 145 which is paired with the if statement on line 109. If we've finished processing all the lines, the dialogue is ended.

The next three methods to add are in Figure 173. In the Update method we called this method on line 152 which just increments the dialogue index and calls "ProcessElement".

```
152     public void ProcessNextElement()
153     {
154         diaIndex++;
155         ProcessElement();
156     }
157
        0 references
158     public void SelectInput()
159     {
160         uiClicked = true;
161         InputWindow.SetActive(false);
162         string inputText = InputWindow.GetComponent<TMP_InputField>().text;
163         FindNextDialogue(inputText);
164     }
165
        1 reference
166     public void SelectChoice(string choice)
167     {
168         uiClicked = true;
169         CleanUpButtons();
170         FindNextDialogue(choice);
171     }
```

Figure 173

The next two methods handle the input field and the buttons and play a critical role. "SelectInput" gets the text from the Input Field and sends it to "FindNextDialogue". "SelectChoice" gets the "arg" we passed in from the buttons in Figure 173 on line 133 to that same method. We will set the input field user interface element to call "SelectInput" when they press RETURN after they type in a string from the keyboard. In "SelectChoice" we can see that the bool "uiClicked" is set here. Since the user just pushed the button, this is the place we need to acknowledge that, so the next dialogue line won't be skipped.

Now the method where the rubber hits the road. Code up "FindNextDialogue" from Figure 174. While it is a short method, it allows us to connect dialogue elements and go back and forth. We use that helper function from the Dialogue script to get the dialogue line that we need, set the dialogue index to it, and go straight to processing the next element. The 'if' statement on line 177 just makes sure that the method returned a valid index, if not the dialogue index just goes to the next line.

```
173 private void FindNextDialogue(string lineName)
174 {
175     int tempIndex = curDia.GetIndexFromDialogueName(lineName);
176
177     if (tempIndex >= 0)
178     {
179         diaIndex = tempIndex;
180         ProcessElement();
181     }
182     else
183     {
184         diaIndex++;
185         ProcessElement();
186     }
187 }
```

Figure 174

> Remember, to destroy game objects you instantiate when you don't need them anymore. Leaving them impacts performance.

Way back in the "ProcessElement" method, about two pages ago, we instantiated a bunch of buttons so the player can make a choice. Well, now we need to clean all of those up. After the "FindNextDialogue" method, add "CleanUpButtons" like Figure 175.

The code simply iterates through the button list and destroys the button. It does check if the button isn't null before it destroys it because otherwise that would cause a run-time error. Finally, it empties the list of all these destroyed buttons by calling the "Clear" method. This gets it ready for the next dialogue where there is a choice.

```
private void CleanUpButtons()
{
    foreach(GameObject button in buttonList)
    {
        if (button != null)
        {
            Destroy(button);
        }
    }
    buttonList.Clear();
}
```

Figure 175

Updates for Dialogue

All these scripts are great practice of the concepts we've learned so far and will let the dialogue flow well. However, there are some changes that need to be made to other scripts to support the dialogue feature. The scripts we're going to update are "ThirdPersonUserControl", "ActorController", and "GameController".

Let's start with "ThirdPersonUserControl". After "lastPos" add a private bool variable named "disableMove" on line 31 shown in Figure 176. This will stop the player from moving during dialogue.

```
30     private Vector3 lastPos;
31     private bool disableMove;
```

Figure 176

Next, scroll down to the Start method and initialize "disableMove" to false as shown in Figure 177 on line 51. This means that the player will start out able to move Moses.

```
48    m_Character = GetComponent<ThirdPersonCharacter>();
49    m_Audio = GetComponent<AudioSource>();
50    InvokeRepeating("PreventWaterWalk", 0.25f, 0.25f);
51    disableMove = false;
```

Figure 177

After that, scroll to FixedUpdate where we need to add code in Figure 178. If movement has been disabled, then we set the horizontal and vertical inputs to zero before they get processed. This will keep Moses from moving no matter how much the player presses the keys.

```
private void FixedUpdate()
{
    // read inputs
    float h = CrossPlatformInputManager.GetAxis("Horizontal");
    float v = CrossPlatformInputManager.GetAxis("Vertical");
    bool crouch = Input.GetKey(KeyCode.C);

    if (disableMove)
    {
        h = 0;
        v = 0;
    }
```

Figure 178

The last change to the Third Person User Control script is to add the method "SetMoveEnable" which you see in Figure 179. This method allows someone to tell Moses whether or not he can move. Notice how we use the '!' or NOT operator to say that "disableMove" will be the opposite of the enable. Be sure not to forget it!

```
public void SetMoveEnable(bool enable)
{
    disableMove = !enable;
}
```

Figure 179

There's only one change we need to make in the actor controller. Open it up and scroll down to the Update method to add the code you see in Figure 180. Every frame, the actor checks if the player has clicked the left mouse button. If the player does AND the actor is highlighted, then that means the actor has been clicked on. Remember that the "savedShaders" list gets populated when the mouse hovers over the actor and cleared when the mouse moves away.

```
if (Input.GetMouseButtonUp(0) && (savedShaders.Count > 0))
{
    Dialogue dia = GetComponent<Dialogue>();

    if (dia)
    {
        GameObject gc = GameObject.FindWithTag("GameController");
        gc.GetComponent<GameController>().StartDialogue(dia);
    }
}
```

Figure 180

Then, if there is a Dialogue component attached to the actor, then get it and tell the game controller to start a dialogue with it. Having the Dialogue attached to the game object means we don't need to add a public variable in the actor class.

If the player clicks a button or presses enter for an input text field then we would also hit that in our update function, so we need to make sure we don't think it's for the next cut scene item by ignoring the first time through the "Update" method.

There are two changes that needs to be made in the Game Controller. First, add a reference to the Dialogue Controller like you see in Figure 181.This will allow us to call into the Dialogue Controller to start a dialogue with the Dialogue component that's been given to us from the actor. Also add the namespace we're going to use called "UnityStandardAssets.Characters.ThirdPerson" so we can more easily refer to that script when we disable and enable movement for Moses.

```
using UnityEngine;
using UnityStandardAssets.Characters.ThirdPerson;

Unity Script (1 asset reference) | 3 references
public class GameController : MonoBehaviour
{
    public DialogueController DialogueCtlr;
    public ZoneText ZoneTextObj;
```

Figure 181

```
public void StartDialogue(Dialogue dia)
{
    uiState = _ui_state.None;
    WorldMapSetActive(false);
    Player.GetComponent<ThirdPersonUserControl>().SetMoveEnable(false);
    DialogueCtlr.StartDialogue(dia);
}

2 references
public void EndDialogue()
{
    Player.GetComponent<ThirdPersonUserControl>().SetMoveEnable(true);
}
```

Figure 182

See Figure 182 for the last bit of code we need to add to get our dialogue system working. There are two methods, one for starting the dialogue and one for ending it.

You can type-cast values between int, float, and char. Also, you can type-cast between child and parent classes.

When starting the dialogue, in addition to letting the Dialogue Controller know what dialogue to start, we disable our UI for the world map and tell Moses to stop moving. When the Game Controller is told by the Dialogue Controller that it's time for the dialogue to end, all it needs to do is tell Moses he can start moving again.

User Interface for the Dialogue

Wow, that was a semi-truck load chock full of C# code! Let's take a break from writing code and make some UI objects. We're going to need a Window to display all the text, a text object to display the speaker's name, another text object for what the speaker says, an input box for the player to enter text, the continue text, and a prefab for the buttons we'll create in choice responses.

Determining the best way to show things to a player or user is called User Experience or UX. It is a field now its own right because having a game or an app that is easy to use is very important to give your project a competitive edge.

We'll create our dialogue window first, so go back into Unity. In the Hierarchy View, right-click the "Canvas" object and select "Create Empty". Rename it to "DialogueWindow". Now right-click on that and select UI > Image to create the background for the window. You can even name it "Background". In the Project View, go to Assets > RPG GUI > Texture > Form > Dialog and drag the "Form" file onto the Source Image variable in the Image component of the inspector. This gets the right look for a dialogue window. Now we need to get the right placement. Check out the Inspector in the Rect Transform component you'll see some squares with "center" written near them at the top-right. When you click it you'll see a pop-up like what's shown in Figure 183. This allows you to tell Unity which side of the screen you want this UI component to stick to. For the Dialogue, we're going to choose the bottom-center. Next, set the Pos Y to '-200', Width to '500' and Height to '300'.

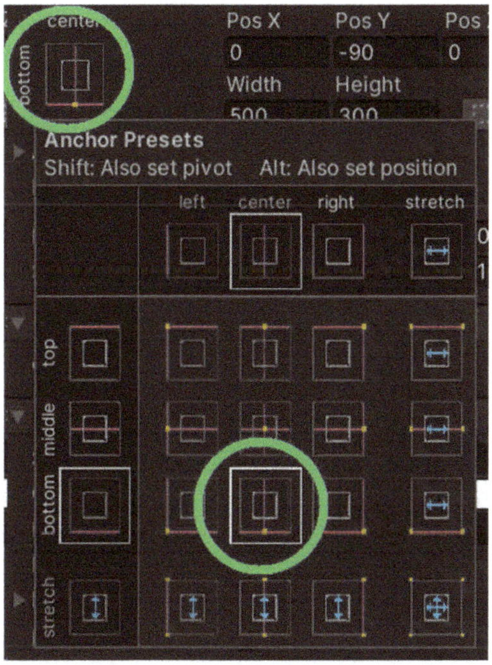

Figure 183

Back in the Hierarchy View, right-click the "DialogueWindow" object and select UI > Text - TextMeshPro to create the text as a child object under the "DialogueWindow". Rename it to "Speaker", set the Font Size to '16' and the Color to white. Set the Pos X to '-135' and Pos Y to '-23'. Copy the "Speaker" object in the Hierarchy View and paste it but rename the new text object to "Dialogue". Set the variables Pos X to '0', Pos Y to '-132', Width to '470', and Height to '200' and make sure it matches Figure 184.

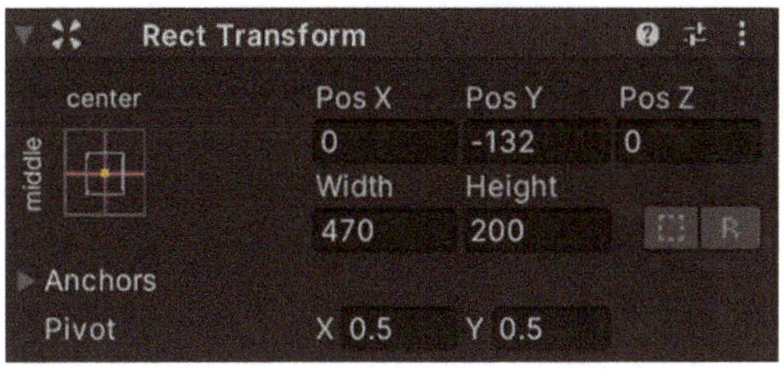

Figure 184

Copy and paste the text again, but this time name it "Continue". This will be our text that prompts the player to advance the dialogue. Set the Pos X to '0', Pos Y to '-265', Width to '250', Height to '30' and set the Text to "Press a key to continue...".

Now create an input field by right-click on "DialogueWindow" and selecting UI > Input Field – TextMeshPro. You don't need to rename it. Set the Pos Y to '-225' and Width to '300'. This Graphical User Interface (or GUI) should look like Figure 185.

Figure 185

The last user interface object we need to create is the button prefab. Right-click on the "DialogueWindow" again and select UI > Button – TextMeshPro. This creates the button right in the center of the screen. Rename it to "ChoiceButton". In the inspector of the button, as the Source Image select the file "Button_1" from Assets > Images > RPG GUI > Button. The Dialogue Controller script sets the position and listener, so we're done. Save it as a prefab in Assets > Prefabs > UI by dragging it in the empty space there. Then you can delete the "ChoiceButton" from the Hierarchy View. The Hierarchy View should show the "DialogueWindow" with the child objects in Figure 186.

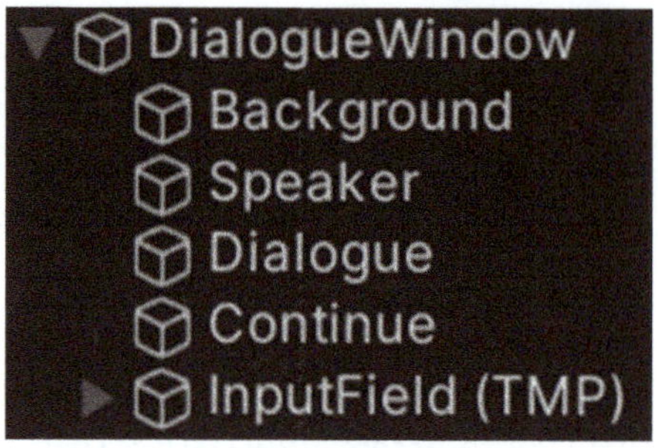

Figure 186

When creating a user interface, its important to think about where you want to direct the player's focus. Keep the interface controls nearby where you want them to focus their attention and don't show too much to minimize distractions.

Hooking up the GUI

The scripts are written, and the GUI is created, so all that's left is to glue it all together. Do "Create Empty" in the Hierarchy View and name it "DialogueController". Then go to where we saved the script with the same name in Assets > Scripts. Drag the "DialogueController" script on the Hierarchy View object with that name. In the inspector, you'll see a bunch of "None" filled into the fields. We're going to connect all of those together in this section.

The next part is going to be a scavenger hunt of sorts. We need to find all the of the objects and prefabs that need to be glued together and put them in the right spot. Are you ready? Let's go!

In the Hierarchy View, keep the "DialogueController" selected. Under Canvas > DialogueWindow, drag the "Speaker" object to the "Speaker Text" field. Drag the "Dialogue" to the "Dialogue Text" field. Drag the "InputField (TMP)" to the "Input Window" field. And then drag the Continue" object to the "Continue Text" field. Now, drag the "DialogueWindow" to the "Dialogue Panel" field.

With the “DialogueController” still selected, drag “MosesPlayer” to the “Player” field. From the Project View, at Assets > Prefabs > UI, drag “ChoiceButton” onto the “Button Prefab” field. And finally, drag the “GameController” to the “Gc” field. The dialogue controller script should now all be hooked like you see in Figure 187.

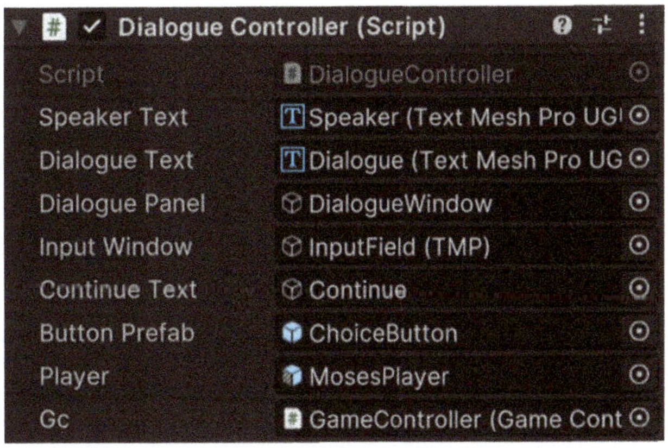

Figure 187

We also need to connect the dialogue and game controllers. Select the “GameController” in the Hierarchy View. Drag the “DialogueController” into the field for “Dialogue Ctlr”. Now, when we call the “StartDialogue” method, it will go to the appropriate script.

Figure 188

We’re not done yet. In the Hierarchy View, go to Canvas > DialogueWindow and select “InputField (TMP)”. Scroll to the bottom of the inspector, press the ‘+’ sign underneath the section that says, “On End Edit (String)” like you can see in Figure 189. This adds a listener slot.

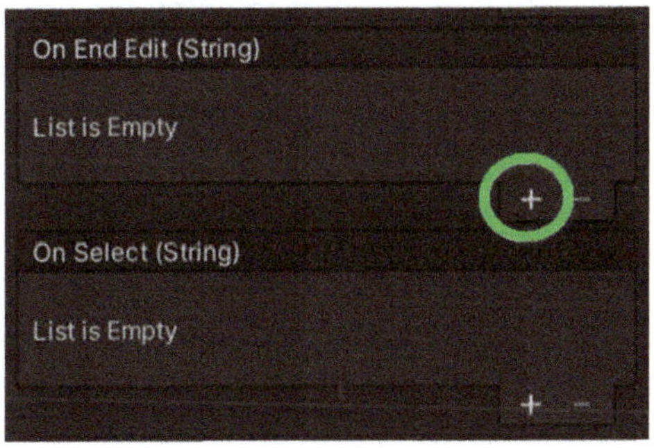

Figure 189

You will then see field where you can drop a game object into. Find the “DialogueController” in the Hierarchy View and drag it in there. The drop-down box in the upper-right corner of the slot changes to say “No Function”. Click it and change it to DialogueController > SelectInput.

Now, when the player is done typing the text into the input field, our method “SelectInput” on the dialogue controller will be called to let it know.

Figure 190

Let’s test it out. But before we can press the play button, we need someone to talk to. Let’s grab the “Embalmer” prefab we used as a guard in the last chapter. Find your Moses character (remember you can click on “MosesPlayer” in the Hierarchy View and press ‘F’ to focus on him) and drag the embalmer nearby. In the Project View, go to Assets > Scripts and drag the dialogue script (make sure it says “Dialogue” and not “DialogueElement” or “DialogueController”) onto the embalmer.

The dialogue will start out empty, like you see in Figure 191. To add a new line of dialogue, click the plus sign '+' at the bottom-right. This adds a brand new, and empty, element to the array.

Figure 191

As you recall, when we coded the dialogue script, we made lines an array and not a list. Those are two different things. While Unity says that the "List is empty", it's an array and not a list in the code.

Add the dialogue like you see in Figure 192. The responses are selected using the drop-down menu. You can add more choices by clicking the inner plus '+' sign that is under "Choices". The first line is a standard greeting. The Guard will say, "Hello" and two buttons will be instantiated for the player response. The player can choose if they want to respond with "Hi" or "Bye".

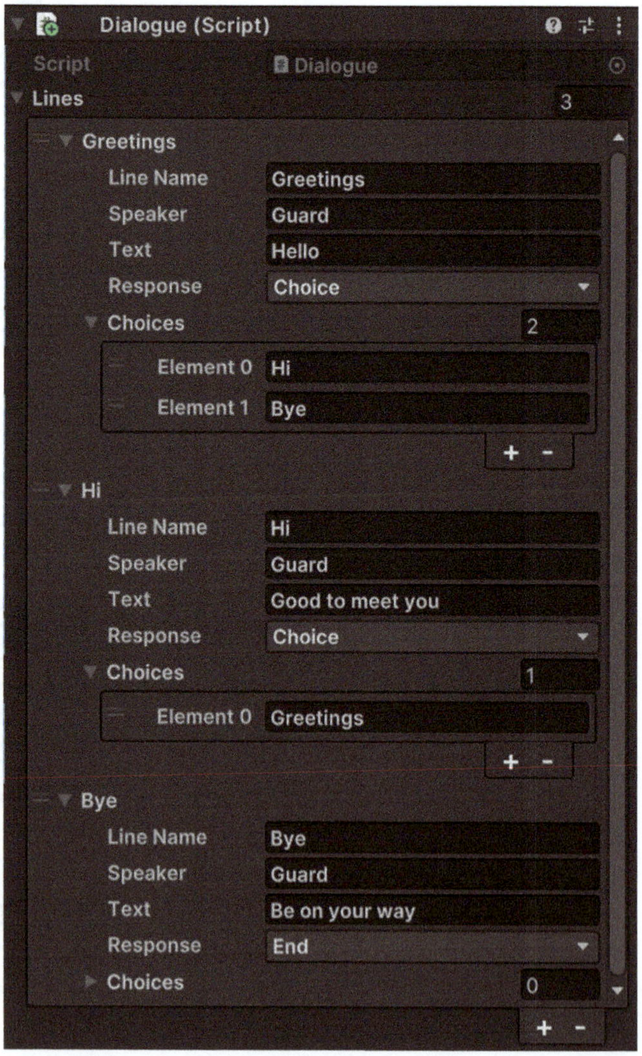

Figure 192

In the code, when the player clicks on one of the choice buttons and the "SelectChoice" method is called where the argument passed in is the text of the choice we have right here. The next line will be whichever choice they make. You can see that the line names are "Hi" and "Bye" respectively.

If the player clicks "Hi", then the guard replies with "Good to meet you". Then we have another choice which sets the next line back to our greeting.

If the player clicks "Bye" then the guard sends Moses along and the dialogue ends. Click the button for play mode and test this out!

If there are no errors and everything was glued together correctly, then you should be able to run over to the embalmer, and, when you hover your mouse over him, he highlights. Then when you click him the dialogue window pops up like in Figure 193. If you click the "Hi" button you can test the loop of greetings. When you get tired of talking to the guard, click the "Bye" button and after telling you to be on your way, the dialogue ends.

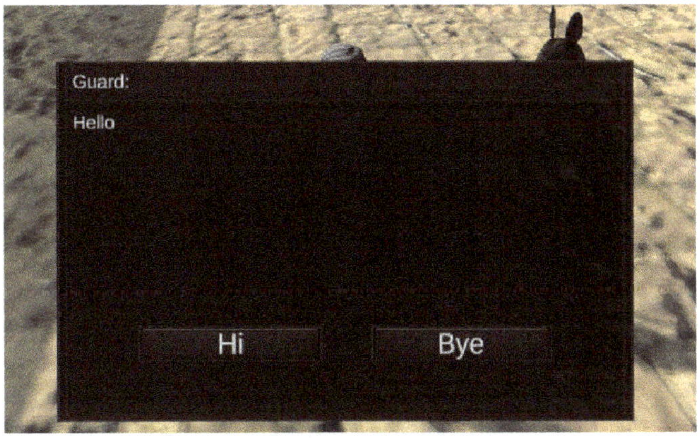

Figure 193

Blinking Text

We will do one more little thing that will require a small amount of code. The text "Press any Key to Continue..." can be brought more to the player's attention. We can do this by making it blink. Create a new C# script named "BlinkText" and open it up in Visual Studio.

Type in the code you see in Figure 194. Instead of using a public variable to get the "TextMeshPro", we're just getting it at the start using the "GetComponent" method. This expects us to put this script on the text mesh object directly.

Two new methods you can see are "OnEnable" on line 18 and "OnDisable" on line 23. These get called when the game object is enabled or disabled. We enabled and disabled the UI objects in the dialogue controller using the method "SetActive". These are like listeners when that happens.

When the object is enabled then we will toggle whether the text can be seen repeating every number of seconds specified by the "Rate" public variable which will be set in the inspector. When the object is disabled, that timer calling "Blink" is canceled.

```
4   using TMPro;
5
6   public class BlinkText : MonoBehaviour
7   {
8       public float Rate;
9
10      private TextMeshProUGUI m_Text;
11
12      // Start is called before the first frame update
13      void Start()
14      {
15          m_Text = GetComponent<TextMeshProUGUI>();
16      }
17
18      private void OnEnable()
19      {
20          InvokeRepeating("Blink", Rate, Rate);
21      }
22
23      private void OnDisable()
24      {
25          CancelInvoke("Blink");
26      }
27
28      private void Blink()
29      {
30          m_Text.enabled = !m_Text.enabled;
31      }
32  }
```

Figure 194

Figure 195

Save the script and go back into Unity. In the Hierarchy View, go to Canvas > DialogueWindow and find "Continue". Put the "BlinkText" script on the object. Set the rate to 0.75. This means every ¾ of a second, the text will change between enabled and disabled. Check it out in play mode!

Writing Dialogue

The dialogue between characters can make the difference between trudging through a book, movie, or game to being completely enthralled. But what makes good dialogue? How can you use dialogue to level up your game instead of making it feel like a grind?

Have you ever been subjected to dialogue where the characters are talking about how something works in the world? Then you start wondering why they're talking about something that they both should already know. This is called exposition. The writer is using the dialogue to explain something about the world to the reader, viewer, or player. Unless it is done very well, exposition should be avoided in dialogue. It is one of the most common ways to make your players bored.

Another great way to make your players bored is through monologue. You can think of dialogue like words going across from different people, whereas monologue is one person doing all the talking. There are some great monologues, out there. But unless you've got a lot of experience or are the next William Shakespeare, I would also steer clear of those too.

With all this talk about what not to do, you may be asking yourself, "How can I write good dialogue?" Well, I'm glad you asked. Good dialogue tells the player how the character feels about something. You can be obvious or subtle. Let's look at some examples of dialogue for a guard greeting Moses.

"Please state your name and business."	- Polite, professional, higher social standing
"Don't cause any trouble here."	- Slightly antagonistic or suspicious
"Did you need something?"	- Helpful, good-natured
"You didn't see that thief, did you?"	- Has a goal, trying to do something good

You can see that by varying how the greeting is worded that we can change the player's perception of the guard. This also makes the guard feel more real and better immerse the player in the game. Below are some guidelines to consider:

- Reveal character traits, emotions, and relationships
- Make it sound natural while avoiding filler words like "um"
- Craft different ways of talking for each character using, for example, vocabulary
- Concise dialogue gets the point across better
- Introduce conflict or tension to keep players engaged

One tool to consider is to use online chat AI to help generate dialogue if you run into a creative block. Check with your parent or guardian if that is something ok for you to use. Of course, you could try to write an AI that would chat with the player very realistically, but that would take a lot of work and is beyond the scope of this tutorial. Maybe, if you tell all your friends about this tutorial, we can sell enough of them to fund writing an AI Game Tutorial! That would be fun.

Engaging in Dialogue

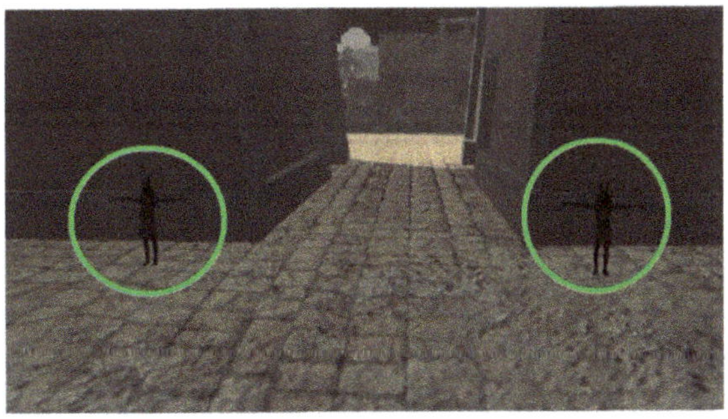

Figure 196

Now that we're ready to put some real dialogue into the game. You can delete the test embalmer you put in the game in the "Hooking up the GUI" section to test the dialogue system. We're going to go around to the different guards and slaves we added during Chapter 6 to give some of them a voice.

Let's start with the 2 guards on the outside of the city gate as shown in Figure 196. For purposes of this tutorial, it doesn't matter which guards say which lines. What does matter is that you use your creativity to think of interesting things for them to talk with the player about, remembering our guidelines for writing good dialogue.

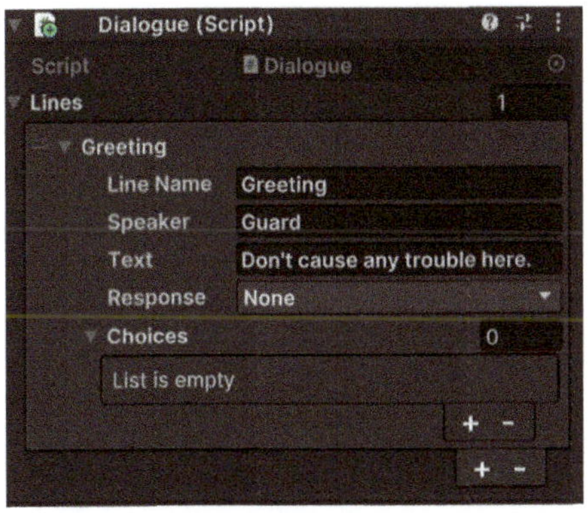

Figure 197

Click on one of them and add the dialogue script. Add a line with the name "Greeting". The Speaker is the "Guard". For the text let's give him something short to say. I'm going to use my example above, but you can make up anything you like. It should look like Figure 197. Feel free to enter play mode and give the dialogue a try as a player would to see if it's what you want.

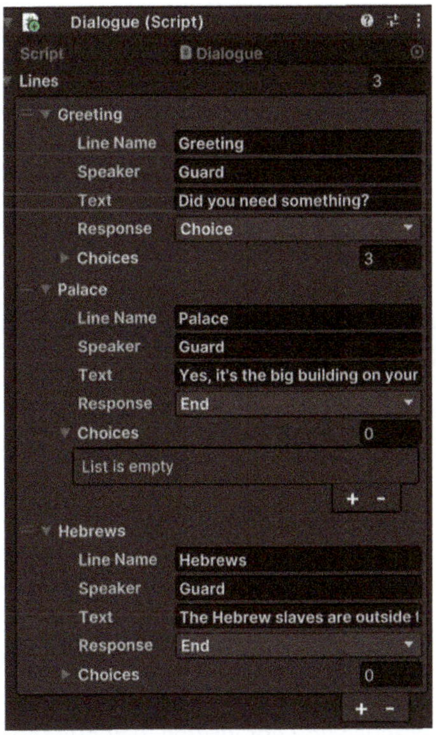

Figure 198

For the other guard, let's add a little more complexity. We'll give the player a choice. I'm going to use my example above again where the guard asks, "Did you need something?" Then the player can choose either the "Palace" or the "Hebrews" and the guard will tell where they are. If the player chooses "Palace" the guard says, "Yes, it's the big building on your left as you enter the city." If the player chooses "Hebrews" then the guard says, "The Hebrew slaves are outside the city on the far island to the right." For the lines after the greeting, be sure you put "End" as the response or the player may read a line you didn't intend.

Now let's leave these two actors to learn their lines while we go to the guards at the other gate. Choose one and let's have this guy give a riddle. If the player guesses it incorrectly, then they can try again or give up. If they try again then the dialogue goes back to the first line that asks the riddle. Guessing it correctly will play a line where the guard acknowledges the player's win. If the player gives up, then the guard will gloat.

You can make up your own riddle, but I'm going to use this one:

"Nobody can guess my riddle! I go without pause between earth's ancient jaws. Around a bend and under the sky. Who am I?"

The first two lines will look like Figure 199. The first line's name "Guess again" matches the first choice in the second line. One thing to note is that the text in the first line only shows "Nobody can guess my riddle!" but the rest of the string is hidden to the right. It's there, you just can't see it in the figure.

If the player clicks "Guess again" they can keep guessing in a loop until they get it or give up.

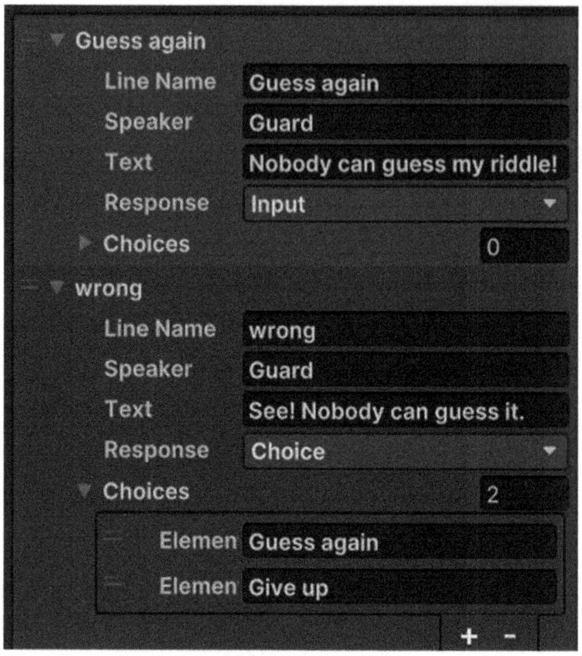

Figure 199

The next and last two lines look like Figure 200. The 3rd line named "river" is the answer to the riddle. If the player guesses it then the guard reluctantly tells them they are right. The response is "End" because there is no line to play after this one.

If the player gives up, then that is the guard's cue to give them the answer and gloat. You can really tell he enjoys asking riddles because of the dialogue.

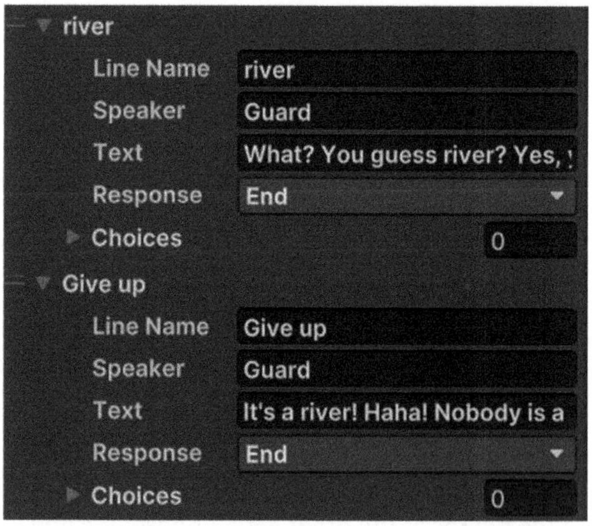

Figure 200

For the last guard at the gate, why don't you choose how he'll respond using your imagination and creativity. We've worked on the scripts and talked about how to write dialogue. You have everything you need. Now come up with something that is yours. Don't be afraid! I'm sure it'll be great. The more practice you get writing dialogue the better you'll be.

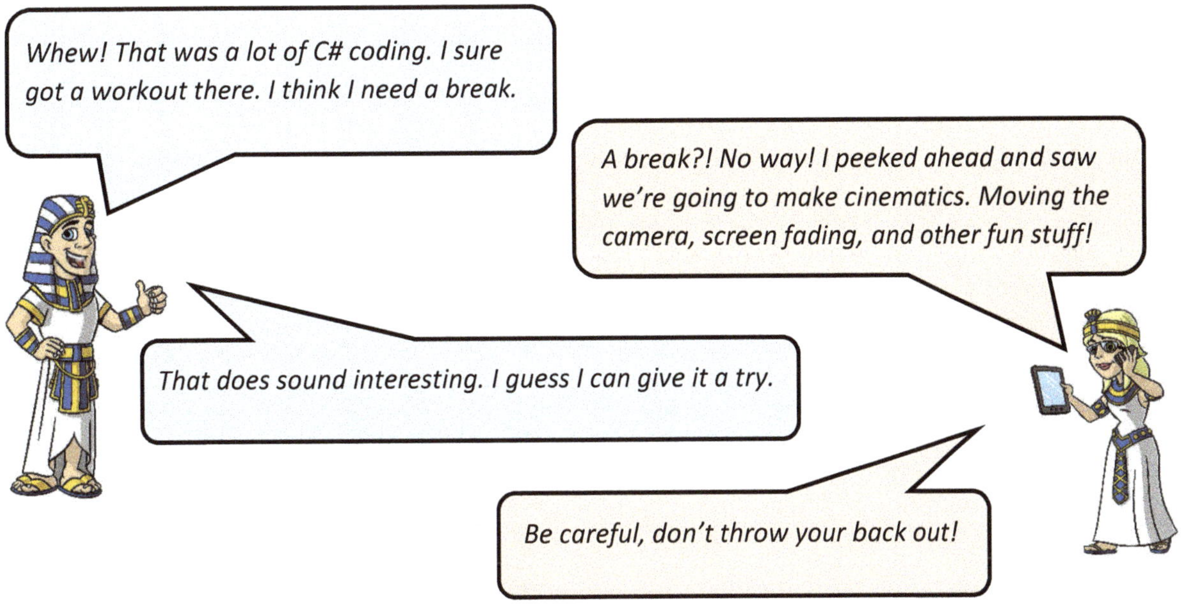
Whew! That was a lot of C# coding. I sure got a workout there. I think I need a break.
A break?! No way! I peeked ahead and saw we're going to make cinematics. Moving the camera, screen fading, and other fun stuff!
That does sound interesting. I guess I can give it a try.
Be careful, don't throw your back out!

Chapter 8 – Cinematics and Cut-scenes

Most people will enjoy a good movie from a genre they like. In addition to entertainment, putting movies inside of a game can enhance the player's experience and further immerse them in the world you are trying to create. It is a powerful tool to tell the story and evoke emotions in players. It also helps to connect one part of the game to another, so it makes sense to the player. It can also be used to teach the player how to play the game or guide them in what they are supposed to do.

Movies you use in your game can also be used out of your game to promote it. Using video editing software, you can cut sections of your game movies together to create teasers and trailers to get potential players excited to play your game. Making your game is half the work but promoting it is the other half.

There are two kinds of movies that games use, and they each have different purposes and are used differently to achieve them. Cut scenes are shorter movies that act as glue between parts of your game and short bursts of information. Cinematics are longer movies that are engaging to the player to provide story and emotional impact.

How long or short should these be? That depends on what you're trying to accomplish. A good rule of thumb is to make it as short as you can to keep the player from losing attention. Of course, you may be thinking of big games you've played that have movies that are many minutes long. Those games will often use common cinematography practices to keep the player's attention. It takes a lot of experience and expertise to make those engaging movies. We'll cover some guidelines that will help you as someone new to creating movies for your game.

Cinematography Guidelines

For reference, here are 9 cinematography guidelines we'll cover:

- Compelling Storytelling
- Character Development
- Effective Dialogue
- Pacing
- Camera Techniques
- Set Details
- Sound and Music
- Originality

Professional storytellers have a hook in every scene. A hook is something very interesting or engaging to keep up interest. Check with family and friends if they can identify them in your scenes. If not, that's ok, it just means you've got more work to do.

Compelling Storytelling draws the player into the narrative of your game in a way that resonates emotionally and intellectually. First, crafting an interesting plot is a subject that other books have already been written about. I recommend reading "The Hero with a Thousand Faces" by Joseph Campbell. The basic idea is the hero of the story goes through a journey that we identify with at a primal level. Great works like the movie Star Wars ™ make extensive use of the hero's journey.

Second, make the characters relatable. That means the player empathizes with the characters' struggles, goals, and growth (we'll talk about that next). Third, add some conflict or struggle to create tension and make sure the stakes are clear. Conflict doesn't need to be fighting. It could be trying to pass a music audition or make a new friend who has trouble trusting people. Stakes are the consequence for failure. The stakes for a music audition might be not getting into the music group. Maybe you need the new friend's help to pass a test in class.

Character Development is how the main character changes over the course of the story. A good hook, or interesting idea to keep people interested, might be a big lesson the character learns that changes what they're going to do that helps them resolve the conflict in the plot. It could be a flaw like pride they need to overcome. Not all characters in the story need development, just the main ones.

We talked about writing **Effective Dialogue** in Chapter 7. Feel free to go back and review it.

Pacing refers to how fast or slow the story progresses through the plot. Changing the pace to make the plot progress a little faster helps to build tension and excitement. Slowing the pace gives people time to think about your story. One common technique is to increase the pace as the conflict arises to build excitement and then have your main character fail at what they were attempting. Then you slow the pace down so that people have a chance to reflect on why the character failed. This helps setup a resolution for the people to resonate with the character better when they succeed later.

Camera Techniques are very detail-oriented about how to use camera angles, movement, and framing to evoke emotions and highlight important details. Moving the camera is necessary if the character or object of focus is also moving, so the camera moves with it. Panning the camera, or moving it from side to side, is good for showing landscape. For things like conversation, camera movement can be too distracting.

Framing the camera refers to how the subjects are placed. This is also called composition. It is good to follow the "Rule of Thirds". This is a fundamental principle of composition where you divide the camera frame into a grid of three rows and three columns. See Figure 201. Objects and characters should be placed on these lines.

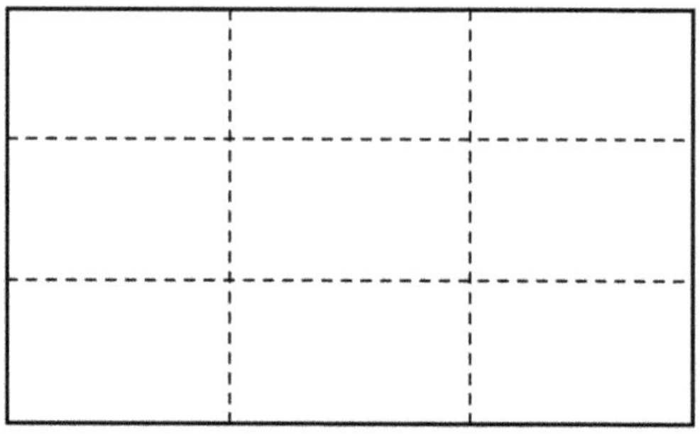

Figure 201

Common Camera Angles:

- Eye Level: Most common for a neutral perspective, use to allow the viewer to connect with the character more on a personal level.
- Low Angle: Below eye-level looking up. Makes the character or object seem more powerful, imposing, or intimidating. Use to create a sense of dominance.
- High Angle: Above eye-level looking down. Make the character or object seem smaller, weaker, or more vulnerable. Use to show submission or highlight surroundings.
- Dutch Angle: Tilted to one side. This diagonal angle creates a sense of disorientation, tension, or unease. Don't use this often, only in very dramatic moments.

- Over-the-Shoulder: The camera looks over the shoulder of a character while focusing on what or who that character is interacting with. Use to establish character relationships or conversation.

Set Details are all about the little things that help immerse the viewer in the movie. It includes what characters wear, objects they have, furniture, decorations, and many other things. These are the things a viewer won't specifically see because they should be focusing on the main objects or characters but has a big impact.

Sound and Music is all of the audio in the scene. Sound could be footsteps, background noises, sword clangs, etc. The music should be chosen to set the feeling that you're trying to portray. A battle scene will have hectic or even dissonant music. A scene with a slow river along a grassy bank may have slow tranquil music.

Originality shows your fingerprint. While it's difficult to give specific instructions to be original, there are some things that help creativity. You can take some time to brainstorm and write down any ideas that come to you, no matter how bad they may seem. You never know if they'll lead you to good ideas. Don't be afraid to explore new ideas or challenge assumptions you've made. If you've racked your brain and can't come up with anything, then maybe it's time for a break. Perhaps play "Exodus Vigil" or read "Exodus: God of the Slaves". Then come back and see if more ideas come to you.

Timeline Sequencing

In prior editions of this tutorial, we scripted our own cinematic and cut-scene system. Typing away for hundreds of lines of code that felt like thousands of lines. Unfortunately, with this edition, you don't get to go through that pain. Nope! Unity has included a package that does it all for us now called Timelines.

The Timeline lets us sequence things together for our cinematics and cut scenes. First, create an empty game object named "Timelines". This will be a parent container object to organize all of our timelines. Then create an empty child object named "IntroCinematic". Looking at Figure 202, go to the main menu and select Window > Sequencing > Timeline.

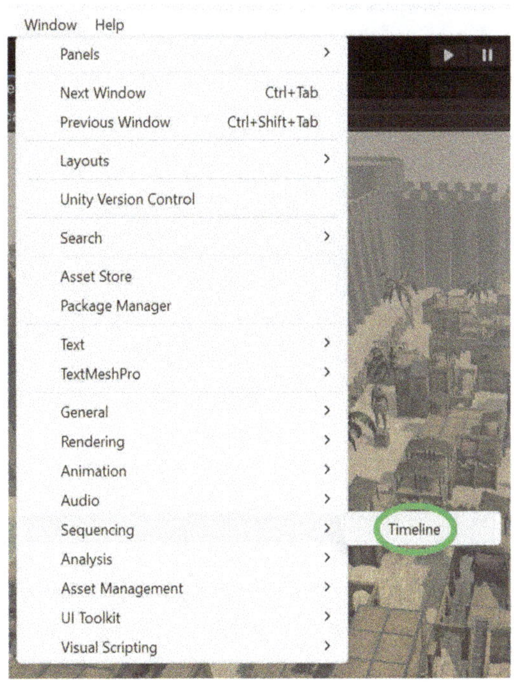

Figure 202

This opens up the timeline editor in the middle pane that you can see in Figure 203. This is the window you will use to edit your cut scenes and cinematics. Making sure you still have the "IntroCinematic" object highlighted, click the "Create" button to make new director and timeline components. This will open a window to save them.

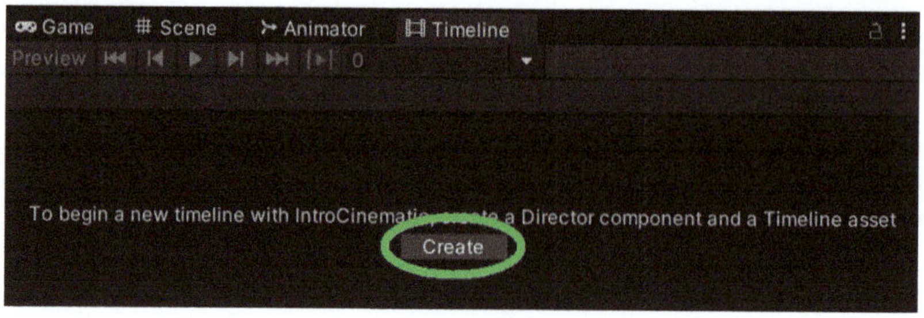

Figure 203

Browse to the Assets folder and create a new folder named "Timelines" as shown in Figure 204. The filename should already be "IntroCinematicTimeline" so you can leave that alone. When it looks good then click the "Save" button.

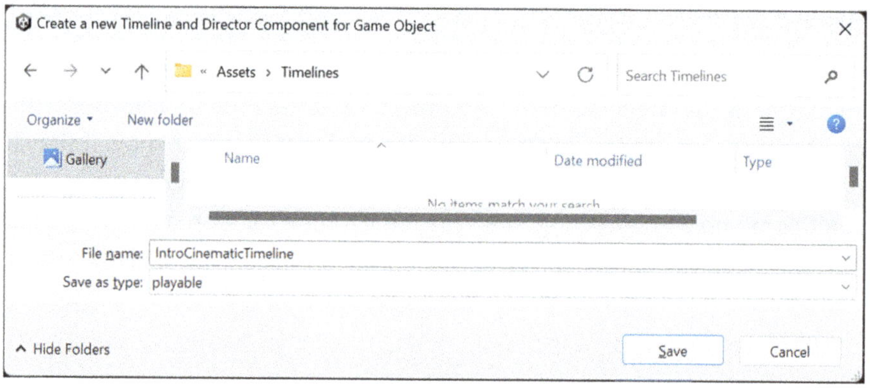

Figure 204

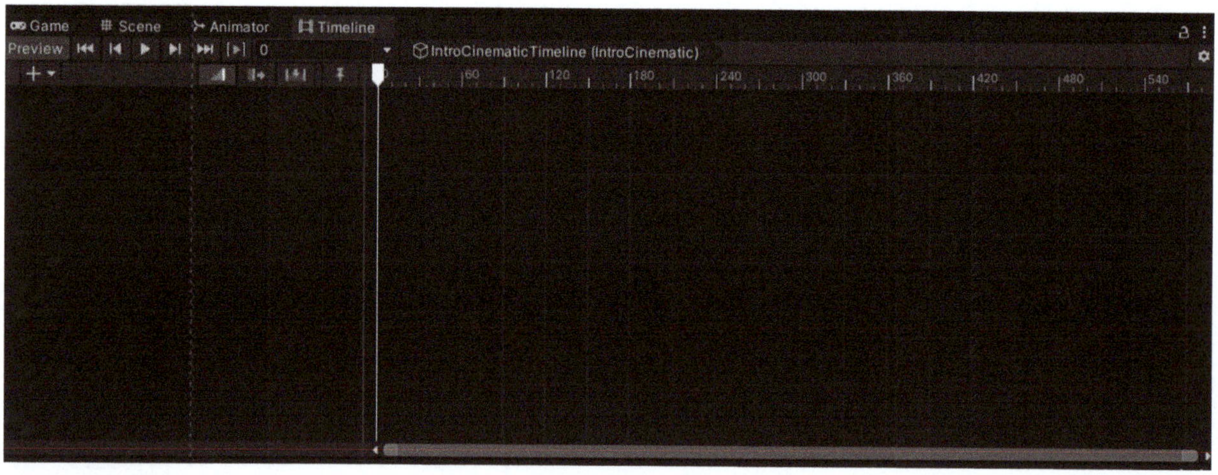

Figure 205

The window will then look like Figure 205 to edit the timeline. The right part is the actual timeline of the... timeline. You can see the time markers which are frame numbers (not seconds). The left empty part of the window will contain all the objects controlled by the timeline. As we scroll around in the right timeline portion of the frame, the left objects portion will remain visible so you can see what the objects are doing in the timeline. The white marker and line indicate the frame's current editing or playback is at. You can click on the marker at the frame numbers and move it around. Just leave it at zero for now.

Looking at the inspector, you can see the "Playable Director" component that was attached to the "IntroCinematic" object. It should look like Figure 206. The Playable field points to the "IntroCinematicTimeline" we created earlier. This is what you looked at in Figure 205. You can click it to have the Project View show its location. We'll leave the Update Method as "Game Time". See below for what the other options mean.

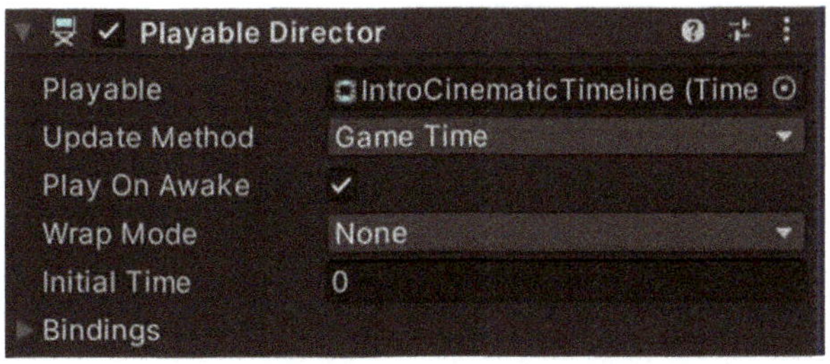

Figure 206

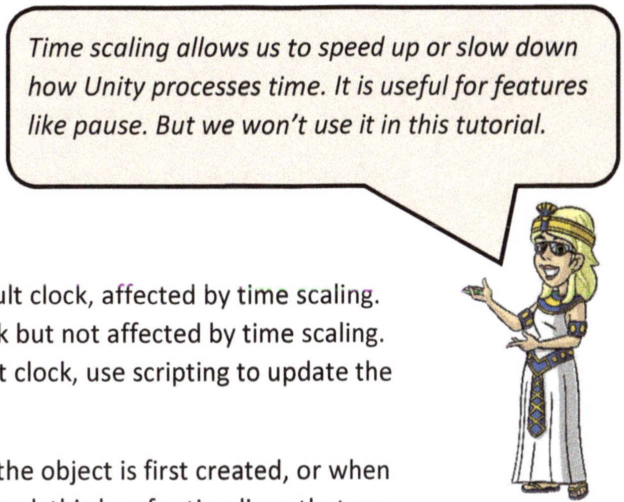

Update Method Options:

- DSP Clock: synchronized to the same clock that audio components are synchronized to. This is useful to make sure those play exactly together if that's important.
- Game Time: Default option using the default clock, affected by time scaling.
- Unscaled Game Time: Use the default clock but not affected by time scaling.
- Manual: [Advanced] Do not use the default clock, use scripting to update the clock time.

The "Play On Awake" check box means that when the object is first created, or when the scene is loaded, it will play automatically. Uncheck this box for timelines that you want to wait until some later time to play. Wrap Mode tells Unity what to do after the timeline completes.

Wrap Mode Options:

- Hold: After the timeline completes playing once, hold the last frame.
- Loop: After the timeline completes playing, play back from the beginning.
- None: After the timeline completes playing, put objects back the way they were.

The "Initial Time" tells Unity how long, in seconds, to start playback. If you want to skip forward, for any reason, you can use this. The Bindings are an advanced feature that allows you to customize the director. We won't be covering that in this tutorial.

Cinemachine for a Smart Camera

A great add-on to Unity's Timeline is Cinemachine. It will allow us to move around cameras very easily. It does not, however, come built-in with Unity. We need to download it as a separate package. Note that you will need a connection to the internet and be logged into your Unity account to successfully download the package.

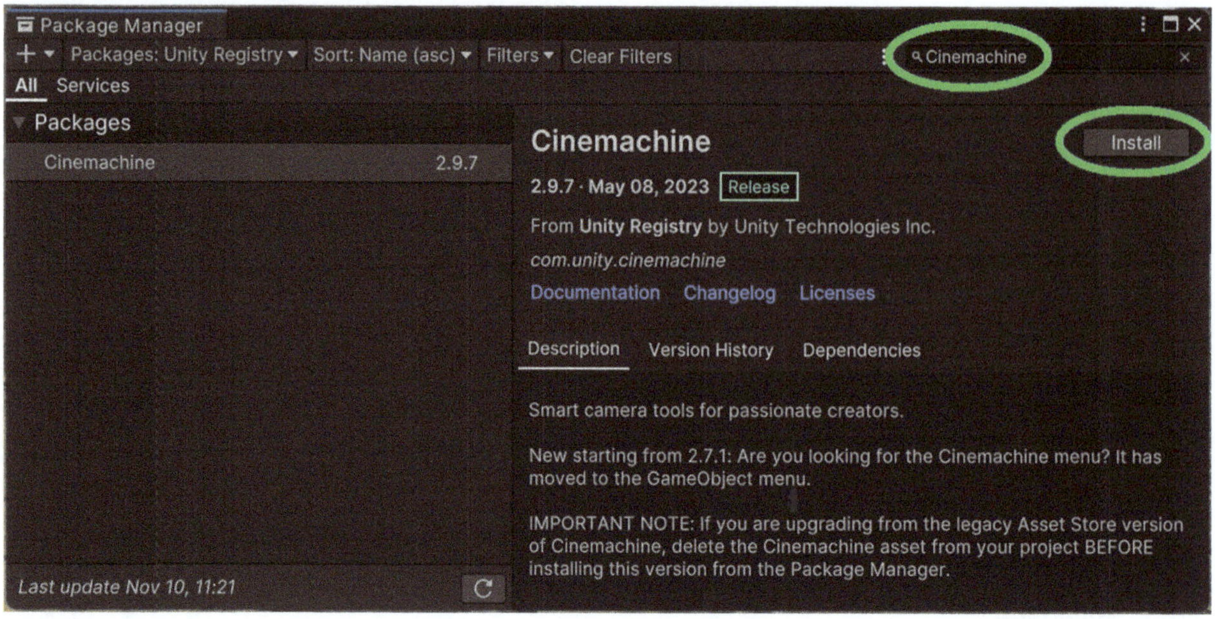

Figure 207

In the Main Menu, select Window > Package Manager. When it pops up, in the upper right corner type "Cinemachine" in the search bar. You can see it come up as shown in Figure 207. The version may look a little different than shown above, but that should be ok. Click the install button. After a short wait, you'll see a window to compile scripts and otherwise load the package. When it disappears, it is done. You may close the Package Manager window. We'll learn how to use it a little later.

Fade in and Start

A nice touch with cinematics is fading in and out from black (sometimes white, but that's only for special circumstances). To do that in our game, we first need a black screen to fade. We're going to create that black screen and then use our timeline to do the fading.

Right-click on the Canvas object in the Hierarchy View and select UI > Image. Name it "BlackScreen". We haven't looked at UI images yet, so with the "BlackScreen" object highlighted, press the 'F' key to focus on it. You will see that it appears as a white square in the center of the screen canvas on top of the other UI objects we created in previous chapters.

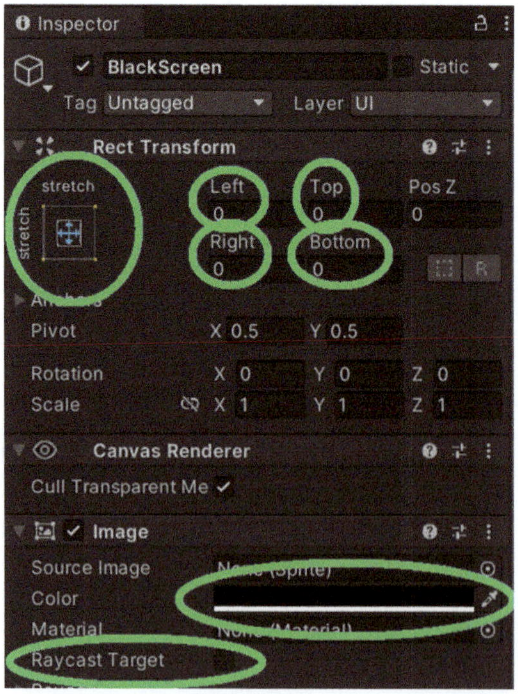

Figure 208

In the inspector, we need to make some modifications. First, we make it cover the whole screen. Set the Anchor Preset to stretch on both the horizontal and vertical axis. This option is on the bottom right of the Anchor Presets pop-up. Then set all the Left, Top, Right, and Bottom attributes to zero. When in the stretch anchor preset, the values for these attributes tell Unity how far from the edge to put the image.

Then we need to make the screen black. We can easily do this by adjusting the color. Click on the white color rectangle to the right of the Color field and a popup window will appear. You can set it to black by dragging the little circle down to the bottom left of the color palate or setting the Hexadecimal value to all zeros. Make sure "Raycast Target" is unchecked so the black screen doesn't block our other UI objects.

When you're done, the inspector Rect Transform and Image components should look like Figure 208. In the Scene View, you should also see the entire canvas covered and the other UI objects not visible. This is what we want because the black screen needs to show over everything else, otherwise the fading won't work right.

Let's add it into the timeline now. Click the "IntroCinematic" object in the Hierarchy View and click the Timeline View in the center panel. To create a new entry for our black screen, press the "+" sign in the upper left and select "Animation Track" as shown in Figure 209. The animation tracks either changes attributes like position, rotation, and color as well as playing animations for 3D models.

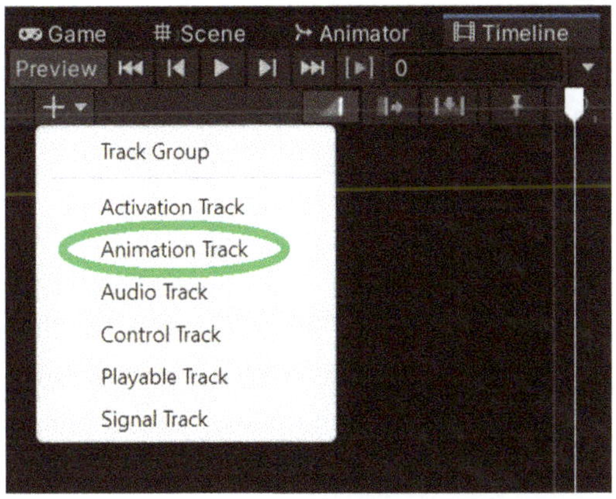

Figure 209

For the black screen, we're going to change the alpha value of the color. Alpha is the transparency of the image. When you changed the color of the screen to black, you may have noticed the color level shown in Figure 210. In addition to 'R' for red, 'G' for green, and 'B' for blue, there is an 'A'. That 'A' means the alpha channel of the color for transparency. When it is 255 or full, then the color is opaque, when it is zero or empty then it is transparent and can't be seen. Anything in between is semi-transparent.

Figure 210

To set the "BlackScreen" to animate, drag it from the Hierarchy View onto the Timeline View where it says "None (Animator)". A little popup will ask you to "Create Animator on BlackScreen" as shown in Figure 211. An animator component is needed for the timeline to perform the animation. Go ahead and click it.

Figure 211

To create the animation, there is a little red record button next to the object name that you can see in Figure 212. Press it to start recording the animation. When you do, the right side of the Timeline View will have a red line appear that says "Recording…" and the recording button will blink.

Figure 212

Now click on the "BlackScreen" in the Hierarchy View. Click the Color field in the Image component to see the popup. Change the A or Alpha value slider just a little bit and then move it back so the value is 255 again. It's a little hard to see, but a small gray diamond appears on the timeline where the white marker line is. It should look like Figure 213. This is called a Key Frame. In animation, key frames tell Unity what value certain attributes need to be at specific frames. When the animation is played, Unity will automatically change the attribute values to smoothly go between the value at the old key frame and the new one. It may seem a little confusing now, but once we get it working you should be able to see what I'm talking about.

Figure 213

Next, move the white marker to frame 30. We're still recording. Then open the color palate again on the "BlackScreen". This time, set the alpha all the way to the left, or zero. This makes it completely transparent. You will also see another key frame created like in Figure 214. We're done recording the animation for the black screen object now. You can click the record button again to stop recording. The right side of the Timeline View will go back to gray, and the recording button will stop blinking. But you should still see the two key frames we created. Press CTRL+S to save the timeline.

Figure 214

Let's take a look at how it worked. Click the play button to test. It may take you a few times of entering and leaving play mode to really notice the fade. But if you watch the color of the "BlackScreen" object in the inspector, you will see the white bar underneath the black color disappear from right to left. That means it's working. Congratulations! You have now created your first timeline cinematic.

I'm sure glad we've got that GDD. Since we already sat down and thought about what is in our game, we just refer to it to figure out what to do.

Moses on the Hill

Now that we have the basic building blocks in place for making our introduction cinematic, let's add a camera and actor. In the main menu, create a new camera as you did for the maps in Chapter 5. Name it "CineCam" and set the Depth to '2'. That will make sure it displays on top of the other cameras.

In the timeline, add a Cinemachine Track and drag the "CineCam" where it says "None", creating a "CinemachineBrain" on the camera. The Cinemachine Brain script controls the position and rotation of the camera, so you get the shot you want. To help with that, it uses something called Virtual Cameras. These Virtual Cameras aren't real cameras, but the Cinemachine Track in the Timeline uses them to set the location of the camera controlled by the brain. Clear as mud? Good! It'll get clearer as we go along.

Let's create our first virtual camera. In the Hierarchy View, when you right-click, underneath "Camera" there is a new entry for "Cinemachine". Select Cinemachine > Virtual Camera and name it "IntroCam1". Set the transform to what you see in Figure 215. When you press 'F' to focus on the camera you will see it is at the top of a hill over some water.

Figure 215

Duplicate this virtual camera by selecting it in the Hierarchy View and pressing CTRL+D. You'll see a new one appears underneath it named "IntroCam1 (1)". Rename to "IntroCam2". Then set the Y position to '50.4' which is just a little higher.

Switch from Timeline View to Scene View. Grab the "Model_Civilian" from Assets > Models > Extreme Adventure characters pack > Characters > Characters and place it on the edge of the cliff, facing toward the city like in Figure 216. Looking through the camera, try to position the "Model_Civilian" to be in the left one-third of the frame. Now when you press the play button, you should see the intro cinematic fade in with Moses' feet with a pyramid in the background.

Figure 216

Switching back to Timeline View, and making sure the "IntroCinematic" is selected, drag the "IntroCam1" object onto the line for the "CineCam" at marker zero. You should see a box appear with the name of the camera. Now drag "IntroCam2" to about frame 15 so it overlaps the other box. It should look like Figure 217.

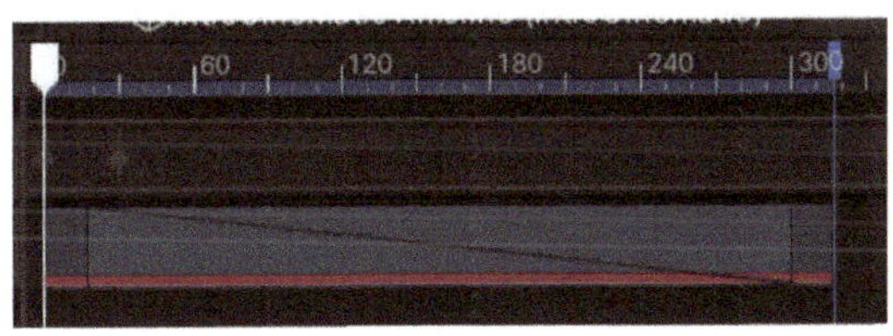

Figure 217

What you're looking at here is Cinemachine blending the two virtual cameras. This means that as the timeline plays, Unity will move the camera between "IntroCam1" and "IntroCam2". Notice the dark gray blocks at the beginning and end. These are the parts where the camera does not move. The blending happens in the middle where you can see there is a diagonal line going from the top left to the bottom right.

If you move your cursor to the border where the blending stops (light gray to dark gray), your cursor will change to a 2-sided arrow. That means you can drag these boxes around to change how the blending happens. Change the box for "IntroCam1" to end at frame 180. Then change "IntroCam2" to end at frame 180 also. It should now look like Figure 218.

Figure 218

Let's test it out. Click the record button again to stop recording and press the play button. You should see the camera pan up from Moses' feet to his knees.

Intro Cinematic Code

One problem you've probably noticed by now is that after the cinematic is done, you're not able to see yourself moving Moses around like before. This is because the camera we created for the cinematics and cut scenes is still showing on top of the third person controller's camera. To fix that, and better optimize our scene, we will make an update to the Game Controller script.

Open the "GameController" script up in Visual Studio and add line 5 shown in Figure 219. This lets us directly reference the director component in the next change.

```
4   using UnityStandardAssets.Characters.ThirdPerson;
5   using UnityEngine.Playables;
```

Figure 219

Add the public and private variables shown in Figure 220. Line 17 is for the introduction cinematic which we'll glue together later. Line 18 is a reference to the cinematic camera which we'll disable when the cinematic is done playing.

The private variable on line 27 helps us keep track of if the cinematic has already played.

```
16      public GameObject Player;
17      public PlayableDirector IntroCine;
18      public GameObject CineCam;
19
        10 references
20      private enum _ui_state
21      {
22          None,
23          WorldMap
24      }
25      private _ui_state uiState;
26      private List<GameObject> ZoneWorldMapTextObjList;
27      private bool IntroCinePlayed;
```

Figure 220

In the Start method, add the lines of code starting on line 46 from Figure 221. We indicate the intro cinematic hasn't played yet and disable the minimap and player. We also make sure the "CineCam" is enabled. We then tell the introduction cinematic to play by calling that method. This is how to play the timeline in code.

```
44          WorldMapSetActive(false);
45
46          IntroCinePlayed = false;
47          CineCam.SetActive(true);
48          MinimapObj.SetActive(false);
49          Player.SetActive(false);
50          IntroCine.Play();
51      }
```

Figure 221

Go next to the Update method and the new lines from 56 to 64 that you see in Figure 222. Once the intro cinematic is done playing, we'll disable the cinematic camera and enable the player as well as the minimap.

```
54      void Update()
55      {
56          if (!IntroCinePlayed)
57          {
58              if (IntroCine.state != PlayState.Playing)
59              {
60                  CineCam.SetActive(false);
61                  Player.SetActive(true);
62                  MinimapObj.SetActive(true);
63              }
64          }
```

Figure 222

Going back to Unity, select the "IntroCinematic" and uncheck the "Play On Awake" box. We don't need this anymore since we're playing it from the game controller script.

Speaking about the game controller, select that object in the Hierarchy View and drag the "IntroCinematic" into the Intro Cine field and then the "CineCam" into the Cine Cam field so it looks like Figure 223. This will glue the introduction timeline and cinematic cameras to the script. Now, when you press the play button, you should be able to see yourself move Moses around after the cinematic is done.

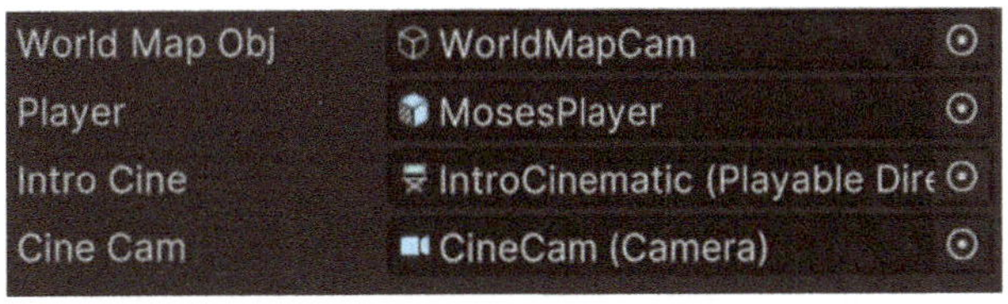

Figure 223

Moses' Details

One detail about Moses that is clear is that he had a staff. We would be remiss if we didn't include one in his wardrobe. Expand the following in the "Model_Civilian" child object Reference > Hips > Spine > Spine1 > Spine2 > RightShoulder > RightArm > RightForeArm > RightHand. This "RightHand" object is the point at which animations for the model's right hand occur. We can put another 3D object here and it will look like Moses is holding it.

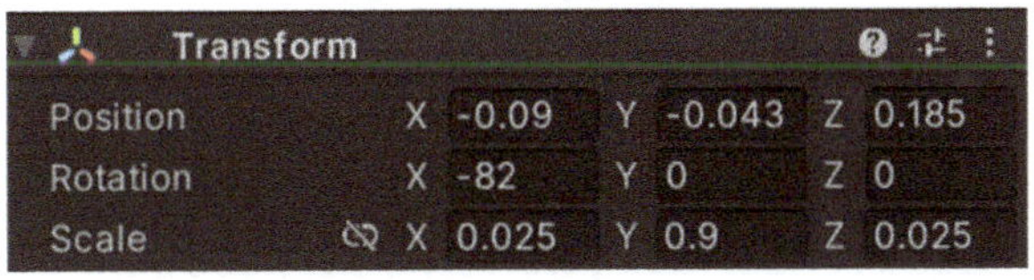

Figure 224

Right-click on the "RightHand" and select Create > 3D Object > Cylinder. This will be the staff we'll use for Moses so name the object to "Staff". Then remove the staff's capsule collider component. Set the transform to have Position, Rotation, and Scale as shown in Figure 224. It should look like a staff now and that Moses is actually holding it.

The last thing we need to do is make it look like real wood. In the Project View, go to Assets > Models > Rustic_Pack > Materials and drag the "Wood" texture onto the Staff object in the Scene View. Now it has a much more "woody" and "natural" look to it as shown in Figure 225.

Figure 225

This is all well and good, but the weird T-pose will not do for a cinematic. We're going to set him up with an animation so he looks a bit less stiff. In the Project View, go to Assets > Animations and create an "Animator Controller" from the right-click menu. Name it "AmbientAnimCtlr". Click that in the Hierarchy View and then open the Animator View in the center pane.

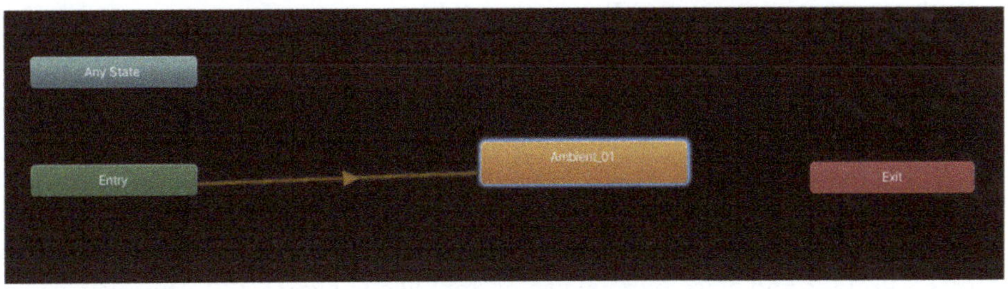

Figure 226

It will be empty except for 3 boxes (you may need to pan around a little to see them). There is a cyan "Any State" box, a green

"Entry" box, and a red "Exit" box. We're going to add an animation that Moses will play. You can find it in Assets > Models > EgyptCharacters > Source > Anims. Drag "Ambient_01" between the Entry and Exit boxes. You will see a new orange box appear with a line going from Entry to it like in Figure 226. This means that when the animator starts up at the beginning of the scene, Moses will play the "Ambient_01" animation. Finally, drag the "AmbientAnimCtlr" on the Controller field of the Animator component on the "MosesStaff" object. With Moses given his nice wooden staff, rename him to "MosesStaff" and save a prefab of him. This way we can reuse it for later.

Making a Big Scene

Looking at the introduction cinematic section in the GDD, we've got 4 scenes:

- Moses on the hill overlooking the city.
- Moses after he killed the Egyptian.
- Moses running away from the city.
- Moses at the burning bush.

Figure 227

We already created the first scene of Moses overlooking the city on the hill. Let's work on the second one. We're going to create the Egyptian that Moses kills next (don't worry, no 3D models will be harmed in the making of this scene, he's just playing dead). Add "Sem" from Assets > Models > EgyptCharacters > Prefabs to the scene. Set the transform to what you see in Figure *227*. Pressing 'F' to focus on him you see this leaves poor old Sem face down in the dirt.

Create another Animator Controller in the Assets > Animations folder named "PlayDeadAnimCtlr". From the Project View, go to Assets > Models > EgyptCharacters > Source > Anims and drag the "Idle" animation onto the Animator View. Then click on the orange Idle box and its attributes will be shown in the inspector. Since most dead people don't move, we're going to set the speed of the animation to zero like you see in Figure 228.

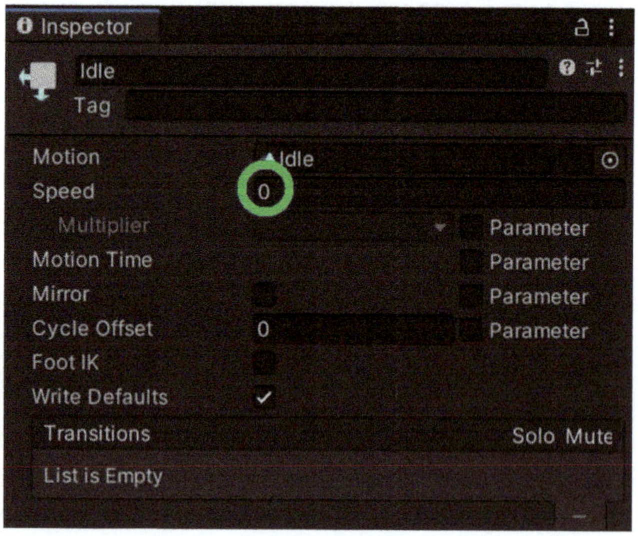

Figure 228

The speed of the animation can change to make the animation play faster or slower. A value of '1' means normal speed. Anything higher will make it play that times faster. Slower than '1' and up to zero will make it go that times slower. A value of '0' will make it only show the first frame of the animation. In our case, it's good to show the dead Egyptian but can also be used to place characters in a pose like a statue. Drag the "PlayDeadAnimCtlr" on the Controller field for Sem.

Now we'll have Moses standing over the Egyptian. Drag a new instance of the "MosesStaff" prefab from Assets > Prefabs and place him next to ol' Sem like in Figure 230. This way we can imply that Moses is

Figure 230

guilty of something bad here without showing any violence. The new Moses will be automatically named “MosesStaff (1)”.

Figure 229

Now let’s move that camera over here to expose this dirty deed. Select the “IntroCinematic” and make sure you can see the Timeline View in the bottom pane. We’re going to do a neat trick. If you press a specific key combination, you will make a selected object move to exactly the orientation of the Scene View. This will make creating the camera shots in our cinematic much easier. First, move the Scene View camera so that you’re looking similar to Figure 229. Notice that I tried to follow the rule of thirds here. I’m also having the camera look up at Moses so that he seems more intimidating and up to no good.

In the Hierarchy View, duplicate the “IntroCam2” again and rename to “IntroCam3". Select the “IntroCam3” in the Hierarchy View and hold CTL+ALT while pressing ‘F’. You remember pressing ‘F’ to focus on an object. This is sort of the opposite where instead of us going to the object, the object comes to us.

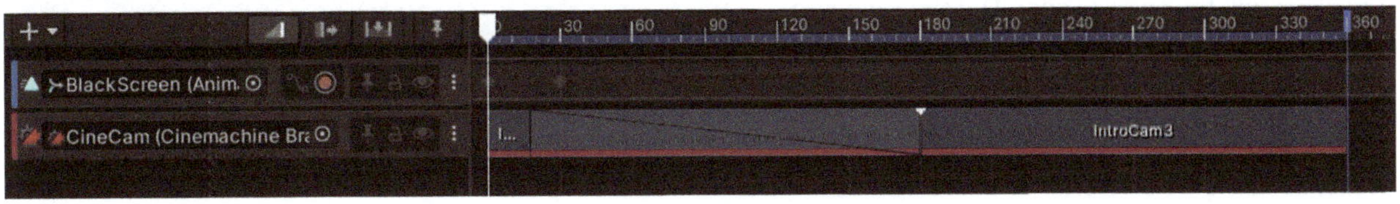

Figure 231

Going back to the Timeline, drag the “IntroCam3” object onto the timeline and arrange like you see in Figure 231. Make sure the box snaps right next to the box to the left of it so there is no gap. The right boundary of the box will be at frame 360.

This Moses also needs an animation, let’s give him a second ambient one. In the Project View, go to Assets > Animations and create another animation controller named “Ambient2AnimCtlr”. From Assets > Models > EgyptCharacters > Source > Anims, drag “Ambient_02” onto the Animator View for this new animation controller.

The next part of the cinematic pans from Moses’ knees to his waist. So, let’s go back to Moses on the hill. In the Hierarchy View, click “MosesStaff” and press ‘F’. Highlight the “IntroCam1” object and press CTRL+D, renaming it to “IntroCam4”. Change its Y position to ‘50.6’. Duplicate “IntroCam4” and name it “IntroCam5”. Set the Y position to ’50.8’.

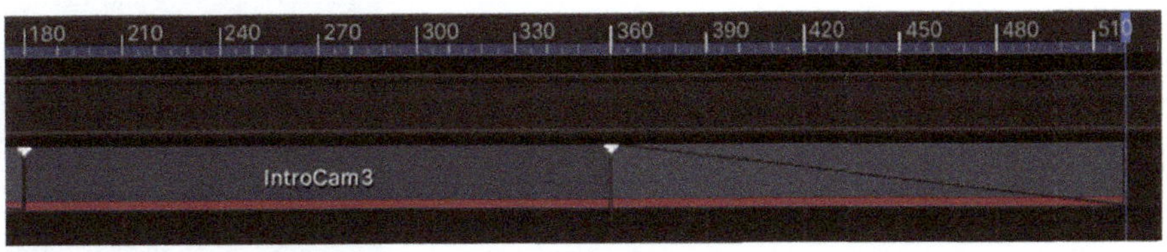

Figure 232

With those created, drag the “IntroCam4” object to snap next to the object “IntroCam3”. Set the end to frame 120. Then drag the object "IntroCam5" onto the timeline and blend them together in a similar way as we did the first 2 virtual cameras. This time, we can have the blending start right away. The timeline should look like Figure 232. Feel free to take a quick break and play the game to make sure everything works.

The next scene is where Moses flees Egypt. So, drag another "MosesStaff" prefab out and set the Transform to Figure 233. Pressing 'F' to focus on the new "MosesStaff (2)", you'll see that he's underneath the palace gate. He's going to have an animation to run out of there.

Figure 233

Create a new Animator Controller in Assets > Animations named "RunAnimCtlr". In the Project View, search for "HumanoidRun" and drag the first result that comes up into the Animator so you see the orange "HumanoidRun" box. Then drag the "RunAnimCtlr" into the "MosesStaff (2)" Animator's Controller field. Moses will be running by default. So, we need to only enable this Moses when it's just the right time. But first we'll add the virtual camera for this scene.

Duplicate the virtual camera "IntroCam6" and set the Transform to what you see in Figure 234. This will be one of those Dutch angle shots to let the viewer know there is tension going on here. Drag the virtual camera "IntroCam6" onto the timeline, snapping to the blend of the previous cameras and ending at frame 660.

Figure 234

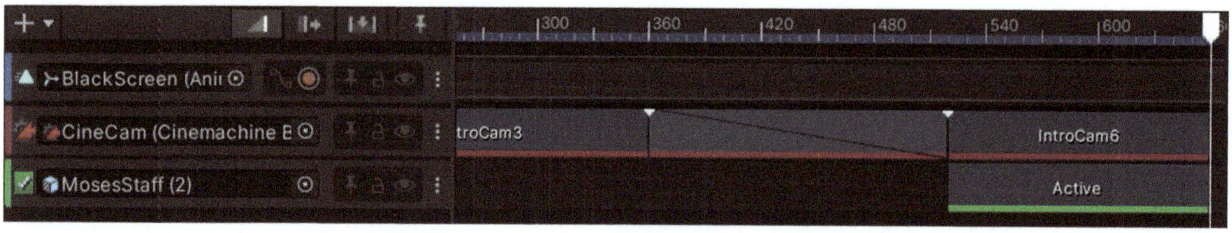

Figure 235

Remember, we need to enable Moses at just the right time. Click the '+' sign on the Timeline and create a new Activation Track. This track tells the timeline when an object I active for. Drag the object "MosesStaff (2)" onto where it says "None". Then change the bounds of the "Active" box to match "IntroCam6" like you see in Figure 235. This will enable Moses when the camera is set, and then disable Moses when we're ready to move to the next scene.

We'll continue moving up Moses' profile next. Duplicate "IntroCam5" and name to "IntroCam7" with the Y position set to '51'. Duplicate that virtual camera and name to "IntroCam8", setting

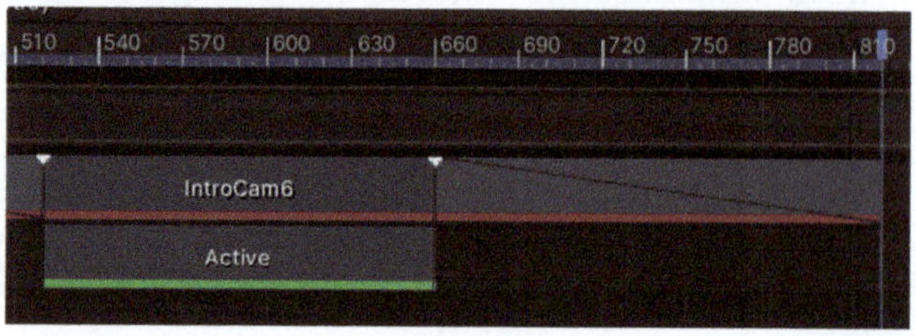

Figure 236

the Y position to '51.2'. Add them to blend like the previous ones, ending at 820. It should look like Figure 236.

If you play the introduction cinematic now, it will show the story of how Moses came to leave the city interspersed with him now confronting the city that he fled from. Figure 237 shows that disorienting Dutch Angle.

Figure 237

A Burning Bush... Sort of

For the next scene, we need a burning bush. To play the part of a bush, we're going to use a tree, but shorter and have a flame going on in it. In the Project View, go to Assets > Standard Assets > Environment > SpeedTree > Palm and drag the "Palm_Desktop" onto the Scene View. Set the transform to Figure 238 and press 'F' to focus on it. Grab another "MosesStaff" prefab and place him nearby the bush. Rotate him so that he's looking at the bush.

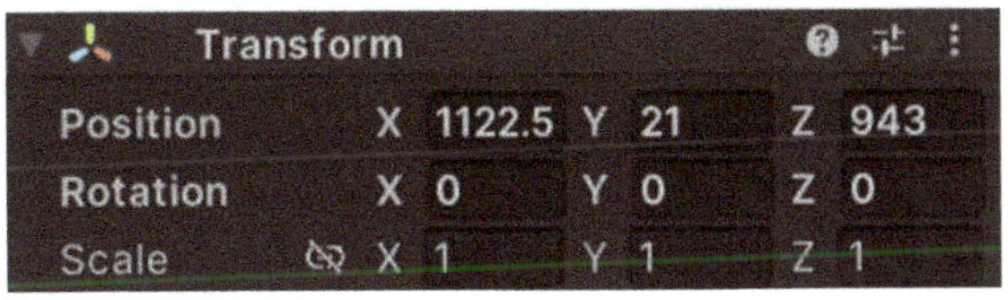

Figure 238

Duplicate another virtual camera and name it "IntroCam9". Using the rule of thirds, place your Scene View to look something like Figure 239. Then drag "IntroCam9" onto the timeline and have it end at frame 960.

We've got Moses and our "bush", now we need to get the burning part. In the Project View, go to Assets > Models > Ancient Egypt > Models > House_Prefabs and find the FireBowl. In addition to having a nice stone bowl, it also has fire, which is what we need.

Figure 239

Drag the FireBowl prefab so that it is occupying the same space as the tree. It should look really weird, like the tree is growing out of the stone. But don't worry, we're going to fix that. Expand the Firebowl object in the Hierarchy View and you'll see two child objects: FireComplex and another FireBowl. Click that second Firebowl and disable it by unchecking the box next to the name in the inspector as shown in Figure 240. You can use this way to enable or disable objects in the scene in addition to the scripts.

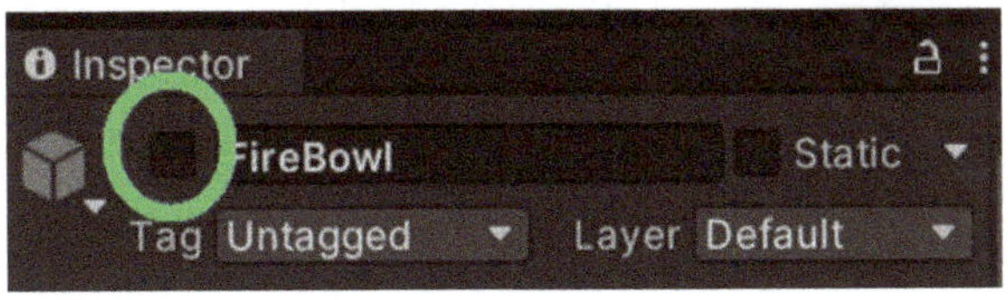

Figure 240

You will also need to remove the two scripts on the FireComplex: Particle System Destroyer and Particle System Multiplier. Remember, you use the 3 vertical dots at the right side of the script component and select "Remove Component". Since this is a prefab, Unity still shows that these components were removed by graying them out. This way, if you change your mind, you can easily add them back.

To finish our climb of Moses' profile, duplicate "IntroCam8" and name to "IntroCam10", setting the Y position to '51.5'. Duplicate it again and set the Y position to '51.7'. Duplicate it one more time but this time set the Transform to what you see in Figure 241. This virtual camera will show Moses in front of the Egyptian city.

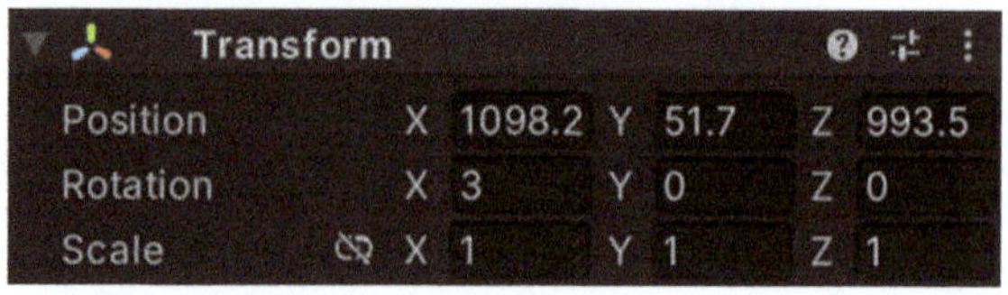

Figure 241

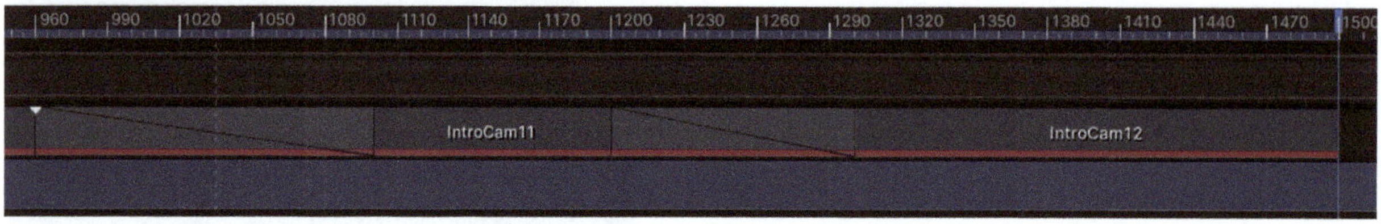

Figure 242

Drag "IntroCam10" onto the timeline, snapping to the previous camera and ending at frame 1100. Now drag "IntroCam11" onto the timeline, blending it from the start, but this time let it end at frame 1300. Finally, drag "IntroCam12" onto the timeline so it starts around 1200 and ends 1500. You may need to expand the box a few times to reach the 1500 mark. The entire sequence should look like Figure 242.

You can use the middle mouse button to pan around the timeline. If there are a lot of tracks then, in addition to panning sideways, you can also pan up and down too! Scrolling the mouse wheel will zoom in and out so you can see transitions easier.

Fade out and End

That is the main part of our introduction cinematic. To let the player know that it is done, we'll fade out to black. In the Timeline View, set the white marker to frame 1350. On the line for the "BlackScreen", click the record button. We'll be changing the alpha back to opaque on the black screen. But first we need a key frame to be added here so that the black screen doesn't change to opaque all throughout the cinematic. So select the object "BlackScreen" and open the Color popup. Change the alpha value a little and then put it back to create the key frame.

In the Timeline View, set the white marker to frame 1450. Then go back to the black screen and set the alpha value to 255 which makes it opaque. We're done with that so you can click the record button to end recording. You'll see that we leave a little time left for IntroCam12 after the fadeout. This gives the player a little time to grasp what's going on before we thrust them into the game.

The final bit of code for the chapter will make sure the black screen is disabled when the cinematic is done. Go back to the Game Controller script in Visual Studio. Start by adding the public variable on line 19 of Figure 243 as a reference to the black screen.

```
18        public GameObject CineCam;
19        public GameObject BlackScreen;
```

Figure 243

Then add the private variable on line 29 in Figure 244 which tells the script if it is supposed to fade out the black screen.

```
28        private bool IntroCinePlayed;
29        private bool FadingOut;
```

Figure 244

In the Start method, initialize the "FadingOut" Boolean on line 49 to false as shown in Figure 245.

```
48            IntroCinePlayed = false;
49            FadingOut = false;
```

Figure 245

The last bit of code is in the Update method to perform the fade out which you can type from Figure 246. If the black screen is supposed to fade out then we perform it by adjusting the alpha on line 73. Then, once the alpha is all zero, we indicate that the fade out is complete.

```
68          }
69
70          if (FadingOut)
71          {
72              Color tCol = BlackScreen.GetComponent<UnityEngine.UI.Image>().color;
73              tCol.a -= Time.deltaTime;
74              BlackScreen.GetComponent<UnityEngine.UI.Image>().color = tCol;
75
76              if (tCol.a <= 0) FadingOut = false;
77          }
78
79          if (Input.GetKeyUp(KeyCode.Escape))
```

Figure 246

All that's left is to hook up the black screen to the script. Go back into Unity and select the Game Controller object. Then drag the "BlackScreen" object into the Black Screen field in the inspector.

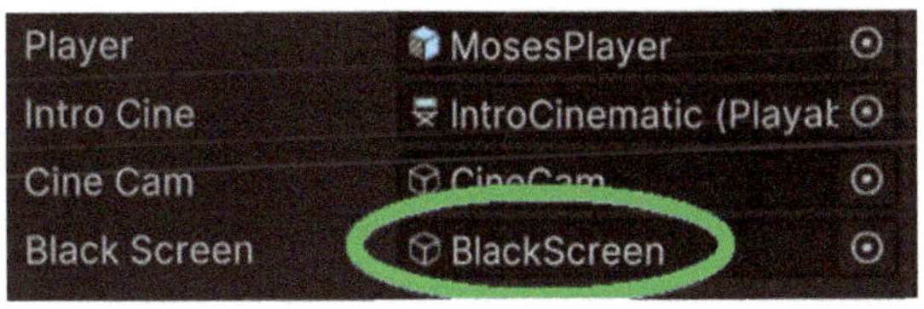

Figure 247

Give the game one more test by pressing the play button. You should see the cut scene fade in from black, play all the scenes showing Moses' flight from Egypt and then his return. It then fades out to black for a small time before fading in where you can now control Moses again.

Music Track

Adding music to the timeline is pretty easy. In the timeline for the introduction cinematic. You can either click the '+' sign or right-click under the other lines and select "Audio Track". Now it is added to the bottom of the timeline.

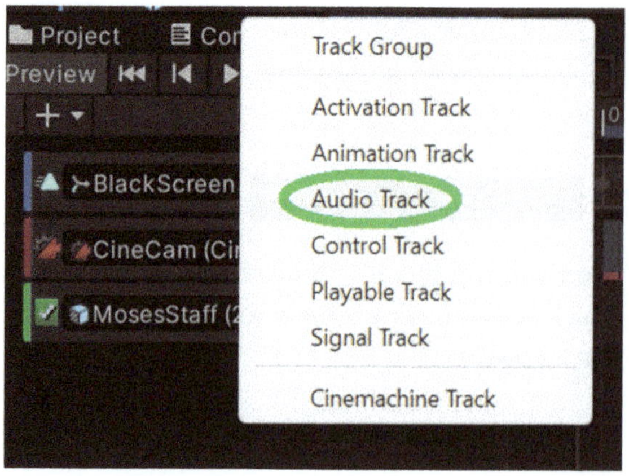

Figure 248

We do need an Audio Source to play the music. To be simple, if you drag the object "IntroCinematic" from the Hierarchy View onto the line, you can have Unity create an audio source on that object for you. There are other audio sources we could have used for this, but having a dedicated audio source is a good practice to make sure you don't cause issues with other objects or things may not work right anymore.

Right-click on the audio track line, where the frame markers are, and select "Add from Audio Clip". It opens a window that lets us choose what to add. In the search bar type "Combat_detected" and double-click it. The audio box will appear starting where you clicked. Drag the box so it starts at the beginning. Then move the white marker to the end of "IntroCam12" which is frame 1500.

To see the full music length, you'll to scroll out on the mouse wheel. Once you see the end, drag it, resizing the box, to also end at frame 1500. Since you put the white marker there, it will snap to it. A little triangle appears at the end of the audio which indicates the original audio file doesn't end there. The new timeline should look like Figure 249.

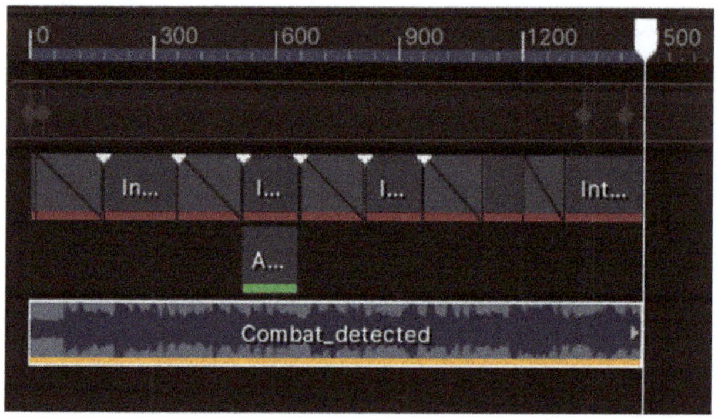

Figure 249

Now when you play the cinematic, you can hear the music play throughout. Then, when the cinematic is done, the music stops. We'll add music to the game play section at chapter 12.

Cleaning up

Having an introduction cinematic is a great way to get the player engaged in the game. However, now we have all these actors and objects laying around. It would be very weird for Moses to meet himself in the game. So, we need to disable them when the cinematic is done. The way we're going to do that put

Not showing objects when you're not using them doesn't only prevent the player from seeing copies of themselves, it also improves performance in the game because the computer is not showing and keeping track of those objects. It is a good practice for larger games to keep the player from experiencing lag.

them all under a parent object, enable the parent object when the cinematic is playing, and disable the parent object after the cinematic completes. To do this, we're going to make some more modifications to the Game Controller script. Don't worry, it's not that much more coding.

First, create an empty game object named "IntroCineObjects". This will be our parent object. Then move all the objects we created so far for the introduction cinematic as child objects underneath it. You can drag each one individually, or click the top object, hold SHIFT, and then click the bottom object to highlight all of them and then drag them over as a group. I like doing that because it saves me time. The arrangement in the Hierarchy View should look like Figure 250.

Figure 250

Go back to the Game Controller script in Visual Studio again. Add a public variable to hold a reference to the introduction objects named "IntroObjects" on line 20 in Figure 251.

```
19    public GameObject BlackScreen;
20    public GameObject IntroObjects;
```

Figure 251

In the Start method, enable the introduction objects as shown on line 54 of Figure 252.

```
54        IntroObjects.SetActive(true);
55        IntroCine.Play();
```

Figure 252

In the Update method, where we disable the cinematic camera, add the code to disable the introduction objects on line 67 of Figure 253.

```
66                IntroObjects.SetActive(false);
67                CineCam.SetActive(false);
```

Figure 253

Going back into Unity, let's glue things together. Drag the "IntroCineObjects" parent object into the Intro Objects field as shown in Figure 254.

Figure 254

Entering play mode, we can test out this change. After you finish watching the cinematic, you should see the "IntroCineObjects" parent object and all child objects underneath it become grayed out. This means they are disabled and now being shown in the scene. They should look like Figure 255.

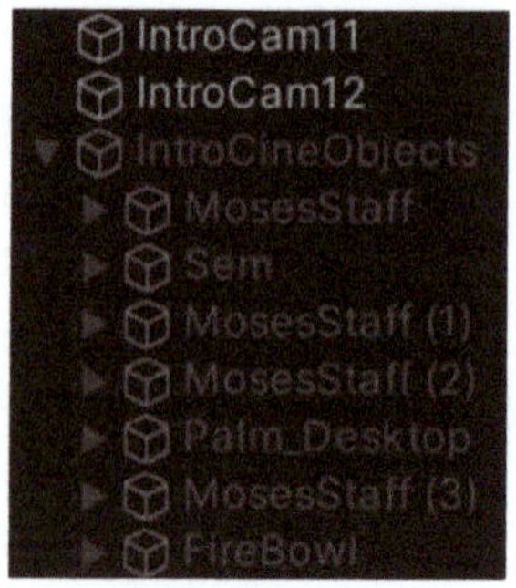

Figure 255

Set Details

The last thing to round out this chapter is to add details to the sets for each of the scenes. Recall from the cinematography guidelines at the beginning of the chapter that having the little details will help to better immerse the player into what's going on. Unlike previously, when I walked you through setting up the cinematic and writing the code, I'm going to give some general guidance and show you the models you can use to build up the scenes you've already created.

There are a number of very high-quality models that come included in the Exodus Adventure Tutorial. First, we'll look at the various models and then talk about how we can decorate our scenes with them.

Here is a reference of all the props you can use:

Description	**Location**
Cliff Rocks	Assets > Models > Ancient Egypt > Models > Prop Environment
Large Rocks	Assets > Models > Ancient Egypt > Models > Rock_Prefabs
Furniture	Assets > Models > Ancient Egypt > Models > House Parts > Additional Addons
Containers	Assets > Models > Ancient Egypt > Models > House Parts > Additional Addons
Boats	Assets > Models > Ancient Egypt > Models > House Parts > Additional Addons
Oil Lamp	Assets > Models > Ancient Egypt > Models > House Parts > Additional Addons
More Furniture	Assets > Models > Rustic_Pack
FireBowl	Assets > Models > Ancient Egypt > Models > House_Prefabs
Cups and Dishes	Assets > Models > Ancient Egypt > Models > House Parts > Additional Addons
Market Table	Assets > Models > Ancient Egypt > Models > House Parts > Additional Addons
Statues	Assets > Models > Ancient Egypt > Models > Statues
Tents and Covers	Assets > Models > Ancient Egypt > Models > Tents
Palm Tree	Assets > Standard Assets > Environment > SpeedTree > Palm

This is a good mix of indoor and outdoor props that you can use. If you just put random items randomly in the scene, they may look out of place. Then again, having some randomness helps the scene to look more natural.

You also want to consider if these objects in the scene should remain in there or disabled when the cinematic is over. If you have a specific set out in the desert, you may want to clean that up. But if you're adding buildings or objects that already looks like it should be there then consider leaving it enabled after the cinematic.

In the first scene, I added a cliff and a couple rocks to provide something nice to look at while panning Moses' profile from Figure 256. Since this is an outdoor scene more in the desert, there won't be much else that would feel natural here. See what kind of rock placements look good to you.

Figure 256

In the scene where Moses stands over the dead Egyptian taskmaster, I added a couple more palm trees and rock to make it look like Moses is trying to hide what he did. See Figure 257 to get an idea.

Figure 257

For the rest of the scenes, see what you can do that adds interest to the scene while still making sense. Something put where it doesn't below will stand out and capture the player's attention. We don't want that with these details. They're meant to enhance the focus objects and characters.

Chapter 9 – Menu System and UI

All of the people and things walking and talking in the game is great. But to have a nice and polished game we need a good user interface (or UI) and menu system so the player can easily do the things they need in the game.

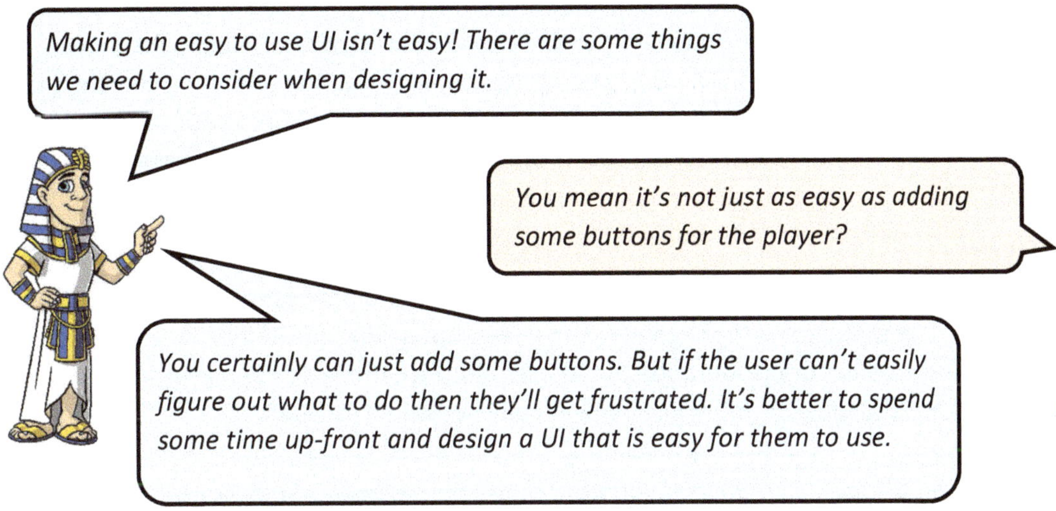

UI design Principles

Before we get started, I want to bring up these things to think about when you go design your user interfaces. These principles apply, not only to games, but to other UI you design for your other programs.

The components on the user interface should be clear. It should be obvious what buttons and boxes do. A lot of times we think things are obvious, and to us as the game developer it is. But for the player, it may not be obvious. Try and put your feet in the shoes of someone who has never played your game before. Forget what you know about your game and come at it, pretending to be a new player.

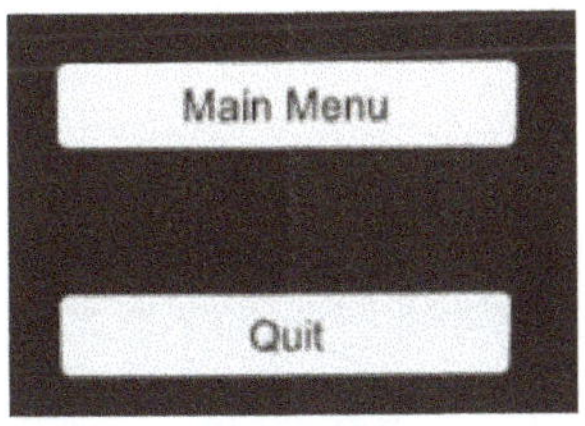

Figure 258

The UI should be designed with **clarity**. That means it is clear to the player what it does. Figure 258 shows 2 buttons. The bottom says "Quit" and the top says "Main Menu". Can you guess which one is clearer? "Quit" does indicate leaving the current mode of play we don't know what we're quitting. Are we quitting to go back to the main menu? Or does it quit the game entirely? Naming the button "Main Menu" tells the player that if they want to go back to the main menu then they should click there. Definitely clearer than "Quit".

If you're playing a game, it can be distracting when you have to look at things outside the game. A good example is trying to make money by showing advertisements at the bottom of the screen or popping them up every once in a while. These disrupt the player's attention on the game and gives them a negative experience. While making money is important for a full-time game developer, you can't sacrifice the player experience.

The UI should be designed to focus player **attention**. When the player is playing the game, the UI should feel almost invisible. This is why many games put the UI in the top, bottom, or corners of the game. Then, when the player needs to interact with the UI, it should focus their attention on what they most likely need to do. If they open the main menu, what are the most common reasons? Do they want to quit? Or edit options? Or something else? Usually, people start looking at UI from the top because that is how we read, top to bottom and left to right. Put the most commonly used features where they look first.

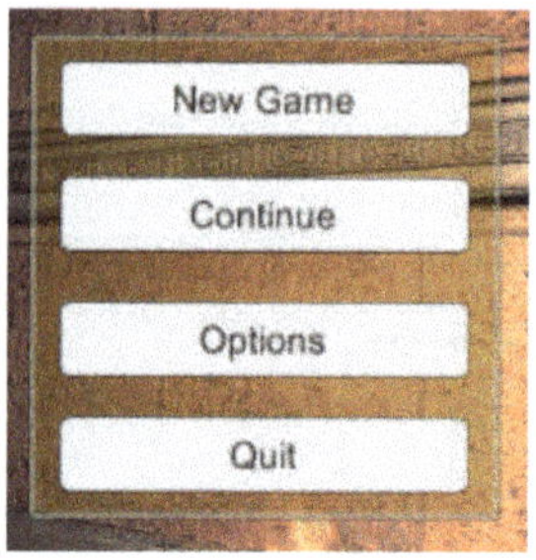

Figure 259

Figure 259 shows a title menu. When the player first sees this they are drawn to "New Game". Next is "Continue" and then "Options". Finally we get to "Quit". Players will mostly need "New Game" the first time they play the game. Every other time they will select "Continue" to play from where they left off unless they want to start over. One improvement could be to instantly launch the player into a new game when there is no saved game. Then the "Continue" button could be shown first, since that is more commonly used.

The UI should be designed with **behavior over appearance**. Having a user interface that looks good is important. But having a user interface that is easy to use is more so. If the graphics or presentation of the user interface distracts the player from what they're trying to do, then the player is more likely to get confused and frustrated.

There's nothing wrong with being creative. If you want to use butterflies for buttons give it a try! But be honest with yourself. Do the butterflies really add something useful? Or do they just distract?

The UI should be **consistent**. Nothing is more frustrating for the player than trying to do something in the UI and not being able to find the button, box, or widget they need to do it. Once you show the player a button to do something on a screen, keep it at the same location for all screens.

Also, use consistent names. Don't use "Exit" in one place and "Quit" in another place. It can confuse the player who may wonder if they do the same thing or something different. Designing for clarity can help resolve these kinds of problems as well.

Unity Scenes

With a basic understanding of how to design a user interface we're ready to get started on our menu system. The first thing we need is a title scene. This will be the first scene that is loaded when the player starts the game.

In the main menu, go to File > New Scene (or press CTRL+N). A new scene window will pop-up leave the defaults and click the button "Create" as shown in Figure 260.

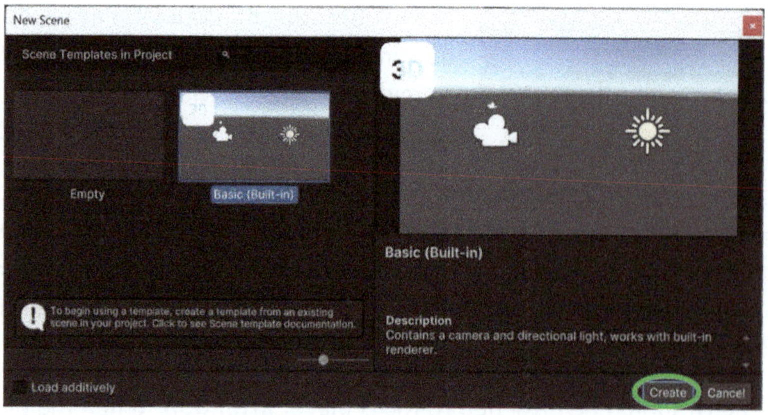

Figure 260

You'll be greeted, again, by an endless horizon. Save the new scene by either going to the main menu and selecting File > Save or pressing CTRL+S. This opens a window to save the scene that you can see in Figure 261. At the top bar, make sure it is set to Assets > Scenes so that it is saved in the right place. Then, at the bottom, set the File name to "Title". Then click Save.

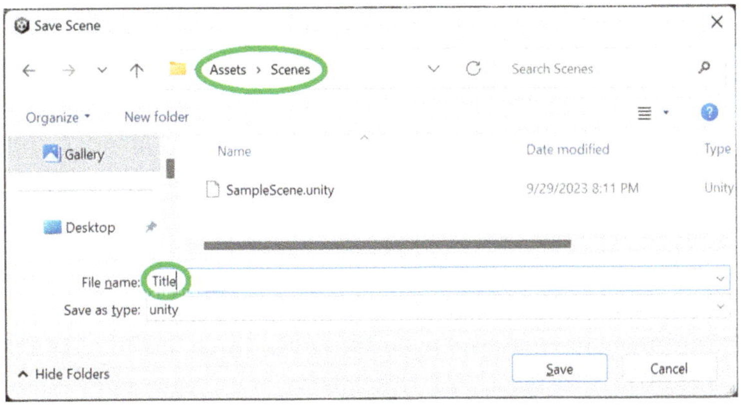

Figure 261

If you go into the Project View, then you'll see we have our very first scene there. We'll put all our game scenes into this folder. That includes the "Egypt_Nile Scene" we've been working on so far. We're going to move it so we can keep our scenes together. Go to Assets > Models and click Ancient Egypt. You should see the "Egypt_Nile Scene" file to the right. Then collapse the Models folder and drag the "Egypt_Nile Scene" file over onto the "Scenes" folder under Assets, like Figure 262. Note that there is also a scene "Egypt_Nile_Scene_Backup" which we're not using. In Chapter 11 we'll create a couple more scenes that we'll put here. But this is good for now.

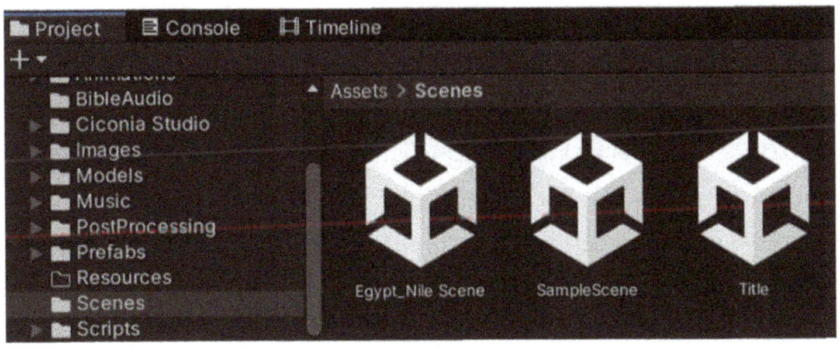

Figure 262

Next, we're going to add these scenes to the build settings in Unity. In the main menu, File > Build Settings. The Window that pops up contains all the scenes that get loaded into our game. The "Scenes in Build" section should be empty. If there are any scenes currently there then click each one and press the DELETE key to remove them.

To add our Title scene, click the "Add Open Scenes" button. You'll see that "Scenes\Title" is added at the top. Click the 'X' button on the top right to close the window. Next, go back to the Project View and double click the "Egypt_Nile Scene" to load it. After it is done loading, open the build settings again and click "Add Open Scenes". It should now look like Figure 263. Open the "Title" again.

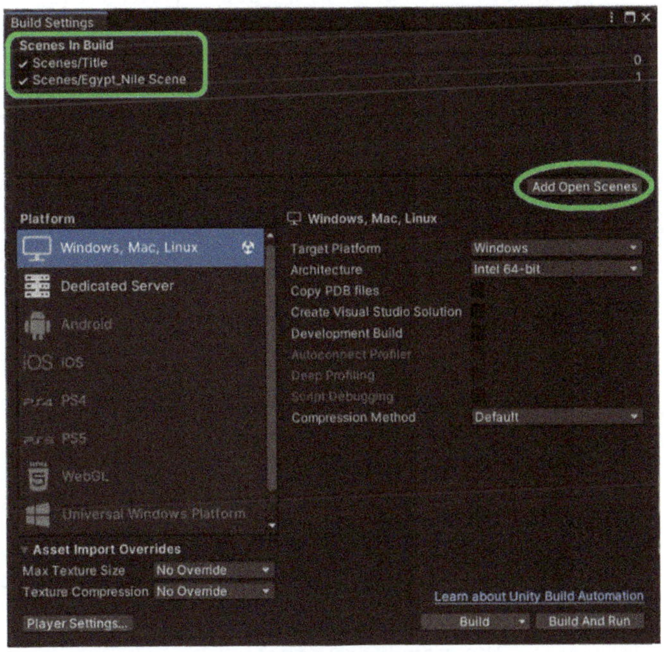

Figure 263

The only order that matters in this list of scenes is which scene is at the top. The scene at the top is always loaded first when the player launches the game, so we need to make sure the Title scene is first. The numbers on the right can be used as an easy way to refer to scenes in C# scripts when loading a different scene. You can either refer to the scene name (i.e., the file name in the "Scenes" folder) or to this number. We're done here, close the Build Settings.

Push Your buttons

We're going to create some buttons now. Open the Title scene again. In the main menu, GameObject > UI > Button - TextMeshPro. Not only will this create a button for you, but also a canvas object and set the button as its child. Name it "ContinueButton".

In the Scene View, press the 'F' key to focus on the button object. You should be able to see your button. Pan and rotate the Scene View so you can see the white rectangle around the button as shown in Figure 264. This rectangle is the canvas and represents the screen the player will see. Everything inside it can be seen by the player while everything outside it cannot.

Figure 264

Let's create our main menu. Right-click the Canvas object in the Hierarchy view and select "Create Empty". Rename it to "MainMenu" and drag the "ContinueButton" underneath it as a child object.

Now we're going to put our custom GUI on the button. With the Button still showing in the inspector, browse the Project View to Assets > Images > RPG GUI > Texture > Button. Drag the "Button_1" file over the existing image of the button's "Source Image" on the inspector in the "Image" script. You will see the button become all black in the Scene View. In the Hierarchy View, expand the button and click the "Text" object. This is the object that shows the letters on the button. In the Text script, change the "Color" to white and the words now show up again on the button.

Here is a cool trick if you want to hide an object but need to keep it active. Just move it out of the canvas rectangle. You can do this by adjusting the Rect Transform.

Our custom GUI also has a cool panel to put our buttons into. On the inspector for the MainMenu click "Add Component" and scroll down to "UI". Click it and then select "Image". A white box appears in the middle of the screen. Now, in the Project View, from Assets > Images > RPG GUI > Texture > Button, drag the "Button_menu" file onto the "Source Image". Set the Width and Height to '200'.

This gives us room for about 4 buttons. Duplicate the "ContinueButton" 3 times with CTRL+D. Notice, you still only see 1 button in the scene view. That is because all the buttons are on top of each other. Let's spread them apart. Give the buttons a "PosY" in their Rect Transform these values from top to bottom, '60, '20', '-20', and '-60'. This spreads them out evenly across the main menu panel.

Let's give them some names now. In the Hierarchy View, expand each of the buttons to reveal the Text objects. Expand the "ContinueButton" and then go to the Text (TMP) child object and set "Text" variable in the component on the inspector to "Continue" as well. Repeat the process for the other 3 buttons using the names "New Game", "Options", and "Quit Game".

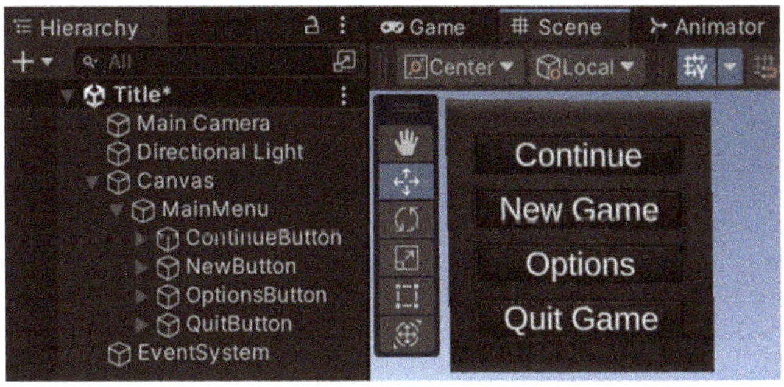

Figure 265

At this point, your Scene and Hierarchy Views should look like that in Figure 265. Go into play mode and check out your cool new buttons. If you click on them then the button changes darker. Of course, nothing happens yet when you push the button because we haven't set up our handler yet. We'll add the C# code to handle the button presses next.

Title Controller Script

We're going to have some cool features on this script. This will be the script that controls what happens in the Title scene. First, the scene will fade in from blackness. This will be similar to how we faded the zone names. Then the player can select from the main menu, potentially change some options, and if they choose "New Game" or "Continue" then the Title scene is faded out and a loading window appears while the next scene is loaded.

```
4   using UnityEngine.SceneManagement;
5
    Unity Script | 0 references
6   public class TitleController : MonoBehaviour
7   {
8       public GameObject LoadingPanel;
9       public GameObject MainMenuPanel;
10      public GameObject OptionsPanel;
11      public UnityEngine.UI.Slider MusicSlider;
12      public UnityEngine.UI.Slider SoundFXSlider;
13      public string GameSceneName;
14      public UnityEngine.UI.Image BlackScreen;
15      public float fadeSpeed;
16
17      private bool selectNewGame;
18      private bool selectContinue;
19      private bool fadedIn;
```

Figure 266

Create a new script in our scripts folder named "TitleController" and open it in

> *The variable for fadeSpeed is technically not needed. We could hardcode a number for the speed in the script. But making that number a variable allows us to easily change the speed in the inspector, so we don't have to change a script if we want to change the speed. It's a best practice!*

Visual Studio. Add the variables shown in Figure 266 to the top of the class. On line 4, we're using the Scene Management namespace for loading scenes.

See below for a description of the variables.

- LoadingPanel: The window that informs the player a new scene is loading.
- MainMenuPanel: The parent object that contains all the buttons for the main menu.

- OptionsPanel: Has all the UI objects for the options the player can set.
- MusicSlider: A UI slider so the player can adjust music volume.
- SoundFXSlider: A UI slider so the player can adjust sound FX volume.
- GameSceneName: Name of the next scene to load.
- BlackScreen: The image for the black screen used to fade in and out.
- fadeSpeed: How fast the fade will be done.
- selectNewGame: True only if the player clicked the button for "New Game"
- selectContinue: True only if the player clicked the button for "Continue"
- fadedIn: This starts out false and turns true after the initial screen fades in

Now add code in the "Start" method as shown in Figure 267. First, we call a method that we'll write later to set the initial state of the screen to be opaque (cannot see through it). Set "fadedIn" to false so we will know we still need to fade in. Set "selectNewGame" and "selectContinue" to false because the buttons haven't been pushed yet. Set the main menu to active because the player will see that the first thing. But set the loading and options panels to inactive. We'll add some code in update to show it next.

```
void Start()
{
    ModifyScreenAlpha(1);
    fadedIn = false;
    selectNewGame = false;
    selectContinue = false;

    MainMenuPanel.SetActive(true);
    LoadingPanel.SetActive(false);
    OptionsPanel.SetActive(false);
}
```

Figure 267

Now add the code to the "Update" method shown in Figure 268. The first "if" block fades the screen from opaque to transparent. On line 40 we set "fadedIn" to true if the screen is fully transparent, so we know we're done. Importantly, if the player starts a new game or continues an old game then we want to stop fading.

The other "if" block handles the fade out for when the player presses the "New Game" or "Continue button. First, we check if we're still fading out. If the image is not fully opaque, then continue fading out. Once the fade out has completed

```
35  void Update()
36  {
37      if (!fadedIn && !(selectNewGame || selectContinue))
38      {
39          ModifyScreenAlpha(-Time.deltaTime * fadeSpeed);
40          if (BlackScreen.color.a == 0) fadedIn = true;
41      }
42
43      if (selectNewGame || selectContinue)
44      {
45          if (BlackScreen.color.a < 1)
46          {
47              ModifyScreenAlpha(Time.deltaTime * fadeSpeed);
48          }
49          else
50          {
51              LoadingPanel.SetActive(true);
52              if (selectNewGame)
53              {
54                  SceneManager.LoadScene(GameSceneName);
55              }
56              else if (selectContinue)
57              {
58                  SceneManager.LoadScene(GameSceneName);
59              }
60          }
61      }
62  }
```

Figure 268

then show the loading window and load the new scene.

Add the private methods shown in Figure 269 named "ModifyScreenAlpha". This is a helper method that allows us to change the alpha of a color with a single method call. The call to the Mathf library for "Clamp01" will force the value to be clamped between 0 and 1. This is useful for making sure variables do not go outside that range. Since the alpha value we change in the script has that restriction, we'll enforce it.

```
private void ModifyScreenAlpha(float deltaAlpha)
{
    Color tCol = BlackScreen.color;
    tCol.a = Mathf.Clamp01(tCol.a + deltaAlpha);
    BlackScreen.color = tCol;
}
```

Figure 269

Lastly, add the 4 button handlers shown in Figure 270. The methods "ButtonNewGame" and "ButtonContinue" will get called when the respective buttons are pressed. Setting their respective "select" bools will trigger the fadeout to a black screen, show the loading panel, and load the next scene.

The "ButtonOptions" method will actually be hooked up to two buttons. We'll attach this to both the options button in the main menu and the button in the options menu to go back to the main menu. This method toggles showing the options panel. If the options menu is currently displayed, then hide it and show the main menu. If the main menu is currently displayed, then hide it and show the options menu.

```
public void ButtonNewGame()
{
    selectNewGame = true;
}

0 references
public void ButtonContinue()
{
    selectContinue = true;
}

0 references
public void ButtonOptions()
{
    OptionsPanel.SetActive(!OptionsPanel.activeSelf);
    MainMenuPanel.SetActive(!MainMenuPanel.activeSelf);
}

0 references
public void ButtonQuit()
{
    Application.Quit();
}
```

Figure 270

Calling "Application.Quit()" while in the Unity editor won't do anything. To test it we'll have to build a game executable and launch that. We'll go over it later.

The last method will be called when the "QuitGame" button is pressed and calls the necessary method to quit and close the game out.

Create an Empty object named "TitleController" in the Hierarchy View and drag the "Title" script onto it. You can see all the empty public variables there now. Next, we'll create the other UI objects we need and then use the Unity glue to paste them together, so they all work together in Unity (Haha! The Unity puns are the gift that keeps on giving).

Title Screen UI Objects

There are a number of objects we need to create for the "TitleController" script. We briefly mentioned them above, but now we'll go over them in greater detail.

- Loading Panel: Indicates the game is loading, often used to remind players of important information like how to use complex features or game lore and story.
- Options Panel: Adjust settings about game input, graphics, and audio. In this tutorial, we're only going to adjust audio levels in the options panel.
- Music Slider: Allows the player to change the music volume in the game from 0% to 100%.
- Sound FX Slider: Allows the player to change the sound volume in the game from 0% to 100%.
- Black Screen: The image we use for fading which is the same as what we created in Chapter 8.

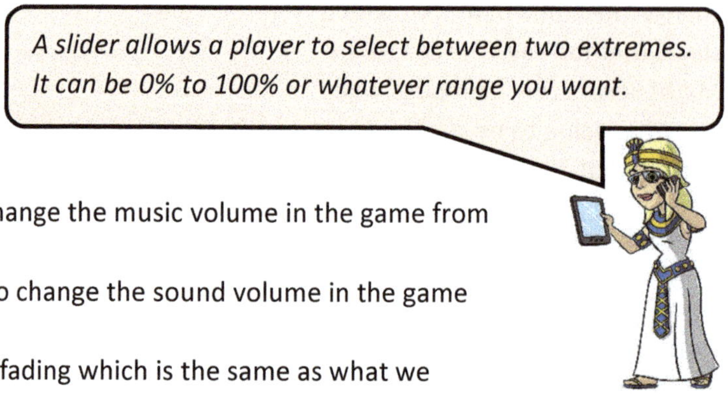

Create a second panel by doing right-click the Canvas object in the Hierarchy View and select UI > Image. Name the object "LoadingPanel". Set the Source Image to the "Button_menu" like with the main menu. You can also add some text that tells the player the game is loading as well as some other text that you want the player to know. Remember that you add text by right-clicking the "LoadingPanel" and selecting UI > Text - TextMeshPro. See Figure 271 for how I created the loading panel.

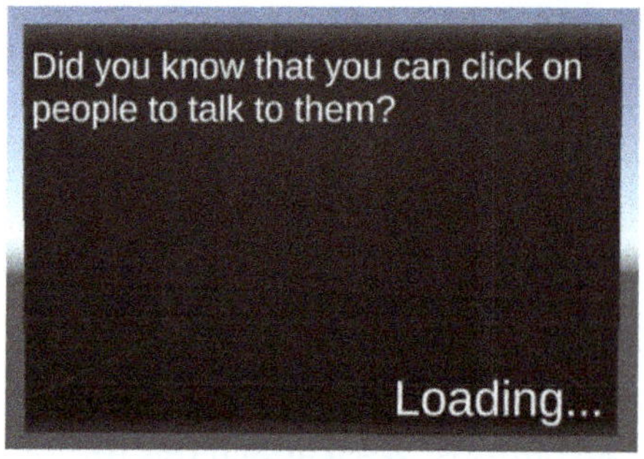

Figure 271

On to the options menu. Create another panel the same way as with the loading window except name it "OptionsPanel". Set the Width to '200' and the Hieght to '250'. Right-click on it and create a Text - TextMeshPro UI object. Set the Pos Y to '100', Text to "Options Menu", Font Size to '28', and Alignment to center.

Right-click on the "OptionsPanel" again and Create > UI > Slider. Name it "MusicVolume". Set the Pos Y to '35'. Right-clicking on the "MusicVolume" slider object create a Test Mesh Pro child object. Set the Pos Y to '20', Text to "Music Volume", Alignment to center, and Font Size to '18'.

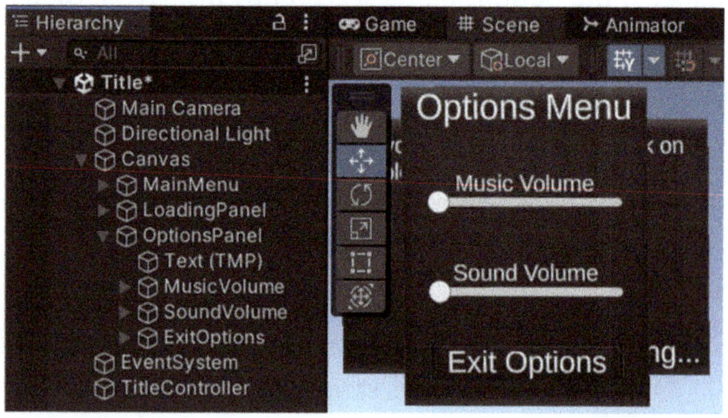

Figure 272

Duplicate the "MusicVolume" slider using CTRL+D and set the Pos Y to '-35'. Rename the slider name to "SoundVolume" and also change the text of the child object label to "Sound Volume". We will hook these up to actually crontrol music and sound volume in Chapter 14.

Now create a button under the options menu named “ExitOptions”. Set the Source Image to “Button_1” as before and the text Child object to “Exit Options”. Then set the Pos Y to ‘-90’ which places the button at the bottom of the panel. The options menu should look like Figure 272.

We will create the Black Screen used for fading the same way we did for Chapter 8. Right-click the “Canvas” and select UI > Image, naming the new object “BlackScreen”. In the inspector, recall that the Anchor Preset is the grid at the top left which says center and middle. Click that and select stretch and stretch which is in the bottom right of the pop up. Then set the Left, Top, Right, and Bottom attributes In the Rect Transform to ‘0’. Change the color to black and, most importantly, uncheck the “Raycast Target” box. Remember that allows us to click on stuff underneath it.

You can tell which UI objects are in front by the order in the Hierarchy View. The child objects closest to the Canvas are in the back while the ones furthest from the Canvas are in the front.

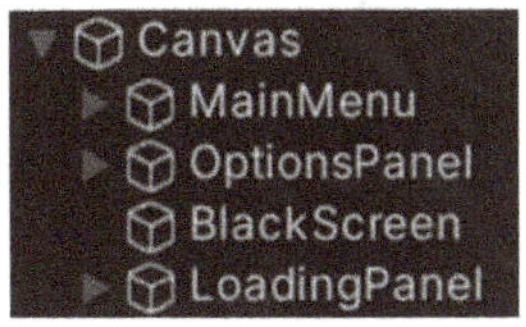

Figure 273

In order to see the loading screen we need to change the order. When dragging objects in the Hierarchy View, you’ll see that if you hover over an object then the object is highlighted in blue. If you hover in-between objects, then there is a blue line. The blue line means that the object will be placed between them. Drag the “LoadingWindow” object down below the “Screen” object. It should look like Figure 273.

Figure 274

The last thing to do is to glue them all together. Click the “TitleController” object in the Hierarchy View to see the inspector. From the Hierarchy View, drag the “Screen” object onto the Screen in the inspector. Then drag the “LoadingWindow” onto the loading variable. Then drag the “MainMenu” onto the Main Menu Panel. Then drag the “OptionsMenu” over to the options panel. Drag “MusicVolume” to the Music Slider and then the “SoundVolume” to the Sound Slider. The Game Scene Name will be set the scene we had been working and we added to the build settings named “Egypt_Nile Scene”. Set the Fade Speed to ‘1’. The inspector should now look like Figure 274.

Figure 275

Now we need to hook up the buttons to their handlers There are five buttons. We’ll start with the “Continue” button. Click it in the Hierarchy View. Scroll to the bottom of the inspector and you’ll see a box that says “On Click ()” with a ‘+’ and ‘-’ underneath.

This is a list of methods that will get called when the button gets clicked. We'll only need 1 method called. Click the '+' and you'll see an entry gets added. From the Hierarchy View, drag the "TitleController" object into the box under "Runtime Only" that says "None (Object)". Click where it says "No Function" and select TitleController > ButtonContinue. You'll see that method is now listed to be called when the button is clicked as shown in Figure 275.

Dragging the object tells Unity to call one of the methods in that object. Then specifying the "TitleController" class narrows it down so you can specify exactly which method. When the player presses the button, that method from that class on that object gets called.

Now do this with the other buttons as well. There are three more buttons in the main menu and then the button in the options controller to exit the options. You can see them highlighted in Figure 276.

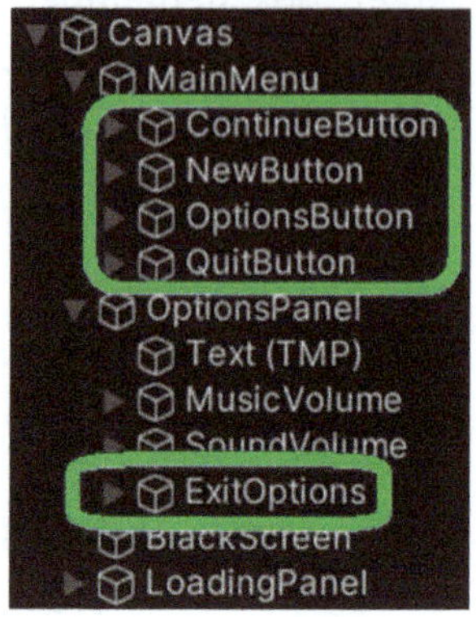

Figure 276

Click the '+' for the "On Click ()" listener and drag the "TitleController" object into the box for all of them. Set the button listeners to the methods shown in the below table. Remember that we coded the "ButtonOptions" method to handle both showing and hiding the options panel.

Button	**Method**
ContinueButton	ButtonContinue
NewButton	ButtonNewGame
OptionsButton	ButtonOptions
QuitButton	ButtonQuit
ExitOptions	ButtonOptions

It is also easy to change the build settings so you can build the game for any platform that Unity supports. But for this game we're only going to build for Windows.

With the objects sufficiently glued, give the title scene a test. Click the options button and make sure it shows the options panel. Clicking the "Quit Game" button will do nothing since we're in the Unity editor. Then try "Continue" it should load the Egypt_Nile scene and you'll be treated to the cinematic you created in the last chapter. If not, check the spelling of the string in the "TitleController" Game Scene Name field. Also, make sure that scene is present in the build options.

Capital Amusement

In order to execute the game (no, we're not going to kill it... yet) Unity will build an executable that players can double-click. This will launch the game so they can start playing it. Luckily, this is a pretty easy thing to do in Unity.

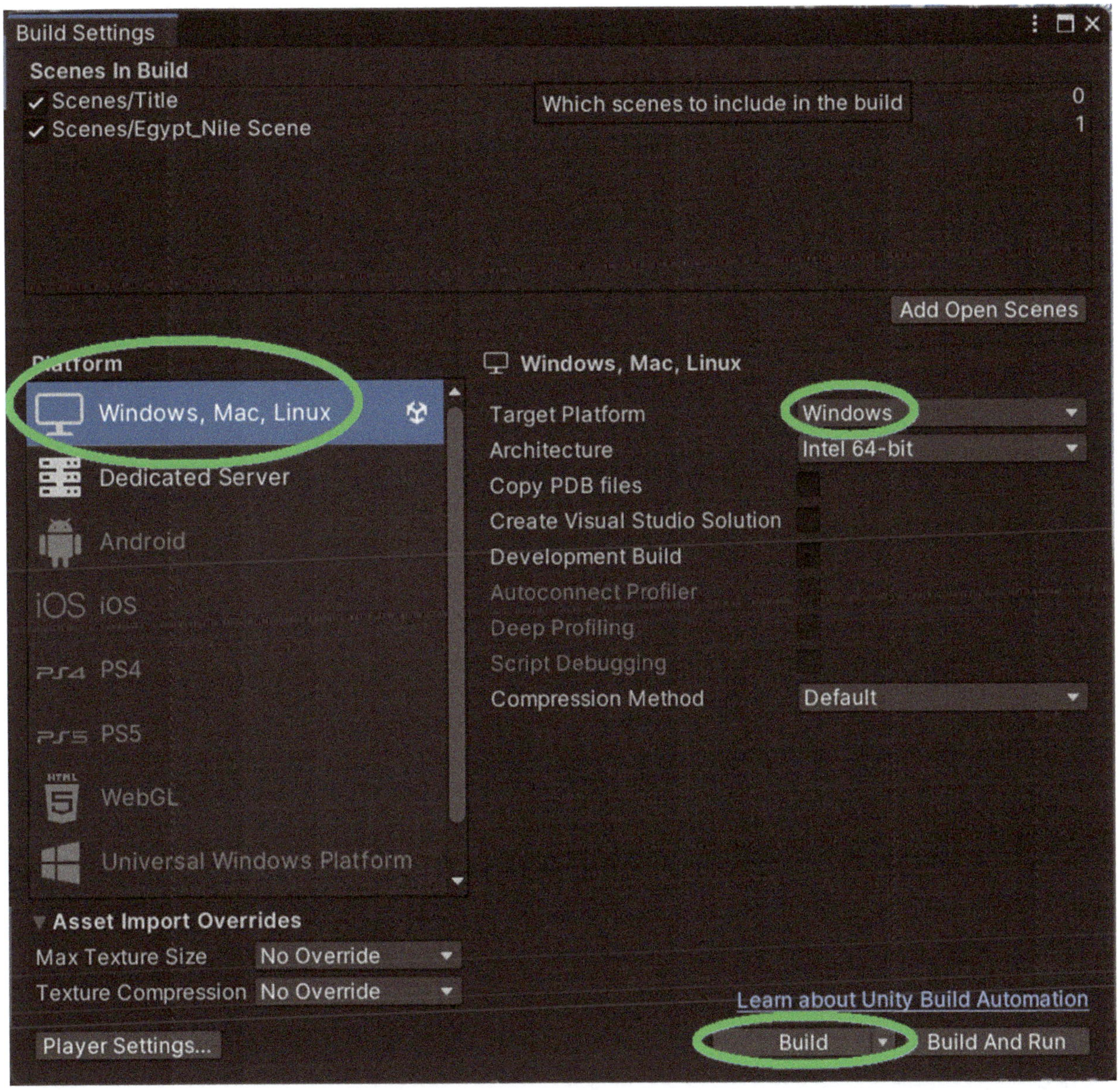

Figure 277

Click File > Build Settings and you'll see the window from before that shows the 2 scenes we added to the game shown in Figure 277. We saw this in a previous section but skipped over the options in the bottom pane. The top, of course, has the scenes that will be included in our build. Whenever you create a new scene for your game you MUST add it to the list, or it will not be included in the build.

One of the great things about Unity is that you can use it to build games for many different platforms. A platform is a piece of computer hardware. You're likely to be using Windows, Mac, or Linux. So, we'll keep that platform set for us. But you can also build the game for phones and tablets using the Android or iOS platform. You can also build for game consoles like Playstation ™ and Xbox ™.

The Architecture is either Intel 32-bit or Intel 64-bit. PDB files are used for debugging problems in your game and often used with the "Development Build" option. The rest are advanced not covered here.

Ensure the Target Platform is set to the OS you're running on, mine is Windows and click the "Build" button. You can also click the "Build And Run" button which will run the game automatically after it is built. A window pops up asking for Folder to Build Windows (or whatever OS you're running). Click the "New folder" button near the top and name it "Build". Then click "Select Folder" as shown in Figure 278.

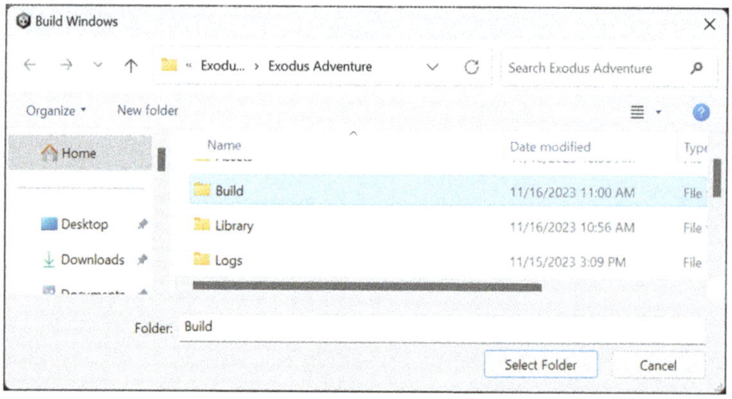

Figure 278

If you haven't saved your changes yet, Unity will prompt you that the Scene was modified. Click "Save" to continue. At this point you need to wait while Unity goes through the process of building the game. Just sit back with a nice cold beverage while the build is in-progress. Except if you're in somewhere cold. Then you may want to sit back with a hot beverage.

There are lots of neat platforms to build for including VR! If you'd like to see more game tutorials for them then tell your friends to consider this tutorial so we can fund more of them.

When it's done a window pops up of the location where the executable was built. If not, then browse to the root "Exodus Adventure" folder and select "Build". Here, you can double-click the executable, as the player would do, to launch the game. Go ahead, double-click it. After a quick splash screen advertising Unity as our engine of choice, you will see the menu panel you created. Or, if you clicked "Build And Run" you don't even need to double-click the executable.

Try clicking "Options" and it will show that menu instead. Try playing around with the sliders. They don't control anything yet. We'll add support for that later in a later chapter. Click "Exit Options" to go back.

Now kill the game by clicking "Quit Game". This will end the game and close the window. Now let's re-open the game and test out the "Continue" button. When you click it, the scene fades out as the "Egypt_Nile Scene" is loaded and our cool Loading window is displayed. When it finishes you can see the opening cut scene you created before. But now we have a problem, there is no button to quit the game! Luckily you can just press the 'X' at the top right to end the game. But we'll add a menu system in-game next.

In-Game Menu

No, we won't design this game so players can't quit. We definitely want players to keep playing our game, but keeping them from exiting is just downright mean. So, next we'll implement the main and options menus as well that the player can bring up while inside the game as well as the loading window.

First, let's make some prefabs. We're going to re-use the main and options menus that we created here so we don't have to do the work twice. Drag the "OptionsPanel", the "BlackScreen", and the "LoadingPanel" objects from the Canvas onto Project View in the Assets > Prefabs > UI folder. Don't make one for the main menu as the game menu is going to be a bit different.

Remember, one of the design principles is to be consistent. So we want to keep our menus in the same location. That way the player won't be frustrated trying to find what they want to do.

We're going to use a nifty trick to create the in-game main menu. Click the "MainMenu" object under the Canvas and press CTRL+C to copy it. In the Project View, go to Assets > Scenes and double-click "Egypt_Nile Scene" so it will load. Be sure to save your Title scene before it unloads. If the canvas isn't visible in the Scene View, then find it in the Hierarchy View and click it. Then move the mouse to the Scene View and press 'F' to focus on it. Scroll and zoom the Scene View so you can see the entire white rectangle (or square) of the canvas.

Expand the canvas and click on one of the child objects inside. Press CTRL+V to paste the Main Menu. Now drag the 2 prefabs we created, "LoadingWindow" and "OptionsMenu" onto the Canvas object in the Hierarchy View. You'll see them appear in the middle of the canvas where it was in the Title scene. Since the scene already has a black screen, we don't need to drag over another one from the Prefabs folder. The Hierarchy View should look similar to Figure 279.

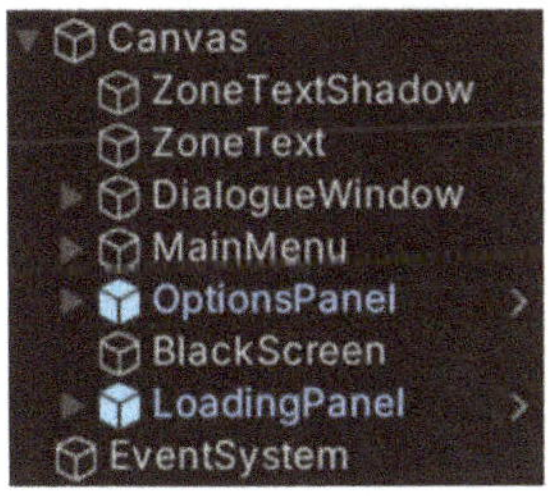

Figure 279

For the main menu, we don't want it to look exactly like the one in the title scene. Instead of "Continue" and "New Game" buttons we need a button to go back to the title scene. And then we need to change the "Quit Game" to "Resume Game".

Click on the "Continue" button under the main menu. Rename it to "ResumeButton" and set the Text of the child object to "Resume". Delete the "NewGame" button. For the Options button, set the Pos Y of the Rect Transform of the buttons to '0'. It should now look like Figure 280.

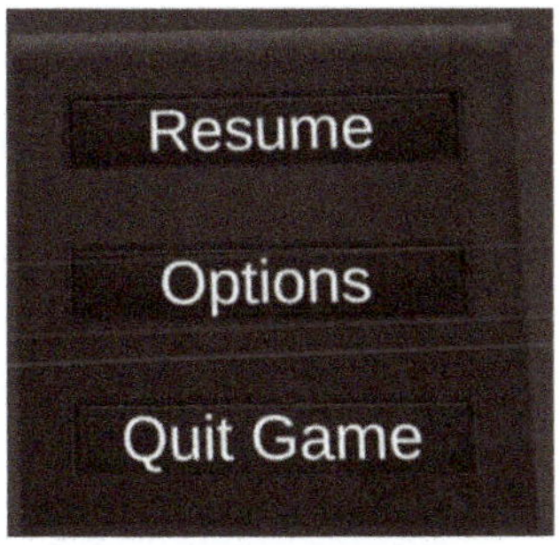

Figure 280

If you cannot see it in the Scene View, it is likely behind the other windows. An easy way to bring it out is to click the "MainMenu" object in the Hierarchy View and drag it, in the Scene View along the X (or red) axis passed the other windows, and the black screen, so you can see it. Just be sure to set the Pos X back to '0' when you're done.

Once it looks right, drag the "MainMenu" from the Hierarchy View to the Project View under Assets > Prefabs > UI to save a prefab of it. We'll make good use of these prefabs when we get to Chapter 11 and design and build our own new levels. It will save us a lot of time.

In-Game Menu Scripting

Now it's time to code up what will happen to these UI objects in the "GameController" script. In the Assets > Scripts folder double-click on that script and let's get back to coding some C#!

Add the new variables shown in Figure 281. The "MainMenuObj", "OptionsMenuObj", and "LoadingPanelObj" store handles to the UI objects we in the scene. In the UI State enumeration, we add 2 new states "MainMenu" and "OptionsMenu". We will use the state variable to determine what windows we need to close.

On line 36, add a bool "fromMainMenu". This is a special variable for our options menu. The player can just press 'O' to get to the options menu or they can press the button from the main menu. If they come from the main menu then if they want to leave they'll expect to go back to the main menu. Because we now have to do something different if the player was at the Main Menu or not, we need a flag. We'll use "fromMainMenu" as a flag to tell us that we need to go back to the Main Menu instead of just hiding the options menu.

```
19      public GameObject BlackScreen;
20      public GameObject IntroObjects;
21      public GameObject MainMenuObj;
22      public GameObject OptionsMenuObj;
23      public GameObject LoadingPanelObj;
24
        27 references
25      private enum _ui_state
26      {
27          None,
28          WorldMap,
29          MainMenu,
30          OptionsMenu
31      }
32      private _ui_state uiState;
33      private List<GameObject> ZoneWorldMapTextObjList;
34      private bool IntroCinePlayed;
35      private bool FadingOut;
36      private bool fromMainMenu;
```

Figure 281

Flags in C# coding are kind of like flags for football or soccer. If something that wasn't expected happens or a rule was broken then a flag is thrown. In C#, we use Booleans to track if a flag was thrown. If was, then we know we need to do something special.

In the Start method, we need to initialize these new variables. On line 57 we initialize our special flag, "fromMainMenu" to be false. That means it is not thrown at the beginning. Then on lines 62 through 64 the new UI components are default to hidden It would look weird to the player to see all those panels laying on screen. Line 63 has a method we will call for the options menu because that will have special handling later. The code should look like Figure 282.

```
55          IntroCinePlayed = false;
56          FadingOut = false;
57          fromMainMenu = false;
58          CineCam.SetActive(true);
59          MinimapObj.SetActive(false);
60          Player.SetActive(false);
61          IntroObjects.SetActive(true);
62          MainMenuObj.SetActive(false);
63          OptionsMenuSetActive(false);
64          LoadingPanelObj.SetActive(false);
65          IntroCine.Play();
```

Figure 282

There are a couple places we need to change in the Update method. The first is in the if statement to handle the ending of the cinematic. We

```
if (IntroCine.state != PlayState.Playing)
{
    FadingOut = true;
    IntroObjects.SetActive(false);
    CineCam.SetActive(false);
    Player.SetActive(true);
    MinimapObj.SetActive(true);
    IntroCinePlayed = true;
}
```

Figure 283

need to make sure the variable "IntroCinePlayed" gets set to true on line 80 as shown in Figure 283. This sets up the following part in the Update method.

After the code to fade the gameplay in, add the if block from Figure 284 starting at line 93. Once the introduction cinematic has played, we will now accept input for the UI. Each UI object will have their own handler that gets called at the appropriate key press. The world map when 'M' is pressed, the main menu when ESCAPE is pressed, and the options menu when 'O' is pressed.

```
93          if (IntroCinePlayed)
94          {
95              if (Input.GetKeyUp(KeyCode.M))
96              {
97                  WorldMapHandler();
98              }
99              else if (Input.GetKeyUp(KeyCode.Escape))
100             {
101                 MainMenuHandler();
102             }
103             else if (Input.GetKeyUp(KeyCode.O))
104             {
105                 OptionsMenuHandler();
106             }
107
108             if (uiState == _ui_state.None)
109             {
110                 MinimapObj.SetActive(true);
111             }
112             else
113             {
114                 MinimapObj.SetActive(false);
115             }
116         }
```

Figure 284

Afterwards, we will do some special handling for the minimap. We only want to show the minimap when the other UI objects are not being shown. So, on line 110, the minimap is being activated only when the UI state is "None". All other times it is hidden from view.

At first glance it may seem like a switch statement would work for the if block on lines 95 through 106, but it won't. We call the method and pass in a different argument each time. Switch statements are only to check values of variables. In this if block, we have method calls for "GetKeyUp" which return bool. Because we're checking for different keys each time, we need to use if instead of switch.

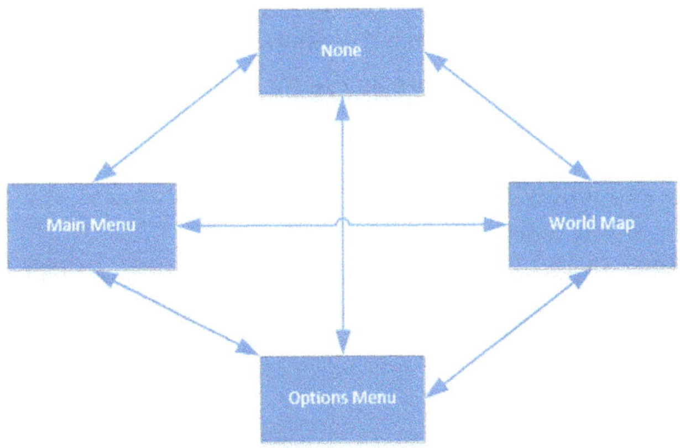

Figure 285

Next is where the complicated part of the UI happens. The code change itself isn't that complicated but understanding how the state changes and what else needs to change with it can be a little overwhelming. Many times, it is helpful to draw a diagram of how things are supposed to change.

Figure 285 shows a basic state diagram of how the UI will work. The state machine starts at the top in the "None" box or state. From there, we can go to any other state depending on what the player presses or clicks. The same thing applies to that state. Depending on what the player clicks, we could go to any of the other states. This gives the player a lot of flexibility in how they navigate the menu system and UI. Having a diagram to map out the states is helpful to understand what the code should do. Now let's write that C# code!

In Figure 286 we've removed the old code and replaced it with a nice clean "switch" statement (Haha! It works here). This goes through the states for the UI. The "None" case is not listed as it is handled in the default section.

For these handler methods we're writing it's important to know what we're trying to do. In this case, the user has pressed the 'M' key and we need to show the world map. The UI State shows what is currently on the screen. So the goal of this method is to hide what is currently there and then show the world map. If nothing is on the screen, then the job is easy, just show the world map.

```
public void WorldMapHandler()
{
    switch(uiState)
    {
        case _ui_state.WorldMap:
            WorldMapSetActive(false);
            uiState = _ui_state.None;
            break;
        case _ui_state.MainMenu:
            WorldMapSetActive(true);
            MainMenuObj.SetActive(false);
            uiState = _ui_state.WorldMap;
            break;
        case _ui_state.OptionsMenu:
            WorldMapSetActive(true);
            OptionsMenuSetActive(false);
            uiState = _ui_state.WorldMap;
            break;
        default:
            // Catch the "None" state here
            WorldMapSetActive(true);
            uiState = _ui_state.WorldMap;
            break;
    }
}
```

Figure 286

Add the method for handling the main menu next as seen in Figure 287. This gets called when the player presses the ESCAPE key. The switch statement here has the same structure as the method for the world map.

Try to follow the logic and see how these methods work with the state diagram. Each time the user presses a key is an arrow going to a new state.

```
public void MainMenuHandler()
{
    switch (uiState)
    {
        case _ui_state.MainMenu:
            MainMenuObj.SetActive(false);
            uiState = _ui_state.None;
            break;
        case _ui_state.WorldMap:
            WorldMapSetActive(false);
            MainMenuObj.SetActive(true);
            uiState = _ui_state.MainMenu;
            break;
        case _ui_state.OptionsMenu:
            OptionsMenuSetActive(false);
            MainMenuObj.SetActive(true);
            uiState = _ui_state.MainMenu;
            break;
        default:
            // Catch the "None" state here
            MainMenuObj.SetActive(true);
            uiState = _ui_state.MainMenu;
            break;
    }
}
```

Figure 287

Next are the methods to handle the Options menu and ending the game you can code up in Figure 288. In a later chapter, we're going to hook up the volume sliders. When we do, the method "OptionsMenuSetActive" will be where we set the sliders to the saved value. But for now, it just enables and disables the options menu panel.

```
public void OptionsMenuSetActive(bool active)
{
    OptionsMenuObj.SetActive(active);
}

0 references
public void EndGameHandler()
{
    MainMenuObj.SetActive(false);
    LoadingPanelObj.SetActive(true);
    UnityEngine.SceneManagement.SceneManager.LoadScene(0);
}
```

Figure 288

The method "EndGameHandler" takes the player back to the Title scene which we placed at index 0 so it will get loaded first. This way we don't need to refer to it by the string name. We also set up the UI so the player sees the loading panel.

Now we write the method for the final state, the options menu, shown in Figure 289. This one is a bit different. On line 235 we set the "fromMainMenu" flag. This tells us that the previous state was the main menu. When this happens, the player expects to go back to the main menu.

Normally, when the player presses the 'O' key or clicks the button to exit the options we just hide the options menu. But if the previous state was the main menu, then we need to go back to it. So, we check if the flag is set. If it is, then we hide the options menu and show the main menu. We also need to clear the flag (by making it false) so that if the player presses 'O' to enter the options menu next time then we don't send them to the main menu.

Other than that, this method looks very similar to the others with the switch statement and all the cases and the default at the end.

```
225 public void OptionsMenuHandler()
226 {
227     switch (uiState)
228     {
229         case _ui_state.OptionsMenu:
230             OptionsMenuSetActive(false);
231             if (fromMainMenu)
232             {
233                 MainMenuObj.SetActive(true);
234                 uiState = _ui_state.MainMenu;
235                 fromMainMenu = false;
236             }
237             else
238             {
239                 uiState = _ui_state.None;
240             }
241             break;
242         case _ui_state.WorldMap:
243             WorldMapSetActive(false);
244             OptionsMenuSetActive(true);
245             uiState = _ui_state.OptionsMenu;
246             break;
247         case _ui_state.MainMenu:
248             MainMenuObj.SetActive(false);
249             OptionsMenuSetActive(true);
250             fromMainMenu = true;
251             uiState = _ui_state.OptionsMenu;
252             break;
253         default:
254             // Catch the "None" state here
255             OptionsMenuSetActive(true);
256             uiState = _ui_state.OptionsMenu;
257             break;
258     }
259 }
```

Figure 289

Connecting the Menu System

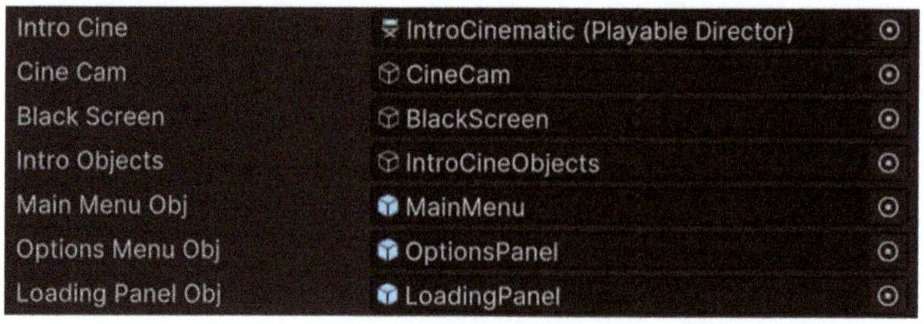

Figure 290

The final part, as always, is to connect our objects together with our script so they can live in Unity. Luckily, this is all stuff we've done before so no sweat!

Go back into Unity and click the "GameController" in the Hierarchy View. With the Canvas expanded, drag the "MainMenu", "OptionsMenu", and "LoadingWindow" onto the respective variables in the inspector as shown in Figure 290.

Now expand the "MainMenu" and "OptionsMenu" under the Canvas and get ready to set the methods for the "On Click()" events on the buttons. Press the '+' for each one drag the "GameController" object over to the box that says "None (Object)".

Set the methods of the "On Click()" event as shown below:

Menu	**Button**	**Method**
Main Menu	QuitButton	EndGameHandler
Main Menu	OptionsButton	OptionsMenuHandler
Main Menu	ResumeButton	MainMenuHandler
Options Menu	ExitOptions	OptionsMenuHandler

With all that Unity glue in place, we're ready to test out our in-game menu system. Click the play button and give it a test drive. Try all the different UI objects like the world map, main menu, and options menu to make sure they work. Also, try going between them. You can even go back and forth between this and the Title scene now. However, when you go back to the "Egypt_Nile Scene" it doesn't put you back where you left off. We'll add that feature in chapter 15.

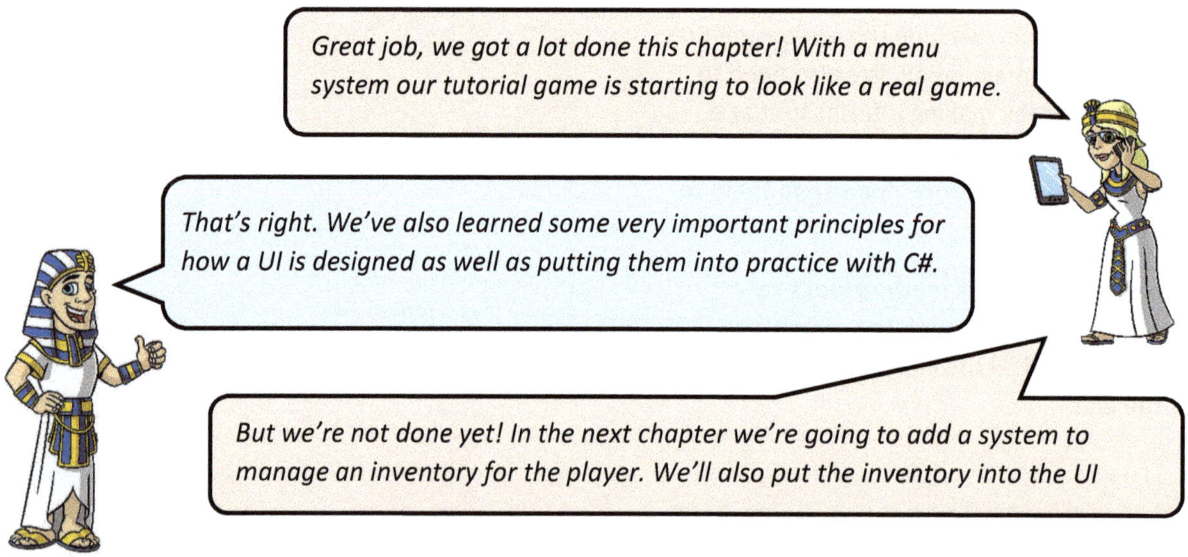

Chapter 10 – Inventory Management

One of the great features in many games including puzzle games is being given or finding items you can use or figure out where to use to progress in the game. It is a feature many players in the puzzle genre of game expect, and one that can add a lot of fun (or frustration, if you're not careful). I encourage you to read through the Inventory section of the GDD to get an idea of where we're going with this feature.

We'll have three C# scripts to code up for this feature. The first will be the class for the items itself. The second will engine to build up the total list of items and track the user's inventory. The last will be code to handle the user interface for the inventory. We'll add this into our menu system we created in the last chapter so it's easy for the player to use.

In addition to writing the code to handle items, we'll need to be able to give them to the player and take them away. This will be done by adding a new "Item" element to the cut scene system.

Create a new C# script named "Item" and open it in Visual Studio. Remove the "Start" and "Update" methods and add the code shown in Figure 291. This class contains all the information we need for the item.

```
public class Item : MonoBehaviour
{
    public string ItemName;
    public string Description;
    public Sprite Icon;
}
```

Figure 291

Every item has a name. The description tells the player what it is and gives them a hint for what the item is used for. The Icon is of a type called "Sprite". This sprite is a 2D image that we'll use to graphically represent the item.

Dictionary Definition

One last thing to talk about before we start coding our cut scene engine is the dictionary class. You normally use a dictionary when you come across a word you don't know what it means. Maybe you go on your phone, or you break out an old-school book, but you go and look it up and the dictionary tells you what it means. A dictionary in C# is the same thing. It's kind of like a list or an array, except instead of using an integer for the index you can use any type you want.

Example:

```
Dictionary<string, string> defs = new Dictionary<string, string>();
defs.Add("C", "Procedural programming language");
defs.Add("C++", "Object-oriented programming language");
defs.Add("C#", "Object-oriented scripting language");
Debug.Log(defs["C#"]);
```

Dictionaries really help out when we have two things we need to connect together. If you just have data you want to store, a list or array is probably what you need. But if you need to access something by its name, then a dictionary would work best.

In the above example, we can see how to declare and define a dictionary. We've declared a variable named "defs" that is a dictionary where you use a string (first parameter in the alligator brackets) to look-up another string (second parameter in the alligator brackets). Then we create a new instance of it, like we do with other classes, using the "new" keyword. The first parameter is called a key.

This dictionary keeps track of the history of the C languages and tells what they are. When you add new elements into the dictionary, you use the "Add" method, similar to lists, and specify both parameters you declared the dictionary with. In this case, they are both strings.

The first parameter is called the "key". Keys must be unique for a dictionary. That means you can't have duplicate keys. A key can only have one definition. Otherwise, the dictionary doesn't know which definition to give you.

Item Engine

Create another new C# script named "ItemEngine" and open it in Visual Studio. Remove the code for the "Update" and "Start" methods and the parent class ": MonoBehaviour" and make this class static to access the public variables and methods from other scripts without needing to create an instance first as seen in Figure 292.

```
public static class ItemEngine
{
    static public bool isInitialized;

    static private Dictionary<string, Item> ItemList;
    static private List<Item> InventoryItems;
    static private Item SelectedItem;
}
```

Figure 292

Sometimes programmers get into the habit of using a certain kind of object or coding style. It is good to keep a varied toolbox so you can adapt to the situation.

Since this class is static, the Boolean for "isInitialized" is needed to find out if initialization has completed. This is initially false and is set to true when all the items are loaded and ready for use. Again, this is needed when we have multiple scenes later on, so we don't initialize the system more than once.

We use a dictionary for the total items in the game but a list for the items in the inventory. The reason is because they are used differently. For the "ItemList" we'll be having the name of the item we want to access and need to get back the item's information. For the "InventoryItems" the player will click on icons that correspond to an item using an index (or integer).

Finally, the "SelectedItem" is the item that the player is currently dragging. The player will click the item in the inventory, drag it to the actor, and unclick. This will be for fulfilling item conditions on the cut scene items.

Underneath the variables, add the static method for "Initialize" as shown in Figure 293. The initialize here gets passed the array of items as a parameter. After some initialization, we create the dictionary using the item name as the key and the item itself as the value.

```
static public void Initialize(Item[] items)
{
    ItemList = new Dictionary<string, Item>();
    SelectedItem = null;

    foreach(Item it in items)
    {
        if (!ItemList.ContainsKey(it.ItemName))
        {
            ItemList.Add(it.ItemName, it);
        }
    }

    if (InventoryItems == null)
    {
        InventoryItems = new List<Item>();
    }

    isInitialized = true;
}
```

Figure 293

Since keys are required to be unique for dictionaries, we'll print an error if the item name is already present. This means you're trying to create 2 items with the same name which isn't allowed here.

After that, we'll initialize the inventory, if it needs it and then indicate that our initialization for items is complete.

Next, add the "GetItem" method shown in Figure 294. This method returns the requested item from the dictionary using its name. If the item is not in the dictionary, then we log an error. This is likely a typo for the item name in either then item list or the condition that uses this item. There is no method to remove items from the dictionary because we don't need it.

```
static public Item GetItem(string name)
{
    Item retItem = null;

    if (ItemList.ContainsKey(name))
    {
        retItem = ItemList[name];
    }

    return retItem;
}
```

Figure 294

The next set of methods will deal with the player's inventory. Code the methods shown in Figure 295. The "InventoryAddItem" method will add an item to the end of the player's inventory. If the item is not in the dictionary, then it is likely a typo.

```
static public void InventoryAddItem(string name)
{
    Item item = GetItem(name);

    if (item != null) InventoryItems.Add(item);
}

0 references
static public bool InventoryCheckItem(string name)
{
    bool check = false;
    Item item = GetItem(name);

    if (item != null) check = InventoryItems.Contains(item);

    return check;
}
```

Figure 295

The "InventoryCheckItem" will return true if the given item name is in the player's inventory and false if it is not. This method is important when we implement the item condition in the dialogue system. We'll mark certain dialogues with item conditions. The player must drag that item onto the actor so the dialogue will take effect. The dialogue controller will call this method to find out if the required item is present in the player's inventory. If it is, then the cut scene item is played. If not, then the cut scene item is not played.

Next, we add the methods to remove items from the player's inventory shown in Figure 296. You might have noticed that both of these methods have the same name. You may be asking; how does C# know which method I'm trying to call?

```
static public void InventoryRemItem(int slot)
{
    if (slot < InventoryItems.Count)
    {
        InventoryItems.RemoveAt(slot);
    }
}

0 references
static public void InventoryRemItem(string name)
{
    Item item = GetItem(name);

    if (item != null) InventoryItems.Remove(item);
}
```

Figure 296

Well, I'm glad you asked. In C#, you can have methods with the same names just as long as either the return type is different, or the parameters are different. C# will figure out which method you're referring to by those.

The next 3 methods, shown in Figure 297, are the last to add to this class. The "InventoryGetItemList" method returns the list of total items which will be useful in later chapters.

```
{
    return InventoryItems;
}

0 references
static public void SetSelectedItem(Item item)
{
    SelectedItem = item;
}

0 references
static public Item GetSelectedItem()
{
    return SelectedItem;
}
```

Figure 297

Then we have methods to "set" and "get" the selected item. The method to set is called when the player clicks on an item in the inventory. The method to get is called when a cut scene item is processed that has an item condition.

The last new script we need to create is "Inventory" that will control the user interface for the player's inventory. So do that and open it in Visual Studio adding the variables shown in the code in Figure 298.

```
public TMPro.TextMeshProUGUI ItemDescriptionObj;
public GameObject InventoryPanel;
public GameObject IconPrefab;

private List<GameObject> IconObjList;
private GameObject SelectedIcon;
private Vector3 IconOldLocation;
```

Figure 298

You'll see the how all these objects work in Unity when we're building the UI, but I'll describe them in some words here. Normally, each icon will be shown in a smaller for that is 50x50 pixels wide and high. This is what the "IconPrefab" is for. We'll instantiate an icon for each item in the inventory so the player can easily see what they have. When the player clicks on an item then the item's icon will be displayed in the big 100x100 image and the item's description will be displayed to the player. These will all be displayed in a special panel or window for the inventory that we'll build later.

The "IconObjList" tracks all the icons we create so we can delete them later. The "SelectedIcon" is used when the player clicks the icon so we know which icon they clicked, the icon will follow the mouse, and will be put back at "IconOldLocation" when they unclick.

Update the "Start" method with the code in Figure 299. We start off by initializing the icon list, hiding the inventory, initializing the item engine, and setting the "SelectedIcon" to null which means that there is no selected item.

```
void Start()
{
    IconObjList = new List<GameObject>();
    if (InventoryPanel) HideInventory();
    SelectedIcon = null;
    ItemEngine.Initialize(GetComponents<Item>());
}
```

Figure 299

We'll create the item icons when the player presses the 'i' key and delete the icons when hiding the inventory.

Now add the code to the "Update" method shown in Figure 300. This is the code that figures out if the player clicked on an icon and moves the icon with the mouse.

```
void Update()
{
    if (InventoryPanel.activeSelf && Input.GetMouseButtonDown(0))
    {
        GameObject foundIcon = null;
        float mX = Input.mousePosition.x;
        float mY = Input.mousePosition.y;

        foreach(GameObject icon in IconObjList)
        {
            RectTransform rect = icon.GetComponent<RectTransform>();
            float lBnd = rect.position.x - 35, rBnd = rect.position.x + 35;
            float bBnd = rect.position.y - 35, tBnd = rect.position.y + 35;

            if ((mX <= rBnd) && (mX >= lBnd) && (mY <= tBnd) && (mY >= bBnd))
            {
                foundIcon = icon;
                break;
            }
        }

        if (foundIcon != null)
        {
            Item item = ItemEngine.GetItem(foundIcon.transform.name);
            BigImageObj.sprite = item.Icon;
            BigImageObj.color = Color.white;
            ItemDescriptionObj.text = item.ItemName + "\n" + item.Description;
            SelectedIcon = foundIcon;
            IconOldLocation = foundIcon.transform.position;
            ItemEngine.SetSelectedItem(item);
        }
    }

    if (SelectedIcon != null)
    {
        SelectedIcon.transform.position = Input.mousePosition;
    }
}
```

Figure 300

First, we make sure that the inventory is being showed. When the player clicks the left mouse button we go through each icon and check if the player clicked on it. We figure out the mouse position on the screen and then check to see if it's inside the bounds of each icon. Another possible implementation would be to put colliders on the icons and raycast to find it. Or you could use the "OnMouseOver" method with a script on each icon. But I choose to implement it this way because looping through each and doing a few "if" statements doesn't get the Unity physics engine involved and helps to improve performance. We can do this since we know exactly where the icons are placed.

If we found that the player clicked on an icon, then we want to mark the item associated with that icon as selected. This means that the icon is shown bigger and the description text for that item is displayed. Then we mark it selected so the icon will follow the mouse by changing the icon's position to be the mouse's position.

Next, we're going to add the "LateUpdate" method shown in Figure 301, which gets called after update. Here is where we handle the button de-press and move the icon back to where it was before the player clicked and dragged it.

```
private void LateUpdate()
{
    if (Input.GetMouseButtonUp(0) && (SelectedIcon != null))
    {
        SelectedIcon.transform.position = IconOldLocation;
        SelectedIcon = null;
        ItemEngine.SetSelectedItem(null);
    }
}
```

Figure 301

```
public void ShowInventory()
{
    float xAdd = -196, yAdd = 165;

    InventoryPanel.SetActive(true);
    ItemDescriptionObj.text = "";

    foreach (Item item in ItemEngine.InventoryGetItem())
    {
        GameObject itemObj = Instantiate(IconPrefab, InventoryPanel.transform);
        Vector3 invPos = InventoryPanel.GetComponent<RectTransform>().position;

        itemObj.transform.name = item.ItemName;
        itemObj.GetComponent<UnityEngine.UI.Image>().sprite = item.Icon;
        invPos.x += xAdd;
        invPos.y += yAdd;
        itemObj.GetComponent<RectTransform>().position = invPos;
        IconObjList.Add(itemObj);

        xAdd += 65;
        if (xAdd > 194)
        {
            xAdd = -196;
            yAdd -= 65; // Add scrolling if > 35 items in inventory
        }
    }
}
```

Figure 302

After that add the method to "ShowInventory" shown in Figure 302. This method shows the inventory window to the player and creates all the item icons in the correct locations.

The "xAdd" variable is the width along the screen to put the icon while "yAdd" is the height up from the middle to put it. The icons will be in a grid layout with 7 icons across and 5 icons down. Then we mark the inventory shown, activate the inventory panel and initialize the description to be blank.

For each (see what I did there?) item in the player's inventory, we instantiate a new icon game object and place it on the inventory panel at the next location in the grid, specified by "xAdd" and "yAdd". Then we add the object to the list so we can clean it up later when the player is done with the inventory. Finally, we update the variables so we can put the icon at the next location. If the row is already 7 elements (we do some math to figure out that is '194') then we reset "xAdd" and move on to the next row.

One way you could improve this code is to make "xAdd", "yAdd" and the row boundaries public variables so you can change them in the inspector so it would be easier to adjust the values.

Note, that if the player is given more than 35 items then the icons will not be displayed correctly. You can either ensure the player will not receive more than that amount or implement scrolling in the inventory so it will be displayed correctly. For this tutorial, we'll ensure no more than 35 items are given to the player.

Playing with the inventory was fun, but we need to clean up our toys when we're done with them. The last method we need to add is to hide the inventory when the player is done with it. You can code up "HideInventory" from Figure 303. We mark the inventory as not shown, inactivate the inventory window, and reset the big image object. Then we go about destroying each of the icons that we created.

```
public void HideInventory()
{
    InventoryPanel.SetActive(false);
    BigImageObj.sprite = null;
    BigImageObj.color = Color.black;
    foreach (GameObject icon in IconObjList) Destroy(icon);
    IconObjList.Clear();
}
```

Figure 303

Game Controller Updates

Now that we've created the scripts necessary to handle inventory management and the inventory user interface, we need to make some changes to the scripts we've already created so we can take full advantage of this feature. We'll start with the "GameController" script.

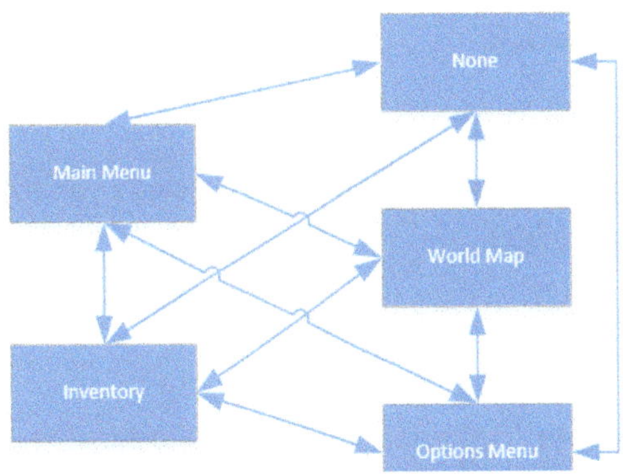

Figure 304

Before we make changes to the script, let's understand how our UI state machine changes by adding this new state. If you remember, our previous diagram looked like a plus sign. The new diagram has 5 states, as seen in Figure 304. We just need to add our "Inventory" state in the bottom left and move things around.

We'll do the same thing when we add our quest journal state later and make this diagram have 6 states. It's good to refresh your memory on the diagram so you can remember how the code works.

First, we need to add the "InvController" public variable so we can get a handle on the inventory user interface as shown in Figure 305. We'll need that when it's time to hide or show the inventory.

```
public GameObject OptionsMenuObj;
public GameObject LoadingPanelObj;
public Inventory InvController;
```

Figure 305

Next, add the "Inventory" value to the UI State enumeration as shown in Figure 306. This is what really adds the new state to the UI state diagram. We'll need to update all the other methods to make sure that they can transition to and from the new state.

```
private enum _ui_state
{
    None,
    WorldMap,
    MainMenu,
    OptionsMenu,
    Inventory
}
```

Figure 306

We can skip the Start method.

We do need to make changes to the "Update method. Add the "else if" statement at the end of the "if" block checking for keyboard depresses as shown in Figure 307. This statement will call the "InventoryHandler" method we will code up in a little bit if the player presses the 'i' key.

```
else if (Input.GetKeyUp(KeyCode.O))
{
    OptionsMenuHandler();
}
else if (Input.GetKeyUp(KeyCode.I))
{
    InventoryHandler();
}
```

Figure 307

In these next set of updates, we'll add the handling for the "Inventory" case when processing the other states. These are the arrows going from the inventory state. Scroll down and update the switch statement in each of these three methods by adding the new case at the end of the other cases but before the default. Keep careful attention to these because they have some key differences.

Update "WorldMapHandler" using code from Figure 308.

```
case _ui_state.Inventory:
    InvController.HideInventory();
    WorldMapSetActive(true);
    uiState = _ui_state.WorldMap;
    break;
```

Figure 308

Update "MainMenuHandler" using code from Figure 309.

```
case _ui_state.Inventory:
    InvController.HideInventory();
    MainMenuObj.SetActive(true);
    uiState = _ui_state.MainMenu;
    break;
```

Figure 309

Update "OptionsMenuHandler" using Figure 310.

```
case _ui_state.Inventory:
    InvController.HideInventory();
    OptionsMenuSetActive(true);
    uiState = _ui_state.OptionsMenu;
    break;
```

Figure 310

After the "OptionsMenuHandler" method add the code for the "InventoryHandler" shown in Figure 311. This is the method that gets called when the player presses the 'i' key on the keyboard.

The actual processing of the method is very similar to the other handler methods for the UI. If the UI is showing the main menu, options menu, or the world map, then we need to hide those windows and show the inventory. If we're already showing the inventory, then hide the inventory. If no window is being displayed, then just show the inventory.

```
public void InventoryHandler()
{
    switch (uiState)
    {
        case _ui_state.MainMenu:
            MainMenuObj.SetActive(false);
            InvController.ShowInventory();
            uiState = _ui_state.Inventory;
            break;
        case _ui_state.OptionsMenu:
            OptionsMenuSetActive(false);
            InvController.ShowInventory();
            uiState = _ui_state.Inventory;
            break;
        case _ui_state.WorldMap:
            WorldMapSetActive(false);
            InvController.ShowInventory();
            uiState = _ui_state.Inventory;
            break;
        case _ui_state.Inventory:
            InvController.HideInventory();
            uiState = _ui_state.None;
            break;
        default:
            // Catch the "None" state here
            InvController.ShowInventory();
            uiState = _ui_state.Inventory;
            break;
    }
}
```

Figure 311

Dialogue Updates

All the code up to this point will track the items and show the player's inventory. But now we need to handle the giving and taking of items to the player. This will happen using the dialogue system. This way, we can give or take items based on choices the player makes in the dialogue.

First, we'll update the "DialogueElement" class so open it up in Visual Studio. Make the changes from Figure 312. We're adding two enumerated types, one starting on line 16 and the other starting on line 22. These will not only support giving and taking items, but also allowing us to require the player use an item on an actor.

If the name of the item matches "CondName" then the condition is met, then the dialogue will start. Likewise, if the action is to give or take an item to or from the player's inventory.

```
10      public string Text;
11      public _cond_type CondType;
12      public string CondName;
13      public _action Action;
14      public string ActionName;
15
        2 references
16      public enum _cond_type
17      {
18          None,
19          Item
20      }
21
        3 references
22      public enum _action
23      {
24          None,
25          GiveItem,
26          TakeItem
27      }
```

Figure 312

```
79      public void StartDialogue(Dialogue dia)
80      {
81          if (!curDia)
82          {
83              bool startDialogue = true;
84
85              string selItem = "";
86              if (ItemEngine.GetSelectedItem() != null)
87              {
88                  selItem = ItemEngine.GetSelectedItem().ItemName;
89              }
90
91              if (dia.Lines[0].CondType == DialogueElement._cond_type.Item)
92              {
93                  if (selItem != dia.Lines[0].CondName)
94                  {
95                      startDialogue = false;
96                  }
97                  else
98                  {
99                      ItemEngine.SetSelectedItem(null);
100                 }
101             }
102
103             if (startDialogue)
104             {
105                 curDia = dia;
106                 diaIndex = 0;
107                 DialoguePanel.SetActive(true);
108                 gc.InvController.HideInventory();
109                 ProcessElement();
110             }
111             else
112             {
113                 gc.EndDialogue();
114             }
115         }
116     }
```

Figure 313

Next open the script "DialogueController" and scroll down to line 79 to update the "StartDialogue" method as shown in Figure 313. We add a bool named "startDialogue" which we will set only if there are conditions and they have been met. If they have been met, the dialogue is started on line 99.

On line 88, we get the selected item if there is one. Then on line 93 we check if that matches the item listed in the condition of the dialogue.

Don't forget! Line 104 adds code to hide the inventory if the dialogue is started. It would look wrong to have the inventory panel covering up the dialogue.

```
167                 case DialogueElement._response_type.End:
168                     waitForClick = true;
169                     ContinueText.SetActive(true);
170                     break;
171             }
172 
173             switch (curDia.Lines[diaIndex].Action)
174             {
175                 case DialogueElement._action.GiveItem:
176                     ItemEngine.InventoryAddItem(curDia.Lines[diaIndex].ActionName);
177                     break;
178                 case DialogueElement._action.TakeItem:
179                     ItemEngine.InventoryRemItem(curDia.Lines[diaIndex].ActionName);
180                     break;
181             }
182         }
183         else
184         {
185             EndDialogue();
186         }
```

Figure 314

Now scroll down to the method "ProcessElement". From Figure 314, add the switch statement starting on line 165. If the dialogue element or line has the action to give or take an item, then use the "ActionName" as the item to add or remove from the player's inventory.

Inventory User Interface

The player's inventory will lay out the items in a grid (7 columns with 5 rows each). The selected item's icon will be shown bigger, and the description will be displayed to the player. We will not implement scrolling in this tutorial so we have a 35-item max that can be displayed.

In the Hierarchy View under the "Canvas", create a new UI > Image as a child object named "InventoryWindow". As shown in Figure 315

, set the anchor to "top" and "left". This keeps the window in the upper-left corner for different screen resolutions. Then set the position, height, and width.

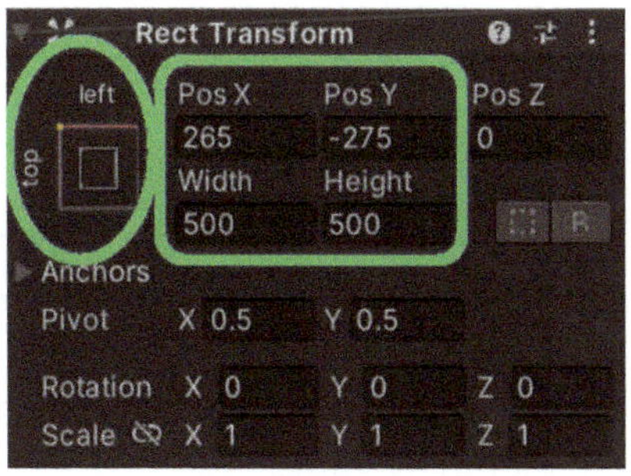

Figure 315

We'll use the RPG GUI for the UI graphics again. In the Project View, go to Assets > Images > RPG GUI > Texture > Form > Inventory and drag the "Form" image to the Source image. It will look similar to the dialogue window but have a lighter section at the bottom.

Create another UI Image as a child object under "InventoryWindow" named "BigIconObj". Set the Rect Transform to Pos X='-180', Pos Y='-185', PosZ='0', Width='100', and Height='100' like in Figure 316. Then set the Source Image to "slots_icon" in Assets > Images > RPG GUI > Texture > Slots. This is the image that shows the selected icon.

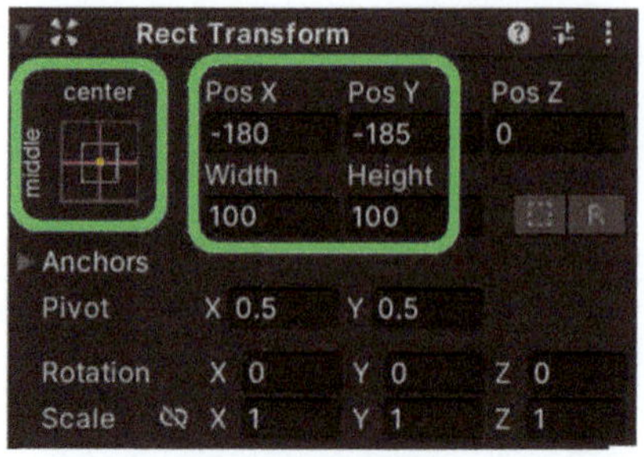

Figure 316

Right-click on the "InventoryWindow" and select UI > Text - TextMeshPro named "Title". Set the Rect Transform to Pos X='0', Pos Y='215', Pos Z='0', Width='200', and Height='50'. Then change the Text to "Inventory", Font size to '36', and set the alignment to center. The rect transform should look like Figure 317.

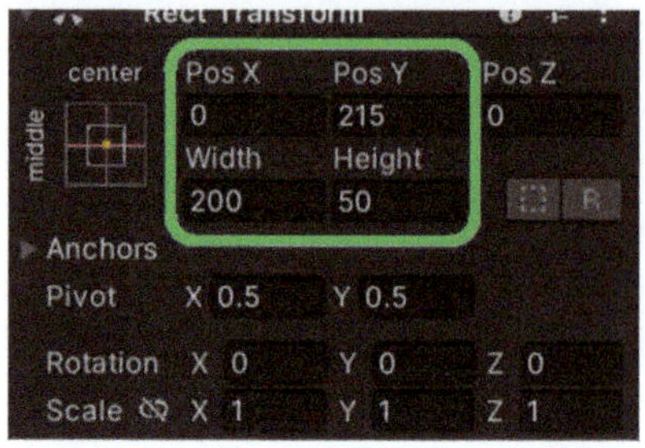

Figure 317

Copy and paste the title and rename the new text object to "Description". Then set the Rect Transform to the values shown in Figure 318 where PosX='58', PosY='-188', PosZ='0', Width='350', and Height='90' like in Figure 318. This text object will be where we display the name of the object and the description, so the player knows what it is and has hints on what it's used for. Set the Font Size of the text to '16'.

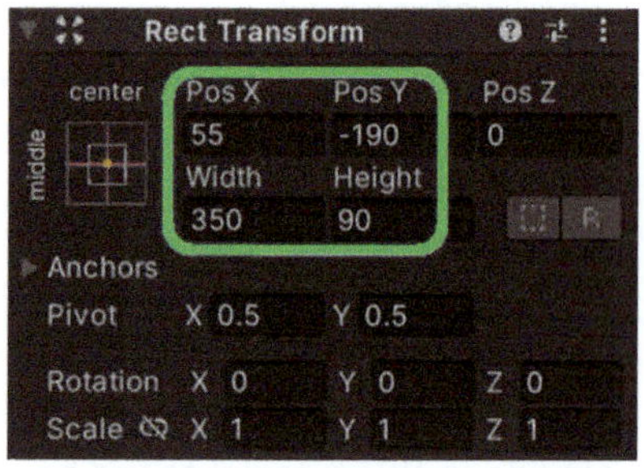

Figure 318

For the inventory slots, we're going to create a prefab that will be instantiated in our inventory panel. Create a new Image named "Slot". Set the Width='50' and Height='50'. The Rect Transform should look like Figure 319. Drag it to Assets > Prefabs > UI to save a prefab. After the prefab is saved you can delete the "Slot" object in the Hierarchy View.

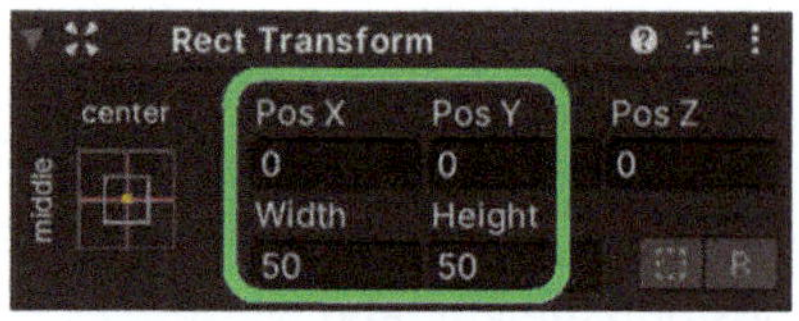

Figure 319

With all the UI objects in place, the inventory panel should look like Figure 320 in the Scene View. The Hierarchy View should have the "InventoryPanel" as a child object of the "Canvas". Then there are three child objects under "InventoryPanel" which are: BigIcon, Title, and Description.

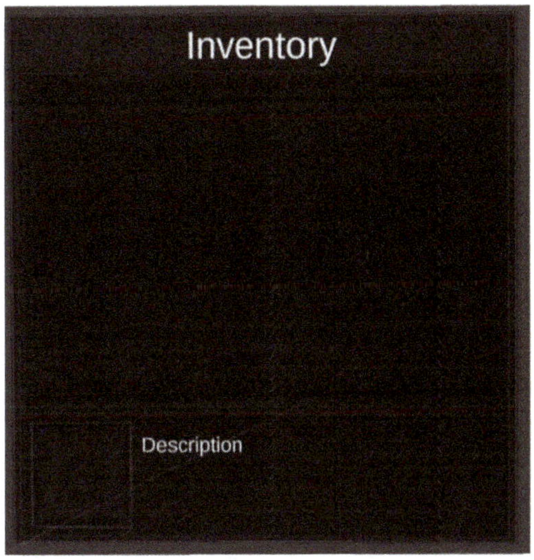

Figure 320

Gluing the Inventory Together

We created scripts and now we're done with the inventory user interface, it's time to bring them all together so they can live in Unity (Yes! Another successful pun). First, we need to create our "Inventory" controller object, so create an empty game object named "Inventory" and drag the "Inventory" script onto it. I like to drag it higher up in the Hierarchy View so that it is next to the other controllers like the game controller and the dialogue controller. Something similar to Figure 321.

Figure 321

Set the Big Image Obj to the Canvas > InventoryPanel > BigIcon object. Set the Item Description Obj to the Canvas > InventoryPanel > Description object. Set the Inventory Panel to the Canvas > InventoryPanel object. And finally, drag the prefab "InventorySlot" from Assets > Prefabs > UI in the Hierarchy View to the Icon Prefab field.

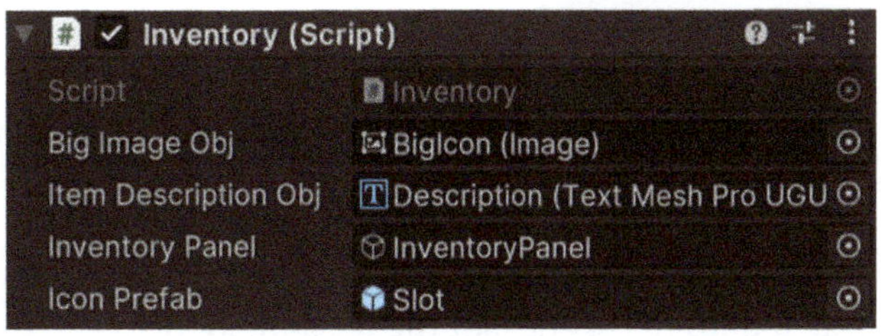

Figure 322

Next click on the "GameController" object in the Hierarchy View. You should see the Inv Controller field appear. Drag the "Inventory" object from the Hierarchy View onto that field. This will let the game controller tell the inventory when to hide and show itself.

With those things glued together, we're ready to create some items. Before we do that, we need to fix some of the images we'll use as icons. Go to Assets > Images > Icons in the Hierarchy View and you'll see some really odd-looking pictures. Click on the "Hyssop1" image and, in the inspector, change the Texture Type to "Sprite (2D and UI)". Scroll down to the bottom of the inspector and click "Apply". Now you can see that the image looks like some of the hyssop plant with red stuff on it. What is that red stuff? No spoilers! You'll have to keep reading to find out.

The textures are set in "Default" mode. This means Unity thinks they are for putting onto a 3D object like a model. Telling Unity to configure the texture as a sprite. Go ahead and repeat the above process for the UnleavenedBread image.

Note that for other icons we want to use as images, we will need to change their texture type too. You can either do that now or will need to do it later when it comes up in the respective chapters. The good thing is that you can highlight all the images while holding the CTRL key and make this change to all of them at the same time to save time.

That sets up the icons we're going to use for our items. Now click back on the "Inventory" object in the Hierarchy View. Drag the "Item" script from Assets > Scripts in the Project View, over to the inspector of the "Inventory". Now do it again. We're creating three different items.

Add the item names and descriptions to these items as shown in Figure 323. Go back to the Assets > Images > Icons folder for the "Jar", "Hyssop2" and "UnleavenedBread" images used as the icons for the respective items.

Description for the Hyssop: "This plant was used to paint the doorframes of the house with the blood of the sacrificed lamb."

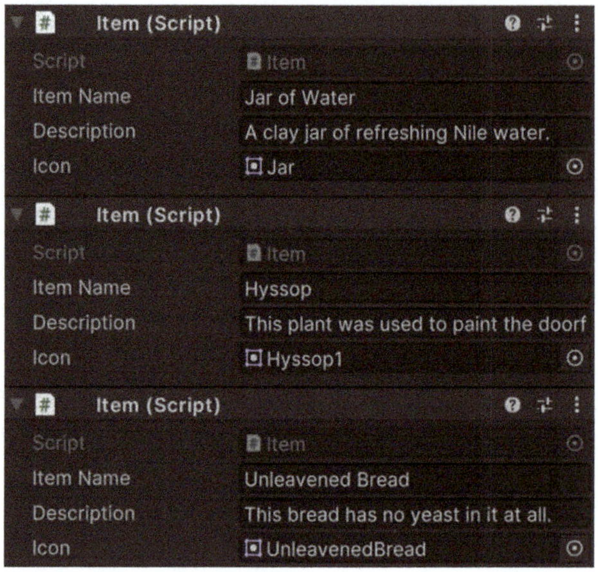

Figure 323

Satisfy your Thirst

The last thing we need to do to test out our inventory is to give the player an item. And of course, we'll want test out item conditions on dialogues. We need to see if this inventory management system can hold water. And what better way than with a clay jar!

In the Project View search bar, type "Pot_1" and drag it onto the scene. Set the position in the transform to Pos X='1062', Pos Y='16.1', and Pos Z ='1556'. Press 'F' to focus on the jar and you'll see that it is placed nearby a river. See Figure 324.

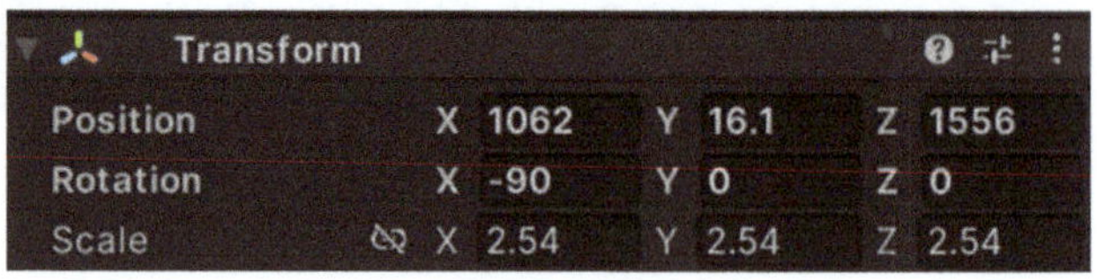

Figure 324

Add a Box Collider to the pot, or jar as we're going to keep calling it. Remember, you can do this by looking in the inspector, clicking the "Add Component" button, and searching for "box", or in the Main Menu choosing Component > Physics > Box Collider. We can leave the default attributes for it.

Next add an Actor Controller script and a Dialogue script onto the jar. We don't need to make any changes to the Actor Controller. For the Dialogue, there will be three lines. The first line asks if the player wants to take the char and gives them a choice. See Figure 325.

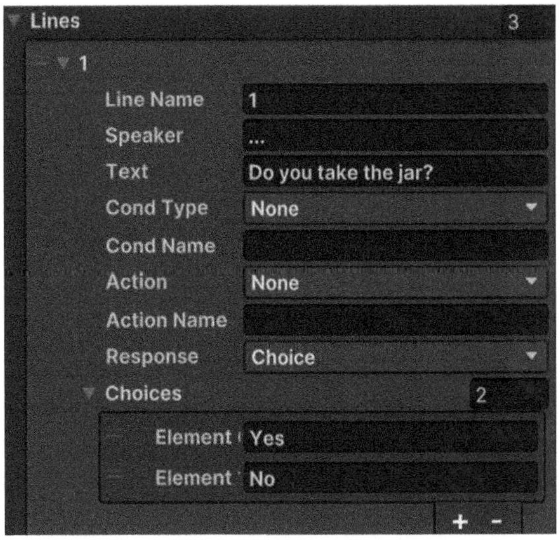

Figure 325

The second line is for the "Yes" response, see Figure 326. It lets the player know that they received the Jar of Water. Then, under actions, we give it to them. The Response is "End" to stop the rest of the dialogue.

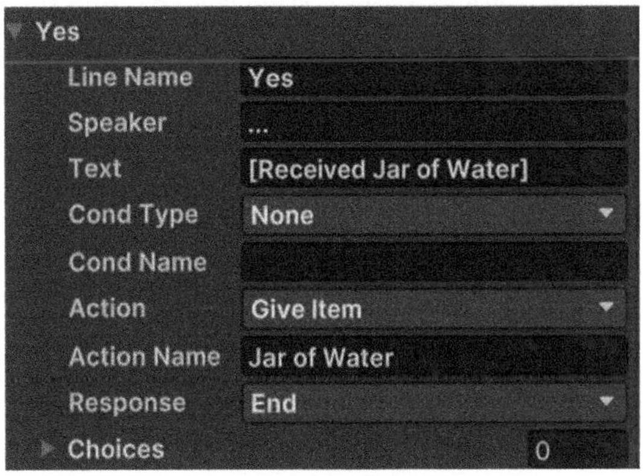

Figure 326

The third and last line is for the "No" response, see Figure 327. We tell the player that they left the jar and just end the dialogue.

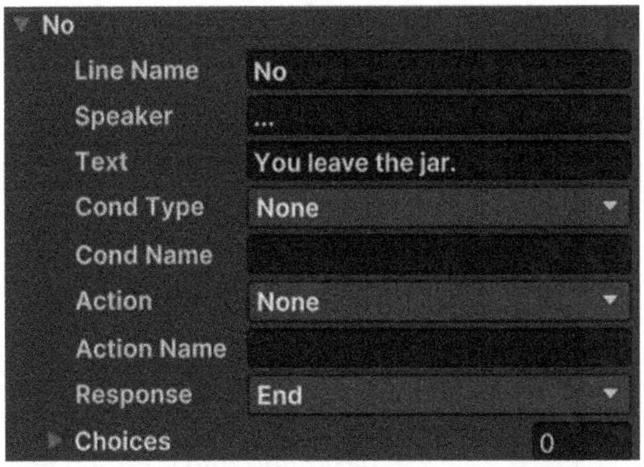

Figure 327

With the jar of water done, let's add a thirsty slave who is waiting for you to give them some refreshment. From Assets > Prefabs, grab the "EgyptianSlave" and place him onto the scene. Set his transform to what you see in Figure 328.

Figure 328

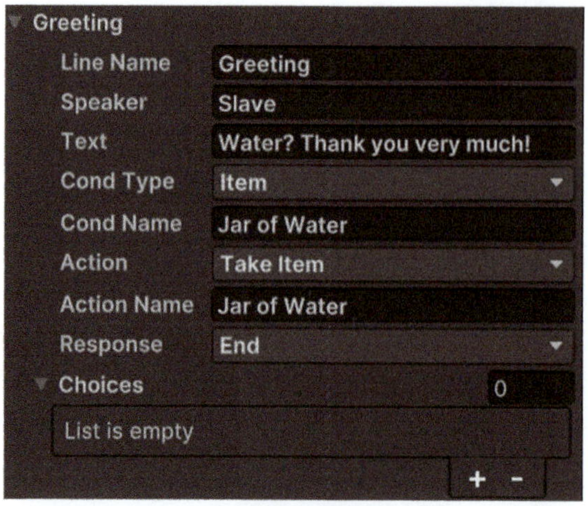

Figure 329

He already has an Actor Controller, but you can set the Action Type to "Idle" and delete the "Painting2" string in the Animation field. Then add the Dialogue script and add the line shown in Figure 329. We set the condition type or "Cond Type" to "Item". Then we name the item in "Cond Name" to the "Jar of Water". The Action is to "Take Item" on the "Jar of Water". Then the slave thanks the player for the water.

Let's test it out. Press play mode and it will show your introduction cut scene. When it is done, walk over to the slave. Don't be afraid to use the Scene View if you're not sure where he is. He should ignore you. Then march on down to the river where we left the jar of water. When you click it, you can select Yes or No. If no, then nothing happens. But if you click yes then the dialogue tells you that you received it. Then when you click 'i' to view your inventory, you will see the jar icon. Clicking the jar icon, it shows up in the big icon and gives you a description of the item.

Press 'i' again to close the inventory. Then walk uphill back to the slave. If you talk to him nothing will happen (definition of insanity, right). But if you open the inventory, drag the jar of water to the slave, and then release the mouse button, he will take away the jar and thank you. You can confirm the jar was indeed taken away by opening your inventory again.

Now Moses can do things with items! One problem, however, is that after Moses picks up the clay jar, it is still there. We'll add the ability to make objects disappear in later chapters. Going further, you can implement all the items described in the GDD. Use the same process to create those as we did for the Hyssop, Jar of Water, and Unleavened Bread above.

Chapter 11 – Building Levels

A big part of developing games is level design. This refers to actually making the floors or terrain, trees, houses, and other things the player walks among. Placing people, puzzles, and obstacles are also part of level design.

You can think of a level as a scene in Unity. For the "Egypt_Nile Scene", much of this level is already designed for us. The terrain has been created with textures painted on to look like desert, grass, stones, and rocks. The city was there for us to walk around in. There just wasn't any people or puzzles or anything else.

In this chapter, we're going to build some levels up from scratch. These will be indoor levels for the pyramid and the Pharaoh's palace.

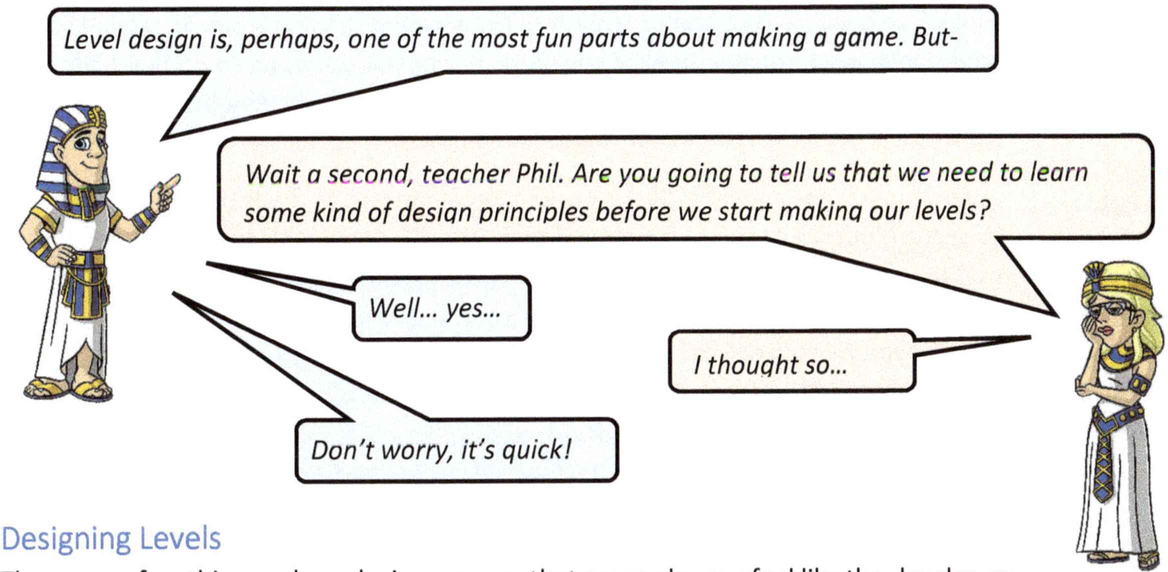

Designing Levels

There are a few things, when playing a game, that can make you feel like the developers didn't spend as much time or money on the game as they should have. Sometimes it may be true, but other times it may just be they didn't think through the level with these things in mind.

The parts of the level should flow together naturally. Or if it doesn't then there ought to be a good reason given to the player as early as possible. Having an old English cottage house in the middle of a modern city is not believable. But if that house is part of a historic district of the city and used for tours, and possibly old secrets to explore, then they are more likely to believe your level design.

Break out a pen and paper or your paint program of choice and draw a map of all the parts of the level. If it's an indoor location where people live in, then try putting yourself in the shoes of people who live there. Where do they sleep? Where do they eat? How about a kitchen? Are there guards? If so, should there be an armory to store weapons?

When you're done mapping out your level and have started implementing it, think about what each area is and what would be inside it. Consider all the resources you have at your disposal to populate the level. What 2D or 3D art assets do you have, or would you need? If you're putting together a throne room then you probably need some of these: 1) a throne, 2) some nice decorations on the wall, 3) lampstands or something else to provide light at night, and 4) others.

One thing that can be hard to balance is creating prefabs and reusing content versus making it all new. If you reuse too much, then the players will see it but if you don't reuse enough then it can take a lot longer to make your levels. It can be hard to find where the right line to draw is on this at first. The best way is to decide up-front what prefabs you will have to reuse.

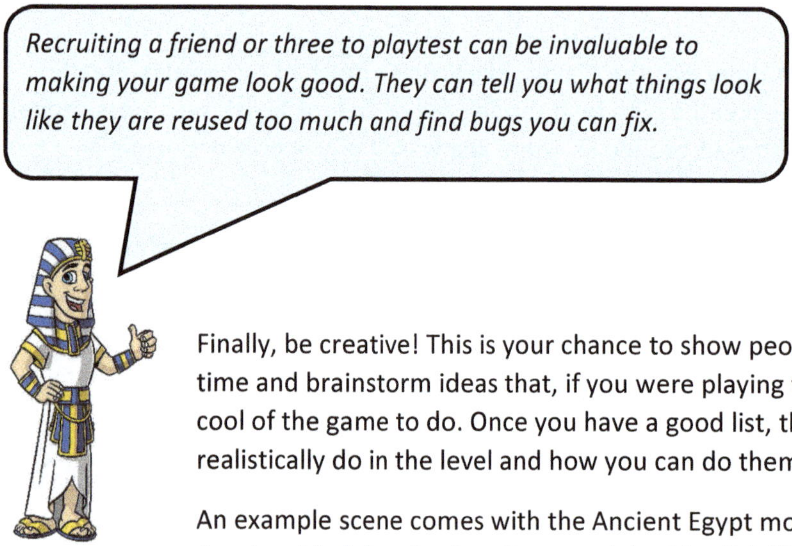

It is important to get the big things in the different areas right, but don't forget the little things. It is usually the sum of the little things that really pull the player into the game.

Finally, be creative! This is your chance to show people what you can do. Spend some time and brainstorm ideas that, if you were playing the game, you'd think are pretty cool of the game to do. Once you have a good list, think about which ideas you could realistically do in the level and how you can do them.

An example scene comes with the Ancient Egypt models. In the Project View, go to Assets > Models > Ancient Egypt and double-click "Dungeon_1". In the Hierarchy View, click the "Parts" object and focus on it in the Scene View. This example gives you an idea of what you can do with the building blocks given. Push the play button and give it a try! The controls are like the FPS that we had in the "Egypt_Nile Scene" before we added our 3rd person controller. Explore the area and try to notice all the objects in the scene. We won't be building this setup; this is just an example. You'll be able to use your creativity to make your own.

Starting from Scratch

Now let's get started building Pharaoh's palace. Create a new scene like we did for the Title scene by going to File > New Scene. When it finishes loading, save it as "Palace Scene" in the Scenes folder under Assets. In the Project View, from Assets > Models > Ancient Egypt > Models > Temple Parts, drag "DT_EndDoor" onto the scene and set the Transform Position to all zeroes.

The models in this folder can be thought of as building blocks, rather literally. We'll be putting these building blocks together to make the palace.

Rotate the Scene View around so you can get a good look at the different sides of it. One thing that you'll notice is that you when you are behind the wall you can see through it (see Figure 330). This isn't a bug, it's a feature! If we couldn't see through the walls from behind it, then it would be much harder to design our level because we wouldn't be able to see anything inside. But now, we can see the mural on the door, the stones, and the other side of the wall.

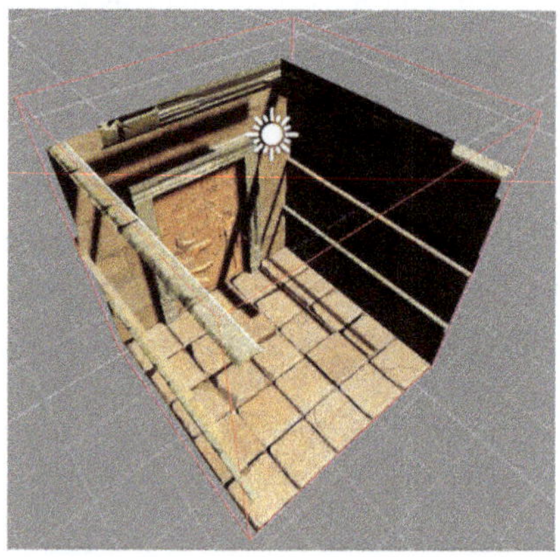

Figure 330

Before we put our Moses player here, we want to change the camera a little bit. Go to Assets > Prefabs and Double-click on "MosesPlayer". This opens the Prefab in Scene View. You can tell if you're looking at a prefab or the actual scene by the blue background as shown in Figure 331. This is how you can edit the child objects in prefabs.

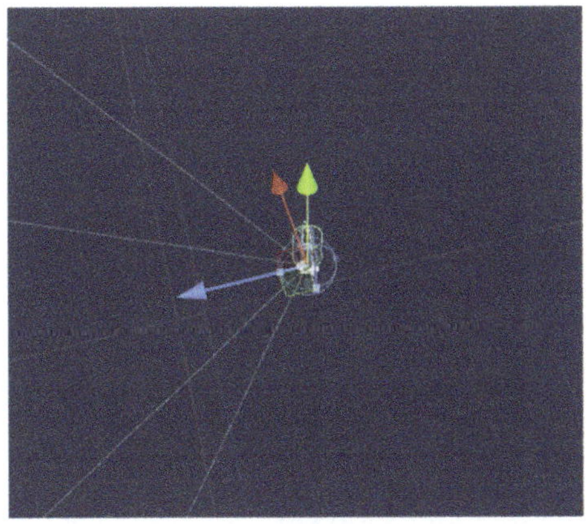

Figure 331

Click the "Camera" child object and, in the inspector, change the "Background" color to black. That field changes the color shown when there is nothing else to show the player. Since black is a very unobtrusive color, it will help to hide where some halls may not align exactly as shadows. Changes are automatically saved.

To exit prefab mode, look to the upper left of the Hierarchy View and click the less than symbol or '<' as shown in Figure 332. This takes you back to the normal Scene View.

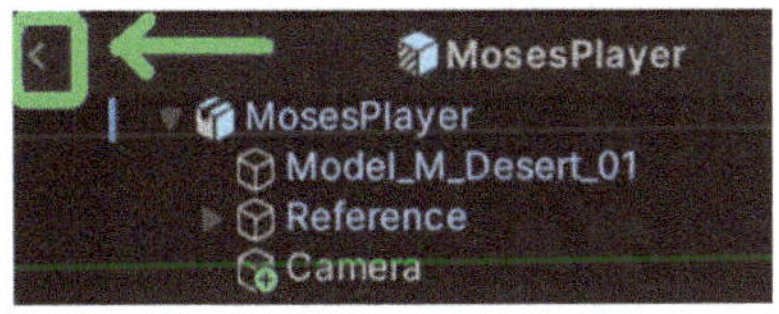

Figure 332

Create a new object called "GameController" and drag the script of the same name onto it from Assets > Scripts.

Glancing at the inspector, you'll see all the public variables that we have been making in our outdoor Egypt scene. But fear not! We don't have to start from scratch. We know what objects we need, so we can minimize our work by creating one prefab to rule them all! This prefab will have everything we need to make a new scene playable. Open the "Egypt_Nile Scene".

The "GameController" object will be the parent for everything. First, reset the transform of the game controller, this sets it back to all zeros and will help other objects act the same. Drag the "Canvas" object as a child object underneath the "GameController" object. Next the "DialogueController", "PlayerPos", "MiniMapCam", "WorldMapCam", "CineCam", and "Inventory. It should look like Figure 333. At this point, save the "GameController" as a prefab in Assets > Prefabs. Let's save the scene and then open the "Palace".

Figure 333

One more thing before we're done! In the "GameController" prefab, set the number of the Zone Objects array to '0'. This will ensure that our game controller for each scene starts with fresh new zones.

When the scene loads, drag the "GameController" prefab onto the Hierarchy View. Make sure the Transform is reset so the position and rotation are all zero. You'll notice that all the variables are set except for three: the Player, Intro Cine, and Intro Objects.

They are easy enough though. For the Player, drag "MosesPlayer" from the Hierarchy View over to fill it. For the Intro Cine, create an empty object named "PalaceIntro", in the Timeline View click "Create", and save it as "PalaceIntroTimeline" in Assets > Timelines. Then drag it into the Intro Cine field. For the Intro Objects just create an empty game object named "PalaceIntroObjs" and drag it into that field. Finally, set the Player object in the "MiniMapCam" object to the "MosesPlayer".

Try playing the scene and you'll see something like Figure 334. Moses is standing at the edge of the abyss! Don't jump down. Don't jump. Don't do it! Hey, I told you not to jump. Now Moses is going to fall endlessly until you stop play mode.

Figure 334

Let's try adding another block to our palace. Go back to the Project View and in Assets > Models > Ancient Egypt > Models > TempleParts drag DT_1 onto the scene. Set the Position to '0', '0', '-6'. You should see that Moses now has a little more room to run.

We can just keep adding more and more building blocks to the scene, but it would soon get overwhelming to find anything in the Hierarchy View. Create an empty object there and name it "Palace". Set the transform position to all 0s. Now make the "DT_EndDoor" and the "DT_1" children of the "Palace" object. We'll keep all our palace models organized there.

Copy and paste the "DT_1" object and set the 'Z' of the new object to '-12'. Do it again and set the 'Z' to '-18'. Now we've got the beginnings of a nice little hallway.

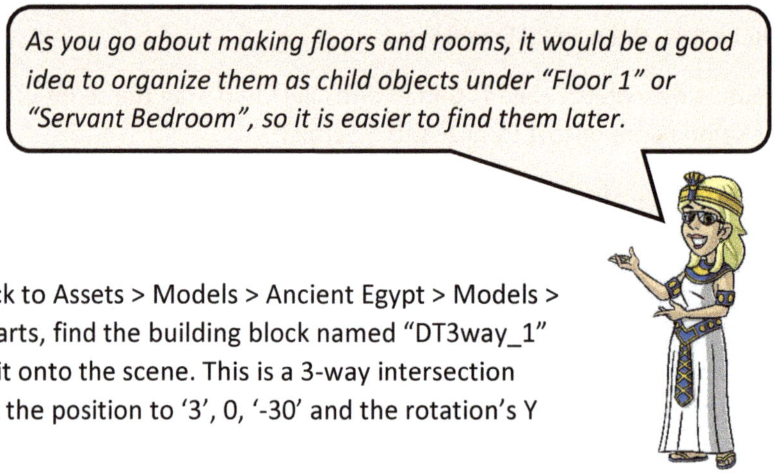

Figure 335

Going back to Assets > Models > Ancient Egypt > Models > Temple Parts, find the building block named "DT3way_1" and drag it onto the scene. This is a 3-way intersection piece. Set the position to '3', 0, '-30' and the rotation's Y to '90'.

If you zoom in on the building block you can see that it doesn't line up very well to the other piece, as seen in Figure 335. We'll have to manually change the position, so it fits. Click the 3-way intersection object in the scene view to highlight it. Then rotate the camera so you can see the biggest gap in the wall. Then click the green arrow to move the transform along the 'Y' axis until the gap is no longer visible. Press CTRL and left click on the object so it isn't highlighted anymore.

This doesn't fix our problem yet. Remember that players could look at the model going either way down the hall. You need to look at the seam between the objects from both sides and make sure there is no gap. Use the transform tool to move the object along the axis as before. Then when it looks good, pop back over to the other angle and look. Bounce back and forth until it looks good from both angles.

Paste another "DT_1" and set the Position to '12', '0', and '-30'. Also, set the Y rotation to '90'. This gets the new building block fitting close to where the intersection veers left. Use the method described above to get it as close as you can.

Luckily, we don't have to do this every time. Once you've lined up a particular model to the others you can copy and paste it to preserve the location. Then when you move it along the axis hold the CTRL key and it will move the object in units of '1'.

Watch out for the 'Y' position of the object when you copy and paste. Sometimes Unity will change it slightly and it won't line up with the rest of the building blocks. If that happens, just check the 'Y' position of a correct building block and copy it over to the new one.

Break out your favorite scissors and white glue because we're going to do a lot of copying and pasting now. Copy and paste the ""DT3way_1" object and try using the CTRL trick to move it in the negative Z direction so the Z position is about '-48'. Give the seams a once over to make sure there are no gaps. Paste another copy and position it the same way to about '-66', making sure there are no gaps in the seams.

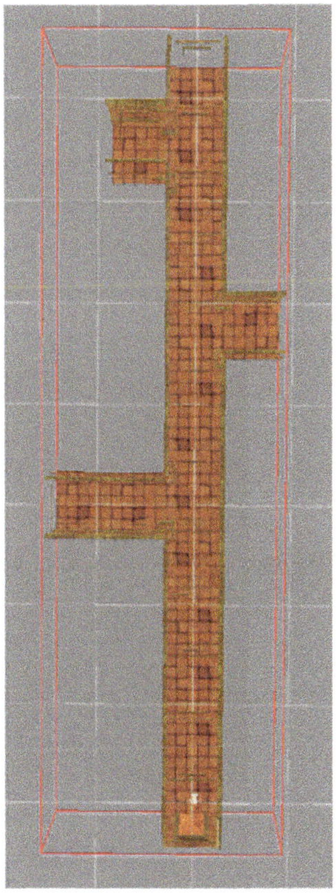

Figure 336

If you zoom out and look at the scene from overhead, it should look like Figure 336. This is going to be a long hallway that leads to the stairs up to Pharaoh's throne room. Give the hallway a play-through to really get a feeling of the work you've done. You may find that there are still some graphics glitches (parts where the gap between the models is visible). These little glitches won't affect gameplay, only how the game looks.

Throne Room

Figure 337

Pharaoh's palace would be pretty poor indeed if it didn't have a throne room, so that's what we'll build next. The throne room will be on the second floor, so we're going to need a staircase to get up there. Go back to the same folder we've been going to for our building blocks (Assets > Models > Ancient Egypt > Models > Temple Parts) and drag over the "DT_Stairs" object. Set the position to '0', '5.5', and '-84' and then adjust the position to fix all the gaps so it looks like Figure 337.

Now let's get started on the actual throne room itself with the floor, so we have something to walk on. From the same folder find the "foundations_floor" prefab and drag that onto the scene with the position '0', '-27', and '0'. Adjust the height (the blue axis going with the arrow going up) of the foundation to line up with the top of the stairs so there aren't any glitches.

We'll need more than a single floor tile to make a throne room. Copy/paste it and drag the new tile up the X axis so that it is flush against the other tile. Be watchful so you don't have a glitch between them. The new X position should be about '8.45'. Do the same thing again and set the new tile around '16.9' on the X axis. Create another copy, but this time copy the X position of the 2nd tile (about '8.5') and paste it into the X position for the new tile and make it negative by putting a '-' in front of the number. This way will save you the time of lining up the tiles. Do the same trick for the next tile which would be about '-16.9'.

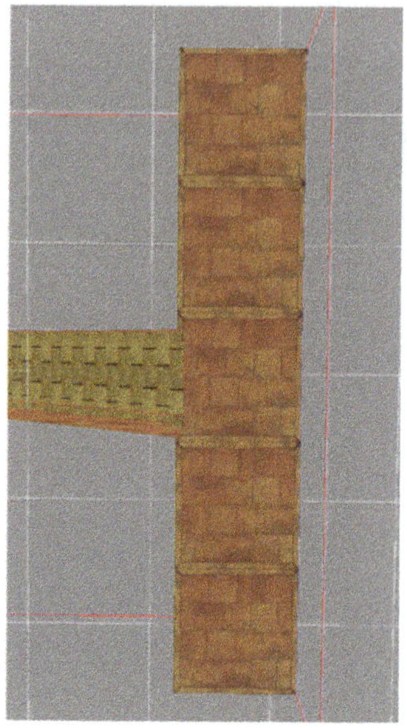

Figure 338

You should now have a column of tiles that look like Figure 338. Put your Scene View in a similar position overhead because now we're going to copy and paste the entire column. Highlight the whole column by clicking on the top tile and then hold down the SHIFT key as you click on each tile underneath. You can see that they all are highlighted in orange now.

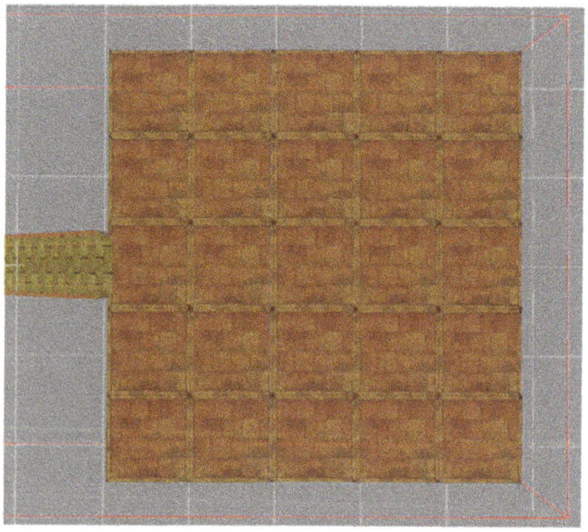

Figure 339

Press CTRL+C and CTRL+V to create a copy of the column. Then, with the new column still highlighted, move it along the Z axis so they fit nice and snug against the other column. You'll likely need to hide the highlighting so you can see any glitches. Just click on the gray part of the scene without any objects to deselect the tiles. If you need to make adjustments, then you can press CTRL+Z (or the undo hotkey) to select the whole column again and drag it where you want it to go.

Do that 3 more times and you'll end up with a square with 5 columns and rows as shown in Figure 339. Go ahead and give it another play-through. As you go through, note any glitches you see so you can fix them later. Enjoy the fruits of your labor now. Next up are the walls and ceiling. As we go through building the rest of the level, feel free to stop and play through what you've made so far.

Raising the Roof

From the same "Temple Parts" folder we've been getting our hallway, stairs, and floor tiles from, find "T_wall2" and place it next to the stairs at about position '7.25', '-31.7', and '6.8'. Then find "T_corner2" and place it next to that wall segment at about position '17.2', '-27.9', and '6.8'. Since the corner isn't facing the right way, we need to rotate it by setting the Y rotation to '180'. Now get "T_ColumnWall" and place it on the other side of the corner piece around position '21', -18', and '6.85'. Set the Z Rotation of it to '-90'. After that, visually inspect the seams for glitches and use the transform tool to fix them. You may find that after you adjust one object to fix a glitch that you'll have to fix other objects. This is normal since the positions are relative to each other. In the end, the corner should look like Figure 340.

Figure 340

With one corner of the room done, we'll use the same trick that we did for the tiles, so we don't have to adjust for glitches on the other side of the stairs. Highlight the "T_wall2" object in the Hierarchy View, copy and paste it, and set the X value to the negative of what you previously set it. Then do the same with the other 2 objects. Once again, the corner isn't the correct orientation. Fix it by setting the Y Rotation to 0. Look over it and make sure there aren't any glitches. If you find one, it is likely also in the other corner too, so you'll want to fix it there. If all went well then it should look like Figure 341.

Figure 341

Next, highlight the 2 "T_ColumnWall" objects in the Hierarchy View and copy them to move the new objects next to the empty objects. Copy one of the corners and move it to the other side of the "T_ColumnWall" objects. You'll need to rotate it and adjust the transform so there aren't any glitches. Do the same for the other corner. At this point you'll notice that the floor keeps going outside the room. This is ok. The player won't be able to see it through the walls.

Figure 342

Now make a copy of one of the "T_ColumnWall" objects and put it next to one of the corners. You'll need to set the Z Rotation to '0' and check for glitches. Make a copy of it and change the sign of the X position (add a '-' or take it away). Finally, make a copy of the "T_wall2" object and place it between the two "T_ColumnWall" objects so it fills the gap right across from the stairs. If it isn't long enough you can adjust the Y Scale to make it fit. The whole wall should look like Figure 342.

The only thing that's left is the space above the stairs. We're going to fill that with some blocks. Go to Assets > Models > Ancient Egypt > Models > Temple Parts > RuinParts and find "Block1". Drag it into the scene and set the transform to what is shown in Figure 343. Move the block so that it lines up against the wall and the stair ceiling.

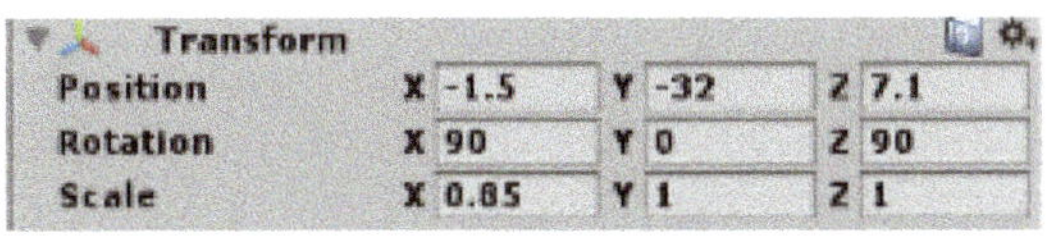

Figure 343

Figure 344

Copy/Paste and move the blocks to fill the gap above the stairs. 8 blocks should be enough to do the trick and will look similar to Figure 344. Setting 3 blocks going up will be enough for the wall above the stairs. 2 more blocks are also needed on the top left and right so that the player cannot look through the molding at the top of the other wall pieces. Since these blocks are squares, if you want to give them a less patterned look you can adjust the Z rotation by '90', '180', and '270' in some of the blocks. This helps avoid the player getting the impression you are reusing the same model for each block.

Next up is the roof (get it?). For that, we're going to use the "T_ceiling" prefab that's in Assets > Models > Ancient Egypt > Models > Temple Parts. Drag it onto the scene and place it at '16', -27', and '14'. It should look like Figure 345. As before, check all the seams for glitches. Once you are satisfied, copy, and paste it, and then move it along the X axis (red arrow) using the transform tool. Check for glitches between the two ceiling tiles.

Figure 345

You may notice that the ceiling tile has no sides. If you position the Scene View to look diagonally down into the room, then it looks like there is a gap between the ceiling and the walls. But if you position the Scene View to look up at the ceiling tiles, then there is no gap. Since these ceiling tiles aren't meant to be viewed from the side (top and bottom only) leaving the sides off helps improve performance by reducing the workload on the graphics card. This is a common trick that 3D modelers use to improve performance in games. And the player doesn't know the difference!

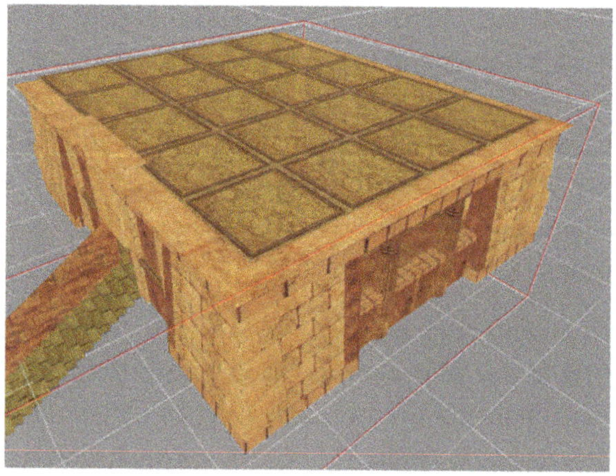

Figure 346

Now copy and paste the rest of the column to have a total of 5 ceiling tiles using this process. Give it another once over with your eyeballs to see if there are any glitches. Now highlight the whole column and copy/paste it 3 times, moving it along the green arrow toward the other side of the room. At this point, it should look like Figure 346 and totally cover the ceiling of the throne room.

The process of going back to make the game look and feel higher quality is called "polishing" and is an important part of making a game.

Whew, that was a lot of work. Give the level a play-through and enjoy running around the new room you created which will look like **Error! Reference source not found.**. Take note of any glitches you see to fix later. Don't feel bad if you keep finding glitches or can't get all of them out. Just do your best. If you spend all your time trying to make the levels look perfect, you won't have time adding the features that make the game fun. It is better to get it looking good enough for now, adding all the features you need, and then going back to fix these things. Get the scene into the game by going to the main menu and selecting File > Build Settings... and click the button to "Add Open Scenes". It should show up as the third on the list, or index number '2'.

Figure 347

Transitioning Scenes

Now that we've had a good warmup by building part of Pharaoh's palace, let's write some C# code to glue this scene to the Egypt scene so they can both live in Unity (Yes! I still got it). In the Project View under Assets > Scripts, create a new C# script named "SceneEngine" and open it in Visual Studio. This script will handle the scene transitions for the whole game.

Add the code shown in Figure 347. Note that we mark the class itself as static. This means that you cannot make an instance of the class using the "new" keyword and the compiler will flag an error for each variable or method in the class that isn't marked as static. This helps prevent bugs from using the class in a way it wasn't intended.

```
using UnityEngine;
using UnityEngine.SceneManagement;

0 references
static public class SceneEngine
{
    static public string NewSceneName;
    static public Vector3 NewPlayerPos;

    0 references
    static public void LoadScene(int index)
    {
        SceneManager.LoadScene(index);
    }

    0 references
    static public void LoadScene(string name)
    {
        if (GetCurrentSceneName() != name)
        {
            SceneManager.LoadScene(name);
        }
    }
```

Figure 347

The variables hold the new scene to load and the position to put the player after the scene is loaded. Being static, they will remain the same value when the scene changes. Only static variables remain the same when the scene changes. This is what we want since this information must be preserved if so, we can spawn the player at the right spot. There will be three methods to change scenes but two of them are written above. The caller of the method can use either the scene name or index. Remember, that is the index in the Build Settings.

```
24      static public void LoadScene(string name, Vector3 pos, GameObject player = null)
25      {
26          if (GetCurrentSceneName() != name)
27          {
28              NewSceneName = name;
29              NewPlayerPos = pos;
30              LoadScene(name);
31          }
32          else if (player != null)
33          {
34              player.transform.position = pos;
35          }
36      }
37
        2 references
38      static public string GetCurrentSceneName()
39      {
40          return SceneManager.GetActiveScene().name;
41      }
42  }
```

Figure 348

The third method to load a new scene is in Figure 348. Notice that the bottom two check if the current scene is the same as the scene the caller wants to load. If it is, we save them the trouble and do not re-load the scene. On lines 28 and 29 of the third method, we will set the position of the player in the new scene. Then on line 33, if it is the same scene and the player object is given then we'll just change the position of the player.

Another way to change scenes is when the player walks through a door or something. This means we need a collider for the player to touch. But first let's write the code. Create another script named "SceneTransition" and add the code in Figure 349. Whenever the player collides with the object that has this script, the "GameEngine" will load the scene we specify here and then the "GameController" will place the player where we specified. Now, you may protest saying, "We never coded the game controller to do that!" Don't worry, we'll do it next.

```
public class SceneTransition : MonoBehaviour
{
    public string SceneName;
    public Vector3 PlayerPos;
    public GameController gc;

    Unity Message | 0 references
    private void OnCollisionEnter(Collision col)
    {
        if (col.transform.tag == "Player")
        {
            gc.LoadingPanelObj.SetActive(true);
            SceneEngine.LoadScene(SceneName, PlayerPos);
        }
    }
}
```

Figure 349

But first we need to initialize the Scene Engine in the Title Controller. Open the "TitleController" in Visual Studio and add lines 33 and 34 shown in Figure 351. Setting the "NewSceneName" to an empty string means there is no scene change which is important, so the first scene doesn't change the position of the player to something we don't intend.

```
31            OptionsPanel.SetActive(false);
32
33            SceneEngine.NewPlayerPos = Vector3.zero;
34            SceneEngine.NewSceneName = "";
```

Figure 351

```
67        IntroCine.Play();
68
69        if ((SceneEngine.NewSceneName != null) && (SceneEngine.NewSceneName != ""))
70        {
71            Player.transform.position = SceneEngine.NewPlayerPos;
72            SceneEngine.NewSceneName = "";
73        }
```

Figure 350

Now open the "GameController" script and add the if statement shown in Figure 350 on lines 69 through 73. If the Scene Engine's "NewSceneName" was set to anything prior to calling the game controller's Start method, then we'll move the player to whatever the position that was intended.

One last thing to do is fix the Bible audio so it doesn't start playing when a cut scene is going on. This is easily done by only playing the Bible audio if the cut scene isn't playing. See Figure 352.

```
public void EnterZone(string zoneName, float offset, float length)
{
    if (IntroCine.state != PlayState.Playing)
    {
        ZoneTextObj.SplashZone(zoneName);
        GetComponent<AudioSource>().time = offset;
        GetComponent<AudioSource>().Play();
        Invoke("StopAudio", length);
    }
}
```

Figure 352

Let's make a scene transition to the palace now. Load the "Egypt_Nile Scene" in Unity, click on the "Big Temple" object in the Hierarchy View, and focus on it in the Scene View by pressing 'F'. Since Pharaoh is using this as his palace, we're going to put some scene transition objects here so that when the player walks inside, the scene changes to the "Palace" scene. On either side of the building are two doorways that you can see in Figure 353.

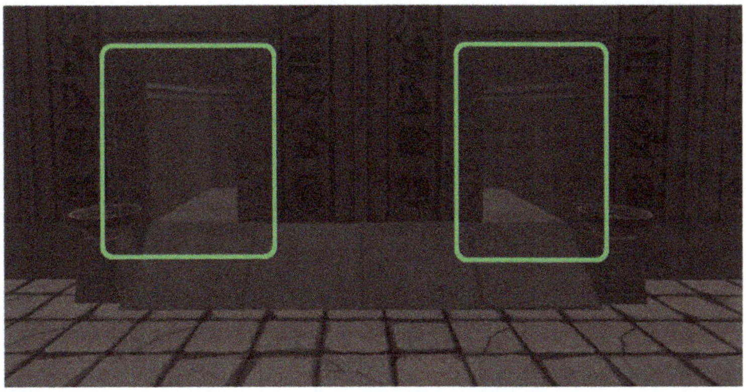

Figure 353

We're going to put our scene transition in front of both these sets of doors. In the main menu select GameObject > 3D Object > Cube. Rename it to "PalaceTransition" and drag the "SceneTransition" script onto it.

Set the transform and Scene Transition script field values to what is shown in Figure 354. Drag "GameController" from the Hierarchy View onto the Gc field. Also, uncheck the box in front of Mesh Renderer to make it inactive. This means the cube is no longer rendered on-screen, but the object is still there invisible.

Let's save this in a prefab. Drag the "PalaceTransition" into Assets > Prefabs in the Project View and rename it to "SceneTrans".

Now, copy and paste this object and move it along the Z axis to about '1561'. This covers both entrances to the palace so that no matter which one the player enters, they get sent to the Palace scene.

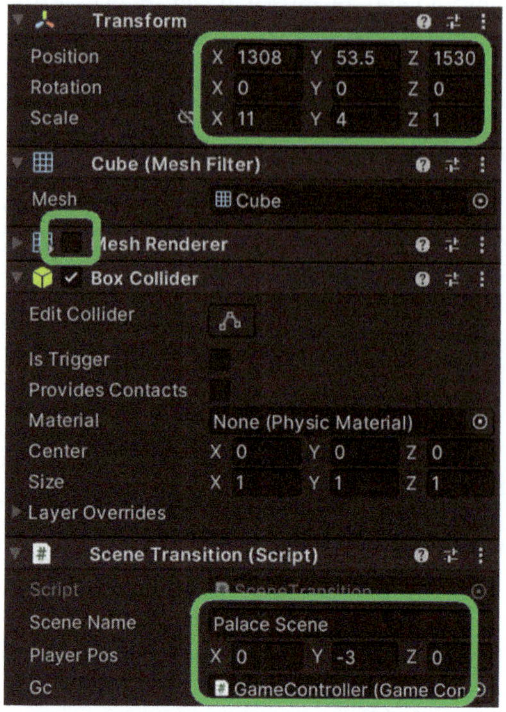

Figure 354

Next we get to hook up the scene transition going back to the Egypt Nile scene. Drag the "SceneTrans" prefab into the Hierarchy View and set the transform and scene transition script to the values shown in Figure 355. You'll see the green collider box appear at close to the wall on the inside of the hallway. Make sure to drag over the "GameController" to the Gc field too.

If you play the scene now, then the player object will be moved to the designated spot and ready for you to test out the scene transitions. Run Moses into the door and you'll see the loading window pop up. Then, when the scene loads, the opening cut scene will display and then you'll find yourself standing next to Pharaoh's Palace. This is because there is no player at the start of the scene. Since the player is created during the first "Update" method call and the mini-map's target is set to it, this error is ok.

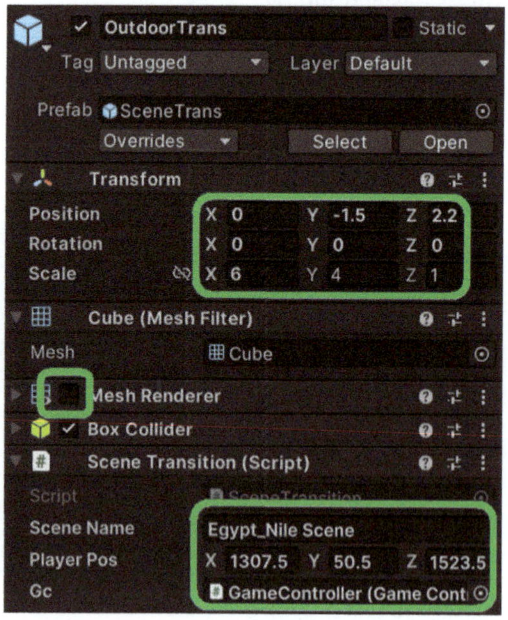

Figure 355

Finishing the Palace

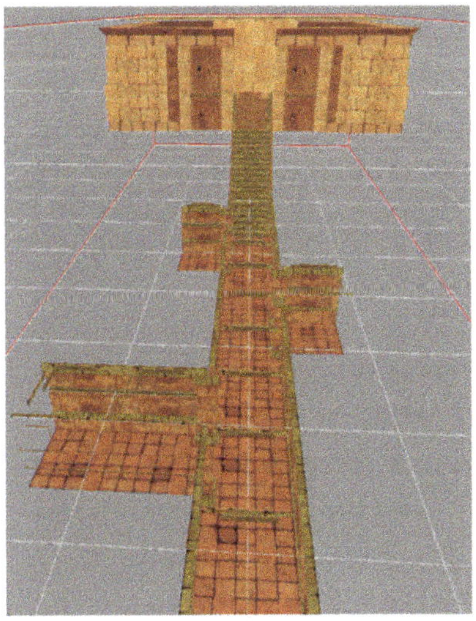

Figure 356

Now let's turn our attention back to the palace. Last we left it, we had a long hallway leading up to the throne room (see Figure 356), with 3 areas for side-passages. Going back over our GDD, we have a puzzle that will be done in the palace. There are 3 guards blocking the player and each require a different seal so the player can pass. We'll the quest later, but now, we need to create the areas the player needs to go through so the seals can be found.

I'm not going to show you how to build the rest of the palace. This is the part where you can show off your creativity to design and implement it for yourself. You have all the tools you need to do it. You know a few of the models from the "Temple Parts" and "RuinParts" folders. I encourage you to go through and really see what else is there. If you go to Assets > Models > Ancient Egypt" you'll see a "Dungeon_Parts_1" scene. This shows you some of the big parts you can use to finish the palace. It also has 2 rooms you can use. You can also go back to the "Dungeon_1" scene and see how the parts fit together again. Use that to get some ideas for how to complete the rest of the level.

But let me give you some advice before you start. Really take stock of all the parts you have to work with. Make a list if you want. Then think of all the different kinds of places to go in the palace. Think of rooms where we can use the ones we found in the "Dungeon_1" scene. Now, take all those places and use them to draw your map of the level. Don't forget that you can use stairs to make multiple floors.

One question to answers is "should I make a new scene for every floor?" The answer to this question, as it is with many questions, is that it depends. There are three reasons why different scenes are often used for separate locations. 1) Including everything in a single scene is impractical. While, trying to fit an indoor location inside its outdoor representation would be realistic, you may find that you need additional space and making a separate scene lets you have as much as you need. There is fine line between realism and practicality you need to walk. 2) Separate scenes improves performance. It reduces the number of objects the system has to track to check if the player can view them or not. 3) Keeping scenes modular makes it easier to maintain them. It is easier to find objects when the list is small.

But I still haven't answered the question well enough. Use the reasons given above as a guide. Simply decreeing that every floor needs a separate scene can be a bad idea if your floors are small. Once the scene gets big enough then it warrants multiple scenes. How big is big enough? The best way to answer that is when it starts getting reduced performance on your target platform. This will differ depending on the quality of your average player's computer.

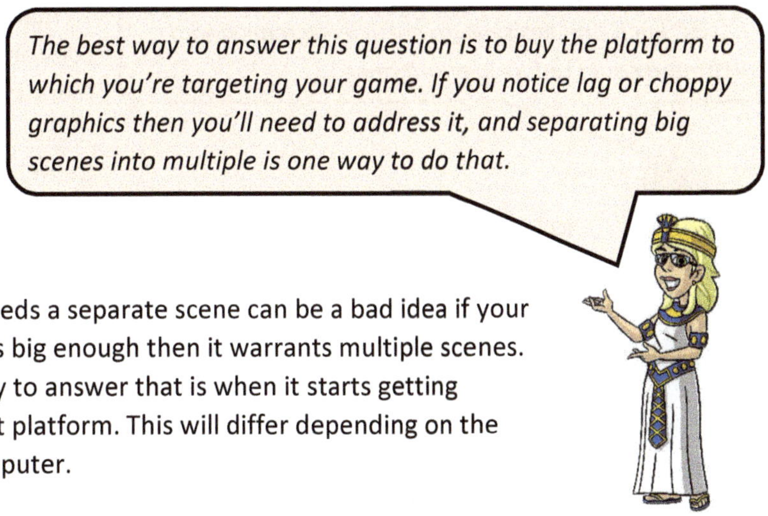

With all that said, have fun building the rest of the palace scene. Remember to take stock of all the resources available to you, draw it out and try to include multiple floors. Most of all, be creative! People love not knowing what is around the next corner.

If you have trouble getting those creative juices flowing, then you can check out the final assets project to see an example of how it could be created.

Laying the First Stone

Figure 357

The time has come for the pyramid. We're going to use very similar techniques and models for the pyramid interior as we did for the Palace. First, we need to understand what we need to accomplish with the palace interior. According to our GDD, the pyramid itself functions as puzzles for the game. We design it like a maze for the player to run through. To be believable, we should make the pyramid feel like the outside is square and then each floor gets smaller the higher up you go and larger as you descend. You can look at the pyramid in Figure 357 for reference.

Create a new scene named "Pyramid Scene". Add a "DT_EndDoor" prefab again and set the position to all 0s like before. Delete the default camera and directional light. This time, however, we won't adjust the lighting. We're going to keep the scene dark and use some point lights to illuminate the passages and rooms. This will give the player a more mysterious feeling as they explore. Grab the "Firebowl" prefab we created several chapters back from Assets > Prefabs > Objects and put it on the side wall as shown in Figure 358.

Figure 358

To make the lighting a bit more "2-sided", copy and paste the "FireBowl" object, in the Hierarchy View, and then use the transform tool to slide it along the X axis (red arrow) to the wall on the other side.

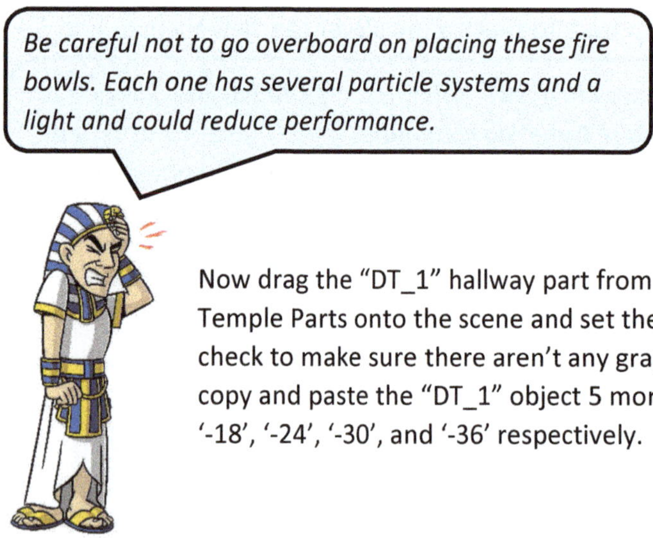

Now drag the "DT_1" hallway part from Assets > Models > Ancient Egypt > Models > Temple Parts onto the scene and set the position to X='0', Y='0', and Z='-6'. Double-check to make sure there aren't any graphics glitches (fix them up if there are). Then copy and paste the "DT_1" object 5 more times and change the Z coordinates to '-12', '-18', '-24', '-30', and '-36' respectively.

Now select the two "FireBowl" object you created and copy and paste 3 sets of them, spreading them across the hallway so every other hallway piece has 2 fire bowls in them. You should see something like Figure 359 where the mysterious lighting and ominously placed bowls of fire contribute to the feeling where you don't know what's going to be around the next corner.

Figure 359

Speaking of what's around the next corner, we're going to add a 4-way intersection next so we can find out what's there. Go to Assets > Models > Ancient Egypt > Models > Temple Parts and drag the "DT4way_1" onto the scene and set the position to X='0', Y='-0.45', and Z='-42' and double check for any graphics glitches.

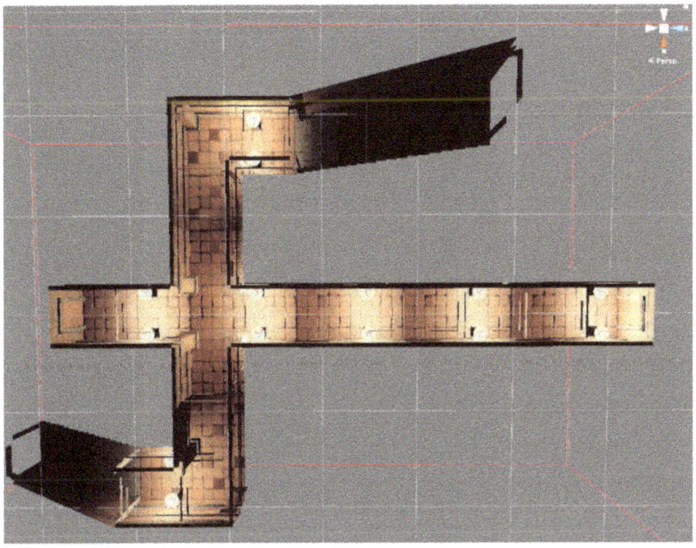

Figure 360

Based on what we've done previously and in previous sections, try to create the rest of this level as shown in Figure 360. At the end of the hallway there is one more "DT_1" block followed by a "DT_EndDoor" block that you'll need to rotate 180 degrees along the Y axis.

The top has a "DT_1" rotated 90 degrees, a "DT2way_1" corner piece and a stairway leading up. The bottom has the same thing except the stairway is leading down. After you're done, move the camera around and carefully look any graphics glitches and fix them.

Next, we'll get this hooked up with the game controller and scene transitions. Drag the "GameController" prefab onto the scene and hook it up like before. That's placing the "MosesPlayer" prefab and adding it to the game controller and minimap. Create an empty game object and add a Timeline component onto it. Remember to save the timeline in Assets > Timelines. Then drag that object onto the game controller's Intro Cine. Lastly, create the placeholder parent object for the Intro Objects and drag it to the respective field in the game controller.

Ok, that wasn't lastly. The lastly lastly thing to do (really lastly this time) is go to the Main Menu and select Build Settings. Then click "Add Open Scenes" so we can load the scene when the game is built.

Let's add the transition objects to go into and out of the pyramid. Drag over the "SceneTrans" prefab, naming it "OutdoorTrans", and fill out the transform and scene transition script details shown in Figure 361. Don't forget to drag the game controller into the Gc field.

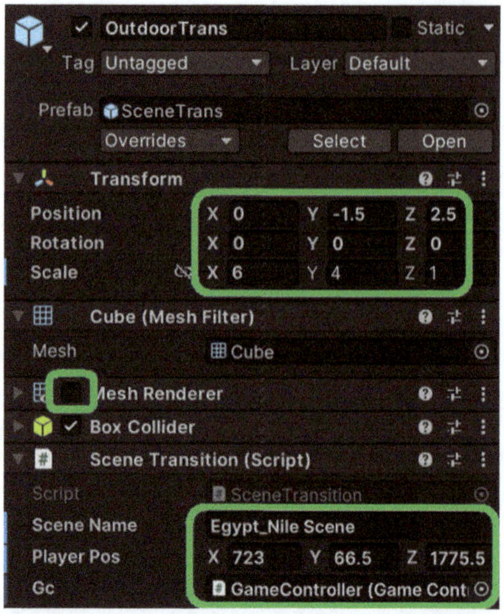

Figure 361

In the "Egypt_Nile Scene", drag the SceneTrans" prefab out into the Scene View and name it "PyramidTransition". Then do the same for it as shown in Figure 362.

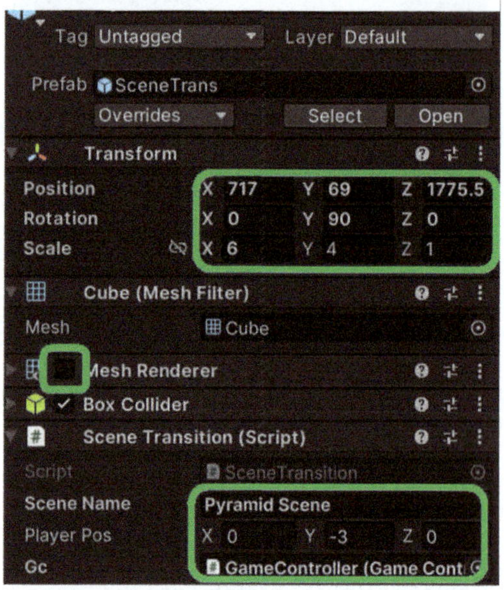

Figure 362

Go back to the "Pyramid" scene and click the play button. Moses will stand at the beginning of the hallway. You can explore a bit in the pyramid interior that we created. Once you're done, go and touch the scene transition. Like with the palace scene, you'll be sent to "Egypt_Nile Scene", but this time you're at the pyramid. Go back to the pyramid entrance and make sure the scene loads back to the pyramid.

As with the Palace, I'll leave the design and implementation of the rest of the pyramid up to you and your creativity. A few things to keep in mind as you go about finishing it are: 1) go through the quests in the GDD and make sure you have all the rooms and everything you need, 2) lighting with the fire bowls can help create different moods like having a royal chamber bright and some storage room dark, and 3) pyramids get bigger at the bottom and smaller at the top or the player may not believe your design.

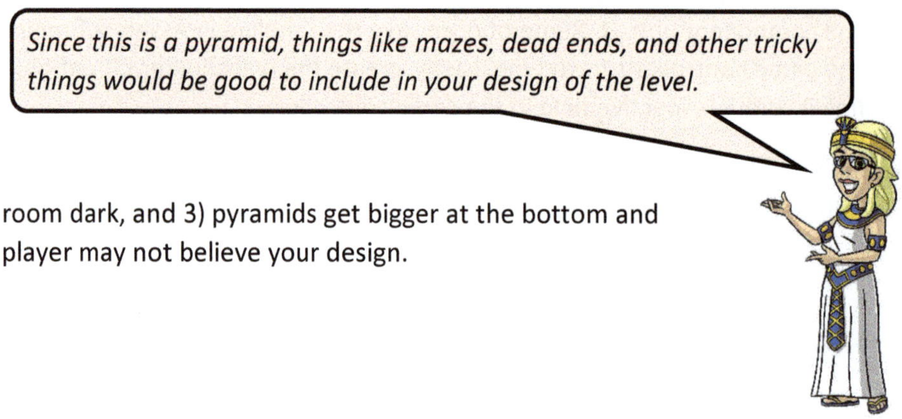

Chapter 12 –Music and Miscellaneous

One of the greatest keys to unlocking human emotion is music. It can make you shed tears of sadness as well as tears of joy, jump in fright, and even uplift your soul. Music can help to create just the right mood to draw the player into the game so they can feel what the characters in the game are feeling.

In this chapter we're going to make sure every scene has music, add support for changing the music in our cut scene system, and also change the music when the player enters different zones. Unity has audio sources to create sounds (music is a kind of sound) which we've already used for footsteps and the Bible audio.

Go to the GDD and read about the music and sound effects section. This will give you an idea of what pieces of music we'll use for the different parts of the game.

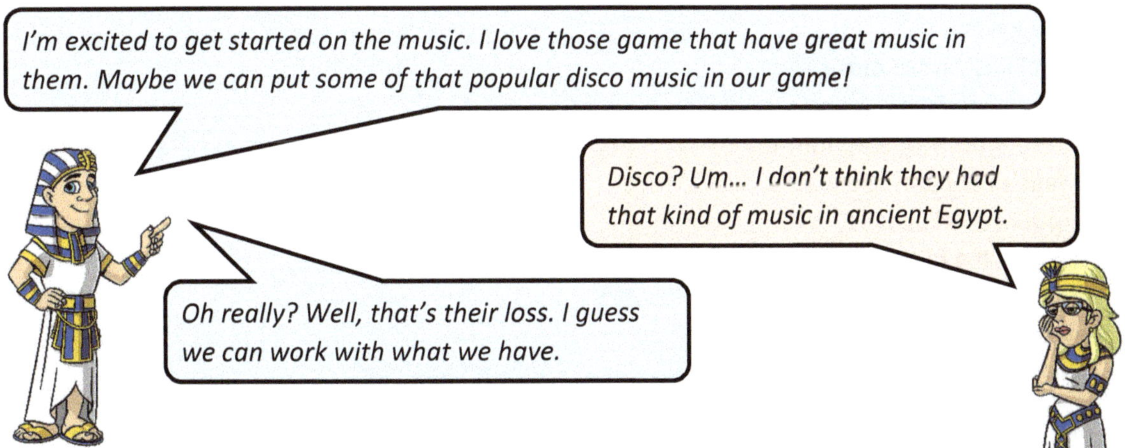

First, let's add music to our title scene. In the Project View go to Assets > Scenes and open "Title". When it loads, go to Assets > Music > Extreme Fantasy Music > Day and drag "Day_Time_3" onto the Hierarchy View. This adds the music to the scene so it will start playing. We do, however, need to check the "Looping" box in the object's inspector. See Figure 363.

Click the Play button to see what this sounds like. Er... I mean... Hear what this sounds like. The music should start as soon as the game loads. This music will always be playing during the title scene. We won't change it like we will for the other scenes.

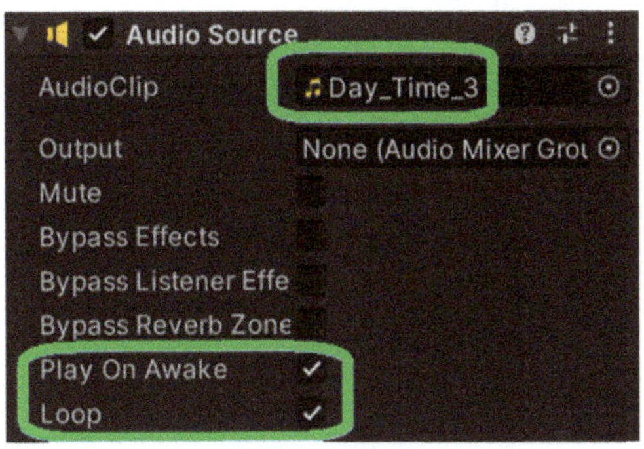

Figure 363

If you don't hear any music, check the top right of the Game View, near the Gizmos, make sure the little speaker does not have an 'x'. Figure 364 shows the sound enabled.

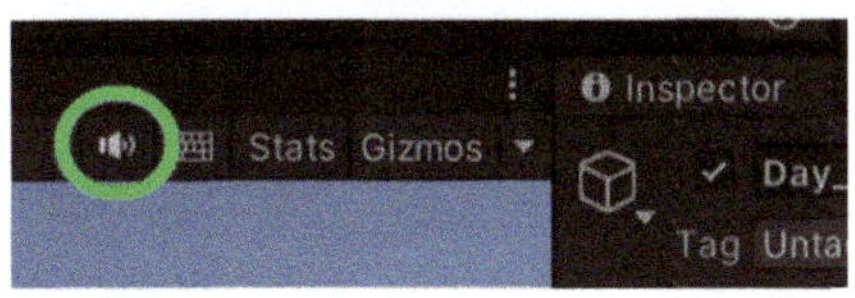

Figure 364

Music Controller

Now we're going to create our music controller, which will oversee what music is currently playing in the scene. Basically, the controller will play a default piece of music until the player enters a zone. Then the music corresponding to that zone will be played. The music can also be faded out, similar to the screen, except using volume instead of the alpha. We also need to delay playing music for a second so that music played for cut scenes has a chance to play.

Create a new C# script named "MusicController" and open it up in Visual Studio. Add the variables and the "Start" method shown in Figure 365.

- StartClip: Music to play when the scene loads.
- MusicClips: List of music clips that can be played.
- FadeLength: How long for music to fade in and out. Default length of 1 second.
- nextClip: If a fadeout is needed on the previous clip, this holds the next one.
- fadeOut: True if the operation is fading out but false if fading in.
- m_Audio: Holds a reference to the audio component.

```
public string StartClip;
public AudioClip[] MusicClips;
public float FadeLength = 1;

private string nextClip;
private bool fadeOut;
private AudioSource m_Audio;

// Start is called before the first frame update
Unity Message | 0 references
void Start()
{
    m_Audio = GetComponent<AudioSource>();
    m_Audio.clip = GetClip(StartClip);
    PlayMusic();
}
```

Figure 365

The start method will just get the reference to the audio source, set the starting music clip, and play it.

Add the code shown in Figure 366 to the "Update" method. The outer 'if' statement checks that there is a clip to fade into and that the audio source is playing. If it isn't playing that means a cut scene or cinematic is playing. We don't want the music controller to play music on top of those since they'll have their own music.

The next 'if' statement checks whether we're fading out or fading in. Fading out lowers the volume while fading in raises the volume. At the end of each section, it checks if

```
void Update()
{
    if ((nextClip != "") && m_Audio.isPlaying)
    {
        if (fadeOut)
        {
            m_Audio.volume -= Time.deltaTime * FadeLength;

            if (m_Audio.volume <= 0.1f)
            {
                fadeOut = false;
                m_Audio.clip = GetClip(nextClip);
                m_Audio.Play();
            }
        }
        else
        {
            m_Audio.volume += Time.deltaTime * FadeLength;

            if (m_Audio.volume >= 1)
            {
                nextClip = "";
            }
        }
    }
}
```

Figure 366

the fading is done. If Fadeout is completed, then set the next clip and start fading it in. If Fade in is done, then we're all done.

After the Update method, add the additional methods shown in Figure 367. The "PlayMusic" method will setup the next clip to be faded. The argument "clipName" has a default value of an empty string so that a call of no arguments means to play the starting clip at line 60. If the clip was already playing, then, in the 'if' block at line 63, simply fade that music back in.

Default arguments for methods are a great way to simplify calling it. In addition, for our case, allowing us to use the starting clip by default, it allows us not to worry about less commonly used arguments in methods with longer argument lists.

Line 70 simply gives a public method to stop the music. We'll use this to stop the music before the introduction cinematic is played.

Finally, we have a helper method called "GetClip" which returns the audio clip given its name. We need to loop through each of the music clips to see if the names match. If so, then return it. If not, then return null.

```
51      public void PlayMusic(string clipName = "")
52      {
53          fadeOut = true;
54          nextClip = clipName;
55          CancelInvoke("PlayMusic");
56          m_Audio.Play();
57
58          if (nextClip == "")
59          {
60              nextClip = StartClip;
61          }
62
63          if (m_Audio.clip.name == nextClip)
64          {
65              m_Audio.volume = 0;
66              fadeOut = false;
67          }
68      }
69
        1 reference
70      public void StopMusic()
71      {
72          m_Audio.Stop();
73      }
74
        2 references
75      private AudioClip GetClip(string name)
76      {
77          AudioClip retClip = null;
78
79          foreach (AudioClip ac in MusicClips)
80          {
81              if (ac.name == name)
82              {
83                  retClip = ac;
84                  break;
85              }
86          }
87
88          return retClip;
89      }
```

Figure 367

The "GameController" script needs to be updated next. Open it up and add a public variable for the music controller on line 25. See Figure 368.

```
23      public GameObject LoadingPanelObj;
24      public Inventory InvController;
25      public MusicController MusController;
26
```

Figure 368

Scroll down to the Start method and add line 68 shown in Figure 369. Before we play the introduction cinematic, we stop the music, so we don't have double music playing.

```
67                LoadingPanelObj.SetActive(false);
68                MusController.StopMusic();
69                IntroCine.Play();
```

Figure 369

Continue scrolling down until you get to the Update method. Add line 91 shown in Figure 370 to play the music again after the introduction cinematic completes.

```
89                    MinimapObj.SetActive(true);
90                    IntroCinePlayed = true;
91                    MusController.PlayMusic();
```

Figure 370

```
143     public void EnterZone(string zoneName, string musicName, float offset, float length)
144     {
145         if (IntroCine.state != PlayState.Playing)
146         {
147             ZoneTextObj.SplashZone(zoneName);
148             MusController.PlayMusic(musicName);
149             GetComponent<AudioSource>().time = offset;
150             GetComponent<AudioSource>().Play();
151             Invoke("StopAudio", length);
152         }
153     }
```

Figure 371

The last edit in the game controller is down in the "EnterZone" method. Add the argument "musicName" as a string on line 143. Then on line 148, add a call to "MusController" to play the zone's music. The code should now look like what you see in Figure 371.

Finally, in the script "Zone", add a string for the "MusicName". Then, in the method when the trigger is entered, on line 16, add that new variable to the method call to enter the zone.

```
7       public string ZoneName;
8       public string MusicName;
9       public float AudioOffset, AudioLength;
10      public GameController gc;
11
        Unity Message | 0 references
12      private void OnTriggerEnter(Collider other)
13      {
14          if (other.transform.tag == "Player")
15          {
16              gc.EnterZone(ZoneName, MusicName, AudioOffset, AudioLength);
17          }
18      }
```

Figure 372

That takes care of all the script changes. Now we'll make all these scripts live together with the objects in Unity (Can keep doing that?). Anyway, in the Project View, go to Assets > Prefabs and open the "GameController". By editing the prefab, we'll change the object in all scenes that the game controller is in which saves us a lot of time later on. You'll see the Scene View showing it now. Right-click on "GameController" in the Hierarchy View and create an empty object. It will show up as a child object. Give it the name "MusicController" and drag the corresponding script onto it.

Expand the Music Clips array and set the Size to '8' as shown in Figure 373. In the Project View, go to Assets > Music > Extreme Fantasy Music > Day and add "Day_Time_1", "Day_Time_2", "Day_Time_3", and "Day_Time_FRONT" to the array. Then go to Assets > Music > Extreme Fantasy Music > Night and add "Night_Time", "Night_Time_Event", and "Night_Time_OUT1" to the list. The last music we'll add is "Combat_detected" from Assets > Music > Extreme Combat Music Pack > Combat. Then set the Start Clip to "Night_Time".

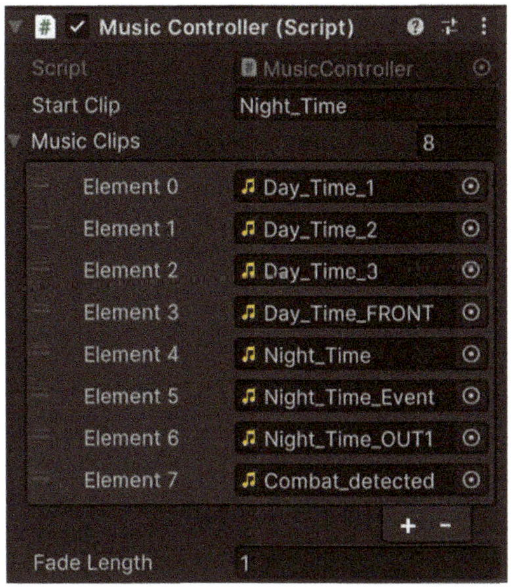

Figure 373

Set the default Start Clip in the prefab to "Night_Time". You'll also see that the Fade Length is already set to '1'. This was because we gave it a default value. That gets all the music we'll use set up with our music controller. If you hear another music clip you like, then you need to add it here before you can use it.

Finally, add an Audio Source component onto the music controller for the script to use. Make sure the "Loop" field is checked as shown in Figure 374.

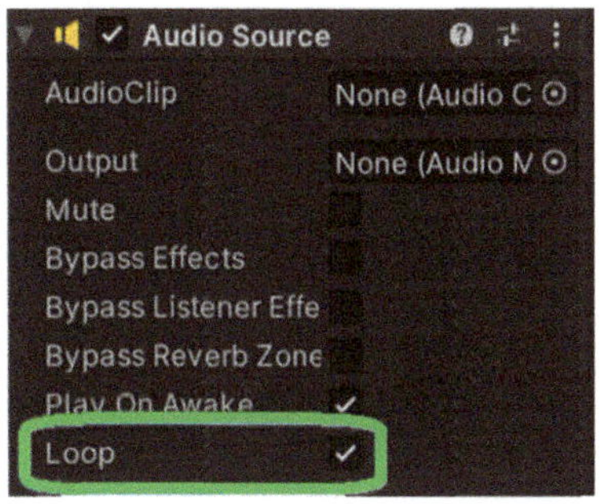

Figure 374

Click over to the "GameController" object and then drag the "MusicController" in the Mus Controller field so the game controller can make method calls into the music controller. That's all we need to change in the prefab. Click the arrow in the top left corner of the Hierarchy View to go back. Recall that the prefab is automatically saved.

Make sure you have the "Egypt_Nile Scene". Expand the "MapZones" object and click the "PalaceZone". The Music Name field will appear. When it does type "Night_Time_OUT1". If you've created the other zones, then use the GDD to cross reference the music name for each of the zones.

Let's test out this feature now. Click the play button and wait for the game to load. When it does, after about a second, you will hear the specified Start Clip. Since there wasn't any music in the cut scene, it played. We'll add music to the cut scene next, which will override the start clip.

Having different music clips for different zones around the map can help create the right mood for that area and is one of those little things that helps immerse the player in the game.

Walk over to Pharaoh's palace next. When you get close you should see the zone text appear, the Bible audio speak, and the new music play. You can exit play mode now.

Skip Cinematics

Quality of life, or QoL, is an idea that speaks to how easy the player can do things and feel in the game. Some examples might be improving the user interface so the player can equip and use items better, redesigning levels so that players don't have to walk all the way back to the beginning where nothing else is going on and adding audio and visual cues to important reflex-based mechanics.

We're going to improve player QoL by allowing them to skip the introduction cinematic. It is important to keep a player's attention. If they've already seen the cinematic then they are less likely to just want to get in and play the game.

```
79  void Update()
80  {
81      bool escapedCinematic = false;
82
83      if (!IntroCinePlayed)
84      {
85          if ((IntroCine.state != PlayState.Playing) || (Input.GetKeyUp(KeyCode.Escape)))
86          {
87              escapedCinematic = true;
88              FadingOut = true;
89              IntroObjects.SetActive(false);
90              CineCam.SetActive(false);
91              Player.SetActive(true);
92              MinimapObj.SetActive(true);
93              IntroCine.Stop();
94              IntroCinePlayed = true;
95              MusController.PlayMusic();
96          }
97      }
```

Figure 375

Let's get back into the game controller script. Scroll down to the Update method and add the bool on line 81 shown in Figure 375. That variable will track which reason why the escape key was pressed. Recall that in Chapter 9 – Menu System and UI, when the player presses escape the Main Menu is shown and hidden. But here we want to skip the cinematic if the escape key is pressed. This flag will let the Main Menu code know that the player pressed Escape because they wanted to skip the cut scene and will not show the Main Menu.

Handling that flag is a simple addition to the 'if' statement checking the press of the Escape key for the Main Menu. See Figure 376 and add the additional condition on line 113. This will only handle the Main Menu if the Escape wasn't pressed because the player wanted to skip the cinematic.

```
110 if (Input.GetKeyUp(KeyCode.M))
111 {
112     WorldMapHandler();
113 }
114 else if (Input.GetKeyUp(KeyCode.Escape) && !escapedCinematic)
115 {
116     MainMenuHandler();
117 }
```

Figure 376

Appear and Disappear

In the last section of this chapter, we're going to make that clay jar (or pot) actually disappear, so it looks like Moses took it. To do that, we will add capability in our dialogue system to activate and inactive (show and hide) game objects.

Open the script "DialogueElement" and make the two changes shown in Figure 377. The first change is on line 15 where a game object variable is added as "ActionObject". This will be the object that we work on. Then on lines 28 and 29, add the two new entries into our enumeration for "ActivateObject" and "InactivateObject".

Next, add the two more cases in the switch statement on line 173 of Figure 378. The case for setting the object to active is on line 181 and inactive is on line 184.

```
14      public string ActionName;
15      public GameObject ActionObject;
16
        2 references
17      public enum _cond_type
18      {
19          None,
20          Item
21      }
22
        5 references
23      public enum _action
24      {
25          None,
26          GiveItem,
27          TakeItem,
28          ActivateObject,
29          InactivateObject
30      }
```

Figure 377

```
173             switch (curDia.Lines[diaIndex].Action)
174             {
175                 case DialogueElement._action.GiveItem:
176                     ItemEngine.InventoryAddItem(curDia.Lines[diaIndex].ActionName);
177                     break;
178                 case DialogueElement._action.TakeItem:
179                     ItemEngine.InventoryRemItem(curDia.Lines[diaIndex].ActionName);
180                     break;
181                 case DialogueElement._action.ActivateObject:
182                     curDia.Lines[diaIndex].ActionObject.SetActive(true);
183                     break;
184                 case DialogueElement._action.InactivateObject:
185                     curDia.Lines[diaIndex].ActionObject.SetActive(false);
186                     break;
187             }
```

Figure 378

Selecting the "Pot_1" in the Hierarchy View, we see the Dialogue script in the inspector. First, change the "Yes" line in the array of Lines so that the Response is None. This means that the dialogue won't end.

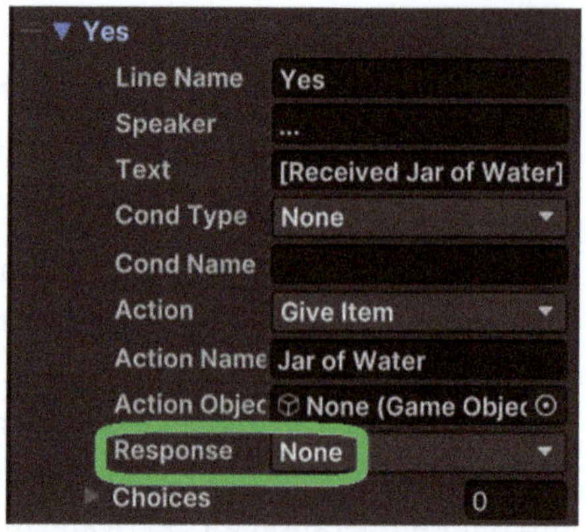

Figure 379

Next, click the '+' symbol at the bottom of the array of Lines to create a new line. It will duplicate the bottom line which is "No". Set the values to that shown in Figure 380. For the Action Object, drag the "Pot_1" from the Hierarchy View onto it. This will cause the dialogue controller to inactivate the pot. Then here is where we "End". Finally, clicking and holding the two lines on the left side of the line, drag it right underneath the "Yes" line. Now it will play right after.

Give the game another test run. Go over to the pot and try picking it up. After you do, you will see that it disappears. Using this same code, we can make other things disappear or appear.

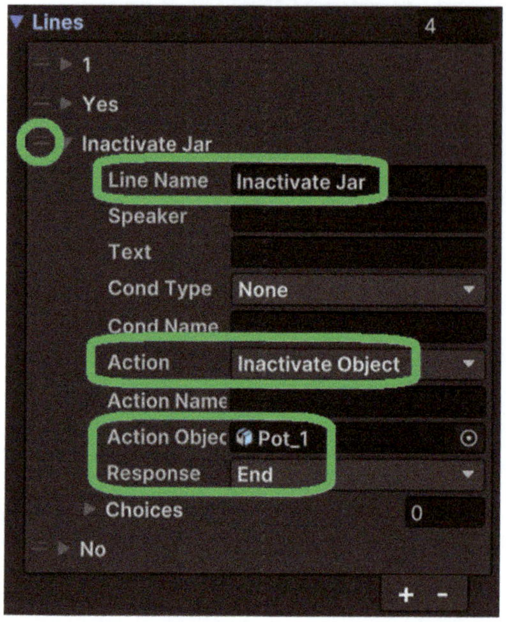

Figure 380

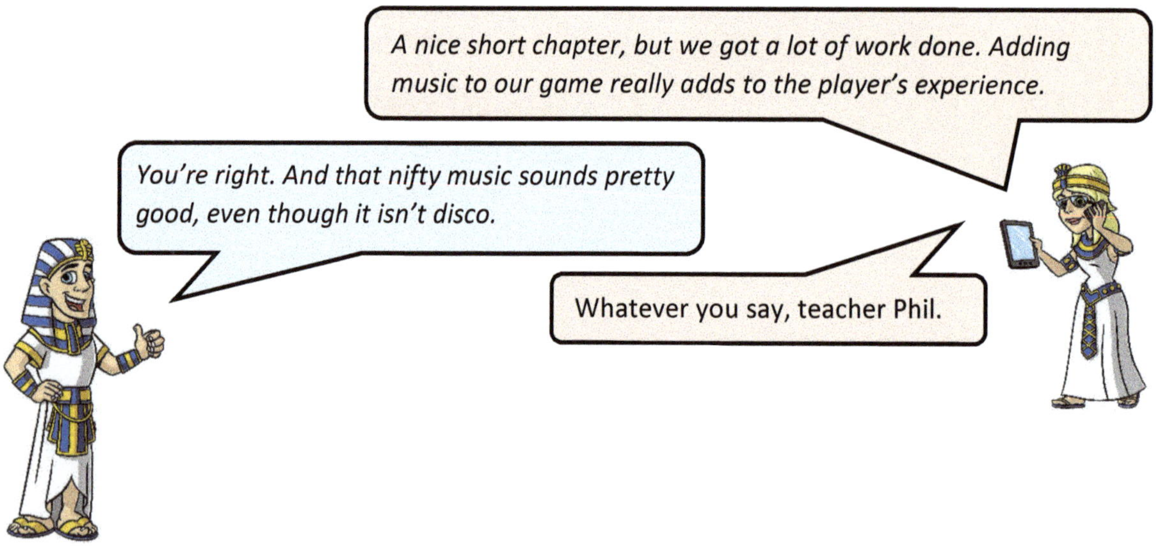

Chapter 13 – Skybox Controller

One piece we're missing in our little land of Egypt is the sky. A pretty big piece, actually. All that blackness when the player looks up, it just plain looks weird, and kind of creepy. We'll fix that now.

We're going to create a sky box and actually have a day and night system. The lighting will increase in the morning and decrease towards nighttime. The position of the sun, in the sky, will also match the time of day. And it will disappear at night.

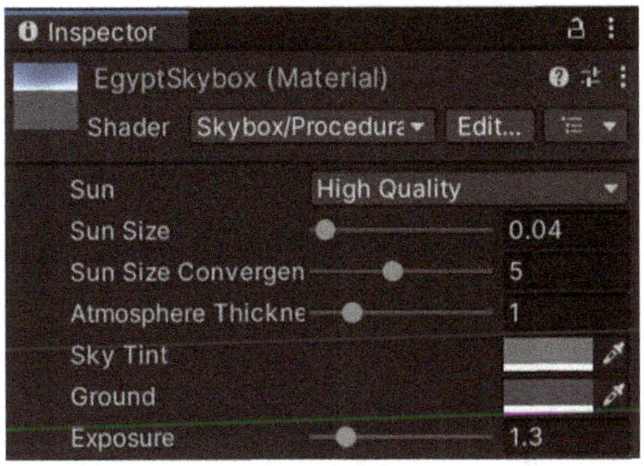

Figure 381

Creating the Sky

In the Project View, go to Assets and create a new folder named "Materials". Then right-click and select Create > Material. Name it "EgyptSkybox" and set the Shader to Skybox / Procedural. You'll see a nice blue sky with an orangish-yellow horizon appear. This skybox is created by Unity using the fields found in Figure 381 as an input.

- Sun: A high quality sun will have a glare around it whereas a simple sun is just a circle or disk. Alternatively, you can choose to have no sun.
- Sun Size: How big the sun is.
- Sun Size Convergence: For "High Quality" suns, allows more customization.
- Atmosphere Thickness: Atmosphere density where higher values absorb more light and give a browner hue. Can be used to simulate particles like smoke in the air.
- Sky Tint: Changes the sky color. You can get all sorts of weird sky colors here.
- Ground Tint: Color for the ground if not covered by a terrain.
- Exposure: Brightness of the sky.

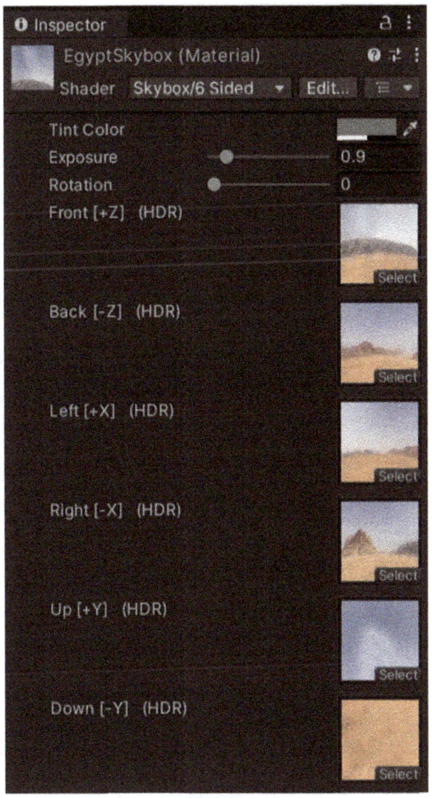

Figure 382

Having a good skybox is important for 3D games. Just a solid color was fine for old-school retro 2D games back in the day. But players expect more from games today.

Feel free to play around with these. We're actually not going to use this kind of skybox shader. But if you want a cool flying game then a procedurally generated skybox may be what you want to use.

Now set the Shader to Skybox / 6 Sided. This kind of skybox treats the sky as an actual box with images on each of the 6 sides where the player is inside it.

In the Project View, go to Assets > Models > Ancient Egypt > Models > Textures > Skybox and use these images to setup the skybox so it looks like Figure 382. Tint Color is like the Sky Tint from before and the exposure is the same. You may want to adjust the rotation, so the skybox image lines up with other models in the scene.

Scene Lighting

We've done some different kinds of lighting for the new scenes we created. In the Palace scene, we made an area light that provides light to the entire scene for a bright day-time look. In the Pyramid scene, we used point lights with the fire bowls for a more mysterious mood. The outdoor scene already has a directional light that we haven't used much yet.

If you haven't already, load up "Egypt_Nile Scene". From the Main Menu, select Window > Rendering > Lighting as shown in Figure 383. A new "Lighting" window will appear. I like to dock it with the Inspector panel. Just click the "Lighting" tab and drag it next to the Inspector panel to dock it. You may need to resize the panel to make it wider so you can see all four tabs in the Lighting panel.

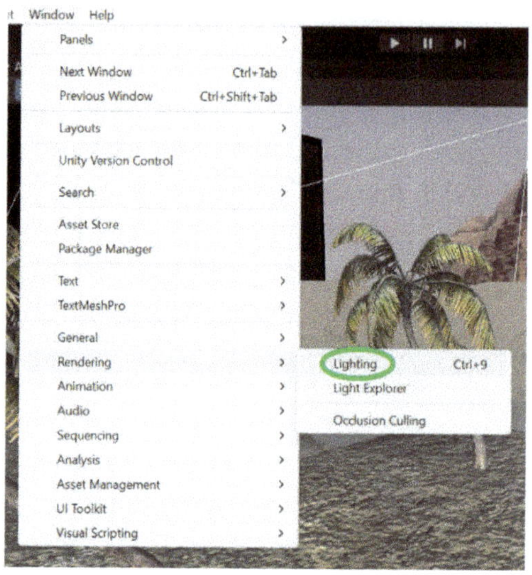

Figure 383

Lighting is a very important, but unfortunately advanced topic in game development. We'll cover it enough to make you dangerous. Meaning you'll understand most of the various knobs, gizmos, and gadgets, but grasping how to put them together to look great and make the game pop can be a whole book unto itself.

Anyway, this briefly describes the lighting tabs:

- Scene: Set realtime and baked lighting mixes and options
- Environment: How light interacts with objects in the scene, also can set fog
- Realtime Lightmaps: Lists all lightmaps for the current scene. Right now, we have none.
- Baked Lightmaps: If the Scene tab has "Baked Global Illumination" checked, then this will show all the generated lightmaps. Right now, we have none.

In the Environment tab, set the "Skybox Material" to the "EgytSkyBox" material we just created. When you do, you'll see the dull black sky change to a real-life-like Egyptian sky complete with mountains in the distance and clouds overhead.

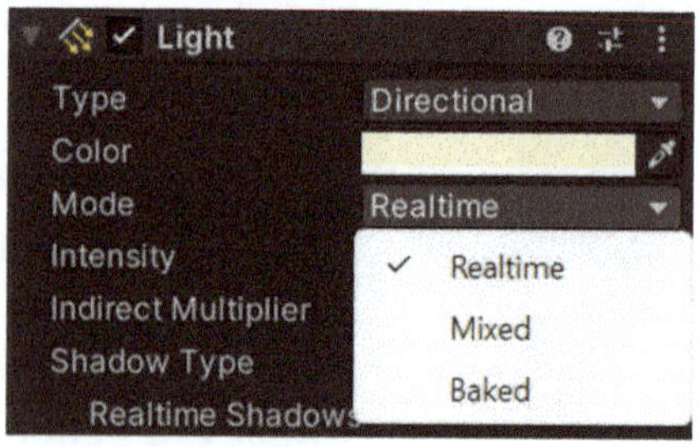

Figure 384

Next, we'll spend a moment talking about the different options in these tabs. But first, it's important to know there are two lighting modes. Each light can be set to Realtime, Baked, or Mixed. We'll talk more about what these mean next.

The first is the Scene Tab which you can see in Figure 385. In the "Lighting Settings" section it just has the Lighting Settings Asset which contains the lighting settings and options for the whole scene. In general, lighting determines how bright the objects appear, how the shadows look, and the tint or color change based on the light.

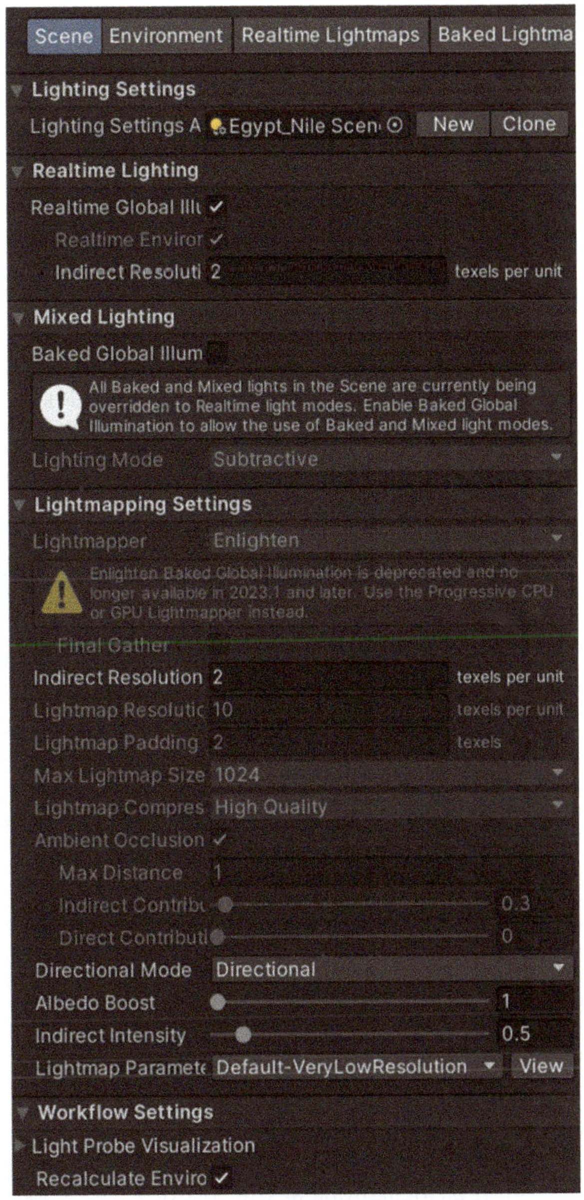

Figure 385

There are two types of lighting, realtime and baked. Realtime lighting is calculated in-game and uses more performance. Baked lighting is calculated before we build the game and saves performance at the cost of a higher file size for the game. You can also have a mix of both to try and find the right balance for your game. Ultimately, the choice of which to use depends on the performance. Nobody likes lag. If the game is laggy, moving more of your lighting to baked may help.

Realtime Lighting Section:

- Realtime Global Illumination: Checking enables use of the lightmapper in the Lightmapping Settings section.
- Realtime Environment Lighting: If both Realtime and Baked lighting are used then this can be checked for mixed lighting.
- Indirect Resolution: Simulating real life, indirect lighting means light that has bounced off surfaces of objects instead of directly from a lighting source. The higher this resolution, the better quality the lighting will be but takes more time when baking lightmaps. Make this smaller to reduce baking times.

Mixed Lighting Section:

- Baked Global Illumination: Use baked lights when calculating indirect lighting.
- Lighting Mode (3 options): The default is Subtractive which models lighting by absorbing or subtracting colors from the light spectrum. Baked indirect uses precomputed values in the lightmaps. Shadowmask is for dynamic shadow movement based on light sources, objects, and camera viewpoint. Subtractive is the best quality, Shadowmask is the best performance, and baked indirect is the happy medium.

Lightmapping Setting Section (Will focus on default changeable options):

- Lightmapper: Which lightmapper to use. Note that this will only be allowed to change if "Baked Global Illumination" is checked. At the time of this tutorial, "Progressive GPU" is in preview mode and "Enlighten" has been deprecated (or not supported anymore). Set this to "Progressive CPU".
- Indirect Resolution: Light bounces from objects for baked lighting.
- Directional Mode: If Directional mode is used then an additional texture is created in the lightmap about how to treat the incoming light. Disable by setting to "Non-Directional" will improve performance.
- Albedo Boost: Adjusts how much color is transferred by the light when bouncing.
- Indirect Intensity: Changes the brightness of indirect lighting.
- Lightmap Parameters: Advanced parameters beyond the scope of this tutorial.

Moving on to the Environment Tab.

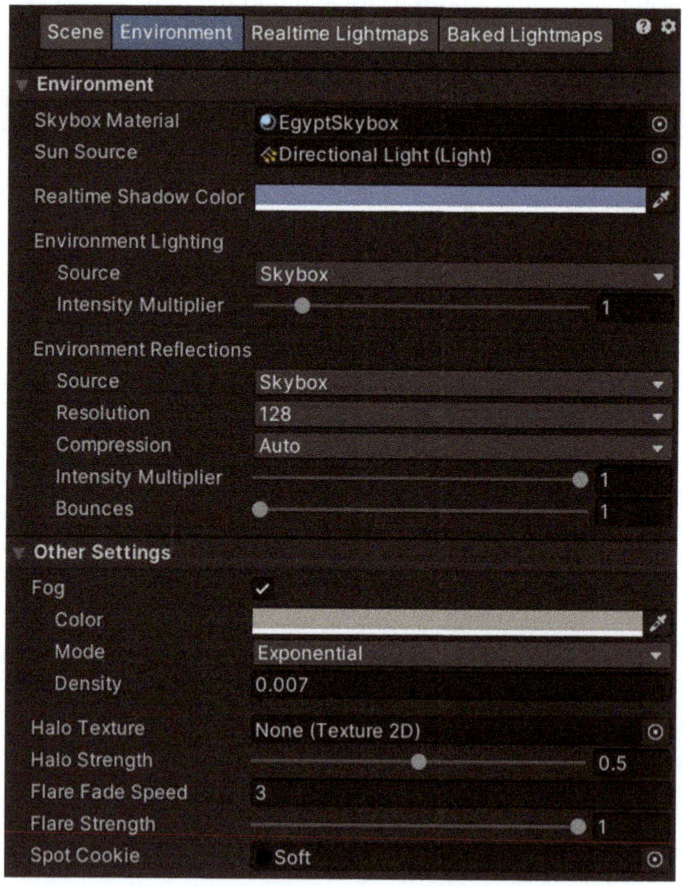

Environment Section:

- Skybox Material: Select the skybox.
- Sun Source: Select light for the sun.
- Realtime Shadow Color: Color used to mix baked and realtime shadows.
- Environment Lighting: Skybox uses colors from the skybox material. Gradient blends two colors for sky, horizon, and ground. Color uses a flat color for ambient light.
- Intensity Multiplier: Adjusts the brightness of the scene.
- Environment Reflections: Settings for Reflection Probe baking. Reflection probes help get more realistic lighting at the cost of performance. This is an advanced feature, and we won't be using it in this tutorial.

Other Settings Section:

- Fog: Obscures objects that are farther away from the camera. The Color changes the color of the obscurity. The Mode and parameters of the mode (i.e., Density for Exponential) impact how much fog there is.
- Halo Texture: Texture shown when looking directly at a light source.
- Halo Strength: How big the halos are.
- Flare Fade Speed: Controls fading on lens flares.
- Flare Strength: How big the lens flares are.
- Spot Cookie: The cookie is like a stencil or template placed in front of spotlights for patterns.

Controlling the Sky

We created the skybox, now we're going to code the C# script for the day and night cycle. This script will adjust the skybox exposure to make it look like the sky is darkening, adjust the directional light intensity so the terrain and objects get darker, and then change the rotation so that the location of the sun in the sky matches the time of day. Warning: There will be some heavy math in this section.

Create a new C# script named "SkyboxController" and open it in Visual Studio. Code the variables and "Start" and "Update" methods shown in Figure 386.

- SunObject: Handle to the directional light
- SkyboxPrefab: Handle to the skybox
- TimeScale: How quickly the sun moves
- StartTime: Time of the day to start, in 24 hours
- GameTime: Current time of the day, in 24 hours

To make the math easy, the script uses a 24-hour time frame. That way we don't have to worry about AM or PM. In the "Start" method we'll initialize the "gameTime" to the specified start time. Then we call the "UpdateDay" method to update the sun and sky to match the time. In the "Update" method, we only need to update the sun and sky.

```
public GameObject SunObject;
public Material SkyboxPrefab;
public float Timescale;
public float StartTime;

private float gameTime;

// Start is called before the
Unity Message | 0 references
void Start()
{
    gameTime = StartTime;
    UpdateDay();
}

// Update is called once per
Unity Message | 0 references
void Update()
{
    UpdateDay();
}
```

Figure 386

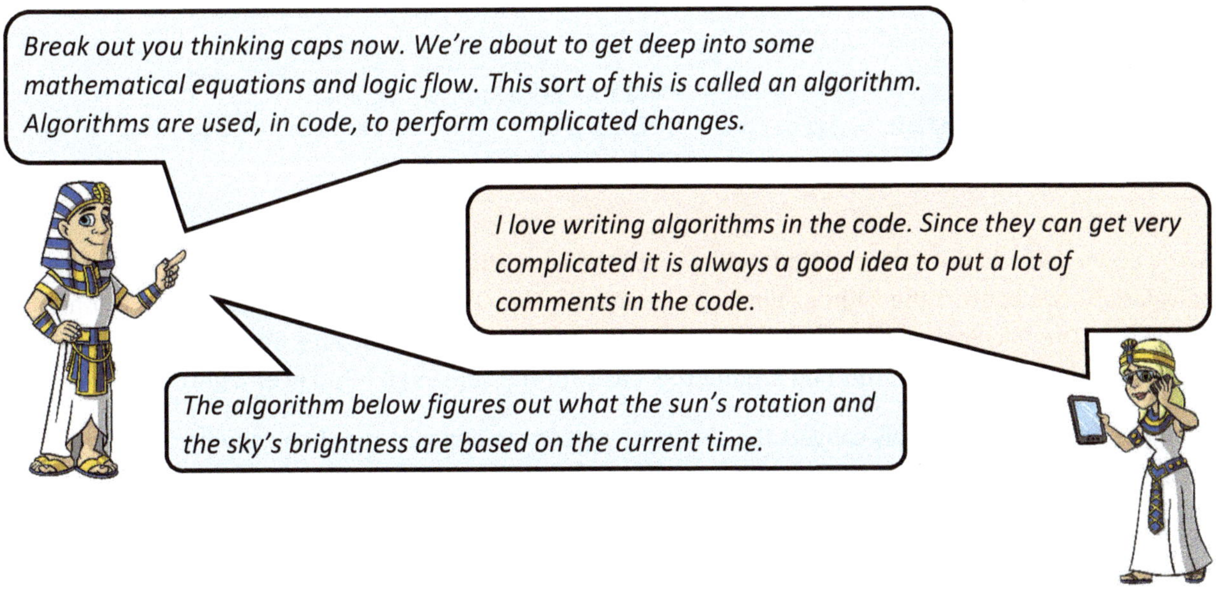

```
27      private void UpdateDay()
28      {
29          // Simply model time between 0 and 1 using a 24-hour clock
30          float timeValue = gameTime / 24f;
31          float sunValue = timeValue - 0.3f;
32
33          if (sunValue < 0)
34          {
35              sunValue += 1;
36          }
37
38          SunObject.transform.rotation = Quaternion.Euler(sunValue * 360, 30, 0);
39
40          // Ensure we don't get light from the other side of the planet
41          if ((sunValue > 0) && (sunValue < 0.5f))
42          {
43              SunObject.GetComponent<Light>().intensity = 1;
44          }
45          else
46          {
47              SunObject.GetComponent<Light>().intensity = 0;
48          }
49
50          if (timeValue < 0.5f)
51          {
52              SkyboxPrefab.SetFloat("_Exposure", timeValue * 2);
53          }
54          else
55          {
56              SkyboxPrefab.SetFloat("_Exposure", 1 - ((timeValue * 2) - 1));
57          }
58
59          // Update game time and roll over after 24 hours
60          gameTime = (gameTime + (Timescale * Time.deltaTime)) % 24;
61      }
```

Figure 387

Scroll down and add the method “UpdateDay” with the code shown in Figure 387. For ease of calculations, we convert the 24-hour time into a percent value 0% is morning and 100% is the last hour of the day. The “skyBoxValue” variable is the value to set the skybox’s exposure. The float for “sunValue” is the percent of rotation around the X axis for the sun and if it is day or nighttime.

On line 38, we can just simply convert the sun value percent to degrees and then convert that from Euler format to a Quaternion. We set the Y rotation to ’30 degrees to give the sun a little bit of a tilt.

Then we figure out if it is daytime or nighttime. If “sunValue” is between ‘0’ and ‘0.5’ then it’s daytime, otherwise it is nighttime. During the daytime let the sunshine, but at nighttime we turn the sun off. Now, the Earth may not be flat, but our game sure is. If the sun is shining up (meaning, the opposite side of the planet), then since our terrain can only be seen from above, the light will shine through and come up from the ground. So, we need to turn off the sun at nighttime.

Then we adjust the brightness of the sky using 2 modes: 1) brighter and 2) darker. We start getting brighter at midnight and darker at noon. Since we divide the 24-hour period up into 2 parts (day and night), we need to multiply "timeValue" by 2 so we can go from a full '0' to '1' on exposure.

To get darker, we start at a value of '1' (fully bright) and subtract "timeValue" from it. Since "timeValue" multiplied by 2 is greater than '1 at this point, we need to subtract '1' so that we can keep our exposure between '0' and '1'.

To access the exposure field of the skybox from the script we use the "SetFloat" and "GetFloat" methods. The first parameter is the name of the field to set. We need to specify the exact right value, or it won't work. For our case, the exact field name is "_Exposure". The 2nd parameter is the float that sets the exposure.

Then we'll increment the game time using the change in the time modified by our time scale value. The last bit of code starts the time back at '0' once the day is done.

Glue the Sky Together

Go back into Unity and create an empty game object named "SkyboxCtlr". Then drag the "SkyboxController" script onto it and set the fields as shown in Figure 388. The same "Directional Light" we set as the Sun in the Lighting tab goes as the Sun Object here. The same thing with the "EgyptSkyBox" material we created. I've done some playing around and feel that a Time Scale value of '0.025' will move the day along at the pace that seems right.

Figure 388

You can play around with this value and see what happens. If you increase it then the day goes faster while decreasing it makes the day go slower. Be ready for one wacky ride if you set it to '1'. If you add a little more programming, you can even control the sky and make it stop in the middle of the battle of the battle with the Amorites for Joshua back in the Old Testament!

There is one more thing you must do before we're ready to play. Open the "MosesPlayer" prefab and click the "Camera" object. Add a "Flare Layer" component. This will show the lens flares.

Click the play button now and let the cut scene run full. Enjoy yourself as you're greeted by the blue sky and models faraway. Marvel at the towering mountains on the horizon. This is much better than the drab blackness from before.

Once the cut scene ends, see if you can spot the sun in the sky. What you see is called a lens flare. This is typically what happens when you go outside and aim a camera toward the sun.

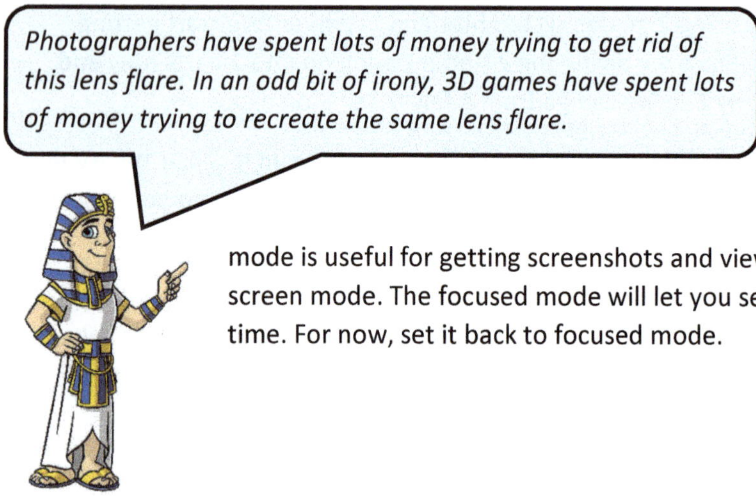

Exiting play mode, go to the Game View and click where it says, "Play Focused". Select "Play Maximized" instead. Now, when you click the play button, you'll see the cinematic fill the entire game window. This mode is useful for getting screenshots and viewing the game as a player would in full screen mode. The focused mode will let you see the console and inspector in real time. For now, set it back to focused mode.

Figure 389

Palace Lighting

The palace scene is an indoor scene, so we don't need to have the skybox controller there. But there are some windows in Pharaoh's audience chamber, and we'll want to give the player something nice to look at. Save the scene and load up "Palace Scene". You're greeted by the same blackness as in the other scene, but now we're armed with the knowledge to make it better.

Click the Lighting tab next to the inspector and set the Skybox to our "EgytSkyBox" in Assets > Materials. As before, you'll notice the scene looks many times better. However, this also comes with a danger. Any graphics glitches that you still have in the hallway parts will become very obvious like in Figure 389. You'll want to spend a little more time walking through the palace to fix these.

Once you have everything looking good (don't worry about perfection right now, just do your best) we'll add some more lighting to the scene. In the main menu, select GameObject > Light > Spotlight.

The directional light acts like the sun, where light falls on the Earth, seemingly, from a single direction. But a spotlight works more like the spotlight on a stage. The light starts from a specific origination point and gets bigger as it goes out in a cone shape. Set values as shown in Figure 390.

- Range: How far the light will go
- Spot Angle: Radius size for the light
- Color: Tint of the light to cast onto the objects
- Intensity: How bright the light will be
- Bounce Intensity: Brightness for light bouncing

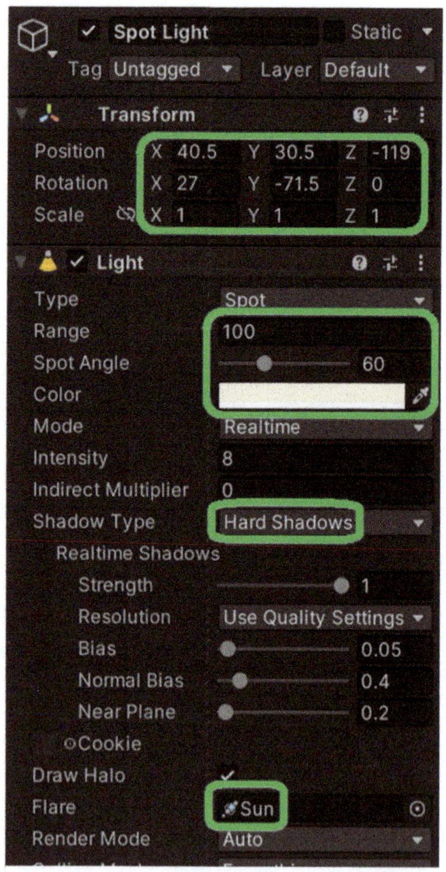

Figure 390

- Shadow Type:
    - Hard Shadows: Shadow edge less blurred
    - Soft Shadows: Shadow edges are more blurred
    - No Shadows: Don't cast shadows
- Draw Halo: Give the impression of dust in the air
- Flare: Use a lens flare with this light

Figure 391

Setting the transform like this will shine the light into Pharaoh's audience chamber. Then when the player goes in there and looks out the window, the sun and its flare will be seen and give the added depth of being inside a building in the daytime.

There is one unintended side-effect from creating this spotlight. If you have any hallway or room parts in the path of the spotlight then they will get the light, see Figure 391. This light from nowhere will look very weird. If you create a cube 3D shape and size and place it in the right spot you can block the light to avoid this problem.

Chapter 14 – Saving Player State

Another very big feature of games is persistence. I'm not talking about bugging your parents until they give you enough money to buy the next great game. I mean persistence rooting from "persist" meaning to continue to exist. In games, and the computer world in general, being persistent is less a personality trait and more a term meaning that the data you have will still be there when you turn the system off and back on again.

The first persistent memory was called a ROM or Read Only Memory. This was because it would be programmed with certain data one time and read the rest of the time. Memory like this was great for saving your code in because the code wouldn't change. Of course, if you did have to change it, it was not very easy. Now we have hard drives and solid state drives that make it very easy.

In this chapter, we're going to create one script to handle the saving data. But we'll also need to modify a few of the other scripts we already coded to take advantage of this feature. We're going to save the player's location, current scene loaded, whether or not the opening cut scene has been played, current game time for the skybox, each actor's state, and the player's inventory. We'll also update the title scene so all this gets reset when the player starts a new game. Finally, we'll add a cut scene item to save information in a cut scene.

Create a new C# script named "PlayerData" and open it up in Visual Studio. Make it a static function and remove the inheritance from the "MonoBehavior" class as well as the "Start" and "Update" methods. Then add the methods shown in Figure 392.

These use the Unity static class "PlayerPrefs" to store data that we want to persist. Since we have a few things we want to do special, we use this to augment it. Keeping those augmentation methods in the same file is a best practice.

PlayerPrefs can store 'int', 'float', and 'string', but not bool. Since we have some Boolean flags to save, we add the methods to store a bool as an 'int'. You can see on line 9 that if the bool is true then we save it as a '1' otherwise it's a '0'. When we check it on line 15 if it isn't '0' then we declare it as true, otherwise it is false.

```
5   static public class PlayerData
6   {
        1 reference
7       static public void StoreBool(string name, bool val)
8       {
9           if (val) PlayerPrefs.SetInt(name, 1);
10          else PlayerPrefs.SetInt(name, 0);
11      }
12
        1 reference
13      static public bool LoadBool(string name)
14      {
15          if (PlayerPrefs.GetInt(name) != 0)
16          {
17              return true;
18          }
19          else
20          {
21              return false;
22          }
23      }
24
        0 references
25      static public void StoreCurrentScene(string curScene)
26      {
27          PlayerPrefs.SetString("CurrentScene", curScene);
28      }
29
        0 references
30      static public string LoadCurrentScene()
31      {
32          return PlayerPrefs.GetString("CurrentScene");
33      }
```

Figure 392

For the methods to store and load the scene the player is at, we could just let the code call "SetString" directly. However, keeping it in the same file lets us make sure the name that we're storing the current scene under is the same for storing and loading. This makes the code less prone to bugs.

Next, add the static methods shown in Figure 393. There is no player preference method to set a Vector3, so we set each float manually in the "StorePlayerLoc" method. Then we have the method "LoadPlayerLoc", which gets each coordinate, places it into a new Vector3 variable which is assigned to the player's position.

```
static public void StorePlayerLoc(GameObject player)
{
    PlayerPrefs.SetFloat("PosX", player.transform.position.x);
    PlayerPrefs.SetFloat("PosY", player.transform.position.y);
    PlayerPrefs.SetFloat("PosZ", player.transform.position.z);
}

0 references
static public void LoadPlayerLoc(GameObject player)
{
    Vector3 tPos = new Vector3();
    tPos.x = PlayerPrefs.GetFloat("PosX");
    tPos.y= PlayerPrefs.GetFloat("PosY");
    tPos.z = PlayerPrefs.GetFloat("PosZ");
    player.transform.position = tPos;
}
```

Figure 393

```
static public void StoreInventory()
{
    List<Item> itemList = ItemEngine.InventoryGetItem();

    PlayerPrefs.SetInt("InventorySize", itemList.Count);
    for (int i = 0; i < itemList.Count; i++)
    {
        PlayerPrefs.SetString("Item:" + i.ToString(), itemList[i].ItemName);
    }
}

2 references
static public void LoadInventory()
{
    int invSize = PlayerPrefs.GetInt("InventorySize");
    for (int i = 0; i < invSize; i++)
    {
        ItemEngine.InventoryAddItem(PlayerPrefs.GetString("Item:" + i.ToString()));
    }
}
```

Figure 394

After those, add the two methods shown in Figure 394. To store the inventory, we first need to save how many items there are, then in the method to load the inventory we read that size and use for the "for" loop. The item keys are saved in the format of "Item0", "Item1", and so on. The value is the actual name of the item itself. When loading, the item engine is queried to find which item it is from the name and add that item to the player's inventory.

Saving Things

With the infrastructure for the saving of our various things that need saving in place, we're ready to actually save them now. We're going to start with the "SkyboxController", so open it up in Visual Studio. This will not only save the game time when the player closes the game, but also when the player moves to a new scene. Remember, whenever the scenes change, the "Start" method will be called, so we need to make sure this case is covered.

```
15    void Start()
16    {
17        if (PlayerPrefs.GetInt("TimeStarted") != 0)
18        {
19            gameTime = PlayerPrefs.GetFloat("GameTime");
20        }
21        else
22        {
23            gameTime = StartTime;
24        }
25
26        UpdateDay();
27        InvokeRepeating("StoreGameTime", 1f, 1f);
28    }
29
      0 references
30    private void StoreGameTime()
31    {
32        PlayerPrefs.SetInt("TimeStarted", 1);
33        PlayerPrefs.SetFloat("GameTime", gameTime);
34    }
```

Figure 395

In the "Start" method, add the code at the beginning shown in Figure 395. If game time has been stored, then we'll load it, otherwise, use the default. On line 27 we invoke the method "StoreGameTime" which is defined on line 30. That method will store the game time every second. We could do this in the Update method, but all that constant saving may impact performance.

```
30    void Start()
31    {
32        if (PlayerPrefs.GetString(transform.name + "Status") == "Inactive")
33        {
34            gameObject.SetActive(false);
35        }
36
37        m_Animator = GetComponent<Animator>();
38        m_Renderers = GetComponentsInChildren<Renderer>();
```

Figure 396

Open the "ActorController" script and add the code shown in Figure 396 at the top of the "Start" method. The if statement on line 32 will check Playerprefs for the actor's name followed by "Status". If it is marked "Inactive" then we mark the game object as inactive. That way when we pick up that clay jar, it will disappear forever! Or until the player starts a new game.

Next, open the "GameController" script because we have a couple of things we need to update here. We added the code to save and restore both the player position and if the opening cut scene has been played. Here, we are going to save both the current player position and scene as well as save that the opening cut scene has been played.

Near the bottom of the Start method, modify the code from Figure 397 starting on line 58. Instead of defaulting the introduction cinematic to not being played, we load it from the player data using "LoadBool" using the name of the scene and adding "Cine onto the end.

On line 64, make a repeating invoke to a method we'll write later named "StorePlayerLoc" which will do what its name suggests.

Then blocks from lines 66 to 70 will activate objects and set flags based on if the value we got earlier on line 59. Finally, on line 72 we will only stop the music and play the introduction cinematic if the flag we loaded is false, which means the introduction cinematic for this scene has not been played yet.

```
58          string sceneName = SceneEngine.GetCurrentSceneName();
59          IntroCinePlayed = PlayerData.LoadBool(sceneName + "Cine");
60          fromMainMenu = false;
61          MainMenuObj.SetActive(false);
62          OptionsMenuSetActive(false);
63          LoadingPanelObj.SetActive(false);
64          InvokeRepeating("StorePlayerLoc", 1f, 1f);
65
66          FadingOut = IntroCinePlayed;
67          CineCam.SetActive(!IntroCinePlayed);
68          MinimapObj.SetActive(IntroCinePlayed);
69          Player.SetActive(IntroCinePlayed);
70          IntroObjects.SetActive(!IntroCinePlayed);
71
72          if (!IntroCinePlayed)
73          {
74              MusController.StopMusic();
75              IntroCine.Play();
76          }
```

Figure 397

```
78          if ((SceneEngine.NewSceneName != null) && (SceneEngine.NewSceneName != ""))
79          {
80              Player.transform.position = SceneEngine.NewPlayerPos;
81              SceneEngine.NewSceneName = "";
82          }
83          else if (PlayerData.LoadCurrentScene() == sceneName)
84          {
85              PlayerData.LoadPlayerLoc(Player);
86          }
```

Figure 398

At the end of the Start method, add the 'else if' block shown in Figure 398 on line 83 to 86. Remember, the 'if' block on line 78 checks if the player got here from another scene. This block will load the player location if the loaded scene name matches this scene's name.

```
90      void Update()
91      {
92          bool escapedCinematic = false;
93
94          if (!IntroCinePlayed)
95          {
96              if ((IntroCine.state != PlayState.Playing) || (Input.GetKeyUp(KeyCode.Escape)))
97              {
98                  PlayerData.StoreBool(SceneEngine.GetCurrentSceneName() + "Cine", true);
99                  escapedCinematic = true;
```

Figure 399

The next code to update in this file is in the "Update" method. Scroll down to it and add it from Figure 399 on line 98. This will save whether the cinematic was played so it won't be played next time.

The last code for this file is to save the player position. After the Update method, add method "StorePlayerLoc" from Figure 400. Recall, this method will get called every second and here you see it will save the current scene name and the player location. Again, it could be in the Update method, but this way minimizes impact to performance.

```
private void StorePlayerLoc()
{
    PlayerData.StoreCurrentScene(SceneEngine.GetCurrentSceneName());
    PlayerData.StorePlayerLoc(Player);
}
```

Figure 400

Open "ItemEngine" because saving the inventory is next. Figure 401 has the code for adding an item on line 51. We use the "StoreInventory" static method we coded earlier. Every time an item is added to the inventory, we will store the inventory so it can be loaded later.

```
46  static public void InventoryAddItem(string name)
47  {
48      Item item = GetItem(name);
49
50      if (item != null) InventoryItems.Add(item);
51      PlayerData.StoreInventory();
52  }
```

Figure 401

We add the corresponding store of the inventory when an item is removed. See Figure 402. In both methods to remove items, either by slot number or by item name, the inventory is stored for later load.

```
static public void InventoryRemItem(int slot)
{
    if (slot < InventoryItems.Count)
    {
        InventoryItems.RemoveAt(slot);
        PlayerData.StoreInventory();
    }
}

1 reference
static public void InventoryRemItem(string name)
{
    Item item = GetItem(name);

    if (item != null) InventoryItems.Remove(item);
    PlayerData.StoreInventory();
}
```

Figure 402

Open the "TitleController" script and scroll down to the Update method and modify the 'if' blocks shown in Figure 403.

When a new game is selected, all the player preferences are deleted. Then the starting items are given to the player.

Then, instead of using the scene manager from Unity to load the scenes for new game and continue, we'll use our "SceneEngine". This way, our code above knows that there was a prior scenes that was loaded.

```
if (selectNewGame)
{
    PlayerPrefs.DeleteAll();
    ItemEngine.InventoryAddItem("Staff");
    ItemEngine.InventoryAddItem("Cloak");
    SceneEngine.LoadScene(GameSceneName);
}
else if (selectContinue)
{
    PlayerData.LoadInventory();
    SceneEngine.LoadScene(PlayerData.LoadCurrentScene());
}
```

Figure 403

```
173                     switch (curDia.Lines[diaIndex].Action)
174                     {
175                         case DialogueElement._action.GiveItem:
176                             ItemEngine.InventoryAddItem(curDia.Lines[diaIndex].ActionName);
177                             break;
178                         case DialogueElement._action.TakeItem:
179                             ItemEngine.InventoryRemItem(curDia.Lines[diaIndex].ActionName);
180                             break;
181                         case DialogueElement._action.ActivateObject:
182                             curDia.Lines[diaIndex].ActionObject.SetActive(true);
183                             PlayerPrefs.SetString(curDia.Lines[diaIndex].ActionObject.name + "Status", "");
184                             break;
185                         case DialogueElement._action.InactivateObject:
186                             curDia.Lines[diaIndex].ActionObject.SetActive(false);
187                             PlayerPrefs.SetString(curDia.Lines[diaIndex].ActionObject.name + "Status", "Inactive");
188                             break;
189                     }
```

Figure 404

Open the "DialogueController" script and scroll down to the "ProcessElement" method. In the cases for "ActivateObject" and "InactivateObject". Add the respective lines 183 and 187 from Figure 404 to mark the object in the player preferences with a blank status or as "Inactive". When the actor controller script looks up the status of the actor's name, they will be able to see if it was last stored as Inactive or not.

With that code done, let's go back into Unity and get it working. If you haven't, open the "Egypt_Nile Scene". In the Hierarchy View, expand the "Timelines" object and select "IntroCinematic". In the inspector under "Playable Director", uncheck the "Play On Awake" box as shown in Figure 405. This will allow us to skip the introduction cinematic if the player has already seen it.

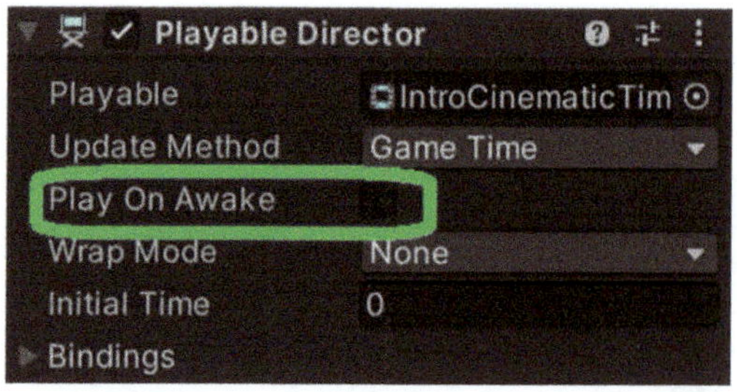

Figure 405

Now we need to add our Cloak and Staff items into the inventory if you haven't already. Go back to Unity and in Assets > Prefabs open the "GameController" prefab. Click the "Inventory" child object to see its inspector. Drag 2 more "Item" scripts onto it and set the Item Name and Description as shown in Figure 406. Use the "Staff image from Assets > Images > Icons and then the "cloaks" icon from Assets > Images > Icons > RPG_inventory_icons.

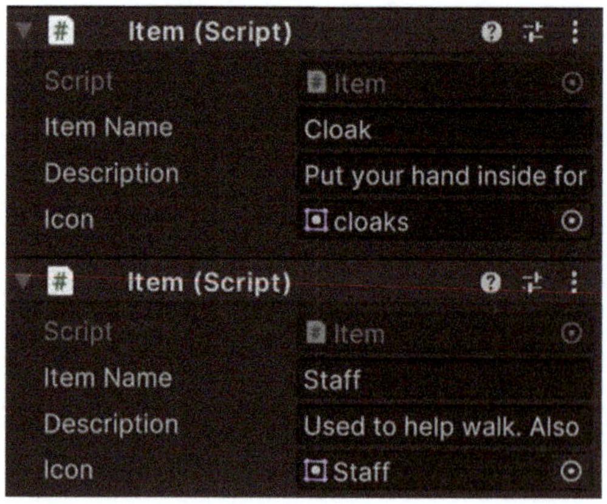

Figure 406

Descriptions:

- Cloak: Put your hand in this for a special surprise.
- Staff: Used to help walk. Also used for some miracles

This will add the items on the prefab for any new scenes you create.

Great! You've now got the new items in the item list. But this only adds them if you start the game in the "Egypt_Nile Scene". You need to add them to all the other scenes you made like "Palace Scene" and "Pyramid" scene.

For the Title Scene, I'm going to show you a neat trick. In one of the other scenes, copy the "Inventory" child object under the "GameController" in the Hierarchy View using CTRL+C, load the Title scene, and then paste it into the Hierarchy View. You'll see that some of the objects in the inspector are missing. That's going to cause a problem, so remove the Inventory script from the object by clicking the 3 dots on the top right of the component and selecting "Remove Component".

Create a new C# script named "TitleInventory" and open it in Visual Studio. We only need to add line 10 in the Start method. You can delete the Update method as we don't need it. The entire class should look like what you see in Figure 407.

```
5   public class TitleInventory : MonoBehaviour
6   {
7       // Start is called before the first frame update
        Unity Message | 0 references
8       void Start()
9       {
10          ItemEngine.Initialize(GetComponents<Item>());
11      }
12  }
```

Figure 407

Playing Persistence

Figure 408

With all that done, we're ready to test out our changes to persist player information. We'll do much of our testing from here. Play the scene and click the New Game button when it loads. The title scene will fade out and the new scene will load. Then you'll be greeted by the opening cut scene. When it is done, press the 'I' key to open the inventory and you'll see the staff and cloak as shown in Figure 408. This verifies our code to give the player those items works, and the opening cut scene still works.

End play mode now. We're going to make sure that the inventory is saved, as well as the player's last scene and position. To do this, we're going to play from the "Egypt_Nile Scene". This will update the player's position to the spawn location nearby the palace. The inventory will be blank here, and that is ok, we're just updating the player position. Since no items are added or removed the inventory won't be saved. Then we'll continue the game from the title scene and verify the player's position and inventory.

> *Just as important as designing and writing the code is making sure you have good testing of your game. We'll talk about playtesting later, but the more you can think of scenarios to test the more your game will stand up to players all sorts of things you never thought of.*

Go ahead and load the "Egypt_Nile Scene" now and click play. When it loads, the player will be at the spawn location nearby the palace. That is all we need. You can end play mode. Now load the Title scene back again and play the scene. Push the continue button. When the scene finishes loading make sure that the player is at the palace. Then open the inventory and make sure the two items' "Staff" and "Cloak" are still there. Then go to the clay jar and pick it up. Then exit play mode and re-enter. You should see the clay jar disappear from the scene and appear in your inventory.

If something isn't working right or there are errors, double-check all the code is typed exactly right. Remember that the errors give the file and line number of each issue.

Music and Sound FX Bonus!

Letting the player adjust the volume of the game gives them a greater sense of control over the game. Other things to let them control are keyboard shortcuts and screen brightness.

Earlier, when we made the title scene, we created a couple of sliders for music and sound effects volume and said that we would hook these up later. Guess what! Later is now. You might be wondering why we didn't code these features in the music section. That is because we were waiting for our persistent storage feature to be completed.

If we're going to update all the music and sound effects, then we need to take stock of every way that they are sent to the player. That means figuring out every object that has an audio source component and making sure it has a way to update the volume based on the player's input.

Create a new C# script named "VolumeControl" and open it up in Visual Studio. Code it up as shown in Figure 409. This script will be attached to all objects with an Audio Source component. When we attach it, we need to tell the difference between music and sound effects. This will happen for each Audio Source in the inspector.

In the "Start" method, we just get a handle to the audio source component. The "Update" method sets volume appropriately based on the audio type.

```
public enum _type
{
    Music,
    SoundFX
}
public _type AudioType;

private AudioSource m_Audio;

// Start is called before the first frame update
Unity Message | 0 references
void Start()
{
    m_Audio = GetComponent<AudioSource>();
}

// Update is called once per frame
Unity Message | 0 references
void Update()
{
    switch (AudioType)
    {
        case _type.Music:
            m_Audio.volume = PlayerPrefs.GetFloat("MusicVolume");
            break;
        case _type.SoundFX:
            m_Audio.volume = PlayerPrefs.GetFloat("SoundVolume");
            break;
    }
}
```

Figure 409

Open up the script "TitleController" in Visual Studio and In the "Start" method, scroll near the bottom and add the code to set the initial values for the music and sound sliders shown in Figure 410. The 'if' block will load the saved values of the sliders if the player has played the game already. If this is the first time then the 'else' will set the defaults to 50%.

```
if (PlayerData.LoadCurrentScene() != "")
{
    MusicSlider.value = PlayerPrefs.GetFloat("MusicVolume");
    SoundFXSlider.value = PlayerPrefs.GetFloat("SoundVolume");
}
else
{
    MusicSlider.value = 0.5f;
    PlayerPrefs.SetFloat("MusicVolume", 0.5f);
    SoundFXSlider.value = 0.5f;
    PlayerPrefs.SetFloat("SoundVolume", 0.5f);
}
```

Figure 410

Scroll all the way down to the bottom of the class and add the 2 new methods shown in Figure 411. We'll use the Unity glue so these methods will get called whenever the player changes the sliders for music or sound. All these need to do is save the value the player changes it to into persistent storage using Player Data.

```
public void MusicSliderChanged()
{
    PlayerPrefs.SetFloat("MusicVolume", MusicSlider.value);
}

0 references
public void SoundSliderChanged()
{
    PlayerPrefs.SetFloat("SoundVolume", SoundFXSlider.value);
}
```

Figure 411

To fully control the volume the player should be allowed to do it in-game. Open "GameController" and add the public variables from Figure 412.

```
public MusicController MusController;
public UnityEngine.UI.Slider MusicSlider;
public UnityEngine.UI.Slider SoundFXSlider;
```

Figure 412

Scroll down to the bottom of the Start method and lines 90 and 91 to set the initial slider value based on what was stored in player preferences in Figure 413.

```
85  else if (PlayerData.LoadCurrentScene() == sceneName)
86  {
87      PlayerData.LoadPlayerLoc(Player);
88  }
89
90  MusicSlider.value = PlayerPrefs.GetFloat("MusicVolume");
91  SoundFXSlider.value = PlayerPrefs.GetFloat("SoundVolume");
```

Figure 413

The "GameController" will need the same methods we coded into the "TitleController" in Figure 411. You can simply copy and paste the code to the bottom of the "GameController" class.

Gluing Volume Controls Together

We'll need to update both the Title scene and the "GameController" prefab. Let's start off by getting the Title scene working with the new volume controls. Go back to Unity, and make sure the Title scene is loaded.

In the Hierarchy View, expand the "Canvas" and then the "OptionsPanel" to reveal the "MusicVolume" and "SoundVolume" child objects. Click the "MusicVolume" object and look at the bottom of the inspector to the section called "On Value Changed (Single)". This is a list of all methods that will be called when the slider changes, similar to how the input UI object works. Click the '+' icon to add a new entry and drag the "TitleController" object from the Hierarchy View onto it and select TitleController > MusicSliderChanged () so it looks similar to Figure 414. Do the same thing for the "SoundVolume" object but set the method to "SoundSliderChanged ()". When the player changes these sliders, the appropriate method will be called and the new slider value will be saved in the player preferences.

Figure 414

Then we need to add our volume control script to the background music in the title scene. Click the "Day_Time_3" object and then drag the script "VolumeControl" onto it. It should appear underneath the Audio Source component. Make sure the Audio Type is set to Music as in Figure 415.

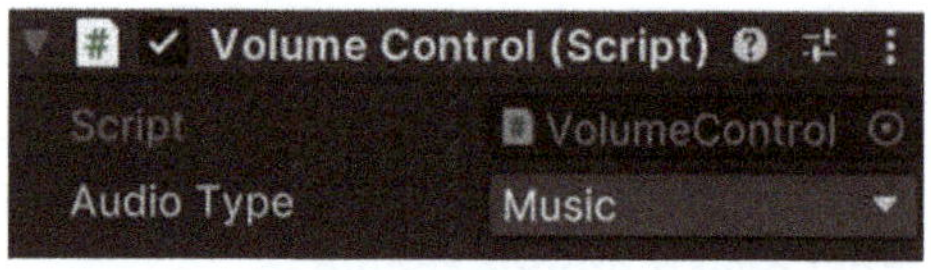

Figure 415

That's all we need to do to test out the volume control for the title scene. Play the scene and let's give it a try. You'll hear the music when the scene fades in. Click the "Options" button so we can see the options menu. You'll see the music and sound volume sliders we just hooked up that are set all the way to the right as shown in Figure 416.

Figure 416

Drag the slider for the "Music Volume" all the way to the left and you'll hear the music stop. Go ahead and play around with it for a little bit. Note that the "Sound Volume" slider won't change anything yet since we haven't hooked it up yet. We'll put this on the player prefab so it will affect things like footsteps, jump, and landing sounds.

Once you're sure it's working, end play mode. In the Hierarchy View, click the "MosesPlayer" prefab from Assets > Prefabs. Drag the "VolumeControl" script onto the inspector and set the Control Type to "Sound FX". This will put our Sound FX control to use with footsteps, jumps, and landing.

Let's update our "GameController" prefab so that volume control works in-game too. As in the Title scene, go to the "MusicVolume" and "SoundVolume" objects in the Canvas > OptionsMenu in the Hierarchy View and click the '+' so we can add a method to listen to when the slider changes. Drag the "GameController" object into the object fields and select GameController > MusicSliderChanged or SoundSliderChanged respectively.

Now click on the "GameController" object and drag the "MusicVolume" and "SoundVolume" slider objects into the respective fields there. It should look like Figure 417.

Figure 417

Then add a "VolumeControl" script onto the inspector for the "GameController" and set it to "Sound FX". This is for the Bible audio. Click the "MusicController" object and add a "VolumeControl" script there as well but leave it set to "Music".

Exit the prefab view by clicking the arrow in the upper left corner of the Hierarchy View and load the "Egypt_Nile Scene". First, in the Hierarchy View, expand "Timelines" and select "IntroCinematic". Add a volume control script to it set to "Sound FX".

That takes care of all the audio sources in this scene. You'll need to do the steps described in the 2 paragraphs above for each scene we have (i.e., Palace, Pyramid, and any others you may have created). Give the game a test run and see how changing the volume levels feels.

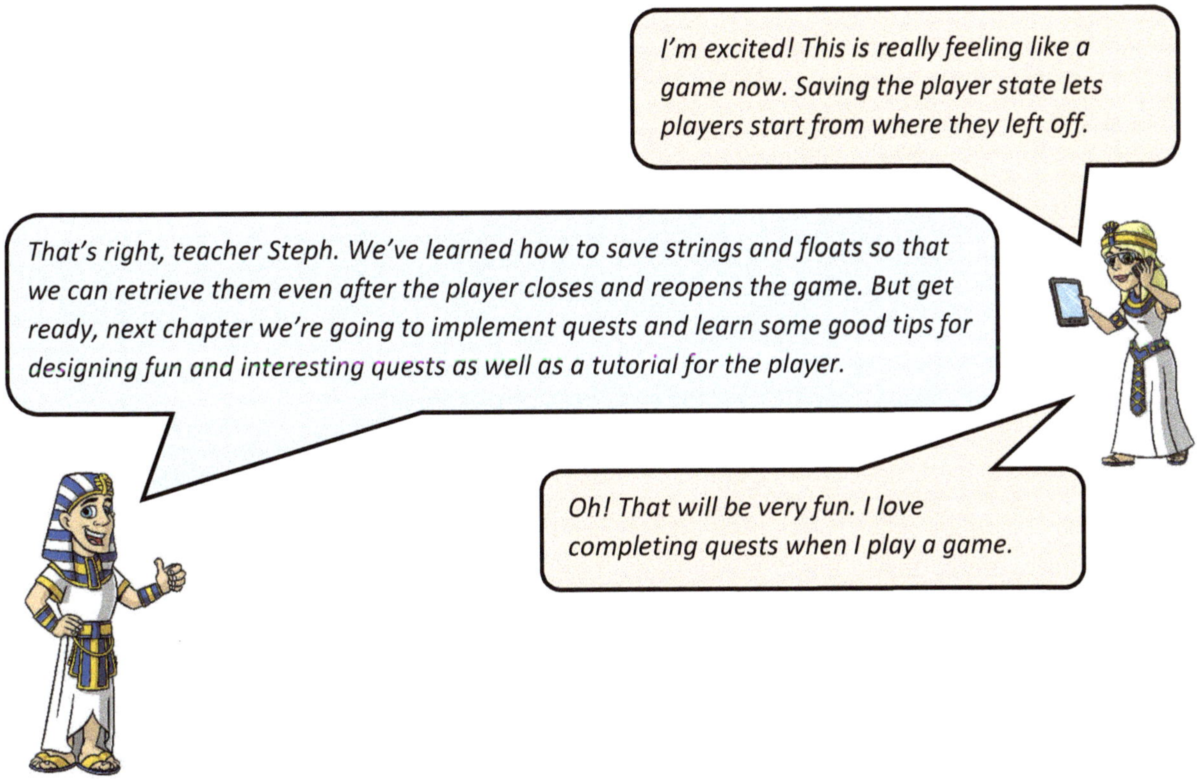

Chapter 15 – Quest Journal

Quests can be the heart of the game that truly immerses the player into the story. They can also be the tedious tasks that the player must endure so they can get to the part of the game they want. Designing fun and challenging quests can be... challenging. It takes experience and careful thinking. Even then, the best of us can still make the player feel like they're slogging through the quests up-hill both ways in the snow with wild wolves chasing them.

In our tutorial, we're going to have a journal that players can look at to see quests organized into books. Each individual quest has information attached to it like its name, description, and so on. The quests in each book are listed sequentially, meaning that you need to complete one quest in that book before moving to the next one. The books may be done by the player in any order they want. They can be at different quests and different chapters for different books. But all the quests within a book must be done sequentially.

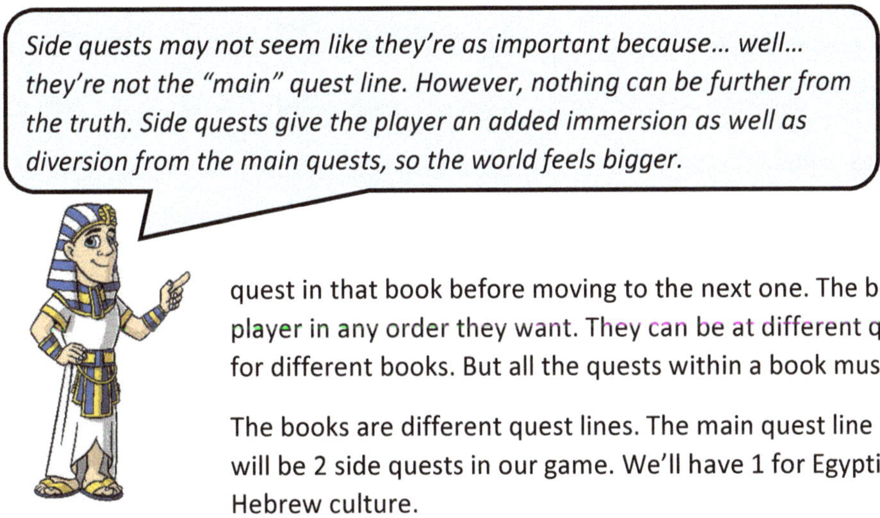

The books are different quest lines. The main quest line is the Exodus story. There will be 2 side quests in our game. We'll have 1 for Egyptian culture and another for Hebrew culture.

The class diagram in Figure 418 shows you how things are going to work together. The Quest Controller will be the hub for all things about the quest. It will contain the quest books which will then, in turn, contain the quests.

Quest Objects are game objects that will only be enabled when a given quest is active. All other times they will be inactive, or not visible to the player.

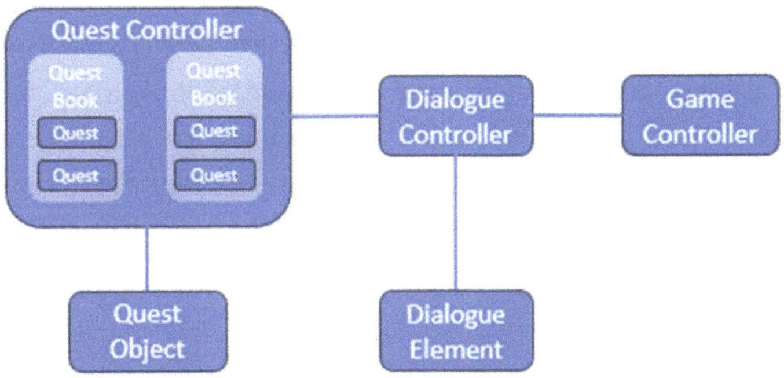

Figure 418

Dialogue Elements will be given the ability to advance or complete quests. This will be the way we allow the player to move the quests and story forward. We'll need to make a few updates the dialogue and game controllers as well.

Later in this chapter, you'll learn how to use dropdown boxes to select books and quests and even program them using scripts. Finally, we'll get started with the beginning of the story, Moses, out in the desert. It's going to be lots of fun!

Quest System Scripts

Let's first add code for the class to hold all the information for our quests. Create a new C# script named "Quest" and open it up in Visual Studio. See Figure 419 for the code.

- QuestName: Descriptive name to display to the player.
- TargetActor: Primary quest actor.
- Location: Name of the area or zone.
- NumReq: Number of somethings required to complete the quest.
- BibleVerse: Verse in the Bible for this quest the player can reference.
- Description: Details about the quest and any instructions to show the player.
- Completed: Whether or not this quest has been completed.
- CurReq: The current number of requirements met.

```
[System.Serializable]
8 references
public class Quest
{
    public string QuestName;
    public string TargetActor;
    public string Location;
    public int NumReq;
    public string BibleVerse;
    [TextArea] public string Description;
    [HideInInspector] public bool Completed;
    [HideInInspector] public int CurReq;
}
```

Figure 419

At the beginning of the class is an attribute "[System.Serializable]" to allow the class to show up in the inspector. The "[TextArea]" attribute tells the inspector to display multiple lines for ease of editing. Also, the "[HideInInspector]" attribute tells the inspector not to show these variables since "Completed" and "CurReq" are not supposed to be changeable there.

The code for the book class is even simpler. Create a new C# script named "QuestBook" and modify it to look like Figure 420. This class has an array of those quests we coded earlier and a name. This class is also meant to show up in the inspector, so we've got the attribute to serialize it as well. Neither inherit from "Monobehavior" and won't attach to a game object.

```
[System.Serializable]
2 references
public class QuestBook
{
    public string BookName;
    public Quest[] Quests;
}
```

Figure 420

Now, let's create the "QuestController" C# script. It'll start before the class declaration by saying we'll be using UI and TextMesh Pro you can see in Figure 421. Lines 9 to 14 are UI objects that the controller will need to display the quests. Line 15 is a handle to the game controller. Line 16 has the array of quest books that will contain all of the quests. Lines 17 and 18 are objects we'll need to refer to when handling quests. Finally, we'll keep a list of the books handy for when we need to build the options in the book dropdown box.

```
4   using UnityEngine.UI;
5   using TMPro;
6
    Unity Script | 1 reference
7   public class QuestController : MonoBehaviour
8   {
9       public GameObject JournalPanel;
10      public TMP_Dropdown BookDropDown;
11      public TMP_Dropdown QuestDropDown;
12      public TextMeshProUGUI QuestText;
13      public Toggle CompletedToggle;
14      public TextMeshProUGUI QuickQuestText;
15      public GameController gc;
16      public QuestBook[] Quests;
17      public QuestObject[] QuestObjects;
18      public GameObject[] TrackedObjects;
19
20      private List<string> questBooks;
```

Figure 421

```
23      void Start()
24      {
25          questBooks = new List<string>();
26
27          // Load Quest Status
28          foreach (QuestBook qb in Quests)
29          {
30              questBooks.Add(qb.BookName);
31
32              foreach(Quest quest in qb.Quests)
33              {
34                  string CompName = qb.BookName + ":" + quest.QuestName + ":Status";
35                  string CurReqName = qb.BookName + ":" + quest.QuestName + ":CurReq";
36                  quest.Completed = PlayerPrefs.GetInt(CompName) == 1;
37                  quest.CurReq = PlayerPrefs.GetInt(CurReqName);
38              }
39          }
40
41          CompletedToggle.interactable = false;
42          BookDropDown.ClearOptions();
43          BookDropDown.AddOptions(questBooks);
44          HideJournal();
45          SetQuestObjects();
46          UpdateQuickQuestText();
47      }
```

Figure 422

Scroll down to the "Start" method and add the code from Figure 422. After initializing the list of quest books on line 25, we load quest completion and the number of current requirements met from player preferences. On line 41, we set the toggle UI object to not be interactable. We'll setup the dropdown box for books. Then we'll get ready for the start of the scene by hiding the journal window, making sure only the quest objects for the current quest are active, and then updating our quick quest text. The quick quest text is a quality-of-life improvement to prevent the player from getting confused.

You can delete the "Update" method as we won't use it in this class. The next two methods shown in Figure 423 are helpers to find what the current quest is from the book. The first method will loop through the quests in the given book number until it finds one that is not completed. If the quest is not completed, then we'll save that quest's index and return it if the next quest has been completed. The

```
public int GetCurQuestNum(int bookNum)
{
    int questNum = 0;

    for (int i = 0; i < Quests[bookNum].Quests.Length; i++)
    {
        if (!Quests[bookNum].Quests[i].Completed) break;
        else questNum = i;
    }

    return questNum;
}

1 reference
public Quest GetCurQuest(int bookNum)
{
    return Quests[bookNum].Quests[GetCurQuestNum(bookNum)];
}
```

Figure 423

"GetCurQuest" method just wraps around the "GetCurQuestNum" method to return the actual quest. Now buckle up because we've got a bunch more methods to add.

The next method shown in Figure 424 will update the text that tells the player what to do next with the current quest's description. We use book number '0' to show the main quest line. When we add our quests, we need to make sure that the first book, or index '0', will be the main quest line.

```
private void UpdateQuickQuestText()
{
    int curQuest = GetCurQuestNum(0);

    if (curQuest >= 0)
    {
        QuickQuestText.text = Quests[0].Quests[curQuest].Description;
    }
    else
    {
        QuickQuestText.text = "";
    }
}
```

Figure 424

The next method shows the player the quest journal in Figure 425. This method activates the quest journal panel. It will default to show the main quest line and proceed to update the quest dropdown box and the text to display.

```
public void ShowJournal()
{
    JournalPanel.SetActive(true);
    BookDropDown.value = 0;
    ResetQuestDropDown();
    SetQuestText();
}
```

Figure 425

The code to reset the quest dropdown box is in Figure 426. To populate the list of quests to select, we need to know how many have been completed. We're only going to show the completed quests and the current quest. That way the player doesn't get overwhelmed with too much quest info. If the quest has been completed, then increment our counter. Once we encounter a quest that hasn't been completed yet, we break and the "lastCompleted" counter will hold the index of the last quest completed. This algorithm only adds the quests that have been completed plus the next quest. Finally, we add the quests to the dropdown menu and set the default quest to view to be the quest the player is currently on. Since that quest will most likely be the one they want to find information about, setting it right away will help improve quality of life.

```
private void ResetQuestDropDown()
{
    List<string> questOptions = new List<string>();
    int lastCompleted = 0;

    QuestDropDown.ClearOptions();
    foreach(Quest quest in Quests[BookDropDown.value].Quests)
    {
        questOptions.Add(quest.QuestName);

        if (quest.Completed) lastCompleted++;
        else break;
    }

    QuestDropDown.AddOptions(questOptions);
    QuestDropDown.value = lastCompleted;
}
```

Figure 426

```
private void SetQuestText()
{
    Quest curQuest = Quests[BookDropDown.value].Quests[QuestDropDown.value];

    QuestText.text = "Quest: " + curQuest.QuestName + "\n";
    QuestText.text += "NPC: " + curQuest.TargetActor + "\n";
    QuestText.text += "Location: " + curQuest.Location + "\n";
    QuestText.text += "Verse: " + curQuest.BibleVerse + "\n\n";
    QuestText.text += curQuest.Description;
    CompletedToggle.isOn = curQuest.Completed;
}
```

Figure 427

The method for "SetQuestText" to be coded next is shown in Figure 427. When the quest journal is opened and the current quest is displayed, or the player selects a different quest to see, the method will set up what the player sees. First, we get a handle to the current quest. Then we proceed to display the name, actor, location, Bible verse, and description in the text object. At the end, we mark if the quest has been completed or not.

Three more methods to help handle UI stuff are in Figure 428. Hiding the quest journal just needs to inactivate the panel. For the next two we'll hook up to the dropdown boxes we'll create later in this chapter when the player changes them. If they change the dropdown for the quest book, then we need to reset what the quest dropdown will show and update the text for the quest shown to the player. If the player changes the quest dropdown, then all we need to do is update the quest text in the journal panel.

```
public void HideJournal()
{
    JournalPanel.SetActive(false);
}

0 references
public void BookDropDownHandler(int changed)
{
    ResetQuestDropDown();
    SetQuestText();
}

0 references
public void QuestDropDownHandler(int changed)
{
    SetQuestText();
}
```

Figure 428

```
public void CompleteQuest(int bookNum, int questNum)
{
    Quest curQuest = Quests[bookNum].Quests[questNum];
    curQuest.Completed = true;
    PlayerPrefs.SetInt(Quests[bookNum].BookName + ":" + curQuest.QuestName + ":Status", 1);
    SetQuestObjects();
}
```

Figure 429

Next, we code the method to complete quests in Figure 429. We simply get the quest given the book and quest numbers and mark it as complete. Then we save that in the player preferences and call "SetQuestObjects" to make sure we have the right quest objects enabled.

```
public void AddQuestCount(int bookNum, int questNum)
{
    Quest curQuest = Quests[bookNum].Quests[questNum];
    string curReqName = Quests[bookNum].BookName + ":" + curQuest.QuestName + ":CurReq";
    curQuest.CurReq++;
    PlayerPrefs.SetInt(curReqName, curQuest.CurReq);

    if (curQuest.CurReq >= curQuest.NumReq)
    {
        CompleteQuest(bookNum, questNum);
    }
}
```

Figure 430

After completing quests, we need to increment the current number of the quest in the method "AddQuestCount" shown in Figure 430. Very similar to the method to complete quests, it gets the current quest, increments the "CurReq" variable, and then saves it in the player preferences. One thing new that we do is check if the current number meets or exceeds the required number. If it does, then we call the method to complete that quest.

```
156     public void SetQuestObjects()
157     {
158         // Build current quest list
159         List<int> curQuestList = new List<int>();
160         for (int i = 0; i < Quests.Length; i++)
161         {
162             curQuestList.Add(GetCurQuestNum(i));
163         }
164
165         // Inactivate all quest objects
166         foreach (QuestObject qo in QuestObjects) qo.gameObject.SetActive(false);
167
168         // Activate only quest objects for the current quest
169         foreach(QuestObject qo in QuestObjects)
170         {
171             bool isForCurrentQuest = qo.QuestNum == curQuestList[qo.BookNum];
172             qo.gameObject.SetActive(isForCurrentQuest);
173         }
174     }
```

Figure 431

Don't give up now! We're almost done. Hang in there. The method shown in Figure 431 will only show the quest objects that are for the current quest. This way we can have special actors and objects that only appear for that quest. First, we get a list of the current quest number in each quest book. This will be used to avoid a nested loop, or a loop within a loop, on line 168. Going back to line 165, we first disable all the quest objects.

The loop on line 168 is a little complicated. It iterates over the quest objects like the one on line 165 but is for activating them. The bool "isForCurrentQuest" uses a conditional, normally used in 'if' statements as its value. This works because it's a bool. If the quest number of the quest object is the same as the book's current quest, then we'll set it to true. We use that to directly set the active state of the object.

It is best to avoid nested loops, when possible. They easily have bugs and are hard to maintain. However, they are a tool in your programming tool belt. Use them sparingly.

```
public class QuestObject : MonoBehaviour
{
    public int BookNum;
    public int QuestNum;
}
```

Figure 432

Whew! To offset all that work on one class, let's have a really small class next. Create a new C# script named "QuestObject" and add the two public variables shown in Figure 432. This holds which book and quest numbers the object is for.

Quest Script Updates

```
7   public class GameController : MonoBehaviour
8   {
9       public DialogueController DialogueCtlr;
10      public QuestController QuestCtlr;
```

Figure 433

Now we have a few updates to make to existing scripts to get everything working in Unity (Ok, to be honest, I think I'm getting tired of that pun now). Open the "GameController" script and add a reference to the "QuestController" on line 10 in Figure 433.

Now scroll down to the "_ui_state" enumerated type. Add "Quest" on line 37 and don't forget to add the comma ',' at the end of line 36 from Figure 434. You may be thinking that means we need to update our UI state machine to incorporate the new quest journal window. And you are right! We'll need to do the same kind of update that we did previously for adding the inventory. In this script we're adding another state to our UI diagram. Like before, we need to make sure that we can get to any state from the journal state and get to the journal state from any other state.

```
30  private enum _ui_state
31  {
32      None,
33      WorldMap,
34      MainMenu,
35      OptionsMenu,
36      Inventory,
37      Quest
38  }
```

Figure 434

Scrolling down to the "Update" method, add the new "else if" statement shown in Figure 435 on lines 145 – 148. Whenever the player presses the 'Q' keys on the keyboard the method "QuestHandler" will be called to show or hide the journal.

```
141 else if (Input.GetKeyUp(KeyCode.I))
142 {
143     InventoryHandler();
144 }
145 else if (Input.GetKeyUp(KeyCode.Q))
146 {
147     QuestHandler();
148 }
```

Figure 435

Scroll down to the "WorldMapHandler" method and add the new case statement for the journal as shown in Figure 436 on lines 216 to 220. So when the player tries to open the world map, the quest journal will hide, the world map will be displayed, and the UI state changes to "WorldMap".

```
211             case _ui_state.Inventory:
212                 InvController.HideInventory();
213                 WorldMapSetActive(true);
214                 uiState = _ui_state.WorldMap;
215                 break;
216             case _ui_state.Quest:
217                 QuestCtlr.HideJournal();
218                 WorldMapSetActive(true);
219                 uiState = _ui_state.WorldMap;
220                 break;
221             default:
222                 // Catch the "None" state here
223                 WorldMapSetActive(true);
224                 uiState = _ui_state.WorldMap;
225                 break;
```

Figure 436

This case also needs to be added for the switch statements in the methods "MainMenuHandler", "OptionsMenuHandler", and "InventoryHandler". You can copy and paste the code but be sure to activate or show the appropriate window and don't forget to set the state accordingly. Otherwise, the menu system won't work right.

Scroll down underneath the method "InventoryHandler" and add the new method for "QuestHandler" as shown in Figure 437. If you want, you can copy and paste from a previous handler like the "InventoryHandler". If you do, make sure you go through each case statement (except the Journal case) to make sure the appropriate window is being hidden and the quest journal is being shown.

```
public void QuestHandler()
{
    switch (uiState)
    {
        case _ui_state.MainMenu:
            MainMenuObj.SetActive(false);
            QuestCtlr.ShowJournal();
            uiState = _ui_state.Quest;
            break;
        case _ui_state.OptionsMenu:
            OptionsMenuSetActive(false);
            QuestCtlr.ShowJournal();
            uiState = _ui_state.Quest;
            break;
        case _ui_state.WorldMap:
            WorldMapSetActive(false);
            QuestCtlr.ShowJournal();
            uiState = _ui_state.Quest;
            break;
        case _ui_state.Inventory:
            InvController.HideInventory();
            QuestCtlr.ShowJournal();
            uiState = _ui_state.Quest;
            break;
        case _ui_state.Quest:
            QuestCtlr.HideJournal();
            uiState = _ui_state.None;
            break;
        default:
            // Catch the "None" state here
            QuestCtlr.ShowJournal();
            uiState = _ui_state.Quest;
            break;
    }
```

Figure 437

It is important to make sure the UI state is changed to be the "Journal" state. In the "Journal" case the quest journal is hidden, and the state is set back to "None" to mean that no windows are being shown. In the default case, where no windows are being shown, show the quest journal window and set the state to "Journal".

That's all for the new state change! It wasn't so bad. This will be the last new UI state change we make in this tutorial. There are other possibilities now that you know how to do it like making a character screen to equip items.

Now open the "DialogueElement" script for a couple of additions there. Add the two new public variables you see on lines 16 and 17 of Figure 438. These will tell our dialogue controller which quest and book to update or complete.

```
14    public string ActionName;
15    public GameObject ActionObject;
16    public int ActionQuestNumber;
17    public int ActionBookNumber;
```

Figure 438

Below that, make the changes to the "_action" enumerated type shown in Figure 439. We're adding an action to complete the quest specified on line 32 in the public variables we added above. Again, don't forget to add the comma ',' on line 31.

```
25    public enum _action
26    {
27        None,
28        GiveItem,
29        TakeItem,
30        ActivateObject,
31        InactivateObject,
32        CompleteQuest
33    }
```

Figure 439

```
185            case DialogueElement._action.InactivateObject:
186                curDia.Lines[diaIndex].ActionObject.SetActive(false);
187                PlayerPrefs.SetString(curDia.Lines[diaIndex].ActionObject.name + "Status", "Inactive");
188                break;
189            case DialogueElement._action.CompleteQuest:
190                int bookNum = curDia.Lines[diaIndex].ActionBookNumber;
191                int questNum = curDia.Lines[diaIndex].ActionQuestNumber;
192                Quest curQuest = gc.QuestCtlr.GetCurQuest(bookNum);
193                if (curQuest.NumReq == 1)
194                {
195                    gc.QuestCtlr.CompleteQuest(bookNum, questNum);
196                }
197                else
198                {
199                    gc.QuestCtlr.AddQuestCount(bookNum, questNum);
200                }
201                break;
```

Figure 440

Now open the "DialogueController" script and scroll down to the "ProcessElement" method. In the switch statement for the current dialogue's "Action", add the new case statement shown in lines 189 to 201 in Figure 440.

On lines 190 and 191, we get the book number and then the quest number in a local variable. Then line 192 gets the current quest. Line 193 checks for only a single number required. If that's the case, then it will complete the quest. If not, then it adds to the current count of the quest.

Remember, up above that in our "QuestController" script, in the method "AddQuestCount", that if the count meets the threshold of the number required then it will complete the quest.

```
204        if (curDia.Lines[diaIndex].Text == "")
205        {
206            if (curDia.Lines[diaIndex].Response == DialogueElement._response_type.End)
207            {
208                EndDialogue();
209            }
210            else
211            {
212                ProcessNextElement();
213            }
214        }
215    }
216    else
217    {
218        EndDialogue();
219    }
```

Figure 441

The last code to update is a quality-of-life improvement. At the bottom of the same 'if' block that the switch statement we just added the case to, we're going to skip showing dialogue that has no text. Before, even though we had actions going on in the dialogue, the controller will still wait for the player's input.

With the code added on line 204 in Figure 441, the dialogue controller will recognize there is nothing to show the player and subsequently skip showing them a blank screen. Line 206 checks if the dialogue needs to end early. If it does then end it, otherwise process the next element.

Quest Journal User Interface

Before we can glue things together, we need to build the user interface for the quest journal. Similar to the inventory user interface, we're going to have a window where we can select the books and quests so that a text object is updated with all the information about the quest including if it has been completed.

Open the "GameController" prefab from Assets > Prefabs in the Project View. Make sure the "GameController" parent object is expanded so you can see the Canvas object. Right-click on the Canvas, select UI > Image, and rename it to "JournalWindow". Move it just above the "Screen" object so the screen hides it. In the Project View, go to Assets > Images > RPG GUI > Texture > Form > Quest and drag the "Form" file to the Source Image in the inspector.

Then set the Rect Transform component to the values shown in Figure 442. This will make the window about the same size as the inventory window but show on the other side of the screen. Also, set the Anchor to the top-right so that it will stay on that side of the screen in all the different screen resolutions.

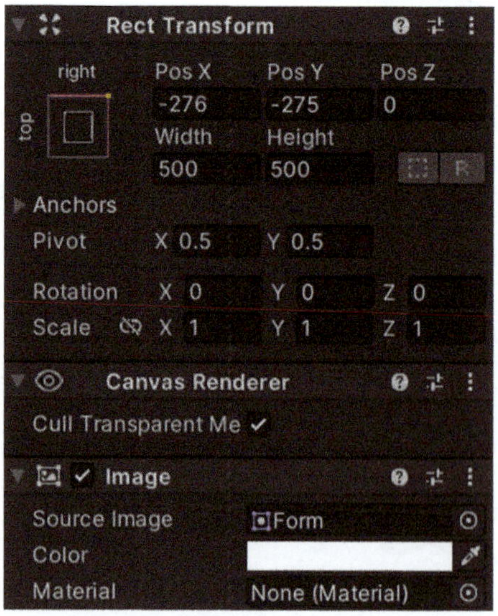

Figure 442

The image itself has 3 panels: 1) top panel for a title, 2) left panel to display the quest, chapter, and book drop-down boxes, and 3) right panel to display the quest information and whether it was completed.

Create the title text for the window by right-clicking on the "JournalWindow" and selecting UI > Text. Rename it to "Title" and set the position to X='0', Y='218', Z='0', Width='250', and Height='50'. For the text type: Quest Journal. Set the Font Size to 36 and the Color to white.

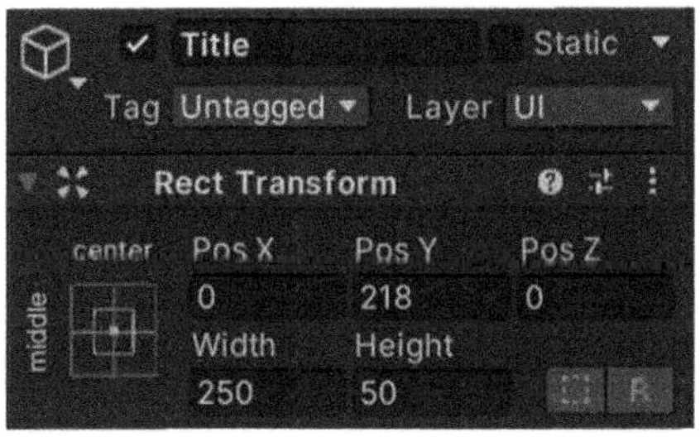

Figure 443

Now we'll create the dropdown boxes for the book, chapter, and quest. Right-click the "JournalWindow" and select UI > Dropdown. Rename it to "BookDropdown" and set the position of it to X='-150', Y='165', and Z='0'. Copy and paste it, renaming it to "QuestDropdown" and set the Y position to '120'.

Implementing the quest selection of book and quest using drop-down boxes is a very space efficient way of doing it. One drawback, however, is that players won't be able to see all the quests at a glance. They'll need to click the boxes to see them. But this is the easiest way.

Now create another text object and name it "QuestDescription". Set the position to X='85', Y='-15', Z='0', Width='275', Height='360' as shown in Figure 444. Then change the Color to white and the Font Size to 18. This is where the quest information will show up that we coded in the quest controller earlier.

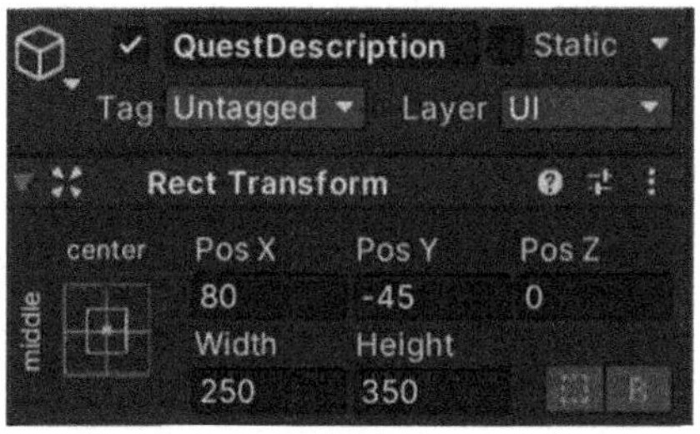

Figure 444

To create the box to show if the quest is completed select UI > Toggle and name it "CompletedBox". Then set the position to X='30', Y='165', and Z='0' as shown in Figure 445. If you scroll down to the "Toggle" component you'll see a number of different colors for the normal case, when the toggle is highlighted, pressed, selected, disabled, and so on. We're disabling the toggle in the code, but the disable causes the check mark to not be very visible. I found by adjusting the color, so the alpha value is set to '255' or totally opaque works for me. Give that a try and see if it works for you when we test it later.

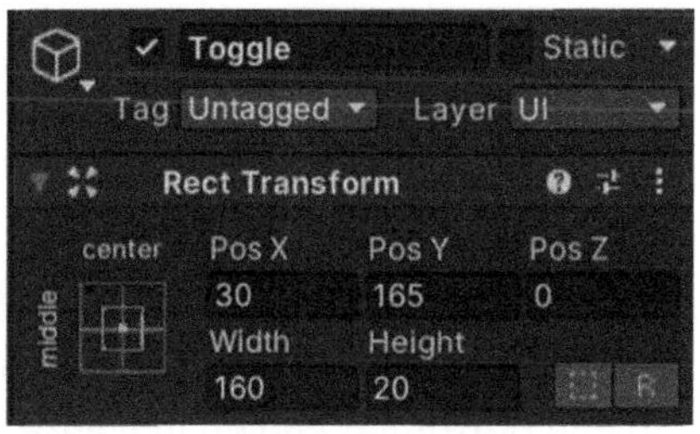

Figure 445

Expand it and inside you'll see 2 child objects. Click the Label and set the Text field to "Completed". Make sure that the Color is set to white.

When you're done, you should see the finished window as shown in Figure 446. We have our two dropdown boxes on the top left side of the quest journal window. The player can use those to select the book they want to read from and which quest from that book.

Figure 446

To the right of those near the top is our toggle or checkbox to show if the quest has been completed or not. If it is completed, then the checkmark will show. Underneath that is the text box showing the description and all the information about the quest. Just what the player wants to know!

For the quick quest text, we'll create another image and attach a text object as a child. Right-click the canvas object and create a new Image named "QuickQuestText". Set the Rect Transform to the values shown in Figure 447, and don't forget to change the layout to left and top. Set the Source Image to "Textbox_1" from Assets > Images > RPG GUI > Texture > Textbox. This will give a good outline box for the description text we'll make next.

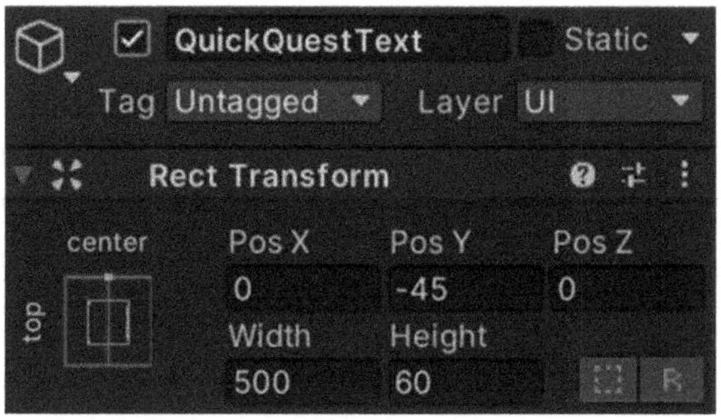

Figure 447

Right-click the "QuickQuestText" object and create a child object under that by selecting UI > Text – TextMeshPro. In the rect-transform, set the Width to '475' and the Height to '50'. The Font Size will be '18' and the color White.

Scrolling down a little further to Alignment. You can set it to center alignment for both left and right as well as top and bottom as shown in Figure 448. This is more of a preference, but I like to see it all centered.

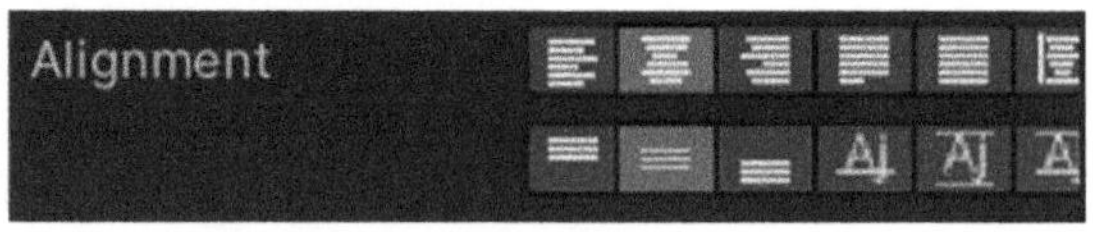

Figure 448

That's all we need for the UI objects! Now we use our special Unity glue to hook them so that they work together in ~~Unity~~ harmony (whew, that was close).

Gluing the Journal

Let's get sticky with it! While still editing the "GameController" prefab, create a new empty game child object under it named "QuestController" and drag the quest controller script onto it. Then fill out the fields as shown in Figure 449. The Journal Panel gets set to the "QuestWindow" object. Then set the appropriate child objects in the journal. For the Quick Quest Text, make sure you grab the actual text and not the background image. Don't worry about the Quests list for now, we'll handle it in the next section for creating quests.

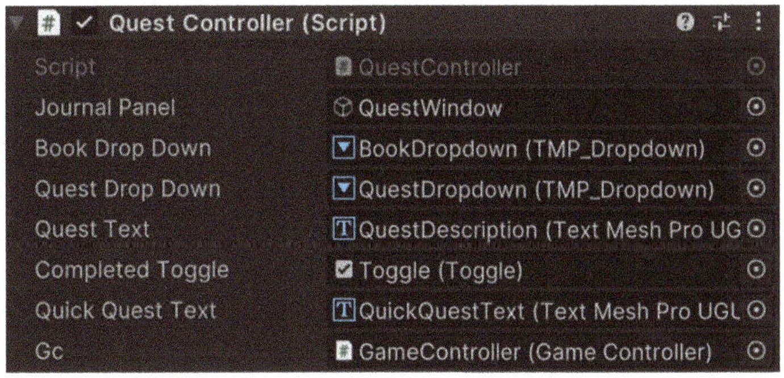

Figure 449

For each of the dropdown boxes, we need to set the "On Value Changed (Int32)" handler. Click on the "BookDropDown" child object and scroll down to the bottom of the dropdown component. Click the '+' symbol to add a new entry and drag our "QuestController" object onto the empty box below "Runtime Only". Then on the box to the left select Quest Controller > BookDropDownHandler. This calls that method whenever the dropdown box gets changed. Go ahead and do the same for the "QuestDropDown" except set the method to "QuestDropDownHandler".

Figure 450

Now click the game controller and look for the Quest Controller field where you'll drag over the newly created "QuestController" object. This allows our game controller easy access to the quest controller.

To test this out, we're going to need some quests and books. Clicking back on the "QuestController" object in the Hierarchy View, look over at the inspector and expand the "Quests" array. Right now, it is empty.

The inspector is great for linking objects together. There is another method if you need to find objects that you can't link there using this:

GameObject.FindGameObjectsWithTag(string);

Take care not to call it often because it can impact game performance.

Add three new elements to the array and give them the book names, "Exodus", "Hebrew", and "Egyptian". To name them, you need to Expand the "Element 0", "Element 1", and "Element 2" and set the "Book Name" field. If you collapse them then you will see the three books shown in Figure 451.

Figure 451

Referring to the GDD (or Game Design Document) in Appendix B, add the first Quest to the Exodus book shown in Figure 452 by clicking the inner '+' symbol. Those nested arrays may get a little confusing so take care. The details section in the GDD is not meant for display to the player. Those are notes for the game developer. That would be YOU. Recording this extra information about the quest reminds us of what it is specifically that we want the player to do.

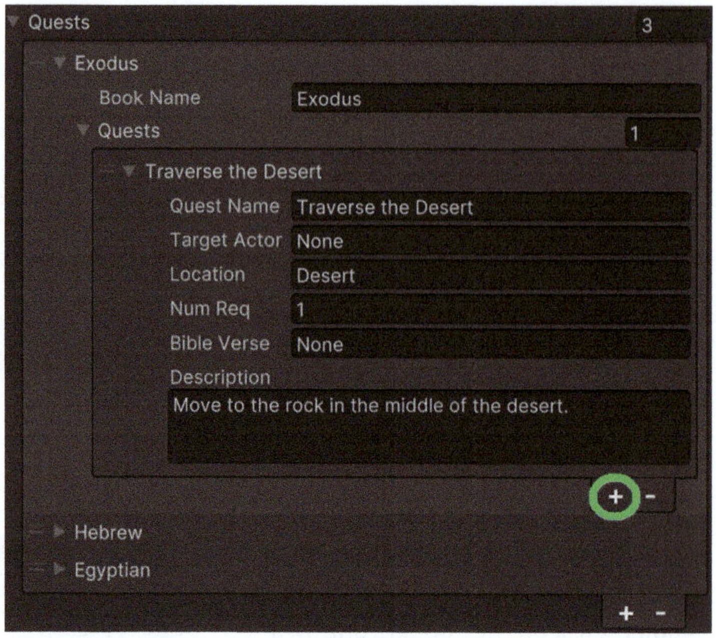

Figure 452

The first quest is a tutorial to teach the player how to move. Moving around is really the basic element of this game. Sure, we have people you can interact, but the player needs to move there first.

Add the second quest in the book. It's in the GDD but I've copied it for you here again in Figure 453. It has similar information, but now we've got an actor and a Bible verse. This is the verse about Moses' meeting with his brother out in the wilderness, which is what the description tells the player. Look at that! You're already teaching your players about the Bible. Give yourself a pat on the back. I'd pat you on the back too but doing it through a book is a little difficult. But I'm patting you on the back in spirit.

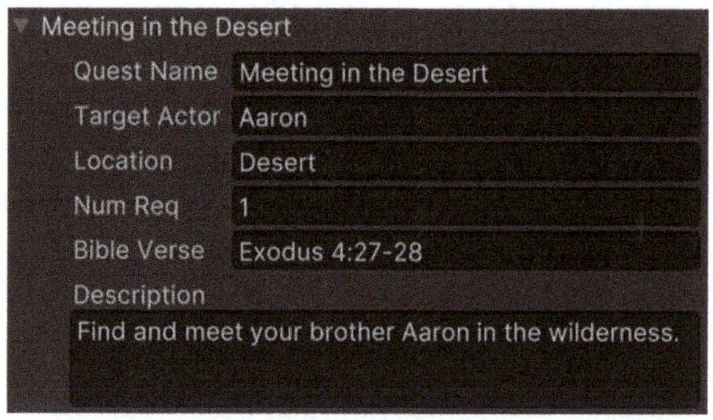

Figure 453

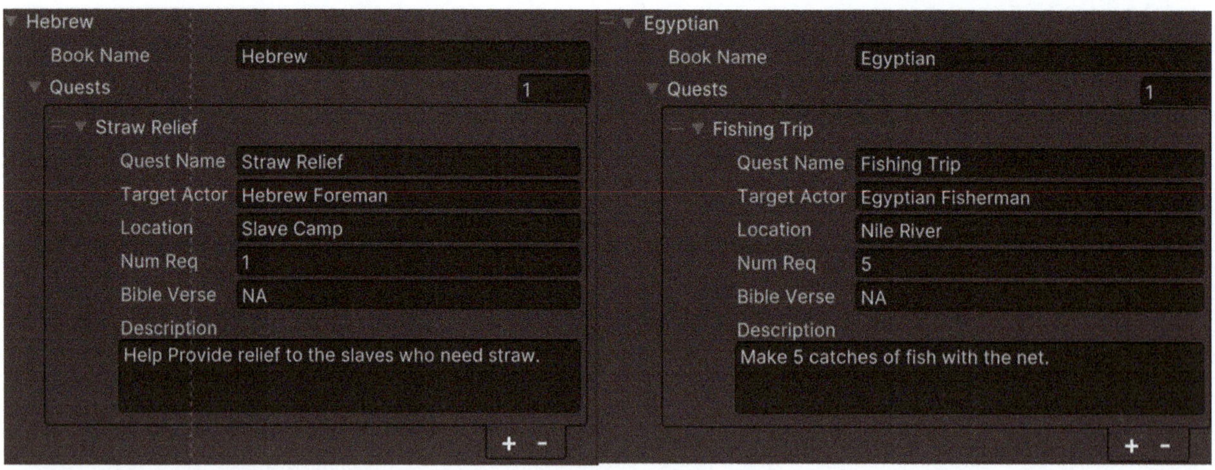

Figure 454

Go ahead and add the quests I've copied here for the Hebrew and Egyptian books in Figure 454. These quests are just the beginning of the books. You can add the rest of the quests from the GDD now.

Now, we're ready to test out what we've done so far. Before you play the game, in the Game View, set the play mode to "Play Maximized" so you can get the full effect of the quest journal. Otherwise, the quick quest text will get in the way. Click the play button and wait for the opening cut scene to complete. When you get in the game press the 'Q' key and you'll see something like Figure 455.

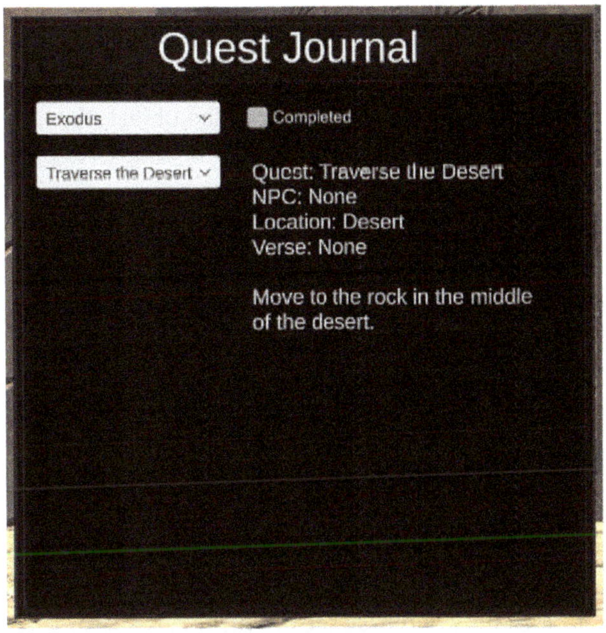

Figure 455

You can select from the three different books and see the quests in each. You'll only be able to select from one of the quests in each book because none have been completed yet.

For the sake of brevity (or keeping things from getting crazy long), we're not going to implement the quests for the Hebrew or Egyptian books in this tutorial. But you can add them on your own using the tools and skills learned. When you're satisfied with the quests you can end play mode.

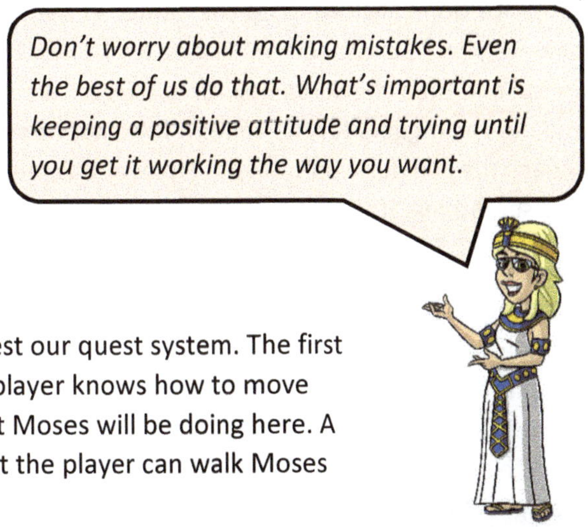

The great thing about creating the quests in the prefab is that it automatically updates all the scenes, so they use the same set of quests.

Creating Quests

We have at least four quests now that we can use to test our quest system. The first two in the main quest line will act as a tutorial, so the player knows how to move Moses around. It also gives the player a clue as to what Moses will be doing here. A rock is mentioned, so let's add that to the scene so that the player can walk Moses over to it.

In the Project View, go to Assets > Models > Ancient Egypt > Models > Rock Prefabs and drag the "Rock_2" prefab onto the scene. Set the transform to what is shown in Figure 456. Then focus on the rock in the Scene View.

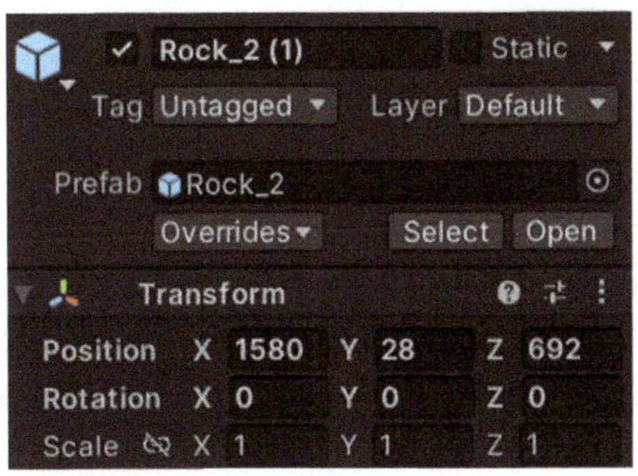

Figure 456

You'll see that the rock was plopped squarely in the middle of the desert. But it will give us a good excuse to have the player walk Moses over there to investigate it.

I do want to mention the "LOD Group" component that is on the "Rock_2" prefab. LOD means Level of Detail. When the camera is at various distances away from the object the model can be swapped with other different models. The idea is that the farther away the camera is from the object, the lower quality the object needs to be. And so we can improve performance by reducing the quality of the object shown.

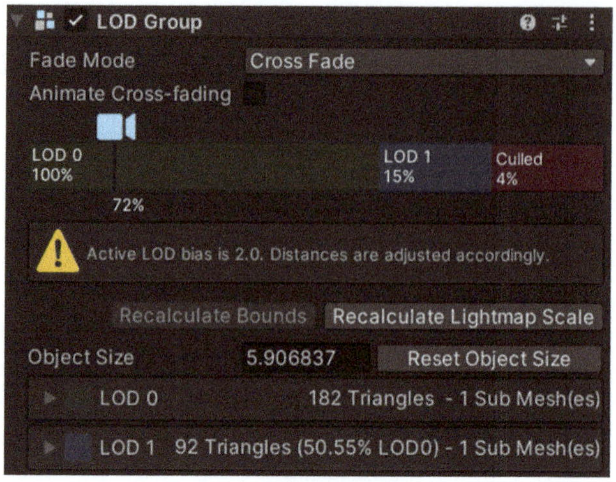

Figure 457

Figure 457 shows an LOD group with 3 different areas. LOD 0 on the left is when the camera is closest to the object. At the bottom, you can see that the sub mesh has 182 triangles. But LOD 1 for the next closest threshold only has 92 triangles. Having enough objects with the LOD groups setup can really add up to improve performance.

Back to the desert. This is the area where the player will start at the beginning of the game. Add a Box Collider to the rock now and drag the scripts for the actor controller and actor dialogue. Check the box in the Actor Controller script for Don't Highlight. Set the Center of the Box Collider at X='-3', Y='3', Z'=0', and the Size to X='10', Y='10', and Z='10' and then check the box for Is Trigger. We set colliders as triggers for the zones a few chapters back. This means the collider won't keep the player out, but the "OnTrigger" method gets called when the collider hits something. It should look like Figure 458.

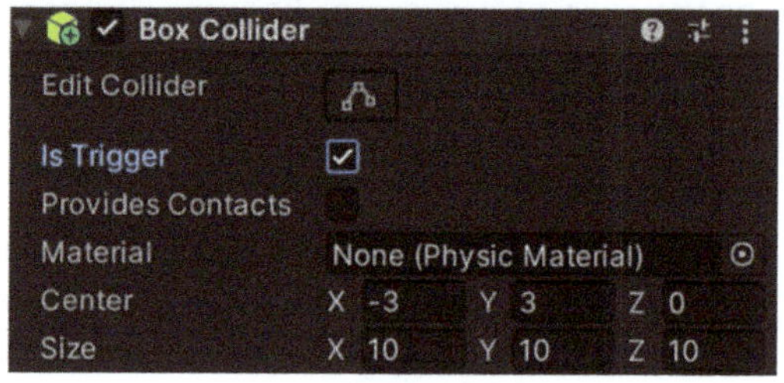

Figure 458

Create a new C# script named "TriggerDialogue". If the player enters the trigger then we'll start the specified dialogue. We could alternatively add this capability into the actor controller, but that class is already pretty big. Having smaller classes is a software best practice. Large files of classes can be hard to maintain. That means longer times adding new features and finding and fixing bugs. A small class like this is easier to understand what is going on and fix bugs and add capabilities.

```
public class TriggerDialogue : MonoBehaviour
{
    public Dialogue Dia;

    Unity Message | 0 references
    private void OnTriggerEnter(Collider other)
    {
        if (other.transform.tag == "Player")
        {
            GameObject gc = GameObject.FindWithTag("GameController");
            gc.GetComponent<GameController>().StartDialogue(Dia);
        }
    }
```

Figure 459

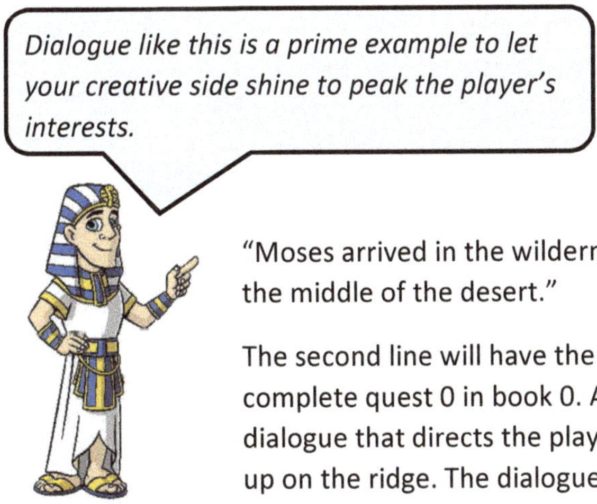

Drag that script over to the "Rock_2" object we created just a little bit ago. Now add a "Dialogue" script into it. This dialogue will have 2 lines. The first will just be some dialogue informing the player about what is going on. I wrote the below:

"Moses arrived in the wilderness looking for his brother. He took a rest at a rock in the middle of the desert."

The second line will have the action to complete quest 0 in book 0. Add some more dialogue that directs the player to find Aaron up on the ridge. The dialogue element should look like Figure 460. I wrote the below:

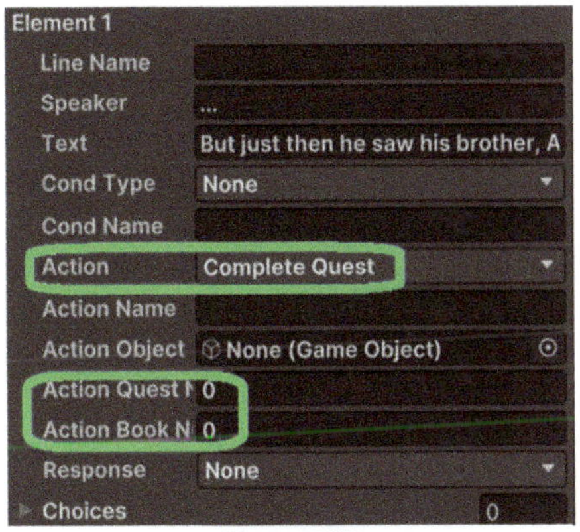

Figure 460

"But just then he saw his brother, Aaron, up on a ridge. He started walking up the hill towards him."

To hook up the dialogue, just drag the "Rock_2 (1)" object onto the "Dia" field of the Trigger Dialogue. Now that dialogue will get started when the player enters the trigger.

Before we can give it a playthrough, we need to put Moses somewhere near that rock. If you set the position of the "MosesPlayer" object to what you see in Figure 461 then it will get him pretty close.

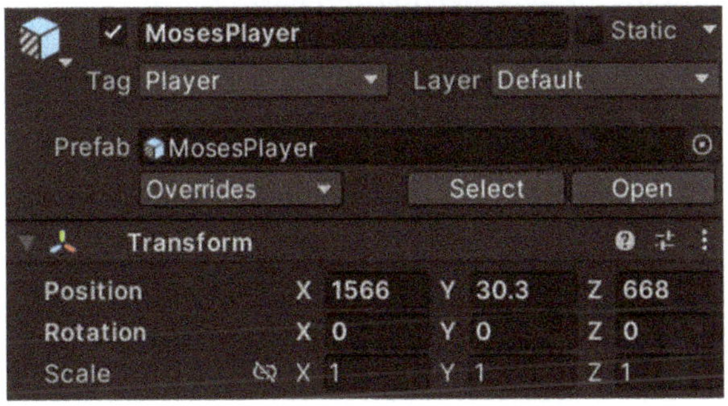

Figure 461

Finally, let's clear the player preferences so the game doesn't load up the last location. In the Main Menu, go to Edit > Clear All PlayerPrefs as shown in Figure 462. This is the way to delete all of them in the editor and useful for testing.

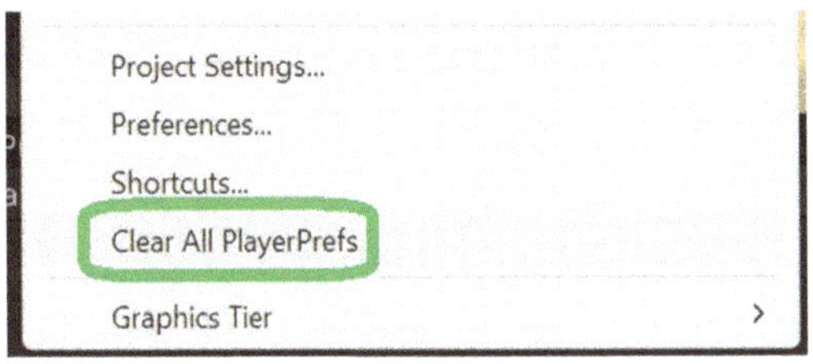

Figure 462

Now enter play mode. You will find Moses nearby the rock. If you press 'Q', you can see the information about the first quest telling you to move to the rock. Press 'Q' again to close the quest journal. When you walk to it, the dialogue will appear. When it is done, press 'Q' one more time to open the quest journal. You should now see that the second quest in our main quest book "Exodus" is displayed. If you use the bottom dropdown box to select the first quest, it should now be marked as completed.

Now, we tell the player that Aaron is on the hill, so we ought to put him there. But we don't want to have Aaron appearing up on that hill all the time. It will only be while this quest is active. Create a new empty game object in the scene and set its position to all 0's. Name it "Exodus_1_Objects". Then drag the "QuestObject" script onto it and set Book="Exodus" and Quest='1'. Now expand the "GameController" in the Hierarchy View and drag "Exodus_1_Objects" onto "Quest Objects".

From Assets > Prefabs > Actors, drag Sem onto the scene and set his position to X='1647.5', Y='50', Z='741', and rotations Y='180'. Rename him to "Aaron". The transform should look like Figure 463.

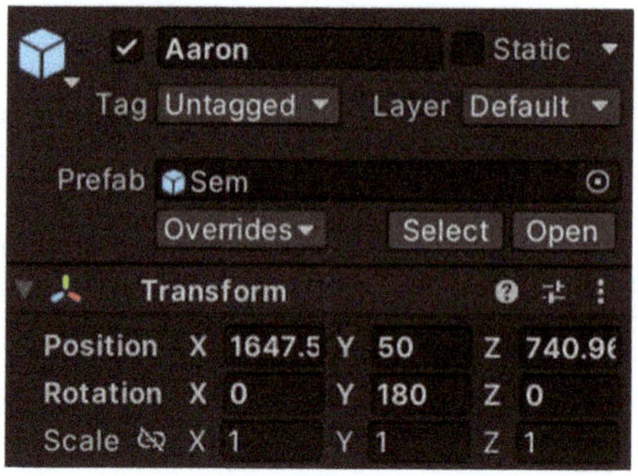

Figure 463

In the Hierarchy View, move him to be a child object under "Exodus_1_Objects". He's only going to be enabled while Quest 1 is active. Do note that after you make the Aaron object a child that his position will change. So don't freak out when you see that. The position is now based on the parent object's position.

Next, we're going to need Capsule Collider and Rigidbody components on the Aaron object.

You can add the new components and setup similar to what we already did on the Egyptian slave and guard prefabs, or we can copy and paste those components and save some effort. I prefer to save the effort. Remember you can copy and paste the components using the 3 vertical dots on the upper right of the component. Finally, in the Animator component, change the "Controller" field to the same "ThirdPersonAnimatorController" as the other actors we made. The inspector should look like what you see in Figure 464.

Figure 464

This sets us up to add the dialogue component on Aaron so the player can walk Moses over to his brother to talk to him. Add the Dialogue script to Aaron now. You can add some conversation between the two brothers. I copied mine below.

Aaron: *It is good to see you, brother.*
Moses: *Yes, Aaron, after all these long years.*
Aaron: *The Lord told me to go into the wilderness to meet you. Why?*
Moses: *The Lord has seen our misery and sent me to rescue His people.*
Aaron: *That is wonderful news! But how will you convince Pharaoh?*
Moses: *Since I'm not very good with words, the Lord wants you to speak for me.*
Aaron: *Me? If the Lord commands, I shall obey. What do we do?*
Moses: *We first go to the elders and perform signs for them.*
Aaron: *What signs?*

We'll stop there for now. You won't need any special actions for this dialogue, just the speaker and the text. When you're done, give it a test to make sure you can see Aaron and that Moses can talk to him.

The last line in the dialogue is Aaron asking what signs to show to the elders. I'm glad he asked! We're going to program those next.

Snake on the Plains

For the miracle where Moses changes the staff to a snake, we gave the staff to the "MosesStaff" prefab. But now the "MosesPlayer" prefab needs a staff. There is an easy way to give the other prefab the same staff in the same position. I'll walk you through it step by step.

1) In the Project View, for "MosesPlayer" and "MosesStaff" prefabs, on the Transform component, click the 3 vertical dots and select "Reset" to change the position and rotation to '0'.
2) Open the "MosesStaff" prefab, focus on Moses if you can't see him, click the staff and press CTRL+C to copy the staff.
3) Open the "MosesPlayer" prefab and press CTRL+V to paste the staff in that prefab.
4) Expand Reference > Hips > Spine > Spine1 > Spine2 > RightShoulder > RightArm > RightForeArm and drag the Staff onto the RightHand child object.

Exit Prefab View and focus back on the "MosesPlayer" object in the Hierarchy View. You should now see that he's carrying his staff in his hand. Now we need to add the snake. Luckily, we've got a nice fancy model of a cobra. Go to Assets > Models > Cobra > Prefab and drag the cobra prefab onto the scene. Set the transform to what you see in Figure 465. This will place the snake right next to Aaron and give him a scare.

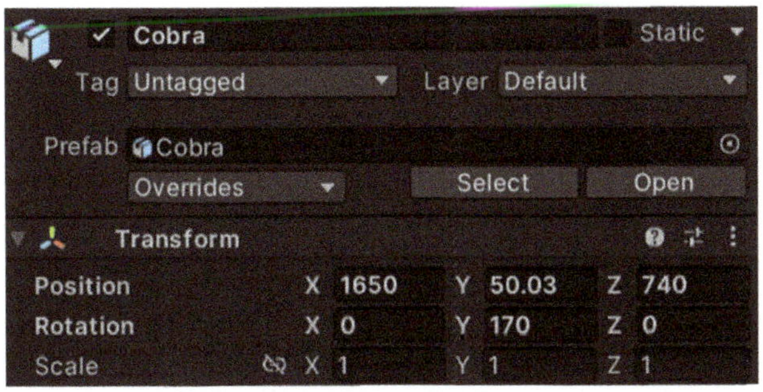

Figure 465

In the same folder as the cobra is a nice animator we can use to make it slither around and give that creepy snake feeling. Drag the "Cobra Animation" into the Controller field of the Cobra's Animator.

The next step is to add the dialogue and include the actions to make these objects appear and disappear. It will effectively look like the staff and snake are being swapped. Now let's add the dialogue elements to make it happen. Select the "Aaron" object again in the Hierarchy View and scroll down to the dialogue script. Add a new line where Moses says he's going to change his staff to a snake.

***Moses**: The first is when I throw down my staff it becomes a snake.*

After that, add two more lines. Make sure to delete the Speaker and Text of each of those because we're going to swap the models. In one line, change the Action to "Activate Object" and drag the "Cobra" onto the Action Object. The element should look like Figure 466. Mine shows as Element 10 because it is at index 10 in the array meaning it is the 11th item in the array.

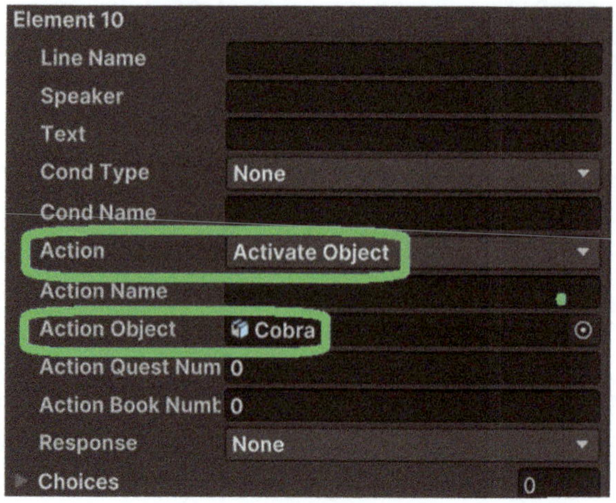

Figure 466

Because we modified the dialogue system to not wait for player input when the Text is blank, the controller will move passed it to the next line without the player needing to press the space bar or click. It will be completely transparent to the player.

On the next line we add the action to inactivate the staff. Set the Action to "Inactivate Object". Then, for the object, we need to into our "MosesPlayer" game object and find the staff. Recall that it is at Reference > Hips > Spine > Spine1 > Spine2 > RightShoulder > RightArm > RightForeArm > RightHand. Drag the Staff over to "Action Object". The line should look like Figure 467.

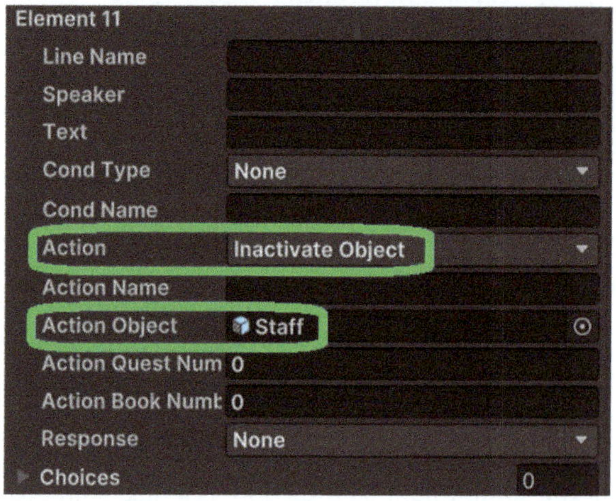

Figure 467

Create another new line in the dialogue that gives Aaron's response. Be sure to set the Action to "None". Set the speaker to "Aaron" and the text to something like being impressed but scared of the snake. Mine is below:

***Aaron**: Whoa! That is a big snake. Can you change it back?*

To swap the models back, just create two more dialogue lines and inactivate the Cobra while activating the staff. Like the above two figures but use the opposite actions. The next line can be Moses responding. You can read the line I wrote for him below:

***Moses**: Fear not. It's a staff again.*

Save the scene and then clear the player preferences by going to Edit > Clear PlayerPrefs. Let's test it out now by clicking the button to go into play mode. Try out the movement tutorial by moving Moses to the rock in the middle of the desert. Then go to Moses' brother and talk to him. You should see the dialogue and in the middle of the dialogue, Moses' staff disappears, and the snake appears. Then they swap back again. Exit play mode once you finish testing.

Leaving the Desert

We're almost done. Now that Moses has met his brother, Aaron, in the desert, they are going to go back to the city and visit the Hebrew elders. There are two steps needed for that. First complete the quest, we already know how to do that. Second is to move the player over there. To move the player, we already have code to do that, we just need to hook it up in the dialogue engine with some code.

Open "DialogueElement" in Visual Studio and add the public variable on line 18 shown in Figure 468. This will be a location to move the player. We will reuse the "ActionName" variable for the scene name.

```
15      public GameObject ActionObject;
16      public int ActionQuestNumber;
17      public int ActionBookNumber;
18      public Vector3 ActionVector3;
```

Figure 468

Now, in the "_action" enumerated type, add a new "SceneTransition" action.

```
        InactivateObject,
        CompleteQuest,
        SceneTransition,
```

Figure 469

In the "DialogueController" script, scroll down to the "ProcessElement" method to the switch statement on the action in the current dialogue. Add the case statement shown on line 202 of Figure 470. This will initiate a transition to a new scene if a scene name other than the one loaded is specified. In our case, we will give the same scene name with the new location and just move the player.

```
202                 case DialogueElement._action.SceneTransition:
203                     SceneEngine.LoadScene(curDia.Lines[diaIndex].ActionName, curDia.Lines[diaIndex].ActionVector3, Player);
204                     break;
```

Figure 470

Go back into Unity and let's hook this code up with three more dialogue lines. Select Aaron and add a line for him saying that it's time to go. I wrote my line below:

***Aaron**: Very Good. Let me take you back to the camp where our elders gather.*

The next dialogue line will be to complete the quest. We're completed quest '1' in the Exodus book, book '0' now. I've copied what it should look like in Figure 471.

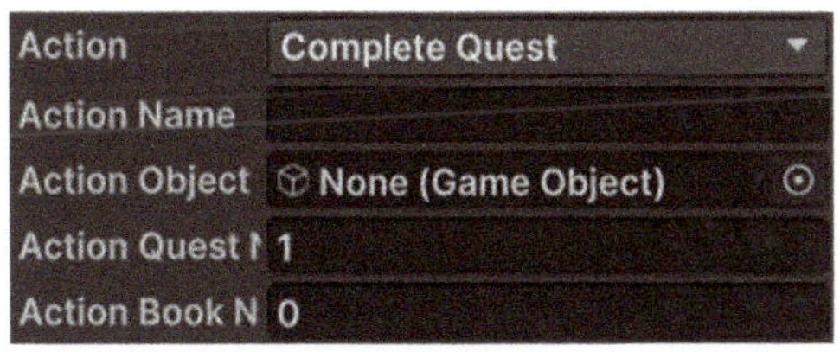

Figure 471

The last line of dialogue will move the player to the place we're going to use for the Hebrew Encampment outside the city. Set the action to "Scene Transition" and the Action Name to "Egypt_Nile Scene". This keeps the scene the same. Then set the Vector to what you see in Figure 472.

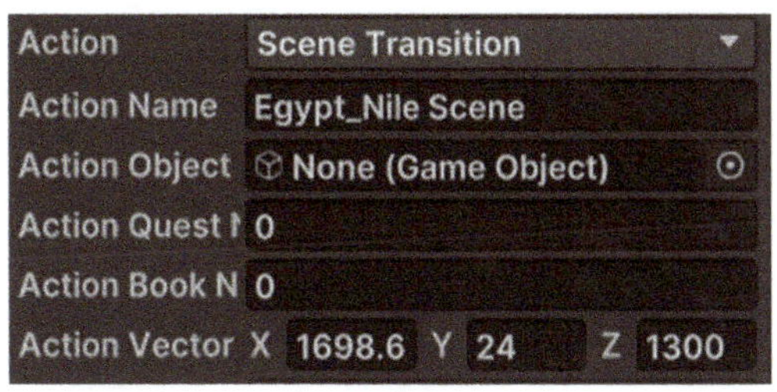

Figure 472

With that done we're ready to test it these changes. First, clear the player preferences and then enter play mode. Make like before and walk Moses to the rock. Once that dialogue completes, you'll see Aaron appear at the ridge. Walk or jump Moses on up there and talk to him. Partway through the dialogue, Moses' staff changes to a snake. Then it changes back again. Finally, the quest completes, and Moses should end up somewhere in the middle of some mudbrick houses. Great work! That wraps up the chapter on creating our quest system. Feel free to follow the GDD in creating the rest of the quests for the game.

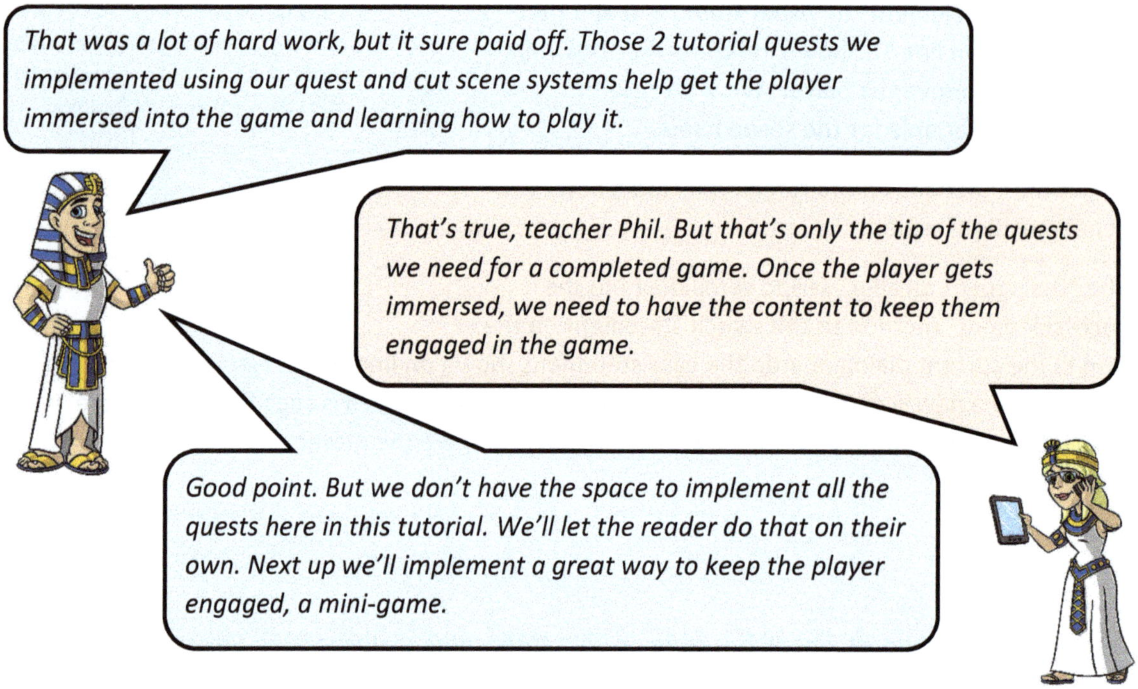

Chapter 16 – Sheep Corralling Minigame

Everybody loves games, right? Even Moses needs a good game to keep his mind sharp and his body in top physical condition. In this chapter, we're going to create a minigame, that is, a game inside a game. Basically, a shepherd challenges Moses' sheep credentials to see how long it takes to bring the sheep back from grazing. Read through the short GDD section for more details.

To implement this minigame we're going to need a number of things. First, we'll get a herd of sheep using the HerdSim package working. Then we'll code some C# scripts for the behaviors in the game. Finally, we'll create a user interface and glue everything together.

> *Minigames have been around in games for a long time. They provide a healthy distraction from the core gameplay and immerses the player deeper into the game.*

Before we get started, drag a second "MosesPrefab" out to the scene and append "Test on the end so the name is "MosesPrefabTest". This way we can easily test features in the game by disabling the real Moses and enabling the test, Moses. We just need to remember to put it back the way it was when we're done. Set the test Moses' position to X='1685', Y='25.5', and Z='1250.5' and then focus on it in the Scene View. This places him next to a small grassy area shown in Figure 473. This is where we'll have our herd of sheep for the minigame.

To get this trick working, Disable the original "MosesPlayer" and set the Player field in all of the "GameController", "DialogueController", and "MiniMapCam" to the new "MosesPlayerTest" object. Clear the player preferences and then enter play mode. Moses should now appear in this pasture.

Figure 473

Following the Herd

The HerdSim package is up on the Unity Asset Store and developed by Unluck Software. It comes with a few different kinds of animals including chickens, cows, pigs, rats, and sheep. It's also easy enough to work with so that if you have your own animated models it can work with them as well. But we'll just use the sheep that is already provided for us.

There are a lot of different scripting languages besides C#. One of them is called Javascript. Unity created their own version of Javascript called Unityscript which is what the HerdSim package is written in. Lucky for us, Unluck Software gave instructions on how to change to C#.

1. Go to Assets > Models > HerdSim > Scripts in the Project View.
2. Delete HerdSimController, HerdSimCore, HerdSimDisabler, and HerdSimScary.
3. Go into the C# folder.
4. Double-click the "HerdSim C Scripts" file.
5. When the Import Unity Package window opens, click "Import".
6. Another window about "Script Updating Consent" may appear, just click the first "Yes" button.

Now, in the Project View, go to Assets > Models > HerdSim > Prefabs and drag the "HerdSim Controller" onto the scene. If the import worked right, then it should have a "Herd Sim Controller" script attached to it. Put it at Position X='1670', Y='25.5', and Z='1207' so it looks like Figure 473 above. The blue rectangle is the boundary for the herd to wander within. They will stay inside this area.

We'll put the sheep here now. Go to Assets > Models > HerdSim > Animal Sheep > Prefabs and drag the "HerdSim Sheep" onto the Scene View but inside the blue rectangle. It doesn't matter where as long as you don't put it on the rocks or the trees. Drag 3 more sheep out there nearby that one. Sheep like to stay in a flock but sometimes wander. Make 2 more groups of 4 sheep inside the blue rectangle.

Click the "HerdSim Sheep" object and look at it in the inspector. In the components section you'll see there is a slot available for a Controller. This is the "HerdSim Controller" that we created earlier. So, drag it over onto this field. Also, you'll need to drag it as the Controller for all the other sheep. This ensures the sheep stay within the blue rectangle.

To get the HerdSim to work properly, we need to jump into Unity's Layer system. Layers are similar to tags in that we can use them to selectively do processing on objects. The Layer is visible in the inspector next to the Tag. For the "HerdSim Sheep", click the drop-down box for the layer and select "Add Layer". The inspector will change to look like Figure 474.

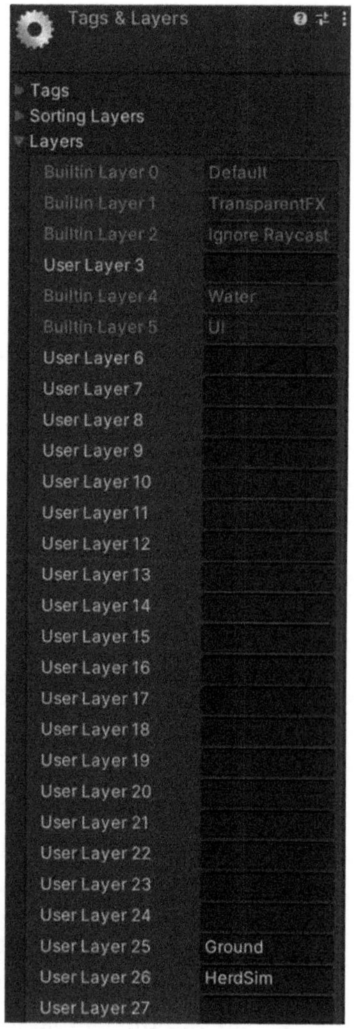

Figure 474

The first 6 layers (except for number 3) are built into Unity and are grayed out so you cannot change them. Everything begins on the "Default" layer which is Layer 0. Nothing special happens on this layer, it's pretty boring. Layer 1 for TransparentFX is used for things like lens flares we used earlier. Layer 2 for Ignore Raycast is when you have an object with a collider that shouldn't block raycasting. Layer 4 is for Water which you'll see if you click the water in the Scene or Hierarchy Views. Layer 5 is for the UI. You can use the rest of the layers for whatever you want.

HerdSim requires the addition of 2 layers to work properly. Go to User Layer 25 and set it to "Ground". Then go to User Layer 26 and set it to "HerdSim". The package uses these layers to manage the various herds that you setup with it. In the Hierarchy View, select the "Terrain" and set the Layer to "Ground". Give it a play test to see the sheep innocently grazing on the "HerdSim" layer.

Now create an empty game object in the Hierarchy View and name it "Herd". Move the "HerdSim Controller" and the various "HerdSim Sheep" inside it as child objects. This helps to keep them organized so it will be easier to handle them.

Let's test this out! Click the play button and wait for the scene to load. Some sheep may be resting on the ground while others may be running around.

A neat little dust cloud gets kicked up when they do run around. This is implemented by the HerdSim package using a particle system. They really are handy for a lot of different uses.

Once you've stood around there and watched the sheep long enough go ahead and exit play mode. We're going to keep going to make this into a mini-game, but if you want to just make a herd of animals then that is all you need to do.

Mini-game Scripts

To get this minigame going we're going to need a couple scripts. First, we'll need custom behavior for the sheep when Moses tags them, so they go to the shepherd. Then there is the controller script for the minigame to track number of sheep tagged, the time, and high score.

Create a new C# script named "SheepTag" and open it in Visual Studio. This script will define what happens when the player "tags" the sheep. Add the code in the class as shown in Figure 475.

```
public GameObject PenObj;
public SheepMinigame MiniGameCtlr;

private HerdSimCore hsc;
private bool tagged;

// Start is called before the first frame update
Unity Message | 0 references
void Start()
{
    hsc = transform.parent.GetComponent<HerdSimCore>();
    Init();
}

2 references
public void Init()
{
    tagged = false;
}
```

Figure 475

- PenObject: Object the sheep runs to when the player tags it.
- MiniGameCtlr: Handle to the minigame controller script we'll code next.
- hsc: Handle to the HerdSimCore script so we can access it easier.
- Tagged: Whether or not this sheep has been tagged by the player

If you're ever grasping for game mechanic ideas, then go back to ones we know work. The game of tag was played by kids long ago, is played today, and likely will continue to be played for a long time after other games fade away. Why? It's simple. So simple a child can play it.

In the "Start" method, the handle for the HerdSim core needs to be obtained. And we initialize the game, which just marks the sheep as not tagged.

In Figure 476 on the following page, add code for the "Update" method. When the sheep is tagged, we need to check if it is close to the pen. If it is, then we tell the HerdSim core script to enable itself (we'll disable it when the player tags it). If the sheep is not near the pen, then we call the "MoveTowards" method from Vector3 to slowly move the sheep there.

```
    void Update()
    {
        if (tagged)
        {
            if (Vector3.Distance(transform.position, PenObj.transform.position) > 1f)
            {
                hsc.transform.LookAt(PenObj.transform, Vector3.up);
                Vector3 tPos = Vector3.MoveTowards(hsc.transform.position, PenObj.transform.position, 0.02f);
                hsc.transform.position = tPos;
            }
            else
            {
                hsc.Enable();
            }
        }
    }

    Unity Message | 0 references
    private void OnCollisionEnter(Collision collision)
    {
        if (!tagged && (collision.transform.tag == "Player"))
        {
            hsc.Disable(false, false);
            hsc._model.GetComponent<Animation>().CrossFade(hsc._animRun, 0.5f);
            hsc._model.GetComponent<Animation>()[hsc._animRun].speed = hsc._animRunSpeed;
            tagged = true;
            MiniGameCtlr.Tagged();
        }
    }
```

Figure 476

Add the "OnCollisionEnter" method so we know when the player tags the sheep. But we do need to check to make sure that it is the player who tagged the sheep. If the sheep collide with each other then they shouldn't be counted as tagged. If the sheep was tagged, then don't let the player tag them again.

The first thing we do is disable the HerdSim Core script. The first false means to disable the model or make it disappear. We don't what that to happen, so we set it to false. The second false is to disable the collider. We also don't want that to happen and also set it to false.

Since we want the sheep to run, we'll call the "CrossFade" method and pass in the run animation. Then we'll set the speed, so the animator knows how fast to run the animation. Then we mark the sheep as tagged and let the controller know that the player tagged a sheep.

Create a new C# script named "SheepMinigame" and open it in Visual Studio. Add the public and private variables shown in Figure 477.

```
    public GameObject MinigamePanel;
    public TMPro.TextMeshProUGUI Timer;
    public TMPro.TextMeshProUGUI SheepCount;
    public SheepTag[] Sheep;

    private int curSheep;
    private float startTime;
    private float score;
```

Figure 477

- MinigamePanel: UI object that is displayed to the player.
- Timer: Display the minigame time.
- SheepCount: Text to display current and max sheep so the player can see their progress.
- Sheep: Array of the "SheepTag" scripts attached to sheep in the minigame.
- curSheep: Number of sheep the player has currently tagged.
- startTime: Game time the player tagged the first sheep and started the minigame.

Figure 478

- score: Time since the player started the minigame which is counted as the score.

Next, add the code in the "Start" and "Update" methods shown in Figure 479. We start by inactivating the minigame panel, so the player doesn't see it until they're supposed to. Then we initialize our private variables.

The "Update" method is also fairly simple. If the "curSheep" variable is zero, then that means the player hasn't started the game yet and there is nothing to do. But once they have tagged a sheep that variable increments to 1 and we can update the game timer to show the player how they are doing in the minigame.

```
void Start()
{
    MinigamePanel.SetActive(false);
    startTime = -1;
    score = 0;
    curSheep = 0;
}

// Update is called once per frame
Unity Message | 0 references
void Update()
{
    if (curSheep > 0)
    {
        UpdateTimer();
    }
}
```

Figure 479

When the player tags the sheep the "Tagged" method in the minigame's controller gets called. The first thing we do is increment the "CurSheep" counter and update the UI object to display to the player. If only one sheep has been found, then that means the game hasn't started yet and we need to start the timer and show the UI so the player can see they've started a new minigame.

Otherwise, all we need to do is check the win condition. If the player has tagged all the sheep, then they win the game, and we stop the timer. The timer is their score so the lower it is the better. We initialize "CurSheep" back to '0' so we can be ready for the next time the player wants to play the game.

```
public void Tagged()
{
    curSheep++;
    UpdateSheepCount();

    if (curSheep == 1)
    {
        MinigamePanel.SetActive(true);
        startTime = Time.time;
    }
    else
    {
        if (curSheep >= Sheep.Length)
        {
            curSheep = 0;
            Invoke("ShowPlayerScore", 2f);
        }
    }
}
```

Figure 480

```
private void UpdateTimer()
{
    score = Time.time - startTime;
    Timer.text = "Timer\n" + score.ToString("F2");
}

1 reference
private void UpdateSheepCount()
{
    SheepCount.text = "Sheep\n" + curSheep + "/" + Sheep.Length;
}
```

Figure 481

The mini-game controller waits for the "Tagged" method call before doing something. This is called event-driven programming and is very common for systems such as Graphical User Interfaces.

After the "Tagged" method, add the two new methods shown in Figure 481. The "Update" method calls the "UpdateTimer" which is the player's score. We call the method "ToString" the parameter "F2" so that it prints the float with 2 decimal places. The "\n" prints another line. Then there is the method to update the sheep count. That way the player knows how many sheep they still need to tag.

The final two methods in the class are in Figure 482. The first method shows the player's score and will let them know if they got a new high score. The high scores are saved in the player preferences.

```
private void ShowPlayerScore()
{
    float savedHighScore = PlayerPrefs.GetFloat("HighScore");

    if ((score < savedHighScore) || (savedHighScore == 0))
    {
        SheepCount.text = "New High Score!!!\n" + score.ToString("F2");
        PlayerPrefs.SetFloat("HighScore", score);
    }
    else
    {
        SheepCount.text = "High Score\n" + savedHighScore.ToString("F2");
    }

    Invoke("HidePlayerScore", 5f);
}

0 references
private void HidePlayerScore()
{
    MinigamePanel.SetActive(false);
    curSheep = 0;
    foreach (SheepTag shp in Sheep) shp.Init();
}
```

Figure 482

This high score will be shown for 5 seconds. The panel will be inactivated so the player can't see it anymore. Lastly, the sheep get re-initialized so that they are ready for when the player wants to play the minigame again.

Mini-game User Interface

The scripting for the minigame is done, but before we glue it together so everything can live in... nope... not going to say it! We need to create the user interface. We'll create a panel, similar to what we did for quests and the inventory, to show the timer and progress toward completing the minigame. We'll also give the player some brief instructions, so they know what to do. Before we get started, you may want to inactivate the other UI objects, so they don't obstruct your view of the UI object we're creating here.

Expand the "GameController" object in the Hierarchy View and right-click on the Canvas Object and select UI > Image to create the background image for our UI object. Rename the new image object to "CorralScore" and set the Source Image to Assets > Images > RPG GUI > Texture > Slots > slots_icon. In the Image component, uncheck the Raycast Target box so that the player can click through the corral score UI object.

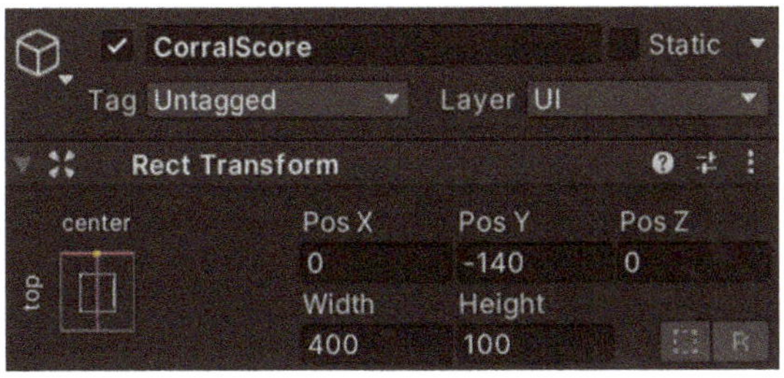

Figure 483

Then set the Rect Transform to the values as shown in Figure 483. Don't forget to set the layout to center and top so the object is in the correct position on the screen for different screen resolutions.

We're going to need four textmesh pro child objects here. One for the title. You can come up with a fun name for the game. I thought of "Sheep Corral" but I'm sure you can do better. The next one will be the instructions. Then create two more that will be at the bottom, one near the left and the other near the right. The left one will be the timer and the right one will be the sheep counter. The UI should look something like Figure 484. I won't go over the details of setting the UI since we've covered how to do it already.

Figure 484

The Hierarchy View of the "CorralScore" panel should look something like Figure 485. Since we're adding new objects onto the prefab, you can see it has a green circle with a plus '+' sign on it. This means that this object is not part of the original prefab. This is an easy way to tell what you've changed to your prefabs and what has not changed.

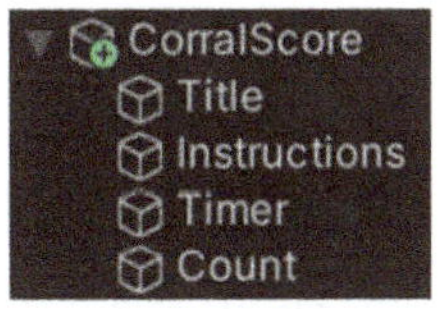

Figure 485

Connect the Objects

Create an empty object in the scene named "Pen" and place it at position X='1685', Y='26', and Z='1239'. This will be the object that all the sheep run to when they are tagged by the player. Then drag the "SheepMinigame" script onto the "Herd" object. Set the "CorralScore" object from the Canvas as the Minigame Panel. Then drag the "Timer" and "Count" objects onto these fields.

In the Hierarchy View, expand the Herd object and each of the "HerdSim Sheep" objects. You'll see that each sheep has a Collider and a Model object. For our method, "OnCollisionEnter" to work, the script needs to be attached to the "Collider" object. Drag the "SheepTag" script onto Collider child objects for each of the sheep. Also, drag the "Pen" object we created before onto the Pen Object field of the sheep tag script on each of the colliders.

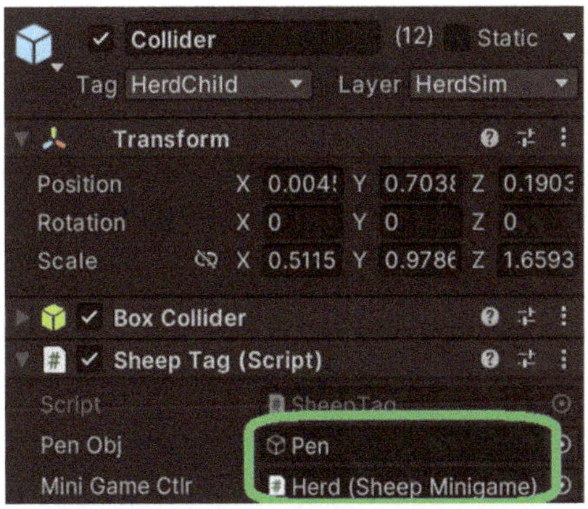

Figure 486

While you have all the sheep expanded with their "Collider" child objects exposed. Let's drag each of those collider objects onto the "Sheep" array of the "SheepMinigame" script on the pen object. I've got 12 sheep, and you can see in Figure 487 that my sheep array has all 12 of them.

Figure 487

With the scripts in place and the objects all glued together, the minigame is ready to be played. But there is one more thing we should add. A cue so the player knows that the minigame exists.

If you've already created a prefab for the "HebrewShepherd" then drag that onto the scene at about position X='1684.5', Y='25.6', and Z='1241' so that it looks similar to Figure 488. If not, you can use the "EgyptianSlave" prefab. Drag the script "Dialogue" onto him. You can have him say something like:

Figure 488

Shepherd: *I've heard of you, Moses. You were a shepherd, right?*

Moses: *Yes, that's right.*

Shepherd: *Really? Prove it! Show me how fast you can tag all the sheep and bring them back to me.*

This Hebrew shepherd tells the player about the minigame in the form of a challenge. This introduces the minigame so that it works well with the story and helps to immerse the player deeper into the game. Then they'll be excited to see the UI pop-up and have fun trying to corral the sheep.

Corralling the Sheep

Now that all the pieces are in place and glued together, let's test out the mini game. Go into play mode and talk to our shepherd guy to make sure he's telling the player what he's supposed to as seen in Figure 489.

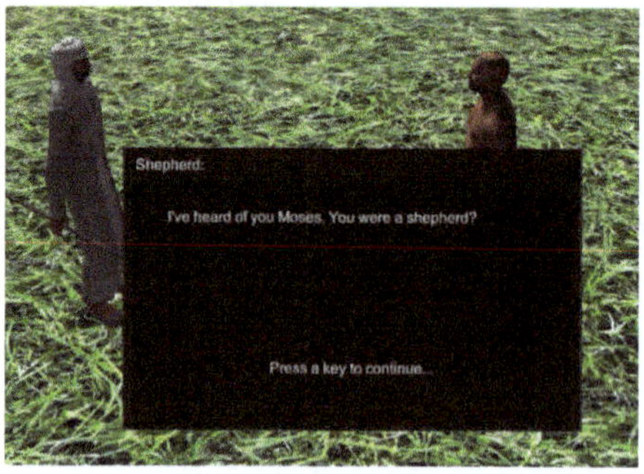

Figure 489

Then find the first sheep to tag. When you do, the sheep will run toward the shepherd. The window should also pop up. You see the timer is going up and the sheep count is at 1 out of 12.

Figure 490

A couple of seconds after you've tagged all the sheep, the high score appears showing that there is a new high score. When it disappears, try to play the minigame again. When you tag all the sheep again, you'll see how you did compared to the last time in the UI Window like in Figure 490.

Now that we're done testing our sheep corralling minigame let's put the player back the way it was. Disable "MosesPlayerTest" and enable "MosesPlayer". Then overwrite the player field on the "GameController", "DialogueController", and "MiniMapCam" objects.

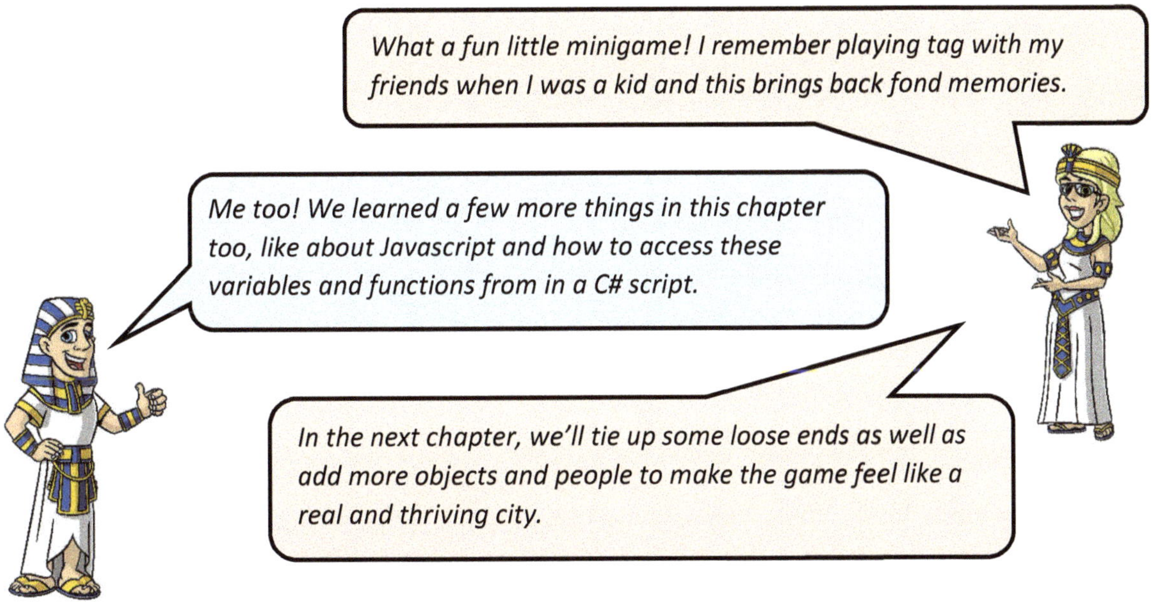

Chapter 17 – Populating the Game World

All that we've talked about right now is the minimum a 3rd person puzzle adventure game requires to be playable. You need to have a character who the player can move around with. You need to be able to interact with objects. You need music and sound effects. You need to have an inventory and puzzles like what is described in the GDD. You need to have nice 3D environments and be able to save the player's progress so they can play it later. You need to have an intuitive user interface or menu system. And then quests and cut scenes are like icing on the cake.

> *As we've been saying, it's the sum of the little things that make a great game. Of course, the gameplay needs to be interesting, user interface intuitive, and the game relatively bug free. Don't neglect the little things.*

That is all well and good to get something up and running to prove to yourself and others that you can do this. You can make a game! But a game needs much more than that to be fun for players. Just running around from one quest or puzzle to another will seem very odd if other things in the game aren't right.

A slave camp needs… you know… slaves in it. A city needs merchants and other regular people so the player feels like it's really a city. What kind of animals are there in the wilderness parts of the game? Why are the trees the same kind of palm tree? Wouldn't people carry tools and use other things in their daily lives?

A 3D adventure game needs questions like these answered. The puzzles and the quests keep the player interested in the game. But all the little things around those quests and puzzles keep the player immersed in the game. So, which should you focus on as a game designer the little stuff or the big stuff? The answer is "yes". The game needs both and time must be spent on both so that one or the other isn't neglected.

Fixing a Computer Bug

What's a computer bug? I'm glad you asked. Let me answer that question in the form of a story. There was a woman named Grace Murray Hopper who worked as an officer for the US Navy in the middle of the 20th century. She did her work on a computer that filled an entire room.

There had been problems with some of the electronics. And then one afternoon in September of 1947, an operator named William "Bill" Burke found a moth stuck between one of the components in the system. Grace recorded the event in her logbook as the "First actual case of bug being found". What was that bug? A moth.

I regret to inform you that we've been walking around with bugs in our game. We implemented quests and the player inventory and saved them so they can persist until the next time the player wants to play the game.

However, if the player is currently in the middle of playing the game and decides they want to start a new game, then their quest progress and inventory will remain what it was in their old game. Go ahead and give it a try! This is not the intended behavior for this game.

Open the "TitleController" script and scroll down to the "Update" method. Inside the 'if' statement when a new game is selected, make a new line after deleting all the player preferences on line 71, writing another new line to clear the player's inventory like in Figure 491.

```
68              if (selectNewGame)
69              {
70                  PlayerPrefs.DeleteAll();
71                  ItemEngine.InventoryGetItem().Clear();
72                  ItemEngine.InventoryAddItem("Staff");
73                  ItemEngine.InventoryAddItem("Cloak");
74                  SceneEngine.LoadScene(GameSceneName);
75              }
```

Figure 491

Save that code and when you go back into Unity to test and see if the bug is gone. You'll find that the inventory works as expected when you start a new game. You didn't even have to get your hands messy with the weird dust on the wings of a moth either!

You are likely to find other bugs in the game as you continue testing. Despite teams of validation engineers, no software or game can be completely bug free. Appendix A includes a list of known issues from the game and how you can go about fixing them.

The Slave Camp

Since Moses goes to the Hebrews first and then to Pharaoh, we'll populate that area first. We're going to add some slaves, equip those slaves with some items and wagons, and then give them a life (meaning some animation or thing to do and some dialogue.

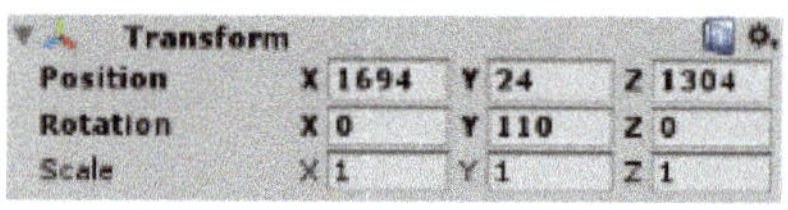

Figure 492

Copy and paste "Aaron" that we created as a child object under "Exodus_1_Objects" and then move the new "Aaron (1)" out so it's no longer a child object. Set his transform to the values shown in Figure 492. Focus on him in the Scene View and he'll be standing right outside a door to one of the houses in the slave camp. This is also right where the player is dropped off after the tutorial quests.

Set the lines to his dialogue to a count of '3'. Update the speaker and text to something like what I have below:

***Aaron**: Welcome to my humble home here in the slave camp.*

***Moses**: I appreciate your hospitality, brother.*

***Aaron**: We should go to the tent of meeting. It is the big one just north of here.*

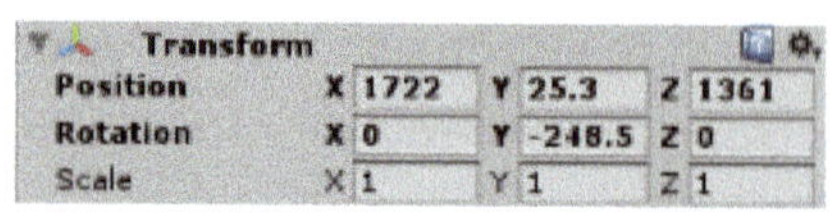

Figure 493

That should be good to get Moses on the right track. For now, we're going to fill out the rest of the slave camp. Choose one of the "Man" prefabs from Assets > Models > EgyptCharacters > Prefabs and drag him onto the Scene View. Set his transform to what you see in Figure 493. Name this guy "PickaxeHebrewSlave". That way we can tell apart slaves that have pickaxes and slaves that use other tools.

In the Project View, go to Assets > Models > Sickleadz Props > Survival Weapons HD Vol. 1 > Models and drag the "Pickaxe" onto the scene nearby the "HebrewSlave". It comes out of the box so big a giant can use it. Set all 3 numbers for the Scale to '0.25' and it becomes much more manageable for a normal person.

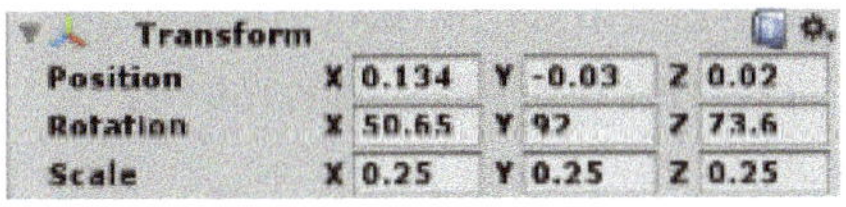

Figure 494

Expand the man for our Hebrew slave and browse to Character > CenterRoot > CenterSpine > CenterSpine1 > CenterSpine2 > RightCollar > RightShoulder > RightElbow and drag the pickaxe onto the "RightHand" child object. Then set the transform of the pickaxe to match Figure 494. This places the pickaxe in his hand.

When you're done, he should look like the guy shown in Figure 495. Like all the other actors, give him a capsule collider, rigidbody, actor controller script, and dialogue script. Remember, you can copy and paste from another actor like Aaron or the shepherd to save time. Also, give him the "ThirdPersonAnimatorController" animator object.

Figure 495

Back in Chapter 6 when we setup our actor animation controller, we added some animations. Go to the Animator tab or open it up if it got closed from the Main Menu at Window > Animation > Animator. Let's add some more! Looking at Assets > Models > EgyptCharacters > Source > Anims shows a bunch of interesting looking animations we can use for our characters.

As we did before, drag the animations "Ambient_01", "Ambient_02", "Ambient_03", and "Dig" onto the animator window. Then create new animation parameters of the same name. Recall that you click the "Parameters" tab in the upper right and then click the '+' sign to add new "Trigger" parameters for each. Then right-click on the orange "Grounded" state to make transitions from that state to each of the other animations. Click the arrows you create and add a condition for the trigger that matches the animation. Then make the transition back to Grounded from each new animation with the condition on the trigger "StopAnim".

Now, you can set the slave's "Animation" in the actor controller component to "Ambient_01". With all the work we did to give him a pickaxe, save him in an original prefab so we can make more of this guy.

Now put this guy around some of the other empty tents, shelters, and work sites. Perhaps put 2 or 3 of them together with some animations to look like they are having a conversation. Show your creative side and make up new dialogues for the slaves so they give the player a more immersive experience. Change up their animations to use a mix of each of the different ambient animations.

If you've created the other Hebrew actor prefabs already, then this would be a good time to add them as well. Groups of slaves have a Hebrew foreman to watch over them. Women and elders would also be there as well. Try putting some people on the second story of some of the houses.

With the Hebrew camp filling up with people, let's add some objects to help with the realism. If you go to Assets > Models > Rustic_Pack then you'll see a number of ordinary objects. There are wooden barrels, buckets, benches, shelves, stools, carts, and tables.

However, wood like this was a precious commodity in ancient times. Sure, trees were common enough, but you needed a skilled carpenter to craft furniture like these. The common folk, especially slaves, couldn't afford much. So be conservative when passing out the wooden furniture.

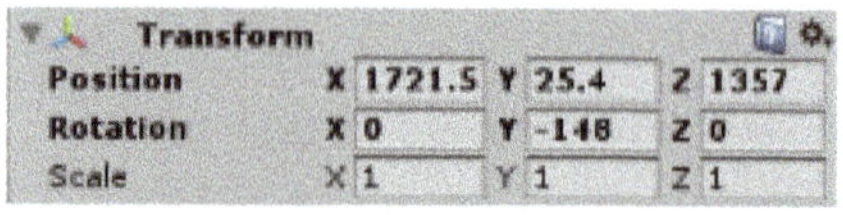

Figure 496

Drag the "Wooden_Cart" onto the scene and set the transform as shown in Figure 496. This places the cart next to the first Hebrew slave we put down with the pickaxe. But there are a couple of problems with this cart.

First, it has no collider. That means the player will be able to walk through it. So, add a Box Collider component to it. Setup the Center and Size of the box so that the cart roughly fits inside of it. It's ok if some of it sticks out. But it is usually best to err on the side of too small rather than too big.

Second, it has straw. Why is that a problem? Well, if you read through the Exodus story then you'll see that Pharaoh banned straw sent to the Hebrews for making bricks. But this happens after Moses has been in Egypt for a little bit. So that's something you'll want to think about as the game progresses.

The Hebrew people were oppressed and mistreated by the Egyptians. See if you can get that message across using the graphics instead of the dialogue.

Now save it in a prefab under Assets > Prefabs > Objects and put carts in some other conspicuous places. You can do the same thing with the tables, benches, stools, barrels, buckets, and shelves. Don't forget to put colliders on them. Just think to yourself where these objects would be put by the people living here.

Save the scene and try it out with the play button. Go to each of the new people that you made and make sure they act and talk the way you want. You may be tempted to think that just because one works the rest must too, but it is folly. Bugs can crawl out from anywhere. We must be vigilant and search for them anywhere they might hide. Feel free to move on when you're satisfied.

Egyptian City Life

Who doesn't love the city life? Lots of people packed into a small area, merchants bartering, animals making noises, and much more to keep the eyes, ears, and nose busy for weeks on end. If you just walk around the city you'll notice a great number of vendor stalls and houses that could be packed with people. But you can add as few or as many people as you want.

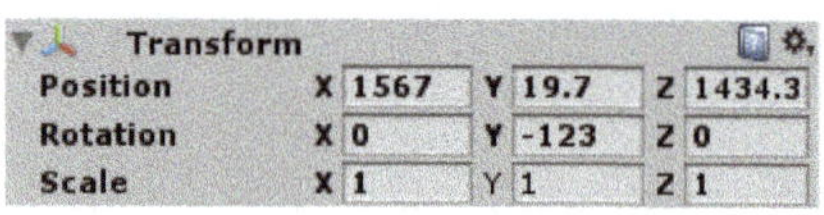

Figure 497

We're going to start putting people on the path leading up to the city. Drag an "EgyptianSlave" prefab onto the scene and set the Transform to what is shown in Figure 497. This puts him nearby some rocks on the road up to the city from the slave camp.

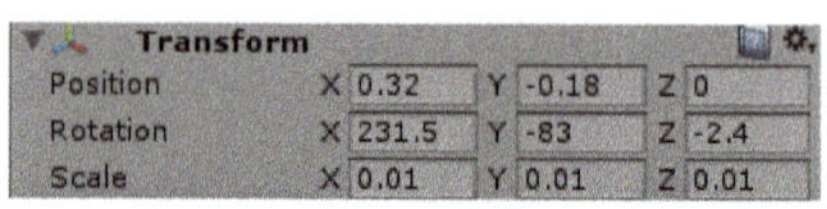

Figure 498

In the Project View, go to Assets > Models > Sickleadz Props > Survival Weapons HD Vol. 1 > Models and drag the shovel nearby the slave. As with the pickaxe, it is really huge. We'll fix that in just a bit. Drag the shovel so it becomes a child object of EgytianSlave >

Man_01 > Character > CenterRoot > CenterSpine > CenterSpine 1 > CenterSpine 2 > RightCollar > RightShoulder > RightElbow > RightHand. After that, set the transform of the shovel to what is shown in Figure 498.

If you've implemented the other animation states in the animator, then you can set the Action Type to "Animation" and the Animation to "Dig". This will make the slave actually look like he is digging with the shovel. Let's check this out! Enter play mode and when the game loads switch over from the Game View to the Scene View (while the game is still playing). You'll be able to see the guy from where you last left the camera, perhaps something like Figure 499.

Figure 499

Although the shovel isn't exactly what they used in ancient Egypt, it gives the idea he's working hard. And only the most detail-oriented players would probably notice. For our game, it should work out just fine.

Rename this guy to "ShovelEgyptianSlave" and make him into a prefab for our Egyptian slave with a shovel. As with the Hebrew slave with the pickaxe, find some other likely places where slaves might be digging and put them there. Where there is one slave digging there is probably a group. And don't forget to give them some interesting dialogue to say that helps the player feel more a part of this world that you're creating which looks a lot like ancient Egypt.

Guard Duty

It can be tough to be a guard. It's your job to make sure nothing bad happens and if it does, you're the first person there with authority to resolve the problem. It's kind of like fixing bugs, but with people.

We've already given the slaves shovels and pickaxes. Let's give the guards a weapon. The "Machete" in the Assets > Models > Sickleadz Props > Survival Weapons HD Vol. 1 > Models is probably about as close as we can get to a period weapon. Don't think they had revolvers back then.

Open the "Guard" prefab and drag the Machete out. Give it a try resizing it and putting it on the guard's "RightHand" object in the Hierarchy View. Now use the scene view to move and rotate the machete so that the handle looks like it fits into his hand. You'll need to move around in the Scene View to look at it from all angles.

Figure 500

Once you think it looks right, exit the prefab view, click the play button, and look at the one of the guards from the Scene View. It should look similar to Figure 500. Look closely at how the weapon fits in his in his hand. If you need to make adjustments then you'll need to do them outside of play mode in the prefab, otherwise your changes to the position won't be saved and propagated to every guard.

The Rest of the City

In this section, we're not going to create any specific objects, but I'll give you some direction on how to fill out the city. If you created the other prefabs for the Egyptian actors, then you can put them around the city. Merchants would be in the various marketplaces. You can use waypoints to make slaves running around to different places.

It can help to zoom out and look at the city from a bird's eye and think about where people would be. Not every vendor booth and house needs to have a person there. But there should be enough so that the player gets the feeling that this is a bustling city with lots of things going on.

The Egyptians also had herds of cows and sheep. Adding a few more herds using HerdSim we made the minigame out of in places outside the city would be a nice touch. They don't need to be another minigame, just wandering around to look authentic. There are also likely to be animals in the city used for labor and barter. You can also use the furniture like the tables, benches, and stools. There would also be carts in various places.

You may want to refer to the chapter about level design for additional tips on how to populate the city.

Again, when placing these actors and objects, don't just put them randomly or haphazardly. Step back and think about where the people would likely be standing or walking. Think about where the people would place the various objects. Put yourselves in the sandals of the people in your game and think about what they would do. Where would it make sense for them to go and put their things?

Bird's Eye View

Talking about the eyes of birds, we have some actual bird models we can use for additional little-thing-immersive-type-stuff. In this section, we'll use some of these models, change up their animations, and have them move about in the sky.

Figure 501

In the Project View, go to Asserts > Models > Flying Birds and drag the "Eagle onto the Scene View. Set the Y position to '100' and then focus on it so you see something like what is shown in Figure 501.

Looking in the inspector, you'll see that this model comes with an "Animation" component. Unlike the animator, it just keeps an array of animation clips and tracks the current clip to be played. There are 2 animations for this bird. The "EagleFly_ANIM" is like an idle animation of the eagle soaring with a little movement on the wings while the "EagleWingsBeat_ANIM" actually flaps the wings.

Go into play mode and change to Scene View and you can watch the animation in action. Clicking on one of the animations will take you there in the Project View.

Exiting play mode, look at the transform to the eagle and set its Scale to 1.5 for each X/Y/Z. Making the eagle bigger will help the player see it from on the ground so when they look up against the sky, they'll see something moving and be interested to look again to see what it is.

Create a C# script named "BirdFly" so we can change animations for it and move the bird around. Add the code shown in Figure 502. In the "Start" method, we get the handle to the Animation component and then make a list of all the animations in the array. Then we update the animation and movement and initialize the timer. The "rotateTimeout" is how long to change direction.

```
public class BirdFly : MonoBehaviour
{
    private Animation animComp;
    private List<string> animNames;
    private float rotateTimeout;
    private int rotDir;

    // Start is called before the first frame update
    Unity Message | 0 references
    void Start()
    {
        animComp = GetComponent<Animation>();
        animNames = new List<string>();
        foreach (AnimationState state in animComp) animNames.Add(state.name);
        UpdateAnimation();
        UpdateMovement();
        rotateTimeout = -1;
    }

    // Update is called once per frame
    Unity Message | 0 references
    void Update()
    {
        transform.position +=
            transform.TransformDirection(Vector3.forward * Time.deltaTime * 4);
        if (rotateTimeout > Time.time)
        {
            transform.Rotate(new Vector3(0, rotDir * Time.deltaTime * 30, 0));
        }
    }

    1 reference
    private void UpdateAnimation()
    {
        int rndAnim = Random.Range(0, animComp.GetClipCount());
        animComp.CrossFade(animNames[rndAnim]);
        Invoke("UpdateAnimation", Random.Range(5f, 15f));
    }

    1 reference
    private void UpdateMovement()
    {
        rotDir = Random.Range(-1, 1);
        rotateTimeout = Time.time + Random.Range(1.5f, 3f);
        Invoke("UpdateMovement", Random.Range(5f, 10f));
    }
}
```

Figure 502

Both the animation and movement update methods heavily rely on random numbers. The animation clip will be randomly chosen from the array, and it will be played for a random amount of time between 5 and 15 seconds. The "CrossFade" method is used to change the animation to keep the transition smooth.

The "UpdateMovement" method will randomly decide whether the bird veers left, right, or straight ahead. While the rotate timer is active the bird will slowly turn in that direction. This slow turning looks much more realistic than just rotating the bird all at once. The "Update" method handles moving forward and making that slow turn.

All you need to do now is drag this script onto the "Eagle" in the Hierarchy View, or onto its inspector. When you click the play button and change the tab to the Scene View, you'll see that it has probably already moved out of your view. Focus on it and you'll see it moving. If you're lucky, going into the Game View, you may be able to spot it when looking up in the sky.

Go ahead and put a few more birds up in the sky. You can copy and paste the eagle and put it in different locations. You'll probably want to rotate them in different directions, so they aren't all flying in the same direction at the start. You can also drag some different birds onto the scene. You just need to add the "BirdFly" script, set the scale to something bigger like 1.5, and change the Y position to something high like '100'. You can have the birds flying at different heights to give more variation.

New Game for a New Player

Let's talk about the experience of a brand-new player. We hinted at it earlier in the tutorial, but we're finally getting back to it. It's important to get the player into the game as soon as possible. The more time spent on the user interface the less fun the player will have. We spent all that time designing and implementing the game, so we might as well get them into it ASAP!

Open the title controller script and scroll down to the "Start" method. As shown in Figure 504, add the code on line 47 to simulate the player pressing the button to start a new game. Recall that the else portion of this 'if' statement means that the player has not played the game before.

```
36        if (PlayerData.LoadCurrentScene() != "")
37        {
38            MusicSlider.value = PlayerPrefs.GetFloat("MusicVolume");
39            SoundFXSlider.value = PlayerPrefs.GetFloat("SoundVolume");
40        }
41        else
42        {
43            MusicSlider.value = 0.5f;
44            PlayerPrefs.SetFloat("MusicVolume", 0.5f);
45            SoundFXSlider.value = 0.5f;
46            PlayerPrefs.SetFloat("SoundVolume", 0.5f);
47            ButtonNewGame();
48        }
```

Figure 504

One more important thing we should do here is consider what the title scene will look like. I've used the "DT_EndDoor" model with a fire bowl and Moses with his staff examining the hieroglyphics in Figure 503. You can make something similar or do something completely different. Perhaps you want to use the terrain from "Egypt_Nile Scene" and show that. If you want to get fancy you can make a script for the main camera to move it through the scene. Be creative with it!

In Assets > Images > Logos there is a title for "Exodus Adventure" that you can use. I've also included the logo for BibleBytle Books but you can make or use your own logo for your game.

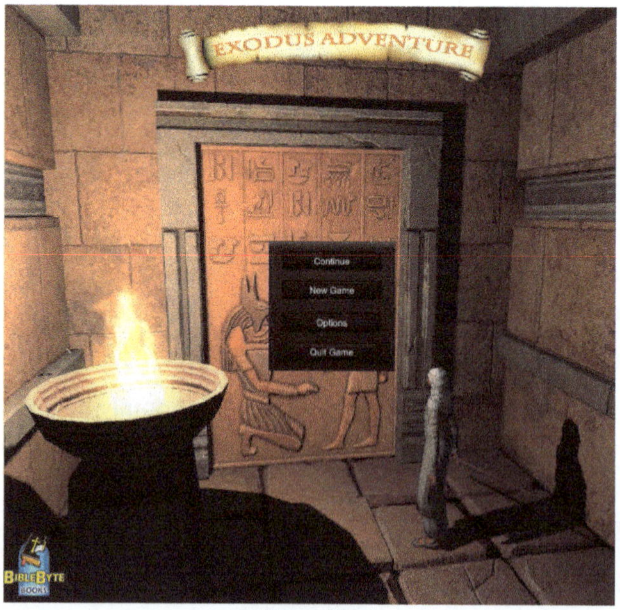

Figure 503

Deploying the Game

Once you're done developing the game or you want to send it out to people to playtest (we'll talk more about that in the next section) you'll want to deploy it. Deploying a game means getting it ready to give out to other people and there are a few steps that need to happen to do that.

The first step is to play through it yourself. Make sure that the basic features work as intended and fix any errors. If there are issues that you can't fix or don't have time to fix, then make a list. A list of known issues in the game or software you deploy is called Errata. This should be given to anyone who plays it so they don't try things you already know don't work and can save them time; they'll appreciate it. After you test be sure to reset the player data to give the tester the new player experience.

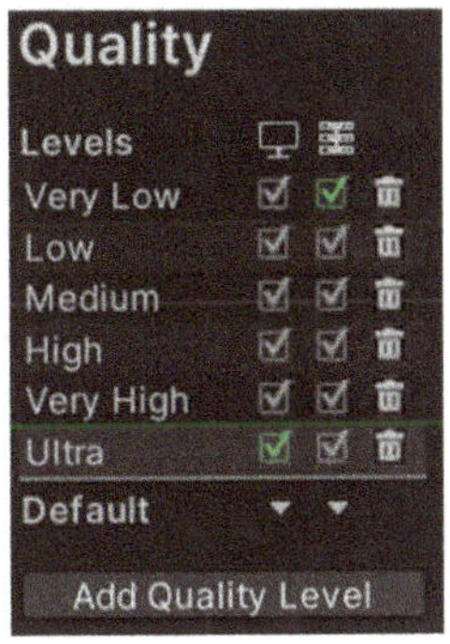

Figure 505

Next, in the main menu select Edit > Project Settings and the window will pop up. Click the Quality page to see and you'll see the different quality levels like in Figure 505. This specifies how good the graphics quality will be for the game. The higher the quality the better the game will look but the more powerful a system the player needs to run that quality at a good performance.

The game defaults to the "Ultra" setting, but you can change it by scripting. The below code is what you use:

```
int qualityLevel = 0;

QualitySettings.SetQualityLevel(qualityLevel);
```

The class QualitySettings contains the static method "SetQualityLevel" which takes an int as a parameter for the quality level index. That indexes into the list of quality levels in this Quality window. There are a lot of options and settings to adjust and fine-tune the quality of the game but that is beyond the scope of this tutorial.

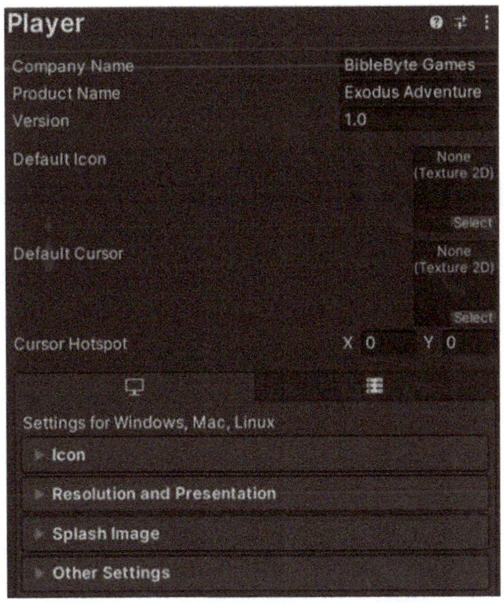

Figure 506

Next, select the "Player" page and you'll see those settings like in Figure 506. See below for descriptions of these.

- Company Name: Name of your company, if you don't have one then think of a cool name nobody else is using.
- Product Name: This is the name of the game.
- Version: string of numbers, usually less than 1.0 is before the official release, 1.0 is your first release, and then it goes up after that.
- Default Icon: This image will be used as the icon for the executable after we've built it.
- Default Cursor: This image will be used as the mouse cursor.
- Cursor Hotspot: Designates the center or pointer of the cursor that the player will point to things with.

There are some other OS specific settings below those but are beyond the scope of this tutorial.

Then open the Build Settings window by going to the main menu and selecting File > Build Settings. The Window shown in Figure 507 will pop up. Make sure all your scenes are added to the "Scenes In Build". The middle left has the Platform, we'll just stick with "Windows, Mac, Linux" for now. Next to that is the "Target Platform". It will default to the OS you downloaded Unity to.

Click the "Build" button. When building the PC version, you'll be prompted with something like what is shown in Figure 507 asking for the folder to save it in. If you have different OS builds, then you may want to save it in different folders. But just a "Build" folder is good enough for us.

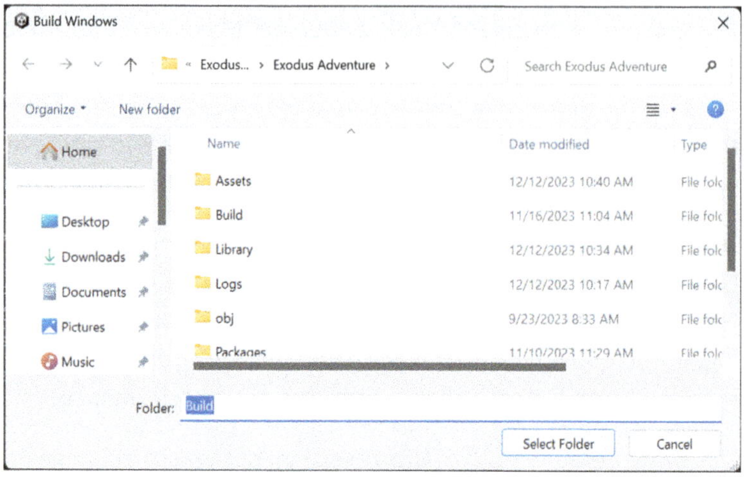

Figure 507

A popup will appear showing that it is "Building Player". This will take a little bit of time since we have quite a few pretty high-quality graphics and models in this game. This is another great time to finish the "Exodus: God of the Slaves" book or play more in "Exodus Vigil.

The resulting build opened as a new window for you when it is done. The "ExodusAdventure.exe" file is present which you can double-click to run the game. There is also a folder named "ExodusAdventure_Data" which is required to be in the same folder as the exe file to play the game. You can distribute the game using these files and folders or you can compress it using your favorite compression program.

Next Steps

Be courteous and polite when asking for favors. Tell them about how cool your game is and ask if they would like to try out an early version in exchange for giving you feedback about how well they liked it.

You've now made your game, built it, and gotten it ready for deployment. However, playing your own game is the worst way to test it. This is because you designed and implemented it yourself and your mind is thinking about what you designed. This is a general rule among software design and programming in general.

Testing software is trying to break it and when you made the system it is hard to think of ways to break it because you don't want the system to break. Family and friends are easy to ask but since they want you to succeed, they unwittingly give you positive feedback which won't help improve your game. Perfect strangers are the perfect testers because they are more likely to give you honest feedback.

If you haven't asked anyone to help you test the game out yet then now would be a good time. You can write up a questionnaire they can fill out after they finish the game that asks for comments about how they liked specific features. When they play the game, watch what they do, where their eyes move, and their facial expressions. If they look frustrated or annoyed about something, then take note of what they were doing in the game. For example, if this happened when the inventory or quest journal was up then start thinking of ways you can improve it.

Going further with the game, there are still a lot of things you can implement from the GDD. You can implement all the main quests, Hebrew culture quests, and Egyptian culture quests. There are also the cut scenes and ending cinematic to do. And even once you complete those you can focus on the little things that will really draw the player into the experience of playing your game.

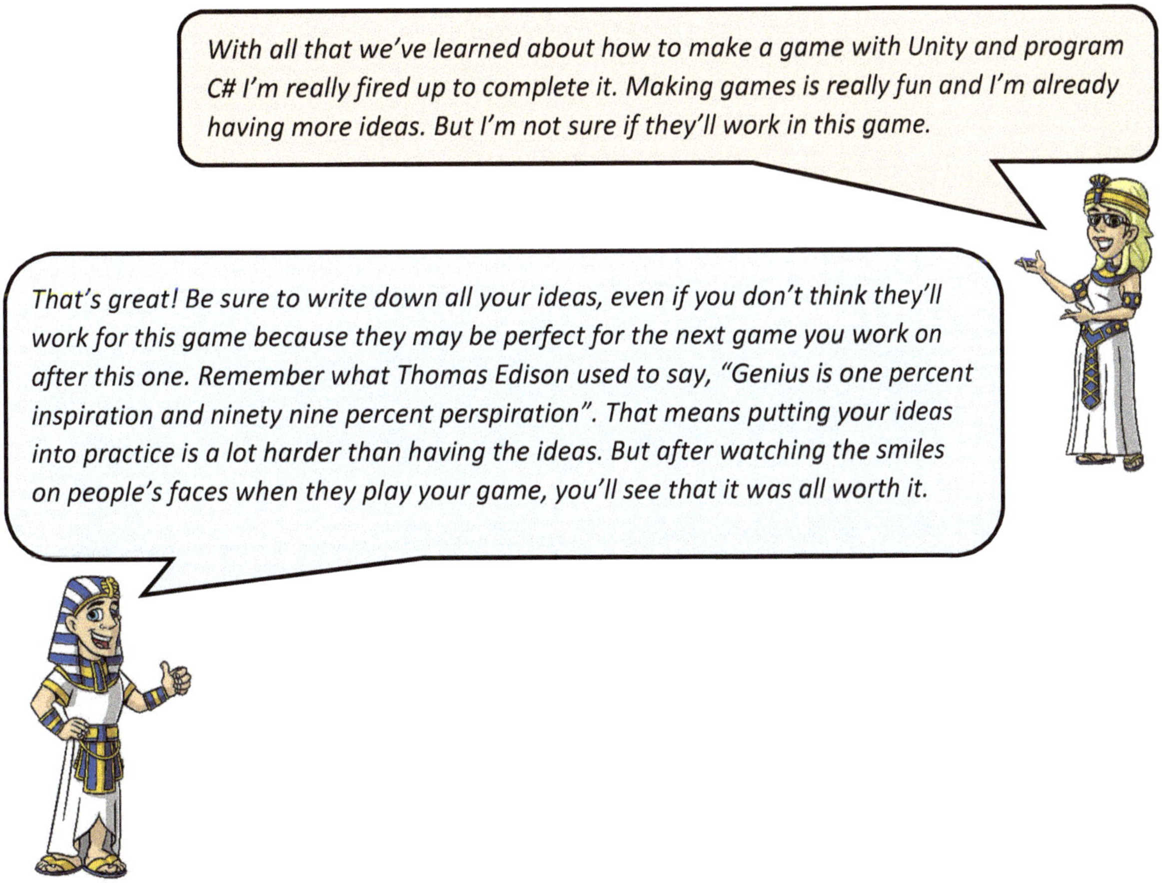

Chapter 18 – The Unity Multipurpose Avatar (UMA)

Filling out the game city and camps with people is great to convince players the game is real and let them experience being immersed in your game. You can have one of your four Egyptian male models be a street trader, another be a guard, another be a different trader, another be a slave walking around, and another be a… Wait a minute, if we only have four male Egyptian models then that means players will run into clones of them and that will hamper the game's realism.

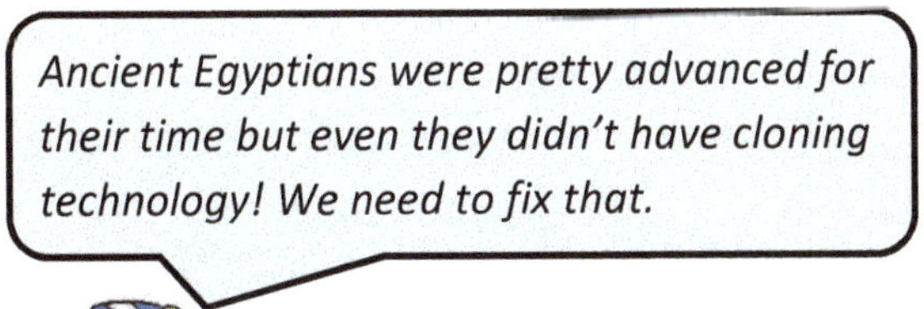

Lucky for us, Fernando Ribeiro developed something called the Unity Multipurpose Avatar, or UMA for short. While working in Rio de Janeiro in Brazil, he wanted to help his 16-year-old students make lots of characters in Unity 3D. He developed the UMA system and provided the source code and base content for free under the MIT license. That means you can use UMA, change it to do what you need, and then send it to whomever you want. All the open-source UMA files are located here: https://github.com/huika. I also want to give a shoutout to Hugo Moraleida who put some basic under-clothing on the avatars for us to give them a 'G' rating.

If Three is a Crowd then what about…

To get our first look at UMA, we're going to check out a whole crowd of characters. In the Project View, expand the folders like this: UMA > Examples > Main Examples. Then click on the "Scenes" folder. You will see seven Unity scenes and a readme file as shown in Figure 508. The first scene should read "UMA Core Demo – Crowd". Double-click to load the scene.

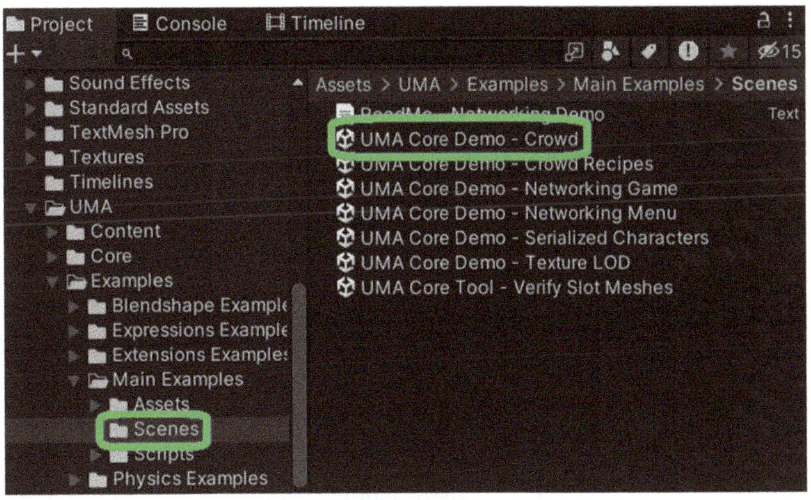

Figure 508

After the scene loads click the play button and let's check it out. When it goes to play mode, you'll just see the empty scene with the floor. Then after a few seconds, characters will pop up out of nowhere and you'll see something like but not exactly Figure 509. What a big crowd that showed up just for you here.

Figure 509

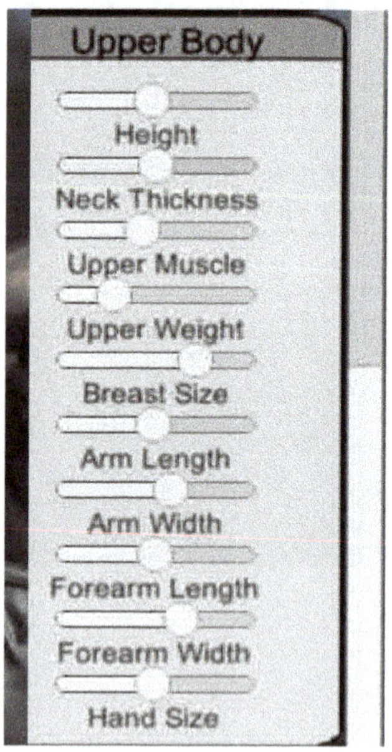

Figure 510

The great thing is that each one of these people are different. Go ahead and look at each one. Click on the Scene View if you want to get a close-up look at them one by one. Their heights, weights, body builds, and hair are all different. Even the eyes, noses, mouths, and ears on their faces are different. They have different clothes with different colors as well.

Go back to the Game View if you haven't already and now move the mouse over one of the characters and click on it. You'll see a bunch of sliders appear on the right-hand side of the screen as shown in Figure 510. Click the round button above "Height" and slide it around to see the character you clicked grow bigger and shrink smaller. Try "Neck Thickness" next and then some other sliders. These characteristics of the various people are called DNA in UMA. These are set up when a character is created and can be changed while the game is running.

There is a scroll bar on the right, and you can see all the different DNA fields UMA allows you to change at run-time. You can click the button "Close DNA Sliders" at the bottom of the Game View to hide them so you can click on another character if you want. Try adjusting the facial features to match that good-looking portrait in the mirror.

One important detail that may seem counter-intuitive is how UMA handles male and female characters which requires a little explanation. In UMA, male and female are different races. I know, I know, you're screaming at me through the pages of this book, "They're not races. They're genders!" And of course, you're right.

Wow! With so many things to change about these characters, we can make a whole town with unique people.

The reason UMA does this is purely technical in the differences between male and female 3D models. UMA gets all the customization by taking a basic 3D model of someone and making changes so the model is taller, has longer arms, or something else like that. But let's say you wanted to make UMA characters for monkeys. You need a different base 3D model for the monkey because the physical differences are so different than, say a male human 3D model, that you cannot make the male 3D model look like a realistic monkey through customization. The same is true about the physical differences between males and females. To make a believably looking female character, you can't customize a male 3D model. Therefore, UMA has males and females as different races because they need different base 3D models, so the characters look right.

You won't find things like hair-style, clothing, or skin tone on these sliders. Those are added to characters as wardrobe recipes. In addition to housing lions and witches, some people also keep their clothes in them. Never mind, that's a different game. Hair color, skin tone, and other colors used on the characters are tracked separately. These things can also change while the game is running but requires some scripting to do it. Why might you want to change something like hair while the game is running? Maybe you want a character to put on a hat. So, you'll need to add the appropriate hat wardrobe recipe using a script.

A wardrobe is a standing closet you use to store clothes like pants, shirts, and your hair. I always make sure I grab a clean wig from my wardrobe to start the day fresh.

In fact, this crowd scene uses a script to create and randomly change the DNA, wardrobe, and other properties of these characters. One of the best ways to learn how to use a new asset is to peek at how it already works, so we're going to open the script that creates this crowd of UMA people and see how they do it so we can learn to do it ourselves. You can exit play mode now. Let's open the UMACrowd script by clicking the UMACrowd game object in the Hierarchy View and then clicking the grayed-out script field named "UMACrowd" (as shown in Figure 511) which takes you to that script in the Project View. Double-click that script to view it in the code editor.

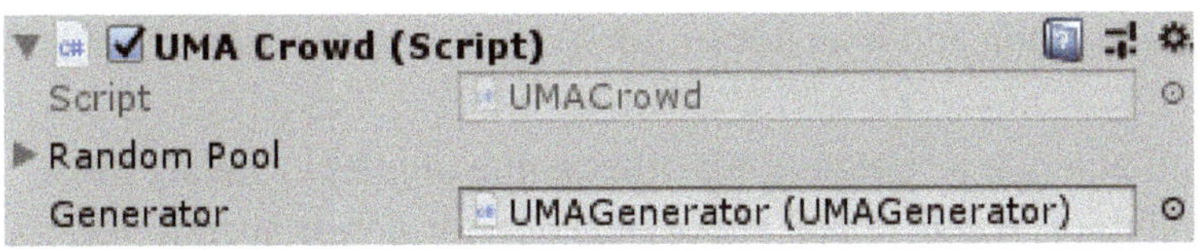

Figure 511

Now, if you scroll through the file, you'll see that there is a truck-load of code here. Don't worry, we won't go through the whole thing. We'll take a highlight of the interesting sections of code that do the heavy lifting to create this crowd of characters. Figure 512 shows the variables at the top of the UMACrowd class.

```
        public UMACrowdRandomSet[] randomPool;
        public UMAGeneratorBase generator;
        public UMAData umaData;
        public UMAContext umaContext;
        public RuntimeAnimatorController animationController;
        public float atlasResolutionScale = 1;
        public bool generateUMA;
        public bool generateLotsUMA;
        public bool hideWhileGeneratingLots;
        public bool stressTest;
        public Vector2 umaCrowdSize;
        public bool randomDna;
        public UMARecipeBase[] additionalRecipes;

        public float space = 1;
        public Transform zeroPoint;
        private int spawnX;
        private int spawnY;

        public SharedColorTable SkinColors;
        public SharedColorTable HairColors;
        // public SharedColorTable EyeColors; TODO: Add support for eye colors
        // public SharedColorTable ClothesColors; TODO: Add support for clothes colors

        public string[] keywords;

        public UMADataEvent CharacterCreated;
        public UMADataEvent CharacterDestroyed;
        public UMADataEvent CharacterUpdated;
```

Figure 512

- **UMACrowdRandomSet[] randomPool:** This array set in the inspector is the pool of races to make the UMA character from. The "UMACrowd" game object sets this array to HumanFemale and HumanMale.
- **UMAGeneratorBase generator:** This is an instance of an UMAGenerator game object that exists in the scene. This generator will do all the heavy lifting to create the customized 3D model as well as the texture that has the skin and everything that wraps around the model.
- **UMAData umaData:** This is created from an UMADynamicCharacter class for each character the script creates. It stores the UMA character's DNA, wardrobe, race, and other characteristics. It also does the heavy lifting for getting the built 3D model from the generator ready to be animated. The process for that is called rigging and is an advanced 3D modeling and animation topic for another tutorial.
- **UMAContext umaContext:** This game object is a container for other game objects including the race library, slot library, and overlay library. We've talked about race but not slot or overlay yet. Don't worry we will, for now, just know that they have to do with creating the UMA character.
- **RuntimeAnimatorController animationController:** This is the animation controller to setup the UMA character with. See Chapter 6 – Actor Animation Controller for more information.
- **float atlasResolutionScale:** This resolution scale lets you decrease the quality of the textures used to make this character. You'd want to do this to keep better performance on older systems that can't keep up.

- **bool generateUMA:** If true, the script builds one UMA characters.
- **bool generateLotsUMA:** If true, the script builds A LOT of UMA characters.
- **bool hideWhileGeneratingLots:** If false, each UMA character is displayed as it is created. If true, all characters are invisible until every character is done being created and they are shown at the same time.
- **bool stressTest:** This is a special mode to test UMA. We won't be using it.
- **Vector2 umaCrowdSize:** Array of how big the UMA crowd gets in terms of rows and columns.
- **bool randomDna**: Whether to change the DNA like height and facial features to random values. If this is false, then the base 3D models are not changed.
- **UMARecipeBase[] additionalRecipes:** This array has any additional things to add to each UMA character. The only element here is a capsule collider recipe which keeps the UMA characters from falling through the floor.
- **float space:** The space between each created UMA character.
- **Transform zeroPoint:** The point in 3D space at which to start creating UMA characters.
- **int spawnX:** Internal variable used to track the current X position of the UMA character.
- **int spawnY:** Internal variable used to track the current Y position of the UMA character.
- **SharedColorTable SkinColors:** Container class of all the colors to use for character skin tone.
- **SharedColorTable HairColors:** Container class of all the colors to use for character hair.
- **string[] keywords:** Optionally change how the characters in the crowd are built. This isn't currently used.
- **UMADataEvent CharacterCreated:** List of methods to call when any character is created. This isn't currently used. This is useful to know when the character was created without having to constantly check.
- **UMADataEvent CharacterDestroyed:** List of methods to call when a character is destroyed. This isn't currently used.
- **UMADataEvent CharacterUpdated:** List of methods to call when a character is changed. This isn't currently used.

```
void Update()
{
    if (generateUMA)
    {
        umaCrowdSize = Vector2.one;
        int randomResult = Random.Range(0, 2);
        GenerateOneUMA(randomResult);
        generateUMA = false;
        generateLotsUMA = false;
    }

    if (generateLotsUMA)
    {
        if (generator.IsIdle())
        {
            int randomResult = Random.Range(0, 2);
            GenerateOneUMA(randomResult);
        }
    }

    if (stressTest && generator.IsIdle() && !generateLotsUMA && !generateUMA)
    {
        RandomizeAll();
    }
}
```

Figure 513

Skipping over the Awake() method we see there are a couple things going on in the Update() method doing in Figure 513. It handles the cases to either generate a single UMA character or to generate lots of UMA characters. In both cases, the method GenerateOneUma() is called with an argument of a random number between 0 and 1. Calling the method Random.Range(0, 2) provides a random whole number between the first number, 0, and the second number minus 1, which is 1. We won't look at the stress test case.

Now I see what happens if you set both generateUMA and generateLotsUMA to true at the same time. Since the 'if' statement for generateUMA is handled first it would execute that code and set both Boolean variables to false. So the script would just generate a single UMA character.

Let's look at the method GenerateOneUMA() now. You can find it on line 604 as seen in Figure 514. It takes in the sex of the character to create as a parameter and returns a GameObject. What is the GameObject that it returns? Sometimes a good method is like a good movie, you need to watch the whole thing for the ending to make sense. But not in this case, if you skip to the end on line 643 you see that the method calls another method GenerateUMA() with the sex of the character and its position and returns whatever that method returns. Looks like we need to go deeper to find the true ending.

```
604         public GameObject GenerateOneUMA(int sex)
605         {
606             Vector3 zeroPos = Vector3.zero;
607             if (zeroPoint != null)
608                 zeroPos = zeroPoint.position;
609             Vector3 newPos = zeroPos + new Vector3((spawnX - umaCrowdSize.x / 2f + 0.5f) * space, 0f,
610                                                     (spawnY - umaCrowdSize.y / 2f + 0.5f) * space);
611 
612             if (spawnY < umaCrowdSize.y)
613             {
614                 spawnX++;
615                 if (spawnX >= umaCrowdSize.x)
616                 {
617                     spawnX = 0;
618                     spawnY++;
619                 }
620             }
621             else
622             {
623                 if (hideWhileGeneratingLots)
624                 {
625                     UMAData[] generatedCrowd = GetComponentsInChildren<UMAData>();
626                     foreach (UMAData generatedData in generatedCrowd)
627                     {
628                         if (generatedData.animator != null)
629                             generatedData.animator.enabled = true;
630 
631                         Renderer[] renderers = generatedData.GetRenderers();
632                         for (int i = 0; i < renderers.Length; i++)
633                         {
634                             renderers[i].enabled = true;
635                         }
636                     }
637                 }
638                 generateLotsUMA = false;
639                 spawnX = 0;
640                 spawnY = 0;
641                 return null;
642             }
643             return GenerateUMA(sex, newPos);
644         }
```

Figure 514

The logic in the middle of the method does have one very important part. To understand it, however, we need to understand the code at the start of the method. The first block on lines 606 to 610 create the new position of the UMA character. The middle block checks if the script is done creating UMA characters. It iterates row and column through the spawn points like a 2D array. Once the 'Y' coordinate is out of bounds of the array then it's done, shows all the characters, and indicates it's done by setting "generateLotsUMA" to false.

In Figure 515, you can see the first part of the method GenerateUMA(). The arguments are the sex of the character generate and the position the character will be created. First thing the method does is create a new GameObject with the name "Generated Character" for the UMA character and setting that Game Object at the specified position. This is the name that will show up in the Hierarchy View.

```
public GameObject GenerateUMA(int sex, Vector3 position)
{
    GameObject newGO = new GameObject("Generated Character");
    newGO.transform.parent = transform;
    newGO.transform.position = position;
    newGO.transform.rotation = zeroPoint != null ? zeroPoint.rotation : transform.rotation;

    UMADynamicAvatar umaDynamicAvatar = newGO.AddComponent<UMADynamicAvatar>();
    umaDynamicAvatar.Initialize();
    umaData = umaDynamicAvatar.umaData;
    umaData.CharacterCreated = new UMADataEvent(CharacterCreated);
    umaData.CharacterDestroyed = new UMADataEvent(CharacterDestroyed);
    umaData.CharacterUpdated = new UMADataEvent(CharacterUpdated);
    umaDynamicAvatar.umaGenerator = generator;
    umaData.umaGenerator = generator;
    var umaRecipe = umaDynamicAvatar.umaData.umaRecipe;
    UMACrowdRandomSet.CrowdRaceData race = null;
```

Figure 515

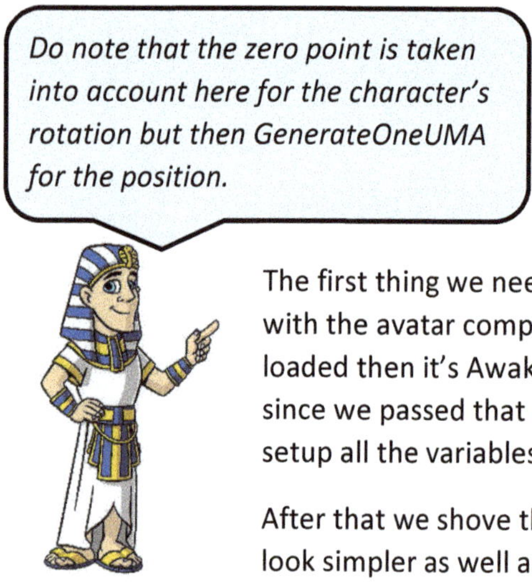

Next, we add an UMADynamicAvatar (I'll just call it avatar for short from now on, because I'm lazy) component on that Game Object. This component has the data we need to make this UMA a customized character. This is the central component required to create an UMA character, when we create a new character, it will have this component.

The first thing we need to do is initialize the avatar. Normally, if the game object with the avatar component is in the scene at the beginning when the scene is loaded then it's Awake and Start methods will get called to initialize everything. But since we passed that point, we need to call it separately. Initializing the avatar will setup all the variables the creation process needs.

After that we shove that avatar's umaData into a local variable. This helps the code look simpler as well as making it run faster since we're not referencing the data through the avatar each time we use it. Sometimes it pays to be lazy. Next it sets up some UMADataEvents. You can think of these like this, when something happens you can specify that a method on a script on an object gets called.

Finally, we give the avatar and the umaData the instance to the UMA generator, get a local variable to old the recipe for the UMA data and another variable to hold the character's race (i.e., sex or gender). The recipe itself stores all customizations like head size. On the next page we'll see what the rest of this method does with this information.

```
        if (randomPool != null && randomPool.Length > 0)
        {
            int randomResult = Random.Range(0, randomPool.Length);
            race = randomPool[randomResult].data;
            umaRecipe.SetRace(umaContext.GetRace(race.raceID));
        }
        else
        {
            if (sex == 0)
            {
                umaRecipe.SetRace(umaContext.GetRace("HumanMale"));
            }
            else
            {
                umaRecipe.SetRace(umaContext.GetRace("HumanFemale"));
            }
        }

        SetUMAData();

        if (race != null && race.slotElements.Length > 0)
        {
            DefineSlots(race);
        }
        else
        {
            DefineSlots();
        }

        AddAdditionalSlots();

        GenerateUMAShapes();

        if (animationController != null)
        {
            umaDynamicAvatar.animationController = animationController;
        }
        umaDynamicAvatar.Show();

        return newGO;
    }
```

Figure 516

Figure 516 is the next part of the GenerateUma() method. When we choose a race from randomPool we first need to make sure it exists and has something in it, so we don't jump off the deep end of the array. If this happens to be the case, then we'll just send the UMA recipe the default race depending on what sex the character is supposed to be.

The call to SetUMAData() just updates umaData with the atlas scale for the UMA texture resolution and sets up the OnCharacterCreated event to call the CharacterCreatedCallback() method defined in this file later on when the character is done being created.

Based on the "race" of the character it will have different slots that make up the 3D model. We're going to look more in-depth into this and the method GenerateUMAShapes() next, but let me finish with this method first. I need to finish something before moving on to something else, I'm just OCD that way.

Way back at the top of the file the animation controller was defined, here is where we tell the avatar to use it. Finally, the avatar is shown to all the world for the marvelous creation that it is. Then the containing game object is returned back to GenerateOneUMA(), which returns it back to the Update() method.

Coming back to the method DefineSlots() shown on lines 584 and 587, we see that there are 2 ways that it is called. The first time, we call it with the chosen random race as a parameter and the second time we call it with no parameters. When we do this with a method name, we say that it is overloaded. It is very useful when you have two methods that do practically the same thing but need to pass in different parameters. In this case, we need to define what the slots are but the code to do that is different if we've chosen a random race or not.

To keep things simple, we're just going to look at the code for the method without parameters. Let me give a little disclaimer, since the code to define the slots is very large, we'll examine it in small sections that have the lines truncated. But I encourage you to have the code up and follow along.

```
102     void DefineSlots()
103     {
104         Color skinColor = new Color(1, 1, 1, 1);
105         float skinTone;
106 
107         skinTone = Random.Range(0.1f, 0.6f);
108         skinColor = new Color(skinTone + Random.Range(0.35f, 0.4f),
109 
110         Color HairColor = new Color(Random.Range(0.1f, 0.9f), Random
111 
112         if (umaData.umaRecipe.raceData.raceName == "HumanMale")
113         {
114             int randomResult = 0;
```

Figure 517

Varying the skin tone and hair colors are a great way to make different characters look different. Lines 107, 108, and 110 in Figure 517 create random colors within a certain range so the colors look somewhat realistic but have enough variability to give each one a unique quality. Colors in Unity use a four-part scheme: red, green, blue, and alpha. Red, green, and blue are kind of easy to understand. These first three just mix the colors together. Remember way back in chapter 4 that alpha refers to transparency. Since we won't have any spirits in this game, the alpha can stay set to '1'.

```
112             if (umaData.umaRecipe.raceData.raceName == "HumanMale")
113             {
114                 int randomResult = 0;
115                 //Male Avatar
116 
117                 umaData.umaRecipe.slotDataList = new SlotData[15];
118 
119                 umaData.umaRecipe.slotDataList[0] = umaContext.InstantiateSlot("MaleEyes");
120                 umaData.umaRecipe.slotDataList[0].AddOverlay(umaContext.InstantiateOverlay("EyeOverlay"));
121                 umaData.umaRecipe.slotDataList[0].AddOverlay(umaContext.InstantiateOverlay("EyeOverlayAdjust",
122 
123                 randomResult = Random.Range(0, 2);
124                 if (randomResult == 0)
125                 {
126                     umaData.umaRecipe.slotDataList[1] = umaContext.InstantiateSlot("MaleFace");
127 
128                     randomResult = Random.Range(0, 2);
129 
130                     if (randomResult == 0)
131                     {
132                         umaData.umaRecipe.slotDataList[1].AddOverlay(umaContext.InstantiateOverlay("MaleHead01"
133                     }
134                     else if (randomResult == 1)
135                     {
136                         umaData.umaRecipe.slotDataList[1].AddOverlay(umaContext.InstantiateOverlay("MaleHead02"
137                     }
138                 }
```

Figure 518

Now, UMA is a great tool for generating your own customized characters. But in our case, since we're dealing with human males and females, the slots will be the same, so I'm only going to cover the first one which is the human male as partly shown in Figure 518. As I mentioned earlier, the 3D character created by UMA uses slots for the different parts; the face is a slot, eyes are a slot, and so on. The recipe in the UMA data has a list that contains all the slots for that character.

Before a slot is usable it must be instantiated, as seen on line 119, with the name of the slot. This is done in the first element of the slot list which is index '0'. After that, an overlay is applied to the slot. The overlay uses a texture to paint around the model for the slot. Line 120 adds the white of the eye with "EyeOverlay" and then the color is added on line 121 using "EyeOverlayAdjust" with a random color mixed in. Different eye colors will help to make the characters look unique.

This code makes creating characters that look different a snap. And if we want to add more face textures we only need to put it in the overlay library and code another 'if' statement.

The next block of code starting on line 123 chooses the face for the model at index '1' of the slot list. The first of which is shown in Figure 518. Again, you see instantiating the slot on line 126 for the face. Then there is a random texture chosen to paint the face with between "MaleHead01" and "MaleHead02". The more variation with different textures we mix in the better.

```
                else if (randomResult == 1)
                {
                    umaData.umaRecipe.slotDataList[1] = umaContext.InstantiateSlot("MaleHead_Head");

                    randomResult = Random.Range(0, 2);
                    if (randomResult == 0)
                    {
                        umaData.umaRecipe.slotDataList[1].AddOverlay(umaContext.InstantiateOverlay("MaleHead0
                    }
                    else if (randomResult == 1)
                    {
                        umaData.umaRecipe.slotDataList[1].AddOverlay(umaContext.InstantiateOverlay("MaleHead0
                    }

                    umaData.umaRecipe.slotDataList[7] = umaContext.InstantiateSlot("MaleHead_Eyes", umaData.u
                    umaData.umaRecipe.slotDataList[9] = umaContext.InstantiateSlot("MaleHead_Mouth", umaData.

                    randomResult = Random.Range(0, 2);
                    if (randomResult == 0)
                    {
                        umaData.umaRecipe.slotDataList[10] = umaContext.InstantiateSlot("MaleHead_PigNose", u
                        umaData.umaRecipe.slotDataList[1].AddOverlay(umaContext.InstantiateOverlay("MaleHead_
                    }
                    else if (randomResult == 1)
                    {
                        umaData.umaRecipe.slotDataList[10] = umaContext.InstantiateSlot("MaleHead_Nose", umaD
                    }

                    randomResult = Random.Range(0, 2);
                    if (randomResult == 0)
                    {
                        umaData.umaRecipe.slotDataList[8] = umaContext.InstantiateSlot("MaleHead_ElvenEars");
                        umaData.umaRecipe.slotDataList[8].AddOverlay(umaContext.InstantiateOverlay("ElvenEars
                    }
                    else if (randomResult == 1)
                    {
                        umaData.umaRecipe.slotDataList[8] = umaContext.InstantiateSlot("MaleHead_Ears", umaDa
                    }
                }
```

Figure 519

The code to handle the second type of head is handled in Figure 519. Notice that the slot '1' is still a head which includes the face. This is a different slot for the head which means it is a different 3D model than previously used. However, it still uses the same two head textures. Effectively, what we have here is two different head slots with two different overlay textures which means (two times two) there are four unique head combinations.

You'll also notice that the next slots are different for this head. The eyes are instantiated in slot '7' and mouth in slot '9'. There's nothing special about which slots go to which index just as long as all the slots get placed and you don't try to put more than one slot in an index.

Next up are the noses. Here it randomly chooses between a normal nose and a pig-shaped nose instantiated in slot '10'. With the pig-nosed option the slot '1' head overlay needs a special texture to make the head look normal, or as normal as possible with a pig-nose. The ears are instantiated in slot '8' with the option to use elven ears if you're making a Tolkien-like Middle Earth themed game.

```
randomResult = Random.Range(0, 3);
if (randomResult == 0)
{
    umaData.umaRecipe.slotDataList[1].AddOverlay(umaContext.InstantiateOverlay("MaleHair01"
}
else if (randomResult == 1)
{
    umaData.umaRecipe.slotDataList[1].AddOverlay(umaContext.InstantiateOverlay("MaleHair02"
}
else
{

}
```

Figure 520

Similar to the other slots, in Figure 520 there are three options for the male hair overlay. Wait a minute. There's something different about it this time. We're adding the overlay to slot '1' but we already instantiated the head to be in this slot. And then the else block is just empty. What is going on here?

While the slot index can only hold a single slot, it can have more than one overlay. So, while it has the head overlay, we add the various hair overlays on top of it. This way, when we animate the model, the hair is attached to the head. That empty else condition handles the case for when the man is bald, which does seem pretty fitting.

The beard options in the next block of code, shown in Figure 521, are done in the same way as the hair. If you look at the second parameter (not shown in the figure) you'll see that this is the hair color and is the same color as the hair on the top of this guy's head. As the next block of code, the beard composition, doesn't have anything special, we'll skip it. Mixing the different beard overlays gives additional uniqueness.

```
randomResult = Random.Range(0, 4);
if (randomResult == 0)
{
    umaData.umaRecipe.slotDataList[1].AddOverlay(umaContext.InstantiateOverlay("MaleBeard01"
}
else if (randomResult == 1)
{
    umaData.umaRecipe.slotDataList[1].AddOverlay(umaContext.InstantiateOverlay("MaleBeard02"
}
else if (randomResult == 2)
{
    umaData.umaRecipe.slotDataList[1].AddOverlay(umaContext.InstantiateOverlay("MaleBeard03"
}
else
{

}
```

Figure 521

```
randomResult = Random.Range(0, 2);
if (randomResult == 0)
{
    umaData.umaRecipe.slotDataList[1].AddOverlay(umaContext.InstantiateOverlay("MaleEyebrow
}
else
{
    umaData.umaRecipe.slotDataList[1].AddOverlay(umaContext.InstantiateOverlay("MaleEyebrow
}

umaData.umaRecipe.slotDataList[2] = umaContext.InstantiateSlot("MaleTorso");

randomResult = Random.Range(0, 2);
if (randomResult == 0)
{
    umaData.umaRecipe.slotDataList[2].AddOverlay(umaContext.InstantiateOverlay("MaleBody01",
}
else
{
    umaData.umaRecipe.slotDataList[2].AddOverlay(umaContext.InstantiateOverlay("MaleBody02",
}


randomResult = Random.Range(0, 2);
if (randomResult == 0)
{
    umaData.umaRecipe.slotDataList[2].AddOverlay(umaContext.InstantiateOverlay("MaleShirt01'
}
```

Figure 522

There are 3 parts in the code segment shown in *Figure 522*. First are the eyebrows which uses the same hair color and attached to the head slot. Then we instantiate the torso in slot '2' and choose between two overlay textures at random for this slot. The last block of code here adds a shirt overlay to the torso slot '2' with a random color.

```
263                 umaData.umaRecipe.slotDataList[3] = umaContext.InstantiateSlot("MaleHands", umaData.umaRecipe.sl
264
265                 umaData.umaRecipe.slotDataList[4] = umaContext.InstantiateSlot("MaleInnerMouth");
266                 umaData.umaRecipe.slotDataList[4].AddOverlay(umaContext.InstantiateOverlay("InnerMouth"));
267
268
269                 randomResult = Random.Range(0, 2);
270                 if (randomResult == 0)
271                 {
272                     umaData.umaRecipe.slotDataList[5] = umaContext.InstantiateSlot("MaleLegs", umaData.umaRecipe
273                     umaData.umaRecipe.slotDataList[2].AddOverlay(umaContext.InstantiateOverlay("MaleUnderwear01"
274                 }
275                 else
276                 {
277                     umaData.umaRecipe.slotDataList[5] = umaContext.InstantiateSlot("MaleJeans01");
278                     umaData.umaRecipe.slotDataList[5].AddOverlay(umaContext.InstantiateOverlay("MaleJeans01", ne
279                 }
280
281                 umaData.umaRecipe.slotDataList[6] = umaContext.InstantiateSlot("MaleFeet", umaData.umaRecipe.slo
```

Figure 523

Figure 523 shows the last segment of code to get the slots setup for our UMA character. On line 263 we instantiate the hands in slot '3' and use the same overlay that we instantiated in slot '2' for the torso. Reusing the same overlay texture helps to cut down on the amount of memory used when playing the game. Lines 265 and 266 instantiate the slot and overlay for the inner mouth. This is what gets shown when the character opens their mouth. That's right! You can animate UMA to open their mouths, close them, and even make them look like their talking.

Continuing South down the body we go for the legs. We'll have two options here, either the UMA guy just wears underwear or sports some tight jeans and give them a random color. Again, we reuse the body overlay for the legs on line 272. The slot for the legs is at index '5' but interestingly we add the underwear overlay to slot index '2' which is the body slot. This is because the underwear paints over the body texture on the slot.

The last slot we instantiate is the feet. This is done in slot index '6' and there isn't anything special that happens here. If you scroll further down, you'll see the creation of the human female slots and you should notice right away that the code looks very different. As I mentioned before, there isn't anything special about where the slots are, just that they're all there. This shows the code for women can do the same thing that the code for men can do, just doing it differently.

```
AddAdditionalSlots();

GenerateUMAShapes();
```

Figure 524

Going back to the method GenerateUMA(), shown in Figure 524, there are two more methods we need to look at: AddAdditionalSlots and GenerateUMAShapes. The first one simply adds what is in the "additionalRecipes" array from the inspector (like the capsule collider). The second one adds the DNA and potentially randomizes it to generate what the shape of the UMA character is going to look like. We'll dive into this one next.

```
protected virtual void GenerateUMAShapes()
{
    UMADnaHumanoid umaDna = umaData.umaRecipe.GetDna<UMADnaHumanoid>();
    if (umaDna ==  null)
    {
        umaDna = new UMADnaHumanoid();
        umaData.umaRecipe.AddDna(umaDna);
    }

    if (randomDna)
    {
        RandomizeShape(umaData);
    }
}
```

Figure 525

Right off the bat the keywords before the method sure hit a homerun in Figure 525. I've mentioned protected before. Both have to do with inheritance. Remember, just like when you inherited that cute nose, adorable dimples, or that silly but slightly annoying habit from one of your parents, any class who inherits from the UMACrowd class will get not only this method but all the other methods and variables in here.

Having methods and variables protected this and virtual that may seem like a waste of time now, especially when we're just trying to get methods to do what we want. But understanding what these are and how to use them can help you better organize your code and keep you from writing bugs into it.

We've also talked about how anyone can call a public method whereas only that class gets to call private methods. Well, a protected method is kind of like a private method except any child class also gets to call it. A virtual method means that when the child class inherits this method from the base class that the child class can make its own implementation of this method, which is called overriding. Let's say we make a child class that inherits from UMACrowd named UMATallCrowd. This class would do the same thing except adjust the height of each created UMA character to be increased by some amount. We could override the GenerateUMAShapes() method and then inside the 'if' block after we call RandomizeShape() we make the change to the DNA. Then, when we instantiate the UMATallCrowd object it would call this new method, that is named the same, instead of the original one.

All of that said, this method is really fairly simple. If there is no DNA in the recipe, then some will be created using the "new" keyword. Then, if random DNA for each character was requested it will be done by calling the RandomizeShape() method.

```
442         public static void RandomizeShape(UMAData umaData)
443         {
444             UMADnaHumanoid umaDna = umaData.umaRecipe.GetDna<UMADnaHumanoid>();
445             umaDna.height = Random.Range(0.4f, 0.5f);
446             umaDna.headSize = Random.Range(0.485f, 0.515f);
447             umaDna.headWidth = Random.Range(0.4f, 0.6f);
448
449             umaDna.neckThickness = Random.Range(0.495f, 0.51f);
450
451             if (umaData.umaRecipe.raceData.raceName == "HumanMale")
452             {
453                 umaDna.handsSize = Random.Range(0.485f, 0.515f);
454                 umaDna.feetSize = Random.Range(0.485f, 0.515f);
455                 umaDna.legSeparation = Random.Range(0.4f, 0.6f);
456                 umaDna.waist = 0.5f;
457             }
458             else
459             {
460                 umaDna.handsSize = Random.Range(0.485f, 0.515f);
461                 umaDna.feetSize = Random.Range(0.485f, 0.515f);
462                 umaDna.legSeparation = Random.Range(0.485f, 0.515f);
463                 umaDna.waist = Random.Range(0.3f, 0.8f);
464             }
465
466             umaDna.armLength = Random.Range(0.485f, 0.515f);
467             umaDna.forearmLength = Random.Range(0.485f, 0.515f);
468             umaDna.armWidth = Random.Range(0.3f, 0.8f);
469             umaDna.forearmWidth = Random.Range(0.3f, 0.8f);
```

Figure 526

In Figure 526, you can see the first 27 lines of the RandomizeShape() method. As you can see, we reference the DNA a lot, so it makes sense to grab it and keep it in a local variable. Most or all of these

Having these kind of numbers in the code like this is often called "Magic Numbers". It doesn't have anything to do with magic, but that if you're looking at the code for the first time, or haven't seen the code in a while, you may ask why "why are these specific numbers here?" The answer isn't there, but it just works, like how a magician pulls of an amazing magic trick. Usually, we try to minimize these magic numbers and use variables instead. But with so many numbers in this code it is hard to do that.

should be very familiar as we were playing around with them above in Figure 512. We're setting the height, size, and width of the head, as well as the thickness of the neck. You can see that these are being set to random values between two numbers. These numbers were determined by the creators of UMA to produce the most realistic-looking unique characters. On line 451, you see we check the race of the character. Since male and female people have different physical characteristics, we'll simulate that by having slightly different ranges in certain DNA variables.

Since going through the rest of the DNA code here would likely give you IBBS (Incredibly Boring Book Syndrome) you can go through the rest of it on your own. It's not that much different than what we've already covered here. There are a few interesting things, however, so I do recommend you check it out.

Picking one out of the Crowd

Now that we've looked at a whole crowd of UMA characters and gone through the basics of how UMA works by deciphering the code in the UMACrowd script, we're ready to create our first one. However, we're going to do it a little differently than in the script. The script gave us a great understanding of how UMA works, but to get a single UMA character in the scene there is a much easier way.

Create a new basic scene in Unity (don't need to save the UMA Crowd scene if it prompts you) by going to the main menu and selecting File > New Scene or using the keyboard shortcut CTRL+N. Once it is done, from the Project View, go to UMA > Getting Started. You'll see a handful of files. Drag the UMA_DCS prefab from the Project View onto the bottom of the Hierarchy View. Then drag the prefab for UMADynamicCharacterAvatar to the bottom of the Hierarchy View.

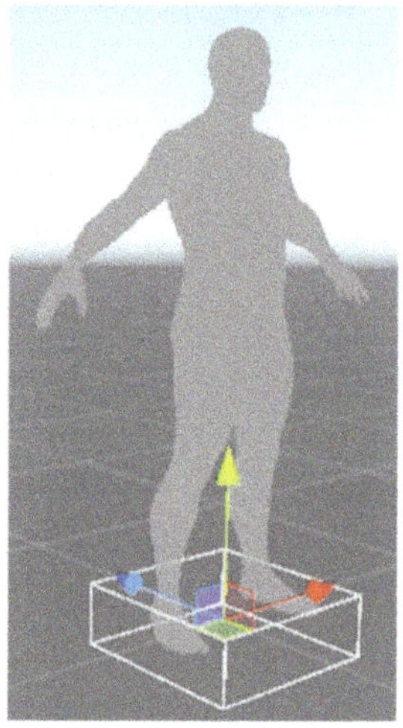

Figure 527

If you click the UMADynamicCharacterAvatar that was created in the Hierarchy View and press the 'f' key, then you should see the silhouette of a person like in Figure 527. Technically, this is all we need to do to get an UMA character displayed in the scene. Much simpler than the gagillion lines of code long file for creating a random crowd. All those slots and overlays will get setup automatically based on the active race of the UMA character.

However, we're not ready yet. If we click the play button now, then he's going to fall into the bottomless void of emptiness where there's weeping and gnashing of teeth. He needs something to stand on so let's create a cube and set the position to 0, -0.5, 0. If you play the scene now, you'll see the guy appear on the cube in his underwear. But we want this guy to dress for success, so we're going to put some clothes on him.

Now, much of what we're going to do next is covered in the "DCS – Getting Started" PDF file in this same folder. It has a lot of great information and I highly recommend reading through it to get more hands-on experience with UMA.

Before we get started, we need to get UMA's global library setup. This library contains each of the races, slots, overlays, and wardrobe recipes we'll need to build our characters. Having a library like that that is global to the whole project makes referencing all the things easier in our different scenes. To access the library, go to the main menu and select UMA > Global Library Window as shown in Figure 528.

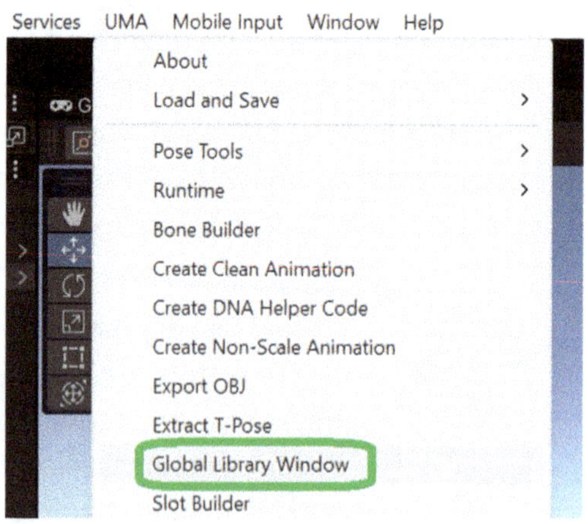

Figure 528

When you do, a window such as Figure 529 will pop up. Click the button that says, "Rebuild From Project (Adds Everything)". This goes through the entire project for all the numerous UMA things like slots, overlays, races, and everything listed at the bottom of the figure and adds them to this global library. Be prepared for a little bit of a wait, so this may be a good time to break out a good book or play a fun game.

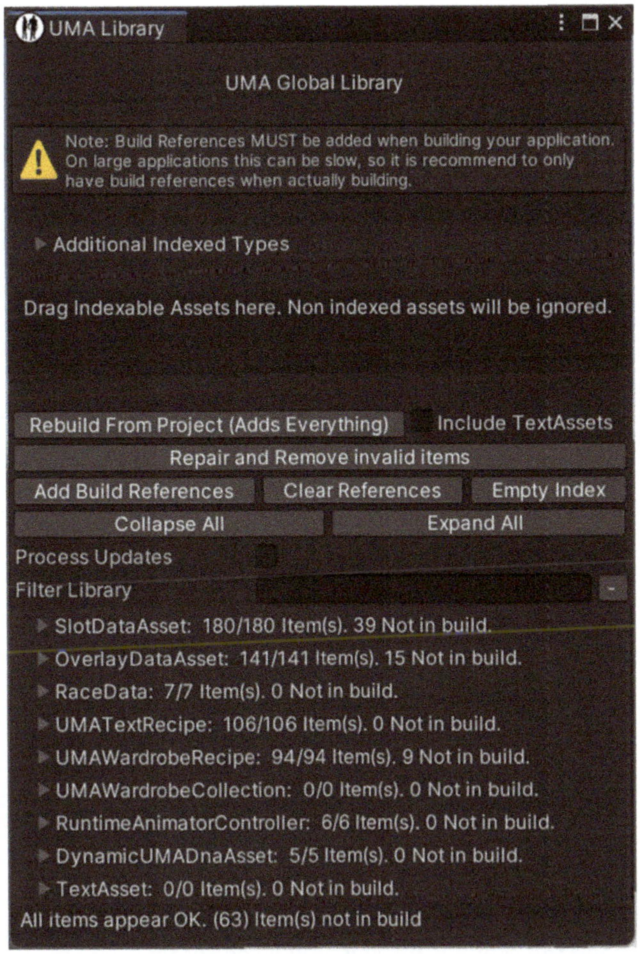

Figure 529

In the Project View, underneath "Project" and to the right of "Create", you'll see a tiny little magnifying glass with some space after it that calls to you to click on it. Many times, when you feel the temptation to do something it is wise to resist. Not in this case. Click it and type in "t:UMAWardrobeRecipe" as shown in Figure 530. This will search through the whole project for files of the *type* "UMAWardrobeRecipe".

This is a pro tip kids, write it down.

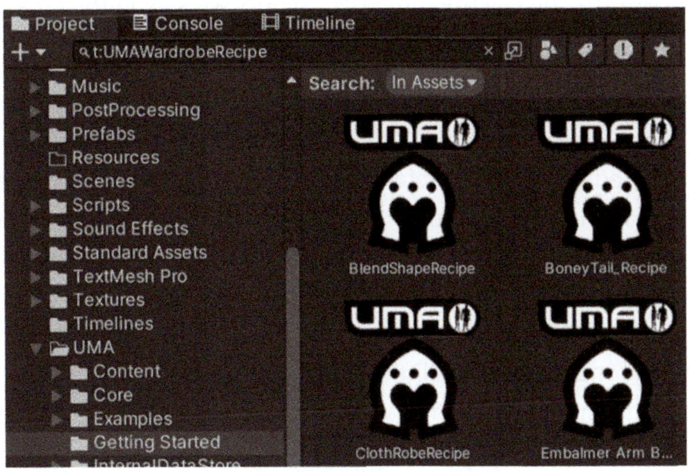

Figure 530

As soon as you finish typing the last letter, you'll see that the files in the Project View fill up with different clothes options. These are all the different Wardrobe Text Recipes in the project, so we get to see the entire wardrobe in one place.

You'll see two different types of Recipes as you scroll down to take a look: Text Recipes and Wardrobe Recipes. As far as we're concerned right now, we can use either type as a wardrobe option for our UMA characters. After you're done looking at some of the different wardrobe recipes, go back to the Hierarchy View and click the UMADynamicCharacterAvatar object. In the inspector, a little way down you'll see "Default Wardrobe Recipes" as shown in Figure 531.

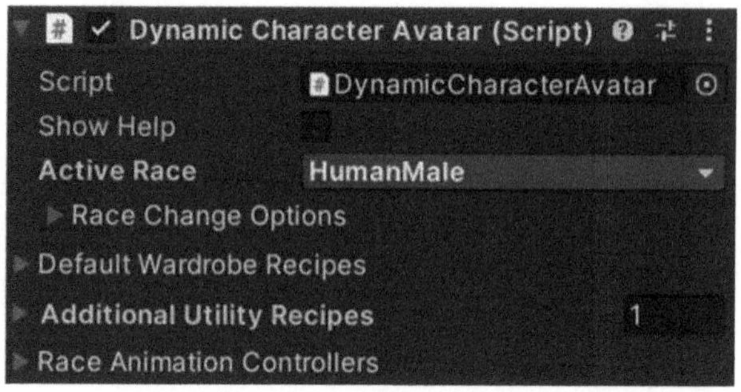

Figure 531

Click the triangle to expand it and you'll see a large box with the text "Drag Wardrobe Recipes Here". In order to clothe our UMA character you drag the wardrobe… recipe… Ok, I'll give kudos to the UMA creators. That was a very well named box. Find the Wardrobe Recipe called "Man1_Shenti_Recipe" and drag it into that aptly named box. You'll see it appear right below the button as shown in Figure 532.

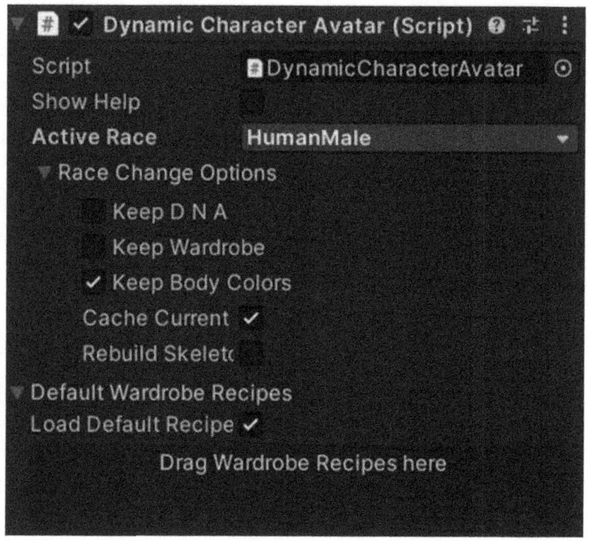

Figure 532

Playing the scene now will let our UMA guy cover up his underwear with what may look like a skirt at first glance but is actually a shenti because Egyptian men don't wear skirts. Looking closer at the inspector while the scene is playing, you'll see that a new component was created on the UMADynamicCharacterAvatar. This is an UMA Data script that has all the same DNA sliders we saw in the crowd script as you can see in Figure 533.

Try changing the Arm Length, you can see that the model is updated in real-time. If you click the "Slots" tab, then you'll all of the same slots with overlays that the UMA Crowd script created on each character. But here in the inspector, you can see all the different texture images associated with the overlay. Some of them look really weird. This is because these images are meant to wrap around the 3D model. We're going to use this model to create a prefab to replace our current Moses with someone who looks a little more… Moses-ish. Next to the Shenti that you added as wardrobe, click the 'X' to remove it.

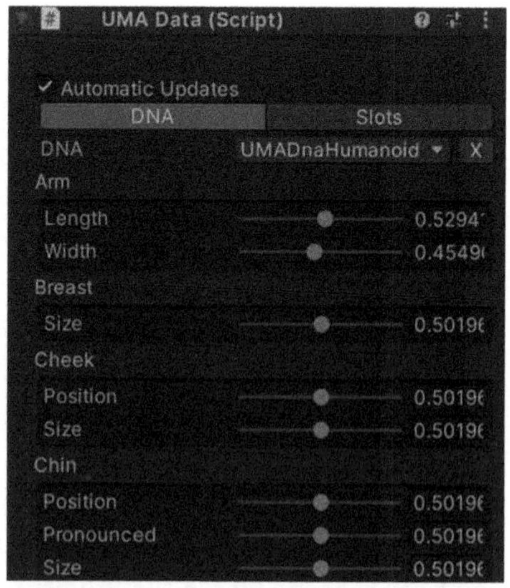

Figure 533

If you scroll down, you'll see that there are four character colors that UMA will use to generate the textures as shown in Figure 534. There are Hair, Eyes, Skin, and Pants. Look at the BaseColor under the Skin section. By making this a darker color we can give Moses a tan (he was Middle Eastern, after all). He was also pretty old, so let's give him gray hair. Click the solid color bar to the right of the "BaseColor" underneath the "Hair" section.

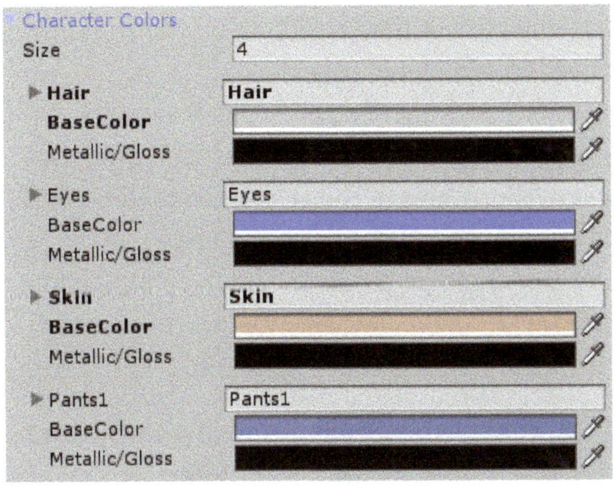

Figure 534

A color window will pop up as shown in Figure 535. At the bottom before the "Swatches" you'll see a field labeled "Hexadecimal". This is the numerical representation of this color. Unity uses this number to know exactly which color you want to use. Set that field to 'C8C8C8FF' and then click the 'X' button in the top-right. Click the solid color next to the BaseColor under skin, set the Hexadecimal value to 'DCA483FF' to give him that tan he got from sunning himself on the bank of the Nile, and close the window. Finally, click the solid color under the Eyes section and use that to find a color you think Moses' eyes should be. Close the window when you're done.

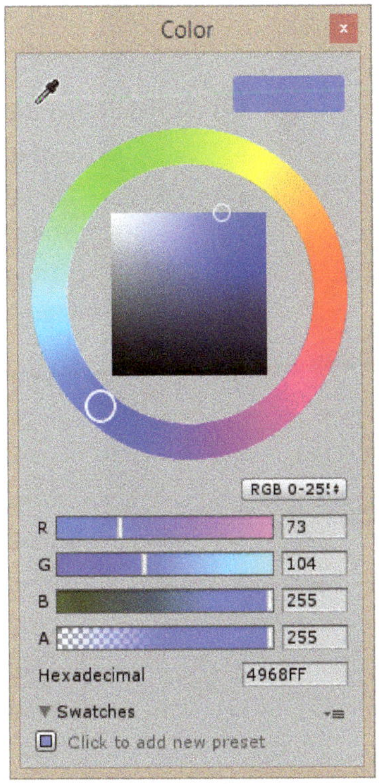

Figure 535

The Swatches are a list of colors you can preset. So if you know you're going to use a particular color a lot then you can click the "Click to add new preset" and the selected color will be saved for you to use later. Much easier than trying to match it or remember the Hexadecimal value each time.

Looking back at the Project View, you should still have the search field set to "t:UMAWardrobeRecipe" to show all the wardrobe recipes. Search the list and drag the following recipes to the character: MaleBrow02, MaleFace_Old, UM_Beard_B_Recipe, UM_HairStyle_G_Recipe, POV_Sandals_Recipe, and ML_A_Dress_Recipe. The list of wardrobe recipes should look like Figure 536.

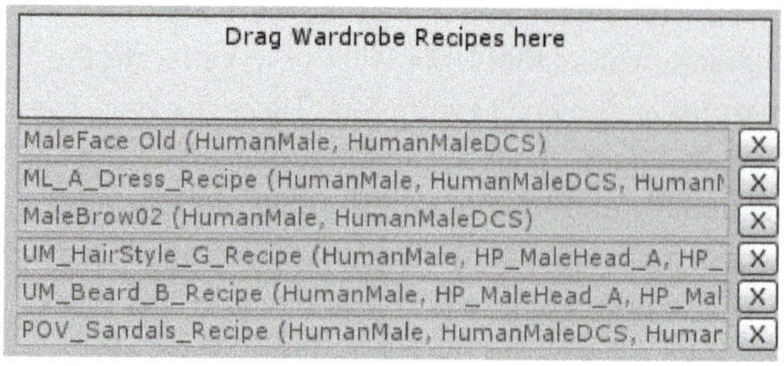

Figure 536

Figure 537

If you play the scene now, you'll see that we've got a pretty convincing looking Moses here as shown in Figure 537. He's got some old robes that were made drab brown by years of walking through the desert. His worn old face reveals determination born from coming in contact with the one true God who gave him his mission. The gray hair, beard, and eyebrows add an air of ancient wisdom.

Underneath the Default Wardrobe Recipes are the Race Animation Controllers. Expand that and you'll see that the default Animation is "locomotion". Let's change that to our Third Person Animator Controller. In the Project View, go to Standard Assets > Characters > ThirdPersonCharacter > Animator and drag the "ThirdPersonAnimatorController" into the Default Animation as shown in Figure 538. Also, add an Animator component using "Add Component".

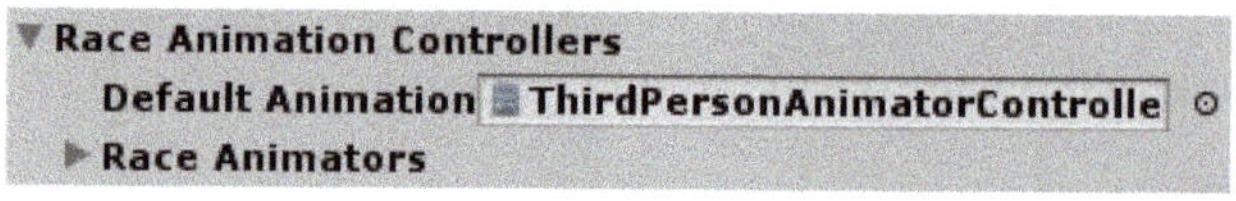

Figure 538

To get him fully ready to be an actor let's add the ActorController script from Assets > Scripts. Be sure to check "Look At Player" and "Change Camera".

It's so easy to dress up the models just the way we like. The only thing to be mindful of is that each recipe is attached to a race. That means races not in the list can't wear the wardrobe recipe. So, clothing for a male can't be put on a female model. You can add the race to the wardrobe item, but since it was made for specific races it may not look right.

See them Face to Face

To give him that unique quality we saw in the UMA crowd (ok, ok, not that elf-ear-unique, but Moses-unique) we're going to change his DNA. If not already, put the scene into play mode because that is how we're going to do this. Each Dynamic Character Avatar script lets you save or load the DNA and slots so that you can setup a character the way you want to a file and not have to worry about rebuilding it later. It's also useful for sharing with your family and friends if they want to load your Moses up on their own Exodus Unity game.

After the game is running and Moses is loitering on his little cube suspended over the vast nothingness of oblivion click the UMADynamicCharacterAvatar and in the inspector, scroll down so you can see the UMA Data script. Change the below parameters as indicated and set the rest to 0.5.

Set these parameters:

- Eye Rotation : 0.75
- Forehead Position : 0.25
- Head Width : 0.506
- Jaw Size : 0.6
- Low Cheek Pronounce : 0.65
- Nose Width : 0.7

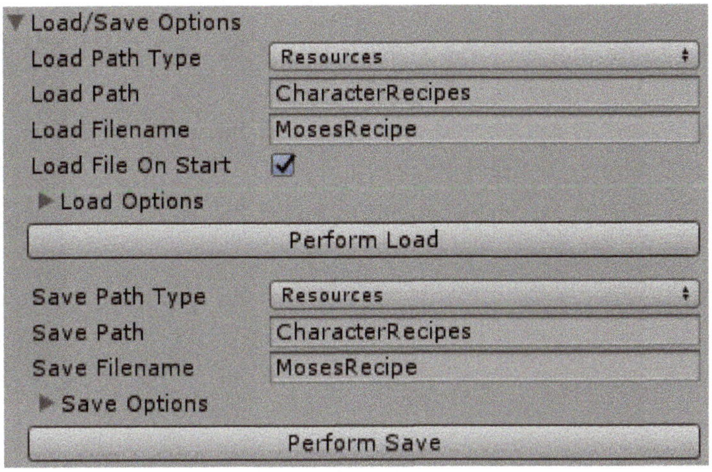

Figure 539

Feel free to play with any other parameters and try to get someone who you think Moses would look like. Once you're satisfied with the facial reconstructive surgery you performed on Moses scroll up in the inspector. Underneath the Character Colors that we set in the previous section are the Load/Save Options. When you expand it you'll see something like Figure 539.

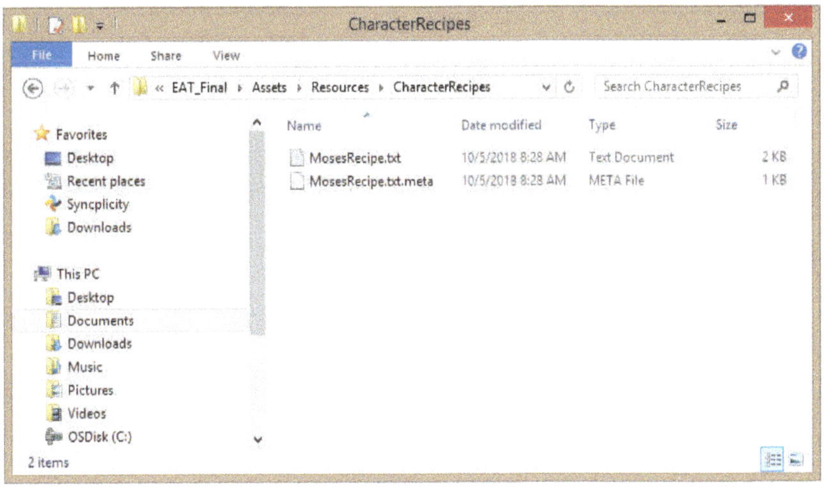

Figure 540

Change the Save Path Type to Resources and give the Save Filename "MosesRecipe". Then click "Perform Save" and the script will take all the wardrobe slots and DNA customizations and shovel them into a file. If you go into your Windows Explorer under the folder "Assets\Resources\CharacterRecipes" then you'll see something like Figure 540. All the character recipes will be stored here. When you exit play mode, the Filenames for the recipes will reset. So set them back to "MosesRecipe". Now let's save this guy by creating a prefab named "UMAMoses" in the Prefabs > Actors folder and drag the

UMADynamicCharacterAvator in there. The DNA and slots are loaded through resources so you don't need to overwrite the prefab when making changes.

Next up is Moses' older brother, Aaron. We've got some different clothes for him as well as a different haircut. And while we're at it, let's change his DNA. While he'll have very similar DNA to his brother, it won't be exactly the same. Let's remove his clothes, hair, and beard by clicking the 'X' on the right side of them. Leave the "MaleFace_Old" and "POV_Sandals_Recipe" as shown in Figure 541. We're going to reuse those for the next UMA character.

Figure 541

Make sure that the Project View's search string is "t:UMAWardrobeRecipe" again and add UM_Beard_C_Recipe, UM_Moustache_C_Recipe, MaleCostume_E_Dress_Recipe, and MaleCostume_E_HeadGear_recipe to the list of wardrobe recipes so you get the complete list of wardrobe recipes shown in Figure 542.

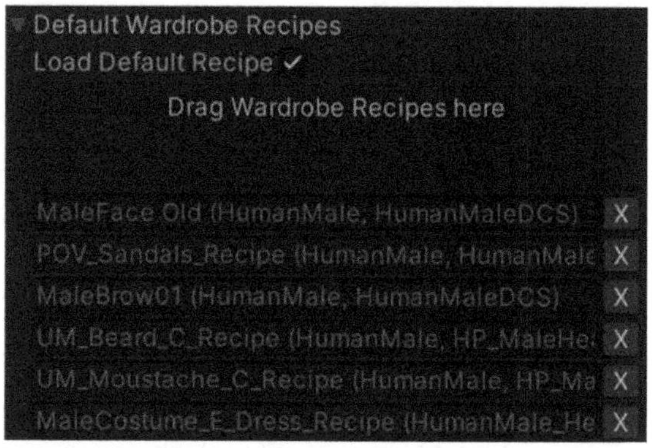

Figure 542

Before we can play and get his DNA setup, we want to make sure that he isn't going to load Moses' wardrobe. If it's one thing that's really annoying is accidentally dressing yourself up in someone else's clothes. In the inspector, scroll doing the "Load/Save Options" and delete the "MosesRecipe" that was in the Load Filename so that it's blank as shown in Figure 543 so that it doesn't load instead of using the specified wardrobe recipes.

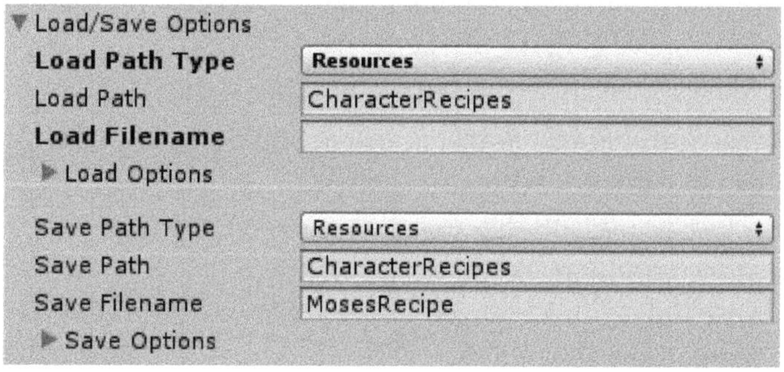

Figure 543

Now when you click play, you'll see a much different looking UMA character. He's wearing a different robe, has a fashionable head covering, and sports a nice beard and mustache combo as shown in Figure 544.

Figure 544

In the same way you changed the DNA for Moses, make the below changes for his brother Aaron to make look distinct. Feel free to adjust any other DNA sliders.

- Eye Rotation : 0.75
- Forehead Position : 0.35
- Head Width : 0.507
- Jaw Size : 0.7
- Low Cheek Pronounce : 0.7
- Nose Width : 0.75

Once you're done go back to the "Load/Save Options" and change the Load Filename and Save Filename to "AaronRecipe" as shown in Figure 545 and then click "Perform Save". Once again, this will create a recipe in the same folder as before to store all of Aaron's wardrobe and DNA.

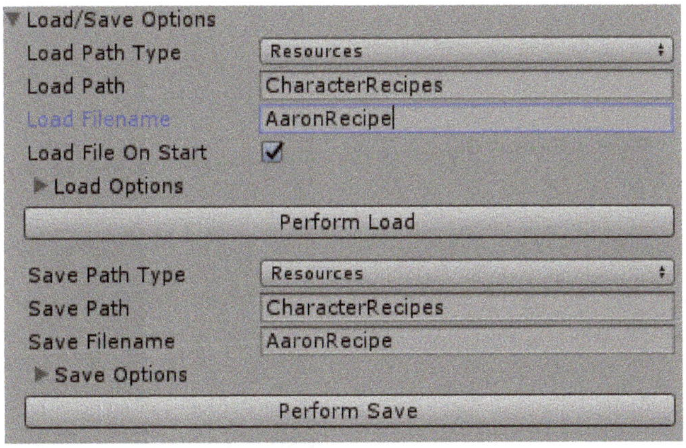

Figure 545

When you exit play mode set the Filenames back to "AaronRecipe", create the prefab for him named "UMAAaron" in the Prefabs > Actors folder and drag the UMADynamicCharacterAvatar on it to save a copy of him for us to use later.

Moses and Aaron also had a sister named Miriam who, in addition to being a prophetess, sang a neat song to celebrate the crossing of the Red Sea and broke out some dance moves as well. She'll be the last unique UMA character we'll create right now.

Normally, it would be slightly difficult to change one's race. However, with UMA, it is very simple. Clicking on the UMADynamicAvatar in the Hierarchy View, go to the inspector and find the "Active Race". Set it to "HumanFemale" as shown in Figure 546 and then remove all the current wardrobe recipes. We'll need to add a completely new wardrobe for her.

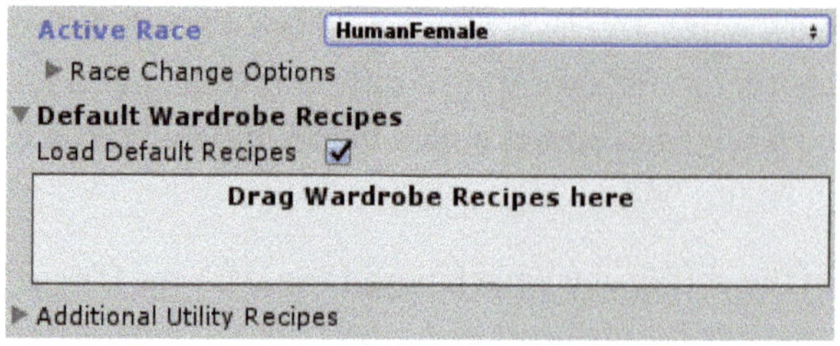

Figure 546

Making sure you've got the project search string set to "t:UMAWardrobeRecipe", add "FemaleCostume_D_Dress_Recipe", "FemaleCostume_D_HeadGear_Recipe", and "Female_Shoes_Recipe" to the wardrobe list as shown in Figure 547.

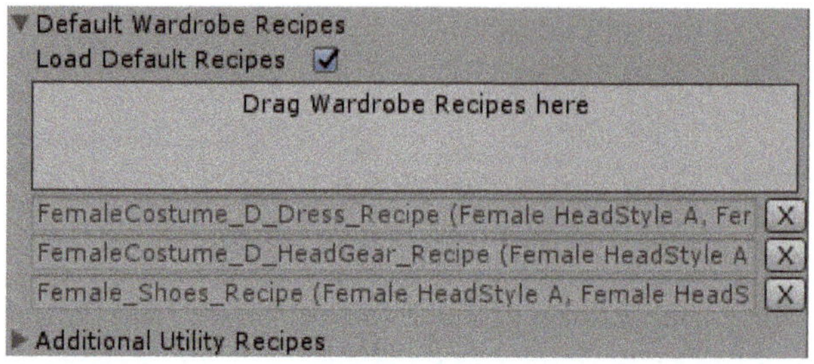

Figure 547

Play the scene and set the DNA as before to the below values as well as adding your own artistic flair to her genetics.

- Eye Rotation : 0.75
- Forehead Position : 0.8
- Head Width : 0.506
- Jaw Size : 0.55
- Low Cheek Pronounce : 0.75
- Nose Width : 0.6

Figure 548

When you're done you should see something that looks similar to Figure 548. Save her recipe off as you did Moses and Aaron by giving the name "MiriamRecipe" into the Save Filename under the "Load/Save Options" and click the Perform Save button. Exit play mode and fix up both the Load Filename and Save Filename to be "MiriamRecipe".

You can make her gray silhouette look more feminine by changing the Placeholder Options in the inspector. Expand it and under Preview Model select "Female". Then create a new prefab in the Prefabs > Actors folder named "UMAMiriam" and drag the UMADynamicCharacterAvatar onto it to save her along with her brothers.

Technically, because we're loading from the recipe file, we don't need to have any of the wardrobe, DNA, or colors set in the prefab. It can be set to anything or nothing and the same person will be loading from the recipe file. But there's no harm in keeping the prefab and the recipe the same.

Go to Assets > Prefabs and open "UMAMoses. Back in the Project View's Prefabs folder, click on the "MosesPlayer" prefab. When you scroll to the bottom of the inspector, you'll see the familiar scripts shown in Figure 549. Our UMA version of Moses needs to have all these components so it works right with the rest of the game.

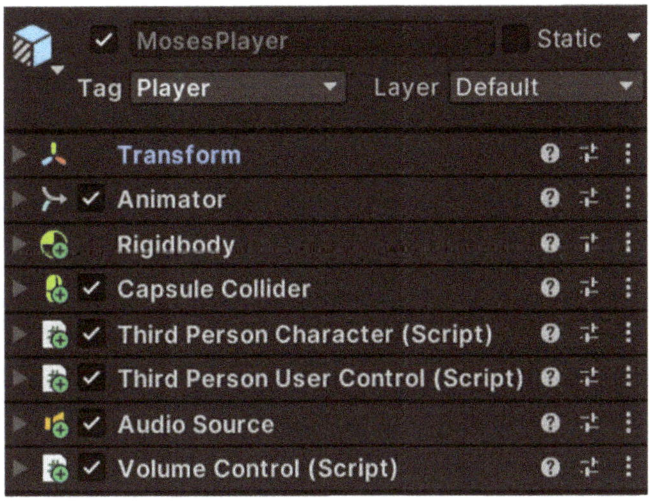

Figure 549

Using the same method, we copied components over when creating the player inventory, for the "Third Person User Control (Script)" click the 3 dots icon and select "Copy Component". In the Hierarchy View, click on the "UMAMoses" game object and, in the inspector on any of the components click the gear icon and select "Paste Component as New". This adds, not only that script, but the Third Person Character script, Rigidbody, and Capsule Collider as well. This is because the script marks them as required components. We do need to change the "Ground Check Distance" to 1.25. Also, on the Third Person Character script make sure the Jump Power is set to 9. In fact, it would be best to double-check that the other values are the same.

Next, you can copy components for the Rigidbody, and Capsule Collider. Then when you paste, select "Paste Component Values" so that the new components use the same values as the other prefab. Then create an Audio Source on "UMAMoses". Finally, paste the "Volume Control" script to "UMAMoses" from the prefab "MosesPlayer". At the top of the inspector, change the Tag to "Player" so other scripts can easily find it. Also, delete the Actor Controller component.

The last thing to add from "MosesPlayer" is the camera, you can expand the object to show it. An easy way is to just copy it over. Open "MosesPlayer" and copy the "Camera". Then open "UMAMoses" and paste. All you need to do now is drag "UMAMoses" onto the "Player" field of the Third Person Orbit Cam script on the Camera.

There's quite a list of components, so here's the list: Transform, Dynamic Character Avatar, Rigidbody, Capsule Collider, Animator, Volume Control, Player Interact, Map Item, Third Person User Control, Third Person Character, and Audio Source.

But Really... UMA

Having the UMA characters saved in prefabs can be really useful. What would be even more useful is to have the UMA really used in a real scene... really. Ok, so the scene isn't really real, but really, it looks really close.

We don't need the scene anymore so you can go to the Project View and from the Scenes folder open up the "Egypt_Nile_Scene". You also don't need to save any changes in the other scene as we've already saved the prefabs that we need. Just discard this scene.

When the scene loads, the first thing we need to do is get the object with all the libraries for UMA in the scene. Like we did for the test scene, in the Project View, drag the "UMA_DCS" prefab into the Hierarchy View from Assets > UMA > Getting Started.

To make the scene use our new UMA player, we just need to swap to the new prefab in the game controller. In the Hierarchy View, find the canvas and expand it. Then click on the GameController object to see it in the Inspector View. At the top you'll see the Player Prefab. Drag the "UMAMoses" prefab there as shown in Figure 550.

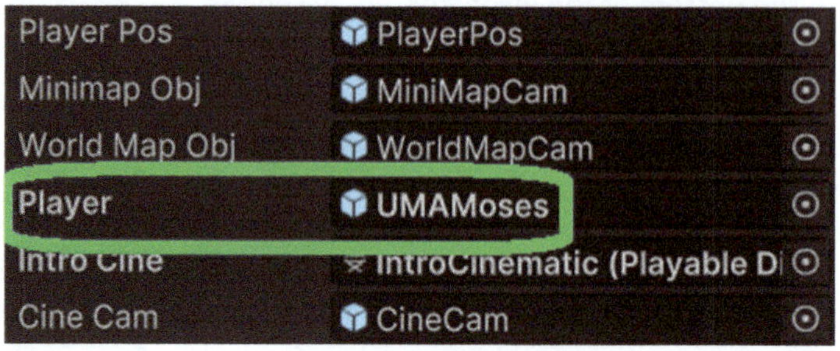

Figure 550

Finally, copy the transform of the "MosesPlayer" object and paste it on the new "UMAMoses" object. You can disable the "MosesPlayer" now. You will also need to go to "PlayerShip" and update the Boat Controller script to use the new "UMAMoses" game object. Otherwise, the ship will go back to the old Moses. When you play the scene, you can now see Moses with all the new style you created for him in the scene like in Figure 551, replacing the other model. There was a lot of hard work to get to this point. Think of all those pages you turned and buttons you clicked! Spend some time running around the scene just enjoying what you've done so far.

Figure 551

Alright, that's enough revelry, we're still not through. We also need to make these changes in the other scenes. Go back through the "Palace Scene", "Pyramid Scene", and "Pyramid2 Scene" to add the "UMA_DCS" prefab and then change the GameController to use the "UMAMosesPlayer".

Going back to the "Egypt_Nile Scene", let's add Aaron and Miriam. After it loads, in the Hierarchy View, scroll down to the "Exodus_1_Objects" and expand it. Click on the "Aaron" object and press 'F' in Scene View to focus on him. Drag the "UMAAaron" from Prefabs > Actors out onto the "Exodus_1_Objects" so that it's a child object along with the other "Aaron". Disable the "Aaron" object and it will darken in the Hierarchy View like the top part of Figure 552. To make the UMA build right, disable the parent "Exodus_1_Objects" so that the build process starts when the parent is enabled like the bottom part.

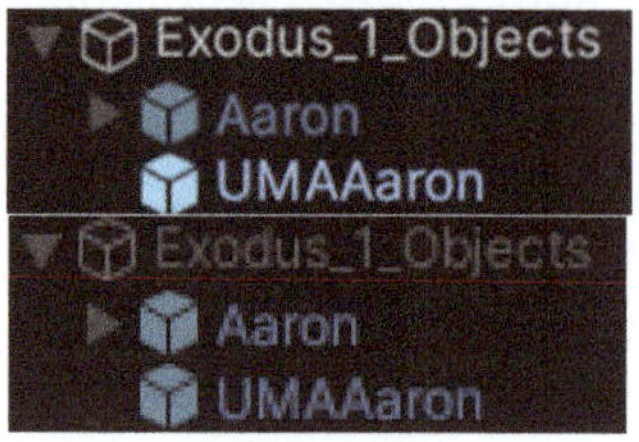

Figure 552

To Swap the Aaron models, copy the transform component using the gear icon. Then go to the new Aaron's transform and select "Paste Component as Values". The transform values get copied and the model goes to the same position as the old Aaron. Using the "Paste Component as New" option, copy over the Animator, Capsule Collider, Rigidbody, Actor Controller, and Dialogue components.

If you play the scene right now and switch to Scene View and try and look for Aaron, you won't find him. If you remember, the "Exodus_1_Objects" parent object will get disabled by the Game Controller at beginning because only the current quest objects are enabled. Go ahead and enable the Exodus_1_Objects game object. You still won't see Aaron show up.

Sometimes it can get frustrating when things don't work. You fix one issue and another one pops up in its place. The key is persistence. Keep trying until you get it. If you can't get it by yourself then ask someone who may know. There are also some good online forums to ask questions about Unity.

Now, now, at this point you may be asking yourself if I'm just trolling you. Do you really think I'm the kind of person who would do that to you? Ok, I may be. But seriously, this time is something different. UMA characters need to have some time to get the characters created. Disabling the game object will disrupt the process and they won't get built. This means that we need to wait to disable UMA characters until the process has been completed.

There are a number of ways to solve this problem. The first option is to avoid the problem. We would move Aaron out of the quest parent object and make sure that no other UMA characters are child objects in them. This would be the easiest option, but also the most restricting as we need to be careful how we design our levels. The second option is to keep all quest groups enabled for a specific amount of time when we're sure that all the UMAs will be done creating. This would require making a timer and waiting on that before disabling the quest group, which would be pretty easy. However, you can run into problems. The player might see some object they aren't supposed to before it disappears.

Also, if the player runs the game on a slower system then it may not be enough time and the UMA character still won't display. A third option is to check each UMA character in the quest group and wait until that one is done building before we disable it's quest group. This would be the most complicated but also let give us the most flexibility. You may be able to think of other solutions too. Each one has pros and cons and it is up to the game designer to figure out which is the best one for this particular situation.

To keep things easy, we're just going to go with our option #1, to avoid the problem. The more complicated our code is then the more prone to bugs to is. Drag the "Aaron" object outside of the "Exodus_1_Objects" game object so that it is no longer a child.

If you play the scene now and switch over to Scene View than, after a short wait, you'll see Aaron appear in his robes and head covering looking something like Figure 553. This is the first appearance that Aaron makes, there is another appearance in the Hebrew camp. We'll also need to change that model to use the new UMA character we created.

Figure 553

You'll run into a similar problem with "UMAMoses". If the introduction cinematic plays then Moses will not display to the screen. An easy fix is to go to the "GameController" script and comment out line 73 which enables or disables the player based on if the introduction cinematic has played or not. A better, and more complicated, fix would be to hold the blackscreen on until the UMA characters are done loading. But for this tutorial we'll stick to the easy fix you can see in Figure 554.

```
72          MinimapObj.SetActive(IntroCinePlayed);
73          //Player.SetActive(IntroCinePlayed);
74          IntroObjects.SetActive(!IntroCinePlayed);
```

Figure 554

After that, remember that we have one more Aaron out there in the slave camp. You'll need to update him too. You should be able to copy and paste the new Aaron. Then copy the old Aaron's transform and paste it onto the new Aaron. For the Dialogue, you can also copy and paste it from the old Aaron to the new Aaron. At that point, you're done with the old Aaron and can delete or inactivate him.

Let's put Miriam there next to Aaron. Maybe they're having a conversation about potential geo-political upheavels in the near-term future. In the Project View, from Prefabs > Actors, drag UMAMiriam out nearby UMAAaron and rotate her so that they are facing each other, something like Figure 555. Remember that she's also going to need an Animator, Capsule Collider, Rigidbody, Actor Controller, and Dialogue.

Figure 555

Since they're talking, let's set their animations to show that. Click "UMAAaron" in the Hierarchy View and scroll down in the inspector until you find the Actor Controller. Then change the Action Type to "Animation" and set the Animation field to "Ambient_01". Then do the same thing for "UMAMiriam" but set her Animation field to "Ambient_02".

We do need to make some script changes for new UMA characters to work right. Open up the script "ActorController" in Visual Studio. Add 3 more "using" statements shown in Figure 556 on lines 4, 5, and 6. These will help us work with the UMA framework to get these animations playing the way they're supposed to.

```
1  using System.Collections;
2  using System.Collections.Generic;
3  using UnityEngine;
4  using UnityEngine.Events;
5  using UMA;
6  using UMA.CharacterSystem;
```

Figure 556

```
49        if (GetComponent<DynamicCharacterAvatar>())
50        {
51            GetComponent<DynamicCharacterAvatar>().CharacterCreated.AddListener(new UnityAction<UMAData>(StartAnimation));
52        }
53        else if (ActionType == _action_type.Animation)
54        {
55            SetAnimation(Animation, Random.Range(0f, 5f));
56        }
```

Figure 557

Scroll down to the "Start" menu and we're going to have to change-up the 'if' statement to handle UMA. The problem is that we can't tell UMA models to start animating until they are done being loaded. Looking at Figure 557, line 49 tells us if the actor is UMA. If it is then we want to have a new method called when the character is done being created. This is accomplished by creating a Unity action using the event system. Suffice to say, the "StartAnimation" method will get called when the character is done being created and ready to animate. Otherwise, we'll check for the action to be an animation and do the normal setting for the animator.

```
public void StartAnimation(UMAData umaData)
{
    m_Renderers = GetComponentsInChildren<Renderer>();

    if (ActionType == _action_type.Animation)
    {
        SetAnimation(Animation, Random.Range(0f, 5f));
    }
}
```

Figure 558

After the "Start" method, add a new method named "StartAnimation" shown in Figure 558. Because we setup as a listener for UMA's "CharacterCreated" event, we need to have the "umaData" argument even though we don't need to use it. Once this gets called, we're free to set our animation like normal. Because the renderers aren't created until the character is created, we need to get those also.

Equipping Moses for the Job

Of course, only God could equip Moses with the skills he needed. But he still needs his staff! In Chapter 8 – Cinematics and Cut-scenes, we first gave our Moses character his staff. If you recall, to get it to move right in his hand we needed to go deep into Moses' bone structure to place it. Figure 559 shows where it went. However, with UMA, the bones are created after the game starts. So, we can't add it to Moses the same way that we did before. We're going to use another Character Created call back method to place a prefab of the staff where it needs to be.

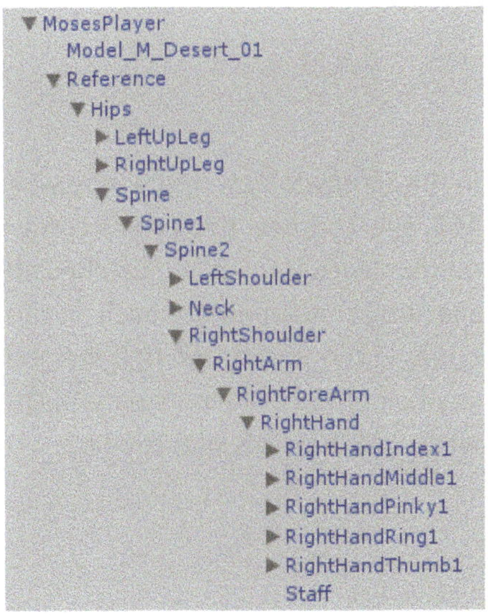

Figure 559

Open the "MosesPlayer" prefab from Assets > Prefabs. Click on his staff in the Scene View to select it without having to browse through the whole skeletal structure. Now drag it to Assets > Prefabs to create a prefab of it.

```
3   using UnityEngine;
4   using UnityEngine.Events;
5   using UMA;
6   using UMA.CharacterSystem;
7
    Unity Script | 0 references
8   public class UmaEquip : MonoBehaviour
9   {
10      public GameObject Equipment;
11      public string BoneName;
12      public Vector3 BonePos;
13      public Vector3 BoneRot;
14
15      // Start is called before the first frame update
        Unity Message | 0 references
16      void Start()
17      {
18          DynamicCharacterAvatar dca = GetComponent<DynamicCharacterAvatar>();
19
20          if (dca) dca.CharacterCreated.AddListener(new UnityAction<UMAData>(EquipItems));
21      }
22
        1 reference
23      public void EquipItems(UMAData umaData)
24      {
25          if (Equipment)
26          {
27              Transform bone = null;
28              Transform[] children = GetComponentsInChildren<Transform>();
29              foreach (Transform t in children) if (t.gameObject.name == BoneName) bone = t;
30
31              if (bone)
32              {
33                  GameObject equip = Instantiate(Equipment, bone);
34                  equip.transform.localPosition = BonePos;
35                  equip.transform.localRotation = Quaternion.Euler(BoneRot);
36              }
37          }
38      }
39  }
```

Figure 560

In the Scripts folder, create a new C# script named “UmaEquip”. Add the code shown below in Figure 560. The only new thing you’ll come across is the “GetComponentsInChildren()” method on line 28. This method goes through all the child objects from the current objects as the parent and returns the specified component for each. In this case, it is the transform. The idea is that we go through all the bones in the rig until we find the one to attach the equipment to. It also needs to be set using the local position of the child to its parent. Otherwise, the object will be placed using the global system and it won’t go where it’s supposed to.

Go ahead and drag our new UmaEquip script onto our "UMAMosesPlayer" prefab. Drag the "Staff" prefab from Prefabs > Objects into the Equipment field. Then set the Bone Pos field to X=-0.08, Y=-0.075, and Z=-0.02. The component should look like Figure 561. As per the script, when the "EquipItems" method is called the "Staff" prefab will be instantiated as a child of the right hand at those coordinates.

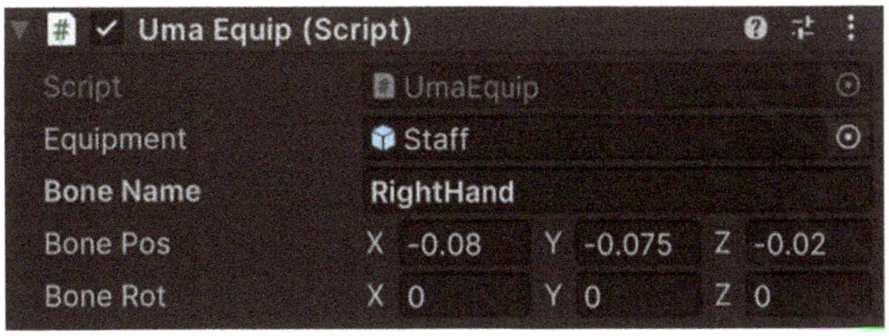

Figure 561

If you play the scene now, then you'll notice that Moses is equipped with his staff so he can go about Egypt doing the miracles that God told him to. Looking back on the code for UmaEquip in Figure 562, you can see that we can also equip something in his left hand. Now, the Bible doesn't say which hand Moses preferred. So, I'm sure any credible scholar out there would say it's ok if you wanted to make him left-handed.

Figure 562

Now that Moses has his staff, we can update the introduction cinematic. If you remember, we created it with the other model. The previous model looks younger, and the new one gives a much older more mature Moses. Hey! You know what? I have an idea that would immerse the player more into the game as well as saving us some work! Let's have the previous model be the young Moses and the new UMA model be the old Moses.

This ability to equip items onto our characters is powerful! In this way, we can combine UMA clothing and flexibility with 3D models already created. We can even add other slots like the forearms if we wanted to equip shields or something.

In this case, we only need to replace one model, the one standing at the rock overlooking the city. From Prefabs in the Project View, drag "UMAMoses" into the "IntroCineObjects" container in the Hierarchy View. Copy the Transform component of the "MosesStaff" object and paste it onto that "UMAMoses" object. Disable the "Third Person Character" and "Third Person User Control" scripts on the "UMAMoses" object by unchecking the boxes for them in the inspector. Then, in the Hierarchy View, expand it and disable the camera by unchecking the box in the inspector at the top near the name. Finally, click the "MosesStaff" object and also disable it by unchecking the box in the inspector at the top near its name. Test it out by clearing the player preferences and clicking Play.

Don't lose your head!

If you like the phrase "Two heads are better than one" then you're going to love the fact that we have ten heads. That's right! In addition to snazzy new robes and stylish hair and beards, we can change out the heads of our UMA characters to something that looks a little different and continue to provide that visual variety our players crave.

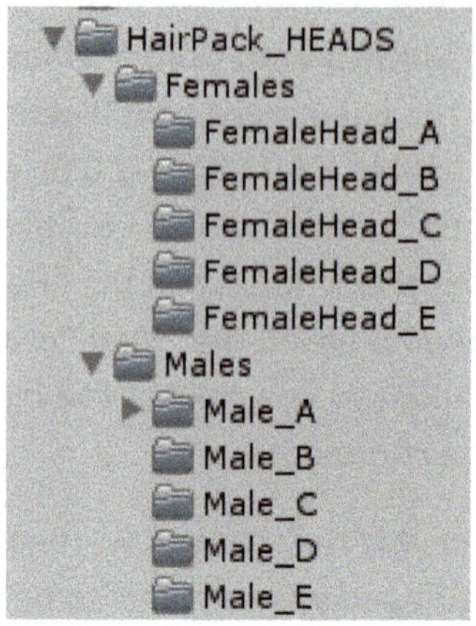

Figure 563

Let's check these heads out! In the Project View, go to UMA > Content > UM_HairPack_Arteria3d > HairPack_HEADS and if you expand the "Females" and "Males" folders then you'll five heads for each of them as shown in Figure 563. Each one of these has a slightly different-looking head.

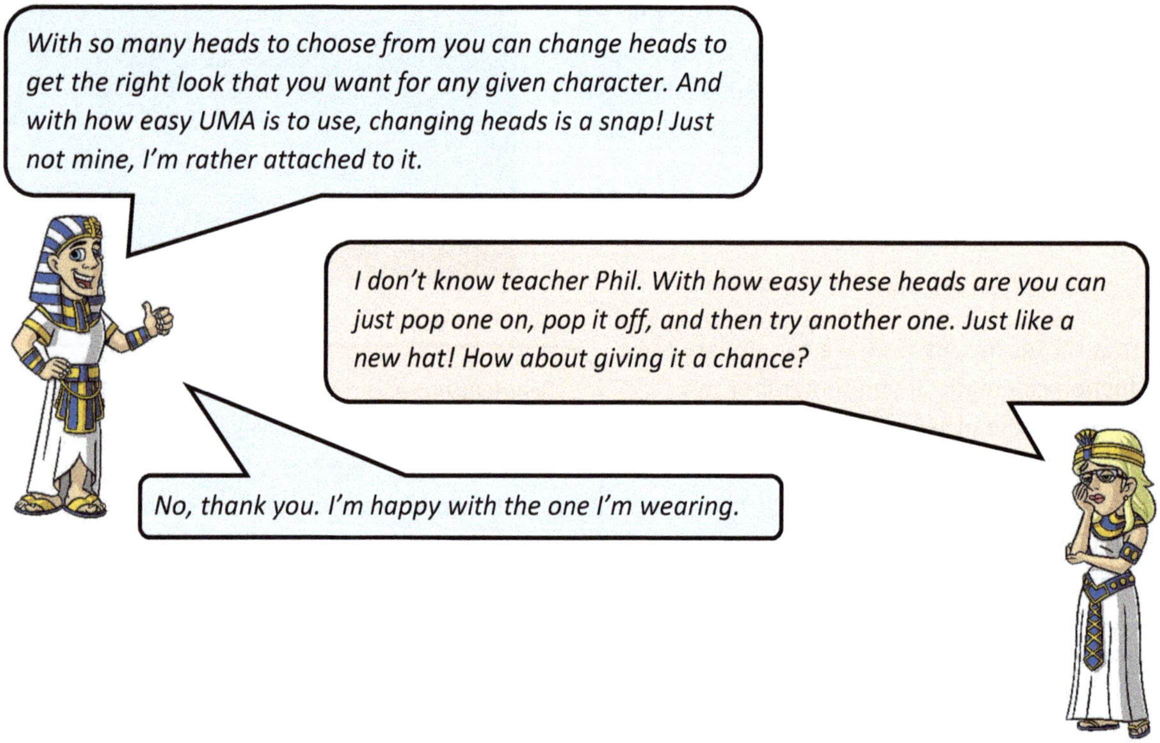

Still in the Project View, click on the "FemaleHead_A" folder and in the containing files select "HP_FemaleHead_A_Recipe". In the Inspector, you'll see tabs, dropdown boxes, and sliders like in Figure 564. This recipe contains both DNA and slots. Now, it doesn't say here, but this is actually a base recipe for a race. In fact, each of these heads is tracked as a different race. Scroll down and you'll see the familiar sliders for the character DNA.

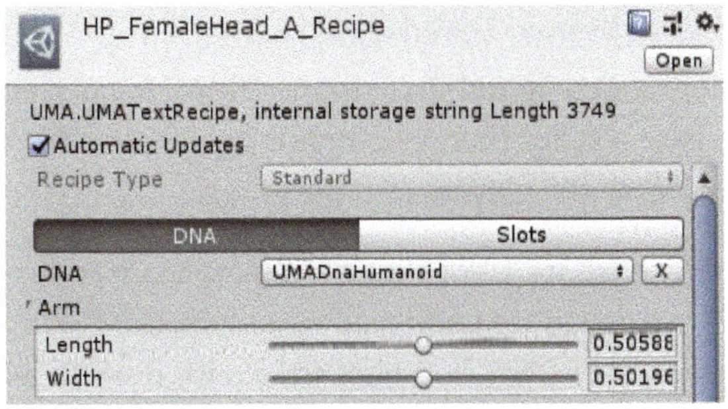

Figure 564

Now click over to the Slots tab. Drawing our attention to the "Shared Colors" section (click the triangle before it if it isn't expanded) you'll see that there are three colors here as shown in Figure 565 for "Skin", "Hair", and "Eyes". You might remember setting these colors just a few pages up to get our characters looking more realistic. Being able to change the colors easily on the UMA character is very convenient.

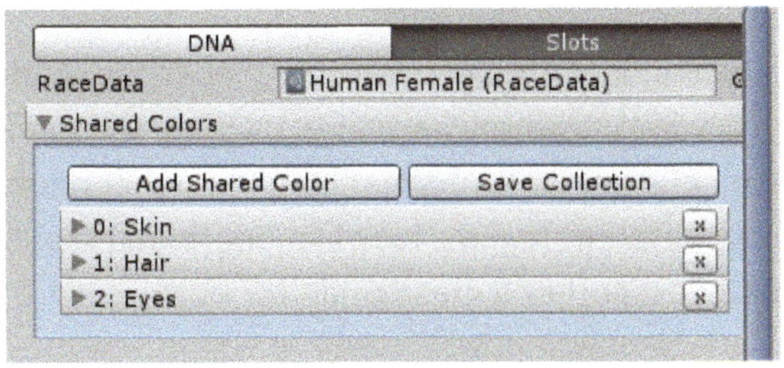

Figure 565

However, there are some shared colors that aren't setup for us, and we'll have to do ourselves. Scroll down under "FemaleEyes" and look for the "Default Eye Adjustment". This is the color that is added to the iris of the eye. But if you look, the box for "Use Shared Color" is not checked. Check the box and set the field to "2: Eyes" as shown in Figure 566.

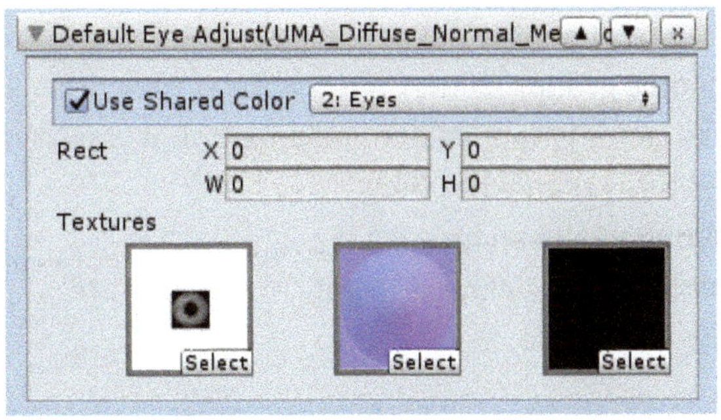

Figure 566

There is one more we need to set, the head itself. Scroll down to the bottom until you find the "HP_FemaleHead_A_Slot". Check the box to "Use Shared Color" for "0: Skin" as seen in Figure 567. This will keep the head and the body the same color selected on the UMA character.

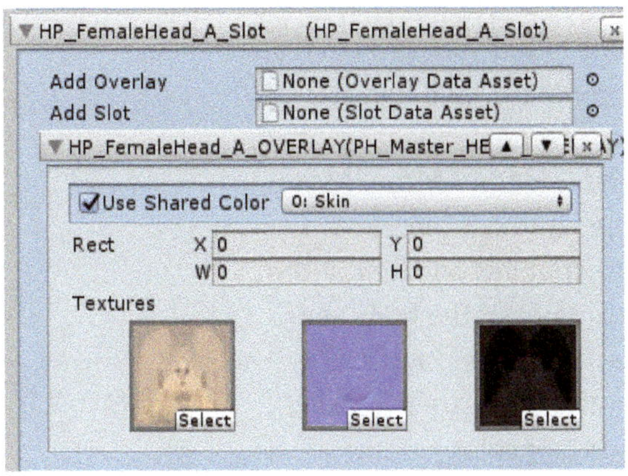

Figure 567

With those changes the shared colors for our UMA characters will work as expected for the HP_FemaleHead_A race. Unfortunately, there are nine other races that need to be changed. These are the same ones you saw in Figure 563. Go through each of those folders and change the "Recipe" file to use the shared colors for the eye and head slots as you did for "HP_Female_Head_A". Once you're done, you'll be ready to use those races with the different heads on your UMA characters.

The Random Townsperson

Now we come full circle to the UMA Crowd scene. With what we've learned thus far, we're going to create a script that will randomize people's DNA so we get that variety of people that will help to immerse the players into the game.

Before we start slogging waist deep in C# code, we have a big question we need to address. That is, "what are these people going to look like?" We know that UMA gives us a lot of control over the character's DNA, but what should we do with all that control?

Ideally, we want the people to look authentic. In this time period, we're talking about Hebrew, Egyptian, and African people. Makes sense. And luckily for us, others have already done the hard work of compiling information about what people from different regions look like. Jourmana Madlej has put together a great guide for us to use:

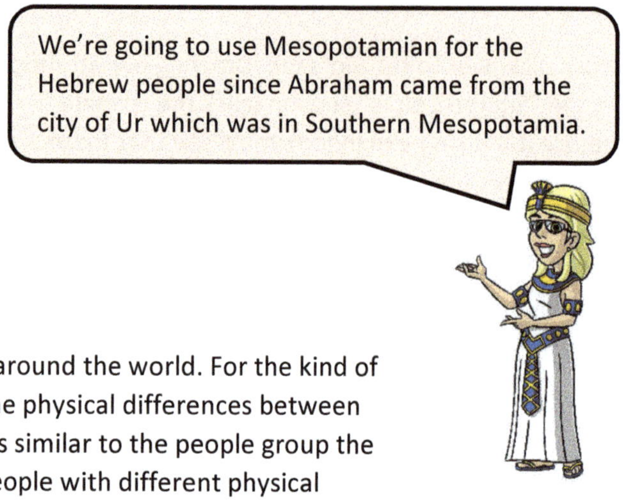

http://cedarseed.com/portfolio/human-types/

This is an artist's guide to different people from all around the world. For the kind of artists who draw people, it is very useful to know the physical differences between people groups so that the character they draw looks similar to the people group the character is supposed to be a part of. If you have people with different physical features than what they should be it can be a big hindrance for players to get into the game.

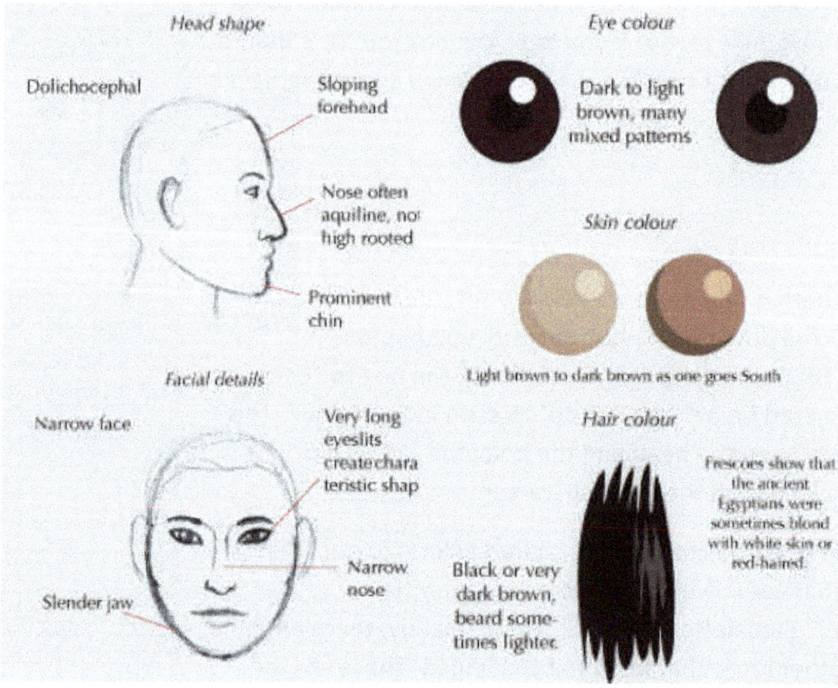

We're going to use this page to help guide what our different types of people will look like. If you scroll to the right then you'll find sections for Mesopotamian, Egyptian, and General African. As you read through the descriptions and look at the diagrams of the body and facial features, you'll also notice there are eye, skin, and hair color.

I've already done the hard work of taking all these features and colors and putting them in the code for you. But keep this in mind for your next game project.

In the Project View, go to the scripts folder and create a new C# script named "UmaRndChar" since it will create a random UMA character. Double-click it to open it up in the code editor. You can type the code shown in Figure 568. Line 4 has a new "using" statement for "UMA.CharacterSystem". This lets us access the Dynamic Character Avatar. Then add the public and private variables declared inside the class.

Since we've got three people groups to create, this fits nicely into an enumerated type. The "Avatar" variable will be a local copy of the Dynamic Character Avatar that normally. The "rebuild" component that normally. The "rebuild" Boolean lets the Update method know to rebuild the UMA character since we've changed its DNA and colors. The other variables are the different colors and color lists for each people-group.

```
1   using System.Collections;
2   using System.Collections.Generic;
3   using UnityEngine;
4   using UnityEngine.Events;
5   using UMA;
6   using UMA.CharacterSystem;
7
8   public class UmaRndChar : MonoBehaviour
9   {
10      public enum _ethnicity
11      {
12          RandomEgyptian,
13          RandomAfrican,
14          RandomHebrew
15      }
16
17      public _ethnicity Ethnicity;
18      [HideInInspector] public bool Built;
19
20      private DynamicCharacterAvatar avatar;
21      private bool rebuild;
```

Figure 568

```
24      void Start()
25      {
26          rebuild = false;
27          Built = false;
28          avatar = GetComponent<DynamicCharacterAvatar>();
29          if (avatar) avatar.CharacterCreated.AddListener(new UnityAction<UMAData>
              (BuildUma));
30      }
31
32      // Update is called once per frame
33      void Update()
34      {
35          // Cannot be done in the same frame as BuildUma()
36          if (rebuild)
37          {
38              rebuild = false;
39              Built = true;
40              avatar.BuildCharacter();
41              avatar.ForceUpdate(true, true, true);
42          }
43      }
```

Figure 569

After that, we fill out the Start and Update methods with the code shown in Figure 569. Start will initialize the bool flag that tells the code to rebuild the UMA, get a handle to the dynamic character avatar, and add a listener to call the method “BuildUma” when the character is created. There is a little bit of a complication that requires this code in the Update method. We’re going to use a callback in the dynamic character avatar to call a method to change the colors and DNA. However, we can’t update the UMA character in that call, so we do it in the Update method.

Figure 570 is the method we’re going to supply to the callback named “BuildUma”. This method gets called when the UMA character creation process is complete. We check the type of character to set the DNA and colors to and call the appropriate method. At the end we set “rebuild” to true indicating to the Update method that it is ready to update the character.

```
public void BuildUma(UMAData umaData)
{
    switch(Ethnicity)
    {
        case _ethnicity.RandomAfrican:
            RandomAfricanDna();
            break;
        case _ethnicity.RandomEgyptian:
            RandomEgyptianDna();
            break;
        case _ethnicity.RandomHebrew:
            RandomHebrewDna();
            break;
    }

    rebuild = true;
}
```

Figure 570

```
private void SetCommonDna(Dictionary<string, DnaSetter> setters)
{
    setters["headSize"].Set(Random.Range(0.45f, 0.5f));
    setters["neckThickness"].Set(Random.Range(0.4f, 0.6f));
    setters["armLength"].Set(Random.Range(0.45f, 0.55f));
    setters["forearmLength"].Set(Random.Range(0.45f, 0.55f));
    setters["armWidth"].Set(Random.Range(0.45f, 0.55f));
    setters["forearmWidth"].Set(Random.Range(0.45f, 0.55f));
    setters["handsSize"].Set(Random.Range(0.4f, 0.5f));
    setters["feetSize"].Set(Random.Range(0.4f, 0.5f));
    setters["upperMuscle"].Set(Random.Range(0.4f, 0.6f));
    setters["lowerMuscle"].Set(Random.Range(0.4f, 0.6f));
    setters["upperWeight"].Set(Random.Range(0.4f, 0.6f));
    setters["lowerWeight"].Set(Random.Range(0.4f, 0.6f));
    setters["belly"].Set(Random.Range(0.35f, 0.65f));
    setters["waist"].Set(Random.Range(0.35f, 0.65f));
    setters["breastSize"].Set(Random.Range(0.4f, 0.55f));
}
```

Now we get into setting DNA for the three different ethnicities. First, we have a method to set common DNA so we don't have to write it three times. You can code it up from **Error! Reference source not found.**. The next three methods, "RandomAfricanDna", "RandomEgyptianDna", "RandomHebrewDna", set the appropriate DNA and colors. Add those methods next.

It may seem like a lot of code, but hopefully it went by quickly. Save the file and go back to the Unity editor. After it reloads after the code, if there are any errors in red displayed in the Console View go ahead and double-click it and make sure the code looks exactly like what's in the above code.

These methods have 3 main parts. First, the colors for the ethnicity's skin, eye, and hair are setup. Then the DNA is set. Finally, the avatar is updated.

It may seem like a lot of code, but hopefully it goes by quickly. When done, save the file and go back to the Unity editor. After it reloads after the code, if there are any errors in red displayed in the Console View go ahead and double-click it and make sure the code looks exactly like what's in the above code.

```
private void RandomAfricanDna()
{
    List<Color> SkinList = new List<Color>();
    Color tCol, eyeColor, hairColor;

    // Setup Ethnicity colors
    ColorUtility.TryParseHtmlString("#7E4031FF", out tCol);
    SkinList.Add(tCol);
    ColorUtility.TryParseHtmlString("#83533CFF", out tCol);
    SkinList.Add(tCol);
    ColorUtility.TryParseHtmlString("#4F3035FF", out tCol);
    SkinList.Add(tCol);
    ColorUtility.TryParseHtmlString("#2B1720FF", out tCol);
    SkinList.Add(tCol);
    ColorUtility.TryParseHtmlString("#290101FF", out eyeColor);
    ColorUtility.TryParseHtmlString("#231F20FF", out hairColor);

    Dictionary<string, DnaSetter> setters = avatar.GetDNA();
    SetCommonDna(setters);
    setters["height"].Set(Random.Range(0.45f, 0.7f));
    setters["headWidth"].Set(Random.Range(0.55f, 0.65f));
    setters["legSeparation"].Set(Random.Range(0.55f, 0.65f));
    setters["legsSize"].Set(Random.Range(0.5f, 0.65f));
    setters["gluteusSize"].Set(Random.Range(0.5f, 0.65f));
    setters["earsSize"].Set(Random.Range(0.35f, 0.45f));
    setters["earsPosition"].Set(Random.Range(0.45f, 0.55f));
    setters["earsRotation"].Set(Random.Range(0.45f, 0.55f));
    setters["noseSize"].Set(Random.Range(0.55f, 0.65f));
    setters["noseCurve"].Set(Random.Range(0.55f, 0.7f));
    setters["noseWidth"].Set(Random.Range(0.6f, 0.9f));
    setters["noseInclination"].Set(Random.Range(0.3f, 0.55f));
    setters["nosePosition"].Set(Random.Range(0.3f, 0.45f));
    setters["nosePronounced"].Set(Random.Range(0.5f, 0.75f));
    setters["noseFlatten"].Set(Random.Range(0.5f, 0.6f));
    setters["chinSize"].Set(Random.Range(0.6f, 0.8f));
    setters["chinPronounced"].Set(Random.Range(0.6f, 0.8f));
    setters["chinPosition"].Set(Random.Range(0.1f, 0.4f));
    setters["mandibleSize"].Set(Random.Range(0.4f, 0.5f));
    setters["jawsSize"].Set(Random.Range(0.6f, 0.9f));
    setters["jawsPosition"].Set(Random.Range(0.45f, 0.55f));
    setters["cheekSize"].Set(Random.Range(0.4f, 0.6f));
    setters["cheekPosition"].Set(Random.Range(0.1f, 0.3f));
    setters["lowCheekPronounced"].Set(Random.Range(0.6f, 0.8f));
    setters["lowCheekPosition"].Set(Random.Range(0.3f, 0.5f));
    setters["foreheadSize"].Set(Random.Range(0.5f, 0.7f));
    setters["foreheadPosition"].Set(Random.Range(0.4f, 0.6f));
    setters["lipsSize"].Set(Random.Range(0.6f, 0.8f));
    setters["mouthSize"].Set(Random.Range(0.7f, 0.9f));
    setters["eyeRotation"].Set(Random.Range(0.5f, 0.75f));
    setters["eyeSize"].Set(Random.Range(0.4f, 0.55f));

    avatar.characterColors.SetColor("Hair", hairColor);
    avatar.characterColors.SetColor("Eyes", eyeColor);
    avatar.characterColors.SetColor("Skin", SkinList[Random.Range(0,
      SkinList.Count)]);
}
```

```
private void RandomEgyptianDna()
{
    List<Color> SkinList = new List<Color>();
    Color tCol, eyeColor, hairColor;

    // Setup Ethnicity colors
    ColorUtility.TryParseHtmlString("#D8AF8FFF", out tCol);
    SkinList.Add(tCol);
    ColorUtility.TryParseHtmlString("#D2946DFF", out tCol);
    SkinList.Add(tCol);
    ColorUtility.TryParseHtmlString("#BD755DFF", out tCol);
    SkinList.Add(tCol);
    ColorUtility.TryParseHtmlString("#83532BFF", out tCol);
    SkinList.Add(tCol);
    ColorUtility.TryParseHtmlString("#290101FF", out eyeColor);
    ColorUtility.TryParseHtmlString("#231F20FF", out hairColor);

    Dictionary<string, DnaSetter> setters = avatar.GetDNA();
    SetCommonDna(setters);
    setters["height"].Set(Random.Range(0.4f, 0.6f));
    setters["headWidth"].Set(Random.Range(0.45f, 0.55f));
    setters["legSeparation"].Set(Random.Range(0.45f, 0.55f));
    setters["legsSize"].Set(Random.Range(0.45f, 0.55f));
    setters["gluteusSize"].Set(Random.Range(0.45f, 0.55f));
    setters["earsSize"].Set(Random.Range(0.45f, 0.55f));
    setters["earsPosition"].Set(Random.Range(0.45f, 0.55f));
    setters["earsRotation"].Set(Random.Range(0.45f, 0.55f));
    setters["noseSize"].Set(Random.Range(0.45f, 0.55f));
    setters["noseCurve"].Set(Random.Range(0.55f, 0.65f));
    setters["noseWidth"].Set(Random.Range(0.25f, 0.5f));
    setters["noseInclination"].Set(Random.Range(0.4f, 0.5f));
    setters["nosePosition"].Set(Random.Range(0.45f, 0.55f));
    setters["nosePronounced"].Set(Random.Range(0.35f, 0.65f));
    setters["noseFlatten"].Set(Random.Range(0.35f, 0.45f));
    setters["chinSize"].Set(Random.Range(0.55f, 0.65f));
    setters["chinPronounced"].Set(Random.Range(0.6f, 0.8f));
    setters["chinPosition"].Set(Random.Range(0.1f, 0.4f));
    setters["mandibleSize"].Set(Random.Range(0.45f, 0.55f));
    setters["jawsSize"].Set(Random.Range(0.65f, 0.85f));
    setters["jawsPosition"].Set(Random.Range(0.45f, 0.55f));
    setters["cheekSize"].Set(Random.Range(0.6f, 0.8f));
    setters["cheekPosition"].Set(Random.Range(0.3f, 0.5f));
    setters["lowCheekPronounced"].Set(Random.Range(0.5f, 0.65f));
    setters["lowCheekPosition"].Set(Random.Range(0.3f, 0.5f));
    setters["foreheadSize"].Set(Random.Range(0.6f, 0.8f));
    setters["foreheadPosition"].Set(Random.Range(0.4f, 0.6f));
    setters["lipsSize"].Set(Random.Range(0.5f, 0.6f));
    setters["mouthSize"].Set(Random.Range(0.5f, 0.65f));
    setters["eyeRotation"].Set(1);
    setters["eyeSize"].Set(Random.Range(0.45f, 0.55f));

    avatar.characterColors.SetColor("Hair", hairColor);
    avatar.characterColors.SetColor("Eyes", eyeColor);
    avatar.characterColors.SetColor("Skin", SkinList[Random.Range(0,
      SkinList.Count)]);
}
```

```
private void RandomHebrewDna()
{
    List<Color> SkinList = new List<Color>();
    Color tCol, eyeColor, hairColor;

    // Setup Ethnicity colors
    ColorUtility.TryParseHtmlString("#B9946AFF", out tCol);
    SkinList.Add(tCol);
    ColorUtility.TryParseHtmlString("#946E4AFF", out tCol);
    SkinList.Add(tCol);
    ColorUtility.TryParseHtmlString("#8A685EFF", out tCol);
    SkinList.Add(tCol);
    ColorUtility.TryParseHtmlString("#684B3BFF", out tCol);
    SkinList.Add(tCol);
    ColorUtility.TryParseHtmlString("#461A17FF", out eyeColor);
    ColorUtility.TryParseHtmlString("#231F20FF", out hairColor);

    Dictionary<string, DnaSetter> setters = avatar.GetDNA();
    SetCommonDna(setters);
    setters["height"].Set(Random.Range(0.4f, 0.6f));
    setters["headWidth"].Set(Random.Range(0.35f, 0.5f));
    setters["legSeparation"].Set(Random.Range(0.45f, 0.55f));
    setters["legsSize"].Set(Random.Range(0.45f, 0.55f));
    setters["gluteusSize"].Set(Random.Range(0.45f, 0.55f));
    setters["earsSize"].Set(Random.Range(0.45f, 0.55f));
    setters["earsPosition"].Set(Random.Range(0.45f, 0.55f));
    setters["earsRotation"].Set(Random.Range(0.45f, 0.55f));
    setters["noseSize"].Set(Random.Range(0.5f, 0.65f));
    setters["noseCurve"].Set(Random.Range(0.6f, 0.75f));
    setters["noseWidth"].Set(Random.Range(0.6f, 0.75f));
    setters["noseInclination"].Set(Random.Range(0.4f, 0.55f));
    setters["nosePosition"].Set(Random.Range(0.45f, 0.55f));
    setters["nosePronounced"].Set(Random.Range(0.35f, 0.65f));
    setters["noseFlatten"].Set(Random.Range(0.45f, 0.55f));
    setters["chinSize"].Set(Random.Range(0.5f, 0.7f));
    setters["chinPronounced"].Set(Random.Range(0.5f, 0.7f));
    setters["chinPosition"].Set(Random.Range(0.5f, 0.7f));
    setters["mandibleSize"].Set(Random.Range(0.45f, 0.55f));
    setters["jawsSize"].Set(Random.Range(0.5f, 0.65f));
    setters["jawsPosition"].Set(Random.Range(0.45f, 0.55f));
    setters["cheekSize"].Set(Random.Range(0.45f, 0.55f));
    setters["cheekPosition"].Set(Random.Range(0.3f, 0.5f));
    setters["lowCheekPronounced"].Set(Random.Range(0.5f, 0.6f));
    setters["lowCheekPosition"].Set(Random.Range(0.35f, 0.5f));
    setters["foreheadSize"].Set(Random.Range(0.2f, 0.45f));
    setters["foreheadPosition"].Set(Random.Range(0.5f, 0.7f));
    setters["lipsSize"].Set(Random.Range(0.45f, 0.55f));
    setters["mouthSize"].Set(Random.Range(0.45f, 0.55f));
    setters["eyeRotation"].Set(Random.Range(0.5f, 0.75f));
    setters["eyeSize"].Set(Random.Range(0.5f, 0.65f));

    avatar.characterColors.SetColor("Hair", hairColor);
    avatar.characterColors.SetColor("Eyes", eyeColor);
    avatar.characterColors.SetColor("Skin", SkinList[Random.Range(0,
      SkinList.Count)]);
}
```

After any red errors are gone from the Console, we're ready to test this script out. Let's make an instance of the UMA Dynamic Character Avatar prefab in our Egypt_Nile Scene. In the Project View, go to UMA > Getting Started and drag the UMADynamicCharacterAvatar onto the Scene View. Then click it in the Hierarchy View so its info is shown in the Inspector. Now, from the Project View, drag "UmaRndChar" script from the Scripts folder onto the bottom blank part of the inspector near the "Add Component" button so that it is added as a component like in Figure 571.

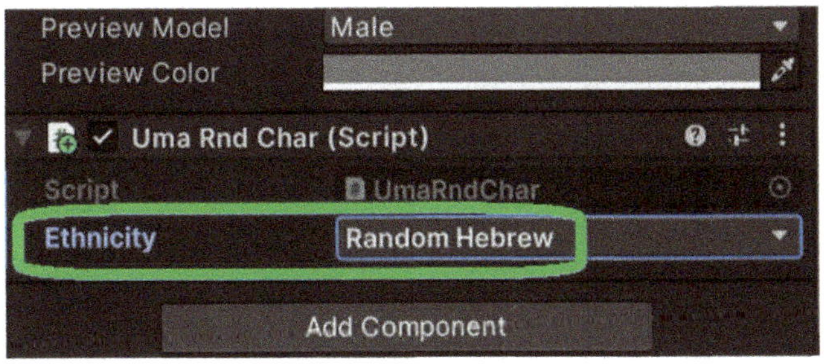

Figure 571

Now, at the very top of the Dynamic Character Avatar component, look for the "Active Race" field. Click the dropdown box and you'll see options like Figure 572. Select the option "HP_MaleHead_A" which is one of the different heads we were looking at in the previous section.

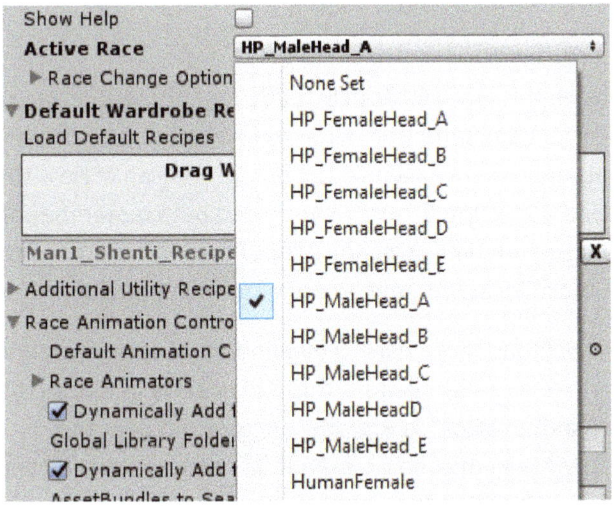

Figure 572

Before we play this scene, let's at least give the guy a shenti to cover up his skin-tight underwear. However, if you remember, you can't just give any race any wardrobe item, we need to add the "HP_MaleHead_A" race to the list of races this wardrobe item can be placed on.

To do that, we go back to the Project View. Go to UMA > Content > EgyptianUMAS > Man_1 > Wardrobe and click the "Man1_Shenti_Recipe". At the top in the inspector, you'll see the list of races. Above the list is another very helpful button that tells us to add new races by dragging it there. And that's exactly what we're going to do.

Still in the Project View, go to UMA > Content > UM_HairPack_Arteria3d > HairPack_HEADS > Males > Male_A > Male_Headstyle_A and drag the "HP_MaleHead_A" race file onto that button so the race gets added to the list as seen in Figure 573. You can do this for each wardrobe recipe you want to add a new race to.

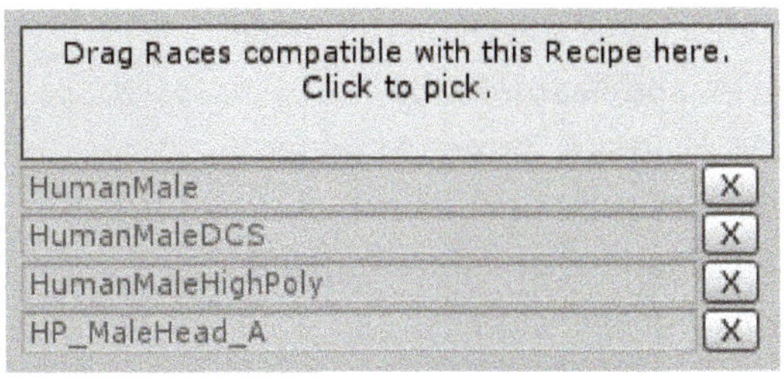

Figure 573

Now we're ready to add the Shenti to our character. Going back to the Hierarchy View, click the "UMADynamicCharacterAvatar". Then drag the "Man1_Shenti_Recip" from UMA > Content > EgyptianUMAS > Man_1 > Wardrobe onto the button that says "Drag Wardrobe Recipes here" so that it is added to as the only wardrobe recipe shown in Figure 574.

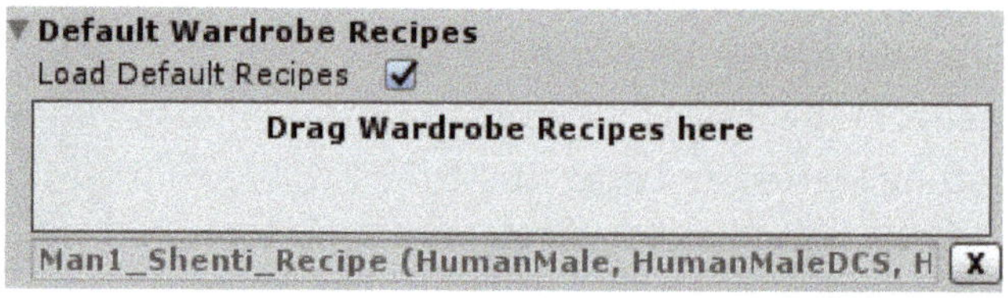

Figure 574

Now he's ready for his big performance debut!
Click the play button and switch to the Scene View. You should see our Egyptian-looking friend shown up right where you put in, similar to Figure 575. Just an average looking dude, right? That's exactly who we want to populate our game with.

Figure 575

Now, this guy isn't totally ready for "primetime" just yet. He still needs the correct animator and actor components so he can behave just like all the other actors we have in the game. You can review the section "Picking One out of the Crowd" if you need help remembering exactly what to do. Make sure he's using the "ThirdPersonAnimatorController", has an Actor Controller script, and an Animator component.

Give it one more play to test and make sure everything works before you create a prefab to store this movie extra in. Create a new prefab named "RandomActor" in Prefabs > Actors and drag the "UMADynamicCharacterAvatar" there to save it. Now, whenever we want any unique random extras in our scenes we can just drag over the prefab, change it to the gender we want, add wardrobe, and set the people-group.

Adding the various head-races to the other wardrobe items in the UMA > Content > EgyptianUMAS folder should be pretty easy with what you've learned so far. The same can be done with the clothes HebrewClothes_10 folder. You can also add them to the hair styles and beards in the UM_HairPack_Arteria3d folder. Make all sorts of different combinations of different people with different clothes.

I'll leave where to put these movie extras up to you. When you get some of them together then you'll really see their differences. Go through the maps and use your intuition for where these extras might be. You can also replace existing actors with these new UMA characters. You have a lot of possibilities, and your only limitation is your imagination!

With UMA there are so many things I can do with the game! This is so exciting. I can't wait to go out on my own and populate the city and camp.

That's the attitude teacher Steph! We've also learned some very useful things with UMA. We can use a script to randomize our characters. But it also goes beyond that. The sky's the limit for what we can use scripts for.

Chapter 19 – Finishing Touches

We've gone through quite a lot of concepts, wrote a lot of code, and made some great progress on the game. Here's a quick recap:

- **Unity Basics:** How to use the editor and get around in it
- **Game Design Document:** Write down our design and requirements in a document
- **Character Controller:** Allow the player to control a character in the game
- **Maps:** Show the player a map of the area
- **NPC Actors:** Animate NPCs to give life to the game
- **Dialogue:** Allow the player to interact with the game
- **Cinematics:** Connect with the player using visual storytelling
- **Menus:** Allow the player to control how they play the game
- **Inventory:** Let the player manage items they pick up
- **Levels:** Build interesting places for the player to go
- **Music:** Give the player something to listen to
- **Skybox:** Create a day and night cycle
- **Save:** Let the player resume from where they left off
- **Quests:** How the player can progress in the game
- **Minigames:** Break up the main gameplay with fun diversions

While we did a ton of work on the game, if you check back in Appendix B, you can see there is still quite a lot more to do. In this chapter we're going to make a dent in that and help get you on your way to complete the rest of it on your own. But first, there's a trick we can use to improve performance.

Into the Details

When deploying on different platforms, it is important to consider how fast it runs. On slower PCs and mobile platforms, having a lot of things going on can cause the game's frame rate to go down. Each time the game screen updates is called a frame. You want to keep the number of frame updates that happen each second at 30 or more. Gamers call this FPS (Frames Per Second). In Unity, if you click the Stats button, then an overlay appears which gives great profiling information about your game. In **Error! Reference source not found.**, you can see the "Stats" circled in green and the FPS circled in red. The "19.0ms" means it takes about 19 milliseconds for each frame update.

Figure 576

UMA is very powerful in letting you create customizable characters but is also very expensive for processing power. If you have too many UMA characters in your scene, then the FPS (Frames Per Second, which is how many times the game updates each second. A good number is between 30 and 60) will drop. How many characters depends on the player's platform.

Unity comes with a feature similar to this called Occlusion Culling. A typical RPG quest might be culling wolves. The wolves are a problem and there needs to be less. Occlusion is where things are blocked. For example, when your mouth is closed the food inside is occluded. Occlusion Culling is where Unity doesn't render objects that won't be in view of the camera. Cameras in Unity enable Occlusion Culling by default with a check box in the inspector.

But there are ways you can improve performance. One such way is called LOD, or Level of Detail. LOD is Unity's way of letting developers show what is shown to the camera based on how far away the object is. Why is that important? Well, I'll tell you! Look at your hand. Go ahead, do it. Now move it closer. Even closer. Closer still. Ok, not that close. But you can really see all the little lines that move in random directions very well. Now move it as far away as possible. Be careful! Don't knock down your monitor. If you look at it now, it's harder to see all those details.

The same is true for games. Because the textures on our models need to be rendered as pixels, the camera approximates the colors. It's not noticeable when models are close to the camera, but when they are far away, they look... well... pixelated. Using this knowledge, we can change the far away models to one that are less performance intensive. They models could have fewer points and the texture a lower resolution.

We can show something that looks similar at a distance but when the player moves up to it, the model is swapped so the player sees the high-quality model up close. This way, you can show the player high quality models while still having better performance. Let's look at how to do it in Unity.

In the Hierarchy View, expand the "Rocks" object and then expand the "Rocks_1" object. Select "Rock_2(2)" as shown in Figure 577.

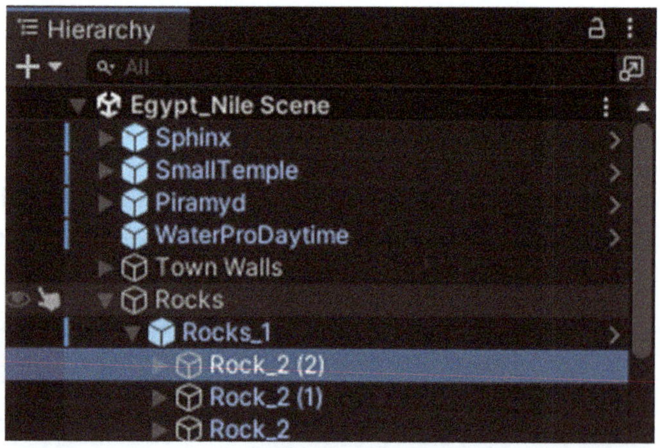

Figure 577

Then look over to the right in the inspector and you'll see an "LOD Group" component attached to the rock object as shown in Figure 578. You'll see a number parts in this component. Take a look at the green, blue, and red boxes close to the top. There is also a lighter blue box shaped like a camera. In fact, this little gadget represents the camera. If you click on it and drag it around, you can see the camera moving closer to and farther from the rock.

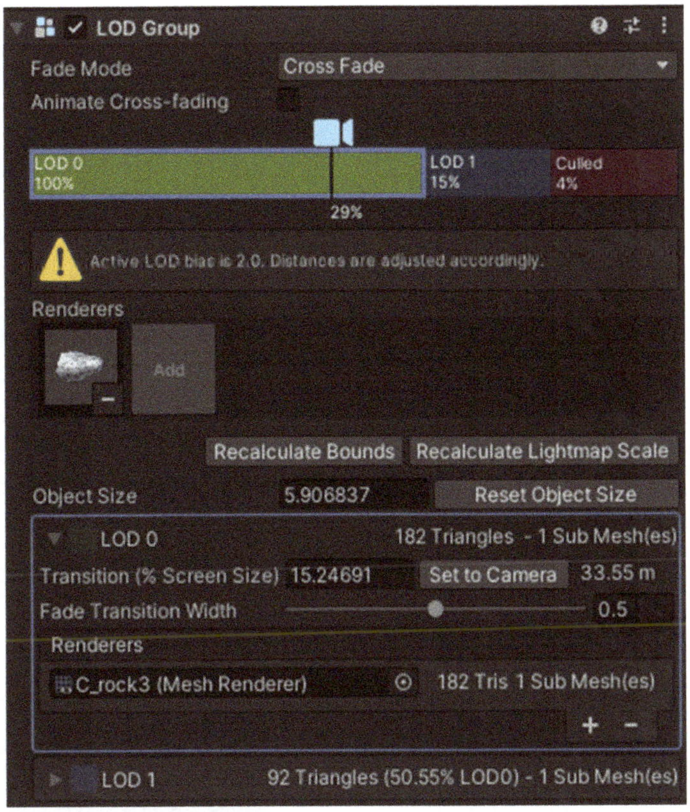

Figure 578

LOD 0 is the highest detail model. You can see near the bottom that it has 182 triangles. Below that you can see another LOD 1 that only has 92 triangles. The 182-triangle rock is higher quality and looks better but the 92-triangle rock performs better.

Looking back at the rectangles at the top, when you drag the camera onto the LOD 1 section it will fade out the 182-triangle rock and fade in the 92-triangle rock simultaneously. This is called "Cross Fade" which you can see in the "Fade Mode" attribute. There is another way of fading they use for speed trees, and you only need to worry about that when you're making your own trees for the terrain.

When you drag the camera into the red zone, it is culled, or not shown at all. This is, of course, the best performance. Cull the object when you think it's at a far enough distance, so the player won't miss it. If you want to improve performance in your game, go through the prefabs with LOD groups and decrease the distances you're showing higher quality models.

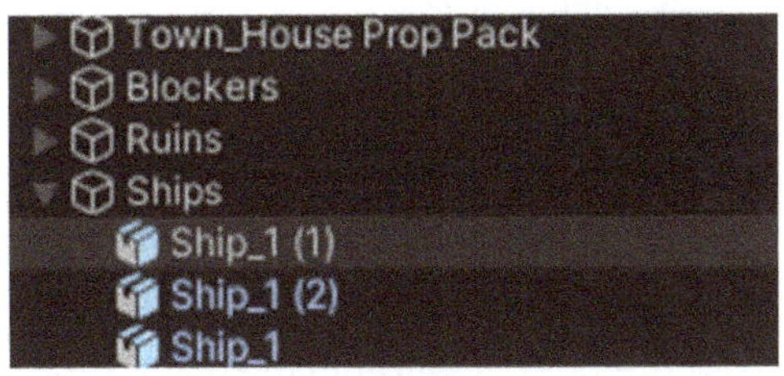

Figure 579

Let's add some of these LOD groups to the ships. In the Hierarchy View, find the "Ships" object and expand it. Then click on the "Ship_1 (1)" object as shown in Figure 579.

In the inspector on the right, add a new "LOD Group" component. It comes with 3 groups planned but we only need 1. Right-click on "LOD 1" and LOD 2" and delete them as shown in Figure 580.

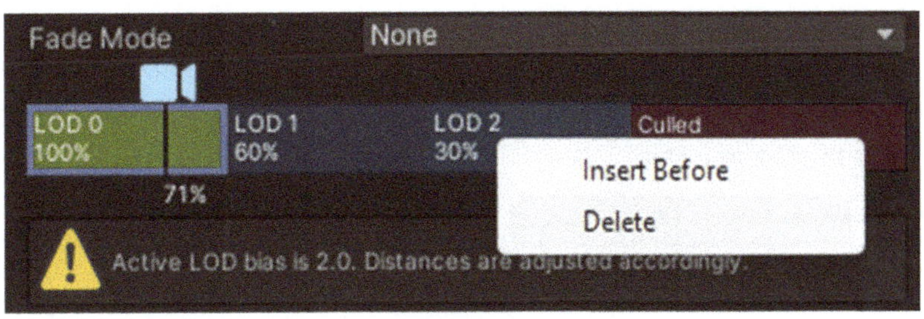

Figure 580

Now, let's set up this LOD group as you can see in Figure 581. First, select "Cross Fade" for the "Fade Mode". Don't change the rectangles yet, the model's renderer needs to be added first. Expand the LOD 0 item and click on the '+' button to add a spot to put the ship's mesh renderer. To Add it to the LOD 0 item, just drag the "Ship_1 (1)" object from the Hierarchy View onto that empty slot. When you do, you'll see that it has 916 triangles with 2 Sub Meshes.

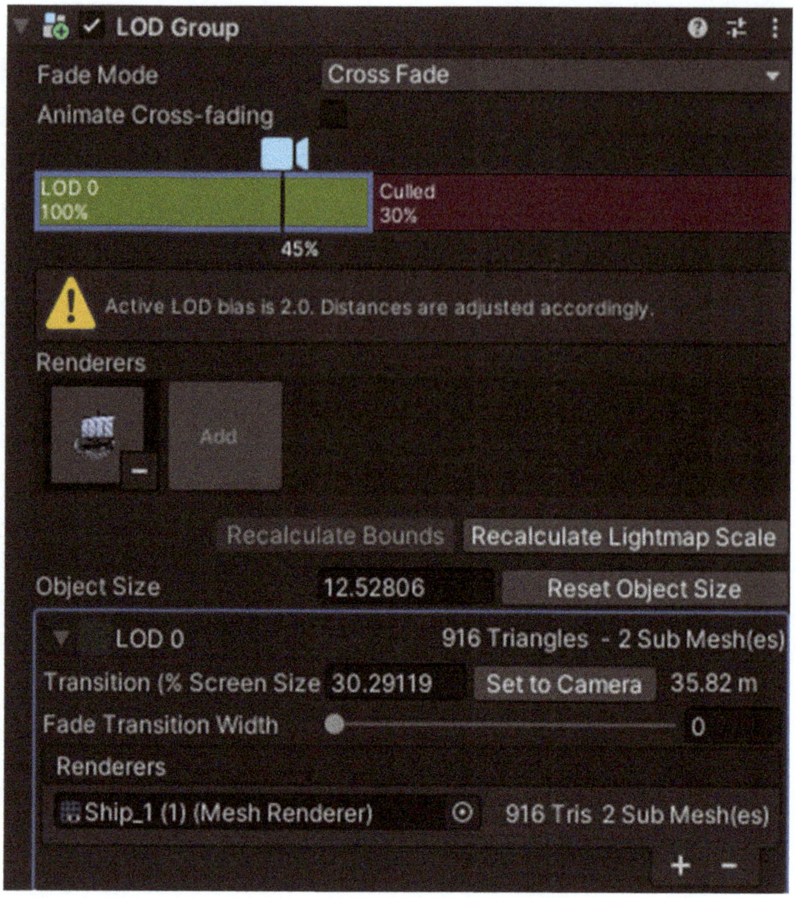

Figure 581

Now click the "Recalculate Bounds" button. Unity automatically sets the Object size based on the size of the object from its renderer. The button will gray out after this is done.

I found that setting culling at 30% seems to feel about right for me when the ship doesn't need to be shown. Maybe you have a different feeling. Go ahead and set the red rectangle for culling the object.

Now click play to play the game and go straight to the Scene View. Make sure the "Ship_1 (1)" is focused on. You should see that LOD 0 is being shown like in Figure 582.

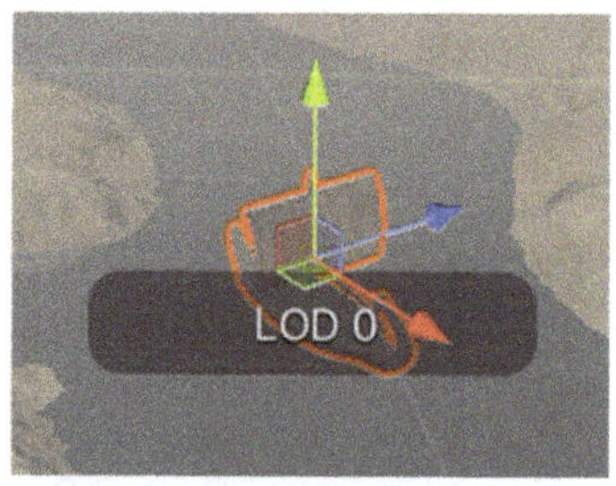

Figure 582

Still in Scene View, either zoom out by scrolling the mouse wheel, or move the camera backward by holding right-click and pressing 'S' on the keyboard. Keep doing it and when the distance gets far enough away from the boat, it will get culled and disappear as in Figure 583.

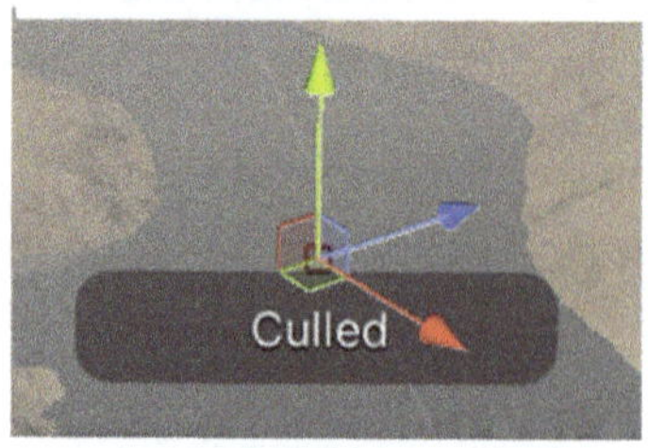

Figure 583

When you exit play mode, you can do the same with the other ships here. A simple copy of the component, highlighting each other ship object, and then from the triple dots on another component, select "Paste Component as New". Do not forget, you need to drag each ship object onto the renderer for LOD 0. Otherwise, all of the LOD groups will only refer to that one ship.

Now You See Me, Now You Don't!

However, there is one object that the LOD Group component can't help with. I'm talking about the UMAs we just added. It won't work because the UMA renderers are created during runtime. There are a couple options, but we'll just create our own script to disable them if they get too far from the camera.

```
using System.Collections;
using System.Collections.Generic;
using UnityEngine;

public class UMA_Culler : MonoBehaviour
{
    public float Distance;
    public float CheckTime;
    public UmaRndChar[] UMAs;

    // Start is called before the first frame update
    void Start()
    {
        InvokeRepeating("CullUMAs", CheckTime, CheckTime);
    }

    private void CullUMAs()
    {
        foreach(UmaRndChar uma in UMAs)
        {
            if (uma)
            {
                CheckDistance(uma);
            }
        }
    }

    private void CheckDistance(UmaRndChar uma)
    {
        Vector3 camPos = Camera.main.transform.position;
        if (Vector3.Distance(uma.transform.position, camPos) < Distance)
        {
            uma.gameObject.SetActive(true);
        }
        else if (uma.Built)
        {
            uma.gameObject.SetActive(false);
        }
    }
}
```

Figure 584

Create a new C# script named "UMA_Culler" and add the code in Figure 584. This script will allow us to cull or disable UMA objects like the LOD group. Unlike the LOD group, this script will disable the game object as opposed to the renderer. This is for convenience. Since UMAs are created dynamically, we would need to add extra code to find the renderer. This way, we can simply disable the object once it is done building.

This script will take a given array of UMAs and periodically check if it's far enough away from the camera to cull or inactivate it. The "Start" method just sets up the repeating invoke call to "CullUMAs".

The "CheckDistance" method loops through each of the UMAs in the array and checks the distance. Those close enough to the camera are marked as active. If not, then if the UMA has been built, it is inactivated. If we inactivate it during the build process the UMA won't build correctly.

Create a few new UMA characters using the steps we just learned in the previous chapter. I put them in the Hebrew slave camp that you can see similar to Figure 585. You can make them whatever you like, but I'm going to have 4 Hebrew women talking with each other.

Figure 585

Remember to give you UMA characters clothes to wear. It wouldn't do to have them running around Egypt in nothing but their underwear. There are some great clothes choices of very high-quality stuff typically worn during that period of time. Would be a shame if it all went to waste. Feel free to thumb through the previous chapter to remind yourself about them.

Next, let's group them together in the Hierarchy View. You can see in Figure 586 that I've got my 4 women as child objects under a "HebrewCampUmaGroup" object. Not only will organizing them Hebrew UMA characters this way keep our Hierarchy View nice and clean, but it will also let us use the parent grouping object to control culling of the UMAs.

Figure 586

Now, add the "UMA_Culler" script to the parent "HebrewCampUmaGroup" object. You can see in Figure 587 that I set the Distance to '50' and Check time to '1'. If performance is a problem, you can make Distance a little lower and Check Time a little higher.

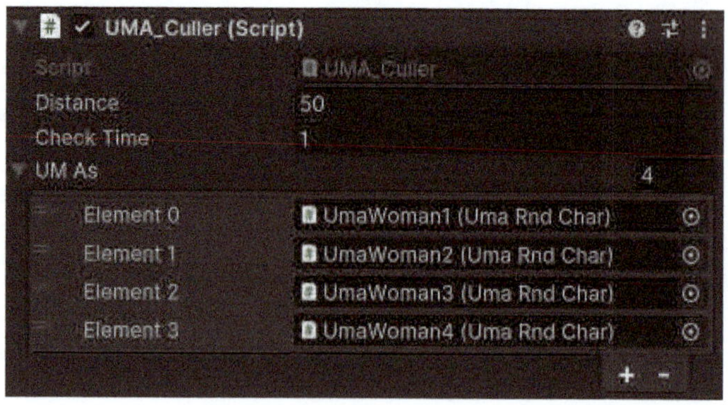

Figure 587

Then add your characters to the "UMAs" list. When you playtest the game, you will be able to see these characters when Moses is up close and when Moses is far away, if you switch to Scene View, you'll be able to see that they've disappeared, or, I guess, not see them.

This is My Quest

As we're nearing the end of our journey together, let's get a few more quests in. If you skipped adding the quests into the "QuestController" child object in the "GameController" prefab, then now's a good time to go back to the Quests section in Appendix B and add the quests in. We'll add the 3 more quests dealing with the signs to the Hebrews.

For the next quest, Moses will change his staff to a snake and back and then make his hand leprous and cured. There are a number of possible places for this to happen. I've chosen a nearby tent down the road, as shown in Figure 588. This tent is around the corner on the hill behind Aaron and Miriam's house. Having it nearby will help the player find it easier and it is on the way to the city where we'll direct them in future quests.

Figure 588

Let's add some the Hebrew elder, now. We'll use UMA! Place the camera inside the meeting tent and find the spot you want to put him. In the Hierarchy View, go to UMA > Getting Started and drag an "UMADynamicCharacterAvatar" into the tent. You can see in Figure 589 that I've placed the elder in between the two long poles of the tent. Rename him to "UMAHebrewElder1" and put the "UmaRndChar" script on him, setting the Ethnicity to "RandomHebrew". Then add the "ActorController" and the "Dialogue" scripts. Also, add an Animator and set the Controller attribute of the component to "ThirdPersonAnimatorController".

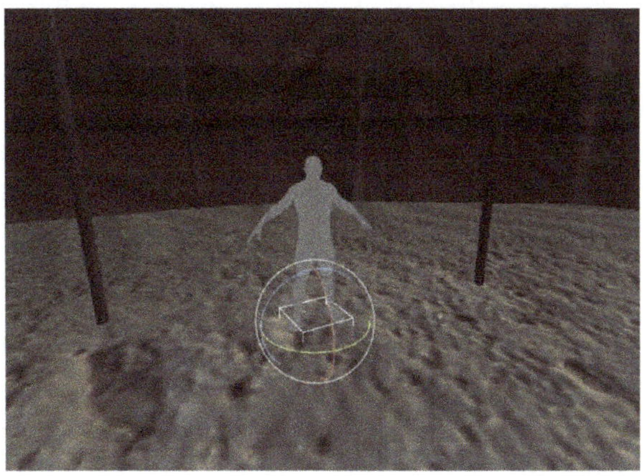

Figure 589

Let's give him some clothes. As we described in the previous UMA chapter, in the search bar of the Hierarchy View, type "t:UMAWardrobeRecipe" and it will show you all of the things that the UMAs can wear. Find some male clothing recipes that fit. I randomly choose "ML_C_HeadGear_Recipe", "ML_B_Dress_Recipe", and "POV_Sandals_Recipe".

When you're done dressing the Hebrew elder, add a basic greeting to the dialogue so we can test and make sure everything works. Something simple like setting "Speaker" to "Hebrew Elder" and setting "Text" to "Hello" will work. Now click play and if you're back at the rock in the desert, just go through the tutorial again quick. Then walk up to him as you can see that I do in Figure 590 and try to talk to him. When you click on him, he will deliver his greeting.

Figure 590

Now that we know that's working, let's add in what he's really going to say. Add 7 lines to the dialogue. The first 4 will have the below speaker and text. We'll talk about the other 3 next.

Hebrew Elder: What do you want, brother of Aaron?
Moses: Watch this sign from the Lord.
Hebrew Elder: Your staff changed to a snake!
Moses: That's right. See the sign and believe the Lord sent me.
Hebrew Elder: That's not enough for me.

With Element 0, set the "Cond Type" to "Item" and the "Cond Name" to "Staff so that the line only plays if the player uses the staff on the elder like I do in Figure 591.

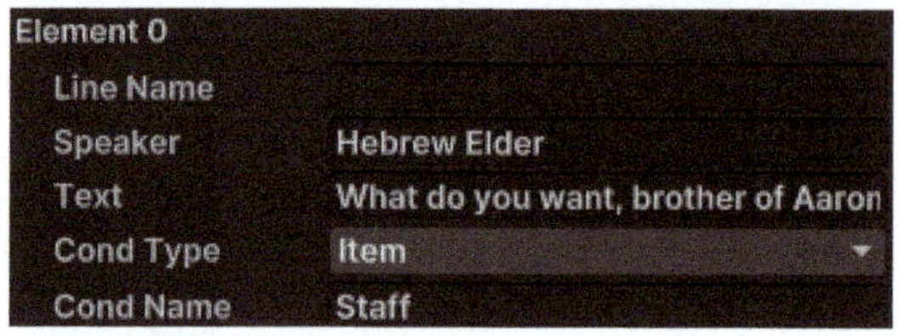

Figure 591

For the last 3 lines, make sure the Speaker and Text are blank to make sure no duplicate lines are shown to the user. For the Element 4, set the Action to "Complete Quest" and the Action Name to "Exodus" to advance the quest line.

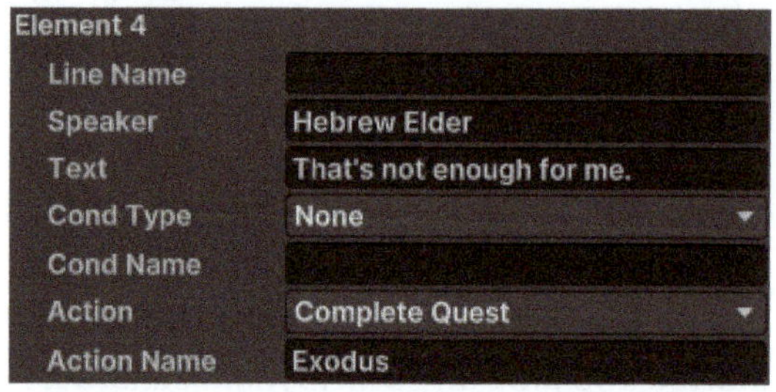

Figure 592

Now, from Hierarchy View, copy the "UMAHebrewElder1" and paste 3 more of him. Name the copies "UMAHebrewElder2", "UMAHebrewElder3", and "UMAHebrewElder4". Make the copies disabled by unchecking the box in the inspector by their name.

Going back to finish up the elder #1 dialogue, set the Action in Element 5 to "Activate Object" and drag the "UMAHebrewElder2" into the "Action Object" like in Figure 593.

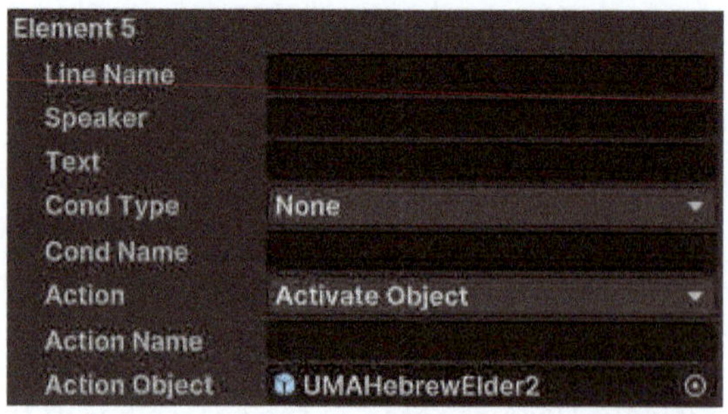

Figure 593

In the last line, Element 6, set the Action to "Inactivate Object" and drag the currently speaking elder #1 into the "Action Object" as shown in Figure 594. This will allow us to have him say different things based on which quest the player is on.

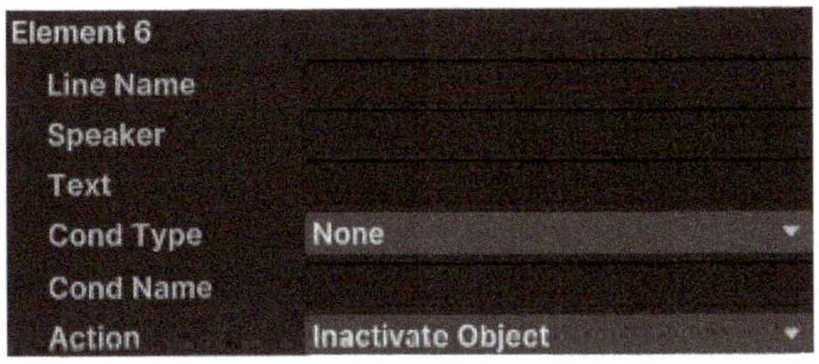

Figure 594

Here is the dialogue for "UMAHebrewElder2":

Hebrew Elder: Did you have something else, Moses?
Moses: I do indeed. Watch what happens when I put my hand in my cloak.
Hebrew Elder: Ah! Stay away, you leper!
Moses: This is the sign! Look! It is normal when I put it back in my cloak.
Hebrew Elder: I see... But it isn't enough to convince me.

On element #0, set the "Cond Type" to "Item" and the "Cond Name" to "Cloak" so that the dialogue only plays when the player uses the cloak on the elder.

Similar to elder #1, for elder #2, we need to complete the quest, activate the next elder, and deactivate this elder. The last line of spoken dialogue is line #5, so go to that line and set the "Action" to "Complete Quest" and the "Action Name" to "Exodus". On element #5, activate "UMAHebrewElder3" and then on element #6, inactivate itself which is "UMAHebrewElder2".

For the next elder, it will trigger on a jar of water. Way back when we learned about inventory management, we created a jar of water that you can use to add to your inventory. Let's move that over to the entrance of the tent so that Moses can use it to turn the water into blood. Find the "Pot_1" object we used and set the transform to what you see in Figure 595. Now it will be easy for Moses to perform the miracle.

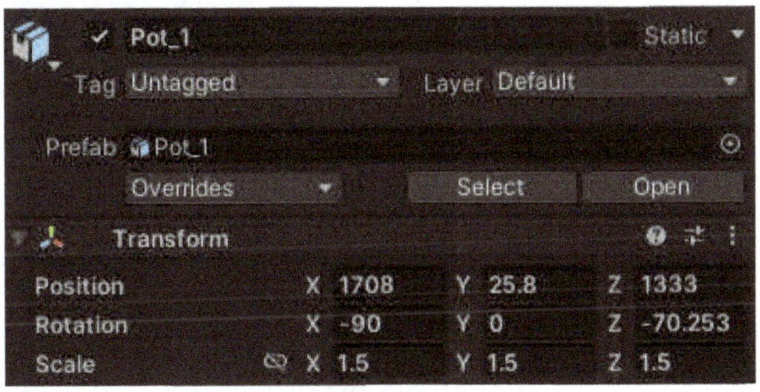

Figure 595

Let's get to the dialogue for "UMAHebrewElder3":

Hebrew Elder: Is there yet more?
Moses: There is. Watch when I pour this jar of water on the ground.
Hebrew Elder: What? Is that? Blood! This can only be the Lord. Very well, I believe now.
Moses: The Lord has seen your misery and will deliver you from Egypt.
Hebrew Elder: Praise the Lord!

Again, set element #0 to have the item condition of the "Jar of Water". Element #4, the last line of spoken dialogue, completes the quest from the "Exodus" quest line. Element #5 Activates "UMAHebrewElder4" and Element #6 Inactivates "UMAHebrewElder3".

The last copy of the elder is going to give a repeated dialogue so the player knows they are done with the elder.

Dialogue for elder #4:

Hebrew Elder: I finally believe the Lord has sent you.
Moses: Very good. He has sent me to deliver you from Egypt.
Hebrew Elder: Praise the Lord!

There needs to be no more actions. So, make sure the dialogue only has 3 lines and they all do not have any conditions or actions. We're all ready to test this out. Click the play button. To reset everything, press escape and click the "Quit Game" button from the main menu which will take you to the title scene. Then click "New Game". You can skip the introduction cinematic and breeze through the tutorial.

Once you get to the Hebrew slave camp, go over to the tent and find the jar of water. You should see it next to the tent entrance like in Figure 596. Then go into the tent and talk to the elder. He should say nothing because you need to perform the miracles for him.

Figure 596

Open you inventory by pressing 'I' for Inventory and drag the staff onto the elder. Now, it will start up the dialogue for the miracle to change the staff to a snake.

After that is done, you'll see the original elder inactivate and the first copy of him activate. Now, when you trade him the "Cloak" from your inventory, you'll trigger the next dialogue. When you trade him the jar of water you just picked up, he will give you the dialogue for the miracle of turning water into blood. Finally, when you continue to talk with him, he will repeat the final dialogue.

A bug you may have seen when testing is that the Quick Quest text at the top of the screen doesn't update when we go to the next quest. Let's fix that now, it's easy. Open up the "QuestController" script and scroll down to the CompleteQuest() method on line 135. If you scan through, you'll notice that the Quick Quest text is not updated with the new quest. Go ahead and add the code you see in Figure 597.

```
135    public void CompleteQuest(int bookNum, int questNum)
136    {
137        Quest curQuest = Quests[bookNum].Quests[questNum];
138        curQuest.Completed = true;
139        PlayerPrefs.SetInt(Quests[bookNum].BookName + ":" + curQuest.QuestName + ":Status", 1);
140        SetQuestObjects();
141        UpdateQuickQuestText();
142    }
```

Figure 597

Do another play through, starting a new game. When walk Moses over to the rock in the middle of the desert, you will now see that the Quick Quest text at the top of the screen does indeed update now.

While we're in the business of fixing quest-related bugs, let's fix another one. If you scroll up to line 67 in the "QuestController", the same file, you'll see the UpdateQuickQuestText() method. On line 71, we check if the current quest is negative, but we don't check if it's beyond the length of the Quests array inside the book for Quests[0]. This will cause a runtime error when the player finishes the last quest.

```
67    private void UpdateQuickQuestText()
68    {
69        int curQuest = GetCurQuestNum(0);
70
71        if ((curQuest >= 0) && (curQuest < Quests[0].Quests.Length))
72        {
73            QuickQuestText.text = Quests[0].Quests[curQuest].Description;
74        }
75        else
76        {
77            QuickQuestText.text = "";
78        }
79    }
```

Figure 598

To fix it, edit line 71 like what you see in Figure 598. This will make sure we only index into the Quests array inside the Quests[0] book of quests if we're not going outside the bounds.

The End

Well, not quite the end for us, but we're going to create the ending cinematic to provide a nice bookend on our game. You can then write the quests that go in between.

Check out the ending cinematic in the "Cinematics and Cut Scenes" section in Appendix B – Game Design Document. Here's a list of the characters we'll need for this cinematic: Moses, Aaron, Miriam, multitude, and an eagle.

Let's get started by creating the timeline object. In the Hierarchy View, create a new object under "Timelines" named "OutroCinematic". If the Timeline View isn't visible, then make it visible by going to the main menu and selecting Window > Sequencing > Timeline. With the "OutroCinematic" selected, click on the create button and in the popup, the default name is fine but make sure it is in the Assets > Timelines folder.

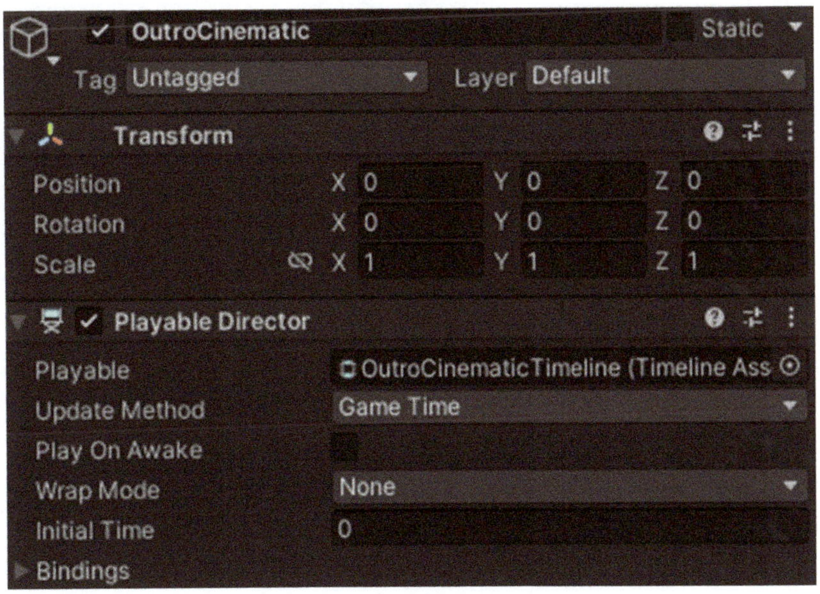

Figure 599

When the "Playable Director" is created, be sure to disable the "Play On Awake" attribute in the inspector. This will prevent it from playing when the scene loads. It should look similar to 601.

Now, we get our timeline ready for what needs to happen. Add the below tracks in the Timeline View.

- Animation Track: for the blackscreen
- Cinemachine Track: for the camera
- Audio Track: for music
- Animation Track: for Moses
- Activation Track: for the Multitude

Figure 600

The timeline should now look like 602. The first thing is to start with the black screen shown and fade in, so the player sees a closeup of Moses' face. Then the camera zooms out to show the Hebrews on the Nile. Then the eagle flies overhead. The camera will cut to Moses, Aaron, and Miriam. Moses raises his staff, and he leads out.

The first couple tracks are easy. In the Hierarchy View find "BlackScreen" and put in the first animation track. Then find "CineCam" and put it in the cinemachine track.

Figure 601

Before we get too far, we need to find a good location for our ending cinematic. There's a number of good possible spots. Figure 603 shows a map of the city and surrounding area. I choose a nice spot on the middle left side which I circled for you with an arrow in green pointing to it.

We're going to add our outro objects, so we'll need a parent object to keep them organized and be able to disable and enable them at the right time. Like how we have an object for "IntroCineObjects", in the Hierarchy View, create a new object called "OutroCineObjects". In the spirit of keeping things organized, I like to move it next to the

"IntroCineObjects" object. When you create the objects for our ending cinematic, but sure to put them in this parent object.

Since we need Moses, Aaron, and Miriam, let's drag the UMA prefabs we made of them onto the scene. I placed Moses at the location shown in Figure 604 and Aaron and Miriam behind him. This location has a good view of the city gate. Nearby is also the island temple and the pyramid.

Figure 602

For the multitude, we're going to use the non-UMA models for better performance. In the Project View, navigate to Models > Egypt Characters > Prefabs and use all except for the embalmer and Pharaoh. Add thirty people. Like what we did with the intro cinematic UMA Moses, in this one, disable the camera child object. Also disable the "Third Person Character" and "Third Person Control" scripts. This will ensure the player doesn't control Moses during the cinematic.

Before the player can see anything, we need to fade in, which means animating the "Blackscreen" from opaque to transparent color. Remember, you can record the animation by pressing the red button on the right of the track, select the "Blackscreen" object, and changing the alpha value in the image color. Set the white timeline marker to 0 and start out opaque with an alpha value of 255. Then around marker 150, set the alpha value to 0.

Figure 605

The closeup of Moses is the first scene, so let's add those shots. Create a virtual camera by either copying and pasting one of the previous virtual cameras for the intro cinematic or going to the main menu and selecting GameObject > Cinemachine > Virtual Camera. Name it "OutroCam1". With it selected, move the Scene View to something like Figure 605 and press CTRL+F to set what the virtual camera will look at. We want it close to his face but not too close because if he shifts weight then his face may not be in view.

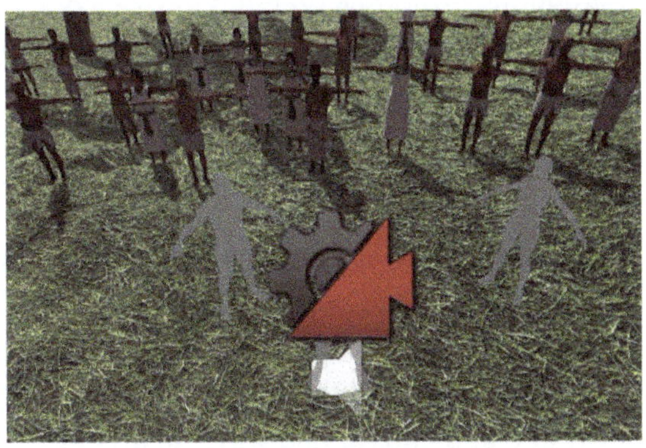

Figure 606

Add a new virtual camera named "OutroCam2". Then zoom out and set it to look at the zoomed-out Scene View similar to Figure . Don't zoom out too much or the player will see you've only got thirty people in the multitude. We want them to think that there are a lot more people behind them to give that multitude feel. Add the two virtual cameras to the cinemachine track.

Have the shots overlap so cam 1 starts transitioning to cam 2 around marker 120 and then the transition completes around marker 270. Then make cam 2 end around marker 850.

Next, drag Moses onto the animation track field where it says "None". If you right-click on the track and select "Add from Animation Clip" a search window pops up. Find "Humanoidldle" and move it so it starts at marker 0. With it selected, duplicate it with a CTRL+D. This is Moses waiting around while we zoom out the camera.

Then look for "IdleGrab_FrontHigh" and put it next. This one has multiple animations in it so we need to reduce the duration. In the inspector, after Start and End you'll see Duration. Set the left 's' part to 4.5. After that, add a final animation "WalkFWD" to Moses.

For the multitude, it wouldn't be very good to add animation tracks for each person. Instead, we're going to code a quick script that the timeline is going to signal to when it's time for them to start walking.

Create a new C# script named "StartWalk" and code it like what you see in Figure 607. We've seen the "OneEnable" method before. It gets called whenever the attached game object is activated. When that happens, all of the actors in the list will have their "MoveActor" method called.

```
public class StartWalk : MonoBehaviour
{
    public Transform WalkLoc;
    public ActorController[] ActorArray;

    Unity Message | 0 references
    private void OnEnable()
    {
        foreach(ActorController actor in ActorArray)
        {
            actor.MoveActor(WalkLoc.position, 0.5f);
        }
    }
}
```

Figure 603

In the Hierarchy View, create an empty game object under "OutroCineObjects" named "MultitudeWalk" and add the "StartWalk" script you just created. Uncheck the enabled box to the left of its name in the inspector so that it will start the game disabled. Create another empty game object that will be the location they will walk to. Put it back a good way behind the virtual cameras. Then fill the script's "Walk Loc" with it. Each actor except for Moses will need to be added to the actor array. Finally, drag the "MultitudeWalk" object over to the Activation Track on the timeline. Move the Active box on the timeline to start around marker 650 and end around marker 850, where the outro cam 2 ends.

Now add an audio Source onto the "OutroCinematic" object and populate our audio track with it. Then choose some music that will play during the cinematic. I choose "Day_Time_POST_INTRO" but feel free to listen to the selections in the Music folder and find the one you think works best. Add it onto the track so it starts at 0 and ends at 850 with the others.

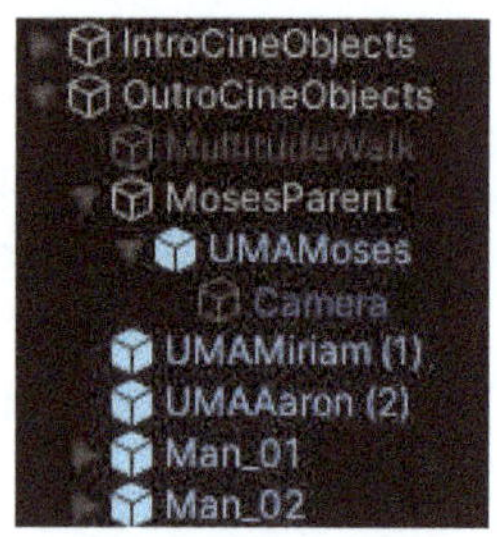

Figure 604

Because having the animation track gives the timeline full control over Moses, it will move him to another location. To get around that, simply right-click on Moses to create an empty game object. Then move them around so that Moses is the child and this empty game object is the parent like what you see in Figure 608.

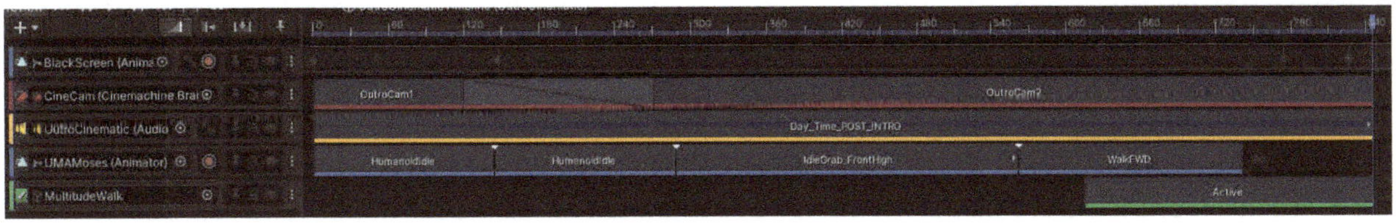

Figure 605

Finally, let's fade the black screen out so that it starts to fade out around 775 and finishes around 825. With all this you should see a timeline like Figure 609. To test the cinematic out, you can go to the "GameController" object, overwrite the "Intro Cine" with the outro cinematic timeline, clear all player preferences, and then click play. Just be sure to change it back to the intro cinematic when done.

To make the outro cinematic available to show, we're going to make some updates to the script "GameController". Add the public variables on lines 19 and 23 to insert the outro cinematic as shown in Figure 610. Remind me we need to hook these up in Unity later.

```
17        public GameObject Player;
18        public PlayableDirector IntroCine;
19        public PlayableDirector OutroCine;
20        public GameObject CineCam;
21        public GameObject BlackScreen;
22        public GameObject IntroObjects;
23        public GameObject OutroObjects;
24        public GameObject MainMenuObj;
```

Figure 606

Scrolling down to the Start() method, add the code to deactivate the outro objects on line 78 as shown in Figure 611.

```
75            //Player.SetActive(IntroCinePlayed);
76            IntroObjects.SetActive(!IntroCinePlayed);
77
78            OutroObjects.SetActive(false);
```

Figure 607

```
    public void StartOutroCine()
    {
        CineCam.SetActive(true);
        MinimapObj.SetActive(false);
        Player.SetActive(false);
        OutroObjects.SetActive(true);
        MusController.StopMusic();
        OutroCine.Play();
        InvokeRepeating("CheckOutroDone", 2, 1);
    }

    0 references
    public void CheckOutroDone()
    {
        if ((OutroCine.state != PlayState.Playing) || (Input.GetKeyUp(KeyCode.Escape)))
        {
            UnityEngine.SceneManagement.SceneManager.LoadScene(0);
        }
    }
```

Figure 608

Now scroll way down to the bottom of the class and add these two new methods "StartOutroCine" and "CheckOutroDone" shown in Figure 612. The "StartOutroCine" method does similar things as when the introduction cinematic starts. Instead of checking whether the cinematic is done in the Update() method, we create a new method and call it every second. Once the cinematic is done, we put the player back to the title scene. Of course, they have the option to skip the cut scene by pressing escape.

To start the ending cinematic, we're going to use a trigger. If you remember, a trigger is a type of collider. However, when it collides with another collider it doesn't interact with it visually. Instead, we can use it to execute code. Go ahead and add this code from Figure 613. When the player enters the trigger collider for the object we put it on, the code will find the "GameController" and call the "StartOutroCine" method.

```
public class TriggerOutro : MonoBehaviour
{
    Unity Message | 0 references
    private void OnTriggerEnter(Collider other)
    {
        if (other.transform.tag == "Player")
        {
            GameObject gc = GameObject.FindWithTag("GameController");
            gc.GetComponent<GameController>().StartOutroCine();
        }
    }
}
```

Figure 609

Before we test it out, we'll need to deactivate the "OutroCineObjects" by unchecking the box next to the name in the inspector. The Hierarchy View should show the object in dark gray like in Figure 614. If we don't, then the UMA character build process will be interrupted, and they won't show up in the game.

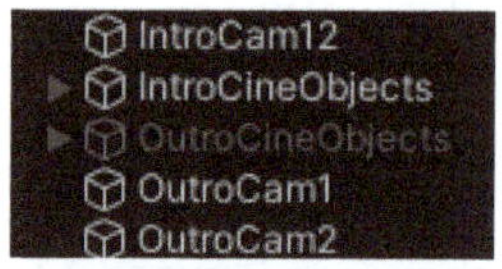

Figure 610

You can test it out by creating a cube, checking the "Is Trigger" checkbox in the Box Collider component, and add the "TriggerOutro" script. Place the cube nearby Aaron and Miriam in the Hebrew sector like in Figure 615 where it's nearby the door.

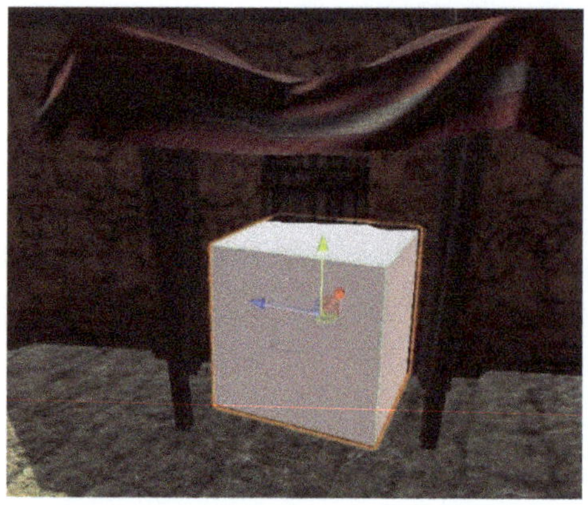

Figure 611

If you clear the player preferences, then moses will be back in the desert, and you need to go through the tutorial before you're sent into the Hebrew section. Once you touch the cube, the outro cinematic should play. Finally, it's the title scene.

Once you're there, you can exit play mode and be thrust back to the Egypt scene. Be sure to delete the cube when you're done testing as you don't want the player to accidentally find it.

We'll leave the rest of the quests as an exercise for you. You can follow the GDD in Appendix B or make your own design! Once you get the quests done, you can put that trigger script on a cube, make the cube's collider a trigger, and tell the player to go to where you place that cube to start the outro cinematic.

Chapter 20 – Deploying your Game

When you feel like your game is ready, you may want other people to play it. Friends and family are good for starters, but like an artist who paints a portrait, you'll want the community to play your game as well. Brightening their day with a little entertainment is very satisfying.

Taking all the game files, putting them together, and placing them somewhere that other people can access them is called deployment. Similar to other software, making games follows a typical "Product Lifecycle". I've alluded to several of these steps, but I'll list them out now.

Product Lifecycle:

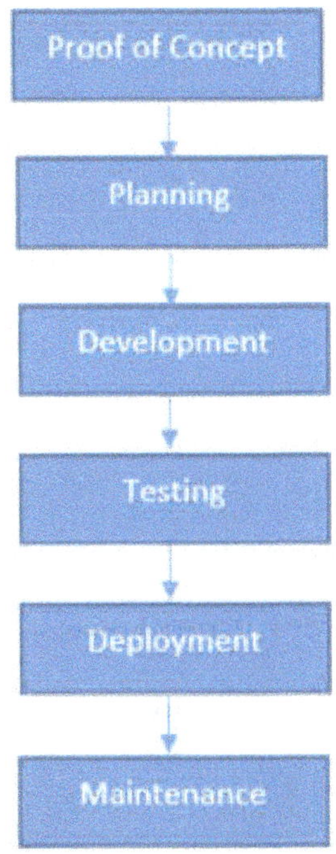

1. **Proof of Concept**: A simple demo that proves the technology works and the idea is sound. For a game, if it requires multiplayer, then the proof of concept is coded for the players to connect. It also shows that the game can be fun. For software, this would show it is useful.
2. **Planning**: What is it going to take to develop this game? Here is where the GDD is developed. Try and think of all the art assets, components, and other necessary things here. Try to guess how long it's going to take given who will work on the project. If it's just you, then that makes it easier.
3. **Development**: This is where you create the art, write the code, and put everything together. It can be helpful to go back and revise the GDD if you make changes. Don't be afraid to make important changes. But remember about feature creep. It's a fine line to walk.
4. **Testing**: Leverage your friends and family to play through the game so you can fix bugs and change the game to make it more fun.
5. **Deployment**: Package your game up and figure out where and how to release your game. Deployment, of course, is the main focus of this chapter.
6. **Maintenance**: Haha! You thought you were done when you released your game? Turns out that when the community starts playing your game, they'll find more bugs. AND THEY WILL FIND MORE BUGS! This happens with every software product. I'm sure you're thinking of a game or piece of software right now where people who played or used it found some major bug.

We've talked about platforms before (i.e., PC, Android, Xbox, etc...) and they should be kept in mind all throughout the product life cycle. The proof of concept may not be done on the target platform, most likely will be done on PC, but there will be a firm grasp on how the game would work on the target platform.

Different platforms have their own deployment methods. For example, to deploy a game or app on Android devices you would use the Play Store. You need to create an account, upload your game, and provide some information as well as some other steps to make your game available.

BibleByte Games Community

So now you're ready to deploy your game! But where can you put it so that other people will know to get it? The great people at BibleByte Games are proud to offer a special hosting service for people who purchased this tutorial and want others to play what they created. Hint: "they" means you.

Here's a high-level view how it works.

1. Choose a mission from the GDD
2. Use the assets provided in this tutorial to build a scene in Unity.
3. Export the Scene as a package
4. Upload the package file the BibleByte Games community
5. Now, anyone can download your scene and play it in Unity

Follow these steps to Export the scene as a package:

1. Right-click your scene file in Unity and select "Export Package..."

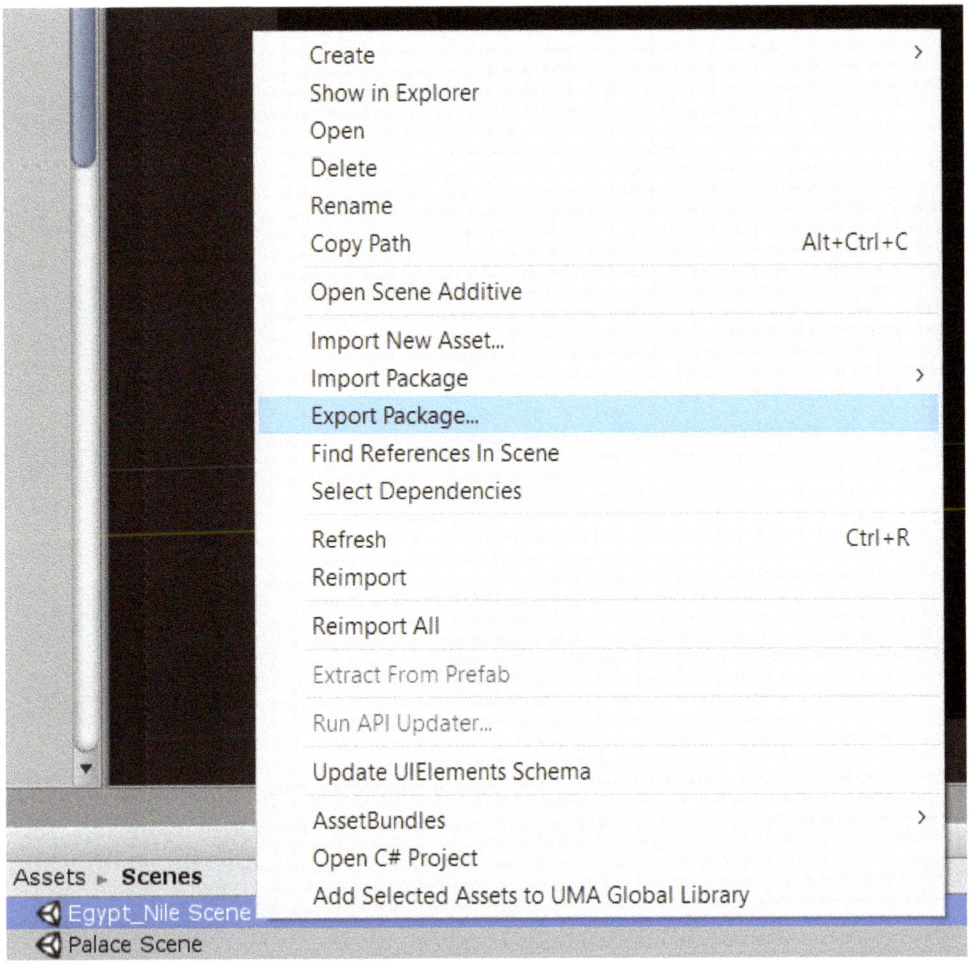

2. When the pop-up appears, check and make sure the files you are exporting are what you intend. Then click the "Export..." button.

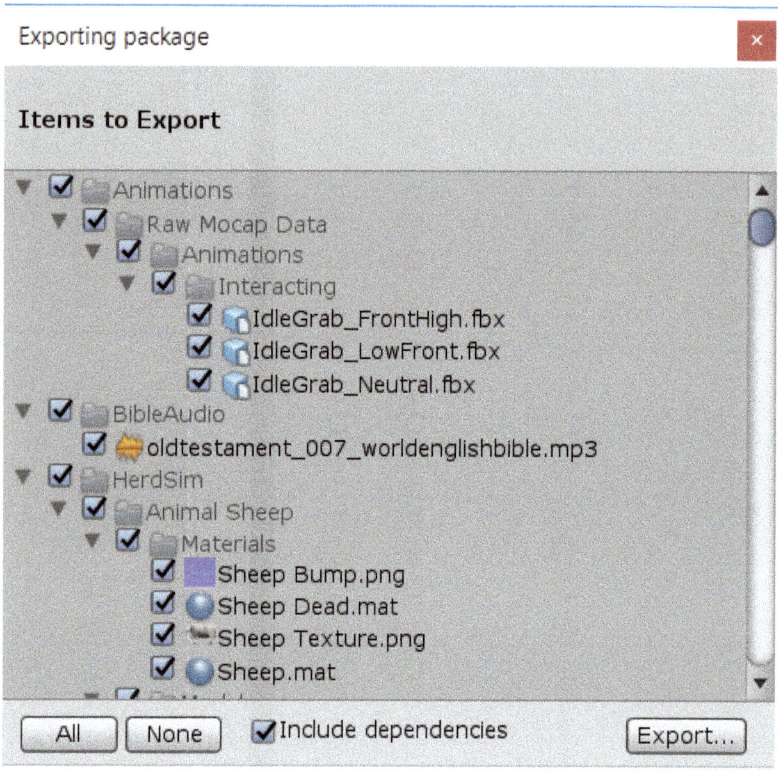

3. Another popup to select the name of the package appears. Choose a descriptive name and click the "Save" button.

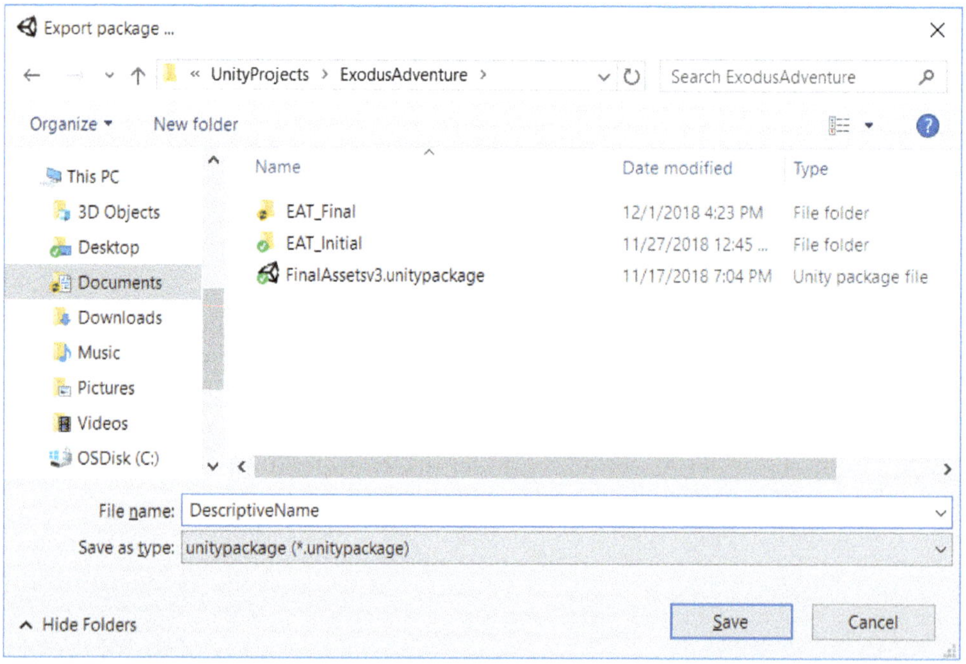

4. When the export completes an explorer window will open to the location

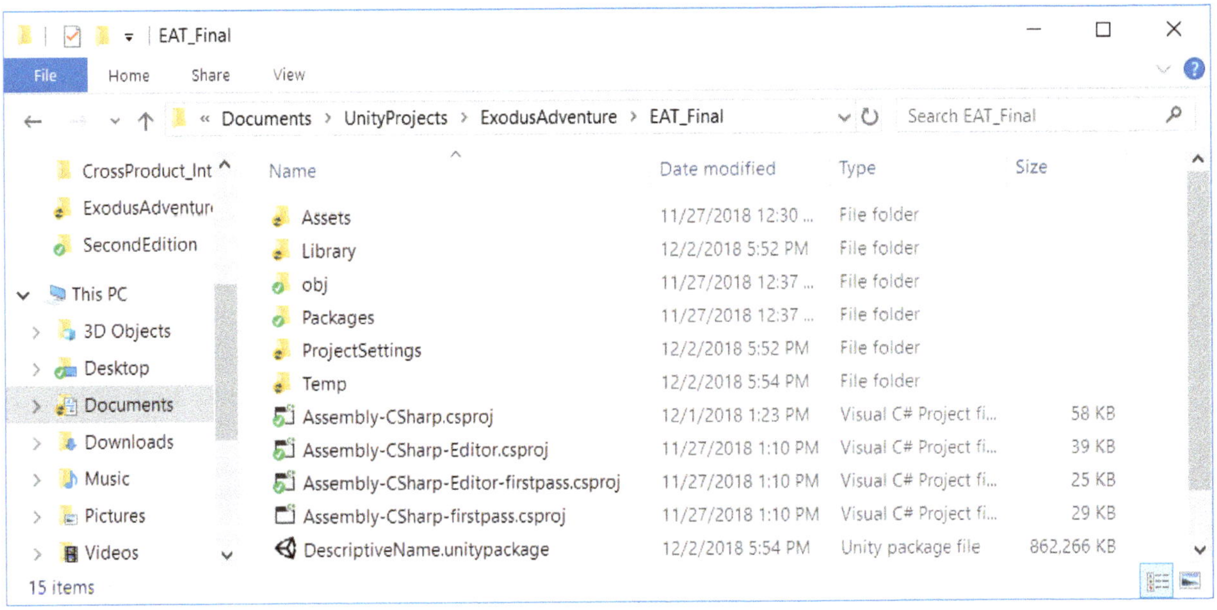

Follow these steps to upload the package file:

1. Send an email to philip@biblebytebooks.com
   a. Subject: Exodus Tutorial Scene Submission
   b. Message: Polite message saying you want to submit a scene
   c. **DO NOT ATTACH YOUR SCENE PACKAGE FILE TO THE EMAIL!**

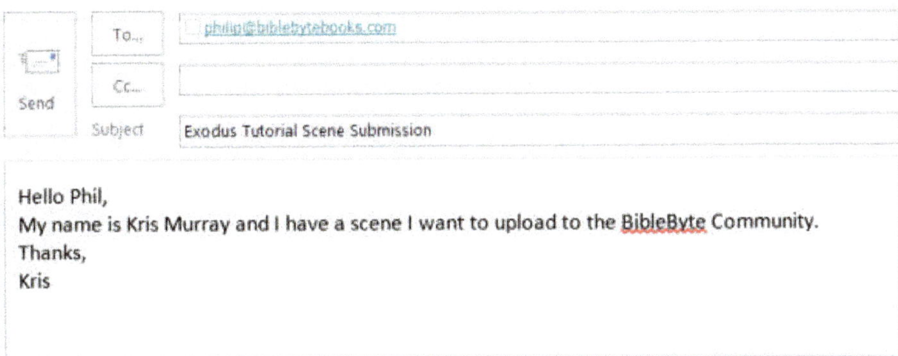

2. Wait for a reply email with a Dropbox Account Link or unique FTP UserID/Password and instructions like the one below.

From: Philip Conrod
Sent: Thursday, December 13, 2018 8:00 PM
To: Murray, Kris R
Subject: Re: Exodus Tutorial Scene Submission

Hi Kris,

Thank you so much for your email. We are very excited that you want to help us expand the Exodus Adventure Game. Please upload your new .unitypackage file to this location on DropBox for review:

Your Link Here!

We will be back in contact with you shortly.

Best Regards,
Philip Conrod
President & Publisher
BibleByte Books & Games
https://www.biblebytebooks.com

3. Upload your Scene Package File according to the instructions given.

Appendix A – Troubleshooting

If you've come to this section, then that means things didn't go smoothly loading the assets. Don't worry! Things go wrong in projects all the time. What matters is that you persevere until you figure out how to resolve the problem. If your purchased textbook did not come with the C# source code and all the Unity 3D multimedia files you can register your original textbook purchase at the following website address https://www.biblebytebooks.com/u3d-exodus/ to download all the files you will need to complete this tutorial.

Go through the table below until you find the problem that you see. Then follow the steps for the solution.

Problem	**Solution**
In Chapter 1, the objects keep falling and don't stop.	Check to make sure that the plane 3D object is created and is underneath the objects
In Chapter 3, if the "Egypt_Nile Scene" doesn't load when you double-click on it.	Make sure you are double-clicking the Unity Scene and NOT the folder.
In Chapter 3, if you can't move Moses when pressing keys.	Make sure you have both the "Third Person Character" and "Third Person User Control" scripts. These are different existing scripts that both need to be on the Model Civilian.
New Scripts don't see MonoBehavior.	1) Open a standard assets script like "ThirdPersonUserControl.cs" 2) Right-click on the "Scripts" folder on the root directory of "Assembly-CSharp-firstpass" and select Add > Add Files from Folder 3) Select the Scripts folder 4) Check all new scripts that you want to add and click OK
Visual Studio doesn't highlight keywords like the pictures and doesn't underline errors in red.	There was a problem creating the Visual Studio Project or Visual Studio wasn't set properly when Unity was automatically configured. 1) In the Main Menu Select Edit > Preferences 2) In the window that pops up, select "External Tools" on the left pane 3) In the right pane, make sure the External Script Editor is set to "Microsoft Visual Studio 2022". There will also be a version number in brackets. 4) Click the button "Regenerate project files" 5) Close the Visual Studio Window and re-open your script by double-clicking on it in the Unity Project View
An actor the player clicks on doesn't have the dialogue pop-up.	This is likely because the actor is placed too close to a zone boundary. The zone collider will intercept the raycast sent by the mouse-click. Try moving the actor away from the zone boundary and retrying.
When the player clicks a button or other UI object and nothing happens.	This could happen for a couple reasons. 1) Check and make sure an "EventSystem" object is present in the Hierarchy View.

	2) There may be other UI objects blocking it (like the screen) so you can try reordering the objects under the Canvas in the Hierarchy View. 3) If you changed the method to handle the UI event (i.e. the name or the parameters) then it breaks the connection to the UI object. You need to go back into the inspector for that object and set the method again.
I get runtime errors when trying to call a method on the game controller when I find it using "FindObjectWithTag" in certain scenes.	This is usually caused by forgetting to set the game controller object to use the "GameController" tag in that particular scene. To resolve this issue, just go to the scene with the problem and set the tag appropriately. This can also happen to other objects that you rely on finding using a tag.
I don't like the current shader for highlighting actors.	Another shader you can try is: "Legacy Shaders/Self-Illumin/Bumped Specular".
When I build the standalone version of the game and play it the highlight for the actors is pink or some other solid color.	Unity tries to save space by not including assets into the build that aren't used. Since the shader we're using for highlights isn't in a Unity scene it won't be included in the standalone build. To resolve this: 1. Create a material in the Project View and set the shader to the one you're using for the actor highlights. 2. Create a 3D object in one of the scenes (like the Title scene) and place it so the player won't see it. 3. Apply the material to the object 4. Rebuild the standalone game and the highlight will now happen as in Unity.
From the Console: NullReferenceException: Object reference not set to an instance of an object ZoneText.SetAlpha (Single alpha) (at Assets/Scripts/ZoneText.cs:68) ZoneText.Start () (at Assets/Scripts/ZoneText.cs:24)	There could be 2 issues here: 1. Ensure the Shadow field in the inspector has an object 2. Make sure no other objects (like the GameController) have the ZoneText script.

Bug	Root Cause & Resolution
When I inactivate the player in a cut scene then nothing shows up on the camera.	This happens because our camera is inside the player prefab. Since the player is set to inactive the camera is inactivated with it. To fix that, when you instantiate the player, change the parent of the main camera to null. Changes are required in GameController.cs.
When I inactivate the player in a cut scene I get an error in the cut scene controller.	Because the cut scene controller will set the player's movement to zero when a cut scene is going on, if the player is set to inactive then this will cause runtime errors. To fix this you can check if the player is active before setting the movement. Changes are required in CutSceneController.cs.
Quests that have more than a single required count will be completed when the first time the quest completion is issued.	This is because the quests were implemented to only be completed or not completed, even though we had a "numReq" variable. To resolve this, the quest needs to get a new variable to store how much progress the player has made. The quest engine must then increment this current count on every "complete" and then if it equals the required the quest becomes completed. Additionally, the player data must be updated so that it saves quest progress instead of quest completion since quest completion can be derived from the progress. Changes are required in Quest.cs, QuestEngine.cs, and PlayerData.cs.
When updating player data so that actors are inactive, disabled, or get out of those states the actual actor doesn't change state when the dialogue ends.	In the actor controller, when the actor is first created it will check the status in the "Start" method, but that is it. When the cut scene ends the status should also be checked and updated. Changes are required in ActorController.cs.
Items in the middle of the inventory are not removed.	In the current implementation, the item is searched for using "GetItem" and then the item itself is removed. However, the removal function doesn't find the item. In order to resolve this, you need to loop through each item in the inventory, check if the item's name matches, then remove it while updating the Player Data and then break out of the loop. Changes are required in ItemEngine.cs.
Animations stop short in dialogue and cut scenes.	This is because the trigger in the animator for "StopAnim" is getting set at the end of each cut scene. So whenever the player or an actor tries to do an animation it will start doing it, but then the animator processes the "StopAnim" and stops animation short. To resolve this, we need to conditionally send the stop animation trigger only if another animation is happening. Changes are required in ActorController.cs and in the animator for the third person controller. 1. Add the "Grounded" tag to the Grounded state in the animator. 2. In the actor controller's "SetAnimation" method, don't set the trigger for "StopAnim" if no animations are playing.

	3. To preserve animations for actors created to start an animation in a cut scene, you'll also need to check if the "m_Animator" is null and get a handle to it if it is. Code to see if no animations are playing: m_Animator.GetCurrentAnimatorStateInfo(0).IsTag("Grounded") This code goes into the animator and checks the tag of the current state. In step 1 we set the Grounded state to Grounded. So if the actor is "Grounded" they are not playing an animation.
After initiating a dialogue using an item, it requires 2 presses of the 'I' key to open the inventory.	This is because the current implementation of starting a cut scene only sends the inventory window the message to hide itself. The UI state in the game controller isn't changed. So the first time the player presses the 'I' key the game controller thinks the inventory is already being shown and needs to be hidden. To resolve this, instead of hiding the inventory window directly, make a call to the game controller's "InventoryHandler" method. This will ensure the UI state gets updated.

Appendix B – Game Design Document

This appendix is for the Game Design Document (GDD) of the Exodus Adventure Tutorial.

Overview

The Exodus Adventure is a 3D 3rd person puzzle adventure game. The player controls Moses and follows the exciting story of God saving His people from slavery in Egypt. The player will travel the land, talk with its inhabitants, collect items, complete quests, and solve a variety of puzzles.

Cut scenes and cinematics will immerse the player in Ancient Egypt and the story. Changing music tracks to match each area's feeling will keep help too. Rewarding the player with cut scenes, story progression, and mini-games will hook them to keep playing.

Target Market

The Exodus Adventure is targeted to Christian teenagers and college students. They will appreciate being able to walk around and experience the familiar Exodus story while learning about ancient Hebrew and Egyptian culture.

The genre of the Exodus Adventure is Puzzle Adventure games. Players of this genre expect puzzles of increasing difficulty that are fun and not tedious. Hints must be available for when they feel stuck so they don't get too frustrated.

Target Platform

The Exodus Adventure will run on PC and Mac computers. Players on this platform expect high quality graphics.

3rd Party Packages

Name	Description
Standard Assets	Free to use assets made by Unity
EgyptCharacters	10x Egyptian themed 3D Character Models by Virtualware
EgyptPack	Egyptian Themed Terrain, Exterior Building Interior buildings, Walls, Temple, Pyramid, Sphinx and many other things by Vlado žabiačan
Extreme Fantasy Music Pack	Day and Night Themed music by Vertigo Games
Extreme Combat Music Pack	Combat themed music by Vertigo Games
Flying Birds	3D birds animated to fly by Virtualware
Raw MoCap Data	https://www.assetstore.unity3d.com/en/#!/content/5330
Rustic Pack	Various rustic themed pieces of furniture and objects by Virtualware
Extreme Adventure characters pack	Using Model Civilian as Moses by Vertigo Games
3rd Person Controller by Vinicius Marques	https://www.assetstore.unity3d.com/en/#!/content/28647
Universal Footstep Sounds by Andrzej Dobrowolski	https://www.assetstore.unity3d.com/en/#!/content/22968

Metal Texture by CrazyTextures	https://www.assetstore.unity3d.com/en/#!/content/23812
Weapons by DSJ	https://www.assetstore.unity3d.com/en/#!/content/46190
Net Materials by Nobiax / Yughues	https://www.assetstore.unity3d.com/en/#!/content/13004
Icons by Alex Ravlik	https://www.assetstore.unity3d.com/en/#!/content/22968
Pharaoh's Throne by 3D Dev	https://www.assetstore.unity3d.com/en/#!/content/17242
Snake by All-Animations	https://www.assetstore.unity3d.com/en/#!/content/19946
Sickle by GamePoly	https://www.assetstore.unity3d.com/en/#!/content/35423
Frog by Junnichi Suko	https://www.assetstore.unity3d.com/en/#!/content/37777
Carpentry Tools by FunFant	https://www.assetstore.unity3d.com/en/#!/content/42010
Fruit & Vegetables by Adventure Forge	https://www.assetstore.unity3d.com/en/#!/content/49035
Sheers by 3D_Mark	https://www.assetstore.unity3d.com/en/#!/content/67789
Pickaxe by GamePoly	https://www.assetstore.unity3d.com/en/#!/content/24367
Herdsim by Unluck Software	https://www.assetstore.unity3d.com/en/#!/content/27134 Chicken, Cow, Pig, Rat, Sheep
Hebrew Icons	3 images for Hyssop and Unleavened Bread

Game Pillars

The Game Pillars are the main high-level points the game tries to be about. These are important to decide what features to include. Many features can be fun but if they don't uphold the game pillars then the features may give the most bang for your buck. Here are the pillars:

- Bible-based: This game is based on the Exodus story in the Bible with the purpose of honoring God, upholding Biblical values, and teaching about the Bible.
- Story-driven: The story of the Exodus and telling how God saves his people.
- Fun and Challenging: Challenge the player with puzzles that are fun to solve.

Gameplay

The primary game mechanic is interacting with the various actors. Clicking on an actor will trigger a dialogue with a list of choices for the player to make. Selecting a choice may have one or more consequences including the following: add an item to the inventory, remove an item from the inventory, trigger a cut-scene, enable a Game Object in the scene, or disable a Game Object in the scene. Each choice can have conditions to appear in the dialogue if these are met: inventory contains one or more specified items, one or more specified items are absent from the inventory, the player has completed one or more specific quests, the player has not completed one or more specific quests.

The reward for interacting with the actors includes the following: progression of the story, viewing cut-scenes, completing quests, and gaining items. When players interact with actors the camera will move to focus on Moses and the actor he is interacting with. After the interaction is complete the camera moves back to the location before the interaction occurred.

Actors

The game has 2 different kinds of actors for the player to interact with: 1) Character Actors who look and move like people and 2) Object actors that are inanimate. Moses will be both a Character Actor and controlled by the player. The Moses who the player controls will be referred to as the Player Character or PC. Actors will be controlled by a common animator and a script that dictates what the default animations are for the actor.

When the player clicks on the actor or uses an item on the actor then the actor may trigger a dialogue. These dialogues will show the player text of what is going on or what the actor is trying to say. The dialogue engine will have the option to pre-program responses the player can make, either button selections, text input, or simple acknowledgement to continue.

Character Actors:

Actor	Description
Angel of Death	3rdPersonController\Models\MaleBaseMesh
Moses	Extreme Adventure character pack\Characters\Model_Civilian
Pharaoh by Virtualware	Man with Pharaoh headdress, one armband, and embroidered loin cloth EgyptCharacters\Prefabs\Pharaoh
Guard	Light skinned man with Anubis head, armbands, and reed-reinforced loin cloth EgyptCharacters\Prefabs\Embalmer
Aaron	Light skinned man with larger lips and white loin cloth EgyptCharacters\Prefabs\Man_01
Miriam	Medium skinned woman with chin-length hair, royal tiara, wristbands, v-neck sleeveless dress, and a green belt EgyptCharacters\Prefabs\Woman_02
Hebrew Slave	Dark skinned man with small stubble for hair and green loin cloth EgyptCharacters\Prefabs\Man_04
Hebrew Woman	Light skinned woman with shoulder-length black hair, royal tiara, armbands, wristbands, neck garment, and long white sleeveless dress EgyptCharacters\Prefabs\Woman_01
Hebrew Elder	Light skinned man with low eye-brows and white loin cloth EgyptCharacters\Prefabs\Man_02
Hebrew Foreman	Medium skinned man with small lips and white loin cloth EgyptCharacters\Prefabs\Man_03
Hebrew Shepherd	Medium skinned man with small lips and white loin cloth EgyptCharacters\Prefabs\Man_03
Pharaoh's Investigator	Light skinned woman with hair between chin and shoulder, neck garment, armbands, white sleeveless dress, and a green belt EgyptCharacters\prefabs\Woman_03
Grain Merchant	Medium skinned man with round hat, wristbands, animal skin sash, and white long skirt EgyptCharacters\Prefabs\Sem
Tools Merchant	Light skinned man with larger lips and white loin cloth EgyptCharacters\Prefabs\Man_01
Metal Refiner	Medium skinned man with small lips and white loin cloth EgyptCharacters\Prefabs\Man_03
Miner Merchant	Medium skinned man with small lips and white loin cloth

	EgyptCharacters\Prefabs\Man_03
Lumber Merchant	Dark skinned man with small stubble for hair and green loin cloth EgyptCharacters\Prefabs\Man_04
Egyptian Fisherman	Dark skinned man with small stubble for hair and green loin cloth EgyptCharacters\Prefabs\Man_04
Egyptian Farmer	Light skinned man with low eye-brows and white loin cloth EgyptCharacters\Prefabs\Man_02
Egyptian Doctor	Medium skinned woman with chin-length hair, royal tiara, wristbands, v-neck sleeveless dress, and a green belt EgyptCharacters\Prefabs\Woman_02
Egyptian Carpenter	Medium skinned man with small lips and white loin cloth EgyptCharacters\Prefabs\Man_03
Egyptian Shipwright	Light skinned woman with shoulder-length black hair, royal tiara, armbands, wristbands, neck garment, and long white sleeveless dress EgyptCharacters\Prefabs\Woman_01
Egyptian Woman	Light skinned woman with hair between chin and shoulder, neck garment, armbands, white sleeveless dress, and a green belt EgyptCharacters\prefabs\Woman_03
Egyptian Overseer	Light skinned woman with shoulder-length black hair, royal tiara, armbands, wristbands, neck garment, and long white sleeveless dress EgyptCharacters\Prefabs\Woman_01
Egyptian Slave	Light skinned man with larger lips and white loin cloth EgyptCharacters\Prefabs\Man_01
Magician	Medium skinned man with round hat, wristbands, animal skin sash, and white long skirt EgyptCharacters\Prefabs\Sem

Object Actors:

Actor	Description
Furnace	Create 3D Object in Unity using the below assets \Ancient Egypt\Models\Textures\TileTex_1 \Ancient Egypt\Models\House_Prefabs\FireBowl
Furnace Door by Hviluvator	Create and shape a cube and apply metal texture https://www.assetstore.unity3d.com/en/#!/content/64240
Lever by Hviluvator	Create and shape a cube and apply metal texture https://www.assetstore.unity3d.com/en/#!/content/64240
Big Rock	Ancient Egypt\Models\Rock_Prefabs\
Fishing Spot	Use in-game strobe-lighting
Leftover Farmland	Highlight a section of the terrain
Egyptian River Boat	Ancient Egypt\Models\House Parts\Additional Addons\Ship_1
Staff	Create and shape a cylinder and apply a wood texture Assets\Models\Rustic_Pack\Materials\Wood
Sheep by Unluck Software	https://www.assetstore.unity3d.com/en/#!/content/27134
Dead Sheep by Unluck Software	https://www.assetstore.unity3d.com/en/#!/content/27134

Frog By JUNNICHI SUKO	https://www.assetstore.unity3d.com/en/#!/content/37777
Snake By All-Animations	https://www.assetstore.unity3d.com/en/#!/content/19946
Swarm of Flies	Create using Particle Effects
Swarm of Gnats	Create using Particle Effects
Swarm of Locusts	Create using Particle Effects

Cinematics and Cut Scenes

These in-game movies will be handled by Unity's Timeline and Director components for sequencing. Two cinematics will bookend this game, one at the beginning and one at the end. The beginning cinematic will catch the player up with Moses' life in Egypt, murdering an Egyptian, exile from Egypt, Life as a shepherd, and the encounter with God in the burning bush. The ending cinematic shows the excited Israelites leaving the land of Egypt with herds and flocks, collecting treasure from the Egyptians, and other Egyptians coming along with them.

Opening Cinematic:

1. Camera fades in. Moses stands on a Hill. Camera pans up from his feet to his knees
2. Moses standing over a dead Egyptian
3. Moses on a Hill scrolling up from his knees to his waist
4. Moses running away from the City
5. Moses on a Hill scrolling up from his waist to his chest
6. Moses standing in front of a burning bush
7. Moses on a Hill scrolling up from his chest to his head
8. Camera pans around Moses to show the city below him
9. Fade out camera.

Ending Cinematic:

1. Fade in from black to a close-up of Moses' face
2. Zoom out to show him standing in front of the Hebrews on the side of the Nile
3. Moses is circled up with Aaron and Miriam
4. Moses raises his staff and starts walking
5. Everyone else starts walking too
6. Fade out to black and roll credits

Table of Cut Scenes:

Name	**Description**
Snake Staff	Based on verses Ex 7:6-13. Pharaoh says "Perform a miracle". Aaron steps forward and throws down his staff. In a brilliant light the staff transforms to a snake. Pharaoh's chief magician throws down his staff and in a puff of smoke it becomes a snake. The two other magicians throw down their staves

	and in puffs of smoke they become snakes. Pharaoh tells Moses he will not let the Hebrews go. Then the magicians shout that Aaron's snake has swallowed theirs. Only show Aaron's snake left.
Water to Blood	Based on verses Ex 7:20-24. Moses and Aaron walk from Pharaoh to the water's edge. Aaron raises the staff and strikes the water with the bottom end. The Nile river changed to blood. Pharaoh commands his magician to reproduce the miracle. The magician steps forward with a bowl of water and after a short while the water turns red. Pharaoh says he won't let the Hebrews go. Then Pharaoh walks, with his entourage back toward the palace.
Frog Army	Based on verses Ex 8:5-7. Aaron stretches his staff up. Frogs appear in the Nile and start marching up onto the land. Pharaoh commands his magician to reproduce the miracle. The magician steps forward and does some incantations and from the other side another smaller army of frogs appears. Pharaoh refuses to let the Hebrews go.
Generating Gnats	Based on verses Ex 8:17-19. Aaron raises his staff up and strikes the ground with it. The ground quakes for a second and the dust rises waist level from the ground. Then clouds of gnats engulf everyone. Pharaoh commands his magicians to reproduce the miracle. The magicians try their incantations but no additional gnats were created. One tells Pharaoh that this is the finger of god. But Pharaoh still refuses to let the Hebrews go.
Boiling Soot	Based on verses Ex 9:10-12. Moses steps forward toward Pharaoh and tosses the handful of soot into the air. The wind takes it up and it quickly spreads to every Egyptian and animal. The magicians are unable to stand. But Pharaoh still refuses to let the Hebrews go.
Incoming Locusts	Based on verses Ex 10:13-15. Moses raises his staff and wind blows from the East bringing a large cloud of Locusts. The Locusts descend onto the city.

Inventory

The game has a list of items the player can collect and use while interacting with NPCs. While not in a dialogue with an NPC or in a cut-scene/cinematic the player can view the items in their inventory and see descriptions of the items with hints about what the item is used for. Items will have a 2D image to show in the player inventory and may have a 3D Game Object to represent it in the game world. Icons will be 256x256 2D graphics.

The inventory is viewable by the player and items will be shown in a grid. The player will be able to scroll down through all the items they have. To use an item on an actor the player will press the mouse button on the item image, which will follow the mouse. Then they will drag it to the desired actor and un-press the mouse button. After the un-press the icon will go back to the inventory slot it was moved from.

Players will be able to sort their inventory manually. There will also be a sort button that will sort the items alphabetically.

Item List:

Name	Icon
Staff	Images\Icons\Staff
Cloak	Images\Icons\RPG_inventory_icons\cloaks
Jacob's Bones	Images\Icons\Box
Straw Bale	Images\Icons\Straw
Empty Jar	Images\Icons\Jar
Jar of Nile Water	Images\Icons\Jar
Outer Palace Seal	Images\Icons\Seal1
Inner Palace Seal	Images\Icons\Seal2
Audience Chamber Seal	Images\Icons\Seal3
Straw Swatter	Images\Icons\StrawSwatter
Sheers	Images\Icons\Sickle
Wool: Dead Sheep	Images\Icons\Wool
Wool: Israelite Sheep	Images\Icons\Wool
Wool: Egyptian Sheep	Images\Icons\Wool
Mud-Bricks	Images\Icons\Mud-Brick
Raw Lumber	Images\Icons\Lumber
Crate of Bronze Ore	Images\Icons\Box
Crate of Bronze Ingots	Images\Icons\Box
Crate of Hand Ploughs	Images\Icons\Box
Sacks of Grain	Images\Icons\Basket
Perfect Lamb	Images\Icons\Sheep
Roasted Lamb	Images\Icons\RPG_inventory_icons\Meat
Lamb's Blood	Images\Icons\BowlOfBlood
Horseradish	Images\Icons\Jar
Sack of Grain	Images\Icons\Basket
Unleavened Bread	Images\Icons\UnleavenedBread
Hyssop	Images\Icons\Hyssop2
Box of Sapphires	Images\Icons\Box
Box of Rubies	Images\Icons\Box
Box of Jasper Stones	Images\Icons\Box
Box of Topaz Gems	Images\Icons\Box
Box of Emeralds	Images\Icons\Box
Box of Malachite Jewels	Images\Icons\Box
Box of Diamonds	Images\Icons\Box
Box of Amber Jewels	Images\Icons\Box
Box of Agate Jewels	Images\Icons\Box
Box of Amethysts	Images\Icons\Box
Box of Lapis Lazuli Gems	Images\Icons\Box
Box of Beryl Gems	Images\Icons\Box
Rock #1	Images\Icons\Rock

Rock #2	Images\Icons\Rock
Rock #3	Images\Icons\Rock
Rock #4	Images\Icons\Rock
Rock #5	Images\Icons\Rock
Rock #6	Images\Icons\Rock
Rock #7	Images\Icons\Rock
Rock #8	Images\Icons\Rock
Rock #9	Images\Icons\Rock
Rock #10	Images\Icons\Rock
Rock #11	Images\Icons\Rock
Rock #12	Images\Icons\Rock
Rock #13	Images\Icons\Rock
Fishing Net	Images\Icons\Net
Basket of Fish	Images\Icons\Basket
Hand Plough	Images\Icons\Plough
Barley Seeds	Images\Icons\Basket
Sickle	Images\Icons\Sickle
Sack of Barley	Images\Icons\Basket
Onion	Images\Icons\Basket
Fig	Images\Icons\Basket
Natron	Images\Icons\Basket
Setseft Seeds	Images\Icons\Basket
Turnip	Images\Icons\Basket
Beet	Images\Icons\Basket
Garlic	Images\Icons\Basket
Jar of Honey	Images\Icons\Jar
Abra Ointment	Images\Icons\Jar
Refined Lumber	Images\Icons\Lumber
Saw	Screenshot Saw Carpentry tool https://www.assetstore.unity3d.com/en/#!/content/42010
Cut Lumber	Images\Icons\Lumber
Chisel	Screenshot Chisel Carpentry tool https://www.assetstore.unity3d.com/en/#!/content/42010
Worked Lumber	Images\Icons\Lumber
Slicer	Screenshot Slicer Carpentry tool https://www.assetstore.unity3d.com/en/#!/content/42010
Wooden Table	Images\Icons\WoodenTable
Drill	Screenshot Drill Carpentry tool https://www.assetstore.unity3d.com/en/#!/content/42010
Finished Wood Table	Images\Icons\WoodenTable
Fresh Baked Bread	Images\Icons\UnleavenedBread
Dirt	Images\Icons\Dirt
Mud Mixture	Images\Icons\Dirt
Brick Mixture	Images\Icons\Dirt
Molded Mud-Brick	Images\Icons\Mud-Brick
Finished Mud-Brick	Images\Icons\Mud-Brick

Map

The player can display a map labeled with all the different locations in the game. There is also a mini-map on the screen that is labeled. The purpose for the two different maps is that the player can get a sense of directions of places far away on the big map and a sense of directions of nearby places on the mini-map.

There are two kinds of locations, outdoor and indoor. Outdoor locations use the main outdoor map, while indoor locations use their own separate maps. These areas will be called zones.

When the player enters an outdoor zone, text will show up on the screen so they know it.

Indoor Locations will have transition points that go between that area and the point on the outdoor location.

Outdoor Locations:

- Wilderness: Ex 4: 27-28
- Sphinx: Ex 9:34
- Slave camp: Ex 3:7
- Nile River: Ex 2:5-6
- Market: Ex 5:4
- Island Temple: Ex 7:6
- City Walls: Ex 2:11-12
- Main City Gate: Ex 1:8
- Nile Farmland: Ex 10:13
- Grazing Grounds: Ex 9:7
- Pharaoh's Palace: Ex 5:2
- Pyramid: Ex 8:15

Indoor Locations:

- Pharaoh's Palace
- Pyramid

Menus and Options

The Main Menu will have 4 buttons: New Game, Continue, Options, and Exit. New Game will clear any saved data and start a new game. Continue will Load the saved data and continue from there. In the options menu the player can adjust volume and toggle mute. The player will be able to go back to the Main Menu from in-game.

The player state will be saved automatically whenever it changes. This eliminates the need for a special save feature. Be sure to notify the player that the game is saved automatically for their peace of mind.

Player State Variables

Name	Description
Location	Current location of the player on the map
Map	Name of the map the player is on
Inventory	What items the player has
Quest Progress	Current progress the player has made for each and every quest
Sky Exposure	Day and night cycle on the skybox

Quest Journal

A quest is not only a goal for the player to achieve but a hint for what to do next so the player never gets stuck. Quests are kept in the player's journal and are separated into books and chapters. The reward for completing quests includes: items, unlocking the next quest in the chapter, and unlocking one or more chapters. The reward for completing a chapter includes: items and unlocking one or more chapters.

In order for the player to see the chapter a quest in it must be active in the Quest Journal. There may be multiple quests from different chapters active at the same time. Each chapter may only have one quest active at a time. Completed quests in the chapter will be displayed in the journal as checked off the list. Uncompleted quests that are not active in that chapter will be greyed out. Some quests will have pre-requisites, meaning that in order to make them ready for completion the player must complete another quest. In this case the pre-requisite will be bolded and colored red so the player knows they need to meet the pre-requisite. When the pre-requisite has been met then the pre-requisite text will not be displayed. Visible chapters may be expanded or collapsed by the player. Chapters with all quests completed will show as 100% completed.

The quest journal will display the following information about each quest: quest name, description, associated actors, and associated location.

Quests

There are three books of quest chapters: Exodus, Egyptian Culture, and Hebrew Culture. The Exodus book will follow the narrative in the Bible from Exodus 4:27 to 12:39 and then pull in 13:19 for Jacob's bones. The Egyptian and Hebrew Culture books will let the player experience what life was like.

Exodus Book, Chapters and Quests:

1. Meeting of Moses and Aaron [Ex 4:27-31]
   1.1. Traverse the Desert

   Actors: Big Rock

   Location: Wilderness

   Items: None

   Description: Move to the rock in the middle of the desert.

Details: Teach the player the controls, how to move and use the map and mini-map to get to a desired location.

1.2. Meeting in the Desert [Ex 4:27-28]

Actors: Moses, Aaron

Location: Wilderness

Items: None

Description: Find and meet your brother Aaron in the wilderness.

Details: Teach the player the controls, how to move and use the map and mini-map to get to a desired location.

1.3. Signs for the Israelites 1 of 3 [Ex 4:29-31]

Actors: Moses, Hebrew Elder

Location: Hebrew Slave Camp

Items: Staff

Description: Perform miracle of the staff to the Hebrew elder.

Details: Use the map to find and go to the tent of meeting. Use the staff and transform it into a snake.

1.4. Signs for the Israelites 2 of 3 [Ex 4:29-31]

Actors: Moses, Hebrew Elder

Location: Hebrew Slave Camp

Items: Cloak

Description: Perform the miracle of the leprous hand to the Hebrew elder.

Details: Use the Cloak to make your hand leprous and then normal again.

1.5. Signs for the Israelites 3 of 3 [Ex 4:29-31]

Actors: Moses, Hebrew Elder

Location: Hebrew Slave Camp

Items: Jar of Water

Description: Perform the miracle of turning water to blood for the Hebrew elder.

Details: Get the jar of water from outside the tent. Pour the water on the ground before the Hebrew Elder.

2. Bricks but no straw [Ex 5]
    2.1. Audience before Pharaoh [Ex 5:1-14]

        Actors: Moses, Aaron, Pharaoh, Pharaoh's guards

        Location: Pharaoh's Palace

        Items: Outer Palace Seal, Inner Palace Seal, Audience Chamber Seal

        Description: Go to Pharaoh's audience chamber and tell him 'Let my people go!'

        Details: Moses must navigate the halls of the palace to find Pharaoh's audience chamber. See Puzzle 1. Once the player solves the puzzle then they are allowed into the audience chamber where there is a cut scene with dialogue based on Ex 5:1-5.

    2.2. Plans of the Foremen [Ex 5:15-19]

        Actors: Moses, Aaron, Hebrew Foremen

        Location: Slave Camp

        Items: Empty Jar, Jar of Nile Water, Bale of Straw, Freshly Baked Bread,

        Description: Calm the rioting Israelite slaves.

        Details: Moses hears of the Israelites complaining about no straw, they are on the verge of rioting. Moses must calm the slaves down. See Puzzle 2. Once the player solves the puzzle the foremen tell Moses they plan to appeal to Pharaoh

    2.3. Just complaints [Ex 5:20-21]

        Actors: Moses, Aaron, Hebrew Foremen

        Location: Main City Gate

        Items: None

        Description: Find out what happened with the meeting.

        Details: Dialogue between Moses and the Hebrew Foremen as per the verses

3. Staff transforms to a snake
    3.1. Conversation with the Lord [Ex 5:22-7:5]

        Actors: Moses, the Lord

        Location: Slave Camp

        Items: None

        Description: Take the Foremen complaints to the Lord.

        Details: Dialogue between Moses and the Lord as per the verses.

3.2. Snakes are a pain [Ex 7:6-13]

Actors: Moses, Aaron, Pharaoh, Pharaoh's guards, Magician

Location: Pharaoh's Palace

Items: Staff

Description: Perform a miracle when Pharaoh asks for it.

Details: Moses needs to elicit the request from Pharaoh to perform a miracle. See Puzzle 3. After solving the puzzle show cut-scene "Staff Snake".

4. Plague of blood
   4.1. Conversation with the Lord [Ex 7:14-19]

Actors: Moses, the Lord

Location: Slave Camp

Items: None

Description: Receive the next plague instructions from the Lord

Details: Dialogue with the Lord to learn what must be done as per the verses.

4.2. Blood is Thicker than Water [Ex 7:20-24]

Actors: Moses, Aaron, Pharaoh, Pharaoh's guards, Magician

Location: Nile River

Items: Staff

Description: Take Aaron and have the Lord turn all the water to blood.

Details: Aaron raises the staff over the Nile and it turns to blood. But now the other water needs to be changed. See Puzzle 4. After solving the puzzle show cut-scene "Water to Blood".

5. Plague of frogs [Ex 7:25-8:14]
   5.1. Conversation with the Lord [Ex 7:25-8:5]

Actors: Moses, the Lord

Location: Slave Camp

Items: None

Description: Receive the next plague instructions from the Lord

Details: Dialogue with the Lord based on the verses.

5.2. Frog Army Advances [Ex 8:5-7]

Actors: Moses, Aaron, Pharaoh, Pharaoh's guards, Magician

Location: Nile River

Items: Staff

Description: Go to the place where Aaron can stretch his hand over the canals.

Details: Moses meets with Pharaoh but needs to go up to a special place so Aaron can put his hands over the streams and canals. See Puzzle 5. After solving the puzzle show the cut-scene "Frog Army".

5.3. Summoned for prayer [Ex 5:8-14]

Actors: Moses, Aaron, Pharaoh, Pharaoh's guard, Magician

Location: Pharaoh's Palace

Items: None

Description: Meet with Pharaoh to discuss getting rid of the frogs.

Details: Meet Pharaoh in his palace and agree to pray to take the frogs away. Then go and pray at the city gate to the Lord and the frogs will be dead.

6. Plague of gnats

6.1. Conversation with the Lord [Ex 8:16]

Actors: Moses, the Lord

Location: Slave Camp

Items: None

Description: Receive the next plague instructions from the Lord.

Details: Dialogue with the Lord based on the verses.

6.2. Annoying Gnats [Ex 8:17-19]

Actors: Moses, Aaron, Pharaoh, Pharaoh's guards, Magician

Location: Sphinx

Items: Staff

Description: Answer the riddles to cross the bridge to meet with Pharaoh.

Details: Moses must go to Pharaoh but in order to cross the bridge he must answer riddles. See Puzzle 6. After solving the puzzle show the cut-scene "Generating Gnats".

7. Plague of flies [Ex 8:20-32]
   7.1. Conversation with the Lord [Ex 8:20-24]

   Actors: Moses, the Lord

   Location: Slave Camp

   Items: None

   Description: Receive the next plague instructions from the Lord.

   Details: Dialogue with the Lord based on the verses.

   7.2. Flight for Pharaoh [Implied]

   Actors: Moses, Aaron, Pharaoh, Pharaoh's guards

   Location: Nile River

   Items: None

   Description: Warn Pharaoh about the flies.

   Details: Warn Pharaoh about the flies and then go back to the Slave Camp.

   7.3. Summons from Pharaoh [Ex 8:25-32]

   Actors: Moses, Aaron, Pharaoh, Pharaoh's guards

   Location: Pharaoh's Palace

   Items: Straw Swatter

   Description: Navigate the flies and get to Pharaoh.

   Details: With the dense cloud of flies in the city Moses needs to figure out how to get to the Palace. See Puzzle 7. Once solved Moses gets to Pharaoh and they dialogue based on the verses. Then Moses goes to the city gate and prays to the Lord and the flies leave.

8. Plague on the livestock [Ex 9:1-7]
   8.1. Conversation with the Lord [Ex 9:1-5]

   Actors: Moses, the Lord

   Location: Slave Camp

   Items: None

   Description: Receive the next plague instructions from the Lord.

   Details: Dialogue with the Lord based on the verses.

8.2. Flocks of Pharaoh [Implied]

Actors: Moses, Aaron, Pharaoh, Pharaoh's guards

Location: Sphinx

Items: None

Description: Report to Pharaoh what the Lord is planning to do

Details: Go to Pharaoh and report what the Lord is planning to do, then go back to the Slave Camp

8.3. Pharaoh's investigation [Ex 9:6-7]

Actors: Moses, Sheep, Pharaoh's Investigators

Location: Slave Camp

Items: Sheers, Wool: Dead Sheep, Wool: Israelite Sheep, Wool: Egyptian Sheep

Description: Prove all Israelite sheep didn't die.

Details: Pharaoh's investigators come and see if any of the Israelite sheep die. They find one dead sheep and Moses must prove it is not from the Israelite flocks. See Puzzle 8. After Moses proves it is from the Egyptian flock the investigators leave.

9. Plague of boils

9.1. Conversation with the Lord [Ex 9:8-9]

Actors: Moses, the Lord, Furnace, Lever

Location: Slave Camp

Items: Handful of Soot

Description: Get a handful of Soot

Details: The Lord instructs Moses to get a handful of soot from a furnace. To get the soot Moses must open the furnace first. See Puzzle 9. Once Moses gets the soot he can go to Pharaoh.

9.2. Boiling soot [Ex 9:10-12]

Actors: Moses, Aaron, Pharaoh, Pharaoh's guards, Magician, Egyptian Overseer

Location: Sphinx

Items: Handful of Soot

Description: Toss the soot before Pharaoh.

Details: Moses goes before Pharaoh and show cut scene "Boiling Soot".

10. Plague of hail [Ex 9:13-35]

10.1. Conversation with the Lord [Ex 9:13-19]

Actors: Moses, the Lord

Location: Slave Camp

Items: None

Description: Receive the next plague instructions from the Lord.

Details: Dialogue with the Lord based on the verses.

10.2. Weather warning [Ex 9:20-26]

Actors: Moses, Aaron, Pharaoh, Pharaoh's guards, Magician, Egyptian Overseers

Location: Pharaoh's Palace

Items: Gate Key

Description: Warn Pharaoh and go to the place to reach up to the sky.

Details: Deliver the warning to Pharaoh. Then go to the correct place. See Puzzle 10. When at the correct place Moses reaches hand up to the sky and hail falls on the city and thunder starts.

10.3. Summons from Pharaoh [Ex 9:27-32]

Actors: Moses, Aaron, Pharaoh, Pharaoh's guards

Location: Pharaoh's Palace

Items: None

Description: Return to Pharaoh.

Details: When Moses gets back to the slave camp, Pharaoh has a summons waiting for him. So Moses must go back to the Palace. Dialogue with Pharaoh based on the verses.

10.4. Hail to the Lord [Ex 9:33-35]

Actors: Moses, the Lord

Location: Main City Gate

Items: None

Description: Go out of the city and make the hail stop.

Details: Moses goes to the Main City Gate and spreads his hands toward the Lord and the hail and thunder stops.

11. Plague of locusts [Ex 10:1-20]

11.1. Conversation with the Lord [Ex 10:1-2]

Actors: Moses, the Lord

Location: Slave Camp

Items: None

Description: Receive the next plague instructions from the Lord.

Details: Dialogue with the Lord based on the verses.

11.2. Locust warning number 1 [Ex 10:3-7]

Actors: Moses, Aaron, Pharaoh, Pharaoh's guards, Egyptian overseers

Location: Island Temple

Items: None

Description: Warn Pharaoh about incoming locusts.

Details: Dialogue with Pharaoh based on the verses.

11.3. Checkpoint [Implied]

Actors: Moses, Aaron, Miriam, Grain Merchant, Tools Merchant, Metal Refiner, Lumber Merchant

Location: Market

Items: Sacks of Grain, Hand Ploughs, Crate of Bronze Ingots, Raw Lumber, Mud-Bricks

Description: Help Miriam barter for grain.

Details: Miriam is trying to barter for more grain, but doesn't have what the grain merchant wants. Moses needs to figure out how to get it so they can buy the grain. See Puzzle 11. Once resolved, Miriam goes back happily and Moses has a summons from Pharaoh.

11.4. Locust warning number 2 [Ex 10:8-11]

Actors: Moses, Aaron, Pharaoh, Pharaoh's guards, Egyptian overseers

Location: Island Temple

Items: None

Description: Go back to Pharaoh to discuss leaving Egypt

Details: Dialogue with Pharaoh based on the verses.

11.5. Locust Invasion [Ex 10:13-15]

Actors: Moses, Aaron, Big Rock

Location: Island Temple

Items: Staff

Description: Go to the Island Temple Roof and stretch staff over Egypt.

Details: Go to the top of the Island Temple to stretch the Staff over Egypt so the Lord will bring the Locusts. See Puzzle 12. When the puzzle is solved, Moses gets up to the roof and uses the staff. Show cut-scene “Incoming Locusts”.

11.6. Pharaoh’s request of forgiveness [Ex 10:16-20]

Actors: Moses, Aaron, Pharaoh, Pharaoh’s guards

Location: Pharaoh’s Palace

Items: None

Description:

Details: Pharaoh summons Moses to the palace. Dialogue based on the verses. Moses goes to the City Gate to pray and the Lord takes the Locusts away.

12. Plague of darkness [Ex 10:21-29]

12.1. Conversation with the Lord [Ex 10:21]

Actors: Moses, the Lord

Location: Slave Camp

Items: None

Description: Receive the next plague instructions from the Lord.

Details: Dialogue with the Lord based on the verses.

12.2. Meeting in the Dark [Implied]

Actors: Moses, Aaron, Pharaoh, Pharaoh’s guards

Location: Pyramid

Items: None

Description: Go to Pharaoh in the Pyramid

Details: Player must traverse the Pyramid to get to Pharaoh. See Puzzle 13. Once solved then Moses gets to Pharaoh.

12.3. Darkness [Ex 10:22-23]

Actors: Moses, the Lord

Location: Market

Items: None

Description: Stretch hands up to the sky and leave the city.

Details: Moses stretches his hand to the sky and darkness fills the whole city. Unfortunately, Moses is still in it and the player needs to use the mini-map (big map is unavailable) to exit the city and go back to the slave camp.

12.4. Summons and threats [Ex 10:24-29]

Actors: Moses, Aaron, the Lord

Location: Palace

Items: None

Description: Go to Pharaoh's Palace and talk to him.

Details: Pharaoh summons Moses to the Palace and there is dialogue based on the verses.

13. The Passover [Ex 11:1-12:30]

13.1. Instructions from the Lord [Ex 11:1-12:20]

Actors: Moses, the Lord

Location: Slave Camp

Items: None

Description: Receive the next plague instructions from the Lord.

Details: Dialogue with the Lord based on the verses.

13.2. Passover Preparation [Ex 12:21-28]

Actors: Moses, Aaron, Hebrew Elders, Hebrew Slaves

Location: Slave Camp

Items: Perfect Lamb, Roasted Lamb, Lamb's Blood, Horseradish, Grain, Unleavened Bread, Hyssop

Description: Prepare for the Angel of the Lord to Pass Over.

Details: With the instructions from the Lord, Moses needs to and collect the items necessary. Out of all the flocks of sheep Moses needs to find the perfect lamb. Moses must also gather Horseradish and grain for the meal and give them to the cooks. Moses will them distribute the Roasted lamb to everyone and apply the lamb's blood to the doorposts.

13.3. The Angel of Death [Ex 12:29-30]

Actors: Moses, Angel of Death

Location: City Walls

Items: None

Description: Watch the Angel of Death from the city walls.

Details: The Lord wakes Moses up in the middle of the night to have him watch as the Angel of Death moves through the city. Moses touches different waypoints which will cause the Lord to do some exposition about the symbolism of what is going on. Afterwards there is great wailing and Moses goes back to the Slave Camp.

14. The Exodus

14.1. Summons from Pharaoh [Ex 12:31-32]

Actors: Moses, Aaron, Pharaoh, Pharaoh's guards

Location: Pharaoh's Palace

Items: None

Description: Pharaoh's final summons to Moses

Details: When Moses gets back to the Slave Camp a messenger from Pharaoh sends his summons. When Moses gets to the Palace Pharaoh tells him to go but also bless him.

14.2. Egyptian Sending [Ex 12:33-36]

Actors: Moses, Egyptian Slaves, Egyptian Overseers, Grain Merchant, Tools Merchant, Metal Refiner, Lumber Merchant

Location: Market

Items: Box of Sapphires, Box of Rubies, Box of Jasper Stones, Box of Topaz Gems, Box of Emeralds, Box of Malachite Jewels, Box of Diamonds, Box of Amber Jewels, Box of Agate Jewels, Box of Amethysts, Box of Lapis Lazuli Gems, Box of Beryl Gems

Description: The Egyptians send the Hebrews off with gifts.

Details: The Egyptians are glad to see the Hebrews go and want to make sure their god doesn't do anything else to them. Collect all the 12 gifts from Egyptians.

14.3. Coordinate the Israelites [Ex 12:38-39]

Actors: Moses, Aaron, Miriam, Hebrew Slaves, Hebrew Foremen, Hebrew Elder, Egyptian Slave

Location Slave Camp

Items: Rock #1, Rock #2, Rock #3, Rock #4, Rock #5, Rock #6, Rock #7, Rock #8, Rock #9, Rock #10, Rock #11, Rock #12, Rock #13

Description: Arrange the line of everyone in the Exodus.

Details: There are twelve tribes of Israel plus Egyptians who want to come with. Determine the order in which everyone will travel. See puzzle 14. When completed the Israelites are ready to go, but one more thing remains.

14.4. Jacob's bones [Ex 13:19]

Actors: Moses, Hebrew Elder

Location: Pyramid

Items: Joseph's Bones, Square Stone, Circle Stone, Star Stone, Triangle Stone, Diamond Stone.

Description: Go to the pyramid and get Joseph's bones.

Details: Moses must travel to the pyramid and go down to where Joseph's bones are kept. See puzzle 15.

14.5. Israelite Exodus [Ex 12:37]

Actors: Moses, Aaron, Miriam, Hebrew Slaves, Hebrew Foremen

Location: Wilderness

Prerequisites: Complete Side Story 1.5 and pilot the boat to where the Israelites are leaving Egypt.

Items: Staff

Description: Go across the Nile and lead the Israelites out of Egypt.

Details: Go to where the Israelites are, which is across the Nile. Moses must complete the Egyptian Shipwright quest so that he has access to a ship. Once across then go to the front and raise the staff high to signal the Israelites to start.

Egyptian Culture Book, Chapters and Quests:

1. Egyptian Culture

   1.1. Fishing trip

   Actors: Moses, Egyptian Fisherman, Fishing Spot

   Location: Nile River

   Items: Fishing Net, Basket of Fish

   Description: Make 5 catches of fish with the net.

   Details: Use the Fishing Net on a Fishing Spot to catch a Basket of Fish. The Egyptian fisherman needs 5 baskets of fish to complete the quest.

   1.2. Farm hand

   Actors: Moses, Egyptian Farmer, Leftover Farmland

   Location Nile Farmland

   Items: Hand Plough, Barley Seeds, Empty Jar, Jar of Nile Water, sickle, Sack of Barley

   Description: Help the Farmer by giving him a Sack of Barley

   Details: The Egyptian Farmer gives Moses the tools necessary to farm and a little plot of land. Moses first uses the Hand Plough to work the soil. Then plant the Barley Seeds. Then fill his Empty Jar in the Nile and water the seeds. The seeds will grow into Barley plants. Moses then uses the Sickle to harvest the Barley and gets the Sack of Barley to give to the Egyptian Farmer.

   1.3. Headache Medicine

   Actors: Moses, Egyptian Doctor, Egyptian Woman

   Location: Market

   Items: Onion, Fig, Natron, Setseft Seeds, Turnip, Beet, Garlic, Jar of Honey, Abra Ointment

   Description: Help a woman ease her headache by collecting the ingredients.

   Details: A woman seeing her doctor for a headache is prescribed some medicine but they don't have it in stock. Moses must collect the ingredients so the doctor can mix them to let the woman's headache get better.

   1.4. Advanced Carpentry

   Actors: Moses, Egyptian Carpenter

   Location: Market

Items: Refined Lumber, Saw, Cut Lumber, Chisel, Worked Lumber, Slicer, Wooden Table, Drill, Finished Wooden Table

Description: Help a carpenter make his orders.

Details: The carpenter is overloaded with many customers coming and asking for items. Moses can help by crafting a piece of furniture for one of the customers and help him get on track again. Moses must use the tools in the workshop. Use the saw to cut the lumber into the right sizes. Use the Chisel for shaping and smoothing the pieces. Use some nails and the Chisel to put them together. Use a Drill to smooth the sharp edges.

1.5. Shipwright

Actors: Moses, Egyptian Ship-builder, Egyptian Carpenter, Egyptian River Boat

Location: Nile River

Items: Lebanese Cedar Plank

Description: Help a builder build a ship.

Details: The Ship-builder was told to make a ship for Pharaoh but is short on materials. To help, Moses needs to find 20 Lebanese Cedar Planks. See Puzzle 16. As a reward, Moses is given a ship to sail on the Nile.

Israelite Culture Book, Chapters and Quests:

1.1. Straw Relief

Actors: Moses, Hebrew Foreman

Location: Slave Camp

Prerequisites: Complete Main Story Quest 2.1

Items: Straw Bale

Description: Help provide relief to the Slaves who need straw to make mud-bricks

Details: Pharaoh has stopped providing straw to the Hebrew slaves to make mud-bricks. Help relieve some of their pressure by collecting 10 bales of straw and giving it to the Hebrew Foreman

1.2. Mud-brick quota

Actors: Moses, Hebrew Slave

Location: Slave Camp

Items: Dirt, Jar of Nile Water, Mud Mixture, Straw Bale, Brick Mixture, Molded Brick, Finished Mud-Brick

Description: Help the Hebrew slaves meet their quota.

Details: The Hebrew slaves are still behind because they need to gather their own straw. They've got the straw now but need to make the bricks. Mix dirt with water to make thick mud. Add straw and stomp on the mixture to knead it. Pour the mud into a brick mold. Remove the brick and let sit. After waiting present, the bricks to the slave.

1.3. Pinch Shepherd

Actors: Moses, Hebrew Shepherd

Location: Grazing Grounds

Items: Staff

Description: Help a shepherd watch his sheep while he looks for a lost one.

Details: The shepherd has lost a sheep and needs to go find it but doesn't want to leave the other sheep unattended. He asks Moses to guard the sheep while he is gone. Moses must go to all the waypoints. There are six points across the meadow and Moses must "watch" at each point. Once all the points have been visited the shepherd returns.

1.4. Stock up grain

Actors: Moses, Hebrew Foremen

Location: Market

Items: Sack of Grain

Description: Gather grain to prepare for the Exodus of Egypt.

Details: To prepare for the journey to leave Egypt, gather 20 sacks of Grain. See Puzzle 17.

1.5. Lost Sheep

Actors: Moses, Hebrew Shepherd

Location: Slave Camp

Items: Sheers

Description: Find the little lost sheep.

Details: The Shepherd is busy with the sheep and realized that the sheep is lost again. Moses must go out and find the sheep for him. The sheep is stuck in some brambles and Moses needs to sheer off the wool that got stuck. The sheep will follow Moses for the rest of the game and the shepherd decides to give the sheep to Moses as a reward, since it won't leave his side anyways.

Puzzles

Puzzle #	Description
1	This puzzle is for Main Story Quest 2.1. Moses enters the palace but the place is like a labyrinth. There are 3 main gates where guards won't allow people without the right seal to enter. Moses must explore the maze and find each seal in order to pass to the next section. The 3rd guard will let Moses into Pharaoh's audience chamber to solve the puzzle. The puzzle should be built so that on future visits to the palace that getting to Pharaoh won't take a lot of time.
2	This puzzle is for Main Story Quest 2.2. There are seven Israelite slaves rioting. In order to get them to stop rioting you need to find an item based on clues in their dialogue and give it to them. The puzzle is solved once all seven slaves stop rioting. Slave 1: Drink of water (Jug of Nile Water) Slave 2: Wife's fresh baked bread (Freshly Baked Bread) Slave 3: Get ahead of the game (Bale of Straw) Slave 4: Give a good word to sweetheart's father (Talk to Israelite Father) Slave 5: Pray with him (Just talk to him) Slave 6: Reassurance from the Elder (Talk to the Hebrew Elder) Slave 7: Look at the snake miracle again (Use the staff to turn it to a snake and back)
3	This puzzle is for Main Story Quest 3.2. There are multiple options in 7 items of dialogue with Pharaoh and the player must get them all right in order to get the right response and solve the puzzle. Aaron, the Magician, and Pharaoh's guard all give hints for how to answer. The player finds out at the end of the dialogue if they got the right selection. If they didn't then make it obvious, they need to try again.
4	This puzzle is for Main Story Quest 4.2. This is a jumping puzzle to get to the correct location for Aaron to stretch his staff over the waters of Egypt. The puzzle should have multiple paths with dead ends and at least one that sends the player to the beginning again.
5	This puzzle is for Main Story Quest 5.2. Moses enters a passage and must navigate the maze to get to the top and solve the puzzle. The maze will have 3 levels and Moses goes up to the next level after each level is solved. Each level requires a key hidden away somewhere in the level.
6	This puzzle is for Main Story Quest 6.2. There are 3 guards on the gate that ask riddles dealing with Ancient Egyptian culture. It is suggested that Moses may be able to find the answers by talking to nearby Egyptian people who will give the answers. To answer the riddle the player types in the correct word.
7	This puzzle is for Main Story Quest 7.3. Dense clouds of flies have descended on the city and Moses needs to figure out how to get to Pharaoh's Palace. The flies are used to block the normal streets in the city. The player needs to find the "Straw Swatter" and then use it to swat down the blocking flies.
8	This puzzle is for Main Story Quest 8.3. Pharaoh's investigators claim that they found a dead sheep in the Israelite encampment. Moses must use some sheers to take a wool sample from that sheep and go compare it to an Israelite sheep and find they don't match. Then he must go to an Egyptian sheep and show they do match. That unmasks the investigators' plot to show the Lord didn't spare the Israelite sheep as He said.
9	This puzzle is for Main Story Quest 9.1. The Lord asks Moses to get a handful of soot. There is a nearby furnace Moses must open. In order to open it 5 levers must be placed in the right positions. Each one has 3 positions it can be in. Spread nearby are papyrus that

	give clues for the positions of each lever. Once all levers are in the correct positions the furnace opens and Moses can get the handful of soot.
10	This is for Main Story Quest 10.2. Moses must go to the right place to reach his hand up to the sky. There is another passage with a maze that Moses must navigate. This maze includes some jumping puzzles as well. There is a locked gate at the end that requires Moses to find a key to open. The puzzle is solved after Moses unlocks and goes through the gate.
11	ThIs is for Main Story Quest 11.2. Miriam is trying to barter for more grain. She has a bunch of extra mud-bricks but the merchant doesn't want those. Moses needs to figure out how to acquire the grain. The grain merchant wants hand ploughs to sell to farmers. The tools merchant wants bronze to make more tools. The metal refiner wants Crate of Bronze Ore to refine. The mining merchant wants wood to make picks. The lumber merchant wants mud-bricks to build bigger warehouses to keep the wood from warping in the sun.
12	This is for Main Story Quest 11.4. This is a jumping puzzle with a big rock in the way that Moses cannot jump over or pass. The staff must be used as a lever to move the big rock out of the way so Moses can go to the roof and solve the puzzle.
13	This is for Main Story Quest 12.2. Moses needs to go to Pharaoh but he is at the top of the pyramid. Moses needs to navigate the pyramid to get to him. There are pressure plates with moving walls and stones to push to open secret doors. Once the puzzle is solved Moses can talk with Pharaoh.
14	This is for Main Story Quest 14.3. Everyone is eager to get out of Egypt but there are many rivalries. Moses must figure out how to arrange each tribe and the Egyptian followers so everyone is happy (or at least not mad). Give numbered rocks to the leader of each group to assign the order. The Elder's give clues for which order they are to be in. Reuben (5) Simeon (10) Judah (2) Issachar (8) Zebulun (6) Ephraim (12) Manasseh (11) Benjamin (1) Dan (13) Asher (3) Gad (9) Naphtali (4) Egyptians Followers (7)
15	This is for Main Story Quest 14.4. Moses must find Joseph's Bones in the lower levels of the pyramid. There are 3 levels that get bigger each time. Pressure plates and levels will open secret doors. The final puzzle to open the compartment with the bones requires five stones of different shape to be placed in the correct order: square, triangle, circle, star, and diamond. There are clues throughout the maze about the order. After the puzzle is solved then Moses gets Joseph's bones and also finds a quick way back out of the pyramid.
16	This is for Side Story Quest 1.5. The 20 Lebanese Cedar Planks are scattered throughout the city with a variety of ways to obtain them. 10 Cedar Planks are lying around and can

	be picked up or rewarded for jumping puzzles. 10 Cedar Planks are obtained by talking to people, bartering with them or helping them.
17	This is for Side Story Quest 2.4. The 20 sacks of Grain are scattered throughout the slave camp with a variety of ways to obtain them. 10 Sacks of Grain are lying around and can be picked up or rewarded for jumping puzzles. 10 Sacks of Grain are obtained by talking to people, bartering with them, or helping them.

Graphic Assets

The 3D art assets will use the Egypt Characters and Ancient Egypt pack. The pre-existing outdoor city scene will be used as-is. Various objects and NPCs will be placed there to populate it. The indoor locations will be built using the building block pieces of the indoor and temple prefabs.

There will also be a skybox. Day/night will be adjusted using the Exposure variable in the skybox material for standard cycles.

List of Object Assets:

Name	**Description**
Column	Ancient Egypt\Models\Temple Parts\Column
Stone Bowl	Ancient Egypt\Models\Temple Parts\FireBowl
Standing Pharaoh Statue	Ancient Egypt\Models\Statues\Statue1
Sitting Pharaoh Statue	Ancient Egypt\Models\Statues\Statue4
Jackal-Head Statue	Ancient Egypt\Models\Statues\Statue2
Bird-Head Statue	Ancient Egypt\Models\Statues\Statue3
Gold and Onyx Jackal-Head Statue	Ancient Egypt\Models\Statues\Statue5
Gold an Onyx Bird-Head Statue	Ancient Egypt\Models\Statues\Statue6
Bowl	Ancient Egypt\Models\House Parts\Additional Addons \Bowl
Rolled up Carpet	Ancient Egypt\Models\House Parts\Additional Addons \Carpet
Stool	Ancient Egypt\Models\House Parts\Additional Addons \Chair_1
Shelves	Ancient Egypt\Models\House Parts\Additional Addons \Closet_1
Shelves: Full	Ancient Egypt\Models\House Parts\Additional Addons \ClosetFull
Metal Cup	Ancient Egypt\Models\House Parts\Additional Addons \Cup
Peach Box	Ancient Egypt\Models\House Parts\Additional Addons \FruitBox1
Green Herbs Box	Ancient Egypt\Models\House Parts\Additional Addons \FruitBox2
Green Herbs Basket	Ancient Egypt\Models\House Parts\Additional Addons \Spice2
Red Spices/Beans Box	Ancient Egypt\Models\House Parts\Additional Addons \FruitBox3
Red Spices/Beans Basket	Ancient Egypt\Models\House Parts\Additional Addons \Spice1
Yam Box	Ancient Egypt\Models\House Parts\Additional Addons \FruitBox4
Bell Pepper Box	Ancient Egypt\Models\House Parts\Additional Addons \FruitBox5
Empty Basket	Ancient Egypt\Models\House Parts\Additional Addons \SpiceEmpty
Stone Oil Lamp	Ancient Egypt\Models\House Parts\Additional Addons \OilLampPrefab

Metal Pitcher	Ancient Egypt\Models\House Parts\Additional Addons \Pitch
Clay Pot	Ancient Egypt\Models\House Parts\Additional Addons \Pot_1
Staff	Create 3D object using a cylinder and a wood texture
Pharaoh's Throne	https://www.assetstore.unity3d.com/en/#!/content/17242
Spear	https://www.assetstore.unity3d.com/en/#!/content/46190
Khopesh	https://www.assetstore.unity3d.com/en/#!/content/46190
Shield	https://www.assetstore.unity3d.com/en/#!/content/46190
Skybox	Ancient Egypt\Models\Textures\Materials\Sky
Eagle	Flying Birds\Eagle
Falcon	Flying Birds\Falcon
Raven	Flying Birds\Raven

List of Maze Assets:

Name	Description
Stairs	Ancient Egypt\Models\Temple Parts\DT_Stairs
Hallway End: Door	Ancient Egypt\Models\Temple Parts\DT_EndDoor
Hallway End: Collapse	Ancient Egypt\Models\Temple Parts\DT_EndColapse
Hallway: Doors at left and right	Ancient Egypt\Models\Temple Parts\DT_3
Hallway: Disrepair	Ancient Egypt\Models\Temple Parts\DT_2
Hallway: Normal	Ancient Egypt\Models\Temple Parts\DT_1
Hallway: 4-way	Ancient Egypt\Models\Temple Parts\DT4way_1
Hallway: T-Intersect	Ancient Egypt\Models\Temple Parts\DT3way_1
Hallway: Corner	Ancient Egypt\Models\Temple Parts\DT2way_1
Hieroglyphics Room	Ancient Egypt\Models\Temple Parts\Room_1
Room with Platform	Ancient Egypt\Models\Temple Parts\Room_2
Dirt Patch	Ancient Egypt\Models\Temple Parts\DungeonSand

List of 2D Assets:

Name	Description
Game Title	Use "Exodus Adventure" Banner from BibleByteGames Opening Scene for Moses in Egypt Exodus PSD file
Inventory Grid	Use stock GUI and Kris to create anything that is needed (may not look the best)
BibleByteBooks Logo	BibleByteBooks_logo.gif

Animation Assets

The PC will use the 3Rd Person Controller to move around and the included camera controller to control the camera. The basic controller supports walking, running, jumping, flying, sprinting, aiming, and strafing. The flying and sprinting will be disabled. The Player Controller will be modified to support footstep sounds as well as grab low, grab medium, and grab high from the Raw Mocap Animations. The footstep sounds will change based on what the player is walking on (stone, dirt, grass). The camera controller will be modified to support zooming in and out using the mouse wheel.

NPCs will also have animations depending on each NPC and what actions they are taking. Some NPCs may have complex or chained animations, each played for a specific length of time.

Music and Sound FX Assets

Music will change based on the location or in cut-scenes. The pyramid and palace will have their own music. Also, the overland locations are divided into the city, wilderness, and slave camp which will change music when the player enters those locations.

Table and Description of Music and Sound Effects:

Name	Description
Title Theme	Extreme Fantasy Music Pack\Day\Day_Time_3
City Ambient	Extreme Fantasy Music Pack\Day\Day_Time_2
Palace Ambient	Extreme Combat Music Pack\Night\Night_Time_OUT1
Pyramid Ambient	Extreme Combat Music Pack\Day\Day\Day_Time_FRONT
Slave Camp Ambient	Extreme Combat Music Pack\Night\Night_Time
Wilderness Ambient	Extreme Fantasy Music Pack\Day\Day_Time_1
Opening Cinematic	Extreme Combat Music Pack\Combat\Combat_detected
Ending Cinematic	Extreme Fantasy Music Pack\Night\Night_Time_Event
Footsteps	StandardAssets\Characters\FirstPersonCharacter\Audio\Footstep01 StandardAssets\Characters\FirstPersonCharacter\Audio\Footstep02 StandardAssets\Characters\FirstPersonCharacter\Audio\Footstep03 StandardAssets\Characters\FirstPersonCharacter\Audio\Footstep04
Jump	StandardAssets\Characters\FirstPersonCharacter\Audio\Jump
Land	StandardAssets\Characters\FirstPersonCharacter\Audio\Land
Footstep Dirt	Footstep Sounds\Example\Sounds\Footstep_Dirt01
Footstep Grass	Footstep Sounds\Example\Sounds\Footstep_Grass01
Footstep Rocks	Footstep Sounds\Example\Sounds\Footstep_Rocks01

Sheep Corralling Mini-game

Inside the game will be another small game for players to divert themselves with. This will be a simple search and find game with a timer and a high score. The goal of the game is to tag all the sheep as fast as they can. A timer will be shown to the player as well as how many sheep they need to tag and the number of sheep they've already tagged.

The first time the player plays the game the score will be saved. Each time they beat that score it will be saved again. The high score will be displayed to the player when the mini-game completes. Also, when the mini-game completes, it will be reset so that the player can play it again.

Other Self-Study and/or Instructor-Led Programming Tutorials By BibleByte Books

Computer Bible Games for Microsoft Small Basic is a self-paced "beginner" programming tutorial for Middle-School students. This tutorial consists of 13 chapters explaining (in simple, easy-to-follow terms) how to build Computer Bible Games in Small Basic. It also includes the Small Basic source code for the several of the original Computer Bible Games. The Computer Bible Games built include: Noah's Ark, Daniel and the Lions, Elijah and the Ravens, The Good Shepherd, The Prodigal Son, The Lost Coin, and Bible Scramble. Other learning projects include a card game, an allowance calculator, a drawing program, a state capitals game, and a video game.

Computer Bible Games with Visual Basic® is a self-study "beginner" programming tutorial consisting of 13 chapters explaining (in simple, easy-to-follow terms) how to build a Visual Basic Express Windows application and Computer Bible Games. The Computer Bible Games built include: Noah's Ark, Elijah & the Ravens, and Daniel & the Lions. Other learning projects include a card game, an allowance calculator, a drawing program, a state capitals game, and a video game. We also include several college prep bonus projects including a loan calculator, portfolio manager, and checkbook balancer.

Computer Bible Games with Visual C#® is a self-study "beginning "programming tutorial consisting of 13 chapters explaining (in simple, easy-to-follow terms) how to build a C# Express Windows applications and Computer Bible Games. The Computer Bible Games built include: Noah's Ark, Elijah & the Ravens, and Daniel & the Lions. Other learning projects include a card game, an allowance calculator, a drawing program, a state capitals game, and a video game. We also include several college prep bonus projects including a loan calculator portfolio manager, and checkbook balancer.

Computer Bible Games with Java™ is a self-study programming tutorial consisting of 7 chapters explaining (in simple, easy-to-follow terms) how to build a Java® Computer Bible Games. The Computer Bible Games built include: Noah's Ark, Elijah & the Ravens, and Daniel & the Lions, Bible Safecracker, Bible Match, and Bible Trivia Tic-Tac-Toe. This advanced GUI tutorial requires a complete understanding of the Java JFC Swing Control Library before attempting. Our parent company, Kidware Software, sells two pre-requisite Java tutorials (*Beginning Java and Learn Java GUI Applications*) that would need to be completed before a student should attempt to complete Computer Bible Games with Java.

More Self-Study or Instructor-Led Computer Programming Tutorials by Our Parent Company, Kidware Software LLC

ORACLE JAVA PROGRAMMING TUTORIALS

Java™ For Kids is a beginning programming tutorial consisting of 10 chapters explaining (in simple, easy-to-follow terms) how to build a Java application. Students learn about project design, object-oriented programming, console applications, graphics applications and many elements of the Java language. Numerous examples are used to demonstrate every step in the building process. The projects include a number guessing game, a card game, an allowance calculator, a state capitals game, Tic-Tac-Toe, a simple drawing program, and even a basic video game. Designed for kids ages 12 and up.

Beginning Java™ is a semester long "beginning" programming tutorial consisting of 10 chapters explaining (in simple, easy-to-follow terms) how to build a Java application. The tutorial includes several detailed computer projects for students to build and try. These projects include a number guessing game, card game, allowance calculator, drawing program, state capitals game, and a couple of video games like Pong. We also include several college prep bonus projects including a loan calculator, portfolio manager, and checkbook balancer. Designed for students age 15 and up.

Learn Java™ GUI Applications is a 9 lesson Tutorial covering object-oriented programming concepts, using an integrated development environment to create and test Java projects, building and distributing GUI applications, understanding and using the Swing control library, exception handling, sequential file access, graphics, multimedia, advanced topics such as printing, and help system authoring. Our Beginning Java or Java For Kids tutorial is a pre-requisite for this tutorial

Programming Games with Java™ is a semester long "intermediate" programming tutorial consisting of 10 chapters explaining (in simple, easy-to-follow terms) how to build a Visual C# Video Games. The games built are non-violent, family-friendly and teach logical thinking skills. Students will learn how to program the following Visual C# video games: Safecracker, Tic Tac Toe, Match Game, Pizza Delivery, and Moon Landing. This intermediate level self-paced tutorial can be used at home or school. The tutorial is simple enough for kids yet engaging enough for beginning adults. Our Learn Java GUI Applications tutorial is a required pre-requisite for this tutorial.

Java™ Homework Projects is a Java GUI Swing tutorial covering object-oriented programming concepts. It explains (in simple, easy-to-follow terms) how to build Java GUI project to use around the home. Students learn about project design, the Java Swing controls, many elements of the Java language, and how to distribute finished projects. The projects built include a Dual-Mode Stopwatch, Flash Card Math Quiz, Multiple Choice Exam, Blackjack Card Game, Weight Monitor, Home Inventory Manager and a Snowball Toss Game. Our Learn Java GUI Applications tutorial is a pre-requisite for this tutorial

MICROSOFT SMALL BASIC PROGRAMMING TUTORIALS

Small Basic For Kids is an illustrated introduction to computer programming that provides an interactive, self-paced tutorial to the new Small Basic programming environment. The book consists of 30 short lessons that explain how to create and run a Small Basic program. Elementary students learn about program design and many elements of the Small Basic language. Numerous examples are used to demonstrate every step in the building process. The tutorial also includes two complete games (Hangman and Pizza Zapper) for students to build and try. Designed for kids ages 8+.

The Beginning Microsoft Small Basic Programming Tutorial is a self-study first semester "beginner" programming tutorial consisting of 11 chapters explaining (in simple, easy-to-follow terms) how to write Microsoft Small Basic programs. Numerous examples are used to demonstrate every step in the building process. The last chapter of this tutorial shows you how four different Small Basic games could port to Visual Basic, Visual C# and Java. This beginning level self-paced tutorial can be used at home or at school. The tutorial is simple enough for kids ages 10+ yet engaging enough for adults.

Basic Computer Games - Small Basic Edition is a re-make of the classic BASIC COMPUTER GAMES book originally edited by David H. Ahl. It contains 100 of the original text based BASIC games that inspired a whole generation of programmers. Now these classic BASIC games have been re-written in Microsoft Small Basic for a new generation to enjoy! The new Small Basic games look and act like the original text-based games. The book includes all the original spaghetti code and GOTO commands!

Programming Home Projects with Microsoft Small Basic is a self-paced programming tutorial explains (in simple, easy-to-follow terms) how to build Small Basic Windows applications. Students learn about program design, Small Basic objects, many elements of the Small Basic language, and how to debug and distribute finished programs. Sequential file input and output is also introduced. The projects built include a Dual-Mode Stopwatch, Flash Card Math Quiz, Multiple Choice Exam, Blackjack Card Game, Weight Monitor, Home Inventory Manager and a Snowball Toss Game.

The Developer's Reference Guide to Microsoft Small Basic While developing all the different Microsoft Small Basic tutorials we found it necessary to write The Developer's Reference Guide to Microsoft Small Basic. The Developer's Reference Guide to Microsoft Small Basic is over 500 pages long and includes over 100 Small Basic programming examples for you to learn from and include in your own Microsoft Small Basic programs. It is a detailed reference guide for new developers.

David Ahl's Small Basic Computer Adventures is a Microsoft Small Basic re-make of the classic *Basic Computer Games* programming *book* originally written by David H. Ahl. This new book includes the following classic adventure simulations; Marco Polo, Westward Ho!, The Longest Automobile Race, The Orient Express, Amelia Earhart: Around the World Flight, Tour de France, Subway Scavenger, Hong Kong Hustle, and Voyage to Neptune. Learn how to program these classic computer simulations in Microsoft Small Basic.

MICROSOFT VISUAL BASIC & VISUAL C# PROGRAMMING TUTORIALS

LEARN VISUAL BASIC is a comprehensive college level programming tutorial covering object-oriented programming, the Visual Basic integrated development environment, building and distributing Windows applications using the Windows Installer, exception handling, sequential file access, graphics, multimedia, advanced topics such as web access, printing, and HTML help system authoring. The tutorial also introduces database applications (using ADO .NET) and web applications (using ASP.NET).

VISUAL BASIC AND DATABASES is a tutorial that provides a detailed introduction to using Visual Basic for accessing and maintaining databases for desktop applications. Topics covered include: database structure, database design, Visual Basic project building, ADO .NET data objects (connection, data adapter, command, data table), data bound controls, proper interface design, structured query language (SQL), creating databases using Access, SQL Server and ADOX, and database reports. Actual projects developed include a book tracking system, a sales invoicing program, a home inventory system and a daily weather monitor.

LEARN VISUAL C# is a comprehensive college level computer programming tutorial covering object-oriented programming, the Visual C# integrated development environment and toolbox, building and distributing Windows applications (using the Windows Installer), exception handling, sequential file input and output, graphics, multimedia effects (animation and sounds), advanced topics such as web access, printing, and HTML help system authoring. The tutorial also introduces database applications (using ADO .NET) and web applications (using ASP.NET).

VISUAL C# AND DATABASES is a tutorial that provides a detailed introduction to using Visual C# for accessing and maintaining databases for desktop applications. Topics covered include: database structure, database design, Visual C# project building, ADO .NET data objects (connection, data adapter, command, data table), data bound controls, proper interface design, structured query language (SQL), creating databases using Access, SQL Server and ADOX, and database reports. Actual projects developed include a book tracking system, a sales invoicing program, a home inventory system and a daily weather monitor.

www.ingramcontent.com/pod-product-compliance
Ingram Content Group UK Ltd.
Pitfield, Milton Keynes, MK11 3LW, UK
UKHW052010041026
15590UKWH00008B/2247

9 781951 077266